Type Right!

Second Edition

A Complete Program for Business Typewriting

Delores S. Cotton
Department Head, Business Education
Henry Ford High School, Detroit

Vito C. Metta
Assistant Supervisor (retired), Business
and Office Education
Cleveland Public Schools

Glencoe Publishing Company
Mission Hills, California

Send all inquiries to:
Glencoe Publishing Company
15319 Chatsworth Street
Mission Hills, California 91345

Library of Congress Catalog Card Number: 85-81376

Printed in the United States of America
ISBN 0-02-830550-7 (Student Text)
ISBN 0-02-830560-4 (Classroom Management Guide)
ISBN 0-02-830520-5 (Transparency Masters)
ISBN 0-02-830570-1 (Stationery Supplies)

2 3 4 5 6 7 8 9 90 89 88 87

PREFACE

The second edition of TYPE RIGHT! is designed and written for teachers who are on the front line—facing students day in and day out. It is a book that makes no claims to any revolutionary breakthroughs in typewriting instruction. Rather, its contents are based on tried and tested methods and materials proven through years of classroom use.

TYPE RIGHT! is a complete instructional program from basic keyboard operation to applied business typewriting. It contains voluminous material for a full two-year course. Not only is there an abundance of exercise material stressing all kinds of on-the-job applications, but, in addition, two complete sections are devoted entirely to drill material—so necessary for the development of speed and accuracy.

Organization

The text is organized into five main sections. Section One introduces the keyboard. The material in this section is presented in 39 *units*, each designed for one classroom period. To accommodate differences in student achievement, 14 of the 39 units provide either review or skill development material to be used at the teacher's discretion.

Sections Two and Three present the main body of instructional matter. Section Two emphasizes the personal, everyday uses of typewriting; Section Three emphasizes the vocational applications. Both sections are organized into *topics* that focus on a single subject, such as *horizontal centering, manuscript typing, proofreading, preparing business letters*, and so forth. Where applicable, information on word processing has been integrated into the discussion of each topic to show the impact that computer technology is having on document production. Topics are arranged in clusters of related learning, and within each cluster the topics are presented in a progression of difficulty. It is not intended that all topics be used in the same sequence as they appear in the text, nor that all exercises in any one topic be done at one time. To achieve variety, the teacher should feel free to move through the text according to class needs and course objectives.

Section Four, *Work Experience Simulations*, consists of 15 projects that simulate on-the-job applications of the learnings presented in Sections Two and Three. The projects are arranged in order of increasing complexity. In the last of these simulations, the setting is a corporate word processing center. Tasks to be done are representative of those that might be given to a correspondence secretary in such a center. The projects are specially designed for students who have learned to use word processing equipment; however, alternative directions are provided for those working on standard typewriters.

Section Five, *Supplementary Practice Exercises*, contains a wealth of drills and timed writings. These are provided for concentrated effort in developing speed and accuracy, for remediation, and for the measurement of speed and accuracy. This material should be interwoven at regular intervals throughout the teaching of Sections Two and Three. It may also be used during the last part of Section One.

Language Arts

With the increased use of transcribing machines and electronic typewriters, language arts has become an important aspect of advanced typing instruction. Special emphasis has been given to developing the typist's ability to find and correct misspelled words, errors in punctuation, and other types of language problems that occur in copy to be typed. Two 100-word spelling lists, detailed rules of punctuation, and rules for typing numbers and abbreviations are included for students' reference and review. Exercises with a language arts emphasis are integrated into several topics and are grouped at the end of the topic for easy identification. Also included are simple composition exercises as well as assignments designed to encourage independent thinking. These appear throughout the text under the headings *Composition at the Keyboard* and *Creative Keyboarding*, respectively.

Exercise Materials

An abundance of exercise material accompanies each topic. Exercises are presented in a variety of formats that become progressively more challenging. The first exercises that students type are usually presented in typewriter face and arranged as finished copy should appear. Afterward, exercises are presented (1) in book type, arranged or unarranged; (2) in handwriting; and (3) in rough draft, both typed and handwritten. The exercises with a language arts emphasis are also presented in different formats that demand more and more of the student's ability to read copy for accuracy and make the appropriate corrections.

Models

Whenever a new learning is presented, an annotated typewritten model accompanies the instruction. Models are numbered consecutively throughout the text and are listed separately after the table of contents for easy reference.

Supporting Materials

A comprehensive *Classroom Management Guide* is available separately. It contains (1) general suggestions for teaching typewriting, (2) lesson plans that outline suggested content for 308 lessons in a two-year course of instruction, (3) instructional strategies for each section of the text, and (4) model solutions for the majority of the text exercises.

Stationery Supplies are also available for classroom use. These working papers consist of letterhead stationery, envelope forms, business forms, legal documents, and other forms needed for the completion of exercises in Sections Three and Four.

Finally, a set of *Transparency Masters* is available for use in producing visual aids. Included are keyboard models with accompanying drill material for individual keys, document models, and selected text illustrations.

CONTENTS

SECTION THREE Typing for Vocational Use 222

SECTION FOUR Work Experience Simulations 382

SECTION FIVE Supplementary Practice Exercises 417

MODELS

SELECTED ILLUSTRATIONS

GENERAL INDEX

Refer to the **Special Index,** page x, for special drills, exercises, and timed writings.

SPECIAL INDEX

This index is provided to facilitate the location of specific *keyboard drills* (for speed, accuracy, and technique development) and *exercises* of a special nature.

KEYBOARD DRILLS

SPECIAL EXERCISES

INTRODUCTION TO THE TYPEWRITER

Type Wheel

Type Ball

Typewriters can be classified by mechanism and by power source.

There are two basic types of mechanisms. The older form is the typebar. On typebar machines, each key is connected to a bar on the end of which is mounted a single piece of type. When a key is depressed, its typebar strikes the paper through the ribbon, leaving an imprint. Since the typebars are stationary, to create a line of typing, the paper must be moved from left to right. This is accomplished by means of a carriage. The carriage is one of the most readily identifiable features of a typebar machine.

Newer typewriters have a different mechanism. Instead of individual typebars, they use a single type element containing all the keyboard characters. The element can be a type ball or a type wheel. In either case, it is the element that moves back and forth to form a line of typing, not the paper. Element machines have no carriages.

The second way to classify typewriters is by power source. Is the machine manual or electric? Electric machines are more common in business and are becoming increasingly sophisticated. They have evolved into electronic machines, microcomputers, and word processors. These types of machines are based on computer chips. The chips increase the number of automatic functions and provide memory and storage capacity.

Despite these differences, there remain many similarities from one piece of equipment to another. Study the following list of typewriter features and locate them in the illustrations. Then find them on your own machine. Consult your operator's manual as necessary.

1. ALIGNING SCALE   Used to locate the typing line when work must be reinserted for correction or completion.
2. AUTOMATIC LINE FINDER   Temporarily disengages the line spacing mechanism and then returns the paper to its original position; used for typing sub- and superscripts.
3. BACKSPACE KEYS   Bring the printing point back one (or one-half) space.
4. CARD HOLDER   Holds cards and labels firmly against the platen.
5. CARRIAGE   On a typebar machine, carries the paper from the left to the right margin.
6. CARRIAGE RELEASE   Allows free movement of the carriage from side to side.
7. CARRIAGE RETURN LEVER   On a manual machine, returns the carriage to the far right and advances the paper to the next typing line.
8. CORRECTION KEY   On some electric machines (those with correction memory and a special carbon ribbon), allows errors to be "lifted" from the page.
9. EXPRESS RETURN   On an element machine, causes the print wheel or type element to return to the left margin without advancing the paper to the next line.
10. IMPRESSION CONTROL   On an electric typewriter, sets the force with which the typebar or element strikes the paper.
11. INDEX/REVERSE INDEX KEY   Moves the machine to the next (or previous) line without returning the printing point to the left margin. (On some machines, moves a half line at a time.)
12. INSERT/EJECT LEVER   Quickly feeds paper into or out of the machine.
13. LINE SPACE REGULATOR   Sets the machine for single, double, or triple spacing between lines.
14. MARGIN-PITCH SCALE   On an element machine, used for selecting margins, counting spaces, and locating the midpoint of the paper.
15. MARGIN RELEASE   Temporarily allows typing beyond the margins that have been set.
16. MARGIN SETS   Used to set the points at which the writing line begins and ends.
17. ON/OFF CONTROL   On an electric typewriter, used to turn the power on and off.
18. PAGE END INDICATOR   Indicates when the desired bottom margin is approached.
19. PAPER BAIL WITH ROLLERS   Holds the paper against the platen.
20. PAPER BAIL LEVER   On an element machine, moves the paper bail forward to prevent the typing sheet from wrinkling during insertion.
21. PAPER BAIL SCALE   On a typebar machine, used for counting spaces and locating the midpoint of the paper.
22. PAPER GUIDE   Guides the left edge of the paper as it is inserted into the machine.
23. PAPER GUIDE SCALE   On a typebar machine, used to set the margins; on all machines, used to position the paper guide.
24. PAPER RELEASE   Frees the paper so that it can be either straightened or quickly removed.

7

Few things taste better than sweet juicy fruit 10
pick fresh from your own trees. 17
The wide vareity of Fruit trees you can have in your 27
own backyard will bring you other joys too. Planting 37
and careing for the trees can give you healthy exer- 48
cise. Their colorful blooms in Spring will please your 59
eyes. And in the warm summer months, your trees will 69
provide cool shade. Fruit trees provide healthful food 81
and they offer all the benefits of a green and natural 90
environment; grow some! It maybe a habit that will 100
grow on you. 102

8

You will offen have occasions to use your type- 10
writing skills to write letters. Aim to maek your let- 20
ters attractive so that they will make a good impres- 31
sion on the readers. 35
In business and in personal life, letters often serve 45
as important records. If there is a dispute about the 58
terms of a transaction for example, a letter may be 69
brought out of a file to provide the evidence to setle 85
it. It is, therefore, essential that the contents of 98
a letter be accurate, complete and clear. 107

25. PAPER TABLE Supports the paper as it is inserted into the machine.
26. PITCH SELECTOR On variable pitch machines, used to set the number of characters that can be typed per inch (usually 10, 12, or 15).
27. PLATEN Provides a hard surface for the typebar or element to strike; the large cylinder around which the paper inserted into a typewriter rolls.
28. PLATEN KNOBS Used to turn the platen by hand when either making corrections or (on most machines) inserting the paper.
29. PRINTING POINT INDICATOR Points to the position either on the paper bail scale (typebar machine) or on the margin pitch scale (element machine) where the next character will be typed.
30. RETURN KEY On an electric machine, automatically returns the printing point to the left margin and advances the paper to the next line.
31. RIBBON CONTROL Determines which portion of the machine's ribbon is struck—the top half (usually black), the bottom half (usually red), or neither (the position for cutting a stencil); on electronic machines, usually found beneath the machine cover.
32. SHIFT KEYS Used for typing capitals and most special characters.
33. SHIFT LOCK Locks the shift mechanism; allows typing of a series of capitals without repeatedly depressing shift keys.
34. SPACE BAR Used to space forward on the typing line.
35. TAB SET AND/OR CLEAR Used to lock in new tab stops and remove those that are no longer needed.
36. TABULATOR Quickly moves the printing point to preselected positions on the typing line; simplifies typing columns and indenting paragraphs.
37. TYPE ELEMENT Device containing the characters an element machine can type; either a ball (a) or a spoked disk (b), variously called a daisy wheel, print wheel, or type wheel.
38. VARIABLE LINE SPACER Releases the line spacing mechanism, allowing the platen to turn freely; permanently changes the typing line.

Electronic Features:

A. AUTO RETURN Causes the printing point to return automatically to the left margin when the end of a line is reached. (*Note:* When this feature is engaged, the return key is used only to space vertically and to end paragraphs or short lines.)
B. CAPS LOCK Allows for the typing of both numbers and uppercase letters without use of the shift keys.
C. CODE KEYS Used simultaneously with other keys to access special features like automatic centering, automatic underscoring, and boldface print.
D. DECIMAL TAB Automatically aligns numbers typed in columns.
E. END KEY Quickly moves the printing point to the end of the document.

TYPEBAR MACHINE (MANUAL)

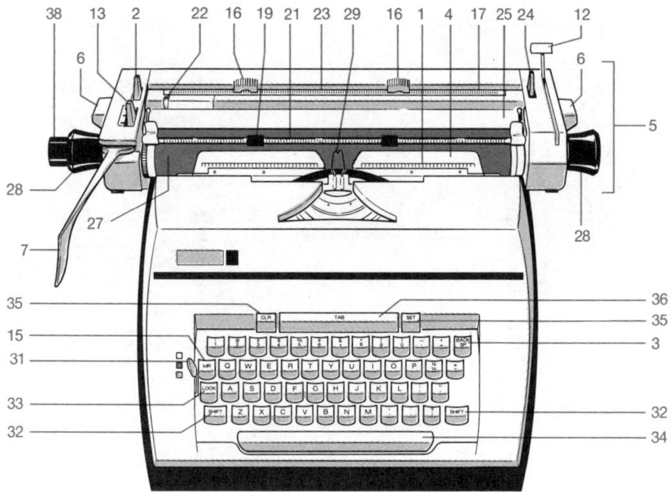

5

We need to understand ourselves as well as others. 11
The observance of holidays, whether they are religious, 23
is one way in which people keep their culture aleve. 34
You may under stand the people of the world better, and 42
be able to accept the difference in others, if you 51
study these holdays. Some American Holidays have 60
brought together customs from many lands. By studing 71
these holidays, you will see how our culture is made up 84
from the contributions of many peoples from many 94
cultures 96

6

There was one many difference between slavery as 11
it existed on the Continent of Africa and the peculiar 22
institution as it came about in the United states. The 33
slave in African life was a status symbol, a isgn of 43
the wealth and position of the owner. People could not 54
afford to own slaves unless they were all ready very 63
wealthy. Therefore, they could not become wealthy on 74
the basis of labor done by slaves. 81
In the Southern U.S., on the other hand, the 92
economy was based upon the free labor supplied by the 101
slaves; and through their slaves, owners could become 113
wealthy. 115

ELEMENT MACHINE (ELECTRIC)

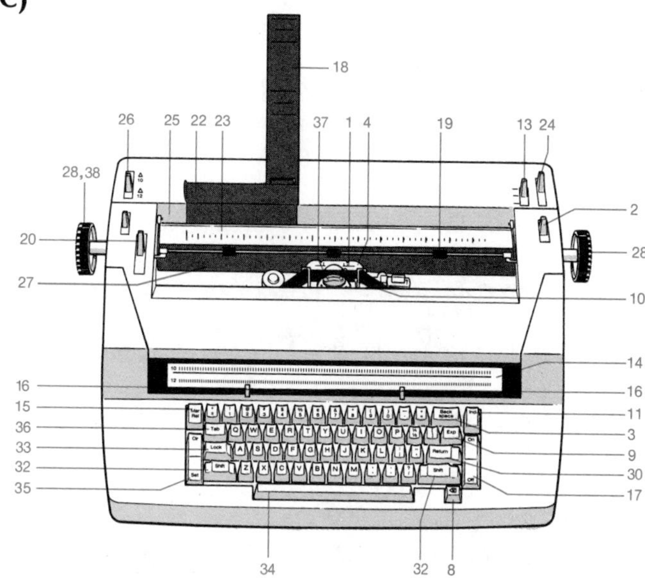

ELECTRONIC MACHINE (XEROX 6010 KEYBOARD)

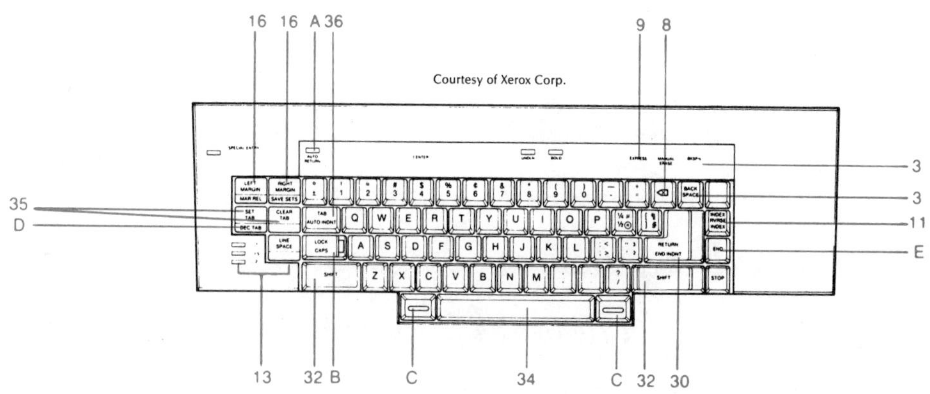

MICROCOMPUTER

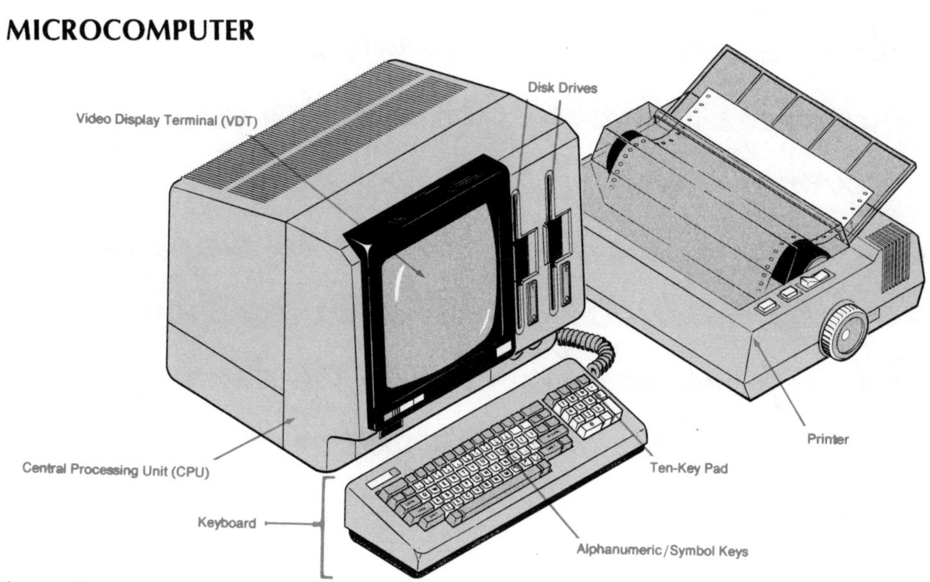

3 A group of us were discussing our jobs, and 10
the talk turned to the subject of tact. We all 19
agreed that tact is one of the important qualities 29
that lead to a successful career. Then we tried to 39
describe what tact means. Someone said that tact 49
is not so much what you say but how you say it. 58
I said that since it comes from a Latin word mean- 68
ing "touch," it suggests a sensitive touch that works 79
with human nature, not against it. The group 88
accepted this. 91

4 Banks will make certain kinds of loans. Other 10
loans will not be made, either because they are 20
barred by law or because they are considered un- 29
sound. In general, banks prefer not to make loans 39
for a long period without return payments at regu- 49
lar intervals. In fact, they usually require loans to 60
be repaid within a short time, except loans on 69
land and buildings. Banks often ask for security 79
for a loan—even from very large companies. 88
As a rule, a bank wants to know the purpose 97
of a loan to help in deciding whether or not to 107
grant it. This information also helps the bank fix 117
the length of time for the loan, as well as the amount 128
of security required. 132

How to Insert the Paper

1. Set the paper guide (22)* at zero on the paper guide scale (23).
2. Rest a sheet of paper lightly against the paper table (25) at the paper guide. Lower the sheet of paper behind the platen (27).
3. a. TYPEBAR MACHINES Raise the paper bail (19). Then grasp the right platen knob (28) and quickly turn it back, away from the keyboard, until the paper is in position. Lower the paper bail.
   b. TYPEBAR MACHINES WITH INSERT/EJECT FEATURE Raise the paper bail (19). Grasp the insert/eject lever (12) and pull it forward. Release. Repeat as often as necessary to bring the paper into position. Use the right platen knob (28) to make any fine adjustments. Replace the paper bail.
   c. ELEMENT MACHINES Pull the paper bail lever (20) forward. Then use either the index key (11) or the return key (30) to feed paper into the machine. When the paper is in place, return the paper bail lever to its original position.
   d. ELEMENT MACHINES WITH AUTOMATIC PAPER INSERTION (electronic only) Pull the insert/eject lever forward. The paper will feed automatically and stop when the lever is released.

Typebar Machines

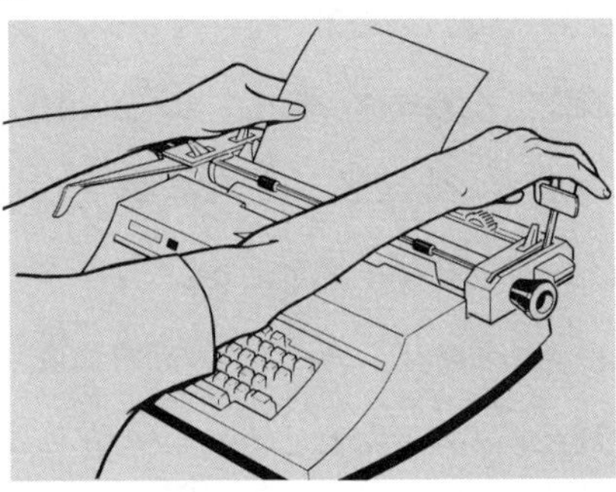

Typebar Machines with Insert/Eject Feature

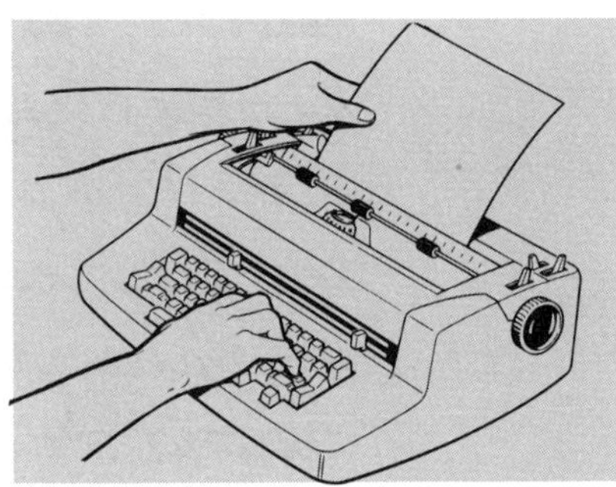

Element Machines

How to Straighten the Paper

1. If the paper is not straight, pull the paper release (24) forward. Then raise the paper bail (19).
2. Adjust the paper. Align the edge of the sheet with the aligning scale (1) or match the left and right edges of the paper as shown in the drawing at the lower left.
3. Restore the paper release and place the paper bail back against the paper.

Straightening the Paper

Removing the Paper

How to Remove the Paper

There are alternate methods of removing paper from a typewriter. Which is used depends on machine features and personal preference.

1. ALL MACHINES Pull the paper release (24) forward. Remove the paper. Restore the paper release to its original position.
2. MACHINES WITH INSERT/EJECT LEVERS Pull the insert/eject lever (12) forward as often (or as long) as necessary to feed the paper out of the machine.

*Numbers in parentheses refer to the list of typewriter parts on pages 1 and 2 and the diagrams that follow.

SCRIPT AND ROUGH-DRAFT COPY

The timed writings in this group are presented in script and rough-draft forms. Since most documents in the workplace are presented in these two forms, it is a good idea to build skill when typing from them. Your speed on such material, however, will probably be lower than your speed on straight typed copy. *Note:* In this group, vertical scales give words per line of edited (or correctly typed) copy. Horizontal scales are not included, as interpolations, corrections, and variations in handwriting would make them virtually unusable.

1

Not too long ago, when the first airplanes 9
were built, some people shook their heads and 18
said that man was not meant to fly. Human skill, 28
however, soon mastered the air, just as once it 38
had mastered the land and the sea. The first 47
small airplanes rose only a few feet in the air 56
and flew slowly over short distances. Modern 65
airplanes rise many thousands of feet and fly 74
around the world in hours. Some are supersonic— 84
they move faster than the speed of sound. The impossibility 96
of yesterday is the commonplace of today. 104

2

America began as a land of immigrants. Some 10
of them left the lands of their birth because there 20
they faced grinding poverty or starvation. Others were 31
driven out by war, the threat of war, or persecution. 42
Today, people from all over the world call America 51
their home. While they have left their native lands 62
behind, however, they have not forgotten their old 72
customs and traditions. 76
The customs and traditions of groups of 85
people are called their culture. The cultures of many 96
countries have mixed to make up America. You 105
might call America a multicultural society. It is 115
a land made up of many groups of people. 123

How to Set Line Spacing

Typewritten lines may be single-, double-, or triple-spaced. (*Note:* Throughout this text, in drills and exercises, these terms will be abbreviated *SS, DS,* and *TS.*) Some typewriters also provide for $1\frac{1}{2}$ and $2\frac{1}{2}$ line spacing.

The line space regulator (13) controls the vertical spacing between lines. When it is set at 1, the cylinder advances one line when the carriage is returned. This results in *no* blank lines between lines of type.

When the line space regulator is set at 2, there is *one* blank line between lines of type. When the line space regulator is set at 3, there are *two* blank lines between lines of type.

```
Single Spacing      Double Spacing      Triple Spacing
Single Spacing
Single Spacing      Double Spacing
                                        Triple Spacing
                    Double Spacing

                                        Triple Spacing
```

How to Set Side Margins

Typed material should be framed by white space called margins. To give typed material an attractive format, top, side, and bottom margins should be approximately even.

There are different types of mechanisms for setting side margins.

1. Spring-Set Margins To set the left margin, press or pull the left set key. Then move the carriage to the desired position. Release the set key. For the right margin, follow the same procedure using the set key on the right side of the carriage.

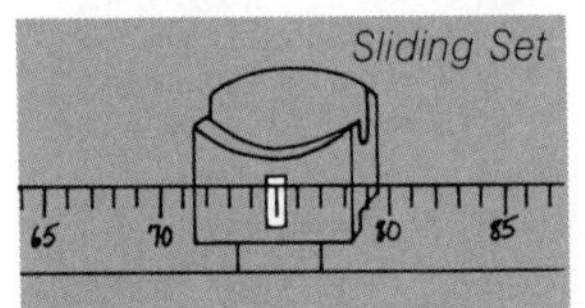

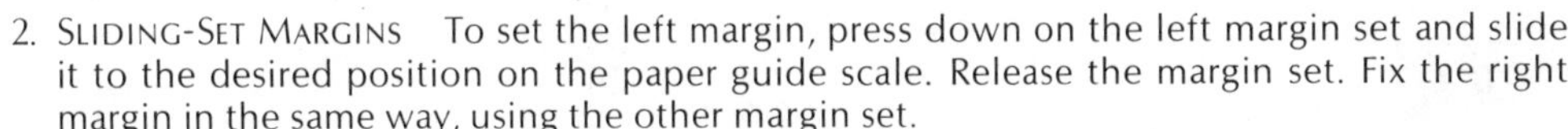

2. Sliding-Set Margins To set the left margin, press down on the left margin set and slide it to the desired position on the paper guide scale. Release the margin set. Fix the right margin in the same way, using the other margin set.

3. Key-Set Margins Some typewriters have a margin reset key (or keys) on the keyboard. On such machines, to set the left margin, first move the printing point to its leftmost position (the previously set left margin). Press the margin reset key (or, where there are two, the left margin reset key) and hold it down as you space or backspace to the position of the new left margin. Release the key. To set the right margin, move the printing point to its rightmost position. Press the appropriate reset key and hold it down as you space or backspace to the position of the new right margin. Release the key. Both margins are now set.

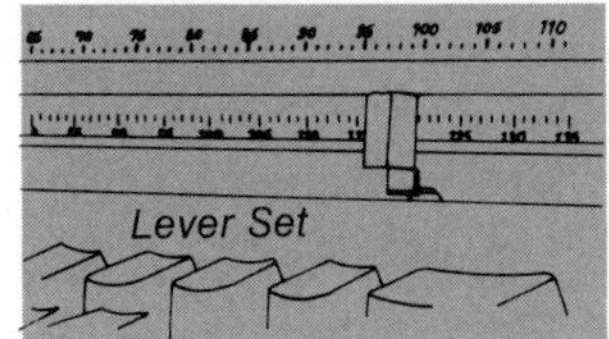

4. Lever-Set Margins First, as a precaution, move the printing point to the center of the margin-pitch scale. (Trying to force either margin set lever past the printing point will damage the machine.) To set the left margin, push in on the left margin set lever and slide it to the desired position. Release the lever. Follow the same procedure with the right margin set lever.

5

309 Words

Even though millions of telephone calls are 10
direct-dialed each day, almost everyone makes 19
some calls that cannot be made without help 27
from an operator. For instance, you may want 36
to reverse the charges on a long distance call, 46
or you may want to find out what a call will cost. 56
Perhaps you need a number that you cannot 64
find in the phone book. In each case, you will 73
need to dial the operator for help. The operator 83
may also be used to call the police or fire depart- 93
ment in an emergency, or to arrange a confer- 102
ence call which will allow three or more people 112
in different places to talk to each other at the 121
same time. 123

These and many other services are supplied 133
by two groups of operators—those at switch- 141
boards in the phone company's office and those 151
at private branch exchange (PBX) switchboards. 160

1 | 2 | 3 | 4 | 5 | 6 | 7 | 8 | 9 | 10 |

Both types of operators may insert and remove 169
plugs attached to cords, or they may make use 178
of keys to connect callers. In a small office, 187
a PBX operator usually receives all incoming 196
calls. In a large office, callers may be able to 206
dial individual offices directly, without going 215
through the central switchboard operator. 223

Telephone company operators are most 232
often called when a person needs their help in 241
order to place a call or to find a number. Most 250
central office operators deal most of the time 260
with long distance calls. They obtain the infor- 269
mation needed to complete the call, make the 278
required connections, and record the details of 288
each call for billing. Directory assistance opera- 298
tors help callers who need local or out-of-town 307
numbers. SI 1.52 309

1 | 2 | 3 | 4 | 5 | 6 | 7 | 8 | 9 | 10 |

6

312 Words

One of the world's most important economic 9
minerals is coal. The first users of coal of whom 19
we have any record were the Anglo-Saxons. They 29
burned lignite, a form of soft coal, as early as the 39
ninth century. In the late seventeenth century, 49
coal was discovered in the United States along 58
the Illinois River. Soon afterward a bed was 67
found near Richmond, Virginia, but mining did 76
not start there until fifty years later. By the mid- 87
nineteenth century, coal was being mined on a 96
scale so great that it was of major importance 105
in shaping the industrial life of our nation. Among 115
its largest users were the railroads that were 124
beginning to crisscross the land. 131

Coal is of vegetable origin. It forms when the 141
vegetable matter decomposes and is subjected to 150
great water pressure, forcing it to give off gases. 161

1 | 2 | 3 | 4 | 5 | 6 | 7 | 8 | 9 | 10 |

This process, when carried on for thousands of 170
centuries, leaves nothing but pure carbon. 179

There are two principal kinds of coal: hard 188
coal or anthracite, and soft coal or bituminous. 198
There are also grades of coal softer than bitu- 207
minous. Anthracite was formed under greater 216
pressure than bituminous, and, thus, it has more 226
carbon and less moisture. It is also generally 235
found deeper in the earth. Supplies of anthracite 245
are much scarcer than soft coals; bituminous is 255
the most plentiful of all. 260

Anthracite is used mainly for home heating, 269
since it produces almost no smoke when it burns. 279
Bituminous is used for heating, too. More im- 288
portant, however, it can be used for fuel in 297
power plants that generate electricity from 306
steam—thus conserving our oil. SI 1.53 312

1 | 2 | 3 | 4 | 5 | 6 | 7 | 8 | 9 | 10 |

SECTION ONE

Introduction to the Keyboard

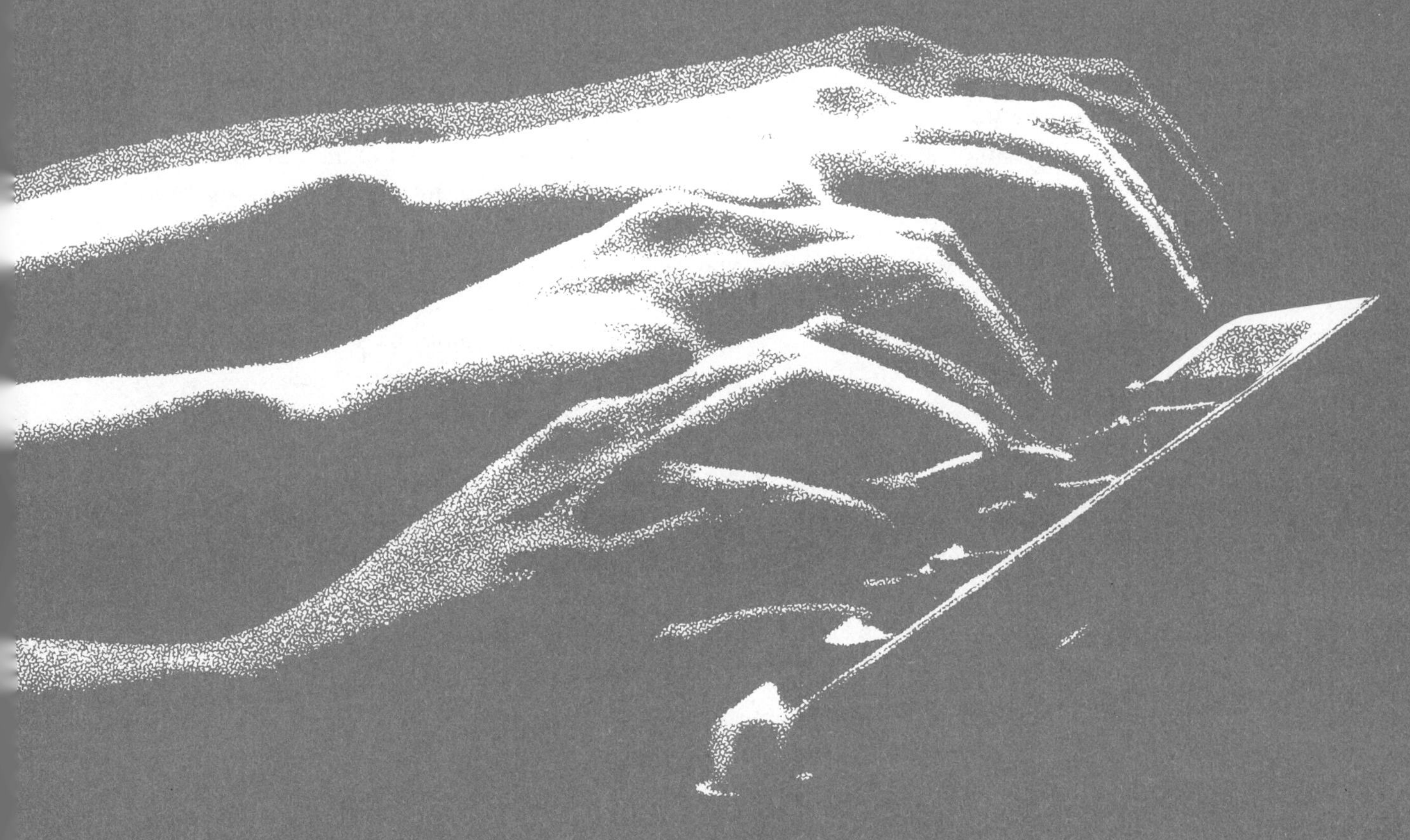

3

300 Words

Most visitors to New York City inform us 9
that they would not like to make it their perma- 19
nent dwelling place. Some of them, coming from 28
small towns with tree-shaded houses set back 37
from the street on green lawns, find the city 46
too crowded. Others become overwhelmed by its 55
huge size. Most of them have a strong attach- 64
ment to the places in which they live. Nonetheless, 75
New Yorkers love their city. 80

New York, with its varied social and business 90
life, is a symbol of America. The city is so enor- 100
mous that the average person does not appreciate 110
all its many attractions. Some find their affec- 120
tions stirred by Greenwich Village. Others enjoy 130
the activity of the Great White Way, the center 139
of the theatrical world. Some people prefer the 149
wide expanse of Park Avenue. Some enjoy the 157

1 | 2 | 3 | 4 | 5 | 6 | 7 | 8 | 9 | 10 |

quiet and beauty of Central Park. Some are moved 167
by the many activities of the harbor, with its 176
stately vessels and its busy tugboats. Others are 186
comfortable in the financial district. Still others 197
are attracted to the exclusive shops, with their 206
dazzling window displays. 211

Seen from a height in the darkness of a 220
velvety summer night, New York is a city of 229
magic. The vista enjoyed from a window high 238
above Manhattan is breathtaking. Decked with 247
patterns of glittering light, the giant city, bounded 257
by two mighty rivers, lies quiet and content, all 267
its shabbiness hidden in a violet haze, all its 277
noise thinned to a faint murmur. Here and 285
there, only moving lights suggest the ceaseless 295
activity throbbing below. SI 1.49 300

1 | 2 | 3 | 4 | 5 | 6 | 7 | 8 | 9 | 10 |

Selections 4–6, SI Range 1.50–1.60

4

328 Words

All of us expect Mother Earth to support us, 10
to provide us with food and drink, and to supply 19
us with the other materials we require. We are 29
meeting our needs by using not only the pro- 38
ductivity of the earth but also its great surplus 47
of capital that has been accumulated during past 57
ages. Generation after generation, this capital 67
becomes less, as we consume it for our needs. 76

We can reasonably expect the productivity 85
of Mother Earth to continue as long as human 94
beings exist. If we take care of the land, it will 104
always provide us with the food necessary for 113
life. But the land may be overworked to such 122
an extent that it loses its fertility. We must allow 133
it to rest for a while so that its fruitfulness will 143
be restored, and we must develop better methods 152
of farming so that the land will not be depleted. 162

The needs of primitive people were few. 171

1 | 2 | 3 | 4 | 5 | 6 | 7 | 8 | 9 | 10 |

They gathered food from the land and the waters. 181
Nature replaced whatever they consumed. Even- 190
tually, however, people began to find the capital 200
that the earth contained. In the course of time, 209
iron was discovered; then coal, oil, and other 219
materials. People learned how to use these to 228
develop greater comfort and more safety for 236
themselves. More and more uses were rapidly 245
found for the capital resources of the earth. 254

There is, however, one aspect of this story 264
that demands serious attention. We are using 273
up the capital that nature took many millions 282
of years to build. We can grow more food, but 291
we cannot replace iron, coal, or oil. We shall 300
have to manufacture substitutes for many nat- 309
ural products that cannot be replaced and at the 319
same time reduce our reliance on such products. 328

SI 1.51

1 | 2 | 3 | 4 | 5 | 6 | 7 | 8 | 9 | 10 |

The standard typewriter has what is commonly called a "qwerty" keyboard. The name comes from the first six characters on the top row of alpha (or alphabetic) keys.

The lessons in this section will teach you how to manipulate a qwerty keyboard without looking at your fingers. In other words, you will learn to keyboard by touch. This is a valuable skill, applicable not only to typewriters but to any machine that enters data through a keyboard (including a computer).

PREPARING TO KEYBOARD

Regardless of the type of equipment on which you are learning, there are certain procedures you should observe before beginning any lesson.

Work Station Arrangement

1. Clear away all books and materials not needed for typing class.
2. Position your book upright, at a comfortable reading angle. If you are using a manual typewriter, place the book at your right so that your view is not obstructed when you return the carriage. With all other types of machines (electric, electronic, or microcomputer), you may place your book on the side that is most comfortable for you.
3. Arrange clean typing paper and other supplies on the other side of the machine.

Machine Adjustments

1. Ribbon indicator on blue or black
2. Line space regulator on 1 for single spacing
3. Paper guide set at 0
4. Margins set for a 40-space line as follows:
   a. On machines with elite type, set margins at 30 and 75. (Elite type allows for the typing of 12 characters per horizontal inch.)
   b. On machines with pica type, set margins at 22 and 67. (Pica type allows for the typing of 10 characters per horizontal inch.)

Position for Typing

POSTURE Sit about eight inches from the typewriter with your feet on the floor and your body bent *slightly* forward.

FINGERS AND THUMBS Curve your fingers, with the tips of the left hand on the *A S D F* keys, and those of the right hand on the *J K L ;* keys. These eight keys are called the **home** keys. The fingers will be referred to by the home keys on which they rest; for example, *A* finger, *S* finger, *L* finger, *Semi* (semicolon) finger, and so on. Keep both thumbs just above the space bar at the bottom of the keyboard.

ARMS, ELBOWS, WRISTS Keep the upper arms and elbows near the body. The forearms and the hands should be parallel to the slant of the keyboard. Do not arch the wrists, but do not let them touch the machine either.

OVER 300 WORDS

The following timed writings are arranged in two groups according to the syllabic intensities of the individual selections.

Selections 1–3, SI Range 1.36–1.50

1

306 Words

Many of the natives of the South Sea Islands 10
still live as primitive people must have lived. 19
They have no idea of personal ownership of 28
property; everything they have is shared. They 37
have no houses and spend their days and nights 46
in the open. One interesting fact about them is 56
that until very recently, they had never seen any 66
form of written language. One can imagine how 75
surprised they were when they first encountered 84
visitors to their islands who could read and 93
write. 94

A health officer relates the following experi- 104
ence. One afternoon, as he was typing in his 113
room, several of the islanders entered. They came 123
nearer and nearer to him, finally touching the 133
paper and the typewriter. The sudden appear- 142
ance of the tiny black characters on the piece 151
of white paper was something entirely unknown 160
to them and beyond their understanding. Even- 169
tually, he had to stop working, clear an area 178
around the typewriter, and show them what he 187
was doing. 189

With the assistance of a boy who understood 198
a little English, he explained that writing is like 209
talking. The marks on the paper were words. But 218
nobody understood what he was attempting to 227
say. He then tried to demonstrate to his listeners 237
more clearly what he meant. He wrote a note to 247
an officer on his ship requesting him to give a 256
blanket to the boy he sent with the message. 265
After the boy had left, he told the islanders what 275
he had written. The boy came back shortly with 284
the blanket. The people were amazed. They called 294
the signs talk marks and wanted to learn how to 304
make them. SI 1.45 306

1 | 2 | 3 | 4 | 5 | 6 | 7 | 8 | 9 | 10 |

1 | 2 | 3 | 4 | 5 | 6 | 7 | 8 | 9 | 10 |

2

300 Words

Over a century ago, a game known as town- 9
ball, the ancestor of baseball, was very popular 19
in New England. It was played on a square field. 29
At each corner of the field was a post that was 38
used as a base. To win, a team had to make one 47
hundred runs. As years passed, the game was 56
modified until it assumed the form that we rec- 66
ognize as baseball. 69

During the Civil War, the soldiers in camp 79
found recreation in playing baseball. At the con- 89
clusion of the fighting, when the soldiers returned 99
to their homes in every area of the United States, 109
they carried the game with them, until it became 119
a national sport. At first, many kinds of teams 128
competed; then clubs were organized; still later, 138
the clubs were combined into the leagues of the 147
present day. 150

There are two major leagues and several 159
minor leagues. The clubs of the major leagues, 168
the National and the American, compete in sched- 178
uled games from April until October. The winning 187
clubs in these leagues then compete in the final 197
series of games for the national championship. 206

The leagues play according to rules estab- 216
lished by a national association, the head of which 226
is the national commissioner of baseball. He has 236
the authority to issue final decisions about any 245
matter in dispute. 249

Interest in baseball has spread from the 258
United States to many other areas in the world. 267
The game is now enjoyed in almost every coun- 276
try. Fans in other countries follow with intense 286
interest the games played by the two major leagues 296
in the United States. SI 1.47 300

1 | 2 | 3 | 4 | 5 | 6 | 7 | 8 | 9 | 10 |

1 | 2 | 3 | 4 | 5 | 6 | 7 | 8 | 9 | 10 |

GENERAL TECHNIQUES

As you do your first keyboarding exercises, try to keep the following points in mind.

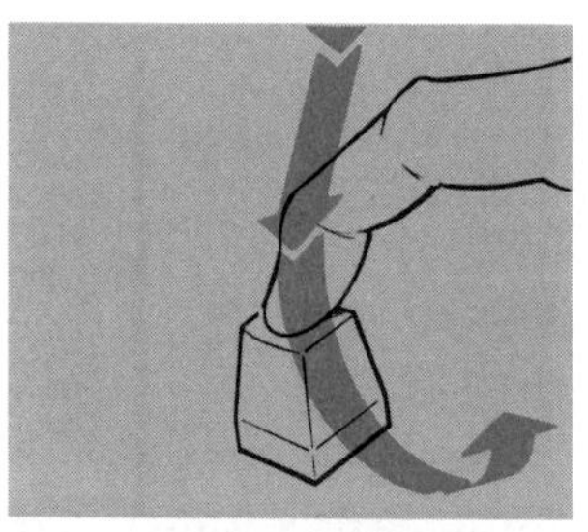

Striking the Keys

1. Hit each key sharply, exactly in the center, and release immediately. Do not push the key or linger on it.
2. Strike keys evenly, with a set rhythm and the same amount of force.
3. Keep your fingers curved.
4. Move your hands and arms as little as possible. Almost all movement should be in your fingers.

Striking the Space Bar

While keeping your fingers on the home keys, strike the space bar sharply with your right thumb. Make it bounce off the bar.

Returning

MANUAL RETURN

1. Keeping your eyes on the printed copy, raise your left hand, palm down and fingers close together, to the carriage return lever.
2. Using your index finger against the lever, move the carriage quickly to the beginning of the next line.
3. Immediately return your left hand to its position on the home keys.

ELECTRIC RETURN

1. Extend your *Semi* finger to the return key.
2. Tap the key lightly.
3. Return your finger to its home position.

Putting It All Together

You are now ready for a trial run. Insert a sheet of paper into the typewriter and get ready to type the lines shown at the bottom of the page.

1. Check your position and posture.
2. Place your fingertips on the home keys as shown in the diagram at the left.
3. Relax, and don't worry about making errors.

Type each line as it appears below. See, say, and stroke each letter. Try not to look at the keyboard unless you lose your home key position.

```
fff jjj fff jjj ff jj fj jf fjf fjf jff      Return
ddd kkk ddd kkk dd kk dk kd kdk kdk kdd      Return twice

sss lll sss lll ss ll sl ls lsl lsl lss      Return
aaa ;;; aaa ;;; aa ;; a; ;a ;a; ;a; ;aa      Return twice

fdsa jkl; fdsa jkl; fdsa jkl; fdsa jkl;      Return
asdf ;lkj asdf ;lkj asdf ;lkj asdf ;lkj      Return twice
```

Turn the page and begin the practice lines for Unit 1.

34

203 Words

Good speech is a mark of good training and 9
good manners. It stamps the speaker as one 18
qualified to deal intelligently with persons and 28
with situations. 31

If you would be understood by others, you 40
should be careful of your speech. You should 49
be sure that the person you are speaking to 58
understands what you are saying. Your words 66
should be spoken very distinctly. Mumbled 75
words convey little meaning to the hearer, and 84
they leave a bad impression, too. 91

There are many business offices where thou- 100
sands of dollars have been spent for modern 109
furniture, equipment, and lighting fixtures in 118
order to impress visitors favorably. All this ex- 128
penditure of money may be wasted if a recep- 137
tionist stationed in such a costly setting fails to 147
make a favorable impression on a caller. The 156
receptionist, or any other employee in charge 165
of the outer office, should have good manners 174
and good speech. This means not only choosing 183
words carefully, but pronouncing them clearly 192
and distinctly, in a tone that is cordial and 201
courteous. SI 1.57 203

1 | 2 | 3 | 4 | 5 | 6 | 7 | 8 | 9 | 10 |

35

289 Words

Advertising appeals are planned around two key 10
considerations. The first is demographics, the de- 20
tailed analysis of a product's market to determine 30
who the potential buyers are. The second is the 40
sales method to be used. Options here include 49
direct retail sales to the public, catalogue and 59
mail-order selling, and telephone sales. 67

Good advertisements are designed to fit the 76
particular class of readers for whom they are 85
intended. When a producer advertises a product, 95
the prospective buyer could be a wholesaler, a 104
retailer, or a consumer. The appeal in each case 114
would be different. A circular letter sent to a 124
retailer might emphasize the advantage of taking 133
a sales agency for the goods. It might offer to help 144
create a demand by preparing window displays 153
or by supplying free samples to customers. On 162
the other hand, an advertisement to a consumer 171
might show how a product can be used, what its 180
qualities are, and where it can be obtained. 189

Good advertisements vary also according to 198
sales methods used. For example, when a drug 207
manufacturer advertises a patent medicine to 216
create a demand for it at the drugstore, the name 226
of the remedy is brought repeatedly before the 235
public. If, on the other hand, an advertiser wants 245
to persuade people to buy a product by mail, 254
the advertisement stresses prompt action. In the 264
former case, the object is to make the name of 273
the product well known; in the latter case, it is to 284
secure an immediate sale. SI 1.60 289

1 | 2 | 3 | 4 | 5 | 6 | 7 | 8 | 9 | 10 |

36

223 Words

In normal times, about one out of every 9
seven retail storekeepers in the United States 18
goes out of business each year. What are the 27
causes of failure among retailers? Some of them 37
are insufficient capital, poor markets, too much 46
optimism, and a lack of business experience and 56
business ability. Although business people who 65
fail in years of depression often attribute their 75
failure to conditions in general, such depressions 85
are not usually the chief cause. 91

A person who invests a fair amount of his 100
or her own capital in a business has a much bet- 110
ter chance of surviving than one who begins with 120
a large proportion of borrowed capital. There is 129
danger in borrowing too much. An analysis of 138
failures in retail stores shows a definite relation- 149
ship between the lifespan of a retail store and 158
the amount of capital invested by the owner. 167
From this evidence, it is safe to say that the owner 177
should invest his or her own funds to the extent 187
of at least 50 percent of the required capital. 196
However, the business will probably be on a 205
sounder financial footing if the owner invests 214
at least 75 percent of the funds required. SI 1.59 223

1 | 2 | 3 | 4 | 5 | 6 | 7 | 8 | 9 | 10 |

Unit 1

Line spacing: single
Line length: 40
Type each line as shown.
Double-space after each pair of lines.

Home Key Location

Check your typing position.

1 fff jjj fff jjj fff jjj fjf jfj fjj ffj
2 fff jjj fff jjj fff jjj fjf jfj fjj ffj

Keep your fingers curved—tips resting lightly on the home keys.

3 ddd kkk ddd kkk ddd kkk dkd kdk dkk ddk
4 ddd kkk ddd kkk ddd kkk dkd kdk dkk ddk

5 sss lll sss lll sss lll sls lsl sll ssl
6 sss lll sss lll sss lll sls lsl sll ssl

Strike the keys sharply and release them quickly.

7 aaa ;;; aaa ;;; aaa ;;; a;a ;a; a;; aa;
8 aaa ;;; aaa ;;; aaa ;;; a;a ;a; a;; aa;

9 asdf ;lkj asdf ;lkj asdf ;lkj asdf ;lkj
10 asdf ;lkj asdf ;lkj asdf ;lkj asdf ;lkj

Word and Phrase Practice

Eyes on copy!

11 as ask; as ask; all all all; sad sad sad
12 as ask; as ask; all all all; sad sad sad

13 fad fad fad; lad lad lad; fall fall fall
14 fad fad fad; lad lad lad; fall fall fall

15 add add add; dad dad dad; asks asks asks
16 add add add; dad dad dad; asks asks asks

17 ask dad lad; ask dad lad; alas lass alas
18 ask dad lad; ask dad lad; alas lass alas

Can't remember the location of a key? Use the keyboard chart.

19 ask a lad; all lads add; a fad; a flask;
20 a salad; as dad asks; a lad falls; alas;

31

250 Words

Shipping and receiving clerks keep track of 10
the goods transferred from place to place by 18
business firms. Before shipments are sent out 28
from a company, shipping clerks check to be 36
sure that the orders have been correctly filled. 46
They prepare the shipping forms, look up freight 55
and postal rates, record the weight and cost of 65
each shipment, and check to see that it is prop- 74
erly addressed. They also keep records of the 84
date and other details about each shipment. 92
Sometimes shipping clerks requisition mer- 101
chandise from the firm's stockroom, wrap and 109
pack the shipment, and direct its loading onto 119
company trucks. 122

Receiving clerks do similar work when ship- 131
ments reach their companies. They find out 140
whether their firm's orders have been correctly 149
filled by checking incoming shipments against 158
the original orders and the accompanying bills 167
of lading or invoices. They also check to see 177
whether the merchandise in each shipment has 185
arrived in good condition. Receiving clerks re- 195
cord all incoming shipments and do the clerical 204
work required for damaged and lost shipments. 213
Routing shipments—to the proper departments 222
of the company, to sections of the warehouse, 231
or to the stockroom—also may be part of their 240
regular duties, especially in smaller companies. 250

SI 1.53

1 | 2 | 3 | 4 | 5 | 6 | 7 | 8 | 9 | 10

32

211 Words

Every telephone user should be familiar 9
with the information provided in the front pages 18
of the telephone directory. These pages give 27
valuable pointers on practically every kind of 37
telephone service. They tell, for instance, how 46
to make local and long-distance calls; what the 56
rates are to many points; how to make emergency 65
calls; and how to call the telephone company 74
regarding repairs, problems in service, and busi- 84
ness matters. These pages also explain how to 93
use the directory itself. 98

You should always look first in the directory 108
for correct telephone numbers. If you cannot 117
find the desired number, you may then dial di- 126
rectory assistance according to the directions 135
given on the first page of the directory. You will 145
find it a great timesaver to keep at hand a special 156
list of the numbers that you frequently call. A 165
list of this kind will be an easy reference and 175
will prevent the confusion and delay that may 184
be caused if you rely on your memory. On re- 193
quest, your local telephone company will supply 202
you with a booklet in which to keep this list. 211

SI 1.57

1 | 2 | 3 | 4 | 5 | 6 | 7 | 8 | 9 | 10

33

226 Words

In most large organizations—and in many 9
small ones—there are receptionists to greet peo- 19
ple and provide them with information. It is the 29
receptionist's job to determine the nature of each 39
caller's business. The receptionist then sends the 49
caller to the proper office, or else contacts that 59
office by telephone to arrange for an appoint- 68
ment. In different types of organizations, recep- 78
tionists have somewhat different duties. In a 87
hospital clinic, the receptionist must direct each 97
patient to the proper waiting room; in a beauty 107
shop, he or she must make an appointment or 115
accompany the customer to the operator's booth; 125
and in a large defense plant, it may be part of 134
the receptionist's job to provide the caller with 144
an identification card and an escort to the proper 154
office. 155

Some receptionists also keep records show- 165
ing the name of each caller, the reason for the 174
visit, the time, and the person to whom the caller 184
was referred. 187

If receptionists have some time when they 196
are not occupied with callers, they often handle 205
other office tasks. They may receive and route 215
telephone calls, sort and open mail, file, or keep 225
books. SI 1.56 226

1 | 2 | 3 | 4 | 5 | 6 | 7 | 8 | 9 | 10

Unit 2

Line spacing: single
Line length: 40
Type each line twice.
Double-space after each pair of lines.

Warmup

Every time you *think* where the key is, you learn its location better.

1 fff jjj ddd kkk sss lll aaa ;;; fff jjj;
2 as ask all sad fad lad dad fall add alas
3 asks a lad; a sad lass; dad falls; flask

New Key Location

***D* finger** 

Return finger to home position after striking **e**.

4 ded ded led led see see fed fed fee fee
5 sell sell deal deal seek seek jell jell
6 seal seal lake lake safe safe fake fake

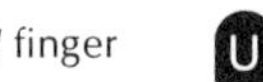

***J* finger** U

Return finger to home position after striking **u**.

7 juj juj sue sue due due use use dud dud
8 dull dull full full suds suds used used
9 dusk dusk fuse fuse dual dual juke juke

Word and Phrase Practice

10 sea sea elk elk elf elf use use due dues
11 self self duel duel fell fell jell jells
12 fall due; sue us; used less; sell seeds;
13 a deal; led us; dusk falls; a sleek elk;

Supplementary Practice

If you finish early, keyboard lines 14–18. Repeat if time permits.

14 jade jade seas seas fade fade fuel fuels
15 skull skull deaf deaf sulk sulk eel eels
16 sell a desk; asks us; used a jade flask;
17 a safe deal; a dead leaf; use less fuel;
18 fell due; a deaf lass; sell a used desk;

28

230 Words

Have you considered the advantages of 8
wearing contact lenses? Millions who must use 18
corrective lenses are now wearing them instead 27
of glasses. 29

Contact lenses are thin, curved, plastic discs, 39
smaller than a dime, that are worn under the eye- 49
lids. They cause no discomfort once the wearer 59
becomes accustomed to them—and most people 67
become adjusted to them quickly. The new "soft" 77
contact lenses take even less time to become 86
adjusted to than the "hard" lenses. 93

Contact lenses are not visible to others; so 102
people who feel self-conscious wearing glasses 112
feel more at ease with the lenses. In some types 121
of work where wearing glasses is a source of 130
danger, contact lenses eliminate the hazard. 139
Athletes also use contact lenses to avoid possible 149
injury from glasses. And people who have had 158
cataracts removed from their eyes see much bet- 167
ter with the lenses than with glasses. 175

Contact lenses are durable, and they do not 185
harm the eyes. They do not "steam up" when the 194
temperature turns from cold to warm, as glasses 203
do. Frequent changes in prescription are gener- 213
ally not necessary; but if vision does change, 222
the lenses in use can often be modified. SI 1.50 230

1 | 2 | 3 | 4 | 5 | 6 | 7 | 8 | 9 | 10 |

29

235 Words

In modern building construction, air en- 9
gineering has become very important. Most large 19
buildings and shops, as well as many homes, 27
now have some form of air control. The desire 36
for comfort and the effect that the quality of the 46
air has on some products account for the great 56
growth in methods of air control. 62

Many materials must be kept at a certain 71
temperature—articles in storage, for instance, 81
such as butter or eggs or fruit. In other cases, a 91
certain temperature must be maintained during 100
the manufacturing process as, for instance, dur- 109
ing the cooling process in the making of chocolate 119
candy bars. 122

A second reason for the great growth in air 131
conditioning is the human factor. Better air 140
means better health for workers. Owners of 149
stores have found that money spent on installing 159
a system of air conditioning is well spent, for it 169
leads to more trade; customers who are comfort- 178
able in a store spend a longer time there and 187
buy more goods. 190

Of late, new designs for buildings are being 200
used that take advantage of natural air flow and 209
temperature gradations. In this way, we are 218
learning to rely less on powered systems of air 228
conditioning that use too much energy. SI 1.50 235

1 | 2 | 3 | 4 | 5 | 6 | 7 | 8 | 9 | 10 |

Selections 30–36, SI Range 1.51–1.60

30

217 Words

In small firms, stock clerks may do the same 10
jobs as receiving clerks, shipping clerks, and in- 20
ventory clerks; but in large firms, stock clerks may 30
be responsible for only one of these functions. 40

The duties of stock clerks also depend on the 50
products they handle. For example, stock clerks 59
working with foods or pharmaceuticals must main- 69
tain proper temperature and humidity conditions. 78
Stock clerks responsible for large construction 88
items may be required to do a lot of walking 97
and climbing to keep track of the condition and 106
quantity of that stock. 111

Stock clerks usually receive and unpack in- 120
coming goods and check the items for quality 129
and quantity. They sometimes make minor re- 138
pairs or adjustments. They also report spoiled 147
or damaged goods and process any papers 155
needed for obtaining replacements or credit. 164

Stock clerks must always keep a record of 173
what enters and leaves the stockroom. They may 182
prepare inventory reports to show what stock is 192
on hand. In addition, stock clerks sometimes 201
order supplies; and they may label, pack, crate, 210
and address goods for delivery. SI 1.51 217

1 | 2 | 3 | 4 | 5 | 6 | 7 | 8 | 9 | 10 |

Unit 3

Line spacing: single
Line length: 40
Type each line twice.
Double-space after each pair of lines.

Warmup

See, say, and stroke each key.

1 ded ded juj juj ded ded juj juj ded jujj
2 led led use use due due sue sue see sees
3 fall due; fed elk; asks us; used a fuse;

New Key Location

F finger 

Return finger to home position after striking **r**.

4 frf frf jar jar are are far far red red
5 dark dark real real jars jars rule rule
6 erase ruler dresses refuse dread reader

K finger 

Return finger to home position after striking **i**.

7 kik kik rid rid lid lid kid kid did did
8 rail rail fill fill jail jail life life
9 silk kill ails ride fail like slid side
10 lid file risk jeer refill residue field

Word and Phrase Practice

Move your hands and arms as little as possible.

11 ill ill sir sir fur fur air air err err;
12 jerk jerk fear fear; side side sale sale
13 fell ill; real full; dark reds; liked us
14 lead us; desk file; a risk; all did less
15 a real sale; fearful air raids; deaf ear

Supplementary Practice

Sometimes, on a typebar machine, the keys will jam. This occurs when you strike a key before the preceding one has been released. To avoid jammed keys, use a quick release. Don't press the keys; snap them!

16 red red air air rid rid fir fir lie lard
17 slur skid sail kiss free sulk deaf skull
18 is rude; real jade; all rules; dull life
19 a deed; is filed; less skill; fill a jar
20 a full skid; refuse all risks; red sails

25

214 Words

You must love justice, and demand it for all, 10
if you would be a true American. You must love 19
equality, and be willing to grant it to all, if you 30
would be a true American. You must love free- 39
dom, not only for yourself, but freedom for all, 48
if you would be a true American. 55

You must be willing to recognize talent, and 65
to help to give it an opportunity to develop, if 74
you would be a true American; not merely the 83
talent that your children and mine may chance 92
to possess, but also the talent of the humblest 101
among us. 103

As a true American, you must practice toler- 113
ance, tolerance of others' religious convictions, 123
tolerance of their social and economic convic- 132
tions, tolerance of their political convictions. You 143
are not a true American, whether you are native- 152
born or foreign-born, if you would deny another 162
the rights that you demand for yourself. 170

As a true American, you must be willing to 179
share—no, demand to share—all the rights and 188
privileges that this free country gives you. You 198
ask them not only for yourself and for your 207
family, but for everyone, everywhere. SI 1.49 214

1 | 2 | 3 | 4 | 5 | 6 | 7 | 8 | 9 | 10

26

213 Words

Nylon is produced, by means of a series of 9
chemical changes, from several natural mate- 18
rials: coal, air, water, petroleum, agricultural 29
by-products, and natural gas. From these can be 38
spun strands of yarn finer than a hair. Nylon first 48
became popular for making the sheerest of hose, 58
since it is as elastic and strong as it is fine. 67

Thousands of useful articles have been made 77
from this synthetic, which was unknown not so 86
long ago, but which has since swept the world. 95
Fabrics, fishing lines, cords for stringing beads, 105
sewing thread, bristles for brushes of all kinds, 115
string for tennis rackets, tents, watch bands, pen 125
tips, tires, rugs, bearings, and gears are just a very 136
few of them. Many beautiful products, such as 145
lace, are also manufactured from nylon. 153

Progressive manufacturers are still experi- 162
menting with nylon and finding many new appli- 171
cations for it. The public continues to be amazed 181
at the ever-increasing number of uses to which 191
it is being put. And there are still so many unex- 201
plored fields where nylon may yet prove to be of 210
great value. SI 1.50 213

1 | 2 | 3 | 4 | 5 | 6 | 7 | 8 | 9 | 10

27

278 Words

On his second voyage to America, Columbus 9
found native boys playing games with high- 18
bouncing balls that were made of a strange sub- 27
stance. This substance was rubber. He took a 36
few of these curios back to Spain with him and 45
presented them to the queen. During the next 54
three centuries, explorers brought back to Europe 64
various rubber articles made by the American 73
Indians, including capes, hats, shoes, bowls, 82
and bottles. Traders returned home with small 91
amounts of crude rubber. 96

Many efforts were made during those early 105
years to adapt rubber to the needs of the civilized 115
world. It is believed, however, that the discovery 126
of the method on which present-day rubber manu- 135
facture is based was the result of a happy 143
accident. 145

Charles Goodyear, a poor inventor, had been 155
experimenting with rubber for years. The story 164
goes that he went to bed one evening, forgetting 174
to remove from contact with a hot stove a sample 183
of rubber-sulfur compound that he had smeared 192
on a piece of cloth. In the morning, he found 202
this sample charred like leather and marvelously 211
changed. It was no longer sticky, but dry and 220
firm. Heat or cold no longer affected it. Its 230
strength had increased. Goodyear found that, 239
just by changing the proportion of sulfur in the 248
mixture, he could make a substance as flexible 258
or as hard as he desired. This was the beginning 267
of the process that later came to be known as 276
vulcanization. SI 1.48 278

1 | 2 | 3 | 4 | 5 | 6 | 7 | 8 | 9 | 10

Unit 4

Line spacing: single
Line length: 40
Type each line twice.
Double-space after each pair of lines.

Warmup

Return quickly without looking up at the end of each line.

1 frf juj ded kik ark ark lie lie due due
2 far far jar jar did did rid rid ill ill
3 is like; did less; is killed; real sale

New Key Location

F finger 

Return finger to home position after striking **t**.

4 ftf ftf sat sat tea tea lit lit its its
5 just just last last jest jest rate rate
6 take take feet feet date date fret fret

 finger 

Return finger to home position after striking **h**.

7 jhj jhj had had his his hit hit her her
8 this this hurt hurt shut shut heat heat
9 that that halt halt half half fish fish
10 thus thus hark hark dish dish here here

Word and Phrase Practice

Don't hump your wrists. Keep them low but not touching the frame of the machine.

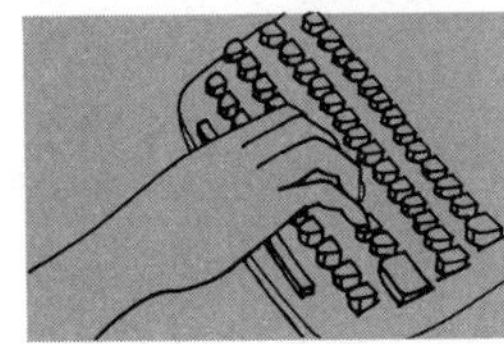

11 sets sets hill hill fret fret task tasks
12 talk talk shirt shirts faith faith three
13 dread shark teeth that jut; half a shelf
14 he hurried; just tell her; fast as usual

Supplementary Practice

15 hid hid jut jutted let let she the these
16 tide tide just just task tasks shut shut
17 seated at the theater; red thread skirts
18 safer at last; a head taller; three feet

22

260 Words

If you are a typist today, you may not fully 10
realize how fortunate you are to have a machine 19
that is a masterpiece of mechanical efficiency. 29
Your typewriter is as different from the first 38
writing machine as the streamlined locomotive 47
is from the first "iron horse." 53

You would find your daily tasks much harder 63
if you had to do your work on one of the early 72
writing machines. One model looked like a toy 81
piano. It turned out letters after a fashion, but the 92
operator broke no speed records. Even stranger 101
was a later model that was worked with one 110
thumb and printed words letter by letter on a 119
long, narrow roll of paper tape. 125

Before 1874, when the first practical type- 135
writer was put on the market in this country, 144
hundreds of patents were issued. Many inventors 153
played with the idea of a machine that would 162
replace writing by hand. The first record of a 171
writing machine is found in the files of the British 182
Patent Office in London. It briefly mentions a 191
device made early in the eighteenth century, but 201
no model has been found. 206

Several thousand patents have been issued 215
by the U.S. Patent Office to inventors who helped 225
speed the day of the modern typewriter. And the 234
end is not yet in sight. Manufacturers are con- 244
stantly trying to turn out machines that will make 254
the job of typing still simpler. SI 1.46 260

1 | 2 | 3 | 4 | 5 | 6 | 7 | 8 | 9 | 10 |

23

217 Words

We like to think that we can make new 8
things. The simple truth, however, is that we 18
actually can make nothing; we just change the 27
forms of materials that already exist. Still, we 36
can do many amazing things by making those 45
changes. 46

For instance, a sculptor takes marble from a 56
quarry and shapes it into a beautiful statue. A 66
farmer places seeds in the ground to grow the 75
plants needed for food. A shipbuilder puts to- 84
gether wood and metal to build ships that sail 93
the high seas. A well driller digs deep into the 103
earth and removes oil millions of years old to 112
run machines and heat buildings. An engineer 121
changes the course of a river in order to store 131
drinking water, irrigate farmlands, and turn 140
waterpower into the electricity needed to run 149
factories. An inventor develops instruments that 158
transmit sounds and pictures through the air 167
around the world. 171

We do not possess the magic of making 179
something from nothing, but we can combine 187
and use in different ways the materials drawn 196
from the earth, the air, and the sea. In so doing, 207
we accomplish wonders that are almost beyond 215
belief. SI 1.46 217

1 | 2 | 3 | 4 | 5 | 6 | 7 | 8 | 9 | 10 |

24

211 Words

The successful operation of a business re- 9
quires accurate and up-to-date records of its 18
financial affairs. Some say that they cannot af- 28
ford the time to bother with records. This is a 38
mistaken idea. It is not shared by the bank and 47
the tax collector, and they have the power to 56
enforce their ideas—the bank when you need 65
a loan, and the tax collector when your income 74
tax figures are checked. Poor accounting can 83
prove to be costly. 87

Moreover, records must be kept and used in 96
the interest of good business management. For 106
instance, records show whether or not a business 115
is yielding a profit, whether there are ample 124
funds for new equipment, and whether credit 133
sales should be reduced or expanded. Even for 142
the simplest business, a record is needed of its 152
cash receipts and payments, its purchases on 160
credit, and its sales to charge customers. 169

The account books may be very simple, 177
but the records must be adequate to meet the 186
owner's needs in trading with creditors and cus- 196
tomers, in dealing with the bank, and in prepar- 205
ing reports to the government. SI 1.49 211

1 | 2 | 3 | 4 | 5 | 6 | 7 | 8 | 9 | 10 |

REVIEW

Unit 5

Line spacing: single
Line length: 40
Type each line twice.
Double-space after each pair of lines.

Warmup

Type evenly and calmly.

1 eat eat see see did did his his red red
2 tree tree fail fail that that just just
3 silk silk lake lake read read hill hill

Word Practice

Strike and release keys in one motion.
Make quick, sharp strokes.

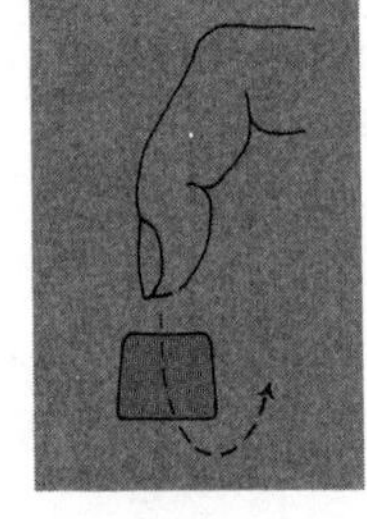

4 did did rid rid jar jar far far lid lid
5 kid kid ill ill red red use use all all
6 led led are are due due sat sat had had
7 his his hit hit has has her her ate ate
8 she she the the hut hut jut jut jet jet
9 rail rail fill fill jail jail kill kill
10 dark dark risk risk fell fell real real
11 shriek fresher rather faith three heard

Phrase Practice

Too many errors?

Try the following:
- Concentrate on each reach.
- Use the keyboard chart when in doubt.
- Practice, practice, practice.

12 red silk; that tall tree; sell this desk
13 fried fish; a fast jet; read that letter
14 just rule; these hard tests; their third

Supplementary Practice

15 life life like like sure sure jell jells
16 sets sets half half hill hill tall tall;
17 desk desk head head left left fast fast;
18 just heard that she hid her head at last

Typing Skill Checkup

Goal: To type lines 19–20 (70 strokes) in 1 minute. Eyes on copy. Two or more tries.

19 he fled just as the fire hit the jailer;
20 she said the desk file is safe ■

19

218 Words

The natives of Australia use a weapon called 10
a boomerang. It is a piece of hardwood, curved 19
like a crescent, with a flat surface on one side and 30
a curved surface on the other. It is used as a 39
weapon of war or as a weapon of the hunt or even 49
as a means of amusement. The skillful boomer- 58
ang thrower can throw the weapon so that it will 67
travel in a curved line up or down, or to the left 77
or to the right. It can be thrown a great distance, 88
high into the air, and it can be made to circle a 98
selected spot. 100

In exhibitions of boomerang throwing, the 110
feat most interesting to the spectator is the throw- 120
ing of the boomerang so that it makes a complete 130
circuit in the air, returning to the point from 139
which it started. When the performer throws 148
several boomerangs in rapid succession, the il- 157
lusion of a flock of birds in flight is created. 167
Because of the peculiar property the boomerang 176
possesses of traveling in a circle, we have come 186
to apply the term boomerang to anything we do 195
that backfires on us; for example, something 203
that is meant to harm another but that results 213
only in injury to ourselves. SI 1.42 218

1 | 2 | 3 | 4 | 5 | 6 | 7 | 8 | 9 | 10 |

20

216 Words

I was part of a once-large family, but only 10
six of us were left—four boys and two girls, all 19
born on the Lower East Side. In the Ukraine, 28
before the turn of the industrializing and ravag- 38
ing century, eight others had been borne by my 47
stolid mother. They had died in infancy in those 57
times of easy dying; but we, Americans all, were 67
tougher, burlier, hardier, and better fed. We were 77
another set of health statistics. We had more 86
possibilities, if less of God. My father, with his 96
stern, fatherly hand, tried to give us, with the 106
bread my mother baked and the wine he made, 115
the guided spiritualism of a man who was as 123
Old Testament as Moses. 128

As children, we were American from the 136
start; but to our parents we were always Jews, 146
never Americans. Our Jewishness came out with 155
the preparation for the Sabbath. It meant going 164
to the baker with a ten-pound iron pot filled with 174
meat and vegetables, the cholent. There the pot 184
remained for twenty-four hours, baking slowly. 193
I would go back there after Saturday's morning 202
service, to take the hot pot back home for the 212
best meal of the week. SI 1.44 216

1 | 2 | 3 | 4 | 5 | 6 | 7 | 8 | 9 | 10 |

21

256 Words

The young Polish soldier, Tadeusz Kos- 9
ciuszko (pronounced Kosh-oo-shko), read the 17
news. The thirteen colonies of America were 26
fighting with Great Britain. They wanted to be 35
independent. They wanted to be free. That was 45
just what Kosciuszko wanted for his country. 54
He wanted Poland to be free from its rulers— 63
Prussia and Russia. But what could he do? He 72
was just a young man, and he had little fighting 81
experience. He had no money to buy guns and 90
powder for an army. 94

But he had an idea. He would go to America 104
and fight. He would help the Americans become 113
free from their ruler. 117

So Tadeusz Kosciuszko came to America. 126
The Revolutionary Army made him captain of 134
an engineers corps. Because he was brave and 143
wise, Tadeusz was soon a colonel. By the end 152
of the Revolution, he was a general. 159

Americans loved the young Polish soldier 168
who had helped them become free. They gave 177
him money. The new United States government 186
made him a citizen, and also gave him 500 acres 195
of wooded land near what is now Columbus, 203
Ohio. But General Kosciuszko was sad. The 212
Americans were now free, but Poland was not. 221
He loved America, but he loved Poland, too. He 230
had to go back to his home. He now had enough 239
money and experience to help him fight for the 249
freedom of Poland, his native land. SI 1.46 256

1 | 2 | 3 | 4 | 5 | 6 | 7 | 8 | 9 | 10 |

Unit 6

Line spacing: single
Line length: 40
Type each line twice.
Double-space after each pair of lines.

Warmup

Keep fingers curved; use a snappy stroke.

1 fed fled sled dust just rust fuss trust;
2 jeer fear dear hear rear dash sash trash
3 fee feet tree free kill hill till skill;

New Key Location

F **finger** G

4 fgf fgf leg leg egg egg keg keg get get
5 girl girl glad glad glue glue huge huge
6 digs digs tags tags high high jugs jugs

J **finger** Y

7 jyj jyj day day gay gay yet yet key key
8 they they rays rays year year yard yard
9 eyes eyes fray fray yell yell fury fury
10 jury jury says says stay stay easy easy

Word and Phrase Practice

Strive for smooth, steady typing.

11 yeast yeast hurry hurry judge judge flag
12 great great agree agree early early tray
13 a great hurry; the girls agree; they try
14 safety first; is easily hurt; great risk

Supplementary Practice

15 glad glad keg keg just just gay gay jugs
16 gray gray yield yield fight fight steady
17 slight delays; she left early yesterday;

Typing Skill Checkup

Goal: To type lines 18–19 (75 strokes) in 1 minute. Two or more tries. Do not look at the keys.

18 he had a great idea later that day; take
19 the three full tall jars after dark ■

16

243 Words

Years ago, when canvas was scarce, artists 9
painted over the works of other artists. Discov- 19
eries have been made of many old masterpieces 28
hidden in this way. 32

When there is a suspicion that a valuable 41
painting has been covered over, an expert goes 50
to work. First, the surface varnish is removed 60
and the back of the canvas is cleaned. The canvas 70
is then studied under ultraviolet lights and by 79
X ray. If it is found that a picture has indeed 89
been painted on top of another one, the next 98
step is to determine the origin of the first work. 108
To do this, the paint on the surface is loosened 117
with alcohol and a sample pigment is chipped off 127
the painting underneath. This is then matched 136
up with samples of pigments used by well-known 145
artists of the time, who had mixed their own dis- 155
tinctive paints. 158

When the identity of the artist has been 167
learned, the work of restoration starts, one sec- 177
tion at a time. The chemicals used for this de- 187
pend on the condition of the canvas and on the 196
kind of paint to be cleaned from the surface. 205
Such work requires the steadiest of eyes and 214
hands in order to avoid damage to the original 223
painting. The reward of all this careful and 232
painstaking work is the reappearance of a lost 241
work of art. SI 1.40 243

1 | 2 | 3 | 4 | 5 | 6 | 7 | 8 | 9 | 10 |

17

243 Words

Few of us pay much attention to the old 9
proverb, "Never put off until tomorrow what 17
you can do today." Many of us seem, in fact, to 27
live by this rule in reverse and never do today 36
what we can put off until tomorrow. Letters re- 46
main unanswered; bills are not paid promptly; 55
the car waits patiently for the time when we shall 65
get around to cleaning it. 70

We have two stock excuses for such behav- 79
ior—lack of time and a poor memory. Neither 88
one of these, however, really holds true. Even 98
the busiest of us wastes a great deal of time; 107
and we never forget what we really want to 115
remember—a party or a pleasure trip. or any- 124
thing else that is fun. The things we put off 133
usually involve doing what we do not enjoy or 142
making decisions we would rather not face. 151

What, then, is the solution? We must start 160
out by facing the fact that all our excuses are 170
without any basis. We should then decide which 179
of our neglected duties, though perhaps not en- 189
joyable in the doing, would yield the most sat- 198
isfying results for us. We should apply ourselves 208
first to the task we have decided upon, without 217
worrying about the others. If we attend to each 227
chore in turn, we shall find our efforts re- 236
warded by a sense of accomplishment. SI 1.41 243

1 | 2 | 3 | 4 | 5 | 6 | 7 | 8 | 9 | 10 |

18

219 Words

Some individuals begin the day's work as if 10
the whole world and its troubles were resting on 19
their shoulders. They arrive at the office in the 29
morning low in spirit or in a surly mood that 38
requires several hours to wear off. 45

In the office, this type of person may lower 55
the general high standard of business efficiency. 65
This is especially true when the office routine de- 75
pends on the cooperation of every member of the 84
group. 86

These morning moods are usually only a 94
matter of habit, perhaps caused by a hasty break- 104
fast or no breakfast at all, or by jostling in the 114
subway or trying to beat the deadline at the time 124
clock. Remove the cause, and the symptoms will 133
disappear. Many office workers have solved such 143
problems sensibly. If the cause is lack of food, 153
they get up earlier so they can eat breakfast. If 163
the cause is discomfort in traveling, they find a 172
better way to make the trip. They may use a slower 183
but more comfortable mode of transportation, even 192
though they may have to walk a little farther or 202
pay a double fare. Measures like these are worth 212
the effort to start the day right. SI 1.41 219

1 | 2 | 3 | 4 | 5 | 6 | 7 | 8 | 9 | 10 |

Unit 7

Line spacing: single
Line length: 50
Type each line twice.
Double-space after each pair of lines.

Start using a 50-space line: 25–80 (elite), 17–72 (pica).

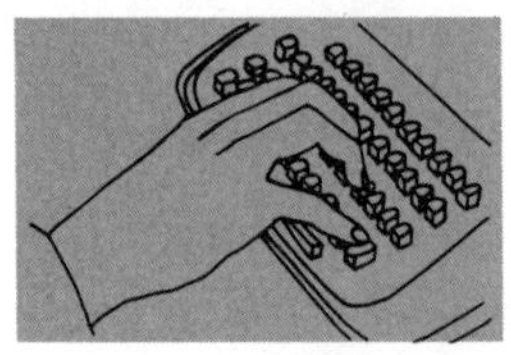

Warmup

1 just just adjust adjust yield yield shield shield
2 leak leak health health fight fight fright fright
3 sure sure surely surely ready ready steady steady

New Key Location

To capitalize a letter typed by a lefthand finger, hold down the right shift key with the semicolon finger and strike the letter.

Semi **finger** RIGHT SHIFT

4 fFf FfF fFf Fred Fred sSs SsS sSs Sue Sue Sue Susy
5 dDd DdD dDd Duke Duke rRr RrR rRr Red Red Red Ruth

To capitalize a letter typed by a righthand finger, hold down the left shift key with the A finger and strike the letter.

A **finger** 

6 jJj JjJ jJj Jay Jay Jay lLl LlL lLl Luke Luke Luke
7 kKk KkK kKk Kurt Kurt iIi IiI iIi Ida Ida Ida Iris

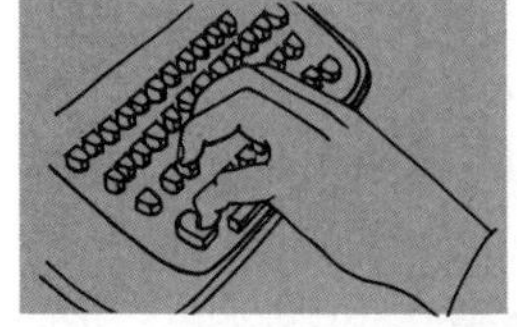

8 UuU Utah; AaA Arthur; HhH Harris; RrR Ray; EeE Ed;
9 GgG Gary; YyY Yale; TtT Terry; EeE Elsie; JjJ Jed;

Space twice after a period at the end of a sentence; once after a period in an abbreviation.

L **finger**

10 l.l l.l; Dr. Dale; I like Dr. Dale. I use a rake.
11 I like his sister Judy. I shall see her Saturday.
12 This is her Easter gift. Ask her if she likes it.

Word and Phrase Practice

13 gay gray hard guard rest gay gray hard guard rest.
14 ask task star start date ask task star start date.
15 a jagged edge; shall start early; right after dark
16 a great desire; the usual results; straight ahead;

13

259 Words

Not long ago, I became of age. To mark the 10
occasion, my father suggested that I open a 18
checking account at a bank, and he presented 27
me with a check to give the venture a good start. 37
He made it clear that it was my responsibility 46
to keep the bank account alive. 52

To open a checking account, I had to sign 61
my name on a card. I believe bank tellers are 71
expected to know the signatures of many regular 80
depositors of their bank; but if necessary, they 90
can refer to the specimen signature. I received 99
a checkbook when I opened the account. In my 108
checkbook I record the deposits I make in addi- 118
tion to recording the checks I issue. Once each 127
month, the bank sends me a statement of my 136
account. In this way, I can check that the bank's 146
records and my records are in agreement. 154

I felt very important the first time I wrote a 164
check, which was made payable to myself. The 173
bank teller was very polite. I have since made 182
a few deposits and have written a number of 191
checks. 192

I learned a great deal about banking practice 202
by having a bank account of my own. I do not 211
need to carry much money with me now. I know 220
that my money is quite safe in the bank—safer 229
than it would be in my pocket. Besides, I have 241
a record of important payments I make and 247
a receipt for each payment in the form of a can- 257
celed check. SI 1.36 259

1 | 2 | 3 | 4 | 5 | 6 | 7 | 8 | 9 | 10 |

14

217 Words

To possess an open mind is to possess some- 10
thing of real worth as we go through life. Because 20
of it, we shall discover much to interest us and to 30
give us pleasure. An open mind means that we 39
are willing to change an opinion if there are good 49
reasons for the change. It means that we are will- 59
ing to consider novel ideas, however strange they 69
may at first seem to be. 74

I am afraid that most of the opinions we hold 84
are the result of general custom rather than the 93
outcome of our own considered thought and 102
observation. Too many people accept an idea 110
only because it has always been accepted. They 120
see no reason for change. That is why improve- 129
ments in living conditions and in industrial con- 139
ditions do not come to pass as quickly as we 148
might desire. We hold fast to what is familiar, 157
and we fear to move forward into something 166
that we do not know. 170

We all want life to be richer and happier. 179
If this happy state of affairs is to come about, 189
we must view facts with clear eyes and judge 198
them not according to set opinions, but accord- 207
ing to their merit. Let us each keep an open mind. 217

SI 1.38

1 | 2 | 3 | 4 | 5 | 6 | 7 | 8 | 9 | 10 |

15

213 Words

Here are some suggestions about the bag- 9
gage to take along on the trip we at Travel Time 19
have planned for you. 23

In the first place, try to reduce the amount 33
of your luggage as much as possible. Take a fairly 43
large suitcase and an overnight bag. The suitcase 53
should not be too large to carry in an emer- 62
gency. Use the overnight bag so that you will 71
not have to open the suitcase if you spend only 80
one night in a place, and so that you may keep 89
together the articles you need every day. Choose 99
baggage that is light in weight, with lock and key, 109
and label it clearly with your name and address. 119

As for clothing, choose slacks and shirts that 129
will not crush easily and that will not need laun- 139
dering too frequently. Use undergarments that 148
you can launder yourself, if necessary. A light- 158
weight coat, a raincoat, and a folding umbrella 168
are also useful. You should have sturdy shoes 177
and a pair of rubbers. 181

It is wise to plan your packing carefully. 191
Sometimes it is difficult to find the things you 200
need while traveling abroad, and often they are 210
very expensive. SI 1.36 213

1 | 2 | 3 | 4 | 5 | 6 | 7 | 8 | 9 | 10 |

Sentence Practice

- Depress the shift key firmly.
- Hold down until *after* the letter key is struck.
- Release the shift key quickly and return your little finger to the home row.

17 Dr. Kessel left Friday. Dr. Harris is still here.
18 Judge Stark is late. I regret that he is delayed.
19 Art asked the judge. There is just a little left.
20 Sue is ready. Ray is glad. Guy trusts Les fully.

Unit 8

Line spacing: single
Line length: 50
Type each line twice.
Double-space after each pair of lines.

Warmup

Two spaces after a period at the end of a sentence; one space after an abbreviation.

1 dust rust fire tire high dust rust just tire right
2 the large shelf; the high shelf; the ledge is high
3 Dr. Glaskel liked the test. Jeff says it is easy.

New Key Location

S finger 

4 sws sws we we we saw saw was was way way jaws jaws
5 why why sew sew what what wait wait were were were
6 walk walk with with wish wish dew dew where always

Semi finger P

7 ;p; ;p; up up gap gap put put apt apt pay pay paid
8 lap lap pass pass swap swap park park ape ape whip
9 paid paid lip lip peep peep reply reply deep depth
10 prepare prepare happy happy party party flap slept

Leave one space after a comma.

K finger 

11 k,k k,k I wish, had tried, after all, if she will,
12 I will get full details, as Lee said, late Friday.
13 Please, Phil, wait a little while with that reply.
14 We like the way it was settled. Keep it up, Kate.

10

234 Words

Suppose a friend said to you, "What difference does it make whether or not you do your schoolwork well? In a few years, you will be out in the working world. That will be the time for you to begin doing your work well." Would you believe such a statement?

If so, you would be making a very serious mistake. It is certainly true that the nature of your work will change when you get out of school. Your habits, however, will probably be about the same; and habits decide the pattern of your life.

Suppose that during your school years you develop the habit of dependability. When you say you will do something, you make certain it is done. When you have work to do, you apply yourself to it and allow nothing to interfere with its completion. You plan to work first and play later. These habits will probably remain with you throughout life.

If, on the other hand, during your school career you keep coming late repeatedly or if you fail again and again to complete your work at the time it is due, you are building a fixed habit that will probably be a handicap to you through the years that lie ahead. Heed that proverb, "As the twig is bent, so the tree grows." SI 1.32

1 | 2 | 3 | 4 | 5 | 6 | 7 | 8 | 9 | 10 |

11

235 Words

Most of us look forward to getting a good new book and finding the leisure hours to read it. As we open the book, what do we hope to find in its pages? Are we planning to read the book simply to enjoy the story it tells? Are we trying to increase our knowledge of some particular subject? Are we seeking beauty in the language of the book and in the writer's expression of his or her thoughts? Sometimes, one of these purposes is uppermost in our minds. At other times, we read for a combination of purposes.

If we are reading just for the story, what kind of story do we hope the book will tell? Do we want a picture of life as it is, or do we want the story to take us away from the real world into a dream world?

Our answers to all these questions will depend partly on the purpose for which we read and partly on our frame of mind at the time. If we read with no set purpose in mind, we shall probably like best those books that tell a story. If we are seeking knowledge, or if we enjoy beauty of expression, our choice can be made from a wider field—science, history, travel, poetry, music, art, and more. Whatever type of book we choose, we can find joy in reading. SI 1.29

1 | 2 | 3 | 4 | 5 | 6 | 7 | 8 | 9 | 10 |

Selections 12–29, SI Range 1.36–1.50

12

203 Words

If you are flying at an elevation of six or seven miles, you are at the level of the highest clouds. There, the tiny drops of water that form the clouds are frozen into very fine snow crystals. Approximately two miles below this level, the swiftest winds are blowing. There, the clouds appear to be most numerous, and they are twisted and stretched into their most feathery configurations.

The clouds from which most of the precipitation falls are usually at a height of two to three miles. These clouds may have a spread of less than half a mile, but they often have a height of four or five miles.

A fog is actually a cloud on the earth. An observer flying above the fog gazes upon a magnificent scene—mile after mile of snow-white, fleecy billows of down. Pilots understand the truth of the saying that every cloud has a silver lining. From below, clouds may look black with the threat of an approaching storm; from above, they seem transformed into silver by the reflection of sunlight on their white tops. SI 1.40

1 | 2 | 3 | 4 | 5 | 6 | 7 | 8 | 9 | 10 |

Figuring Your Speed

In the lessons from now on you will be taking timed writings; that is, you will be typing for a set period of time and trying to reach a better speed, with control, than in previous attempts.

In figuring typing speed, every five strokes (spaces included) are counted as one word. To assist you in figuring the number of words you typed, a cumulative word count is shown at the end of each line. Immediately below the timed writing is a word scale that shows the word count at various points throughout a line.

For example, suppose you typed the following for 1 minute:

Word count

```
15 Yes, Pat liked the first test.  It was truly easy. 10
16 As a result, he was paid                            15
       1|   2|   3|   4|   5|   6|   7|   8|   9|  10|
```

If you completed both lines, you would have typed 15 words (10 + 5) a minute. If you had typed only to the word "a" in line 16, you would have typed 11 words (10 + 1) per minute (wpm).

Typing Skill Checkup

Goal: To type 17 wpm. Two or more tries.

Don't worry about errors, but try to keep them to a minimum.

```
15 Yes, Pat liked the first test.  It was truly easy. 10
16 As a result, he was paid Friday.  He left Tuesday. 20
17 If Wiley will study a little harder, he will pass. 30
                                               SI 1.30
       1|   2|   3|   4|   5|   6|   7|   8|   9|  10|
```

Unit 9

Line spacing: single
Line length: 50
Type each line twice.
Double-space after each pair of lines.

Warmup

Strike each key with equal force.

```
1 kit wit fit jut; day gay way play; art start parts
2 law raw paw thaw; wide pride jury; we three agreed
3 See if Dr. Kyle is here.  If he is, I shall start.
```

7

243 Words

When you go on a camping trip into the 9
mountains and forests of British Columbia, it's 18
a good idea to have a pack pony to carry your 27
equipment. Distances between settlements are 36
often so immense that you cannot carry with you 45
all the supplies you will require on the journey. 55

Before I set out on my trip, therefore, my 65
first task was to locate a suitable pony. Any pony 75
would not do; it had to be a very gentle one. I 84
had seen packs thrown off by ponies, with the 93
result that frying pans, eggs, and sugar were 102
hurled to the four winds; and I wanted to avoid 112
that. Moreover, I required a pony that was not 121
too tall. I am short, and I did not want to carry 131
a ladder with me in order to place the pack on 140
the pony's back. 144

It took me a week to locate the right pony— 153
a little dark brown mare with a white stripe on 163
her nose. There were a few slight misunderstand- 173
ings when we began; but by the end of another 182
week, we knew each other well. A strong friend- 191
ship had even developed between us. I did dis- 201
cover that there was one thing she did not like, 210
and that was a bear. When we were in bear 219
country, I hung a bell around her neck to keep 228
bears away from her. Incidentally, the bell kept 238
the bears away from me, too. SI 1.30 243

1 | 2 | 3 | 4 | 5 | 6 | 7 | 8 | 9 | 10 |

8

248 Words

The strand of cotton that we cut from a spool 10
and deftly thread through the eye of a needle 19
is the product of one of the greatest industries 29
in the world—the cotton industry. 35

We may see cotton growing first in the fields 45
of our own southern states; or we may trace it to 55
Egypt, where a plant very similar to our cotton 65
plant grows. The seeds are sown in February or 74
March, and within ten days the green shoots are 83
up. Before the middle of June, the plants have 93
grown well and are covered with showy yellow 102
or purple flowers. These quickly fall, and in their 112
place appears the fruit, which contains the seeds. 122
Around the seeds are many downy fibers—cotton 131
in its first stage. 135

These fibers must be separated from the 144
seeds, a task that was once performed by hand. 153
Today it is done by the cotton gin, a machine that 163
tears the cotton away from the seeds. Then the 172
cotton is tightly packed by machine into bales 182
weighing approximately 500 pounds each. 189

Most of this product is spun into yarn, and 199
most of the yarn is made into cotton materials. 208
The cotton on our spools of thread is more dif- 218
ficult to make. When the little strands of cotton 228
have been spun into yarn, two or three strands 237
are twisted together, doubled, and wound onto 246
bobbins. SI 1.32 248

1 | 2 | 3 | 4 | 5 | 6 | 7 | 8 | 9 | 10 |

9

215 Words

Wild animals wage a continual struggle 9
against one another, and only the most crafty of 18
them survive. The small creatures of the country- 28
side are masters of disguise and concealment. 37
Every meadow and every wood has its share of 46
small creatures; yet how seldom we see them! 55

It is mainly because our wild creatures know 65
where and how to hide that they are so seldom 74
seen. When they hear noisy human beings 82
coming, they do not start dashing about; if they 91
did, we should certainly see them. They do not 101
hide, as we should do, behind a tree or a bush; 110
they stand dead still at the least sound. 118

Some wild creatures change their color with 128
the seasons of the year. Many others choose a 137
background with coloring similar to their own 146
so that they may escape notice. A toad sits on a 156
mossy stone where it will not be seen. A bat hangs 166
like a cobweb from a beam. The deer stands still 176
and relies on the background to hide him. By 185
covering our faces and hands and dressing in 194
drab clothes, we can become nearly as invisible 203
as the wild creatures, increasing our chances of 213
spotting them. SI 1.34 215

1 | 2 | 3 | 4 | 5 | 6 | 7 | 8 | 9 | 10 |

New Key Location

A finger **Q**

4 aqa aqa aqa quit quit quit equal equal quiet quiet
5 quart quart quart quite quite quite quay quay quay
6 Quality quart jade jars; requires quiet; was equal

L finger **O**

7 lol lol lol old old old low low low told told talk
8 does does does words words words quote quote quote
9 Follow the quay as far as it goes or you will pay.

Sentence Practice

Eyes on copy!

10 Fill this quart jar with water for yourself, Ross.
11 Take a ferry for your trip; a ride is quite short.
12 High quality paper is required for work like this.
13 Let us show you how to get a profit without risks.

Capital Practice

On typebar machines, to avoid "flying" capitals (capitals that are above the line), hold the shift key down firmly until *after* the letter has been struck.

14 Delaware, DE; Georgia, GA; Hawaii, HI; or Ohio, OH
15 Joe, Walt, Pete, Roy, Si, or Kate will go to Utah.
16 Laura will take quite a trip to Italy this August.
17 Fred left for Hawaii Friday. George will go also.
18 You should go to Quail Hill or Key Largo Thursday.

1 | 2 | 3 | 4 | 5 | 6 | 7 | 8 | 9 | 10 |

REVIEW

Unit 10

Line spacing: single
Line length: 50
Type each line twice.
Double-space after each pair of lines.

Do not let your fingers slant or slouch. Keep the correct alignment as shown above.

Warmup

1 your your equip jugs tour poor quote foul owl jowl
2 At her request, he took Dorothy to the Ford Hotel.
3 George refused our request to pay us what he owes.

4

203 Words

As soon as we saw the old house, we wanted 9
to own it. Every consideration of common sense 19
was against the idea. The house had none of the 28
modern conveniences that make life so much 37
easier. It was badly in need of repair, and we 46
would have to spend a good part of our savings 55
to make it habitable. It was miles from town, 65
and there was no good road leading to it. This 74
would mean difficulty in getting service people 83
to come out our way. 87

We understood all this, and we tried to tell 97
ourselves that this was not the place for us. Yet 107
there was something about the old house that 116
reached out to us and urged us to take it on. It 126
was a charming house, beautifully situated on a 135
small piece of land with water on three sides. 144
A feeling of peace and a quiet loveliness lingered 154
about the whole place, and we longed to be part of 164
it. 165

In spite of all our misgivings, we purchased 175
the old house; and we have lived in it for many 184
years. As we had hoped when first we saw it, we 194
had found the haven we had been searching for. 203

SI 1.26

1 | 2 | 3 | 4 | 5 | 6 | 7 | 8 | 9 | 10 |

5

290 Words

The Indian rope trick is one of the most 9
puzzling things in the world. It has existed for 19
ages—travelers to India hundreds of years ago 28
reported seeing it. We are not sure of how this 38
trick is done. The man who performs the trick 47
takes a long rope and throws one end of it into 56
the air. It unwinds and unwinds until the end 65
is high up in the air. Some say that the end can 75
go so far that it is out of sight. Then a small boy 86
climbs up the rope and disappears at the top. 95

Some explain this as a trick of the mind. 104
People think they see what they are told they 113
see. For example, tie a cork to a long black cotton 123
thread, trail it quickly across the carpet in a dim 133
light, and make it disappear behind some article 143
of furniture, crying out, "Look, a mouse!" Most 153
people will then believe that they have seen a 162
mouse. 163

A story is told of a man who was walking a 172
few steps behind a native of Bhutan. The native 182
suddenly turned and cried out a warning about a 191
snake. The traveler thought he saw a large snake 201
glide quickly past his foot, and he jumped back. 211
Then the native laughed and explained that there 220
was really no snake. He went over to the long 230
grass at the side of the road and picked up an 239
ordinary walking stick. He had skillfully used 248
the stick to make the traveler imagine that he 257
had seen a snake. 261

In the same way, we may be led to imagine 270
we have seen things that really do not exist. In 280
this may lie the explanation of the Indian rope 289
trick. SI 1.26 290

1 | 2 | 3 | 4 | 5 | 6 | 7 | 8 | 9 | 10 |

6

200 Words

Right now, the one thing we all seem to want 10
is more energy. We are not sure that America has 20
enough energy reserves to meet our needs for the 29
next century; so we are thinking again of coal, of 39
which there is still an enormous supply. 47

Unfortunately, coal is a dirty fuel. It is 57
black; and when you touch it, your hands get black 67
and dirty. That kind of dirt, however, is only on 77
the surface of the coal. It won't hurt your hands; 87
you just have to wash it off. 93

The real dirt in coal comes out only when it 103
burns. When that happens, it gives off a black 112
smoke, much of which consists of waste chemicals 122
that are lost in the air. If you breathe this 131
smoke, it is harmful to your lungs. 138

For this reason, some companies are building 148
factories to "clean" coal. When coal is cleaned, 157
the harmful chemicals are removed before the coal 167
is burned. They are then used to produce plastics, 177
insulation, and other helpful things. Thus, coal 187
is not only turned into clean energy, but we get 197
extra use from it. SI 1.30 200

1 | 2 | 3 | 4 | 5 | 6 | 7 | 8 | 9 | 10 |

- Select a sentence you feel you can complete in 30 seconds. Do a timed writing.
- If you do not finish or if you make more than 3 errors, select a shorter sentence on the next try.
- If you do complete your sentence, select a longer one for the next timing.

Skill Building

4 I said it was quite easy. 5
5 They will go to see the house. 6
6 He would like to see the jail yard. 7
7 We felt that we really had to look hard. 8
8 It is a pleasure to supply you with the help. 9
9 While she was out, two people were here to see it. 10

Double-Letter Word Practice

Type continuously. Don't pause between strokes or at the ends of lines.

10 pp supports ll Stella ss assure pp supply equipped
11 gg suggest ff Jeffrey ll really ee agreed oo goods
12 ll shall rr ferries ss passed tt Seattle gg ragged
13 rr hurry ll equally ee freed oo shooter dd ladders

Typing Skill Checkup

Goal: To type 17 wpm.

14 Rudolf or Pat will go to Dallas this week. Walter 10
15 hopes to go with his sister. They look forward to 20
16 the trip with great pleasure. SI 1.24 26

1 | 2 | 3 | 4 | 5 | 6 | 7 | 8 | 9 | 10 |

Unit 11

Line spacing: single
Line length: 50
Type each line twice.
Double-space after each pair of lines.

Warmup

1 old old, quell quell; top top, quit quite; jog jog
2 why why lip lip reply reply walks walks pays pays;
3 Dr. Starr offered us the property at a low figure.

200 TO 300 WORDS

The following timed writings are arranged in three groups according to the syllabic intensities of the individual selections.

Selections 1–11, SI Range 1.20–1.35

1

205 Words

A walk on the beach can be full of interest 10
every step of the way. To begin with, it is along 20
the seashore that we can best sense the great 29
wonder of creation. The sea is older than any- 38
thing else in the world. It has always been there 48
and—just think of it—it has always been in mo- 58
tion. The motion of the sea that attracts your 67
eyes, the noise of it that fills your ears, existed 77
thousands and thousands of years before anyone 86
walked the earth and wondered where the sea 95
had come from. Stop and think about the roar 104
of the ocean going on for thousands of years 113
before there were any people on the earth to hear 123
it. How grand, but how lonely it must have been! 132
Then think about the sands. Take up a hand- 142
ful of dry sand, and it runs through your fingers 152
like powder. Go near the waves where the sand 161
is wet, and you will see in it tiny grains of various 172
colors. Once the sands were shells and stones. 181
The sea has ground them into fine particles. 190
Every year the stones on the beach grow smaller 199
as the ocean wears them away. SI 1.23 205

1 | 2 | 3 | 4 | 5 | 6 | 7 | 8 | 9 | 10 |

2

243 Words

My friend Jack is a fox terrier. He is really 10
not my best friend, but he thinks he is, which 19
amounts to much the same thing. I am not his 28
master, and I do not want to take him away from 38
his owner; but his idea is that I am his master 47
and that I want him very much. 53
I blame myself for having made the first 62
advances, although nothing came of them then 71
except a growl. I met him in his master's house, 81
where I was paying a visit. After we had looked 90
at each other for about a minute, I spoke a few 100
kind words to him, and he growled. I thought he 109
was a surly dog and paid no more attention to 118
him that day. 121
About a week later, when I again visited his 131
master, I learned that Jack had had a serious 140
accident. I saw him lying there, a very sick dog 150
indeed. He allowed me to stroke him, opening 159
one eye very slightly. 163
For some time, I did not see Jack at all. Then, 174
as I was taking a walk one evening, I saw his head 184
poking out of a hedge. I said hello to him, and 193
that was enough. He followed me on my walk, 202
and he has been walking with me ever since. He 211
does not really walk with me—he races around 220
me and then away from me and back. I played 229
with him out of sympathy at first, but now I be- 239
long to him completely. SI 1.23 243

1 | 2 | 3 | 4 | 5 | 6 | 7 | 8 | 9 | 10 |

3

206 Words

I have recently been making a list of all the 10
things that I wouldn't have missed. It has been 20
fun—something like going through a lot of old 29
photographs and choosing some to put into an 38
album. My list has grown and grown. The more I 47
think about my life, the more my mind seems 56
to scamper from one thing to another—from 64
Scotland to China, from this year and last year 74
to my boyhood days, backward and forward, 82
forward and backward. 86
Many of the things on my list consist of the 96
first time I did something—the first time I rode 106
a bicycle, my first day at school, the first speech 116
I gave, the first time I had a book published. 125
There was a thrill in all of them. 132
From my college days, I remember very viv- 141
idly the times when I went home for the holidays. 151
I remember my home and all that it stood for— 160
the familiar front door, the rooms that seemed 169
so small and cozy in contrast to the large, bare 179
classrooms and halls. I remember, too, returning 189
from the noise and mud and pain of war to the 198
same room in which I had slept as a child. SI 1.23 206

1 | 2 | 3 | 4 | 5 | 6 | 7 | 8 | 9 | 10 |

Alternate Hands Practice

Goal: To speed up finger movements.

4 the for rug did she due got fit eye fork also duty
5 lap oak dot pry pal the girl held for she got paid
6 sit with tight quake tutor shelf world their digit

Tabulator Key or Bar

The tabulator makes the printing point move multiple spaces in one motion. It is easier, for example, to use the tabulator to make a 5-space paragraph indention than to strike the space bar five times.

To set tab stops, follow this procedure.

CLEAR

SET

TAB BAR *or* TAB KEY

1. Clear all previously set stops. Use the total tab clear mechanism (if your machine has one), or tab to each stop and press the tab clear key.
2. Set new tab stops. Move the printing point to each of the desired positions and press the tab set key.
3. Test the new tab stops. Start at the left margin. Depress the tab key or bar and release. Repeat. Does the carriage or type element stop at the desired positions?

Paragraph Practice

Set a tab stop for a 5-space paragraph indention.

At your own speed, type the first paragraph with no more than 3 errors. If you succeed, move to the second paragraph. Otherwise, retype the first paragraph. Continue the same way on the following paragraphs.

7 We feel that our request is justified, as you 10
8 had agreed to pay. Please pay what you owe today. 20
9 Perhaps you would prefer to write the reports 10
10 yourself. If so, please go ahead after four days. 20
11 If you require a supply of household goods, I 10
12 will gladly help you to prepare your orders today. 20
13 The store is large. It is well equipped with 10
14 all sorts of supplies for those who like hardware. 20
15 I should like to suggest that you let us fill 10
16 all your orders for leather goods. Just write us. 20

SI 1.29

Supplementary Practice

17 Without further delay, they paid all that he owed.
18 Joe took a short trip last April for that purpose.
19 We hope the sale of the house will yield a profit.
20 History supports this theory; perhaps it is right.
21 Philip was glad that his star pupil got the award.

Typing Skill Checkup

Take two or more 1-minute writings on this paragraph.

Goal: Speed–18 wpm
Error limit–3

22 If she swore to a false report, she is guilty 10
23 of perjury. It is quite justified that she should 20
24 go to jail. SI 1.27 22

1 | 2 | 3 | 4 | 5 | 6 | 7 | 8 | 9 | 10 |

22

112 Words

Meteoroids are celestial bodies, possibly as- 10
sociated with comets, that move through space 19
with velocities up to 40 miles per second. When 29
they reach the earth's atmosphere, they are va- 38
porized by the heat caused by the friction of their 48
passage into the atmosphere, and then they are 57
seen as meteors. 61

An unusual number of meteors in a short 69
period of time is called a meteor shower. Meteors 79
are popularly known as falling stars or shooting 89
stars. While most of them are consumed, a few 98
fall to the earth as fused metal or stone and are 108
called meteorites. SI 1.54 112

1 | 2 | 3 | 4 | 5 | 6 | 7 | 8 | 9 | 10 |

23

115 Words

Modern industry has been built upon meth- 9
ods of mass production, which were made pos- 18
sible by machinery. Mass production has put 27
many articles within the reach of everybody and 36
raised our standard of living. Luxuries of past 46
eras have now become commonplace goods. 54

Books are an excellent example of the ad- 63
vantages of mass production. When books had 72
to be written by hand, they were rare works of 81
art that only a very few people could afford. 90
Now books, as well as newspapers and maga- 98
zines, are published by the thousands; and nearly 108
everybody can afford to buy them. SI 1.55 115

1 | 2 | 3 | 4 | 5 | 6 | 7 | 8 | 9 | 10 |

24

118 Words

Our natural environment is formed from 9
chemical elements which join in different ways 18
to form minerals, rocks, soils, water, air, and 27
organic matter. In past years, this natural en- 37
vironment has been much changed by the effects 46
of chemical pollution, at least in some regions. 56
Some of the chemical pollutants might be bene- 65
ficial to human and animal health, and some 73
might be neutral, but many of them are harmful. 83
The task now is to remove pollutants from the 92
environment, and to prevent further pollution. 101
The task will be difficult and expensive. But in 111
the long run it will pay for itself. SI 1.55 118

1 | 2 | 3 | 4 | 5 | 6 | 7 | 8 | 9 | 10 |

25

135 Words

Bookkeeping and accounting workers keep 9
a daily financial history of a business. Records 19
of business dealings, such as the sale or purchase 29
of merchandise, are kept in books called jour- 38
nals or ledgers. 41

In most small firms, one general bookkeeper 51
does all the recording, analysis, and other ac- 60
counting work. Large firms may have many 68
bookkeeping and accounting clerks, each spe- 77
cializing in one or two kinds of accounting work. 87

Bookkeeping and accounting workers also 96
file, answer the telephone, use adding, calculat- 105
ing, and bookkeeping machines, and prepare 113
and mail bills. Some also do payroll work. They 123
record and write checks, too, but they usually 132
do not sign them. SI 1.55 135

1 | 2 | 3 | 4 | 5 | 6 | 7 | 8 | 9 | 10 |

26

148 Words

One of the most important factors in the suc- 10
cess of a business is the attitude of the man or 20
woman who manages it. The ability to get along 29
with people and inspire trust is vital. The owner 39
of a business must develop a good relationship with 49
both customers and employees. A moment's reflec- 59
tion will bring to mind men or women who, by their 69
warm manner, have attracted and held customers. 78
You will recall others who have driven customers 88
away by being abrupt and rude. 94

Another factor that contributes to business 104
success is responsibility in money matters. The 113
store owner has a financial obligation to both 122
employees and creditors. Before the business 131
can clear a profit, the payroll must be met and 141
bills must be paid as they come due. SI 1.57 148

1 | 2 | 3 | 4 | 5 | 6 | 7 | 8 | 9 | 10 |

Unit 12

Line spacing: single
Line length: 50
Type each line twice.
Double-space after each pair of lines.

Warmup

Sit up straight. Keep your wrists low and your elbows loosely at your sides.

1 jagged jaws; please pleasure; quire require, fires
2 Kurt took a trip west last April for that purpose.
3 Louis, please write us if you require further aid.

New Key Location

D finger 

4 dcd dcd dcd cat cat cat car car car jack jack lack
5 call call call each each each case case case space
6 quick quick quick reduce reduce reduce clear clear

F finger 

7 fvf fvf fvf eve eve eve vat vat vat save save save
8 have have have give give give very very very prove
9 vivid vivid vivid velvet velvet velvet valve valve
10 We have to leave quickly for the drive over there.

Leave 2 spaces after a question mark at the end of a sentence.

Semi finger ? *and* ***A*** finger to shift

11 ;?; ;?; ;?; Who called? Did he go? Where is she?
12 What have you to say? What does that prove, Carl?
13 How did you do it, Vi? Will Dr. Davis drive over?
14 Shall I do it today? Do you prefer check or cash?
15 We provide delivery service. Could that help you?

Skill Building

- Select a sentence you feel you can complete twice in 1 minute. Take a 1-minute writing.
- If you don't complete the sentence twice or you make more than 3 errors, select a shorter sentence.
- If you complete a sentence twice easily, select a longer one.

16 Are we required to do it? 5
17 Work for quick, sharp strokes. 6
18 Sit up, erect; type without pauses. 7
19 Try to strike each key with equal force. 8
20 You will type well if you practice regularly. 9
21 Do strive to reach for the key with little effort. 10

1 2 3 4 5 6 7 8 9 10

18

162 Words

A great many people still think that a secre- 10
tary is a kind of machine who turns out perfect 19
letters from nine to five. Some use the title to 29
mean one who is employed as a stenographer or 38
clerk in an office. It is true that typing and short- 49
hand are two of the basic skills of the secretary, 59
but it is also true that a secretary's duties cover 69
a much wider area than those of a typist, stenog- 79
rapher, or file clerk. 83

The secretary, as we use the term today, 92
often does this kind of work, but he or she is 102
much more like an assistant to an executive. The 111
secretary often knows a great deal about many 120
of the confidential matters relating to the com- 130
pany's business. Knowing how to use this infor- 140
mation helps avoid delays and clears the decks 149
for the "boss" in a score of other ways through- 158
out the working day. SI 1.44 162

1 | 2 | 3 | 4 | 5 | 6 | 7 | 8 | 9 | 10 |

19

176 Words

It is hard to realize that there ever was a time 11
when a typewriter was not a necessary piece of 20
equipment in every business office. At first, the 30
greatest appeal a typewritten letter had was the 39
ease with which it could be read. In the early 49
days, typed material did not always look attrac- 58
tive; but it was legible. Misstruck characters and 69
strikeovers were common. 73

Because everyone expected these faults in a 83
typewritten letter, form letters were sent out 92
purposely with such errors, in order to give the 102
impression that the letter was especially written 112
for the individual to whom it was addressed. 120
Today an employer demands that a typist do 129
work that measures up to a high standard of 139
performance. Typed work must meet three re- 146
quirements: (1) it must be done quickly; (2) it 156
must be accurate; and (3) it must be well arranged 166
so that it makes a good impression on the reader. 176

SI 1.49

1 | 2 | 3 | 4 | 5 | 6 | 7 | 8 | 9 | 10 |

Selections 20–26, SI Range 1.51–1.60

20

137 Words

The history of Japanese Americans is in 9
many ways similar to that of Jewish and Afro- 18
Americans. As a people, each has cultural roots 27
that go far into the past. Each has experienced 37
both power and oppression. Each has suffered 46
rejection in our country where all, it is said, are 56
free and equal. 59

Each, too, has a unique and ancient heritage 69
in both oral and written poetry. In Japan, written 79
poetry first appeared at the end of the 700s. 88
There are more than 4,000 poems from that pe- 97
riod. The poems deal mainly with life in the 106
emperor's court, rather than with the life of the 116
common people. But like most Japanese poetry, 125
the poems deal with the closeness of the people 135
to nature. SI 1.52 137

1 | 2 | 3 | 4 | 5 | 6 | 7 | 8 | 9 | 10 |

21

177 Words

Money is the lifeblood of business. The lack 10
of it has brought failure to thousands of business 20
people who had everything else they needed— 29
personality, courage, willingness to work hard, 38
ability, and experience. 43

This does not mean that you must, before 52
starting a business, amass all the money that you 62
will need. Most businesses finance their opera- 71
tions by borrowing funds from time to time. For 81
example, they borrow to purchase inventory. Then 91
they repay the loan with receipts from sales. 100

To obtain a loan for a business operation, 109
a manufacturer or merchant must show that he 118
or she is a good risk. The bank's cash funds come 128
from the deposits of other people, and so the 137
banker must be quite sure that the borrower 146
will pay back the loan. The banker is influenced 155
most by the past record of the applicant, either 165
as a responsible employee or as a successful 174
business person. SI 1.52 177

1 | 2 | 3 | 4 | 5 | 6 | 7 | 8 | 9 | 10 |

Unit 13

Line spacing: single
Line length: 50
Paragraph indention: 5
Type each line twice.
Double-space after each pair of lines

Warmup

Return quickly without looking up.

Leave 2 spaces after a question mark.

1 wave waves; vest request; serves service; discover
2 voice rejoice juices quick plaque grace face facts
3 The price is high. Could you, perhaps, reduce it?

New Key Location

***S* finger** X

4 sxs sxs sxs tax tax tax fox fox fox exit exit exit
5 flax flax flax fix fix fix lax lax lax sex sex sex
6 expect expect expect sox sox sox sixth sixth sixth

***J* finger** M

7 jmj jmj jmj my my my me me me am am am mix mix mix
8 firm firm firm arm arm arm may may may times times
9 came came cave dam dam dam same same game fame jam
10 Who came? What time was it? May they expect you?

***F* finger** B

No space is left after the period in an abbreviation when a semicolon or comma follows.

11 fbf fbf fbf box box box bad bad bad lab lab lab be
12 bake bake bake job job job bid bid bid mob mob mob
13 back back back tub tub tub blue blue blue beam big
14 Mrs. Butler expects a reply by mail this February.
15 September is abbreviated to Sept.; Friday, to Fri.

Typing Skill Checkup

Two or more 1-minute writings.

Goal: Speed—19 wpm
Error limit—3

16   For today, try to put aside worries or doubts 10
17 you may have about yourself. Have thoughts about 20
18 success. Start each day with thoughts of success. 30
SI 1.32

19   I require good quality paper for these works. 10
20 I would like to order it today. Perhaps you would 20
21 prefer that I wait for your approval. SI 1.35 27

1 | 2 | 3 | 4 | 5 | 6 | 7 | 8 | 9 | 10 |

14

152 Words

Once you are in the business world, you will 10
learn many things that are not to be found in 19
books. When you meet people at close range in 28
the office, you tend to get deeper insight into 37
human nature. And the longer you are engaged 46
in business, the more respect you will have for 56
the dignity of labor. 60

You will soon learn the importance of spend- 70
ing wisely the money that you earn and of mak- 79
ing good use of your leisure time. You will learn 89
that your rate of progress depends on your own 98
efforts. You will learn to accept tasks that are 108
boring and even unpleasant, and to face, at times, 118
unreasonable attitudes that your employer may 127
take. In short, you will learn to adapt yourself 137
to other people and to deal intelligently with any 147
situation that may arise. SI 1.37 152

1 | 2 | 3 | 4 | 5 | 6 | 7 | 8 | 9 | 10 |

15

186 Words

The choice of a line of business calls for 9
good judgment. You should select a field that 19
you know, and one that is growing or for which 28
there is a steady demand. Sometimes it is pos- 37
sible to provide some service that does not exist 47
but for which there is a real need. For example, 57
one person thought of a service for supplying 66
box lunches to factory workers—something new, 75
something needed. Now there are many trucks 84
that carry food to workers in districts with few 93
eating places. 96

You might go into business producing in 105
wholesale quantities some article of food that 114
you prepare especially well and that is not al- 124
ready on the market. You might have some spe- 133
cial training of which you can make use. There 142
are other considerations to be kept in mind 151
when choosing a business. You should know the 160
amount of capital you require and the amount 169
available. And you must be careful not to enter 178
a field that is already overcrowded. SI 1.43 186

1 | 2 | 3 | 4 | 5 | 6 | 7 | 8 | 9 | 10 |

16

199 Words

The buyer for a store must use a buying plan. 10
The following practices related to planned buy- 19
ing have stood the test of time. 26

In the first place, the buyer should make 35
purchases often, so that fresh stock is always on 45
hand. This practice will also prevent stock from 55
running out and will avoid the need for a heavy 64
investment at any one time. In a falling market— 74
that is, when prices are going down—purchases 83
should be on as small a scale as possible. Other- 93
wise lower prices will force markdowns and 102
losses. In a rising market, on the other hand, 111
enough goods must be bought to meet competi- 120
tion. The buyer, however, should not yield to the 130
temptation of speculating and overloading. 138

In the second place, the buyer must pur- 147
chase only needed merchandise and not be in- 156
fluenced by high-pressure sales talks, clever 165
advertising, or attractive displays. If he or she 175
buys because the salesperson is persuasive rather 185
than because the goods fill a need, the unwanted 194
stock will prove a burden. SI 1.47 199

1 | 2 | 3 | 4 | 5 | 6 | 7 | 8 | 9 | 10 |

17

148 Words

Printing is a good business. It is an honorable 11
and respectable kind of work. It has prepared 20
many for high stations in life. It has its own in- 30
spiring traditions and legends. The printer must 40
have a knowledge of almost everything under the 49
sun—mechanics, language, color, salesmanship. 58
There is no end to the skills required, because 68
the printer is brought into contact with all other 78
trades and professions. 82

Whether it be a reading primer or a college 92
textbook, a handbill or a newspaper, a ticket or 102
a poster, a folder or a magazine, a box label or 111
a legal document—its message is told to the world 121
by means of the printed word. In this modern 130
age, no business or other organized activity could 140
get far without the art of the printer. SI 1.49 148

1 | 2 | 3 | 4 | 5 | 6 | 7 | 8 | 9 | 10 |

Unit 14

Line spacing: single
Line length: 50
Paragraph indention: 5
Type each line twice.

Warmup

Remember to double-space after each pair of lines.

1 job move love above; same came blame; rough slough
2 Dec., ox fox box, whim make bake; me my myself mix
3 You will get a job if you prepare yourself for it.

New Key Location

***A* finger** 

4 aza aza aza lazy lazy lazy zoo zoo zoo seize seize
5 zeal zeal zeal size size size zero zero zero seize
6 jazz jazz jazz, raze raze raze, dazed dazed dazed;
7 quiz quiz quiz; zebra zebra zebra; doz. doz. doz.;

***J* finger** 

8 jnj jnj jnj no no no net net net on on on ten tens
9 pen pen pen zone zone zone new new new men men men
10 oxen oxen oven been been been many many many dozen
11 Dr. Dorfs ordered a dozen copies of the new books.

Up and Down Reach Practice

Make reaches between the third and the first row without having your fingers pause on the home row.

12 ice ice ice mud mud mud sum sum sum curb curb curb
13 much much much debt debt debt must must must nerve
14 jump jump jump curve curve curve funny funny funny
15 sun sunny numb number brow brown unbend unbendable
16 I must quickly select the clothes to pack my bags.

Typing Skill Checkup

Take two or more 1-minute writings.

Goal: Speed–20 wpm
Error limit–3

17 Stop and think back over your past. What are 10
18 the things you have done at home, at school, with 20
19 friends that you enjoyed doing? What you like can 30
20 enable you to recognize careers worth exploring. 40

SI 1.32

1 | 2 | 3 | 4 | 5 | 6 | 7 | 8 | 9 | 10 |

Selections 9–19, SI Range 1.36–1.50

9

119 Words

Halloween is short for All Hallows Even, the 10
evening before All Saints' Day. Halloween was 19
meant to be a religious time, but our celebration 29
grew from the customs of people who believed in 38
ghosts, witches, and goblins. 44

People all over the world are afraid some- 53
times. They look for sources to explain their fear. 64
For example, people once thought that gods in 73
the sky threw lightning at the earth. In the same 83
way, people thought up ghosts, witches, and gob- 92
lins. If an animal died, they believed that a witch 103
or goblin made it happen. They were afraid, but 112
at least they had an explanation. SI 1.39 119

1 | 2 | 3 | 4 | 5 | 6 | 7 | 8 | 9 | 10 |

10

95 Words

People once moved to the suburbs to get 9
clean air, but there is no place there to hide any- 19
more. Many surrounding communities are as 27
polluted as the central cities and as hazardous 37
to health, even though the pollutants may be 46
invisible. 48

Now there is talk of minimizing clean air 57
standards, of easing enforcement so that more 66
coal can be burned as an answer to the energy 75
shortage. This could delay our goal of clean air 85
for quite a few years. There are no easy answers. 95

SI 1.42

1 | 2 | 3 | 4 | 5 | 6 | 7 | 8 | 9 | 10 |

11

138 Words

Jewish-Americans have a holiday called 9
Hanukkah. Hanukkah is the celebration of the 18
victory of Judas Maccabaeus. Judas and his 26
small band of patriots defeated the Syrians in 35
165 B.C. But before the Syrians left the land of 45
Israel, they destroyed the Jewish temple. 53

When the Jews built a new temple on the 62
ruins of the old one, a strange thing happened. 72
As the workmen were clearing stones from the 80
floor of the temple, they found a jar of holy oil. 90
The holy oil was used for the burning of the 99
Eternal Light in the temple. The jar they found 109
held enough oil for only one day's light. For some 119
reason, the oil burned for eight days and nights. 129
So Hanukkah lasts for eight days and nights. 138

SI 1.43

1 | 2 | 3 | 4 | 5 | 6 | 7 | 8 | 9 | 10 |

12

113 Words

Fruit-bearing trees can be important parts of 10
a landscape plan. Whether planted in a row to 19
mark borders or grouped orchard-style or set 28
out as specimen plantings, they enhance the gar- 38
den year after year. They add to the value of your 48
property, too. 51

Because fruit trees usually last a long time, it 61
is important to choose the best trees when you 70
are buying. A nursery, garden center, or land- 80
scape specialist can give advice on the different 90
varieties and on the best places for planting 99
them. These sources can also give advice for 108
proper planting and upkeep. SI 1.44 113

1 | 2 | 3 | 4 | 5 | 6 | 7 | 8 | 9 | 10 |

13

140 Words

Students frequently do poor work in school 9
because they do not know how to develop good 18
study habits. Trying to read or do homework 27
while you are watching television or listening to 37
the latest recording by your favorite singers is 46
not studying. 49

When questioned about the problem of 57
studying, one student replied, "I don't need a 66
course in how to study; I need a course in how 76
to stop watching television." The solution is really 86
very simple. Just turn off the television set, put 96
one foot in front of the other, and keep moving 106
until you find a quiet place. Then go to work! 115
This is the first and probably the most important 125
step in getting started. You can't be atten- 134
tive to two things at one time. SI 1.46 140

1 | 2 | 3 | 4 | 5 | 6 | 7 | 8 | 9 | 10 |

REVIEW

Unit 15

Line spacing: single
Line length: 50
Paragraph indention: 5
Type each line twice.

Warmup

Spacing review:
- Two spaces follow a period or a question mark at the end of a sentence.

1 men ten mind dent envy rent open went enjoy manner
2 zeal zest haze fix tax next quit quiz quote mosque
3 Shall I exchange these gloves? Size six is small.
4 We must sell them now. Tomorrow will be too late.

Up and Down Reach Practice

- One space follows a comma, a semicolon, and a period used in an abbreviation.

5 sum sum sum deny deny deny sung sung sung fund fun
6 zinc verb live myth uncle exert winds begin breaks
7 Mr. Zed must be present, or else they cannot vote.
8 Judy denied that any amount of the funds was lost.
9 He could not play; music never came easily to him.

Alternate Hands Practice

Type lines 10–18 twice. Then take two or more 1-minute writings: If your goal is speed, select lines 13 and 14 for your copy; if your goal is accuracy, select any line from 15 to 18 for your copy.

10 so is to if me of or to he am go am by is us to do
11 but an man sit eye got dig may dog fur did tie sue
12 down also lake auto city keys make firm hand worms
13 The women may go with Susie to help with the work.
14 An auditor paid for an ornament and got it for us.

Alphabetic Sentence Practice

Keep your wrists low!

15 A brown fox quickly jumps over the big, lazy dogs.
16 Joe packed five boxes of frozen quail in my trunk.
17 Quick, Jay, fix my two big zinc valves which drip.
18 The six brave women do quick flying trapeze jumps.

Tabulator Review

- Clear all tab stops.
- Set new stops 5, 10, 15, and 20 spaces to the right of the left margin.
- Begin line 19 at the left margin.
- Use the tab bar or key to indent the other lines.

```
19 Just put some zip in your work; use sharp strokes.
20      As you hit the keys, do not move your elbows.
21           See, say, and stroke the letter quickly.
22                Never rest your wrist on the frame.
23                     Sit up straight when you type.
```

5

197 Words

Do you have a typebar machine? If you do, you 10
should spend at least some time at the end of each 20
workday caring for it. This will keep the machine 30
in good working order. 35

First, clean the type with a short brush that 45
has straight bristles. To dislodge ribbon ink and 55
other dirt, use a jabbing motion. Finish by wiping 65
the type with several thicknesses of cloth 73
wrapped around the brush, using a side-to-side 82
motion. You may also use a plastic cleaner, which 92
is rolled back and forth over the type. It should 102
be kneaded after each use so that it will absorb 112
the dirt it has picked up. 117

Second, use a long-handled brush to clean 126
the frame, keys, key levers, typebars, and car- 136
riage. Move the carriage right and left to reach 146
underneath. Then brush the back. 152

To finish up, clean the surface under the 161
machine. (If it is fastened, put paper under it 171
while performing the first two steps.) Center 180
the carriage, so no one will bump it and throw 189
it off its rail; then cover the machine. SI 1.30 197

1 | 2 | 3 | 4 | 5 | 6 | 7 | 8 | 9 | 10 |

6

139 Words

It was a cold midwinter evening. Four 9
friends sat near the fire for warmth and comfort. 18
They had enjoyed a good dinner, and now they 27
were ready to spend the rest of the evening in 36
pleasant company. One of them turned on the 45
radio. They listened to a short talk about people 55
who were out of work and about others who 63
were employed at wages that were too low to 72
support them and their families. 78

The little company of four was moved by the 88
troubles that beset some of their neighbors. 97
When the radio program came to a close, the four 106
friends began to discuss what might be done to 116
provide for the needs of their less fortunate 125
neighbors. The next morning, the Mutual Aid 133
Society of our town was born. SI 1.33 139

1 | 2 | 3 | 4 | 5 | 6 | 7 | 8 | 9 | 10 |

7

171 Words

Perhaps the best way to give you an impres- 10
sion of the sport of sand yachting is to take you 19
on an imaginary trip along the beach on a glori- 29
ous summer day. As a pleasant breeze blows off 38
the sea, we travel over ground where probably no 48
one has been before. The sails are pulled in, and 58
the big wheels are coasting over the hard sand. 67
The first sensation is one of surprising speed, 77
with a complete absence of noise or vibration. 86

As we gain speed, you may have your first 95
misgivings as you see the windward front wheel 104
leave the ground. A glance at the speedometer 114
shows that we are moving at forty miles an hour. 123
When you consider that the fastest racing yacht 133
has never exceeded half this speed, you realize 142
how fast a sand yacht is. There is absolute si- 152
lence, except for the sound of the wheels splash- 161
ing through the puddles left by the receding tide. 171

SI 1.33

1 | 2 | 3 | 4 | 5 | 6 | 7 | 8 | 9 | 10 |

8

168 Words

It has long been the custom for people, on 9
the first day of April, to play friendly tricks on 19
each other. The origin of this is unknown. Ac- 29
cording to one version, people are sent on fruit- 39
less errands in memory of the mistake Noah 47
made on the first of April when he sent the dove 57
from the ark before the flood had eased up. 65

Another version traces the custom to a Ro- 75
man tale. A mother, hearing the echo of her 84
daughter's voice calling her, went in search, guid- 94
ing herself by the echo. This, of course, was a 103
fool's errand. 106

Another story says the custom began in 115
France. Formerly the New Year came at the end 124
of March. The height of the holiday occurred on 134
the first of April, when people made visits and 143
gave gifts. When the New Year was changed to 152
the first of January, the custom was kept up as 161
a joke, with mock visits and gifts. SI 1.34 168

1 | 2 | 3 | 4 | 5 | 6 | 7 | 8 | 9 | 10 |

Unit 16

Line spacing: single
Line length: 50
Paragraph indention: 5
Type each line twice.

Warmup

Type evenly and smoothly.

1 jaw car coal yard want, high stands; quick markets
2 It gives us pleasure to forward seven sample jars.
3 Six dozen boxes burned. Frequently zero boxes do.

Up and Down Reach Practice

Make reaches between top and bottom rows without stopping to return to home keys.

4 fund face pony menu fume lump lung hymn muff erect
5 twice check human broad count voice lunch no brain
6 I continue to serve my country every chance I get.
7 You must understand that I expect you much sooner.

Alternate Hands Practice

Try to type short words as a whole instead of letter by letter. Think or say the word; type it.

8 to do the, to do that, to do the, to do work, goal
9 and the, and then, and this, and that, and did, so
10 It is his duty to do the work as well as possible.
11 Down the lane is an old office in which she works.

Corrective Practice

Lines 12–15 reinforce the locations of **o** and **i** so that errors caused by confusing these keys can be reduced.

12 oil into iron omit noise obvious involve inclusion
13 folio obtain occasion indication invoice imitation
14 Importing more oil is going to increase inflation.
15 We will obtain action tonight at the union office.

Alphabetic Paragraph

Take two or more 2-minute writings.

Goal: Speed–20 wpm
Error limit–5

To obtain your speed, divide the total number of words you typed by 2.

16 There is a time for everything; and this is the 10
17 time to buy a new car. You will certainly be amazed 21
18 at our attractive offer on your present car. Just 31
19 examine our stock of new models. We have never seen 41
20 their equal. We look forward to seeing you. SI 1.33 50

1 | 2 | 3 | 4 | 5 | 6 | 7 | 8 | 9 | 10

Group 5 TIMED WRITINGS

The selections in this group serve two purposes. They can be used (1) to develop greater speed and accuracy and (2) to measure progress toward attaining these goals.

The selections are arranged by both length and syllabic intensity (SI). (There is also a group of script and rough-draft selections.) If you want to increase speed, select easy copy—copy with a syllabic intensity in the lower ranges (1.20 to 1.35). If your goal is to improve accuracy, select difficult copy—copy with a syllabic intensity in the higher ranges (above 1.50). For measuring speed *and* accuracy, select copy that falls between these two extremes. *Note:* Use a 70-character line and double spacing for all timings.

UNDER 200 WORDS

The following timed writings are arranged in three groups according to the syllabic intensities of the individual selections.

Selections 1–8, SI Range 1.20–1.35

1

107 Words

Throughout the world, people seem to have 9
always felt the need to tell the time of year. In 19
most regions, time was told by the changes in the 29
moon or the changes in the seasons of winter, 38
spring, summer, and fall. 43

The moon passes through its changes from 52
new moon to new moon in twenty-eight days. 60
It goes from a bright circle in the sky, to a little 71
slice of light, to no light at all. Then it goes back 82
to a bright circle. Native Americans reckoned 91
their time of year by these changes in the moon, 100
which they called the Night Sun. SI 1.20 107

1 | 2 | 3 | 4 | 5 | 6 | 7 | 8 | 9 | 10 |

2

94 Words

The world pays everyone in his or her own 9
coin. If you smile, the world smiles at you in 19
return; if you frown, you will be frowned at. If 28
you sing, you will be invited into musical com- 38
pany; if you think, you will be sought by thinkers. 48
If you love the world and truly seek for the good 58
that is in it, you will have loving friends, and 67
nature will pour into your lap the wealth of the 77
earth. If you blame and criticize, you will be 86
blamed and criticized by your fellows. SI 1.22 94

1 | 2 | 3 | 4 | 5 | 6 | 7 | 8 | 9 | 10 |

3

106 Words

I live in my car. I drive it everywhere, but 10
this week I am leaving it home. There is nothing 20
wrong with my car, but rush-hour traffic keeps 29
getting worse, and the cost of driving keeps 38
going up. 40

So last week I made a decision. I'd leave my 50
car in the garage for a week and give public trans- 60
portation a chance. After all, I am the public. 69
It has been an experience. Instead of watching 79
the brakelights of the car in front of me, I get a 89
chance to look at some scenery for a change or 98
to read a newspaper or just to relax. SI 1.27 106

1 | 2 | 3 | 4 | 5 | 6 | 7 | 8 | 9 | 10 |

4

99 Words

We live in what we regard as a very advanced 10
state of culture. We seldom recall that each age 20
must have seemed just as advanced to those who 29
lived in it. 31

On the other hand, is it not just as likely that 42
in a hundred years from now, new generations, 51
in their turn, will look back on us and, in the light 61
of their increased comforts, think our present 71
way of life incomplete? We have no way to know 80
what new discoveries and inventions may en- 89
tirely change the standards of living in the future. 99

SI 1.30

1 | 2 | 3 | 4 | 5 | 6 | 7 | 8 | 9 | 10 |

Unit 17

Line spacing: single
Line length: 50
Paragraph indention: 5
Type each line twice.

Warmup

1 jets yet keg zoo been being veal vile pen park far
2 What size? Who came next? Did Fred quit quickly?
3 He can do the job, but he should go with them now.

1| 2| 3| 4| 5| 6| 7| 8| 9| 10|

Margin Release and Double Spacing

To type beyond the point where the right margin locks, press the margin release key. This must be done each time the margin locks.
To double-space material (each typed line will have a blank line above and below), set the line space regulator on 2.

Semi **finger or** ***A*** **finger** MAR REL

Set line space regulator on 2. Set a tab for paragraph indentions. Type lines 4–12 line for line. Each time the carriage locks, use the margin release key to complete the line. (Your copy will not have an even right margin.)

4 The next time our family goes camping, we will take our
5 new camper bus. It is a good way to relax. It is the most
6 versatile and comfortable vehicle ever made, as well as the
7 most civilized. You can quote me on that.
8 You can go anywhere in comfort. It has everything,
9 including the kitchen sink. In fact, it also has an icebox,
10 a water pump, closets, and a dining table, plus room enough
11 for beds for two adults and a child. It is quite an
12 enjoyable way to go on a carefree vacation.

Corrective Practice

Lines 13–17 reinforce the locations of **r** and **t** so that errors caused by confusing these keys can be reduced.

Goal: To type line 16 or 17 twice in 1 minute with not more than 2 errors.

13 rot tar rate tear rust trap rent later ratio water
14 trip rest hurt repeat trade report right term tree
15 great there third rebate tenure thereafter theater
16 Try to rotate tires at intervals for better tread.
17 The rate the rat traps were returned was terrible.

1| 2| 3| 4| 5| 6| 7| 8| 9| 10|

Paragraph Practice continued

9 ACKNOWLEDGMENTS: The picture on the cover, entitled "The 12
Open Door," appears through the courtesy of White & Lyons Studios. 26
The cartoon "Good News" (page 69) is printed by special permission 39
of the Carson Women's Club. We are indebted to Mr. John O'Connor for the 53
photographs on pages 28, 30, and 74. 61

10 The Lewis & Haley Toy Shop is conducting a word-building contest. The 15
following sign is displayed in the window: "Prizes of $25, $15, and $10 29
to the girls or boys who prepare the longest lists of words, four letters 44
or more, using the letters in Lewis Haley Toys. Come inside for a circular 65
giving details." 69

11 Henry Bolton of Cleveland, Ohio, reported to the police today that his 15
wife's jewels had been stolen. He said that the jewels, valued at $3,200, 30
were taken from a wall safe in his home. They included a pearl necklace 44
valued at $1,500; a diamond and ruby ring, $900; and an emerald and 58
diamond brooch, $800. The ring was inscribed, "H. B. to L. B.— 70
6/14/66." 72

12 We have just published our handy pocket edition of A Citizen's 18
Guide to the City, size 5½″ × 3¼″. It contains 124 pages of informa- 38
tion about our city—its public buildings, restaurants, hotels, theaters, 53
transit lines—and costs only 95¢. A similar guide, size 10″ × 7½″, has 67
been selling for $2.50. 72

13 BERNARD & FRENCH stores rugs on its premises at a charge of 13
3% of the appraised value. A minimum charge of $7.50 is made for rugs 27
9′ × 12′ or smaller. Small rugs are accepted as scatter rugs in groups of 42
four, at a $9 minimum for the group. In addition, the store offers a 55
cleaning service—80¢ per square foot for domestic rugs and 90¢ per 69
square foot for Oriental rugs. 75

14 At the low cost of only $5 a month, our life insurance policy pays up to 15
$5,500 to your beneficiary if death is due to natural causes. Death 29
benefits are increased for loss of life due to (1) an automobile or bus 43
accident or (2) an accident while traveling in a train or in an airplane. 58
Our policies are issued to men and women, ages 21 to 60 years. Don't 72
delay! Write for full information TODAY! 80

15 NOTICE IS HEREBY GIVEN that the twentieth annual meeting of 13
stockholders of the Regal Gas & Electric Corporation will be held on 26
Monday, November 25, at 2:30 p.m. for (1) the election of directors 40
and (2) the transaction of all other business that may properly come 53
before the meeting. Stockholders who do not expect to attend are urged 68
to sign and return the enclosed proxy. 89

Unit 18

Line spacing: single
Line length: 50
Paragraph indention: 5
Type each line twice.

Warmup

Strike the keys with a quick, light movement.

1 just equal; five copies; size six; too much ground
2 night flight bright quaint acquaint joke woke yoke
3 Mr. Foy; above zero; below zero; tax expert; What?

1 | 2 | 3 | 4 | 5 | 6 | 7 | 8 | 9 | 10 |

New Key Location

The hyphen is used to connect parts of a compound word, like *up-to-date*, and to divide a word at the end of a line.
Two hyphens typed in succession are used to make a dash. Leave no space before, between, or after typing hyphens.

Semi finger -

4 ;-; ;-; a self-made man; fifty-two weeks in a year
5 ;--; ;--; a set-back--no defeat; strike three--out
6 Mrs. Day needs twenty-one change-of-address cards.
7 I hate to ask--you know me--but we need your help.
8 Pins, needles, thread--the store has many notions.
9 Her son-in-law had the right-of-way on the street.
10 We gave that know-it-all a good send-off Saturday.

Up and Down Reach Practice

11 opener opener music music curb curb once once much
12 expect expect noisy noisy cent cent verb verb debt
13 In May the fare was raised from five cents to ten.
14 Tommy expects to travel to France and Switzerland.

Corrective Practice

Lines 15–18 reinforce the locations of **m** and **n** so that errors caused by confusing these keys can be reduced.

15 men men mine mine minor minor mind mind manner man
16 money money numbers numbers manage manager mariner
17 For a nominal sum, we can maintain numerous names.
18 Many minors are mailing money to merchant marines.

Group 4 NUMBERS AND SPECIAL CHARACTERS

PARAGRAPH PRACTICE

Select a paragraph you feel you can type in 1 minute. If you complete the paragraph before time is called, select a longer one for the next writing. Continue this way until you find the longest paragraph you can complete—or almost complete—in 1 minute.

PARAGRAPH PRACTICE

Note that underscored words in these paragraphs have been given triple value in the word counts at the right.

70-space line.

1 James sang "Ol' Man River" in a deep, rich voice. In response to the 15
applause of the audience, he sang, as an encore, "When Twilight's Here" 29
(his own composition). 33

2 Here's a spray that's guaranteed to protect woolens against moths. 14
Buy now, before the moths do any damage. ANTIMOTH sells for $1.95 a 28
pint, $3.45 a quart, and $6.00 a half-gallon; special sprayer, $1.89. 42

3 The corporation's records show that 96% of its 58,000 shares are held 15
by stockholders with addresses in the United States and only 4% are held 29
by stockholders with addresses in foreign countries (chiefly England). 43

4 Color bulbs for lamps are of three types: (1) natural colored glass, 15
(2) glass coated outside, and (3) glass coated or enameled inside. Bulbs 29
may be clear or frosted. Bulbs frosted on the inside absorb only 1% or $1\frac{1}{2}$% 44
of the light. 47

5 On March 1, Cromwell & Company had on hand orders amounting to 13
$68,000—40% more than a year ago—with prospects of an additional 26
increase by April 1. Ms. Yates (in charge during Mr. Cromwell's absence) 41
was very much pleased with the report. 49

6 The farmer ordered three #6 spades at $5.75 and a #41 hoe at $4.50. 14
He said, "I can use more tools than I can afford to buy. I'm hoping for a 29
sale in the spring (or possibly in the early summer) when I can buy at prices 45
that I can afford." 49

7 Our accident insurance policy costs you only $9\frac{1}{2}$¢ a day. Isn't the 14
protection it gives you well worth that amount? Read what Ms. Ellen 28
Burgess writes: "I have received your check for $225 in payment of my 42
claim on Policy #4110. I certainly appreciate your prompt settlement." 56

8 Kearny & Bell, a manufacturer of children's sweaters, has rented 14
6,750 square feet of floor space (75 feet by 90 feet) on the 16th floor of 29
the Lincoln Building, 2834 Clinton Street. They are paying a monthly 42
rental of $3,375. The lease runs for five years, with the option of a five- 58
year renewal. 60

Typing Skill Checkup

Take two or more 2-minute writings.

Goal: Speed–21 wpm
Error limit–5

To obtain your speed, divide the total number of words you typed by 2.

19   As a young worker, you will be trading your 10
20 time and energy and skills for wages--for money. 19
21 Working is really your way of paying the employer 29
22 for all the wages he pays you. 35
23   Wages help determine the place you live, the 45
clothes you wear, and the food you eat. SI 1.30 53

1 | 2 | 3 | 4 | 5 | 6 | 7 | 8 | 9 | 10 |

SKILL DEVELOPMENT — Unit 19

Line spacing: single
Line length: 50
Paragraph indention: 5

Warmup

Type each line twice and double-space after each pair of lines.

1 ice ice run run curb curb zinc zinc next next much
2 They will deny; care-free week; seven-page article
3 Is my service satisfactory? Yes, it is excellent.

1 | 2 | 3 | 4 | 5 | 6 | 7 | 8 | 9 | 10 |

Typing from Script

Typing from handwritten copy is an important part of many jobs. Studies have shown that most copy given to office typists is in this form. Begin to build skill in this vital area by typing the sentences below.

Set margins for a 40-space line: 30–75 (elite), 22–67 (pica).

4 *I must pack all the clothes in my trunk.*
5 *In April the fare was raised five cents.*
6 *He expects to travel to Spain and Italy.*

Speed Paragraphs

Use these paragraphs for 1- and 2-minute writings.

Push for a new level of speed by applying the proper typing techniques learned in earlier units.

1   Here are a few hints on the use of the phone 10
when customers call. Answer the call at once and 20
start by giving the name of your company. In this 30
way you save time. SI 1.18 33

1 | 2 | 3 | 4 | 5 | 6 | 7 | 8 | 9 | 10 |

(Continued on next page)

MOVING FROM BANK TO BANK

In this drill, you will get additional practice in making long reaches. Reach from the first to the third bank of keys, and from the third to the first, without stopping to return to the home keys.

MOVING FROM BANK TO BANK

65-space line.

1 my fun face pony menu fume lump lung hymn muff erect thumb break 13
2 twice check human broad count voice lunch brain pound broil round 26
3 brick elect price under since brush bring humor found bread uncle 39
4 enemy force place sound clung brass piece doubt music ounce amuse 52
5 forbid chance harbor Sunday record junior affect mutual numeral 65

6 amount barber branch immune hunger recent advice murmur central 13
7 recent lumber sprung ground tumble select autumn success account 26
8 receive breathe laundry science mystery counsel subject brought 39
9 economy certain observe brother connect balance perfect country 52
10 service advance destiny maximum because harmony precede proceed 65

11 We expect to continue manufacturing brass plumbing until August. 13
12 We have recently had an opportunity to effect certain economies. 26
13 I assume that you will respect my advice and check the account. 39

14 I remained at the office until six trying to balance the account. 13
15 I found it necessary to obtain insurance on my new car at once. 26
16 No doubt your brother will volunteer to connect our large radio. 39
17 Under the circumstances, this place will serve as my art studio. 52

18 The sound of the tuning of the musical instruments was annoying. 13
19 My uncle expects to succeed in paying off the debt by December. 26
20 They have recently had great success by using a special process. 39
21 Unless we deny the rumor at once, it is certain to affect prices. 52
22 We shall continue to serve our government at every opportunity. 65

23 The office manager found that a number of changes were necessary. 13
24 The laundry announced a slight reduction in price for the summer. 26
25 You must understand that they expect all of you to be punctual. 39
26 My brother and I spent all last summer on a farm in the country. 52
27 Since you have brought up the subject, you must face the truth. 65
28 We have found the lumber we received yesterday of poor quality. 78

29 The balance of his account shows he is too heavily in debt to us. 13
30 The junior partner told the clerk to issue a summons immediately. 26
31 I have no doubt that she will object to the amount of the bill. 39
32 With our new process, we can produce a hundred copies a minute. 52
33 I have found a great difference in the number of copies produced. 65
34 I have checked my count twice, and my answer is certainly correct. 78

1 | 2 | 3 | 4 | 5 | 6 | 7 | 8 | 9 | 10 | 11 | 12 | 13 |

2 Always use a pleasant tone of voice. Speak 10
clearly, so that whoever is at the other end can 19
understand what you are saying. When the person 29
who is wanted is not in, offer to take a message. 39
SI 1.35

3 If you are able to take care of a matter, do 10
it yourself. Be brief and clear. When the other 20
person rambles on and on, try to bring the talk to 30
an end without being too abrupt. End on a cordial 40
note, so as to leave a friendly impression. SI 1.27 48

4 All of our employees must stamp a time clock 10
when they arrive in the morning and when they go 19
at the close of the day. In this way, we have a 29
record of the number of days and hours each person 39
has worked. We need this record for our payroll. SI 1.18 49

Eyes on copy!

5 When you learn keyboarding, you gain a skill 10
that you will never forget even if you do not use 20
it for some time. The good techniques you have 29
learned always remain. Because they do, any speed 39
you lose can easily be rebuilt with just a little 49
practice. It is possible for you to build accuracy 59
in the same way. SI 1.32 62

1 | 2 | 3 | 4 | 5 | 6 | 7 | 8 | 9 | 10 |

SKILL DEVELOPMENT

Unit 20

Line spacing: single
Line length: 50
Paragraph indention: 5

Warmup

Type each line twice.

1 sun sun any any verb verb seize seize yield yields
2 full-time workers; part-time work; Is he a member?
3 What is the amount of discount on the list prices?

1 | 2 | 3 | 4 | 5 | 6 | 7 | 8 | 9 | 10 |

ALTERNATING HAND WORDS

In this drill, each word contains letters typed by alternating hands. This arrangement of letters permits you to type faster than your normal rate. Use this drill whenever you have reached a barrier in your speed and cannot break into new, higher levels.

ALTERNATING HAND WORDS
65-space line.

1 and big man for end pay six air own cut sir the may but sit did 13
2 girl work make turn coal name them such hand duty when down paid 26
3 than both pair town sign land firm with half city goal also held 39
4 corn dish rich hang lake melt ivory eight shake panel shelf field 52
5 right usual spend laugh world slept quake chair shape panel fight 65
6 their sight rifle slant burns civic bushel chapel embody formal 78
7 social handle dismay quench sleigh profit enamel island emblems 91
8 visual penalty auditor problems entitle ancient memento signals 104
9 quantity neighbor chairman ornament busybody amendment proficient 117

1 | 2 | 3 | 4 | 5 | 6 | 7 | 8 | 9 | 10 | 11 | 12 | 13 |

DOUBLE LETTERS

When you strike the same key twice in succession, use equal force each time. To do this, be sure that you release the key before making the second stroke.

DOUBLE LETTERS
65-space line.

1 good beef deep roof cool miss wood ebbs need soon adds door odds 13
2 steep annul cheer feels fully alley annex spool apply berry stood 26
3 sweep allow tooth arrow essay utter troop error asset flood witty 39
4 steel annoy bloom offer added broom carry ditto upper occur funny 52
5 follow common manner supply horror matter appeal errand assistant 65
6 accept afford beggar teller winner ballot effect alleged borrower 78
7 little coffee summer occupy lesson vacuum cotton piazza attentive 91

8 accent canned affair differ dagger sullen effort wallet schooling 13
9 attack attach appear barrel tissue assert arrive attend excessive 26
10 bazaar robber stucco sudden suffer access esteem waffle illogical 39
11 rubbing succeed account address fifteen taffeta suggest trolley 52
12 baggage swallow million ammonia current vanilla suppose appoint 65
13 collect stammer shipped support command channel apparel connect 78
14 approve correct dresser affects planned battery possess proceed 91

15 terrible assemble allotted tomorrow dissolve blizzard occasional 13
16 announce applause surround opposite pressure currency procession 26
17 accuracy struggle alliance commerce druggist collapse biannually 39
18 different efficient aggravate beginning immediately surrendered 52
19 dismissal committee necessary attribute accommodate predecessor 65
20 supplement correspond expression accumulate remittance bookkeeper 78
21 abbreviate commission disappoint appreciate difficulty challenged 91

1 | 2 | 3 | 4 | 5 | 6 | 7 | 8 | 9 | 10 | 11 | 12 | 13 |

Typing from Script

Set margins for a 40-space line: 30–75 (elite), 22–67 (pica).

4 *We organized committees to represent all.*
5 *Barbara made a brief but adequate reply.*
6 *I am paid in full; I expect delivery now.*

Alphabetic Paragraphs

Use these paragraphs for 1- and 2-minute writings.

Concentrate on the reaches that are difficult for you.

1 Have you a picture you would like us to take 10
and exhibit in our gallery of modern art? We try 20
to invite only artists whose work is recognized by 30
well-known judges of art as superior in quality. 39
SI 1.45

2 Here at Green Meadow Inn, vacation dreams do 10
come true. If you want relaxation, you may enjoy 20
quiet, lazy hours stretched out beneath big sunny 29
skies. If you prefer activity, you may prefer to 39
swim, fish, or play tennis and golf. SI 1.41 46

3 Pay all your bills with a personalized check. 10
Our special checking account saves you time and a 20
lot of money. You receive a monthly statement of 30
deposits and withdrawals. Your canceled checks 39
are a record of your major expenses. SI 1.49 46

4 All authorized employees of our company must 10
carry a card showing their name and their picture. 20
We expect them to show this card upon request. We 30
are justified in refusing to admit persons who say 40
they work for us but will not identify themselves. 50
SI 1.50

Return quickly without looking up at the end of each line.

5 On this, our fiftieth anniversary as a large 10
organization, we wish to express our thanks to the 20
many good friends who patronize our service. We 29
hope you will join us in celebrating this event on 39
next Saturday. We shall be happy to mail you two 49
tickets upon your request. SI 1.51 54

1 | 2 | 3 | 4 | 5 | 6 | 7 | 8 | 9 | 10 |

Letter Y

1 any why boy only play body story party young system employ beyond 13

2 They always carry completely equipped bags of the best quality. 13
3 I have really not yet had an opportunity to pay you the money. 12
4 Early in the day, he is generally busy getting the mail ready. 12

5 Every time you give us an order, you are in a hurry for delivery. 13
6 We have a supply of gray yarn at the factory ready for delivery. 13
7 We are very sorry it is necessary to reduce your supply of coal. 13

8 The youthful style of this dress is typical of the stock we buy. 13
9 Everybody is fully aware of the necessity of an early delivery. 13
10 The lawyer says he does not yet know why you had to pay so much. 13

Letter Z

1 zone size dozen seize prize razor hazard realize citizen organize 13

2 We realize that they were not authorized to seize the property. 13
3 The organization offered a dozen prizes for the best suggestions. 13
4 We must familiarize the public with the two sizes of our razors. 13

5 We recognize the great power of an organization of this size. 12
6 The citizens were puzzled by his zeal and amazed at his energy. 13
7 The authorized agents in this zone sold dozens of these razors. 13

8 We realize the size is wrong, but we are puzzled about the error. 13
9 An organization of this size must systematize all its records. 12
10 The citizens asked the officials to recognize their organization. 13

1 | 2 | 3 | 4 | 5 | 6 | 7 | 8 | 9 | 10 | 11 | 12 | 13 |

LEFT- AND RIGHT-HAND WORDS

Each word in this drill is made up of letters typed entirely by either the left hand or the right hand. Left-hand and right-hand words alternate. Use this drill to strengthen fingers of each hand.

LEFT-HAND AND RIGHT-HAND WORDS
65-space line.

1 red you war him tax ill set lip bad oil get joy was pin are mop 13
2 safe look case noon rest upon were pull grew kill best lion read 26
3 text July rate milk dear only feet join date lump fact link card 39
4 poppy trade imply state onion serve pupil exact union brave hilly 52
5 regret million exceeded opinion career minimum addressed monopoly 65
6 plump estate uphill baggage poplin steadfast pumpkin afterwards 78

1 | 2 | 3 | 4 | 5 | 6 | 7 | 8 | 9 | 10 | 11 | 12 | 13 |

Unit 21

Line spacing: single
Line length: 60
Paragraph indention: 5
Type each line twice.

Warmup

Start using a 60-space line: 20–85 (elite), 12–77 (pica).

1 double-spaced, twenty-seven forget-me-nots, up-to-the-minute
2 How quickly were the jackets sent? We shipped them express.
3 Jose—and three men—did not see Van at the end of the path.

1 | 2 | 3 | 4 | 5 | 6 | 7 | 8 | 9 | 10 | 11 | 12 |

New Key Location

A finger **1**

If your machine has no **1** key, use the small **l.**

4 aqa aqa aqa aql aql aql ala ala ala alla alla alla
5 zone l, l television, l jet plane, l taxi, l quart
6 The sheik has ll wives and ll planes and lll cars.

F finger **4**

7 frf frf frf fr4 fr4 fr4 f4f f4f f4f f44f f44f f44f
8 area 4, 4-point grade average, 4 players, 4 houses
9 Mabel is 4 years of age. Her brother Frank is l4.

Number Practice

Keep contact with the home keys as you make direct reaches to the numbers **1** and **4.**

10 l and 4; 4 and ll; l4 and l; l and l4; ll4 and l; l and ll4;
11 These ll4 men won l44 prizes in five days in the llth month.
12 I need ll or 44 blue, 4 or l4 white, l4l or 4l4 red, 4 pink.

Corrective Practice

Lines 13–16 reinforce the locations of **a** and **s** so that errors caused by confusing these keys can be reduced.

13 as safe said seal soap ages scale shape staff state assassin
14 stake areas arise swear space spare speak small smash arrest
15 atlas answer assure standards special adjust surpass assault
16 After the assault, an assassin was arrested by small squads.

Alphabetic Paragraph

Take two or more 1-minute writings.

Goal: Speed–23 wpm
Error limit–2

17 Are you looking for a luxury apartment? If so, apply to 12
18 our authorized agency. The homes we offer, equipped with the 24
19 best modern improvements, are just what you will like. SI 1.50 35

1 | 2 | 3 | 4 | 5 | 6 | 7 | 8 | 9 | 10 | 11 | 12 |

Letter V

1 even very have move drive voice leave every serve provide improve 13

2 We see your point of view and shall be governed by your advice. 13
3 Whenever it is to our advantage to leave, we will move to Denver. 13
4 On several occasions, we have been able to give you this service. 13

5 We believe, moreover, that we can save several hundred dollars. 13
6 We take advantage of every opportunity to improve our service. 12
7 My visit to the governor evidently proved to be a very good move. 13

8 We advise you to give us an order for our new improved varnish. 13
9 We believe you must have received delivery early in November. 12
10 We have, however, investigated their service very carefully. 12

Letter W

1 low own way away view wish power owing where toward follow window 13

2 We know who wrote the letter, and we will answer the complaint. 13
3 A few of the workers went away without waiting for an interview. 13
4 It would be well worth our while to watch them work tomorrow. 12

5 The lawyer wants to know how much power is wasted in this way. 12
6 We know that we owe you the money, but you must wait awhile. 12
7 We would be willing to make an allowance on the damaged pillows. 13

8 Within the next two weeks, we will install a powerful new motor. 13
9 Deposits which are made now will draw interest at seven percent. 13
10 While you were away last week, I did whatever work was necessary. 13

Letter X

1 tax six box next exit exist exact exert extra mixed luxury except 13

2 We expect to send six boxes of canned goods by express next week. 13
3 He explained that he wished to exchange the sixty wax candles. 12
4 She examined the electric fixtures on display at the exposition. 13

5 We ordered textbooks containing the maximum number of exercises. 13
6 Next week we shall begin recording extra charges on index cards. 13
7 She expressed the opinion that we should expand our export market. 13

8 The expert explained that expensive luxuries were subject to tax. 13
9 We expect to be extremely busy with income tax reports next week. 13
10 The extra fixtures were forwarded by express in two large boxes. 13

1 | 2 | 3 | 4 | 5 | 6 | 7 | 8 | 9 | 10 | 11 | 12 | 13 |

Unit 22

Line spacing: single
Line length: 60
Paragraph indention: 5
Type each line twice.

Warmup

Use firm, sharp, brisk strokes.

1 enjoy enjoys enjoyed; quick quickly; offices official; saves
2 expect expert express; seize prizes realizes; sack Jack back
3 He applied 4 times--in 14 days. Give him 1 day and 4 hours.

1 | 2 | 3 | 4 | 5 | 6 | 7 | 8 | 9 | 10 | 11 | 12 |

New Key Location

***F* finger 5**

4 ftf ftf ft5f ft5f ft5f ft5f f5f f5f f55f f55f f55f
5 Code 5, 5 slips, 5 men, 5 dollars, 5 boys, 5 girls
6 He lives at 5 Park Avenue and works 5 blocks away.

***K* finger 8**

7 kik kik ki8k ki8k ki8k ki8k k8k k8k k88k k88k k88k
8 8 seconds 8 minutes 8 hours 8 days 8 weeks 8 years
9 An airplane flew the route in 8 hours, 18 minutes.

Number Practice

10 1 and 4; 5 and 8; 14 and 55; 11 and 4; 15 and 88; 15 and 18;
11 On May 5, the 18 women boarded Flight 85 and flew 584 miles.
12 The 15 boys and 8 girls had a picnic at a park 8 miles away.

Corrective Practice

Lines 13–16 reinforce the locations of **e** and **i** so that errors caused by confusing these keys can be reduced.

13 tie lie ice edit emit irate edible either elicit ignite nice
14 indeed earlier easiest eligible eminent engineer inefficient
15 Efficient service and delicious food are our chief concerns.
16 The eminent engineers said that the evidence was sufficient.

Alphabetic Paragraph

Take two or more 1-minute writings.

17 Wreckers will attack an abandoned building at 58 Smythe 12
18 Street next Friday. A wrecking company at 814 Quinault Road 24
19 has just received a permit to raze the property. SI 1.50 34

1 | 2 | 3 | 4 | 5 | 6 | 7 | 8 | 9 | 10 | 11 | 12 |

Letter S

1 was his set also last wise sweet start trust person answer custom 13

2 I must express my personal disapproval of his course of action. 13
3 First consider the cost before starting to act on her suggestion. 13
4 It is impossible to please this customer; he refuses to listen. 13

5 The advertisement in the last issue caused a sharp rise in sales. 13
6 This store sells shoes, slippers, and socks at reasonable prices. 13
7 Perhaps he considers it advisable to ship these goods by express. 13

8 I assure you that the suggestion is the subject of careful study. 13
9 For several reasons we suspect his answer is not an honest one. 13
10 We wish you would test our service to see how satisfactory it is. 13

Letter T

1 put get art list both test built doubt after health commit better 13

2 It is about time for you to stop trying to control every detail. 13
3 I doubt whether conditions will be any better in the near future. 13
4 Thank you for taking the trouble to investigate the situation. 12

5 The president thought their objections were of little importance. 13
6 After missing the train, they returned from the station together. 13
7 In order not to waste time, ship twenty additional bolts at once. 13

8 If it is not too much trouble, please wait until next Tuesday. 12
9 We operate the factory at great cost and with many difficulties. 13
10 Part of the time was spent in pointing out the faults in style. 13

Letter U

1 out cut buy much your upon about trust usual summer bought future 13

2 Unless your products improve, we must close our account with you. 13
3 Under the circumstances, you should have no serious difficulty. 13
4 He thought that you do not carry enough insurance on your house. 13

5 You will be surprised to see how much better our results are now. 13
6 Unless you have a discount card, we must charge our usual price. 13
7 Let us support the young folk in their drive for a building fund. 13

8 We trust that you can furnish us with double the number of tubes. 13
9 During the summer, we usually offer wonderful values in furs. 12
10 The usual business circular could be drawn up in about an hour. 13

1 | 2 | 3 | 4 | 5 | 6 | 7 | 8 | 9 | 10 | 11 | 12 | 13 |

REVIEW

Unit 23

Line spacing: single
Line length: 60
Paragraph indention: 5
Type each line twice.

Use a sharp, bounce-off stroke on the space bar.

Warmup

1 banks rank; nests jest quest; size prizes; carry marry Jerry
2 If they flee to prevent the exams, she may go to Washington.
3 48 kilograms, 15 grams, 85 liters, 41 centimeters, 58 quarts

1 | 2 | 3 | 4 | 5 | 6 | 7 | 8 | 9 | 10 | 11 | 12 |

Before typing lines 4–7, reset the margins to 25–80 (elite) or 17–72 (pica). Use the margin release to complete each line.

Margin Release Key Practice

4 Under the circumstances, this place will serve as my studio.
5 The office manager found a number of changes were necessary.
6 My brother and I spent last summer on a farm in the country.
7 Tom realized very quickly that jumping was excellent for us.

Clear previous tabs. Set left margin at 30 and tab stops at 45 and 60. Type **across** rows 8–11, not down the columns.

Tabulator Key Practice

	Left margin 30 ↓	First tab 45 ↓	Second tab 60 ↓
8	bad	worse	worst
9	good	better	best
10	much	more	most
11	little	less	least

Did you remember to reset your margins for a 60-space line?

Number Practice

12 He assigned us pages 8 and 15 in our math book for homework.
13 She scored 48 and 55 on the seventh series of English tests.
14 He made 8 home runs in 14 different games during the season.
15 See page 14 in Pamphlet 18 for old—but less costly—models.

Take two or more 2-minute writings.

Goal: Speed–23 wpm
Error limit–4

Alphabetic Paragraph

16 When you are in Europe, make sure you visit Switzerland, 12
17 famous for its majestic snow-clad mountains. Our agency will 24
18 provide up-to-date, luxurious quarters, with the skill born 36
19 of experience. When you travel on Sky-Line Airways, you will 48
20 enjoy both safety and comfort. We have never had an accident. 61

SI 1.50

1 | 2 | 3 | 4 | 5 | 6 | 7 | 8 | 9 | 10 | 11 | 12 |

Letter P

1 pay cap lip deep hope open place cheap speak employ report people 13

2 What we plan to do depends on what happens at the open meeting. 13
3 These samples represent only part of our complete line of paints. 13
4 The present policy of the company prevents our accepting returns. 13

5 We expect a special shipment of paper the latter part of April. 13
6 Our shop hopes to supply superior products at popular prices. 12
7 Our report on the property is based on the opinion of our expert. 13

8 We expect prompt payment for purchases when bills are presented. 13
9 We simply cannot depend on a cheap product to serve our purpose. 13
10 They probably plan to put these imported platters on special sale. 13

Letter Q

1 quite quote equal quick equip liquid inquire frequent acquainted 13

2 I question whether it is worth quoting on so small a quantity. 12
3 Consequently, we requested a large quantity of new equipment. 12
4 A quart of the liquid is required to wax the equipment properly. 13

5 We frequently find it necessary to submit quotations quickly. 12
6 An inquiry into her qualifications proved her equal to the task. 13
7 He inquired about the quantity and the quality of the stock. 12

8 In consequence, we can quote values you cannot equal anywhere. 12
9 We frequently require several months to get adequate equipment. 13
10 Six and a quarter yards are not quite adequate for the quilt. 12

Letter R

1 air are nor care part burn cover front large direct master rather 13

2 The experiment proves that direct advertising is worth the cost. 13
3 Whenever there is serious trouble, they try to win our support. 13
4 We cannot grant further credit before you pay the previous bill. 13

5 Certainly our course is clear; we must look for other markets. 12
6 Unless we approve his report, the treasurer will surely resign. 13
7 Our ready-to-wear winter dresses have been reduced for clearance. 13

8 In March we distributed samples of our product from door to door. 13
9 Under the circumstances, we regret we cannot accept your order. 13
10 As a rule, we try not to censor articles appearing in our paper. 13

1 | 2 | 3 | 4 | 5 | 6 | 7 | 8 | 9 | 10 | 11 | 12 | 13 |

SKILL DEVELOPMENT

Unit 24

Line spacing: single
Line length: 60
Paragraph indention: 5
Type each line twice.

Warmup

1 tax, lax, axes, vex, exists, zeal, zone, zero, zinc, buzzard
2 Math is fun--4 and 4 is 8; 5 less 1 is 4; and 8 less 4 is 4.
3 What did Mr. Gant say? He said he will consider my request.
4 Jorge and Bob did not get their pay for walking off the job.

1 | 2 | 3 | 4 | 5 | 6 | 7 | 8 | 9 | 10 | 11 | 12 |

Alternate Hands Sentence Practice

To develop speed, type smoothly and continuously.

5 She is busy with her work, but is to go to town for the bow.
6 His wish is to go to the city to talk to the man about gold.
7 He may wish to bus them if and when they go to work for her.

Alphabetic Sentence Practice

Goal: To type lines 8–10 with no more than 2 errors.

8 Yesterday, Jo quietly picked six zippers from the woven bag.
9 Please pack my boxes with five dozen jugs of liquid varnish.
10 Jack Farming realized the big, yellow quilts were expensive.

Number Practice

11 1 and 4; 51 and 8; 11 and 4 and 5; 48 and 1; 15 and 8; 4 and
12 a house 15 years old; less than 48 hours; 45 gallons of milk
13 They ordered 18 quilts, but they liked only the 5 blue ones.
14 The accident occurred on July 18. He returned on August 14.
15 Our bill dated November 5 covered your purchase of 48 cases.

Typing Skill Checkup

Take a 2-minute writing on lines 16–21. If you make 4 errors or less, practice lines 5–7. If you make more than 4 errors, practice lines 8–10. Then take two more 2-minute writings. Compare with the first timing.

Goal: Speed—24 wpm
Error limit—4

16 Office jobs are found everywhere—not just downtown in 12
17 cities and towns, but in the country, too. Every business— 24
18 no matter whether it is in the city or whether it is in the 36
19 country—needs office workers. 42
20 When you begin searching for a job, do not skip any place 54
21 because it does not seem like an ordinary business. SI 1.36 64

1 | 2 | 3 | 4 | 5 | 6 | 7 | 8 | 9 | 10 | 11 | 12 |

Letter M

1 met arm rim firm time warm admit limit mimic moment number common 13

2 I remember many remarks he made that seemed strange at the time. 13
3 It is important to have most of the motors completed by tomorrow. 13
4 We may, for example, employ more people in autumn than in summer. 13

5 The company has adopted a modern, improved method of manufacture. 13
6 You must take as much time as you need to match the material. 12
7 Inform him that the men will meet me at the same time tomorrow. 13

8 It may be as much as a month or more before we hear from them. 12
9 Remember that our firm will meet a great deal of competition. 12
10 I recommend this as a modern home, with a good plumbing system. 13

Letter N

1 man not win mean sign turn learn round train within reason nation 13

2 It is my opinion that we need not be concerned about competition. 13
3 Your answers to our questions were neither frank nor friendly. 12
4 Since the situation has changed, I want to reconsider the plan. 13

5 I cannot understand why he did not engage in that discussion. 12
6 It is now nearly a month since we sent the prints on approval. 12
7 The president did not know that the money had been spent. 11

8 Many men have obtained personal or business loans at this bank. 13
9 Kindly notify them that I cannot obtain the information sooner. 13
10 The purchase of savings bonds is a sound financial investment. 12

Letter O

1 for you too work stop move motor short could ought profit dollar 13

2 The road to town has been closed on account of flood conditions. 13
3 Only this afternoon I discovered another error in your accounts. 13
4 I doubt whether the property would altogether suit your purpose. 13

5 We shall, of course, continue to employ some people all year round. 13
6 If you cooperate, we can dispose of our old stock without loss. 12
7 Everyone knows that the spot remover we recommend is a good one. 13

8 You acknowledge that you owe the amount shown on the invoice. 12
9 You owe it to yourself to take advantage of this opportunity. 12
10 Our colored cotton is sold at notion counters in most stores. 12

1 | 2 | 3 | 4 | 5 | 6 | 7 | 8 | 9 | 10 | 11 | 12 | 13 |

Unit 25

Line spacing: single
Line length: 60
Paragraph indention: 5
Type each line twice.

Warmup

Return quickly without looking up at the end of each line.

1 box boxes; size sizes; dozen dozens; checks checked; wrecked
2 These 154 new fliers flew 58 planes at the 18th annual show.
3 The man cut up the six gray furs just the way you had asked.

1 | 2 | 3 | 4 | 5 | 6 | 7 | 8 | 9 | 10 | 11 | 12 |

New Key Location

L finger **9**

4 lol lol lol lo9 lo9 lo9 191 191 191 1.19 1.19 1.19
5 9 cents; 9 nickels; 9 dimes; 9 quarters; 9 dollars
6 All of the meetings will be held on July 19, 1991.

Semi finger **0**

7 ;p; ;p; ;p; ;p0 ;p0 ;p0 ;0; ;0; ;0; ;00; ;00; ;00;
8 10 whites 40 blues 50 greens 80 browns 100 oranges
9 After 50 men gave 100 talks in 90 days, they quit.

Number Practice

Be careful of slanting reaches.

10 10 and 40; 50 and 80; 90 and 100; 10 and 80; 40 and 50 and 9
11 The skillful athletes lost only 15 of their 94 tennis games.
12 The 18 students drove 549 miles in one day and 498 the next.

Skill Building

Use lines 13–20 for 30-second writings to develop speed. Select a line you feel you can complete *twice* in 30 seconds. If you succeed, select a longer line on the next try. If you do not, select a shorter line.

		wpm twice in 30 sec.
13	I wish to burn it down.	18
14	Wrap these for the women.	20
15	Get the right form to sign.	22
16	When both men land, we may go.	24
17	The bank ought to use a new form.	26
18	The man made a big hit in the city.	28
19	They will go there today if they can.	30
20	It is their duty to do this work for me.	32

1 | 2 | 3 | 4 | 5 | 6 | 7 | 8 |

Letter J

1 joy job jar just jump join judge major juice object junior injury 13

2 The majority of the men have no objection to joining the group. 13
3 The judge instructed the jury to deal justly with both parties. 13
4 On account of this prejudice, he misjudged the junior partner. 12

5 He rejected the offer of an adjustment for personal injuries. 12
6 The major object of the demonstration is to combat prejudice. 12
7 Subject to her approval, I will pay interest in January and July. 13

8 These jars contain jams and jellies judged worthy of prizes. 12
9 He jumped and struck his hand, injuring the joint of his finger. 13
10 The junior class joined us to celebrate this joyous jubilee. 12

Letter K

1 ask sky oak book knew week black drink check market thanks remark 13

2 He knew the background of the kind of people to whom he spoke. 12
3 The sick man was too weak to take anything but a drink of tea. 12
4 I will not keep the blankets, as there is no market for them now. 13

5 She would like us to make another attempt to take stock next week. 13
6 We know that our stock of cookbooks will be sold within a week. 13
7 First, I should like to thank the speaker for her kind remarks. 13

8 Kindly ask the clerk whether this skirt material will wrinkle. 12
9 The driver of the truck was asked to take the milk to market. 12
10 I shall go back to the bank at two o'clock to make a deposit. 12

Letter L

1 law fly let rule talk will while until value follow public simple 13

2 We told you it would be difficult to sell the lot at full price. 13
3 We should all be capable of living together in a friendly world. 13
4 The doctor told Len he could get well and live to be an old man. 13

5 It is likely that the usual quality will no longer be available. 13
6 It finally developed that the buildings were sold to a realtor. 13
7 The delicious flavor of our apple jelly appeals to all children. 13

8 Let me call Nell on the telephone and tell her about the deal. 12
9 We will not offer it for sale unless the quality is excellent. 12
10 We cannot possibly deliver the coal until early in the fall. 12

1 | 2 | 3 | 4 | 5 | 6 | 7 | 8 | 9 | 10 | 11 | 12 | 13 |

Unit 26

Line spacing: single
Line length: 60
Paragraph indention: 5
Type each line twice.

Warmup

Strike each key with equal force.

1 view reviews reviewed; acquit acquires acquaint; lacks likes
2 pay way—next text—daze haze graze—juice June—sings swing
3 The first 89 people received 89 prizes at the 140th meeting.
4 Who is Gale Perog? Who is Aimee Robbuff? Are they seniors?

1 | 2 | 3 | 4 | 5 | 6 | 7 | 8 | 9 | 10 | 11 | 12 |

New Key Location

S finger **2**

5 sws sws sws sw2 sw2 sw2 s2s s2s s2s s22s s22s s22s
6 2 cows 2 pigs 2 dogs 2 cats 2 sheep 2 bats 2 birds
7 Today 12 boys and 2 girls won prizes in 22 events.

J finger **7**

8 juj juj juj ju7 ju7 ju7 j7j j7j j7j j77j j77j j77j
9 7 towns 7 cities 7 counties 7 countries 7 planets;
10 In 1987, 7 astronauts may travel 77 million miles.

Number Practice

11 1 and 2; 4 and 5; 7 and 8; 9 and 10; 7 and 2; 5 and 7 and 12
12 Ship it March 27 to 72 West Kinney Street, Newark, NJ 07102.
13 Please check the orders numbered 127-172, as well as 90-101.
14 Change the address from 75 Huron Street to 987 River Street.
15 His committee will meet on Thursday, August 14, in Room 180.

Corrective Practice

Lines 16–19 reinforce the locations of **s** and **d.**

16 sad dash sand skid dust suds sedan reside salad seduce squid
17 seldom sledge smudge soldier solid speed daisy debris design
18 Sidney should send the dress goods to the designers Tuesday.
19 The slender sardine looks delicious with the salad and soda.

1 | 2 | 3 | 4 | 5 | 6 | 7 | 8 | 9 | 10 | 11 | 12 |

Letter G

1 big ago get sign gave page large again begin danger figure regret 13

2 The engineer regarded crossing the bridge as far too dangerous. 13
3 We ought to begin making arrangements for our regular meeting. 12
4 During the morning, they agreed among themselves to charge less. 13

5 The judge thought that the paper ought to be signed that night. 13
6 We generally get a great many packages that contain glassware. 12
7 The eggs are packed in large cartons for shipping to groceries. 13

8 I shall be glad to go again, as the house shows signs of neglect. 13
9 We thought that the girls might get along very well together. 12
10 The messenger gave both packages to a guard, who signed for them. 13

Letter H

1 who had why help both show happy which north method should though 13

2 When the weather permits, the ship will sail to the north shore. 13
3 Though he saw how the accident happened, he did not wish to sign. 13
4 I should be happy to help him, but I do not have the right size. 13

5 We happen to have on hand a hundred reams of heavy white paper. 13
6 These three boxes should be sent to the branch office by freight. 13
7 Each of these machines is worth more than a thousand dollars. 12

8 They themselves wish him to investigate the theft thoroughly. 12
9 Neither of these chairs is worth as much as the man is charging. 13
10 He will show you how to use the polish to obtain a high luster. 13

Letter I

1 oil sit air live idea fine field issue begin differ winter engine 13

2 The firm provided quick repair service by a skilled mechanic. 12
3 If you do not require an immediate answer, I can get his opinion. 13
4 I should like to renew this insurance policy, if it is possible. 13

5 I received a bit of reliable information about his activities. 12
6 If I had any such intention, I have long since given up the idea. 13
7 In my opinion, he is responsible for providing us with an office. 13

8 You might have informed him of the difference in selling price. 13
9 This paint may be high in price, but it is worth the difference. 13
10 It is impossible to find a safe investment that will yield more. 13

1 | 2 | 3 | 4 | 5 | 6 | 7 | 8 | 9 | 10 | 11 | 12 | 13 |

Alphabetic Paragraph

Type lines 20–24 once. Practice three times all phrases in which you typed a word incorrectly. Then take two 2-minute writings.

Goal: Speed–24 wpm
Error limit–4

20 When you get a chance, relax and read about the trials 12
21 and work of Christopher Sholes, the printer who invented the 24
22 first typewriter. Reading the story will not quicken your 35
23 pulse, but it will make you admire the vision and zeal of this 48
24 man. Just why did he desire to help his fellows communicate? 60

SI 1.35

1 | 2 | 3 | 4 | 5 | 6 | 7 | 8 | 9 | 10 | 11 | 12 |

Unit 27

Line spacing: single
Line length: 60
Paragraph indention: 5
Type each line twice.

Warmup

Type continuously, not hurriedly.

```
1 causes because; insures insured insurance; respects inspects
2 How could 24 men and 25 women use up 178 tickets in 19 days?
3 This is a matter on which I am unable to express an opinion.
```

1 | 2 | 3 | 4 | 5 | 6 | 7 | 8 | 9 | 10 | 11 | 12 |

New Key Location

D finger **3**

```
4 ded ded ded de3 de3 de3 d3d d3d d3d d33d d33d d33d
5 3 letters 3 words 3 phrases 3 sentences 3 chapters
6 33 divided by 3 is eleven.  133 minus 133 is zero.
```

J finger **6**

```
7 j6j j6j j6j j66j j66j j66j j67j j67j j67j j67j j6j
8 6 balls; 6 tennis balls; 6 baseballs; 6 golf balls
9 East 6th Street becomes Highway 66 at Main Street.
```

Number Practice

```
10 we 23 yew 632 try 546 pop 090 writ 2485 riot 4895 peep 0330;
11 to 59 wry 246 ewe 323 pup 070 tire 5843 rout 4975 purr 0744;
12 Deliver these 2 packages May 9 to 7860 45th Avenue by 3 p.m.
```

Letter D

1 and had red side hard food spend field under second around indeed 13

2 Although the day was cold, windows and doors were left wide open. 13
3 He was told that his credit depended on his keeping his word. 12
4 You should provide for your old age by building up a fund now. 12

5 We find the goods were shipped yesterday, according to schedule. 13
6 Dine and dance at the Roadside House every Saturday and Sunday. 13
7 We should like to have a hundred dresses delivered immediately. 13

8 Edna needs a dictionary so that she can look up difficult words. 13
9 The goods you ordered were forwarded Tuesday for delivery today. 13
10 The dealer was driving a red sedan that she planned to deliver. 13

Letter E

1 new she let cent near week weigh after never beyond people before 13

2 They spent a little more money than they had intended to invest. 13
3 Competition in this business is keen, but I believe I can meet it. 13
4 If the machine breaks, we must finish sewing the dress by hand. 13

5 It appears certain that some change in their system will be made. 13
6 I believe that we had better let her see the letter we received. 12
7 A great deal of money was needed to get the necessary equipment. 13

8 Early yesterday morning, we sent a telegram rejecting the offer. 13
9 You need never for one moment fear that we shall overcharge you. 13
10 Perhaps you expect prices to rise, but I believe they will fall. 13

Letter F

1 far off few left self half often after chief inform profit effect 13

2 Left to himself for a few hours, he finally found a solution. 12
3 We are satisfied with the offer, for we consider the figure fair. 13
4 We are fully aware of how difficult it is to effect this change. 13

5 In the future, find out first how much you can afford to pay. 12
6 We were informed a few days ago that the first half is finished. 13
7 If you feel sure the fund is sufficient, get gifts for all four. 13

8 Keep them fully informed of all efforts to confirm the facts. 12
9 First of all, I refuse to allow friendship to affect my decision. 13
10 In fact, you will often find it profitable to offer free samples. 13

1 | 2 | 3 | 4 | 5 | 6 | 7 | 8 | 9 | 10 | 11 | 12 | 13 |

Corrective Practice

Lines 13–16 reinforce the locations of **r** and **e.**

13 are wear read more beer dear rather rebel recent eager refer
14 effort enroll enter exert repeat recede rotate celery ordeal
15 Their remarks about the irresponsible engineer were correct.
16 Request three large pears there before they refuse to serve.

Word and Phrase Practice

Think and type each short word as a unit.

17 an so us we or me the you our his may she and this them wish
18 my do am if it is in to by now her him for out that like who
19 it is, to do, to go, to do it, if he is, it is to, if it is,
20 and if the, if we go, for it, for me, and did it, and if he,
21 It will still pay you to do a job as well as it can be done.

1 | 2 | 3 | 4 | 5 | 6 | 7 | 8 | 9 | 10 | 11 | 12

Unit 28

Line spacing: single
Line length: 60
Paragraph indention: 5
Type each line twice.

Warmup

1 forms forgets forever; others another mother brother; dreams
2 taxes wax; boys joy; oak cloak; queer steer; tone zone; live
3 Mr. Polk ordered 3 dozen––or 36––6 oz. bottles of champagne.
4 Practice keeping your eyes on the printed copy while typing.

1 | 2 | 3 | 4 | 5 | 6 | 7 | 8 | 9 | 10 | 11 | 12

New Key Location

The # sign stands for the word *number* if it precedes a numeral, and the word *pound,* or *pounds,* if it follows a numeral. Leave no space between the # sign and the numeral that precedes or follows it.

D finger; right shift 

5 ded ded ded d3d d3d d3d d#d d#d d#d #3 #4 #5 6# 7#
6 Serial #314; Flight #67; Claim ticket #34; Gate #9
7 If you want pinto beans, buy a few 1# or 5# sacks.

Letter A

1 has car pay coal yard want trade stand shall market happen regard 13

2 A few days ago, we again advertised a sale of coats and capes. 12
3 We attempted to ascertain the reason for the failure of the bank. 13
4 All the repairs had been made, and the car was ready for delivery. 13

5 About a month ago, we called attention to a small balance due us. 13
6 A sale of heavy aluminum ware was announced last Saturday. 12
7 We are glad to be able to announce these great savings today. 12

8 I can assure you that the quality is as good as it has ever been. 13
9 It gives us great pleasure to forward several samples of paper. 13
10 Each patient is given the same careful attention as in the past. 13

Letter B

1 cab buy big able both best above doubt about number object become 13

2 Our object is to establish better business relations between us. 13
3 I doubt whether they can possibly publish the book by September. 13
4 Both buildings burned, but they are probably not a total loss. 12

5 Avoid trouble by careful inspection before you buy bargains. 12
6 It will probably be impossible to bring him back before December. 13
7 The fabric of which the blue blouse was made was thin but strong. 13

8 His bank balance was low, but he believed it would be sufficient. 13
9 My brother Ben thought it best to subscribe to the building fund. 13
10 When we publish the book, we shall probably use a brown binding. 13

Letter C

1 act can cut much once each piece force touch school record direct 13

2 I can credit your account or send you a check for the difference. 13
3 The fact is that cheap products do not give satisfactory service. 13
4 The company carried accident insurance on all trucks and cars. 12

5 Once we reach a decision, it is difficult to change our course. 13
6 We offer a choice of attractive lace curtains in white and cream. 13
7 The case has become so difficult that we scarcely expect to win. 13

8 The inspector recommended no change except a new concrete cover. 13
9 The fact is the company cannot give this service free of charge. 13
10 Once officers are elected, we let them exercise complete control. 13

1 | 2 | 3 | 4 | 5 | 6 | 7 | 8 | 9 | 10 | 11 | 12 | 13 |

Leave no space between the $ sign and the number that follows it.

F finger; right shift $

8 frf frf frf f4f f4f f4f f$f f$f f$f $4.00; $34.00;
9 costs $4; a bill for $41; pay him $67; pay her $68
10 Do not pay more than $8 for the concert on May 16.

Leave no space between the % sign and a number.

F finger; right shift %

11 ftf f5f f5f f5f f5%f f5%f f5%f f%f f%f f%f 45% 35%
12 5% tax; a profit of 15%; 10% discount; reduced 25%
13 The discount was 20%. The finance charge was 12%.

Corrective Practice

Lines 14–16 reinforce the locations of **v** and **b.**

14 brave bevel verb adverb beaver vibrant beloved believe blvd.
15 Beverly verbal beloved brevity visible proverb vagabond bevy
16 I believe Beverly drank lots of potent beverages in Bavaria.

Alternate Hands Practice

For speed, keep your wrists and arms almost motionless.

17 paid also duty city envy when name fork make lamb held girls
18 firm spent right shape gowns widow auditor blame chair risks
19 social ancient haughty visible bicycle thrown dismal emblems

Typing Skill Checkup

Type lines 20–23 once. Practice three times all the phrases in which you typed a word incorrectly or which caused you to stumble. Then take two 2-minute writings.

Goal: Speed–25 wpm
Error limit–4

20 When you buy the things you need, you may sometimes buy 12
21 unwisely, but you will almost always get something of value 24
22 for your money. For example, you may buy too much junk food 36
23 and not get enough meat and vegetables. SI 1.33 44

1 | 2 | 3 | 4 | 5 | 6 | 7 | 8 | 9 | 10 | 11 | 12 |

REVIEW

Unit 29

Line spacing: single
Line length: 60
Paragraph indention: 5
Type each line twice.

Warmup

1 tire hires quires; ever never; towns down gowns; flame blame
2 except expects; lights night bright; wave knave brave; fines
3 July 6, 9 boxes of #7 size jars were sent--50% of the order.
4 The typist must always check the accuracy of the final copy.

1 | 2 | 3 | 4 | 5 | 6 | 7 | 8 | 9 | 10 | 11 | 12 |

Group 3 REMEDIAL DRILLS

LETTERS AND PUNCTUATION MARKS

These drills provide material for corrective practice on each letter of the alphabet and on punctuation marks. If you often make errors in typing a particular letter or punctuation mark, or if you slow down in striking a particular key, practice the appropriate drill. *Use a 70-space line.*

Comma

1 You want a comfortable home, good food, and time for recreation. 13
2 I set out at once, making my way slowly, carefully, over the ice. 13
3 In another ten years, in fact, we shall be firmly established. 12

Semicolon

1 The neighborhood was poor; the house was old; the room was small. 13
2 The family is gone; the old house is closed; now all is quiet. 12
3 The change has been beneficial for us; it has also helped you. 12

Question Mark

1 Is he the right man for a position of so much responsibility? 12
2 What qualities make a good leader? Does this woman possess them? 13
3 Why did the account not balance? What mistake had he made? 12

Colon

1 I need the following information: name, date, age, file number. 13
2 I have only one question to ask: Why are you so eager for the change? 13
3 His reasoning was as follows: he had never meant to stay there. 13

Exclamation Point

1 How slowly they moved! At what cost was each step forward taken! 13
2 Oh, you have let them go without me! Stop them! Call them back! 13
3 I looked for one rare stamp—I found three! What a surprise! 12

Dash

1 You and I have a great heritage—the heritage of a free democracy. 13
2 The piano was very, very large—too large to fit into the room. 13
3 That method—trial and error—was the only one he had ever tried. 13
4 I promise—and you can believe me—that I will be there at noon. 13

Parentheses

1 We rose bright and early (or at any rate, early) that morning. 12
2 That is the main purpose (perhaps the only purpose) of his visit. 13
3 They referred to the house (our house) as their legal property. 13

1 | 2 | 3 | 4 | 5 | 6 | 7 | 8 | 9 | 10 | 11 | 12 | 13 |

Capital Practice

On typebar machines, to avoid flying capitals, hold the shift key down firmly until *after* the letter has been struck.

5 Shirley and Betty-Lou took the Southland Express to Raleigh.
6 Mr. and Mrs. Herrera bought tickets to the Houston Symphony.
7 Jack leased his red car from U-Drive-Em Rents last Saturday.
8 Aunt Bea told Lena that Uncle Victor would visit Boston in May.
9 The thirst for fuel has taken drillers to Idaho and Wyoming.

Hyphen and Dash Practice

10 one-half; hit-skip; back-to-school; mid-Pacific; well-suited
11 fifteen-mile limit; up-to-date equipment; cross-country race
12 His brother-in-law was selected vice-president--would I lie?
13 Their devil-may-care attitude was obvious--no self-reliance.
14 Ms. River was well-intentioned, I think--but he thought not.

Number and Symbol Practice

15 I have only $1.30, but I need a 5# bag of the sugar on sale.
16 Did you save 10% of $79.50 you earned last week for college?
17 I want a 10# sack of #1 potatoes and a 3# box of #2 raisins.
18 Every payday, I pay 2% as city taxes and 4% for state taxes.

Alphabetic Sentences

In lines 19–23, type each line until you type it perfectly.

19 One day the quick brown foxes jumped over all the lazy dogs.
20 Max and Francis quickly vowed to seize the good job opening.
21 Every exam with puzzling questions baffled Jackie as always.
22 A jovial workman quickly fixes the blue azalea planting box.
23 The squad has asked Jim to give a box of candies as a prize.

Corrective Practice

Lines 24–28 reinforce the locations of **f** and **g**.

24 fog fig gift golf gulf flag frogs foggy feign forgo frontage
25 figure fixing filing forget frigid godfather gainful gratify
26 lifelong kingfish graft forge filling infringe fudge gainful
27 Four fleeing firebugs took a foreign flight across the gulf.
28 Forgive him if he again forgot to give the gift to Mr. Ferg.

1 | 2 | 3 | 4 | 5 | 6 | 7 | 8 | 9 | 10 | 11 | 12 |

Speed Paragraph

Type lines 29–33 once. Then take two or more 2-minute writings.

Goal: Try to break your wpm record. Ignore errors this one time only.

29 All look to the time when they can do just as they like 12
30 to do. Some like to read books. Some like to go in the woods 24
31 to hunt and fish. Some like to hike or take part in sports. 36
32 Then there will be times when all you want to do is rest, and 48
33 this may be a wise thing to do. SI 1.00 54

Alphabetic Sentences continued

		Words	Cum. Words
	shade of the maple; however, realizing there was work to be done,	26	86
	he jumped up quickly.	30	90
39	The junior partner authorized a well-qualified older member of the	13	103
	firm to vote in her place by giving him her proxy for the stock	26	116
	which they held jointly.	31	121
40	At the inquiry Monday night, the janitor was somewhat hazy as to	13	134
	whether the fire started on the stairway next to the elevator or in	26	147
	the book closet opposite.	31	152
41	The house next door was small, containing five rooms and bath; but	13	13
	it took our fancy because it had an adjoining garage, a wide piaz-	26	26
	za, and a quaint rock garden.	32	32
42	At the banquet, the hotel served an appetizer, jellied consomme,	13	45
	roast chicken and gravy with potatoes and green peas, a mixed salad,	26	58
	ice cream and cake, and coffee.	32	64
43	When the bookkeeper asked him for two assistants to investigate	13	77
	fully all delinquent accounts, whatever their size, the owner ob-	26	90
	jected because of the expense involved.	34	98
44	Make both speed and accuracy your objectives because both are re-	13	111
	quired of the expert typist and everybody must recognize that each	26	124
	has little value without the other.	33	131
45	Although the four sisters did not like to relinquish their claim	13	144
	to the jewels, they realized that the next move would probably be	26	157
	a court action that they could not win.	34	165
46	The even ticking of the clock could be heard quite clearly in the	13	13
	silence that followed his explanation, when the people realized	26	26
	the grave injustice the man had suffered.	34	34
47	Most of the people were accustomed to the luxuries of civilization	13	47
	and found difficulty in relinquishing them and making the adjust-	26	60
	ments necessary to life in a barren wilderness.	35	69
48	Try this gentle soap, which is kind to your hands and yet so effec-	13	82
	tive that you will get many hours of lazy enjoyment and relaxation	26	95
	because you will finish your washing so quickly.	36	105
49	In addition to an excellent stock of canned goods, jellies, dairy	13	118
	products, breads, and cakes, the grocer had the equipment to carry	26	131
	frozen meats and vegetables, if he wished to do so.	36	141
50	The production of large quantities of canned and frozen foods has	13	154
	stabilized the market and made many vegetables and fruits, former-	26	167
	ly seasonal luxuries, just as available in winter as in summer.	38	179

1 | 2 | 3 | 4 | 5 | 6 | 7 | 8 | 9 | 10 | 11 | 12 | 13 |

SKILL DEVELOPMENT

Unit 30

Line spacing: single
Line length: 60
Paragraph indention: 5
Type each line twice.

Warmup

```
1  excel excellent; over cover quiver; life wife knife; special
2  January in Phoenix; April in Kalamazoo; October in Cleveland
3  Lou and Marge did not get all their pay for the one day off.
```

Call-the-Return Practice

Take several 15-second writings. Your teacher will call "Return" at the end of each 15-second interval. Change sentences until you find the one you can complete as time is called. Then take several 1-minute writings on that sentence.

```
                                                              wpm in 15 sec.
4  He said it is very easy to do.                                   24
5  I can show you how to do that well.                              28
6  The man will pay him now for all he did.                         32
7  That was a happy day when she was able to go.                    36
8  She was right, and we shall type all the work now.               40
9  Time is on the side of those who plan their work fully.          44
       1|  2|  3|  4|  5|  6|  7|  8|  9|  10|  11|
```

Corrective Practice

Lines 10–12 reinforce the locations of **w** and **e.**

```
10 we wet ewe were wade weep weak well where wager waste wallet
11 water elbow endow write waiver winter wrench weather whoever
12 Where were the new winter sweaters they wanted on Wednesday?
```

Lines 13–15 reinforce the locations of **d** and **e.**

```
13 die dear dent deep date head lead debt dance feed dread edit
14 bed debit damage danger deaden debate credit edible expedite
15 Mildred developed a different method of dealing with delays.
```

Phrase Practice

Think and type each phrase as a unit.

```
16 if he, if an, if so, on it, if it, if I, to be, to do, in it
17 or if, or to, as it, will be, or not, we were, so we, on the
18 to see, in the, ask us, to the, at this, he will, by the way
```

Typing Skill Checkup

Type lines 19–22 once. Then take two or more 1-minute writings.

Goal: Speed–26 wpm
Error limit–2

19 As a citizen, it is your duty to learn something about 12
20 your environment. Someday you will be the adult members of 23
21 your towns and cities. As voters you will make many choices 35
22 which will affect your surroundings. SI 1.49 43

1| 2| 3| 4| 5| 6| 7| 8| 9| 10| 11| 12|

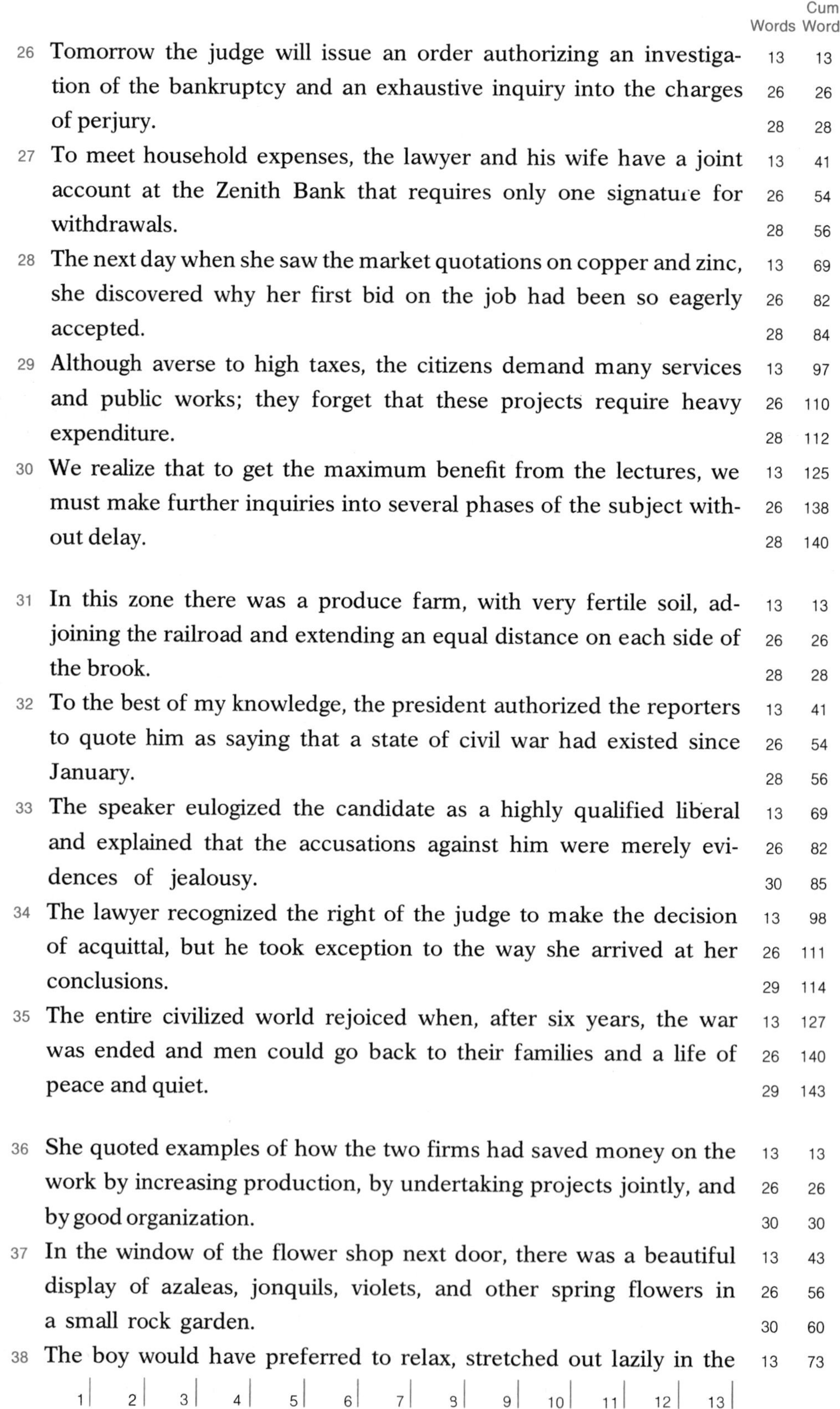

Alphabetic Sentences continued

		Words	Cum. Words
26	Tomorrow the judge will issue an order authorizing an investiga-	13	13
	tion of the bankruptcy and an exhaustive inquiry into the charges	26	26
	of perjury.	28	28
27	To meet household expenses, the lawyer and his wife have a joint	13	41
	account at the Zenith Bank that requires only one signature for	26	54
	withdrawals.	28	56
28	The next day when she saw the market quotations on copper and zinc,	13	69
	she discovered why her first bid on the job had been so eagerly	26	82
	accepted.	28	84
29	Although averse to high taxes, the citizens demand many services	13	97
	and public works; they forget that these projects require heavy	26	110
	expenditure.	28	112
30	We realize that to get the maximum benefit from the lectures, we	13	125
	must make further inquiries into several phases of the subject with-	26	138
	out delay.	28	140
31	In this zone there was a produce farm, with very fertile soil, ad-	13	13
	joining the railroad and extending an equal distance on each side of	26	26
	the brook.	28	28
32	To the best of my knowledge, the president authorized the reporters	13	41
	to quote him as saying that a state of civil war had existed since	26	54
	January.	28	56
33	The speaker eulogized the candidate as a highly qualified liberal	13	69
	and explained that the accusations against him were merely evi-	26	82
	dences of jealousy.	30	85
34	The lawyer recognized the right of the judge to make the decision	13	98
	of acquittal, but he took exception to the way she arrived at her	26	111
	conclusions.	29	114
35	The entire civilized world rejoiced when, after six years, the war	13	127
	was ended and men could go back to their families and a life of	26	140
	peace and quiet.	29	143
36	She quoted examples of how the two firms had saved money on the	13	13
	work by increasing production, by undertaking projects jointly, and	26	26
	by good organization.	30	30
37	In the window of the flower shop next door, there was a beautiful	13	43
	display of azaleas, jonquils, violets, and other spring flowers in	26	56
	a small rock garden.	30	60
38	The boy would have preferred to relax, stretched out lazily in the	13	73

1 | 2 | 3 | 4 | 5 | 6 | 7 | 8 | 9 | 10 | 11 | 12 | 13 |

(Continued on next page)

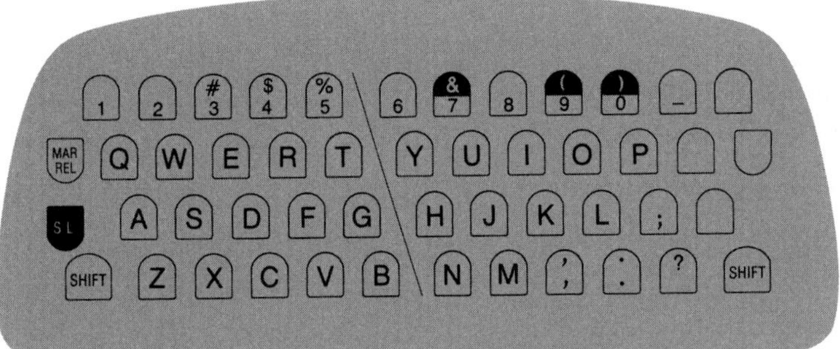

Unit 31

Line spacing: single
Line length: 60
Paragraph indention: 5
Type each line twice.

Warmup

1 tone bone zone known zinc; coin joins; ox fox proxy; qualify
2 1 vat 2 mat 3 bat 4 jam 5 van 6 gun 7 fun 8 low 9 Joe 10 hoe
3 Thinking words rather than letters will help increase speed.

New Key Location

Leave a space before and after the & sign (ampersand), except in abbreviations consisting of all capital letters.

J finger; left shift &

4 juj juj juj j7j j7j j7j j7&j j7&j j7&j j&j j&j j&j
5 James & Conklin; Payner & Russell; Hatter & Lipton
6 AT&T is a famous name in the communications field.

Leave no spaces between parentheses and the material they enclose.

L finger; left shift

Semi finger; left shift)

7 lol lol l9l l9l l(l l(l ;p; ;p; ;0; ;0; ;); ;); ( )
8 (1) one (2) two (3) three (4) four (5) five (6) six
9 Carl is (1) a good typist, and (2) a fine wrestler.
10 Ship four microwave ovens (price $379.98 less 10%).

The Shift Lock

Use the shift lock when you wish to type a series of capital letters. To return to small letters, strike the shift key to release the lock.

A finger

SHIFT

11 Use the shift lock when you want to stress A WORD OR PHRASE.
12 I was minding my own business when--CRASH--the picture fell.
13 Capital letters are sometimes used for book titles--IVANHOE.

Corrective Practice

Lines 14–17 reinforce the locations of **o** and **l**.

14 low oil only foul loyal allow close colon alone novel pillow
15 lot pilot couple balloon conceal formal hollow lovely double
16 toll locale payroll prolong propel outlay absolute pollution
17 Once a pilot and balloonist, he is now in pollution control.

1 | 2 | 3 | 4 | 5 | 6 | 7 | 8 | 9 | 10 | 11 | 12 |

Alphabetic Sentences continued

		Words	Cum. Words
12	The president, who spoke next, appealed to all citizens to avoid	13	38
	quarrels that might easily lead to prejudice and bad feelings.	25	50
13	The firm gave her an exquisite jeweled watch valued at four hun-	13	63
	dred and fifty dollars as a prize for submitting the best sketch.	25	75
14	The pewter box, which had a design of oblique lines, contained over	13	88
	a dozen keys, but none of them exactly fitted the jewel case.	26	101
15	In our July sale we featured exceptional values in garments of all	13	114
	sizes, in black or light colors, superior in quality and design.	26	127
16	Faced with many perplexing problems on this puzzling question, the	13	13
	directors held several sessions last week to discuss the subject.	26	26
17	When the excitement of the quarrel was over, the guard had only a	13	39
	hazy recollection of the specific remarks to which he had objected.	26	52
18	In the open square adjoining the exchange, an outdoor market was	13	65
	organized, at which articles of various types were bartered and	26	78
	sold.	27	79
19	The most puzzling feature of his reckless perjury during the exam-	13	92
	ination at the inquest was that there seemed to be no motive for	26	105
	it.	27	106
20	If you freeze the vegetables until you require them next month,	13	119
	they will keep as well as if they had been purchased just before	26	132
	using.	27	133
21	After the two organizations were joined and an extra dividend was	13	13
	declared, the market quotation rose to nearly double the former	26	26
	price.	27	27
22	He will be glad to know our branch is fully equipped to handle his	13	40
	export shipments just as soon as we receive the authorization from	26	53
	him.	27	54
23	The teacher explained that by seizing every opportunity to practice	13	67
	and by using effective technique we can enjoy improved typewrit-	26	80
	ing skills.	28	82
24	In our judgment, both the salve and the powder are excellent for	13	94
	the treatment of eczema, and they are backed by our unqualified	26	107
	guarantee.	28	109
25	The objective of advertisements of this kind is to familiarize the	13	122
	public with the fine quality of goods produced by our exclusive	26	135
	process.	28	137

1 | 2 | 3 | 4 | 5 | 6 | 7 | 8 | 9 | 10 | 11 | 12 | 13 |

(Continued on next page)

Typing Skill Checkup

Type lines 18–26 once. Practice three times all the phrases in which you typed a word incorrectly. Take a 2-minute writing.

Goal: Speed–26 wpm
Error limit–4

18 Being well dressed but poorly groomed is something like 12
19 putting a beautiful photo into an ugly frame—the total effect 24
20 is poor. When you choose your clothing, you hope to make your- 37
21 self as attractive and appropriately dressed as your budget 49
22 will allow. 51
23 Now, to set these clothes off to the best advantage, you 63
24 must be certain that all the other parts of your grooming are 75
25 the best possible. As a matter of fact, careful grooming, even 88
26 more than proper clothes, will make you an attractive person. 100

SI 1.39

1 | 2 | 3 | 4 | 5 | 6 | 7 | 8 | 9 | 10 | 11 | 12 |

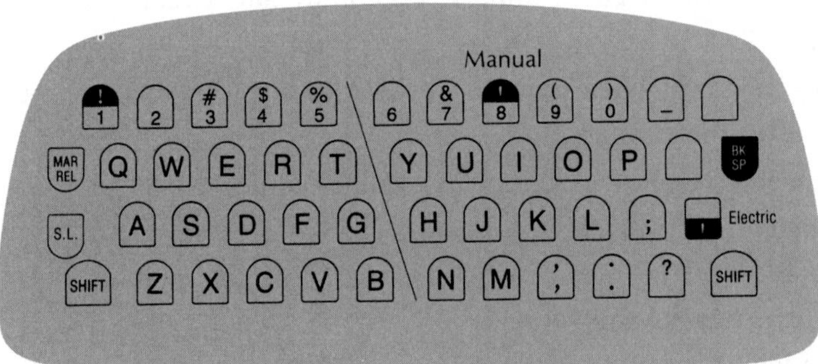

Unit 32

Line spacing: single
Line length: 60
Paragraph indention: 5
Type each line twice.

Warmup

1 Thirteen women work for the chairperson of the bicycle firm.
2 The lazy man worked diligently because he expects something.
3 His novel (QUIET JOVE, published by Vos & Zap) did not sell.

1 | 2 | 3 | 4 | 5 | 6 | 7 | 8 | 9 | 10 | 11 | 12 |

New Key Location

There is no space before or after an apostrophe within a word.

Manual: *K* finger; left shift
Electric: ***Semi*** finger

M4 kik k8k k8k k'k k'k k'k it's, don't, Mary's, Tom's
E4 ;'; ;'; ;'; can't, don't, doesn't, Ed's, Kennedy's
5 Nine 5's; three 6's; four 2's; five 3's; seven 4's
6 I've been wanting to see your Dad's new power saw.

(Continued on next page)

One-Minute Speed Drives continued

16 We must make things; we must be active. Our energy must have an outlet. 14
The human race would die of boredom if we could not find work to do. 28
The industrial world satisfies these needs in part; but it becomes less 42
and less satisfactory as the power of machines displaces human labor. 56
A reduction in the number of working hours gives time for other activi- 70
ties in which we can find satisfaction after our main wage-earning 84
work is done. Such activities give us a chance to do things for sheer 98
pleasure. 100

1 | 2 | 3 | 4 | 5 | 6 | 7 | 8 | 9 | 10 | 11 | 12 | 13 | 14 |

ALPHABETIC SENTENCES

Each of these sentences contains every letter of the alphabet. Type them at a rate that is slower than your best speed. This will help you concentrate more closely on the difficult reaches and improve your accuracy. You may use these sentences periodically for 1- or 2-minute writings to check yourself on the number of errors you make per minute.

ALPHABETIC SENTENCES

65-space line.

		Words	Cum. Words
1	The pink grapefruit was of excellent quality, very juicy and sweet,	13	13
	but small in size.	17	17
2	The citizens openly rejoiced when their brave king and queen re-	13	30
	turned from exile after many years.	20	37
3	This inexpensive bleach makes clothing a dazzling white; try it	13	50
	and judge its quality for yourself.	20	57
4	Jack took a taxicab after the party, since the warm drizzle had	13	70
	quickly changed to a heavy, chilly rain.	21	78
5	A knife or a razor which is made of flexible steel of good quality	13	91
	should never be used to pry open a jar.	21	99
6	Prizes were given for the best experiment described in the quar-	13	13
	terly journal, which the workshop published.	22	22
7	As the visitor was too busy to make up his own speech, he quoted	13	35
	exactly the major part of a magazine article.	22	44
8	The young executive and his wife had a party on the Queen Elizabeth	13	57
	just as the huge vessel was about to embark.	22	66
9	I know that the beef and the veal are of excellent quality, as the	13	79
	cattle grazed on the rich pastures adjoining my farm.	24	90
10	The adjoining room was equipped with parquet flooring, bronze elec-	13	103
	tric fixtures, a brick fireplace, and heavy storm windows.	25	115
11	I realize that the janitor, who has previously had experience as	13	13
	a carpenter, will unquestionably make good use of his skills.	25	25

1 | 2 | 3 | 4 | 5 | 6 | 7 | 8 | 9 | 10 | 11 | 12 | 13 |

(Continued on next page)

The backspace key is used to move the printing point back toward the left margin. You would use the backspace key to return and fill in a letter that was omitted, to make a correction, to construct certain symbols, and to underscore.

The backspace key is also used to center words or phrases horizontally. Study the basic procedure:

1. Move the carriage or element to the center of the paper—50 (elite) or 42 (pica).
2. Silently spell out each line to be centered, backspacing once for every two strokes. (The term *stroke* includes not only all characters—letters, numbers, and symbols—but all internal spaces as well.)
3. Begin to type at the point where you finished backspacing.

Try centering the copy on lines 7–9 using this procedure.

Semi finger BK SP

7 John S. Farley
8 17100 Harvard Ave.
9 Philadelphia, PA 19144

Leave two spaces after an exclamation point at the end of a sentence, one space if within a sentence.

A finger; right shift !

If your machine has no exclamation point, construct one:

- Type a period.
- Backspace once.
- Type an apostrophe.

10 I shall return! Don't give up the ship! Help me!
11 Suddenly, KAWUMP! went the cannon. It was scarey!
12 What a beautiful day! Let's enjoy it in the park!

Centering Practice

Center each line.

13 Freemont Unified High School
14 Typing Awards Assembly
15 Thursday, June 1
16 9 a.m.
17 Auditorium

Typing Skill Checkup

Type each paragraph (lines 18–22 and 23–27) once. Use double spacing. Practice three times all the phrases in which you typed a word incorrectly. Take a 2-minute writing on each paragraph.

Goal: Speed–26 wpm
Error limit–4

18 Over 70 years ago the Wright brothers made history with 12
19 the first airplane flight ever to be made. In all, the plane 24
20 was off the ground for 13 seconds and traveled a little more 36
21 than 100 feet before it crashed into the sand, but a human 48
22 had flown for the first time in a flying machine. SI 1.25 58

23 In southern California, there is a turkey ranch that has 12
24 some interesting office jobs. You might think that office 24
25 workers would not be needed in a place like that. But there 36
26 are typists, order clerks, billing clerks, and payroll clerks, 48
27 to mention a few. The ranch is a good place to work. SI 1.35 59

1 | 2 | 3 | 4 | 5 | 6 | 7 | 8 | 9 | 10 | 11 | 12

One-Minute Speed Drives continued

10 There are always people among us who would rather turn their eyes to the 14
future than look at what is good in the present. Tomorrow, next week, 28
next year, life will be wonderful; and so they forget about today. How- 42
ever, if they do not get some small pleasure from each day as it comes 56
along, it is probable that they will never find it in the days ahead. 70

11 We believe it will interest you to learn that during the three years of 14
our existence as an association, the number of our members has increased 28
from less than one hundred at the end of the first month to nearly three 42
thousand at the present time. As a direct result of the wide support 56
that the public has given us, we have been able to effect great improve- 70
ments in our servicing. 75

12 The time may come when some countries will find it difficult to get 14
enough electricity to meet all their needs because they depend upon coal 28
to produce it, and their supply of coal is limited. In other countries, 42
however, water power is used to produce electricity. There, the supply 56
should last forever, for as long as water continues to fall from high 70
ground to low ground, electricity can be produced. 80

13 Boys and girls are full of interest in life; and for this reason, they 14
have a questioning attitude. The questions that they ask are chiefly 28
of three types. In the first place, they ask questions about the world 42
around them and about human nature. Secondly, they ask questions that 56
have to do with their relationships with other people. Finally, they 70
ask questions about their work and what they will have to do to make a 84
living. 85

14 Ms. Brown had a business appointment in Chicago Monday afternoon. The 14
plane that she took early in the morning was scheduled to make the trip 28
in less than two hours, but it took more than two days. About an hour 42
after leaving, the plane was forced down by bad weather conditions. As 56
the weather did not improve, the passengers finally had to cover the 70
rest of the distance by railroad. Ms. Brown arranged by telephone for 84
a change in her appointment. 90

15 Throughout its past and up to the present time, Wall Street has main- 14
tained its position as a business and financial center. Wall Street 28
will always be a short and narrow canyon. The sweeping changes are in 42
its skyline, as bigger and taller buildings have replaced the old, small, 56
bulging buildings with their carved and gilded domes. Yes, the bankers, 70
the underwriters, the big stock exchanges, all have their roots dug in 84
and around Wall Street, and all are here to stay forever. 95

1 | 2 | 3 | 4 | 5 | 6 | 7 | 8 | 9 | 10 | 11 | 12 | 13 | 14 |

Four-Letter Words continued

14	case	form	just	mean	rate	sure	west
15	cent	free	keep	meet	read	take	what
16	city	from	kind	mind	real	talk	when
17	cold	full	knew	mine	rest	tell	whom
18	come	gave	know	miss	road	than	will
19	copy	girl	land	more	room	that	wish
20	cost	give	last	most	rule	them	with
21	date	good	late	move	safe	then	word
22	dear	grow	lead	much	said	they	work
23	door	half	left	must	sale	this	year
24	down	hand	less	name	same	time	your

FIVE-LETTER WORDS

Left margin at 15. Single spacing.

1	about	could	labor	place	spent	until
2	above	cover	large	plain	stand	usual
3	after	doubt	learn	point	start	value
4	again	dress	least	power	state	voice
5	agree	drink	leave	price	still	waste
6	along	drive	light	quick	store	water
7	among	early	might	quite	story	weigh
8	begin	equal	money	reach	teach	where
9	black	every	month	ready	thank	which
10	board	field	never	right	their	while
11	break	final	night	round	there	whole
12	bring	first	north	serve	these	whose
13	build	force	offer	shall	thing	woman
14	carry	found	often	short	think	women
15	cause	front	order	since	third	world
16	cheap	fully	other	small	those	worth
17	check	great	ought	sound	today	would
18	clean	happy	paper	south	trade	write
19	clear	house	party	speak	trust	wrong
20	color	issue	piece	spend	under	young

SIX-LETTER WORDS

Left margin at 20. Single spacing.

1	affect	degree	expect	method	regard
2	amount	demand	family	minute	regret
3	answer	depend	figure	modern	report
4	appear	desire	follow	nation	result
5	become	detail	friend	number	return
6	before	direct	future	object	second

(*Continued on next page*)

Set margins for a 50-space line: 25–80 (elite), 17–72 (pica).

Typing from Script

5 In choosing a career, first consider your interests,
6 then your natural abilities, and finally the skills
7 you've gained through classes and training programs.
8 Talk with your school's career guidance counselor.
9 Perhaps he/she will see more possibilities than you.
10 Business students should be aware of the concepts
11 and terminology used in the word processing field.

Paragraph Practice

Note: Underscored words are given triple value in the word counts of these paragraphs.

1 My hobby is traveling. I haven't really traveled yet-- 12
except to and from school, and to the lake during the sum- 24
mer. I'd like to visit Spain. I'm quite good at Spanish; I 36
have just won first prize, a medal which I shall always keep 52
and treasure. 54

2 Tonight, John, Hazel, and I went to see "Sink or Swim" 12
at the Roxy Theater. The performance was quite delightful. 24
Don't miss it! Tickets are available at prices ranging from 38
$4.20 to $8.60. Theater parties of twenty-five or more are 50
allowed a 20% discount. 54

3 One 17-year-old boy was captain and driver of a four- 12
person bobsled team that made a record run. After a week's 24
practice together, the four (all under 18) made the twenty- 36
five dangerous turns on Lake Placid's bobsled run at speeds 48
of over 70 miles an hour. They plan to enter a race for a 59
$500 prize. 61

4 Mr. Zims always pays his rent promptly. A few days ago 12
he received a notice from his landlords, Linden & Son, say- 24
ing that the rent was late. He was not worried or anxious, 36
because he had the canceled check, #345, proving he had paid 48
$225--the full amount owed. 53

5 We have two slogans used to discourage jaywalking and 12
hazards due to careless driving. For pedestrians, the 27
slogan is: "Cross at green, not in between!" For drivers, 41
it's: "Drive carefully; the life you save may be your own!" 53

1 | 2 | 3 | 4 | 5 | 6 | 7 | 8 | 9 | 10 | 11 | 12 |

Six-Letter Words continued

7	better	divide	happen	office	should
8	bought	dollar	indeed	people	simple
9	change	during	inform	person	street
10	charge	effect	insure	please	strong
11	common	either	letter	profit	supply
12	course	employ	little	rather	system
13	credit	enough	market	reason	toward
14	custom	except	matter	record	within

SEVEN-LETTER WORDS

Left margin at 15. Single spacing.

1	account	control	hundred	present	special
2	another	country	improve	product	station
3	balance	deliver	inquire	provide	subject
4	because	develop	machine	purpose	success
5	believe	example	measure	quality	suggest
6	between	express	morning	receive	thought
7	brought	forward	neither	regular	through
8	certain	further	nothing	require	weather
9	company	general	perfect	service	whether
10	connect	however	perhaps	several	without

LONGER WORDS

Left margin at 20. Single spacing.

1	attention	consider	pleasure	question
2	business	gentlemen	position	straight
3	complete	important	possible	thousand
4	condition	interest	probably	together

PHRASE PRACTICE

Practice the following phrases several times until you can type them rapidly, without thinking of the individual letters in each word.

PHRASE PRACTICE

Type these phrases in groups of three as directed by your teacher.

	A	B	C
1	to us	by the way	from them
	to be	in the way	from that time
	to do it	in the past	from time to time
2	if it is	you sent us	on your part
	if he is	he must be	to take part
	if you will	they must do	on the part of
3	to be sure	agree with you	our letter
	we feel sure	you will agree that	in this letter
	you may be sure	we have agreed that	no longer than

(Continued on next page)

Paragraph Practice

1 He began dictating the contract as follows: "AGREEMENT 12
made on the fifth day of May, 1984, between Arthur Lewis, of 24
Cincinnati, Ohio (hereinafter called the SELLER), and Bonnie 36
Dix, of Dayton, Ohio (hereinafter called the PURCHASER)." 47

2 Tonight will be Ms. Whalen's 250th performance as Laura 12
in Polk's play "Happy New Year!" Next week the play moves 24
from the Washington Theatre to the Columbus, on 39th Street. 36
The play's success led the producer to plan for a long run. 48

3 We offer household appliances at very low prices. Our 12
special this week is an automatic L&R washer, reduced from a 24
list price of $299 to $249--you save $50! You can save even 36
more by presenting the enclosed card, which offers you an 47
additional 5% discount. Hurry--this offer ends Sunday. 58

4 Word processors are having a great effect on the way in 12
which business documents are produced. As you keyboard on 24
these new machines, words appear on a screen instead of on a 36
sheet of paper. Words can then be corrected, deleted, and 48
moved around in blocks from one spot to another with almost 60
no retyping. When you like the way your copy reads, you can 72
print it out with great speed at just the touch of a switch. 84

1 | 2 | 3 | 4 | 5 | 6 | 7 | 8 | 9 | 10 | 11 | 12 |

SKILL DEVELOPMENT

Unit 38

Line spacing: single
Line length: 60
Paragraph indention: 5

Sentence Practice

Practice keyboarding at an even pace. Try to avoid long pauses between keystrokes.

1 The helpful men held the forms for them to sign their names.
2 The job requires extra pluck and zeal from all young people.
3 Ms. McCreery teaches English as well as typing at Lowe High.
4 Let us show you how to do this work a new way and save time.

1 | 2 | 3 | 4 | 5 | 6 | 7 | 8 | 9 | 10 | 11 | 12 |

Phrase Practice continued

	A	B	C
4	all of them one of these a few of those	as soon as as soon as we can as soon as possible	please ship please send us please let me hear
5	we are not we are not able we shall not be able	now and then again and again more and more	just now not just yet just in time
6	as much as as well as as we have seen	I hope you will I think you are I know you will be	some time today some time next week in the morning
7	once more many more more or less	on sale sale price special sale	for this reason any other reason within reason
8	at some time some time ago at the same time	I am glad glad to hear I am very sorry	I have received you will receive we have just received
9	in a year in a few days a few days ago	out of the way out of town not very long ago	we regard this with regard to we regret that
10	so much very much much more than	they wish to know should like to know should be glad to hear	in all sizes large sizes only a very large number
11	let us hear I have not said we have not seen	please accept please write us please let me know	I do not doubt without any doubt there is little doubt
12	of this kind in this way in every way	in reply to in your reply a prompt reply	good enough whether or not whether you can
13	next week next month during the week	quite a few quite certain not quite ready	your request your account charge account
14	on hand on the one hand on the other hand	I suggest that may we suggest that should like to suggest	your attention special attention as early as possible
15	six weeks ago about six weeks six months ago	express charge free of charge without charge	at your service in question in addition to

Typing Skill Checkup

One way to measure the success of a business is to look at how it handles money. Does the firm pay its bills on time? Does it always meet its payroll? Is money for growth there when it's needed? If the answer to all of these questions is yes, then the business is probably well run. The owners know how to exercise control over their spending. SI 1.29

Students who wish to learn a skill that is sure to be in demand when they graduate from high school should consider taking some business courses. These classes teach students to do office work at the entry level. The need for people who have clerical, keyboarding, and similar skills is great and should grow over the next ten years. This is why most job surveys show a rise in the white-collar work force. SI 1.32

1 | 2 | 3 | 4 | 5 | 6 | 7 | 8 | 9 | 10 | 11 | 12 |

SKILL DEVELOPMENT

Unit 37

Line spacing: single
Line length: 60
Paragraph indention: 5
Type each line twice.

Sentence Practice

Work toward accuracy and speed.

1 Send it to us if they do not want to spend the money for it.
2 She may pay the men to fix her car, but it still won't work.
3 She owes it to you to try to write or to type up her report.

1 | 2 | 3 | 4 | 5 | 6 | 7 | 8 | 9 | 10 | 11 | 12 |

Typing from Script

Set margins for a 50-space line: 25–80 (elite) or 17–72 (pica).

4 Could you use a luxury vacation in the Caribbean?
5 Why not consider our fun-and-sun Jamaican holiday?
6 Round-trip charter fares to Kingston start at $250.
7 All rooms feature beachfront lanais and full baths.
8 Dancing and live entertainment are provided nightly.
9 Reservations required at least two weeks in advance.

SENTENCE PRACTICE

These sentences may be used for developing greater keyboard fluency. They may also be used as 1-minute writings for speed forcing. Practice aimed at helping you to break out of your existing speed level may cause you to make more errors, but don't let this bother you. As you get accustomed to typing at a new level, your errors should decrease.

SENTENCE PRACTICE

70-space line. Double spacing.

		Words
1	We are no longer free to act as we wish.	8
2	The repair shop said it would not start.	16
3	We shall be happy to serve him any time.	24
4	If they must go, they should go tonight.	32
5	Thank you for your attention to this problem.	9
6	As the sale is over tomorrow, you must hurry.	18
7	They will agree that quality must come first.	27
8	In the future, please inform us of your aims.	36
9	We expect to learn more about the matter tomorrow.	10
10	We assure you that we process all orders promptly.	20
11	We all know that words have a great deal of power.	30
12	This is a matter on which I have a strong opinion.	40
13	I am sorry that I will no longer require your services.	11
14	I will give you a full account of the progress we make.	22
15	We must be ready to act when the time for action comes.	33
16	Those machines have reduced costs and increased output.	44
	1 | 2 | 3 | 4 | 5 | 6 | 7 | 8 | 9 | 10 | 11 |	
17	We are glad to learn that you have so high an opinion of us.	12
18	I made an application a while ago, but I have not heard yet.	24
19	Often people allow their emotions to get the better of them.	36
20	I should like to make it clear that the change is desirable.	48
21	No one fights reform so bitterly as people who need it most.	60
22	I am sure that you will be surprised by the results of this test.	13
23	Audiences will find jokes amusing only when they are in the mood.	26
24	People are often judged by their words rather than by their acts.	39
25	The rain stopped quickly and the skies were clear for the parade.	52
26	If delivery is not made by Friday, we shall not accept the goods.	65
27	Hour after hour, the goldfish swim about in their calm world of water.	14
28	Monday was sunny, with no sign of the storm through which we had come.	28
29	We all want to protect our personal liberty and keep our country free.	42
30	The glow of the setting sun clearly outlined the barn against the sky.	56
31	On one side, the slope is gentle; on the other, there is a steep drop.	70
	1 | 2 | 3 | 4 | 5 | 6 | 7 | 8 | 9 | 10 | 11 | 12 | 13 | 14 |	

(Continued on next page)

Corrective Practice

Lines 17–20 reinforce the locations of **i** and **u.**

17 suit unit input build bruise audit union suite tuition until
18 juice buried caution illusion causing uplift council utilize
19 busiest required auditors burial circuit injuries continuity
20 The council was cautious, requiring only qualified auditors.

1 2 3 4 5 6 7 8 9 10 11 12

SKILL DEVELOPMENT

Unit 36

Line spacing: single
Line length: 60
Paragraph indention: 5
Type each line twice

Sentence Practice

Accuracy is the mark of a good typist.

1 Marty gave my excited boy quite a prize for his clever work.
2 The four women she got from the firm can solve the problems.
3 We are very pleased with the work that you have done for us.

1 2 3 4 5 6 7 8 9 10 11 12

Typing from Script

Set margins for a 50-space line: 25–80 (elite) or 17–72 (pica).

4 You can buy personal stationery at a great saving.
5 The notebook comes in three sizes and three colors.
6 Our low price includes embossing with your initials.
7 Trains were delayed hours as a result of the tie-up.

Symbol Practice

8 She invested $1,900 in the bonds offered by Sloane & Tuttle.
9 With a 60% price cut, our goods would be selling below cost!
10 The heavy-duty model weighs $1\frac{1}{4}$ tons and uses 30% more power.
11 The bill listed both black-and-white and color photographs.*
12 *17 black-and-white @ $3 each; 8 color @ $5 each; total $91.
13 Only our "Easy-Tread" shoes, sizes 4 to $9\frac{1}{2}$, will be on sale.
14 The box said, "One dozen #2 pencils (soft) without erasers."
15 The ad in the Chronicle featured tomatoes (#2 cans) for 55¢.

Sentence Practice continued

32 In the long run, we shall all suffer if farmers cannot make a decent living. 15

33 During the next three years, we hope to make a considerable amount of money. 30

34 The directors have considered this matter carefully, but they have no ideas. 45

35 We suggest that when you again make your calls, you pay this dealer a visit. 60

36 There is no truth in the rumor that the manager of this company will resign. 75

37 When you listen at noon to a broadcast from London, it is late afternoon there. 16

38 Again we appeal to our staff to join the effort to reach our quota in this drive. 32

39 We have been compelled to limit production because we cannot get enough material. 48

40 An efficient road system is essential to the well being and growth of our nation. 64

41 His attention was suddenly attracted to a door on the opposite side of the house. 80

1 | 2 | 3 | 4 | 5 | 6 | 7 | 8 | 9 | 10 | 11 | 12 | 13 | 14 |

Group 2 SPEED AND ACCURACY DRILLS

These practice drills and timed writings are designed to increase your speed and improve your accuracy. Use them as directed by your teacher or as independent practice whenever time permits. To get the greatest benefit from your practice, set a goal for each drill you type and always observe the rules of good technique. Check yourself on these points:

1. *Maintain a good posture.* Sit back in the chair and lean slightly forward. Your body should be about 8 to 10 inches from the typewriter, both feet on the floor.
2. *Keep your eyes on the copy.*
3. *Strike the keys quickly and sharply.* Try to strike and release each key with one motion.
4. *Type with rhythm.* Allow your fingers to speed up on short, easy words and phrases. Allow your fingers to slow down when typing more difficult words and letter combinations.
5. *Choose a speed goal.* See if you can add another 3 *wpm* to your existing rate on a 1-minute writing.
6. *Set an accuracy goal.* Set a limit of 1 error for each alphabetic sentence. If you make more than 1 error, repeat the sentence.

Unit 35

Line spacing: single
Line length: 60
Paragraph indention: 5
Type each line twice.

Warmup

1 Next week Hank will buy twenty dozen pies for his busy shop.
2 The woman is to go to town and then make six signs for them.
3 1 2 3 4 5 6 7 8 9 10 11 12 13 14 15 16 17 18 19 20 21 22 23.

1 | 2 | 3 | 4 | 5 | 6 | 7 | 8 | 9 | 10 | 11 | 12 |

New Key Location

Leave no space between a number and the ¢ sign.

Manual: ***Semi*** **finger** ¢
Electric: ***J*** **finger; left shift**

M4 ;¢; ;¢; Candy bars are priced at 15¢, 20¢ and 25¢.
E4 j6j j6j j¢j j¢j Bread prices rose from 49¢ to 56¢.
5 He paid 10¢ but charged me 28¢ and Susan 10¢ more.
6 I think that 56¢ is a lot; 38¢ is more reasonable.

Leave a space before and after the @ sign.

Manual: ***Semi*** **finger; left shift** @
Electric: ***S*** **finger; right shift**

M7 ;@; ;@; The sign @ is used to bill--3 pounds @ $5.
E7 sws s2s s@s s@s 78 bushels of potatoes @ $12 a bu.
8 The bill included 4 roses @ 96¢ and 3 shrubs @ $5.
9 Save 11¢ on Swiss cheese, selling regularly @ 30¢.

Leave no space between a whole number and the signs ½, ¼. Leave 1 space after the ½, ¼ when a word follows.

Semi **finger** ½
Semi **finger; left shift** ¼

10 ;½; ;½; 9½¢ a pound; 4½ inches thick; 8½ feet long
11 ;¼; ;¼; 12¼ inches; 30¼ feet; 61¼ yards; 87¼ miles
12 Bill us for 20¼ dozen knives and 30½ dozen spoons.

Double Letter Practice

13 equal equally whip whipping zigzag zigzagged visual visually
14 ton tonnage sum summarize run runner quit quitter let letter
15 zip zipper hop hopping over overrule net netting kid kidding
16 infer inferring off office less lesser fun funny lap lapping

1 | 2 | 3 | 4 | 5 | 6 | 7 | 8 | 9 | 10 | 11 | 12 |

TEN-SECOND SPEED DRIVES

Select a sentence you feel you can type in 10 seconds. If you complete the sentence before time is called, select a longer sentence for the next writing. Continue this way for several 10-second writings until you find the one you can complete just as time is called.

TEN-SECOND SPEED DRIVES

70-space line.

		wpm in 10 sec.
1	I will try to come over at nine.	39
2	We wish you would tell them now.	39
3	Get her team to work like yours.	39
4	The show was a big hit in the city.	42
5	My car may be in the garage a week.	42
6	We can plan on your taking one pie.	42
7	They wish to have the bill paid today.	46
8	In the next few days we shall send it.	46
9	He does not plan to give a large gift.	46
10	I suddenly noticed a woman in the window.	49
11	Perhaps it is too early to make a report.	49
12	I had to stop in the office on the sixth.	49
13	If you agree with us, we shall act at once.	52
14	You asked me to try to get you two tickets.	52
15	Two seats are yours, in back of third base.	52
16	We are very sorry that we are out of that size.	56
17	It may be just what we require for our project.	56
18	Thank you for inviting me to stop at the plant.	56
19	We shall send you a check on the first, as usual.	59
20	I wish to thank you for the party you had for us.	59
21	We are glad to hear that you have both recovered.	59
22	Reginald refused our request to pay us what he owes.	62
23	We will purchase several vases, if you allow credit.	62
24	Mr. Soo expects you to reply to his inquiry by mail.	62
25	There is very little chance of getting a better price.	65
26	They hope you will notice the progress they have made.	65
27	I found that he did not bring up the subject of price.	65
28	She could not repair the broken box; so she sent it back.	68
29	If you are a good typist, you can always be sure of work.	68
30	The men in the club believe they should offer their help.	68
31	They want to purchase the land by the old dam, if they can.	71
32	The first step in any operation is to review all the steps.	71
33	They may make a big profit if they reinvest the money soon.	71
34	They spent most of their money for an audit of their business.	74
35	This is the plan they told us to follow for touring the plant.	74
36	They do not wish to continue without hearing from their banks.	74

Leave 1 space between a whole number and a fraction made with the diagonal, or slash.

Semi finger /

9 ;/; ;/; 1/2 and 1/3 and 1/4 and 1/5 and 1/6; 7 3/8
10 The sum of 5/8 and 7/8 is 1 1/2. Is that correct?
11 Contact them at 216/845-2630 any day after 10 a.m.

Leave a space on either side of both the plus sign and the equal sign.

Semi finger; left shift for + (+ / =)

12 ;=; ;=; ;+; ;+; 2 + 3 = 5; 4 + 6 = 10; 7 + 8 = 15;
13 He wrote the equation "(a + b + c/d) = e" quickly.
14 I know A = L + C is the basic accounting equation.

Three-Minute Timed Writing

Take a 3-minute writing on lines 15–23. If you make 3 errors or less, practice the speed drills, lines 24–26. If you make more than 3 errors, practice the accuracy drills, lines 27–29. Take another 3-minute writing and compare the results with your first timing.

Goal: Speed–27 wpm
Error limit–4

15 We live in what we regard as a very advanced state of 12
16 civilization. We seldom remember that each age must have 21
17 seemed just as advanced to the people who lived in it. We 33
18 look back at the life led by people a hundred years ago and 44
19 wonder how they found it possible to live. 53
20 On the other hand, is it not just as likely that in a 64
21 hundred years from now new generations, in their turn, will 77
22 look back upon us and, in the light of their increased com- 88
23 forts, consider our present way of life incomplete? SI 1.33 99

1 | 2 | 3 | 4 | 5 | 6 | 7 | 8 | 9 | 10 | 11 | 12 |

Speed Drills

24 we in as age who led by it in to for as our on from way upon
25 do not in the in what at the in it to live of our as a is it
26 live very that each must just look they take part hand their

Accuracy Drills

27 advanced civilization remember possible comfort conveniences
28 hundreds generations increased inventions present incomplete
29 I regard too advanced is responsible to control a suggestion

Number and Symbol Practice

30 The title of Ian Brume's essay was "2 Against 20."
31 Joe Dru, an end, ran for 4 touchdowns (135 yards).
32 Interest charged on a $5,000 loan is 19% (not 9%).
33 I want a copy of the book, <u>Run & Hide</u> (Cat. #136).
34 The "bid" price was $98, with 9% annual interest.*
35 The problem was easy: 49 + 6 + 24 + 8 + 19 = 106.
36 Rowe & Baron advertised in <u>Time</u> (the May 1 issue).

THIRTY-SECOND SPEED DRIVES

Use these sentences for 30-second writings. Remember to double the word count to get *wpm*. If, for example, your goal is 32 *wpm*, choose two sentences from the group numbered 1–5; for a goal of 40 *wpm*, choose two sentences from those numbered 11–15.

THIRTY-SECOND SPEED DRIVES

70-space line.

		Words
1	Let me see. She may go in a day or two.	8
2	Buy the set. We will need it this week.	8
3	Try some, and let me hear from you soon.	8
4	Do not go. He lives very far from here.	8
5	We are no longer free to act as we wish.	8
6	The man said that he is ready to start today.	9
7	Ask for an exchange. You got the wrong size.	9
8	If they must go, they ought to leave at once.	9
9	I shall act as soon as he gives his approval.	9
10	I am very sorry that we are out of that size.	9
11	Thank you for your prompt attention to our letter.	10
12	The sale ended; so you must pay the regular price.	10
13	Please inform us in the near future of your plans.	10
14	We shall send you a check on the second, as usual.	10
15	The women object to the systems in use at present.	10
16	We note what you say. The idea seems to be a good one.	11
17	There is very little chance of getting any other color.	11
18	We hope to learn from the hospital about her condition.	11
19	He expects to receive a supply by the end of next week.	11
20	I brought this matter to your attention seven days ago.	11
21	This is a matter on which I am unable to express an opinion.	12
22	I shall give you a full account of the work that I am doing.	12
23	The question is whether I can make any profit at that price.	12
24	Everybody knows that words have power for good and for evil.	12
25	If you desire more details, we shall be glad to supply them.	12
26	We must be ready to act at once when the time for action arrives.	13
27	In all they said and all they did, they were moved by one motive.	13
28	We are glad to learn you have so high an opinion of our products.	13
29	We can assure you of our prompt attention to all customer orders.	13
30	The new machines have reduced our costs and increased our output.	13
31	No one fights reform so much as someone who stands most in need of it.	14
32	I made application a while ago, but I have not received any answer yet.	14
33	I would like to make you see that this change is a very desirable one.	14
34	So often we allow our emotions to get the better of our good judgment.	14
35	The fact is that we are too slow. We will let you know in a few days.	14

1 | 2 | 3 | 4 | 5 | 6 | 7 | 8 | 9 | 10 | 11 | 12 | 13 | 14 |

Typing Skill Checkup

Type each paragraph (lines 16–19 and 20–24) once. Use double spacing. Practice three times all the phrases in which you typed a word incorrectly. Take two 2-minute writings on lines 20–24.

Goal: Speed–27 wpm
Error limit–4

16 I used to make up boxes of strawberries in an Ann Arbor 12
17 store in 1978. Each box contained 560 to 567 grams of straw- 24
18 berries in a liter box, approximately 12 cm × 12 cm × 7 cm. 36
19 The berries were zesty and would nicely serve 4 or 5 persons. 48
SI 1.33

20 As you gain knowledge about the environment, you may find 12
21 that you would like to work at a job dealing with plant life. 25
22 Landscape companies, greenhouse operators, florists, nurseries, 37
23 and the parks all employ people who are interested in working 49
24 at jobs that are helping to preserve our environment. SI 1.55 60

1 | 2 | 3 | 4 | 5 | 6 | 7 | 8 | 9 | 10 | 11 | 12 |

Unit 34

Line spacing: single
Line length: 60
Paragraph indention: 5
Type each line twice.

Warmup

1 Quietly pack all the crates with five dozen blue gift boxes.
2 We all think it would help if we have you talk to our child.
3 After May 1, Stock Nos. 37 and 38 will no longer be carried.
4 "I can't decide if 1984* or Jaws** is the best," said Marge.

1 | 2 | 3 | 4 | 5 | 6 | 7 | 8 | 9 | 10 | 11 | 12 |

New Key Location

Leave 2 spaces after a colon, except in indicating time.

Semi finger; left shift 

5 ;; ;:; ;:; two aims: accuracy and speed; example:
6 Items to be ordered: soap, towels, powder, brush.
7 The movie, Wizard, will be shown at 7:15 and 9:45.
8 Quotations were as follows: 90 at $50; 10 at $47.

(Continued on next page)

ONE-MINUTE SPEED DRIVES

Select the passage you feel you can type in 1 minute. If you complete it before time is called, select a longer one for the next writing. Continue this way for several 1-minute writings until you find the one you can complete—or almost complete—as time is called.

ONE-MINUTE SPEED DRIVES

70-space line.

1 Too much importance should not be attached to these figures, since it 14
is not possible to make an accurate estimate at this time. 25

2 This is the second annual meeting of the company, and I know that you 14
will be very happy to learn that the report I am about to make is a fa- 28
vorable one. 30

3 The woman wrote a few words on a piece of paper and rang a bell. A girl 14
appeared, took the paper without saying a word, and returned in a short 28
time with a heavy load of books. 35

4 We want to make it easy for the person with a small income to own his or 14
her own home. For this reason, we are willing to grant a loan up to 28
sixty percent of the value of any house that you wish to buy. 40

5 It is much harder to avoid censure than to gain applause; for applause 14
may be earned by one great or wise action, but a person must pass his 28
or her whole life without saying or doing one wrong or foolish thing to 42
escape censure. 45

6 The iron and steel industry is one of the basic industries of this coun- 14
try, with a great influence on many others. For this reason, business 28
people everywhere watch for reports on the wage and price changes in the 42
big companies that make iron and steel. 50

7 Much of the craze for amusements is due to the fact that people are not 14
able to live easily with just themselves. They do not know how to oc- 28
cupy their time if they happen to have a spare hour; so they look around 42
eagerly to see what they can purchase in the form of amusements. 55

8 How fast should you type? It is fairly certain that you can and should 14
type much faster than you are able to do now. Much of the speed you at- 28
tain during this course will depend upon your desire to improve and upon 42
your typing form and style. Now is the time to renew your effort to 56
increase typing speed. 60

9 The storm burst upon us with its great fury. It was all we could do to 14
stand up against it. The night was pitch dark and very cold. Deep down 28
below us, we could hear the thunder of the surf upon the rocks, but we 42
could see no sign of the vessel for which we had come to search. Per- 56
haps the storm had already torn her to pieces. 65

1 | 2 | 3 | 4 | 5 | 6 | 7 | 8 | 9 | 10 | 11 | 12 | 13 | 14

Unit 33

Line spacing: single
Line length: 60
Paragraph indention: 5
Type each line twice.

Warmup

When keyboarding, move your hands and arms as little as possible. Use finger movement only.

1 Jovial Peggy dances badly to mazurkas with that quiet Felix.
2 You must stay awake and work to make those dreams come true.
3 Jot down a list of 11 friends to come to the party August 9.

1 | 2 | 3 | 4 | 5 | 6 | 7 | 8 | 9 | 10 | 11 | 12 |

New Key Location

To underscore copy, first type the word or phrase in question. Then return to the first letter, either by backspacing (on an element machine) or by using the carriage release (on a typebar machine). When underscoring only a few letters, hold down the shift key; otherwise, employ the shift lock. Use a continuous line to underscore a series of words.

Manual: ***J*** finger left shift
Electric: ***Semi*** finger; left shift

M4 j6j j6j j6j j_j j_j j_j; do it now; it's very hot!
E4 ;p; ;p; ;p; ;_; ;_; ;_; so sorry; the London Times
5 This coverage is for a lifetime--not just till 65!
6 Have they started reading The Adventures of Zorro?
7 Please put your name and address on the blue card.

The asterisk may appear before or after a word. Leave no space between the asterisk and the word.

Manual: ***Semi*** finger; left shift
Electric: ***K*** finger; left shift

M8 ;-; ;-*; ;-*; ;*; ;*; credited*; her recent novel*
E8 kik k8k k8k k*k k*k k*k Ford V-8*, famous*, meter*
9 An (*) may be used to call attention to footnotes.
10 For 8 days nothing happened on the Eastern Front.*
11 Use ** for a second footnote. I like her books.**

Leave no space between quotation marks and the material they enclose.

Manual: ***S*** finger; right shift
Electric: ***Semi*** finger; left shift

M12 sws sw2s s2s s2s s"s s"s s""s "Oh yes, of course!"
E12 ;"; ;"; ;"; "Strike three, you're out!" he called.
13 The stock's "high" and "low" is in today's Herald.
14 "Go back at once--there's danger ahead!" he cried.
15 Anne wrote an essay entitled "My Happiest Moment."

SKILL DEVELOPMENT

Unit 39

Line spacing: single
Line length: 60
Paragraph indention: 5

Warmup

Eliminate waste motions and increase your speed.

1 You must return the coupon if you want to get a cash refund.
2 All of the goods damaged by the fire will be placed on sale.
3 Max and Charles did not receive pay, but Joe did pay Lizzie.
1 | 2 | 3 | 4 | 5 | 6 | 7 | 8 | 9 | 10 | 11 | 12 |

Manipulative Key Practice

4 What's a shift key? Where is it? When do you use it? How?
5 Cities listed were Boston, Denver, San Diego, and St. Louis.

6 Push the SHIFT LOCK to keyboard a SERIES OF CAPITAL LETTERS.
7 The sign read NO PARKING, 8 A.M. TO 6 P.M. WEDNESDAY-FRIDAY.

Type lines 8 and 9 as shown. Backspace to fill in the missing letters.

8 Wh_t are all these b_anks d_ing in ou_ key_oar_ing e_ercise?
9 Back_pace to fil_ th_m. Use _our eye_ and _our i_aginat_on.

Set margins for a 50-space line: 25–80 (elite), 17–72 (pica).

10 She wanted the sentences to fit, but they were all too long.
11 The error forced her to press the margin release repeatedly.

Typing from Script

Use lines 12–18 to review spacing before and after punctuation marks.

12 She taught the class; the department head observed.
13 Locate these keys: tab set, tab clear, and return.
14 Can you change the ribbon? Fantastic! Show me how.
15 Shorthand (Mrs. Li's class) is a two-semester course.
16 "See, say, and stroke—that's a good rule to use,"
17 said Amy. "Let's try it before class ends at 3 p.m."
18 Which class has the electric machines—yours or mine?

Group 1 FLUENCY DRILLS

WORD PRACTICE

When you read, your eyes see whole words rather than the individual letters that make up the words. Skilled typists apply the same principle in typing. They type each word as a whole, rather than as a series of individual letters.

Type each of these words as a unit (a word-whole), without thinking of the individual letters. When you come to the longer words, you may find it helpful to use syllables or letter groups as typing units. *Type lines across, not down, in columns. Space once after each word.*

TWO-LETTER WORDS

Left margin at 30. Single spacing.

1	an	be	he	it	of	to
2	am	by	if	me	on	up
3	as	do	in	my	or	us
4	at	go	is	no	so	we

THREE-LETTER WORDS

Left margin at 25. Single spacing.

1	act	ask	far	law	oil	saw	try
2	add	bad	few	let	old	say	two
3	age	big	for	low	one	see	use
4	ago	boy	get	man	our	set	was
5	air	but	has	may	out	she	way
6	all	buy	had	men	owe	sir	who
7	and	can	her	met	own	sit	why
8	any	car	him	new	pay	six	yes
9	are	day	his	not	put	the	yet
10	arm	end	how	now	run	too	you

FOUR-LETTER WORDS

Left margin at 15. Single spacing.

1	able	each	hard	life	near	seem	told
2	also	east	have	like	need	seen	true
3	away	easy	head	line	next	send	turn
4	back	even	hear	list	note	sent	upon
5	bank	ever	help	live	once	shop	very
6	best	face	here	long	only	show	view
7	blue	fact	high	look	open	side	wait
8	body	fall	hold	lose	over	size	walk
9	book	fear	home	love	part	some	want
10	both	feel	hope	made	pass	soon	week
11	call	find	hour	make	plan	sort	well
12	came	food	idea	many	play	stop	went
13	care	foot	into	mark	poor	such	were

(*Continued on next page*)

Supplementary Practice

Reinforce locations of the following keys:

i, r, e, h

sad kid slid; if I did; jar a rail; drill a cliff; skids far
she held her fare; he hid his; she shared freshly fried fish
Half his ideas are hers. He hires and fires. Sell dresses!

g, t, w, y

gather glass; take tests; lift gates; jet lag; Greek letters
say why; try yes; walk away; key years; wise as we are witty
Gray sky, wet weather. Yearly wages grew. Do you know why?

q, u, o, p

query; quite a quick quake; quiet quarrel; qualify quarterly
hope to do so; proof of progress; postal pool; spoke praises
How do you plead? A jury would acquit. Poll people to see.

n, x, m, v

no exit; xerox six; noise annoys; fixing in an annex; Texans
more vim; vast view; main valve; values vary; maximum volume
Many tax moving expenses. Never expend extra money on trim.

b, c, z

call back; carbon copy; branch bank; balance Bob's checkbook
a dozen quizzes; ZIP codes; ozone haze; zigzag to the zenith
Don't be fazed by his zeal. He's zany but capable and nice.

1 | 2 | 3 | 4 | 5 | 6 | 7 | 8 | 9 | 10 | 11 | 12

Typing Skill Checkup

Do you know that you have mastered one of the first steps 12
in learning how to run a word processor or a microcomputer? 24
You gained that skill when you learned to operate a qwerty 36
keyboard by touch. You will have to make only a few minor 48
adjustments when you first sit down to try your hand at word 60
processing. 62

For one thing, you will have to get accustomed to not 74
striking the return key at the end of each line. When the end 86
of a line is reached, the machine knows to carry to the next 98
line any word that will not fit. Also, you will come to love 110
the ease with which changes in copy can be made. 120

One thing will not change, however. You must still be 132
able to proofread your copy. Copy must be completely error- 144
free to be acceptable. SI 1.30 148

1 | 2 | 3 | 4 | 5 | 6 | 7 | 8 | 9 | 10 | 11 | 12

SECTION FIVE

Supplementary Practice Exercises

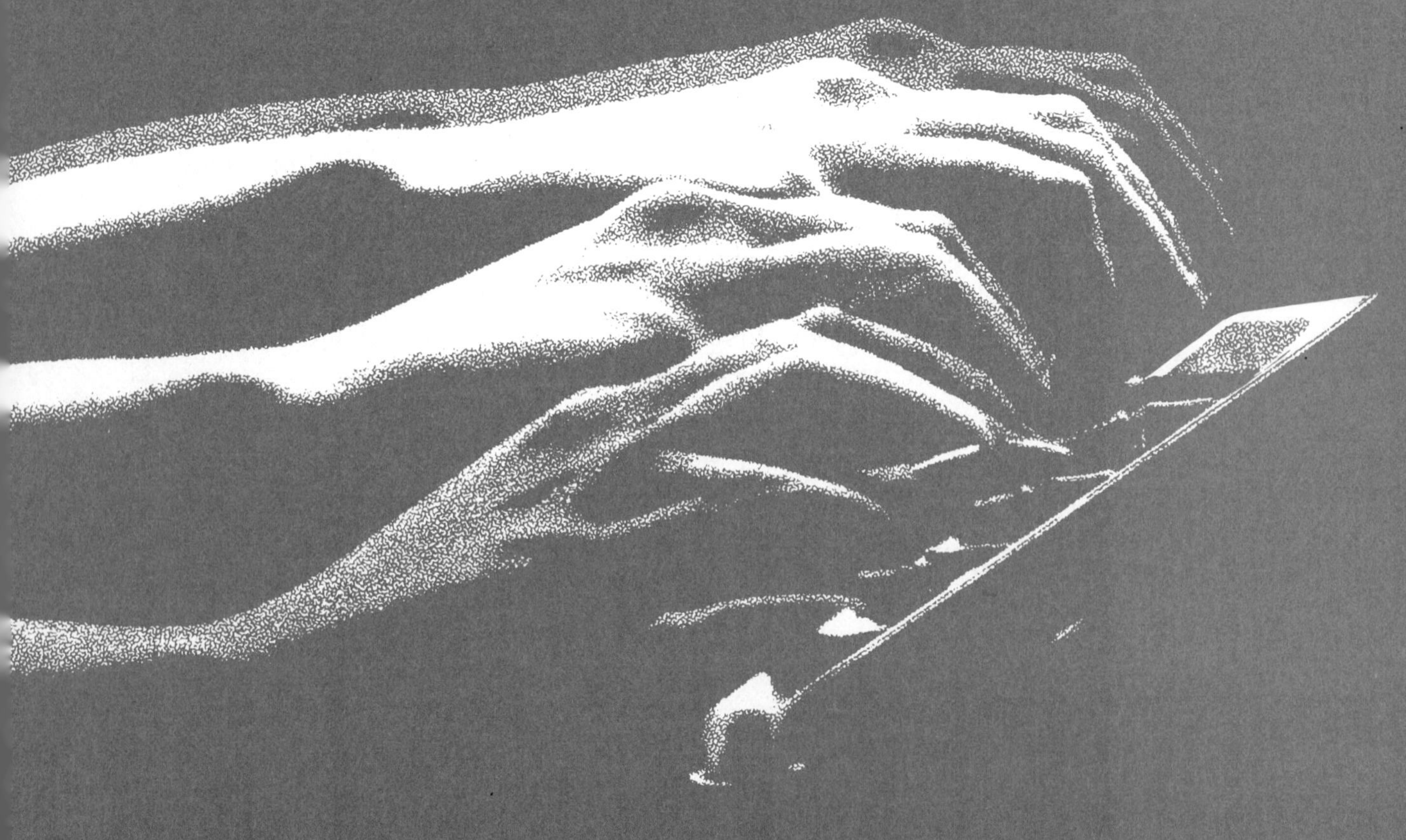

SECTION TWO

Typing for Personal Use

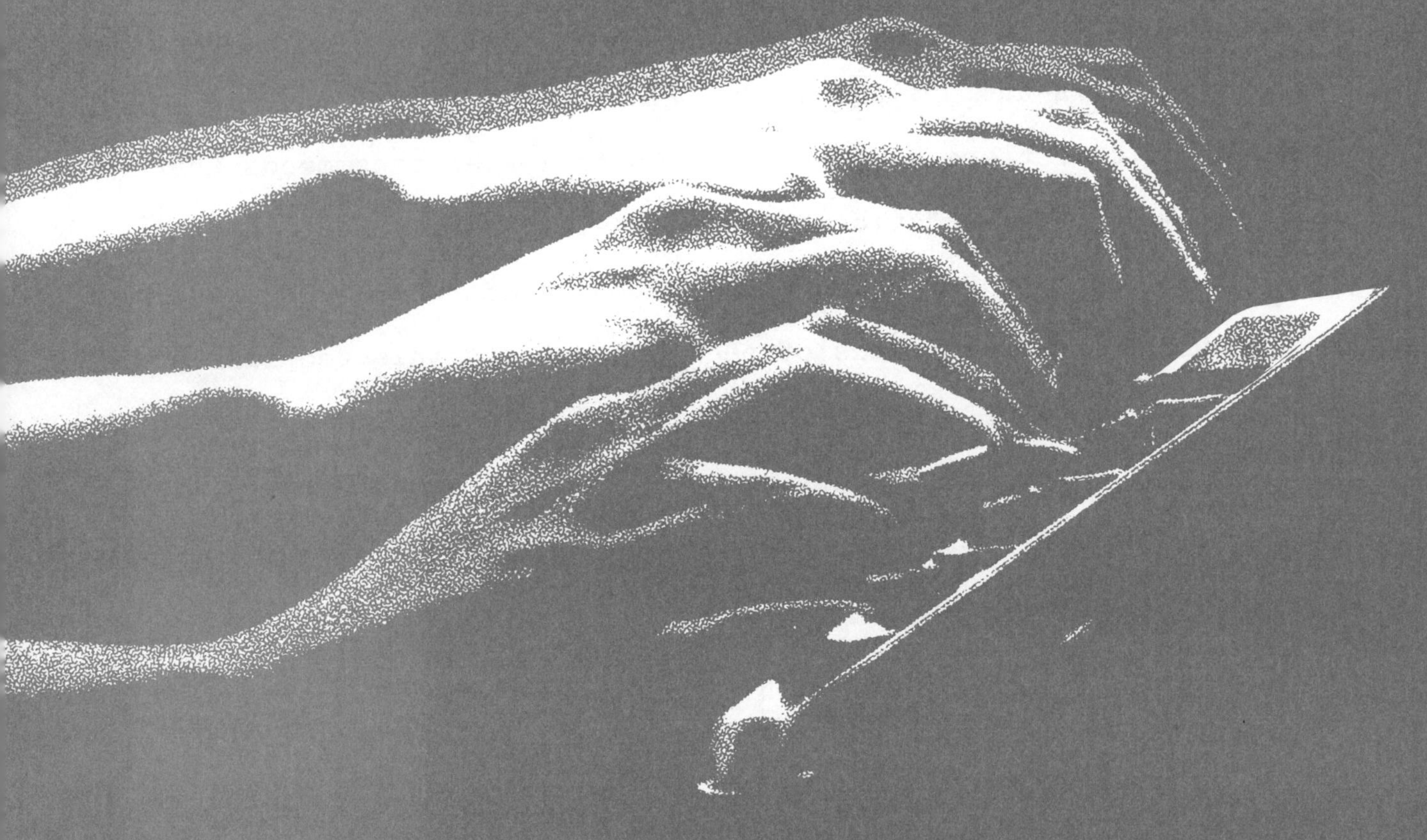

While IPC utilization has remained constant there has been a 67 percent increase in the average benefit payment per admission over the years of the survey to ~~an average of~~ $220 per patient day. In comparison, national hospital payments per member for medical and surgical admissions ~~for this same group~~ averaged $289. Overall, the data suggests that costs could best be controlled ~~by (1)~~ reducing ~~the~~ OPC utilization ~~and (2)~~ reducing IPC costs per patient day.

Plan Recommendation

The trend of increasing ~~OPC~~ utilization and costs ~~can be tied directly to~~ increases in the number of facilities offering OPC services. Unfortunately, very few of those states with Certificate of Need (CON) legislation ~~include the review of~~ OPC facilities. Also, ~~all~~ Health Systems Agencies ~~(HSA)~~ are presently faced with dwindling financial resources, it is doubltful that they will perform voluntary reviews when CON is not applicable.

As a result of these concerns, ~~the Control Plan~~ recommends that all plans ~~should~~ have an "evidence of necessity" requirement in their contracts with OPC's. For those plans in ~~the~~ state where CON laws apply, issuance of certificates of need can satisfy this requirement. However, the absence of a certificate of need, all plans should have a contractually established right to make need decisions, regardless of whether or now that right is exercised.

PART 1

KEYBOARD SKILL BUILDING

Topic 1 TECHNIQUE PRACTICE

You can improve both your speed and your accuracy by developing better typing techniques. For example, by training yourself to hold the shift key all the way down, you can eliminate capital letters that hang above the line. By returning without taking your eyes from the copy, you can avoid wasting time on finding your place again.

The drills in the next ten pages provide practice material designed to help you improve your technique when using the various manipulative keys—the return, the backspace, the tab, the shift keys, and the margin release. Practice these drills frequently. Use them at the beginning of a class for a warmup or at the end of the class whenever you have a few minutes to spare.

RETURNING

A quick, smooth return will add to your typing speed.

Drill 1

CALL-THE-RETURN DRILLS

Select the sentence that will require you to type a little faster than your normal rate. The drill will last for 1 minute, with your teacher calling the return at the end of either a 20- or 30-second interval. If you finish the sentence before the call, wait so that everyone returns at the same time. Change sentences after each 1-minute timing until you find the one you can complete just as the return is called.

65-space line. Single spacing.

		wpm in 20 sec.	30 sec.
1	We wish you would tell him how.	19	12
2	Get her team to work like yours.	19	13
3	Larry will send you a check soon.	20	13
4	My car may be in the garage a day.	20	14
5	We can plan on your taking one boy.	21	14
6	He wishes to have the bill paid now.	22	14
7	In the next few days I shall send it.	22	15
8	He does not plan to give a large gift.	23	15
9	Maybe it is too early to make a report.	23	16
10	Try a few and let me hear from you soon.	24	16
11	I had to stop in the office on the sixth.	25	16
12	Marian filed an application some time ago.	25	17
13	You asked me to try to get you two tickets.	26	17
14	I am very sorry that we are out of that pie.	26	18
15	We wish to sign the note and send it to them.	27	18

1 | 2 | 3 | 4 | 5 | 6 | 7 | 8 | 9 |

(Continued on next page)

CONTROL PLAN RECOMMENDATIONS ON PLANNING CONTROLS ON

OUTPATIENT PSYCHIATRIC CARE (OPC) SERVICES

The Proliferation of Outpatient Psychiatric Care (OPC) Services

According to the National Center for Mental Health, health facilities offering outpatient psychiatric care services were introduced with the passage of the Community Mental Health Center Act. Since its passage, the number of new facilities offering such services has continued to increase.

Employee utilization of psychiatric services was surveyed for the five year period ending in 1985. Data was analyzed for both Outpatient Psychiatric Care (OPC) and Inpatient Psychiatric Care (IPC). It was found that both statewide and nationwide there have been slight increases in the percentage of insurance company payout associated with psychiatric services. Combining OPC and IPC payments represented 11 percent of payments made in the last year compared to 8 percent in the first.

While IPC utilization (both admissions and length of stay) has remained constant over the five years, however, OPC utilization has increased dramatically. The national figures show a five percent increase (from 139 to 218 OPC visits per 1,000 members) and the state figures show a 50 percent increase (from 295 to 442 visits per 1,000 members). Since the average benefit payment per OPC visit has shown only a slight increase, increases in utilization explain increases in OPC benefit payments. Also, national data shows a 41 percent increase in the percentage of member using the OPC benefits.

Drill 1 continued

		wpm in 20 sec.	30 sec.
16	The money is due and I can pay it if you wish.	28	18
17	We are very sorry that we are out of that size.	28	19
18	In the future, send their money to them by wire.	29	19
19	We shall send you a check on the first, as usual.	29	20
20	I wish to express my thanks for the time she gave.	30	20
21	Charles refused our request to pay us what he owes.	31	20
22	He will purchase several vases, if you allow credit.	31	21
23	Mr. Mack expects you to reply to his request by mail.	32	21
24	There is very little chance of getting a better price.	32	22
25	I found that she did not bring up the subject of costs.	33	22
26	He could not read the type on the map; so I returned it.	34	22
27	If you are a good typist, you can always be sure of work.	34	23
28	She may go there today if she can get them to go with her.	35	23
29	They do not own the land by the high dam, but they rent it.	35	24
30	Send it to us if they do not want to spend the money for it.	36	24
31	If they desire more details, we shall be glad to supply them.	37	24
32	They spent half of their money for an audit of their business.	37	25
33	Some of them felt that the man did not know how to do the work.	38	25
34	I can assure you of our prompt attention to all customer orders.	38	26

1 | 2 | 3 | 4 | 5 | 6 | 7 | 8 | 9 | 10 | 11 | 12 | 13 |

TAB MECHANISM

Learn to use the tab key or bar without pausing before or after.

Drill 2

TABULATOR

Type the columns of words at the right across each line.

Left margin at 10. Single spacing. Tab stops at 20, 30, 40, 50, 60, and 70.

```
it        is        to        if        by        an        am
the       for       and       did       due       the       for
is        if        by        to        an        me        it
for       the       did       and       did       for       the
is        if        by        it        is        if        to
and       did       the       did       and       the       for
```

Drill 3

TABULATOR

Practice smooth, quick indentions on the sentences at the right and on the following two pages.

60-space line. Single spacing. 5-space paragraph indention.

1	Less than a hundred years ago, humans made their first	12	12
	attempt to fly with an airplane.	18	18
2	Many people responded by shaking their heads and saying	12	30
	that we were never meant to fly.	18	37
3	In time, however, people grew to accept air travel much	12	49
	as they had accepted travel by water.	19	56

1 | 2 | 3 | 4 | 5 | 6 | 7 | 8 | 9 | 10 | 11 | 12 |

(Continued on next page)

SACRAMENTO LIFE AND CASUALTY INS. CO.

PAYROLL DEDUCTION CODE	AMOUNT OF COVERAGE LIFE		AD&D*	DEPENDENT	CURRENT PREMIUM RATE
40700	$25,000	+	$12,500	none	~~$12.92~~ 14.47 monthly
40702	$25,000	+	$12,500	$5,000	~~16.52~~ 18.50 monthly
40740	$25,000	+	$12,500	$5,000	~~20.70~~ 23.18 monthly
40730	$25,000	+	$12,500	$5,000	~~18.98~~ 21.26 monthly
40720	$25,000	+	$12,500	none	~~15.00~~ 16.80 monthly
40745	$20,000	+	$10,000	$5,000	~~14.05~~ 15.74 monthly
40744	$20,000	+	$10,000	$1,000	~~11.77~~ 13.18 monthly
40743	$20,000	+	$10,000	none	~~11.20~~ 12.54 monthly
40742	$10,000	+	$ 5,000	none	~~7.79~~ 8.72 monthly
40747	$12,500	+	$ 6,250	none	~~9.27~~ 10.38 monthly
40746	$12,500	+	$ 6,250	$5,000	~~14.25~~ 15.96 monthly

*Accidental Death and Dismemberment (paid in addition to Life)

Task

The report on the following two pages was previously typed in the word processing center. After being returned to Jantzen, the word originator, it has been recycled to the center for additional changes. Type the final draft. *Note:* After seeing the final draft, Jantzen unexpectedly requests some major alterations in format. See your instructor for details.

Procedures Manual notes: 1-inch side and bottom margins; title on line 10 (all other pages start on line 7); single-space body; titles in all capital letters, internal headings flush left and underscored in capitals and lowercase.

WORK REQUISITION
Sacramento Life and Casualty Insurance Co.
Word Processing Center A-2

Originator: Robert Jantzen, Director   Date: 2/12/—

Department: Cost Control   Extension: 4316

Item: Report   Input: Stored G-1002-B   Priority: Rush

Special Instructions: Final copy, please

Drill 3 continued

4 You can become whatever you want to be. You can make 12 12
yourself into almost any kind of person. 20 20
5 In the future, please make sure that you get a receipt 12 31
from the person to whom you make the delivery. 21 41
6 I am pleased to be able to tell you that the financial 12 52
position of this company is a very strong one. 21 62
7 As we expect to be very busy next month, we should ap- 12 74
preciate it if you would give us your order now. 22 83

8 All office workers should know how to consult reference 12 12
books in order to get the information they need. 22 22
9 When you apply for a job, you should submit a neat and 12 33
clearly formatted resume to make a good impression. 22 44
10 We should be grateful if you would consider this offer 12 55
at once and let us have your decision within a few days. 23 67
11 We suggest you increase the size of your order so that 12 78
you may take advantage of the special discount we offer. 23 90

12 We are pleased to inform you that we plan to open a new 12 12
branch of our store in your neighborhood within six weeks. 24 24
13 They hope to complete the new plant early next year and 12 36
to have the machines in full production before the beginning 24 48
of fall. 26 49
14 Since tomorrow is going to be sunny, why don't we go on 12 61
a picnic? We can pack a basket of cheese, sausages, bread, 24 73
and brownies. 26 76

15 In choosing a place to live, people usually consider the 12 12
advantages for their children. They prefer neighborhoods 24 24
with good schools. 27 27
16 Experts haggle over precise definitions, but most agree 12 39
word processing is basically the use of automated equipment 24 51
to manipulate words. 28 55
17 You can now take care of all your financial needs, both 12 67
business and personal, at a savings and loan institution as 24 79
well as at a bank. 27 82

1 | 2 | 3 | 4 | 5 | 6 | 7 | 8 | 9 | 10 | 11 | 12 |

(Continued on next page)

¶1 The above medical claim has been presented for payment. Unfortunately we cannot process the claim through our benefits department.

¶2 Where two carriers cover a single policyholder, benefit payments must be coordinated. You should, therefore, first submit your claim to (Stop Code), your other insurance carrier, and send us a copy of their statement of benefits. Upon receipt of this documentation, the balance of the covered expenses can be computed and paid.

¶3 Our records show that we have already paid benefits on this expense. Your doctor, however, has submitted another bill for the same service and same date. Naturally we cannot honor this second billing.

¶4 Our records show that you are entitled to individual coverage only. The medical expenses in question were incurred by a dependent. If you wish to extend your coverage to include such situations in the future, we suggest that you contact your group representative at your earliest convenience.

¶5 The claim is covered under your Major Medical benefits. Such benefits cannot be paid, however, until the policy deductible has been received--a condition that has not been met in this instance.

¶6 If you have any information that would help clarify this situation, please contact us immediately.

¶7 If you have any further questions, please feel free to contact us.

Task

Keyboard and store the table that appears at the top of the next page, revising the premium figures as indicated. Print out a hard copy for preliminary approval by Simonds, the word originator. *Note:* Simonds does, in fact, return the document to the word processing center, requesting two more key changes. Ask your instructor for details.

Procedures Manual notes: Tables centered vertically and horizontally; titles and column headings centered; footnotes flush left with no end punctuation; typist's initials (lowercase) and document code as reference line.

WORK REQUISITION
Sacramento Life and Casualty Insurance Co.
Word Processing Center A-2

Originator Jim Simonds, Account Rep. Date 2/12/–

Department Employee Contributions Extension 4223

Item Table Input stored F-3492-A Priority Routine

Special Instructions Insert revised premium rates. Also tighten up presentation; make heads easier to read.

Drill 3 continued

18 If you have any more trouble with your stereo after we 12 12
return it to you, please let us know and we shall make any 24 24
necessary adjustments. 28 28

19 For millions of industrial workers, the time clock is a 12 40
way of life. It checks the attendance of employees and it 24 52
records the hours they work. 29 57

20 When you have decided on a career goal and the path that 12 69
leads to it, you have really settled on a way of looking at 24 81
life, a blueprint for living. 30 87

21 We have acknowledged the receipt of their order but have 12 12
advised them that we cannot make shipment until we complete 24 24
our investigation of their financial standing. 33 33

22 If you cultivate an agreeable personality, you will not 12 45
only become a happier person but you will also find friends 24 57
and co-workers more helpful in whatever you do. 33 66

1 | 2 | 3 | 4 | 5 | 6 | 7 | 8 | 9 | 10 | 11 | 12 |

Drill 4

COMPOSITION AT THE KEYBOARD

Type your name and today's date three times across as shown at the right.

Left margin at 15. Single spacing. 5 spaces between columns.

1 *Your name* *Your name* *Your name*
2 *Your name* *Your name* *Your name*
3 *Your name* *Your name* *Your name*

4 *Today's date* *Today's date* *Today's date*
5 *Today's date* *Today's date* *Today's date*
6 *Today's date* *Today's date* *Today's date*

BACKSPACE KEY

Operate the backspace key without looking up.

Drill 5

BACKSPACE KEY

Remember that to center a line horizontally, start at the center of your paper and backspace once for every 2 letters or spaces in the line. Center horizontally all the lines at the right.

Double spacing.

SOME INTERESTING OCCUPATIONS

TS

Graphic Artist

Tour Guide

Soil Conservationist

Forester

Copywriter

Computer Analyst

City Planner

Surveyor

Travel Agent

Project C-3

SKILLS COVERAGE
1. *Assembling composite letters*
2. *Applying English language skills*
3. *Typing reports*
4. *Formatting tabular material*
5. *Manipulating data electronically*
6. *Setting priorities*

You are employed as a correspondence secretary in a satellite word processing center at Sacramento Life and Casualty. The center processes a variety of documents from managers in the group life and group health insurance areas. Each document arriving in the center is accompanied by a work requisition form. The center supervisor reviews both the document and the form, records the time of receipt, and assigns the project to a particular operator. The supervisor also notes any special handling or priority requested. (Documents are generally processed in order of receipt. The only exceptions are documents marked "Urgent," which are completed first.) Processed documents are circulated back to the center supervisor for recording of completion time and return to the word originator. *Note:* The company's word processing procedures manual specifies the formats to be used in typing company documents. Relevant excerpts from the manual have been provided for each task.

Task

Store the standard paragraphs that appear on the next page. Then use them to assemble the form letters requested below. (If you do not have word processing equipment, type each letter individually.)

Procedures Manual notes: Block style; open punctuation; standard (6-inch) line; date on line 13; subject lines (3) single-spaced and blocked; typist's initials (lowercase) and document code as reference line.

WORK REQUISITION
Sacramento Life and Casualty Insurance Co.
Word Processing Center A-2

Originator Patricia MacIntyre, Supervisor Date 2/12/–

Department Group Benefits Extension 4302

Item Claims letters (3) Input Stored J-2411-B Priority Routine

Special Instructions ① Spencer Kraft, 158 Alva Dr., Phoenix, AZ 85023; Subject: Group #3-4072-116; Service Date—Jan. 16; Attending Physician—Dr. R. Vanuski; ¶s 1, 4
② Isiah Lawson, 5436 Parker Ave., Fullerton, CA 92632; Subject: Group #2-6736-551; Service Date—Jan. 27; Attending Physician—Dr. F. D. Rosen; ¶s 1, 3, 6
③ Carmela Estrada, 815 Bend Blvd., Santa Fe, NM 87501; Subject: Group #4-8838-792; Service Date—Jan. 30; Attending Physician—Dr. I. Komal; ¶s 1, 2 (Mutual Health Ins.), 7

Drill 6

BACKSPACE KEY

Type the sentences at the right. Immediately after typing each italicized word, backspace, spelling out each letter in the word as you do. Then underscore the word. (*Note:* Each underscored word is given a triple word count.)

65-space line. Double spacing.

1 I cannot be your *friend* and your flatterer, too. 12
2 This is the *first* annual meeting of the company. 12
3 Let your elbows hang loosely, *close* to your body. 12
4 Learn to return your carriage *without* looking up. 13
5 The visitor was *too* busy to make up his *own* speech. 13

6 The spoken word is *more* powerful than the written word. 13
7 Our agents inform us that *you* wish to take out a policy. 12
8 The average life of a paper bill is less than *two years.* 14
9 You understand, of course, that *we shall* expect payment. 14
10 The *pink* grapefruit from Florida is of excellent quality. 13

Drill 7

BACKSPACE KEY

When composing a rough draft at the typewriter, it is faster to X-out an incorrect word or phrase than to erase it. As you type the sentences at the right, backspace and X-out the incorrect (italicized) words. Then supply the correct word and complete the typing of each sentence.

65-space line. Double spacing.

1 Listen for the end-of-line cue for an even *write* margin. 14
2 Everyone *accept* Bristol will go to the picnic on Sunday. 15
3 Carla will chair the student *counsel* meeting this week. 15
4 Mail your job application to the *personal* director. 15
5 Did you *loose* a red wallet in the locker room yesterday? 14

6 Kensington Park is the *cite* chosen for the annual picnic. 14
7 Our profits are greater this year *then* they were last year. 14
8 The dog stopped for a few minutes to lick *it's* injured paw. 14
9 Fast foods generally include *to* many empty calories. 12
10 I was happy to learn that I *past* algebra with a B average. 15

Drill 8

DELETE/CORRECTION KEY

Keyboards on microcomputers, word processors, and self-correcting typewriters have a key that causes the machine to backspace and delete at the same time. Using this key is faster than X-ing out and produces fully corrected copy, with no trace of earlier errors. Type the paragraphs at the right and on the following page. If your machine has a delete/correction key, make your corrections as you type. Otherwise use the X-ing out procedure described in Drill 7.

70-space line. Double spacing. 5-space paragraph indention.

1 The composition of copy is easier on a personal computer than on a 14
typewriter. No longer is there a need to backspace and X-out unwanted 28
copy. The delete key and the cursor control key are used to delete 42
and revise rough draft copy with no retyping. 51

2 For years scientists and laymen alike have wondered about what makes 15
some whales and dolphins suddenly strand themselves on the beach. One 29
theory is that environmental conditions in the water interfere with the 43
natural sonar system used by these creatures to navigate and that they 57
confuse direction. 61

3 Children should be encouraged to form the habit of saving a small sum 15
every week until they reach a definite goal. They should then be guided to 29
select wisely the item they want to buy and helped to make the purchase. In 44
this way they will receive training both in keeping money and spending their 59
savings wisely. 62

1 | 2 | 3 | 4 | 5 | 6 | 7 | 8 | 9 | 10 | 11 | 12 | 13 | 14 |

(Continued on next page)

Task

Prepare a master mailing list of sales representatives. The list is to be used for addressing sheets of adhesive-backed labels. (Ask your instructor for the guide, or backing, sheet that you will need to format the list.) Correct any obvious errors or omissions. (For example, use the appropriate directory to supply any missing ZIP Codes.) Run your list through a photocopier and use the labels as necessary to prepare envelopes for the memorandums.

CLAIRAINE HAIR AND BEAUTY PRODUCTS, INC.
Sales Representatives, Districts 1, 2, and 3

District 1

Thomas A. McLain, 44 e. Roanoke Avenue, Bellaire, Michigan 49615, (616) 661-2347

John Diaz, 132 Newport, Petoskey, Mich. 49770, (616) 381-1109

Joyce Digue, 205 W. Longwood, Alpena, MI 49707, (517) 821-9266

Robert G. Ander, 25245 Five Mile Road, Traverse City, MI. 49684, (616) 872-3553

Mary Brode, 435 Dover, Gaylord, Michigan 48935, (517) 731-3456

District 2

Luke L. Page, 191 Snow, Dearborn, Michigan, 48110, (313) 321-7662

Ann Smith, 2885 Joplin, Detroit, Mich. 48235, (313) 435-6172

Selden Fogel, 8230 Roylat Avenue, Pontiac, MI 48011, (313) 226-1734

R. Patrice Adams, 7634 Edgewood Dr., Ann Arbor, (313) 839-1377

District 3

Chas. Jos. Harvey, 850 Lincoln Court, Lansing, MI, (517) 482-5213

Lynn Holt, 1976 Riveria Drive, Marshall, Mi. 49068 (616) 351-7044

Rita A. Maier, 3232 Alden St., Flint, MI 48517, (313) 882-9736

Rex Ray, 1203 Hall, S.W., Grand Rapids, MI, (616) 339-9183

Task

Ms. Ackroyd wants you to prepare a telephone directory of the sales representatives under her supervision. The list is for her own as well as department reference. Ackroyd's only requirements are that the directory be arranged alphabetically by surname and that the names of the district managers (Digue, Smith, and Harvey) stand out. She leaves other details up to you but cautions that the format will have to be flexible, as the sales staff is expanding rapidly and frequent revisions will have to be made. When you have completed your directory, store it and print out a hard copy for Ackroyd's (your teacher's) preliminary approval. *Note:* You have heard Ackroyd on the phone making job offers to at least two people and suspect there may already be some changes.

Drill 8 continued

4 Many students find that homework assignments and notes that are 14
typed are easy to use for study and review. This is not always true of 28
handwritten notes, which are often difficult to read. Such notes also 42
tend to blur and fade with time and repeated handling. 53

5 Important characteristics of successful real estate salespersons include 15
a pleasing personality, honesty, and a neat appearance. Dealing with pros- 30
pective customers requires maturity and tact as well as enthusiasm for the 45
job. Agents also should have a good memory for names and faces and for 59
business details such as prices and zoning regulations. 69

6 Some years ago a man had the idea that we should all begin our day 14
earlier in the summer than in the winter. From this idea grew the plan of 24
daylight saving time. The proposal to move the hands of the clock ahead in 43
the early spring and to move them back in the fall was one of those obvious 58
yet daring suggestions that rarely occur to anybody. 68

7 Typing and shorthand are two skills that are basic to the efficient 14
operation of an office; however, the duties of office workers cover a 28
much wider range of skills. The increased use of word processing equip- 43
ment has not diminished the need for persons trained in such common 56
office procedures as filing, handling mail, greeting clients, preparing 70
reports, and using the telephone. 77

8 Salespeople who travel try to make calls at the time most convenient to 15
their customers. Frequently, they spend their evenings and weekends writ- 30
ing reports and planning itineraries. However, some salespeople are able to 45
schedule their time off when they want it. When on business trips, sales- 59
people are reimbursed for expenses such as transportation, food, and 72
lodging. Some companies provide a car or pay a mileage allowance to those 87
who use their own cars. 91

1| 2| 3| 4| 5| 6| 7| 8| 9| 10| 11| 12| 13| 14|

SHIFT KEY

Depress the shift key firmly when you type a capital letter. Release the shift key quickly after the letter is struck.

Drill 9

SHIFT KEY

Type each of the sentences at the right.

70-space line. Single spacing.

1 J. W. Fisher ran for Attorney General of Florida. 10 10
2 Daryl called Caroline and invited her to the dance. 10 20
3 Business declined in June but will be better in July. 11 31
4 The next sales meeting will be held in May in Hawaii. 11 41
5 George Landers was elected Senator of North Carolina. 11 52

1| 2| 3| 4| 5| 6| 7| 8| 9| 10| 11| 12| 13| 14|

(Continued on next page)

Task

Recall the form letter from storage and print out a copy for each of the schools listed below. (If you are using a stencil instead of word processing equipment, duplicate the correct number of copies and type in the variable information on each.) *Note:* The last name of the sales representative in whose territory a school is located appears in parentheses after each entry. Full names and telephone numbers can be found in the master mailing list at the end of this project.

1 Mrs. Edward Boyd, Boyd's Beauty College, 232 Maine, Detroit, MI 48236 (Smith)

2 Mr. Cecil R. Prince, Star Institute of Hair Design, 1533 Wildemere, Marshall, MI 49068 (Holt)

3 Mr. Alfred K. Woods, Michigan School of Beauty, 486 Maple, Bloomfield Hills, MI 48013 (Fogel)

4 Mrs. Janice McKean, Northern Academy of Cosmetology, 13667 Woodstock, Petoskey, MI 49770 (Diaz)

5 Miss Alice Dean, Excelsior School of Hairstyling, 1429 Crescent Drive, Saginaw, MI 48604 (Maier)

Task

Keyboard this interoffice memo, correcting any errors you may find in spelling, punctuation, grammar, and style. Store the memo and print out a copy. (If you do not have word processing equipment, simply keyboard an original.) At this point, Ms. Ackroyd requests some last-minute changes (ask your instructor for these). Once the memo has been edited into a final draft form, print out (or photocopy) one for each sales representative in the appropriate district.

TO: District 1, Sales Reps
FROM: Diana Ackroyd, Michigan Sales Director
SUBJECT MCA Convention

The Michigan Cosmetology Association is holding it's convention next month at the Waterford Inn in Alpena, Michigan. The convention will run for 3 days beginning Friday, ____________, 19--. As usual, our co. will set up a booth to display our products.

The exhibit will have to be staffed by XXXXXX our District 1 representives on Fri. & Sat. from 8:30a.m. to 4:30 p.m. and on Sunday from 8:30 to 12 o'clock noon. I have asked Joyce Digue to prepare a schedule of coverage, assigning each rep to the booth for a 4-hr period. She will make personel contact with the other District 1 reps to finalize the arrangements for the coverage. If any of you will be unavailable for booth coverage, Joyce will request asisstance from Reps in Dist. 2 & 3.

Drill 9 continued

6 Did you see the new Sphinx motorcycle at Norton Motors? 11 11
7 I heard that a new Burger Shack is opening on Arrow Lane. 11 22
8 Last year we vacationed in Miami; this year, in San Francisco. 12 34
9 Worldwide Products will open a new warehouse in New Jersey. 12 46
10 Ms. Zuchs plans to visit Zaire, Egypt, and Libya this summer. 12 58

11 Tom R. Busher was promoted to Assistant Vice President today. 12 12
12 A benefit show will be given for the United Appeal of Dayton. 12 24
13 Allen Forbes will not be City Council President as of Friday. 12 36
14 Lake Tahoe is located on the border of California and Nevada. 12 48
15 The Princess Inn Hotel in Quebec City is a nice place to stay. 12 60

16 Our bank has branch offices in England, Canada, and the Bahamas. 13 13
17 Our employees plan to give blood to the Red Cross next Wednesday. 13 26
18 You can buy annuities from the International Mutual Fund in Peoria. 13 39
19 The training director will hold the seminars in the Ocean View Room. 14 52
20 Tom McBride of the Accounting Department was transferred to Montreal. 14 66

21 You can get some of the best land buys from Richey Land Co. in Ocala. 14 14
22 The Sleepy Hollow Club will present Thornton Wilder's play on Tuesday. 14 28
23 Investment advice is available at Thompson, Garafoli, and Sweeney, Inc. 14 42
24 James Ford Rhodes High School won the state meet in Toledo last year. 14 56
25 Interest rates are lower at Holmes State Bank than at Fargo Finance Co. 14 70

26 Hale Brothers will be open on Friday, which is Martin Luther King Day. 14 14
27 Trade between Israel and Europe's Common Market will be increasing. 14 28
28 Ida and Randy are going to New Orleans for the Mardi Gras in February. 14 42
29 We shall send you the latest prices no later than Tuesday or Wednesday. 14 56
30 Amy and Bob wrote letters to colleges in Denver, Dallas, and San Diego. 14 70

1 | 2 | 3 | 4 | 5 | 6 | 7 | 8 | 9 | 10 | 11 | 12 | 13 | 14 |

Drill 10

SYMBOL PRACTICE

This drill will give you practice in typing numbers and the more commonly used symbols that require the use of the shift key.

70-space line. Single spacing. 5-space paragraph indention.

1 A business card is usually 3½" x 2" (though some people use larger sizes). 16 16

2 Will you telephone Mr. Berry and let me know if lunch on Tuesday is convenient? 17 33

3 Somewhere along the line someone has "goofed" in the shipment of your purchases. 17 50

4 Of the 53 people treated, 34% were cured and another 17% reported partial relief. 17 67

5 The ANNUAL STOCKHOLDERS' REPORT for the Benson Division was completed last week. 17 83

1 | 2 | 3 | 4 | 5 | 6 | 7 | 8 | 9 | 10 | 11 | 12 | 13 | 14 |

(Continued on next page)

Project C-2

Skills Coverage
1. *Preparing form letters with variables*
2. *Applying English language skills*
3. *Typing interoffice memos*
4. *Manipulating data electronically*
5. *Reproducing labels from a mailing list*
6. *Using standard office references*

You are employed in the office of Ms. Diana Ackroyd, Michigan Sales Director for Clairaine Hair and Beauty Products, Inc., 11372 Palmer Road, Detroit, MI 48220. Ms. Ackroyd is responsible for communicating with the owners of beauty schools in the area. She also supervises the company's sales representatives in three districts in the state.

The Michigan Cosmetology Association convention is planned for the last weekend of next month, and Ms. Ackroyd needs your help in notifying both her representatives and the beauty school owners. The following tasks are to be completed for her approval and signature as soon as possible.

Task

Keyboard and store this form letter, inserting stop codes for the variables indicated and any others you feel are necessary. If you do not have word processing equipment, prepare a mimeograph stencil instead. Correct any errors you find as you type.

Let us introduce you to an exiting new line of hair care products. Clairaine Soft and Silky can actually help your students ~~do~~ acheive professional looking ~~work~~ results — and bring your school's customers back again and again.

Our sales rep in your area is (full name + phone #). (1st name) would be glad to show you the ~~whole~~ full line of Soft and Silky Products, and provide you with brosures describing their use. Our rep will ~~come to~~ call at your school or, if you perfer meet with you at the Annual Convention of the Mich. Cosmetology Assn.

As I'm sure you aware this year's convention will be held next month in Alpena Mich. at the Waterford Inn. The Clairaine exibit is in room 2133 and free sample of the ~~new product~~ S+S line will be available. We invit you to stop by, talk with our reps, and try Clairaine's new S+S Hair Products. We feel sure you'll find them to your liking, as will ~~so~~ your students and your customers.

Sincerely,

Drill 10 continued

6 My letter to the Credit Department (outlining your proposal) apparently went astray. 18 18

7 Will you be kind enough to give us information (in confidence) about June's qualifications? 19 37

8 Here's to you—Marion and John! Congratulations on becoming the proud parents of a boy! 18 55

9 Endicott is out with a new paint called COLONIAL WHITE which sells for only $8 a gallon! 18 73

10 Will you please, at your earliest convenience, give me a Dun & Bradstreet report on them? 19 92

11 For the sanity of your accounting department (as well as ours), we shall invoice ten times a year. 20 20

12 The ATTUNED EAR, a magazine for music listeners, places the accent on quality instead of quantity. 20 41

13 Interest rates at Phoenix Savings & Loan dropped from 13.75% to 12.75% in less than a week. 19 60

14 The so-called "coffee break," a firmly established custom in millions of offices, takes many forms. 21 81

15 I've just been notified by our accounting department that your refund of $50 will be mailed tomorrow. 21 102

16 Our new copier, which has a 15-month warranty, gives us a range of copy sizes from 5½" x 8½" to 11" x 17". 22 22

17 Companies have rules about points of behavior that could properly be called etiquette (promptness, for example). 23 45

18 The price for the entire group of concerts will be $76 (plus the usual 10% entertainment tax), or a total of $83.60. 24 69

19 The enclosed Request Card entitles you to a free copy of Bulletin #72, HOME GARDENING AND CANNING FOR THE HOMEMAKER. 24 93

20 Will you send your letter of recommendation to Ms. Nancy Kelso at Adams & Bilsky, 22 Park Place, Austin, Texas 78710? 24 117

21 We must now call a halt to any further purchases until the balance shown on the enclosed statement ($3,460.00) is paid. 25 25

22 I realize that a simple "thank you" isn't very much, but I hope you'll understand that it comes from the bottom of my heart. 26 50

23 Should you pick up an extension telephone and discover you've interrupted a conversation, quickly say, "I'm sorry," and hang up. 26 77

24 If you'd like to receive the newsletter every month, just drop me a note, and I'll put your name on our regular mailing list—no charge, of course! 30 107

1 | 2 | 3 | 4 | 5 | 6 | 7 | 8 | 9 | 10 | 11 | 12 | 13 | 14 |

Task

Design an attractive format for the formal announcement of the PMCU's luncheon meeting. You may rearrange copy elements and delete words in order to make essential information stand out. If you are using word processing equipment, employ the automatic centering feature and at least one print enhancement (boldface, italic type, etc.). *Note:* Mr. Downing has indicated that a reproducible original must be delivered to the photocopy center by 2 p.m. if the announcement is to be duplicated in quantity by tomorrow.

The Pittsburgh Musician's Credit Union cordially invites you to attend its 48th Annual Meeting and Luncheon, Saturday, ____________, at the Reynolds house, 25300 West Ten Mile Road, Pittsburgh, Pennsylvania. Luncheon at 12 o'clock noon (tickets $6.50), Speaker and Meeting after luncheon

Please detach & return the bottom part of this form to purchase luncheon tickets.

Enclosed is $_______ for _______ ticket(s) (limit 2 per member) for the PMCU Anual Luncheon Meeting at the XXXXX Reynolds House.

Member Name ________________ Address ____________________________

City ___________________ State _______________ ZIP Code __________

Credit Union Account No _________________

Send no cash. Send checks or money orders only, payable to Pittsburgh Musicians' Credit Union.

Task

Compose a short memo for Ms. Byer, giving her the important details of the letter to Mr. Ferrette. She will need to know that Ferrette has agreed to speak at the luncheon meeting and that a confirming letter has been sent. Be especially sure to provide all information that Byer will need to make correct arrangements for Ferrette's trip, including choice of airline and type of ticket. *Note:* Byer's office is located in Room 132A of the same building.

Task

Assemble all of the materials you have prepared for presentation to Mr. Downing. Include all necessary envelopes and copies.

Drill 11

SHIFT LOCK

Type each line across. Use the shift lock for the state abbreviations. Release the lock immediately after each use without taking your eyes from the copy.

Left margin at 15; tab stops at 35 and 50. Double spacing.

1	Denver	CO	80201
2	Las Vegas	NV	89101
3	Miami	FL	33139
4	Mobile	AL	36601
5	Topeka	KS	66601
6	Memphis	TN	38101
7	Lincoln	NE	68501
8	Baltimore	MD	21215
9	Milwaukee	WI	53228
10	Boston	MA	02138
11	Salem	OR	97302
12	Pittsburgh	PA	17109
13	Mobile	AL	36608

MARGIN RELEASE

Learn to use the margin release smoothly, without hesitation.

Drill 12

RELEASING THE RIGHT MARGIN

As you type the paragraphs at the right, end each line exactly as it appears in the printed copy. Use the margin release when necessary.

Margins at 20 and 85 for elite; 10 and 75 for pica. Single spacing. 5-space paragraph indention.

1 We are sorry that we cannot guarantee early delivery. We have 13
none of these parts in stock. As soon as we get a complete supply 27
from the factory, we shall fill your order. 35

2 If we do not hear from you before October 10, we shall assume 13
that you are no longer interested in our plan and we shall feel free 27
to make a similar offer to some other agent. 36

3 An ice cap that averages five thousand feet in thickness now 13
covers the Antarctic region. Millions of years ago, however, this 26
region had a mild climate and a rich vegetation. 36

4 I found myself in a large room in which there were several 13
long tables. These were occupied by a number of men who were read- 26
ing and taking notes. The room was quiet, except for a rustle now 39
and then as a reader turned a page. 46

5 Our function is to manufacture and to sell electric equipment 13
of all kinds. If we are to be equal to that task, we must be ready 27
to meet every demand that will be made on us as a result of new 39
inventions and improved facilities. 46

6 Division of labor in modern methods of production has come to 13
be an accepted practice. One worker may be employed all day, year 26
after year, in sewing buttons on coats; other workers may make one 40
small part of a machine day in and day out. 48

1 | 2 | 3 | 4 | 5 | 6 | 7 | 8 | 9 | 10 | 11 | 12 | 13 |

Mr. Ralph Lewiston, a personal friend of Mr. Downing, calls and asks to speak to him. When you explain that Mr. Downing is away from the office for the day, Mr. Lewiston asks for five tickets to the annual luncheon meeting. This creates a dilemma for you. You do not want to disappoint Mr. Downing's friend, but you have specific instructions to limit ticket sales to two per member. You tactfully explain the situation to Mr. Lewiston. He then asks that you take a message for Mr. Downing. Mr. Lewiston wishes Mr. Downing to call him at his office at 327-3459, Extension 114, before 3:30 p.m. tomorrow.

Task

The letter below is to be sent to Mr. Irwin Ferrette, the scheduled speaker for the luncheon meeting. His address is shown at the right. The letter was prepared hurriedly by Mr. Downing, who trusts your ability to find and correct errors in spelling, punctuation, and grammar. *Note:* Standard letter format is block style with open punctuation.

Executive Hotel
237 Park Avenue
New York, NY 10039

Dear Irwin

This letter will confirm our telephone conversation of yesterday in which you graciously accepted ~~our~~ my invitation to speak at our cr. unions' annual luncheon meeting. As you know ~~it's~~ the meeting being held on ~~Sat.~~ ———. ¶ Jane Byer, our Public Relations Director is helping with ~~the~~ your travel arrangments and accomodations. As you requested, we will book you on a non-stop ~~diner~~ flight that will allow you to depart New York after 5:30 P.M. on the Friday evening before the luncheon. (Your ~~plane~~ airline tickets will be mailed to your home address. Ms. Byers will meet your plane here and ~~take~~ drive you to your hotel. You'll most likely be staying at the Squire's Inn ~~since it's~~ which is very close to the luncheon cite. We are of course taking care of all your expenses.

On the morning of the luncheon, I will pick you up at your hotel ~~to~~ and drive you to the restarant where the meeting is being held. I am really looking foreward to seeing you again, and to renewing our debate one the greatest Wagnerian sopranos. Yours Sincerly

Drill 13

RELEASING THE LEFT MARGIN

To begin each paragraph, depress the margin release and backspace 5 spaces into the left margin. Make your line endings the same as those in the printed copy.

60-space line. Single spacing.

1 There were dozens of little boys in the main street of the town. When
a tourist came near them, they would run up with palms outstretched,
crying for a coin.

2 The employees in this department deserve a special tribute for the very
fine way in which they have all worked. Through their unfailing
efforts, they have maintained the desired production.

3 As you will see in our report, we have enough contracts to keep our plant
in full operation for several months. Our facilities may be fully
employed throughout the year.

4 In relation to body size, the eyes of small animals are much larger as a
rule than are the eyes of human beings. On the other hand, with
large animals the opposite is true.

5 The ship was seaworthy, but she was slow under sail. As it was important
to reach our destination, it was necessary to use the engines more
than expected.

6 It has been said that young people lack a sense of purpose. I believe
that they very definitely have purposes, but those purposes are not
apt to be the same as those of adults.

Topic 2 SPEED PRACTICE

Select practice lines from the drills in this topic as directed by your teacher. Follow the technique hints given with each drill. As your technique improves, so will your speed.

WORDS

Read, think, and type short, easy words as whole units instead of letter by letter.

Directions:

Type each line twice. 60-space line. Single spacing. DS after each pair of lines.

1 it we or my is us by so of up as be in go if at on to an do 12
2 he in be no go on if at to an do ox or we it is us by so of 24
3 she too ask buy run ago two can end its may get one got eye 35

4 old lot and due how but not now use boy hay her way try for 12
5 out let pay cot day sir own and has new big the any who off 24
6 some here work paid mail such able duty well they your send 35

1 | 2 | 3 | 4 | 5 | 6 | 7 | 8 | 9 | 10 | 11 | 12 |

(Continued on next page)

SERIES

WORD PROCESSING SIMULATIONS

The simulations in this series are intended for use in advanced typing classes. They differ from earlier simulations in three respects.

First, they are more complex. The various projects are longer, and all the work is presented in rough-draft form. Much of the material contains errors that must be corrected, and all of it must be formatted.

Second, the projects in this series are less structured. Directions are kept to a minimum, and tasks are not numbered. This means you will have to read ahead, think carefully, and prioritize—arrange the work for yourself in order of importance.

The third difference is the most significant: all the simulations in this series are designed around word processing equipment and its software. The projects use such word processing capabilities as storage and retrieval, text editing, automatic centering, special print enhancements (like boldface and italics), and semiautomatic document assembly. (*Note:* For those who do not have access to word processing equipment, it is still possible to do all of the activities in the series by using standard typewriters and alternate procedures.)

Project C-1

SKILLS COVERAGE

1. *Typing business letters*
2. *Applying English language skills*
3. *Formatting announcements*
4. *Preparing envelopes*
5. *Taking telephone messages*
6. *Composing memos*

You are working in the offices of Mr. J. D. Downing, Board Chairman of the Pittsburgh Musicians' Credit Union (PMCU), 7480 Duquesne Avenue, Pittsburgh, PA 15218. One of your employer's responsibilities is to plan and coordinate the credit union's annual luncheon meeting. This year, the meeting will be held six weeks from this coming Saturday. Mr. Downing is out of the office for the day, but he has left several tasks for you to complete by tomorrow.

Task

From the information at the top of page 407, create and type the script of a telephone conversation as you imagine it might develop. Use proper telephone answering techniques and manners. Then type a telephone message for Mr. Downing, giving him a report of the conversation. Use plain paper if no message form is available.

Words continued

7 list this just glad more bill very much note like last with 12
8 make what must city will know them name next have good sent 24
9 half soon time made envy line part hand fork wish same been 35

10 right chain until going wrote other cover write sorry early 12
11 would first above taken books check favor these delay claim 24
12 about could again mouth small thank stock three money short 35

1 | 2 | 3 | 4 | 5 | 6 | 7 | 8 | 9 | 10 | 11 | 12 |

PHRASES

Curve your fingers directly over the keys. Use a snappy stroke—strike and release the key in one motion.

Directions:
Type each line twice. 60-space line. Single spacing. DS after each pair of lines.

1 it is, to go, to do, by us, to it, of us, to us, is it, he is 12
2 to do, he is, by it, to go, or if, is to, if it, if he, is he 24
3 to do this, of the, to do that, by the, to do the, to do work 37
4 if the, with them, to do such, and the, with both, with which 49

5 for them, and then, of them, and this, for the, and that was 12
6 and did, and them, and for, by them, and work, they wish for 24
7 they wish, and they, and wish, to them, and shows, got there 36
8 and do, of the, and name, that man, and both, for their good 48

9 with the, to make, with them, when it, with both, and is the 12
10 for them, and their, with me, and they, with that, they make 24
11 did make, for the, did work, for they, and so, for which the 36
12 and if, the big, and if they, go to the, they make, to their 48

13 if they take, as it is, of our, she owns, if they show those 12
14 all of them, one of these, one of our men, as soon as we can 24
15 a few of those, as soon as, we are not, now and then, for he 36
16 as soon as you are, we have been, here and there, as much as 48

17 please send us, by the way, in the past, from them, we asked 12
18 from that time, in this letter, you sent us, he must be here 24
19 you will agree that, to take part, not later than, she feels 36
20 I feel sure, if you agree with us, for a long time, to do so 48

21 as she said, it was done, when it is ready, in the beginning 12
22 around the world, during the week, so to speak, to the right 24
23 if possible, and we quote, last name first, give and receive 36
24 jumps the gun, return a call, join the group, every so often 48

1 | 2 | 3 | 4 | 5 | 6 | 7 | 8 | 9 | 10 | 11 | 12 |

introduce some of our new products, and this, I hope, will lead to increased interest in our company's exhibit.

I am enclosing a copy of my proposed itinerary for your information and reference.

Exercise 2

Type the itinerary for Mr. Suroyal's trip to New York as outlined below. Remember to make an extra copy for enclosure with the memo to Mr. Dryer.

Itinerary
L. M. Suroyal
April 1–4, 19—

<u>WEDNESDAY, April 1</u>	
7 p.m. EST	Leave Cleveland, American Airlines Flight 274, Hopkins Airport.
8:40 p.m. EST	Arrive New York, LaGuardia Airport. Confirmed accommodations at Gotham City Hotel; 280 East 48th Street; Telephone: (212) 988-1072.
<u>THURSDAY, April 2</u>	
9 a.m.	Formal opening of NABE Convention, Dewey Auditorium, Gotham City Hotel.
12 noon	Presentation at luncheon, Empire Room.
3 p.m.	At company's exhibit. Make final arrangements for our hospitality hour.
6 p.m.	Hospitality Hour, Suite 3478.
<u>FRIDAY, April 3</u>	
12 noon	Luncheon meeting with our exhibit staff.
7 p.m.	Formal banquet of convention.
<u>SATURDAY, April 4</u>	
12 noon	Closing luncheon of convention.
3:30 p.m. EST	Leave New York, LaGuardia Airport, American Airlines Flight 208.
4:50 p.m. EST	Arrive Cleveland, Hopkins Airport.
<u>MONDAY, April 6</u>	In office.

SENTENCES

Maintain a good posture. Sit erect, with feet on the floor and body bent slightly forward. Keep the upper arms and the elbows near the body. Let the forearms and wrists slant upward to the machine. Do not hump or arch the wrists; on the other hand, do not let them touch the machine.

Directions:
Take a series of 30-second timed writings on lines 1–20. Explore a new level of typing by reaching for two words more than your regular 1-minute rate. (To figure wpm on a 30-second writing, double the total words you typed.)

60-space line. Double spacing.

1 Both of them may rush to the ancient city for the festivals. 12
2 Elaine wants to move from the crowded town into the country. 24
3 When my best friend Robert asked for help, I gave it to him. 36
4 Those who are masters of themselves are the leaders in life. 48

5 Those who have climbed to the top often began at the bottom. 12
6 People never know the worth of water till the well runs dry. 24
7 The name of the firm they own is to the right of the window. 36
8 Many schools now offer a placement service to some students. 48

9 The judge made sure the lady got just what she ought to get. 12
10 People take more vacations in the summer than in the winter. 24
11 He did the work of five men today, and this is not his duty. 36
12 At the end of the year the firms gave each employee a bonus. 48

13 I had the form with me when I took down the name of the man. 12
14 We wish you would please send us a copy of your fall prices. 24
15 This is the first time we have been able to make our quotas. 36
16 I was happy to find your name was listed in the top quarter. 48

17 There will be many price changes before the end of the year. 12
18 We promise to press just the tip of each finger when typing. 24
19 Eyes on the road at all times; do not drive at a high speed. 36
20 We received notice that a second meeting would be held soon. 48

1 | 2 | 3 | 4 | 5 | 6 | 7 | 8 | 9 | 10 | 11 | 12 |

ONE-MINUTE SPEED DRIVES

Keep eyes on copy, not only while you type, but also when you return.

Directions:
Use these sentences for 1- or 2-minute timed writings. For additional selections, use the Supplementary Practice section at the end of this book.

60-space line. Double spacing. 5-space paragraph indention.

1 The history of humanity, both in the far past and in the 12
recent past, is largely a history of war. SI 1.40 20

2 The extremely mild weather that we have enjoyed this 11
spring has had a favorable effect on our business. SI 1.50 21

3 Our new pen writes as smoothly and naturally as a pencil. 12
The more you use it, the better you will like it. SI 1.27 22

1 | 2 | 3 | 4 | 5 | 6 | 7 | 8 | 9 | 10 | 11 | 12 |

(Continued on next page)

6 Mr. Conrad D. Boyd, Goodwill Hardware, 942 New Street, St. Paul, MN 55116
7 Mr. Louis F. Swarthmore, 709 West Tenth Street, St. Paul, MN 55107
8 Miss Barbara Krantz, 721 McKibbin Street, St. Paul, MN 55115
9 Mr. Leonard D. Nielson, 494 Wellman, St. Paul, MN 55103
10 Dr. Eugene M. Ryan, School of Medicine, Stillwell University, St. Paul, MN 55118
11 Mr. Robert A. Ostmann, Jr., 195 S. Chatsworth, St. Paul, MN 55103
12 Dr. Valerie J. Clappison, 2852 Colby Avenue, St. Paul, MN 55101

Exercise 5

Prepare 12 self-addressed No. 6 envelopes to be used as enclosures with the letters typed in Exercise 3. The envelopes should be addressed to the Children's Club.

Project B-7

This project covers:
1. Interoffice memo
2. Itinerary

Review the general directions on page 394 before you begin.

Exercise 1

The typewritten draft of the memo below contains three spelling errors and two punctuation errors. Find and correct the errors as you type the memo.

SUBJECT: Itinerary for Proposed Trip DATE: March 19, 19--

TO: C. V. Dryer, District Director

FROM: L. M. Suroyal, Manager, Educational Marketing Division

As we discussed prevously, I have been invited to be the luncheon speaker on April 2 at the annual convention of the National Association of Business Educators in New York City. I think that you will agree that my presence at this convention will give me an exellent opportunity to make friends for our company.

My topic "Building Office Skills" should be of great interest to those who attend. During my talk, I will have an opportunity to

(Continued on next page)

One-Minute Speed Drives continued

4 One of our objectives should be to offer employment to 12
all people who wish to work and who are able to do so. SI 1.30 23

5 One day during the summer, we noticed that the trim lawn 12
was no longer trim and that weeds were appearing in the path. 24
SI 1.26

6 People have learned to fly. Parting company with their 12
friend, the horse, they've sailed high into the sky with the 24
eagle. SI 1.27 25

7 As he walked along, he noticed, at the side of the road, 12
a few stones that marked the foundation of what had once been 24
a house. SI 1.15 26

8 We are taking the matter up with the clerk who waited on 12
you and wish to assure you that you will have no further cause 25
for complaint. SI 1.22 27

1 | 2 | 3 | 4 | 5 | 6 | 7 | 8 | 9 | 10 | 11 | 12 |

Beginning with 9, your typed lines will not end at the same point as those shown in the text. If you are using a standard typewriter, listen for the end-of-line cue warning you that you are approaching the right margin. If you are using an electronic typewriter, microcomputer, or word processor, the machine's wordwrap will turn lines for you.

9 In the spring the garden was a beautiful picture. The tulips were 14
a mass of bright colors, red and yellow. The lawn became a soft green. 28
SI 1.31

10 Within the next few weeks, we plan to place on the market a new 13
type of motor, which will undoubtedly find a ready sale both at home 26
and abroad. SI 1.28 28

11 We regret to have to inform you that work on your order is being 14
delayed because Bob cannot obtain delivery of the materials that we 27
need for it. SI 1.50 29

12 A business of our standing is under an obligation to do every- 13
thing in its power to preserve its proper share of the export trade in 27
the next two years. SI 1.40 31

13 It has become the custom in recent years at our open meetings 13
to make a few remarks in regard to general business conditions, as 26
well as those in our own field. SI 1.39 32

14 The spoken word is more powerful than the written word. Today, 14
because we have the radio and can make recordings, the spoken word 27
is limited by neither time nor space. SI 1.42 34

1 | 2 | 3 | 4 | 5 | 6 | 7 | 8 | 9 | 10 | 11 | 12 | 13 |

(Continued on next page)

Exercise 2

This letter was dictated by Gerald T. Horner, Chairman of the Fund-Raising Committee for the St. Paul Children's Club. Supply the salutation and complimentary closing. Determine paragraphing.

October 2, 19– / Mr. Harvey N. Nugent / Nugent Paints / 815 Forge Street / St. Paul, MN 55112 / I wish to thank you on behalf of the Children's Club for the advertisement you placed in the program of our Annual Sports Show. This year, through the support of all our area advertisers, we will again be able to provide many unfortunate young people of St. Paul with assistance ranging from food and clothing to college scholarships. We hope that you will be able to attend a performance of the sports show. We shall be happy to send you a complimentary ticket if you will let us know which performance you would like to attend. If you wish additional tickets, please use the enclosed order form. We will see that your order is filled promptly.

Exercise 3

Type this form letter, which was prepared by Edith W. Wise, Director of the Children's Club. Determine paragraphing. Duplicate 12 copies of the letter for use in Exercise 4.

October 3, 19– / Dear Friend / At this time every year, the Children's Club of St. Paul begins to make plans for its Annual Sports Show. The main objective of the club is to improve the lives of the needy children in this city by providing them with milk and other foods, clothing, and medical and dental care. We sponsor several youth clubs, too, and every summer, we send hundreds of children to a camp where they stay for a week. In recent years, we have also been able to offer scholarships to several institutions of learning. The Annual Sports Show provides the major part of the funds for these activities, and we hope you will help us by attending. We are sure that this year's show has something for everyone to enjoy. We are enclosing a scale of ticket prices with an attached order form. Please fill in the form and mail it to us with your check in the self-addressed envelope. / Cordially

---

Exercise 4

Type address labels from the mailing list below for envelopes in which to mail the form letters prepared in Exercise 3.

1 Ms. Catherine Ives, 66 Newton Avenue, St. Paul, MN 55107

2 Mrs. Rona Willis, 254 Central Avenue, St. Paul, MN 55110

3 Mr. Samuel F. Jeffries, 52 Kingsbridge Street, St. Paul, MN 55103

4 Mrs. Flora Cuneo, Sunrise House, 175 Henry Street, St. Paul, MN 51123

5 Dr. Howard Fishbein, 505 Buckminster Building, 291 Stapleton Plaza, St. Paul, MN 55101

(Continued on next page)

One-Minute Speed Drives continued

15 I have placed a lot of stress on the important problems facing us 14
because I believe that our course of action must be decided in rela- 28
tion to the facts that I have presented. SI 1.40 37

16 To those of us who spend their lives in the light of open spaces, 14
it may be strange to think that there are men who spend a large part 28
of their lives moving about under the ground. SI 1.14 37

17 I am sending you two lists of books that I recommend. The 13
lists have several divisions, each containing a group of books of 26
one type (for example, books of adventure, books on sports). SI 1.36 37

18 Nothing here seems to change. The river still runs over its bed 14
of stones, just as it has been doing for many years. The house is the 28
same as ever. Even the people do not seem to change. SI 1.21 39

19 The average price of most stocks has fallen considerably during 14
the past several months, but the experts say prices will rise again in 28
a week or two. As a matter of fact, some are up already. SI 1.39 39

20 Reading is one of the cheapest and yet one of the most profitable 14
of pleasures. It may even be enjoyed without cost in a public library. 28
Reading offers a storehouse of pleasure which need never end. SI 1.45 40

21 Many boys and girls of high school age spend a great deal of time 14
thinking about which college they should enter. It seems to me that 28
the first question they should decide is whether to go to college at all. 43
SI 1.23

22 All of us have met people who will conceitedly explain to anyone 14
who will listen how to manage the finances of this country, and then 28
they will try to borrow a dollar or two to keep them until the next 41
payday. SI 1.39 42

23 A Frenchman once said that, although the people of other nations 14
could not be expected to agree that France is the greatest nation in 28
Europe, it was enough that they all allowed the French nation to claim 42
second place. SI 1.39 44

24 Once Daisy, our dog, finds a trail, she will follow it no matter 14
how many other paths cross it—unless it enters a body of water. Since 28
water carries no scent, she has to try to pick up the trail again on the 42
other side. SI 1.29 44

1 | 2 | 3 | 4 | 5 | 6 | 7 | 8 | 9 | 10 | 11 | 12 | 13 |

Project B-6

This project includes the preparation of:
1. *Order form with duplicated copies*
2. *Business letter*
3. *Form letter with duplicated copies*
4. *Address labels*
5. *Self-addressed envelopes*

Review the general directions on page 394 before you begin.

Exercise 1

Prepare a ticket order form from the information given below. Then duplicate 13 copies to use as enclosures in Exercises 2 and 3.

CHILDREN'S CLUB
318 Central Avenue
St. Paul, MN 55106

Scale of Prices—Annual Sports Show

Evenings: November 15, 16, and 17, 19—
Matinees: November 15 and 16, 19—

	Matinee	*Evening*
Orchestra, rows 1 to 15	$7.00	$8.00
Orchestra, rows 16 to 30	5.50	6.50
Mezzanine	4.50	5.50
Balcony, rows 1 to 3	3.00	4.00
Balcony, rows 4 to 10	2.50	3.50

--------- *Detach here and return order form below with your check.* ---------

TO: Children's Club
318 Central Avenue
St. Paul, MN 55106

DATE: ____________________

Please send me tickets for your Annual Sports Show as indicated below:

a) ________ tickets @ $ ________ for the matinee performance on November ____

b) ________ tickets @ $ ________ for the evening performance on November ____

If tickets are not available for the date or performance requested, my second choice is: ______________________________

Name ______________________________

Street ______________________________

City, State ______________________________ ZIP __________

Telephone ______________________________

THREE-MINUTE SPEED DRIVES

There are times in your practice work when you should try to break through your speed level. You should do this when you have gained control and can't seem to type at a higher rate of speed. When this happens, forget errors temporarily and concentrate on typing at a new high rate. Each time you hit a new high in your speed, the slower rates will become more natural and your control will return.

Directions:

Use the paragraphs at the right for 3-minute writings. For additional selections, refer to the Supplementary Practice section at the end of this book.

60-space line. Double spacing. 5-space paragraph indention.

1 The paper used for printing paper money of the United 12
States is supplied by a firm that has a secret process for 23
producing a kind of paper that nobody can counterfeit. Only 36
the owner of the mill knows the secret of the process. He 48
received it from his father; he will pass it on to his child. 59
SI 1.39

2 The electric typewriter has made things so much easier 12
that it is hard to understand why the busy typist wishes to 24
use a manual. The finished work always is so much neater. 35
Many more clear copies may be made by just regulating a 47
control for the number of copies that you want. The copies 59
produced will all be clear. SI 1.43 64

3 The state plans to take over part of your land in order 12
to widen the state road which runs past it. The enclosed map 24
shows the part which the state intends to acquire. We shall 36
send a representative from our department shortly to confer 48
with you. She will arrange by next week to adjust your claim 60
for an amount satisfactory to you and to the state. SI 1.32 70

4 I have your letter and the map on which you have marked 12
the part of my property which the state plans to acquire in 24
order to widen the present state road. I shall make a careful 36
study of the map so that I may be in a position to talk the 48
matter over with your representative when she comes. Please 60
ask her to telephone and let me know when she will call at my 72
home. SI 1.25 73

5 Two weeks ago I sent you an order, with check enclosed, 12
for a dozen linen guest towels, listed in your catalog at ten 24
dollars a dozen. I said that I prefer the towels in tan with 36
red border; but that if you do not have these, I would accept 48
them in orange. Since then I have not heard from you. Will 60
you please send the towels promptly or write or call me and 72
explain the delay. SI 1.22 76

1 | 2 | 3 | 4 | 5 | 6 | 7 | 8 | 9 | 10 | 11 | 12 |

(Continued on next page)

Exercise 2

This letter is a reply to Mr. Kahn's letter in Exercise 1. It is written by Rupert C. Pennington, District Sales Manager. Supply the salutation and complimentary closing for this letter. Date the letter August 14, 19–, and send it to the attention of Mr. Kahn at the address shown at the right. Send a copy to Ms. C. L. Trenton, Sales Representative, Suite 326, Danville Bank Building, Danville, VA 24541.

Danville Area Vocational Center
2935 Grover Road
Danville, VA 24541

I am ~~We are~~ sending you under separate cover, our illustrated catalog, which gives descriptions and prices for *all* our folding auditorium chairs.

~~I believe that you will find~~ model No. 28372, *shown on* page 65, ~~especially~~ *appears to be especially* suitable for your purposes. The cahirs are luxuriously padded, with armrests between them. They are easily folded and unfolded in a single movement to allow for *quick and compact* storage. Since they have no nuts, bolts, or scres*w*s, ~~unnecessary~~ *costly* manpower is not ~~wasted in moving the chairs~~ *required to assemble and disassemble them.* Generally we require a shipping time offifteen days after receipt of an order.

A copy of this letter is being forwarded to our sales representative in your area, ~~Ms. C. L.~~ *Constance* Trenton, so that she can follow through on your inquiry. Her office is located in the Danville Bank Bldg. in your city. You ~~will~~ *can expect to* hear from her this week to arrange ~~for~~ a convenient time to meet ~~with you~~ to discuss your order.

Thank you for giving us the op*p*ortunity to serve you.

Exercise 3

Compose a letter from Constance L. Trenton to Albert T. Kahn. Date it September 1, 19–, and include the following information, using your own words:

a. **Thank Mr. Kahn for placing an order for 600 folding auditorium chairs. (He placed the order after you suggested that he visit the office to see showroom samples.)**
b. **Tell him that his order has been put on rush and that the shipment should arrive within ten days.**
c. **Thank him for his business and ask him to call Ms. Trenton if he does not receive a confirmation copy of the shipping order in the next day or two.**

Three-Minute Speed Drives continued

6 This morning we received a telegram from our factory, 12
telling us that there will be a slight delay in shipping the 24
two clocks that you ordered. We regret this delay very much, 36
but it is due to conditions beyond our control. We hope that it 48
will not cause you any trouble. We have instructed the fac- 60
tory to send the shipment to you as soon as possible. It will 72
be shipped by express at our expense. SI 1.37 79

7 It is easier to find fault with the world as it is than 12
to set the world straight. There is no doubt that many of our 24
complaints are well founded; but our duty lies not so much in 36
finding fault with the world as in trying to make the world 48
what it ought to be. If we gave our best strength all day 60
long to setting the world straight, we should not be so likely 72
to sit up far into the night complaining of what is wrong with 84
it. SI 1.15 85

8 Throughout our lives we are spending time. We can go 12
through a day now and then without breaking into our store of 24
money, but we cannot live at all without using some of our 36
store of time. Minute by minute we are spending our time, 48
and the way in which the minutes are spent makes up our way 60
of living. If we let the days slip idly by, we are likely to 72
lead incomplete lives. If we spend our time wisely, we shall 84
lead happy and productive lives. SI 1.25 90

9 Typists who wish to build up their speed should use copy 12
that is easy to type and simple to read. Also, the copy should 25
contain words that they can type at a high rate. 35

Many words should be typed as though they were just one 47
unit, for this is what typists must do when they want to raise 59
their rates to a new high. Some words may be hard to type 71
even though they are short. These words the typist should try 83
to stroke at a pace slow enough to typewrite them without mis- 95
takes. SI 1.14 96

10 We went into the village grocery. It was not a large 12
place—in fact, it was only twelve feet square—but it was 24
filled with a variety of good things. There were hams and sides 36

1 | 2 | 3 | 4 | 5 | 6 | 7 | 8 | 9 | 10 | 11 | 12 |

(Continued on next page)

Exercise 4

This letter was dictated by Lila Stallworth, Supervisor of the Customer Service Department. Determine paragraphing. Note the itemized list.

Mrs. Alice Gardiner / 1482 Bay Road / Milwaukee, WI 53217 / Dear Mrs. Gardiner / Thank you for trusting your fur coat to us for summer storage. We are certain you will be satisfied with our service. At your request, our fur experts have completed an examination of your coat, and they have found it in need of the following repairs: 1. The buttons and the fur around them are worn and should be replaced. 2. The edge of the right cuff is frayed and a new piece of fur should be substituted. 3. The fur lacks luster and would be greatly improved by our Hollanderizing treatment. This gives new life to furs that have received years of wear. It removes grime from beneath the surface and restores natural oils. If you wish the repairs to be made, we shall be happy to give you a quotation. We urge you to have the work done, as it will prolong the life of your beautiful coat. / Sincerely

Project B-5

This project covers the preparation of:
1. *Business letter*
2. *Letter with special notation*
3. *Letter composed from notes*

Review the general directions on page 394 before you begin.

Exercise 1

This letter was written by Albert T. Kahn, Purchasing Agent for Danville Area Vocational Center. Supply the salutation and complimentary closing. Date the letter August 9, 19—, and send it to the address shown at the right.

Institutional Furniture Suppliers
62 Myrtle Street
Richmond, VA 23222

We are in need of approximately six hundred auditorium chairs ~~seats~~ for a dining-forum area in our ~~a~~ new building. We are looking for portable ~~interested in purchasing~~ chairs ~~which are portable~~ since the area will be used for different ~~multi~~purposes. ¶ The chairs should be of a type that can be easily assembled and disassembled and they should fold quickly for storage. We would prefer a model that has ~~chairs with an~~ interlocking padded armrests between every two chairs ~~seats~~. ¶ What have you to offer that meets these ~~our~~ requirements? Please quote us prices and give us an ~~some~~ idea of the time ~~usually~~ required for delivery after an order has been ~~is~~ placed and approved.

Three-Minute Speed Drives continued

of bacon hanging from the ceiling. The floor was crowded with 48
barrels of sugar and flour. The shelves were piled high with 60
tins of coffee and canned foods, with cheese and crackers, 72
loaves of bread, and bags of dried fruits. It was a wonder 84
that so many things could fit into so small a shop, but there 96
they were. SI 1.20 97

11 Typists today find their work much more simple than did 12
those in the past. They can now do rapidly what they would 24
have found at one time to be a long and tiresome job. 35
There were many long years of hard and persistent work 47
on the part of those who wanted to make the job of a typist 59
easier and more pleasant. At that time they realized 70
that typists would one day make up a vital part of the 81
nation and they wanted just the right machine for the job. 93
The copier is one such machine that makes the typist's work 105
easier. SI 1.26 106

1 | 2 | 3 | 4 | 5 | 6 | 7 | 8 | 9 | 10 | 11 | 12 |

Topic 3 ACCURACY PRACTICE

When you wish to type with a high degree of accuracy, the best thing to do is slow down a little. This deliberate reduction in speed reduces tension and permits you to type with confidence and control.

Another way to improve accuracy is to analyze your errors and do corrective practice. You will find corrective drills for substitution errors on pages 74–78 of this topic. In the Supplementary Practice section in the back of this book, there are also remedial drills for every letter of the alphabet and every punctuation mark.

ALPHABETIC SENTENCES

Each of the following sentences contains every letter of the alphabet. Type the sentences more slowly than your normal rate and concentrate on each reach.

Directions:
65-space line. Double spacing.

1 Tomorrow we shall have our junior clerk type a list of expenses, 13
including prizes given at the banquet. 22
2 I am certain that with the addition of just five extra squares each 35
your bigger puzzles would work. 42
3 After briefly questioning the embezzler who stole the funds, the 55
banker rejected his vague explanation. 64

1 | 2 | 3 | 4 | 5 | 6 | 7 | 8 | 9 | 10 | 11 | 12 | 13 |

(Continued on next page)

may telephone for this service. Promptly on receipt of your order, we shall send you a confirmation card that shows the signature of the bonded driver who will call for your furs and the date on which you should expect him. Make certain that the driver signs the call slip and that you compare the signature with the one on the confirmation card. This precaution is taken to protect you against fraud or theft in transferring your furs. / Very truly yours

---

Exercise 2

Prepare a self-addressed postal card for enclosure with the letter in Exercise 1. Use the address shown at the right. Type the information given below on the message side. Leave enough space for the customer to fill in the required information.

Milwaukee Fur Company
Attention Fur Storage Department
809 Grange Street
Milwaukee, WI 53206

______________________, 19__

Gentlemen

Please have your bonded driver call for my ______________________ within one week following receipt of this card. These furs are valued at $ ________________.

____
Name

____
Telephone

____
Street Address Apt. No. City, State, ZIP

Exercise 3

From the information below, prepare a list of fur storage rates for enclosure with Exercise 1. Give the table a title and use the current year. Type leaders between columns for ease in reading.

FUR COATS

Valuation	Rate
Up to $750	$ 15.00
$751 to $1,500	44.50
$1,501 to $3,500	51.00
$3,501 to $5,000	57.50
$5,001 to $6,500	67.00
$6,501 to $9,000	78.00
$9,001 to $12,000	85.00
$12,001 to $15,000	107.00
$15,001 to $20,000	137.00

STOLES

Valuation	Rate
Up to $1,000	$30.00

FUR-TRIMMED COATS

Valuation	Rate
Up to $300	$12.00

Alphabetic Sentences continued

4 Without a doubt, many thousands have joined our organization 12
because of our quick exposure of the plot. 21
5 We recognize the justice of your claim for adequate damages, but 34
you are making charges that appear excessive. 43
6 An industrious worker of average ability frequently accomplishes 56
more at his job than one who is expert but lazy. 66

7 We require five dozen blue glass cups to replace the mixed 12
lot, damaged in packing, which we rejected last Friday. 23
8 We expect to keep the major portion of our heavy equipment in large- 35
sized storage vaults because of lack of floor space. 47
9 My cousin enjoys an inexpensive hobby; he likes building small- 60
sized models of railway equipment, made chiefly of matches. 72

10 A vast crowd at the banquet eagerly awaited the announcement of 13
the lucky exhibitor to whom the jury had awarded the prize. 25
11 The accountant required very little time to examine the journal and 38
find the errors which had so long puzzled the bookkeeper. 50
12 The superintendent of the factory developed a unique plan, with the 63
object of systematizing the work and eliminating excessive motion. 76

13 I recognized the handwriting of the Mexican in the journal that he 13
kept, which I had recently acquired with several other books. 25
14 Mr. Zimmer has been offering excellent values in mink coats, but 38
upon inquiry we find that the sale will be over in just a week. 51
15 The citizens joined in advocating a tax cut of a quarter of a million 65
dollars, but they did not know any feasible way of reducing expenses. 79

16 Another reason for advising you to patronize our store is that we 13
quickly exchange unsatisfactory goods and make liberal adjustments. 26
17 Some of the natives were paralyzed with fear; others, less excited, 39
ran back to join the king and queen and warn them of the danger. 53
18 The governor familiarized himself with every part of the text in the 67
appeal so as to be prepared to make an equitable adjustment in the 80
case. 81

19 At the bazaar, the children will present a musical skit or review in 13
which a five-year-old boy will play a banjo and a mixed quartet will 27
sing. 28

1| 2| 3| 4| 5| 6| 7| 8| 9| 10| 11| 12| 13|

(Continued on next page)

Exercise 3

Prepare a boxed table from the copy below. Figure the vertical and horizontal totals first. In the secondary title, use the date for Monday in the current week.

WEEKLY SALES ANALYSIS

(Week of ———)

	Hardware	Housewares	Linens	Total
Monday	$ 38.95	$ 56.80	$ 16.50	$ XXX
Tuesday	32.60	29.40	68.45	XXX
Wednesday	94.20	38.65	59.55	XXX
Thursday	73.85	43.82	48.16	XXX
Friday	25.15	18.25	89.00	XXX
Saturday	110.50	56.75	98.95	XXX
Totals	$ XXX	$ XXX	$ XXX	$ XXX

Project B-4

This project covers the preparation of:
1. *Business letter*
2. *Self-addressed postal card*
3. *Table with leaders*
4. *Business letter with numbered insert*

Review the general directions on page 394 before you begin.

Exercise 1

This letter was dictated by Randall McKinney, Manager of the Milwaukee Fur Company's Fur Storage Department. Determine paragraphing.

March 19, 19— / Mrs. Alice Gardiner / 1482 Bay Road / Milwaukee, WI 53217 / Dear Mrs. Gardiner / If you value your furs, you will want to give them the protection they need. All furs should be put into storage for the summer, to avoid the drying effects of the warm air and the danger of damage by moths. Our storage service includes not only housing in vaults that are cold, dry, and completely free from moths, but also insurance against fire and theft, and a treatment that removes surface dust. We are enclosing a table showing our rates. We invite you to fill in and mail the enclosed form, postage free. If you prefer, you

(Continued on next page)

Alphabetic Sentences continued

20 The crew disembarked from their ship in a heavy drizzle, after an 41
exciting journey that had taken them halfway around the world along 54
the equator. 57

21 Although the dealer had only a hazy idea of the current quotations 70
in woven textiles, he rejected the price they offered for the valuable 84
damask. 85

22 The woman was puzzled by the directions for operating the vacuum 13
cleaner and asked the salesman to explain briefly the adjustment 26
of the equipment. 29

23 The envelope contained a note politely asking for the loan of a razor 43
and a pair of pajamas, but not a word of explanation for this unusual 57
request. 59

24 By making an adequate gift to this organization, you may share the 72
joy of sending to camp next summer youngsters who very badly need 85
fresh air and sunshine. 90

25 The thousands who patronize our store unquestionably approve of 13
our good judgment in the choice of stock, our exceptionally courteous 27
service, and our reasonable prices. 34

26 As a consequence of the talk which exposed the fraud, a large group 47
of citizens demanded an investigation to establish responsibility and 61
bring the criminals to justice. 67

27 The members of the searching party returned quite exhausted but 80
happy, for in the maze of trees and bushes in the dark jungle they had 94
found the lost child, weary but alive and well. 103

1 | 2 | 3 | 4 | 5 | 6 | 7 | 8 | 9 | 10 | 11 | 12 | 13 |

PAIRED LETTER DRILLS

If you are making many errors, you may want to analyze them to see how many are of a substitution type (that is, substituting *m* for *n*, *i* for e, and so on). If you have this difficulty, the drills that follow will be helpful. Select and type those that are applicable.

Directions:

Type each line twice. 60-space line. Single spacing. DS after each pair of lines.

1 **a/s** assassin standards statements situation separate absenteeism
2 specials assaults assure assign shares arrest adjust surpass
3 We hope the bank will send our statement to our new address.
4 Speakers of all ages will be assigned to answer the charges.

5 **b/n** urban sensible balance nab knobs snubbing subpoena benefited
6 stubbornly rebellion probation mountable honorable crumbling

1 | 2 | 3 | 4 | 5 | 6 | 7 | 8 | 9 | 10 | 11 | 12 |

(Continued on next page)

Project B-3

This project calls for:
1. *Interoffice memo*
2. *Ruled table*
3. *Boxed table*

Review the general directions on page 394 before you begin.

Exercise 1

Prepare an interoffice memo from the handwritten copy below. Use today's date.

Subject: Departmental Reports
To: J. Goodman, President
From: M. Niles, Sales Manager

The two enclosed reports provide the information you requested about sales in the departments under my supervision. I am sending them to you now to allow you time to examine them at your convenience before our next meeting.

Exercise 2

Prepare a ruled table from the copy below. Figure the amounts for the *Net Sales* column by subtracting the sales returns from the gross sales. Provide totals for each column.

ANALYSIS OF SALES RETURNS

Department	Gross Sales	Sales Returns	Net Sales
Cosmetics	$857.74	$12.18	$ XXX
Hardware	375.25	42.45	XXX
Housewares	243.67	76.55	XXX
Jewelry	375.25	10.25	XXX
Leather Goods	455.60	6.55	XXX
Linens	380.61	19.20	XXX
Sporting Goods	995.35	26.75	XXX
Totals	$ XXX	$ XXX	$ XXX

Paired Letter Drills continued

In the bank basement there was a bundle of bonds on a bench.
The husband was being stubborn, ungovernable, and maddening.

c/d exclude idiotic deceased candid confidence deduction conduct
cardiac childhood educate decay cards handicap incident dice
Indicate on cards if the candidates are candid and decisive.
She decided that the accident was due to a cardiac handicap.

c/v invoice vocation excavate conclusive advocate excessive vice
conserve evacuate conceive advance verdict collective active
A convict held Victor captive in a cavern below the convent.
Two vicious convoys advanced on the evacuated town of Vichy.

d/e endure exceed extend eldest emerald evidence deathbed damage
deceased definite deferred delayed expedient explode educate
The college degree made a difference to the eldest daughter.
His case was deferred when new evidence was presented today.

d/k thanked weekend worked stockades attacked keyboard crackdown
breakdown kicked liked provoked skilled backwards blackheads
I thanked the duke for the haddock and vodka I had Thursday.
After darkness the kid locks the stockade and looks skyward.

d/s reside sardines scandals disorder decrease darkness sideline
deserve dress sandy dismissed describe despise dessert sides
He was dismissed speedily when a scandal showed he deserted.
Decreases in deposits caused considerable disorder in banks.

e/i legitimate evidence hygiene implied leisure itemize receipts
indeed eliminate illegible imbecile impatient indicate irate
The differences in the itemized receipts require attention.
Either the irate children were impatient or they were tired.

e/r effort concern charter reserve receipt recover elector reads
operate explore inherit engineer encircle rationale response
What concerns the engineer is the rationale of her argument.
Great pressure was exerted as the operator jerked the crane.

e/t absent execute citizen credit deposit complete accept detect
expect attend matter excite interfere interest dictate tempt
The jet emitted exhaust fumes over the flowers in the field.
An executive ignited a cigarette before he dictated letters.

1 | 2 | 3 | 4 | 5 | 6 | 7 | 8 | 9 | 10 | 11 | 12 |

(Continued on next page)

Project B-2

This project covers:
1. *Business letter*
2. *Tabulated price list*
3. *Telegraph message*

Review the general directions on page 394 before you begin.

Exercise 1

This letter was dictated by Daniel P. Torres, Marketing Manager for Rally CB's. Determine paragraphing.

December 1, 19— / Norwood Electronics / 143 Snyder Avenue / Rochester, NY 14614 / Gentlemen / Why not offer your customers mobile Citizens' Band radios that have all the extras at prices they can afford? Let us put our Rally CB's on display for a week in your store. The enclosed leaflet illustrates and describes the five models in our line; the price list shows the profit margin you can expect on each one. We hope that you will take the time to examine both the leaflet and the price list carefully. If you are interested in our trial offer, a sales representative will be happy to bring a display CB of each type to your shop and demonstrate their many unique features. At the end of one week, we are sure that customer response will convince you to place an order. If you wish to have one of our representatives visit you, please call this office and ask for Lotte Simms. / Sincerely

---

Exercise 2

Prepare a table from this unarranged price list copy. Figure the last column by subtracting the cost price from the list price.

RALLY CB's / Price List

(Subject to Change Without Notice)

<u>Model</u> / <u>List Price</u> / <u>Cost Price</u> / <u>Your Margin</u>

68-P / $48.95 / $20.00 / $*xxxx*

69-P / $70.50 / $45.50 / $*xxxx*

70-T / $110.00 / $89.50 / $*xxxx*

71-C / $149.50 / $99.50 / $*xxxx*

72-C / $248.95 / $198.00 / $*xxxx*

Exercise 3

Type a record of this telegraph message submitted by telephone. (For review of this procedure, refer to pages 296 and 299.)

Night Letter / January 4, 19— / 4:50 p.m. / Charge Sender / Daniel P. Torres / Rally CB's / 4763 Crest Drive / Philadelphia, PA 19119 / (716) 422-6137 / CB's are selling well. Send following immediately: 4, Model 68-P; 5, Model 70-T; and 3, Model 72-C. Bill according to usual credit arrangement. / O. Lawler, Chief Buyer / Norwood Electronics

Paired Letter Drills continued

41 **f/d** field defeat friend defend fender definite confidence afford
42 afraid offend farmlands clarified difficult defended confide
43 It was difficult to defend Ford who benefited from the deal.
44 We offered food to my friend who fled because he was afraid.

45 **f/g** glorify fixing finger grapefruit foreign fights fidgety gift
46 fitting firebug frontage frightful goldfish foggy figure fog
47 I shall begin fixing my home or seek glory on a golf course.
48 A fragile gift arrived from a foreign land for a frugal man.

49 **f/r** refuse firm brief differ effort conform certify offer inform
50 familiar officer perfect ratify portfolio refrain profit for
51 Fred was afraid the firm could not afford the artful affair.
52 The kind officer refused to fire me from the firm for fraud.

53 **g/b** bigamy governable gamble baggage garbage beggars grumble big
54 grab bag agreeable bandage begrudge beg cabbage embargo bugs
55 I was flabbergasted at the gabby grumblings from the beggar.
56 With a meal of cabbage and gingerbread, he became agreeable.

57 **g/h** hedge ghetto fright thing change graph right weight hydrogen
58 length extinguish gather hanging foghorn haggard fights high
59 I was aghast at the frightened, haggard women in the ghetto.
60 We gathered at night to haggle over hamburgers and hot dogs.

61 **g/t** might regret greet sight suggest together struggle gentlemen
62 originate mortgage exaggerate integral sergeants recognition
63 The sergeant went abroad together with his teenage daughter.
64 It was a great night as recognition was given the graduates.

65 **i/u** antiques beautiful community inclusive illuminates ultimate
66 impurity inequity insulted requisition premium minimum build
67 The alumni inquired about equipment issuing in universities.
68 To correct injustices, audits are conducted by seven unions.

69 **k/l** nickel black booklet luck shakily likable cocktail blackball
70 leak bilk kill lifelike checklist bookshelf buckle blackjack
71 We will be lucky if we find a likable bricklayer with skill.
72 Chuckling, the lanky girls knelt beside the playful kittens.

73 **m/n** minimum names meeting nighttime mechanism manuscript numb
74 number machine magazine mailing maintain magnify namely name

1 | 2 | 3 | 4 | 5 | 6 | 7 | 8 | 9 | 10 | 11 | 12 |

(Continued on next page)

will be to implement, on a national level, the policies that have worked so well for us in the southeastern states. In her new position, Marianne will report to Chris Dahl, Vice-President, Marketing. David Santos is appointed Executive Vice-President. Most of you already know David and the fine job he has done as controller for the past nine years. As a direct result of the management controls that he instituted, corporate profits have enjoyed a steady growth for nearly a decade. In his new position, David will be reporting directly to me. Please join me in welcoming Marianne and David to their new positions.

Exercise 2

This memo is from Olga Ghequiere, Office Manager. It announces a temporary change in working hours to take advantage of daylight saving time. Date the memo April 15, 19–, and address it to all office employees. Determine the paragraphing.

Next month we will be adopting "summer" hours. Last year's response to this change was so favorable that we decided to make the change a month earlier. Beginning May 1, our working hours will be from 8:00 a.m. to 4:00 p.m., with 30 minutes for lunch. These hours will apply through the end of August. Anyone who finds that the new hours will create a serious hardship should see me personally before the end of this week.

Exercise 3

This memo is from Lee Anderson, Director of Marketing, and deals with a sales incentive program. Date it March 15, 19–, and address it to all field representatives. Copies are to be sent to Edna D'Or and Bill Capote. Determine paragraphing.

Last year was our best year ever. Sales were up a record 37 percent over the previous year. Those of you who had 12 months' service or more as of December 31 of the past year will share handsomely in this growth, as you will see when you receive your bonus checks later this month. Those of you who were not eligible to participate in last year's program will be pleased to know that, effective immediately, all field sales personnel will now participate in the incentive program from their date of hire. Not only has the incentive program for this year been expanded to include all field representatives, but it has been further modified to provide even greater rewards to those who surpass the budget targets set for their territories. By separate letter, each of you will receive full details of how this plan will affect the bonus you will receive next year. Some of the key points in the new program are as follows: 1. On sales that exceed budget by 10 percent or less, a bonus of one-quarter of one percent of the amount over budget will be paid. 2. On sales that exceed budget by 11 percent to 25 percent, a bonus of one-half of one percent will be paid on the excess over 10 percent. 3. On sales that exceed budget by more than 25 percent, a bonus of three-quarters of one percent will be paid on the excess over 25 percent. I look forward to our making this another record year. / LA

Paired Letter Drills continued

75 For a nominal sum, I can maintain many accounts in his name.
76 Many magazines were missing after going through the machine.

77 **o/i** objective offering office opening opinion opportunity option
78 optimistic inclusion organization import outline iron obtain
79 Opening bids on the stock options were low in their opinion.
80 His office is optimistic that the omission was not intended.

81 **o/l** follow pillow collection foreclose formerly accomplish close
82 tolerate toolroom allow overlook lower solve velocity fellow
83 Those boys have the only double allowances of the whole lot.
84 A couple of decades from now we will be low on domestic oil.

85 **p/o** opinions approve protest bishop hypnotize prompt dispose top
86 approximate popular compact apropos program cooperate oppose
87 Pat and Les prefer purple, compact cars imported from Paris.
88 Temporarily, a popular bishop was appointed to the top post.

89 **r/t** react truck treat third relate terrific tariff thrift report
90 return rotary repeat theater right tenure rebate rents ratio
91 I reacted hysterically when the truck accident was reported.
92 This is the third time I turned right on my new truck route.

93 **r/u** further incur culture frustrate construct accrue bureau turn
94 quarrel acquire absurd curve century argue mature pursue fur
95 Burty, a builder, has constructed some popular homes for us.
96 A true soldier was assured a furlough for the inaugurations.

97 **s/c** scene abscess checks access confuse excess obscene recession
98 facsimile sarcasm discount politics process sincere services
99 I remember picnics where we ate delicious and luscious food.
100 Do not discount reckless schemes by politicians on occasion.

101 **s/w** wash sweet west swell news guesswork towards whereas windows
102 renewals lawless disallow awesome twosome waste whose cashew
103 We saw hundreds of little brownish glowworms on the windows.
104 I wish the housewives would sew all the snowsuits very soon.

105 **u/y** young unity busily annually auxiliary budgetary buying unify
106 yule actually fully adequately equality quality nullify buoy
107 Usually the youthful Mr. Burgyman knows quality when buying.
108 Lucy carefully counted the number of boys beyond your truck.

1 | 2 | 3 | 4 | 5 | 6 | 7 | 8 | 9 | 10 | 11 | 12 |

(Continued on next page)

SERIES B

MINI INTEGRATED PROJECTS

The work of the typist who handles correspondence is not limited to just typing letters. Often, there are accompanying tables, schedules, business forms, or other information that must be typed also. Each of the following mini projects is designed to give you practice in following through on the preparation of the total package of typed materials that centers around a single transaction.

Directions for Series B

1. Prepare at least one carbon copy of each assignment.
2. Type envelopes as necessary.
3. Vary the letter styles from project to project.
4. Determine paragraphing before beginning to type exercises in which the paragraphs are not shown. Remember that a paragraph is a group of sentences that develops one central thought. A new paragraph should begin where an obvious change in thought occurs.
5. Use eye judgment as much as possible to determine the placement of each assignment.

Project B-1

This project covers the preparation of interoffice memorandums.

Review the general directions above before you begin.

Exercise 1

This memo is from John MacMillan, President. It concerns the promotion of two employees. Date it March 1, 19–, and address it to all members of the staff. Determine paragraphing.

I am very pleased to announce the promotion of two of our employees, effective March 1, 19–. Marianne Gilbert, formerly Media Manager for the Southeastern Region, will be joining us in Phoenix as Director of Advertising. Marianne brings to this position twelve years of experience in all phases of our corporate advertising. One of her first responsibilities

(Continued on next page)

Paired Letter Drills continued

109 v/b vibrating vagabonds brevity vocabulary bevels visible beaver
110 valuables avoidable verbal above beverages combative bravery
111 Beverly is well known for her brevity and verbal vocabulary.
112 In the vestibule of the house on the boulevard stood a vase.

113 w/e widower entwine eyebrow edgeways elsewhere wreckage bewilder
114 worthwhile whether eyewitness between newspaper white beware
115 We watched Eyewitness News and later read the old newspaper.
116 Whether it's worthwhile to remarry is up to the old widower.

117 y/t yesterday hypnotic typify ability analyst history rhythm toy
118 thrifty warranty validity technology synthetic treasury type
119 Try to type the story on the history of synthetic dyestuffs.
120 Yesterday a witty analyst with fifty yachts became a martyr.

121 z/a zodiac agonize sizable penalize jazz hazard serialize razors
122 quartz revitalize trapeze paralyze dazzle bizarre liberalize
123 Can you visualize a meal of zesty pizza accompanied by jazz?
124 A zealous zebra zigzagged after a tranquilizer dazzled him.

1 | 2 | 3 | 4 | 5 | 6 | 7 | 8 | 9 | 10 | 11 | 12 |

ERROR CORRECTION DRILLS

Sometimes an error is triggered by the word preceding or following it. Use the paragraphs below and on the next page as practice copy for developing greater control over these types of errors.

Directions:

Type the paragraphs at the right at your own speed. When you make an error, stop and retype the preceding word, the word which contains the error, and the word immediately after the error. For instance, in the first line of the first paragraph, if you make an error on the word *job,* stop and type *right job can* and then continue. After previewing the paragraphs in this way, take a 3-minute timed writing. Your goal is no more than 3 errors.

70-space line. Double spacing. 5-space paragraph indention.

1 Getting the right job can make the difference between a happy, 13
successful life and a life of disappointment and failure. The right job 27
can mean good food and clothes and a comfortable home for you and 40
your family. 42

It can mean time and money for recreation and vacations. It can 56
mean the respect of your friends. Today millions of men and women 69
are enjoying careers in clerical and sales work. SI 1.46 79

2 Many of us have seen television programs in which people on the 14
street are questioned by the inquiring reporter. On one of these programs, 29
the question asked was whether people liked their work. The various 43
answers all pointed to the fact that if they did, it was probably because 58
they were good at it. 62

There is a great deal of truth in this conclusion. You will not meet 77
experts in any trade or art who are not deeply interested in their work. 91

1 | 2 | 3 | 4 | 5 | 6 | 7 | 8 | 9 | 10 | 11 | 12 | 13 | 14 |

(Continued on next page)

Please include these two points when you draw up the formal contract. If you will then send the contract to us, we will forward it toour client for signature.

Very truly yours

Exercise 3

This letter was dictated by Elizabeth L. Hartley. It is to be sent to the address shown at the right. Send a copy of the letter to Walter S. Farley. (There are 143 words in the body.)

Municipal Transportation System
64 Penn Street
Madison, WI 53714

November 22, 19--

Gentlemen

My client, Walter S. Farley, reports an injury sustained by him as he was in the act of stepping off a southbound bus operated by one of your drivers. The bus started suddelny, throwing my client to the ground and injuring his back. The accident occurred last Monday at about 5:30 P.M. at the north west corner of Harvard Avenue and Day Street.

No doubt you have a complete report of this case, including a copy of the police and hospital records and copies of the statements of three witnesses.

Before taking any legal action, we shall be pleased to consider an amicableadjustment that will fully compensate Mr. Farley for the suffering, medical expenses, and loss of employment he incurred due to this accident. Please let us known when we can meet to discuss this matter with you and your attoreys.

Yours very truly

Error Correction Drills continued

People who excel at the work they are paid to do are certain to enjoy it 105
and are well on the road to a happy life. SI 1.33 113

3 A person who takes out a loan and does not repay it on time gets a 14
bad credit rating. If you are in high school, chances are you have not 28
taken out any loans and you have no large debts to repay. In terms of your 43
credit rating, that's an advantage. 50
On the other hand, chances are you do not have any record of good 64
credit either. Most likely, you have no credit rating at all. One bank mana- 80
ger says that she cannot automatically give loans to people with no credit 95
rating because that would be like saying it will be sunny all day when you 110
have seen only five minutes of the day. SI 1.32 118

4 I once asked a group of friends what work is. Most of them considered 15
the question a joke. One spoke of it as the only means he had discovered 29
of getting money. A second defined it as something she was paid to do by 44
someone who got more just for telling her to do it. A third said it is trying 60
to sell something to people who do not want it. 69
Still another took the question seriously. He said that by work we mean 85
using the labor of people in such a way that something is produced that 99
is needed or desired. That answer made me realize the true purpose of work. 114
SI 1.29

5 Sales work offers career opportunities for young people who have 14
not completed high school, as well as for those who have a college degree; 28
for men and women who like to travel and those who do not; and for 42
people who want salaried employment, as well as those who aspire to run 56
their own business. 60
Workers in this occupational group may sell for manufacturers, insur- 74
ance companies, and other producers of goods and services; for whole- 88
salers who stock large quantities of goods so that smaller lots may be 102
purchased and resold by retail stores; and for drugstores, dress shops, 116
and other retailers who deal directly with the public. SI 1.50 127

6 The real source of all the rivers of the earth is above our heads. A vast 16
amount of water is flowing into the many seas of the world and the flow 30
seems to go on forever. Every year fourteen of the largest rivers pour into 45
the seas five billion tons of water; yet the seas never seem to change 59
their level. 62
All rivers flow from the land to the sea, but they must return in another 77
form. When we look up and see masses of moving clouds, we are looking 91
at the constant flow of rivers back to the air. From the seas all over the 106
world, the sun turns water into vapor, which rises into the air until at some 122
time it falls again as rain to renew its ceaseless cycle. SI 1.29 133

1 | 2 | 3 | 4 | 5 | 6 | 7 | 8 | 9 | 10 | 11 | 12 | 13 | 14 |

with the terms of the court order by then, it will be necessary to apply for an extension of time in which to settle the estate.

Please inform us immediatly whether you require additional time. We must make formal application for an extension at least 5 days prior to the final date set by the Surrogate's Ct.

Sincerely

Exercise 2

This letter was dictated by Lloyd F. Gwynn. The letter is to be sent to the address shown at the right. Send a copy of the letter to Bradley Coombs. (There are 127 words in the body.)

Dodge & Bordeau
Building Contractors
206 Ryder Avenue
Madison, WI 53710

November 21, 19--

Gentlemen

We have examined the draft of the agreement between you and our client that you sent us last week. There are two points that should be added before the contract is signed.

In the first place, no time limit for the completion of the work is specified. It is so important that the work should be finished by the end of the month, that our client feels he cannot put his signature to any contract which omits this provision. In the second place, no mention is made of the repairs to the garage. Although they are of minor importance, they should nevertheless be specified in the contract.

(Continued on next page)

Topic 4 NUMBER AND SYMBOL PRACTICE

KEY LOCATION REVIEW

Select lines from these drills and practice them for brief periods to build your confidence in typing numbers and symbols by touch.

Drill 1

NUMBER REVIEW

These drills are designed to give you a review in typing numbers.

Type each line twice. 60-space line. Single spacing. DS after each pair of lines.

1 we 23 quo 179 yew 632 try 546 writ 2485 riot 4895 your 6974
2 to 59 wry 246 ewe 323 pup 070 quip 1780 tire 5843 rout 4975
3 up 70 yip 680 out 975 ire 843 quay 1716 tout 5975 yore 6943
4 wee 233 too 599 woo 299 putty 07556 error 34494 quite 17853
5 yee 633 you 697 root 4995 quire 17843 peep 0330 query 17346
6 pop 090 poor 0994 putt 0755 quote 17953 weep 2330 writ 2485
7 quit 1785 pipe 0803 wept 2305 purr 0744 tree 5433 poet 0935
8 rope 4903 were 2343 quay 1716 your 6974 pope 0903 ripe 4803
9 were 2343 joke 6983 inch 8736 tight 58465 moon 6997 box 592
10 pride 04833 stove 24953 quake 16183 zip 180 yuck 6738 cup 360

Drill 2

SYMBOL REVIEW

These drills are designed to give you a review in typing symbols on manual and electric typewriters.

Left margin at 15. Single spacing.

		Manual	*Electric*
1	$	fr4f fr$f f$f $4 $4	fr4f fr$f f$f $4 $4
2	/	;/; ;/; 1/3 3/4 4/5	;/; ;/; 1/3 3/4 4/5
3	%	f%f f%f 6% 7% 8% 9%	f%f f%f 6% 7% 8% 9%
4	-	;-; ;-; 3-cent 10-60	;-; .-. 3-cent 10-60
5	( )	191 l(l ;0; ;); (9)	191 l(l ;0; ;); (9)
6	'	ki8k ki'k k'k don't	;'; ;'; can't don't
7	"	sw2s sw"s s"s "go"	;"; ;"; 6'2" tall
8	_	j6j j_j can't don't	;-; ;_; can't don't
9	#	de3d de#d d#d #7 8#	de3d de#d d#d #7 8#
10	&	ju7j ju&j j&j 2 & 4	ju7j ju&j j&j 2 & 4
11	¢	;¢; ;¢; 20¢ 15¢ 38¢	j6j j¢j 20¢ 15¢ 38¢
12	@	;@; ;@; ;@; 7 @ 49¢	sw2s sw@s s@s 6 @ 9¢
13	*	;*; ;*; * (asterisk)	k8k k*k * (asterisk)
14	½	;½; ;½; 4½# 6½' 7½"	;½; ;½; 4½# 6½' 7½"
15	¼	;¼; ;¼; 7¼# 8¼' 9¼"	;¼; ;¼; 7¼# 8¼' 9¼"
16	=	;=; ;=; 9 = 8 A = B	;=; ;=; 9 = 8 A = B
17	+	;+; ;+; 21 + 3 = 24	;+; ;+; 21 + 3 = 24

interest in the house after your inspection of it last week, I wanted to notify you of the situation immediately. ¶There has already been a definite interest shown in the property by several parties, and I think you will have to act quickly if you want to purchase it. I know that the Carmines have already received one offer of $190,000. ¶I suggest that we get together on Saturday and sit down with Mr. and Mrs. Carmine to make them an offer of their asking price. I feel confident that they will accept a full-price offer. (130 words)

Exercise 4

June 18, 19— / Boynton Pattern Company / 260 Purdy Street / Schenectady, NY 12318 / Attention Carl L. Boynton / Since you have informed us that you are looking for a new business location, we are writing to you about the Eliot Building at 300 North Berkeley Street. ¶We believe that this building, located in the heart of the commercial district, is particularly suited to your needs. It offers 30,000 square feet on the ground floor at a very attractive rate. ¶We suggest that you see it immediately. Please call me for an appointment. (74 words)

Project A-5 LAW FIRM

You are working for the firm of Hartley, Gwynn, & Hartley, Attorneys-at-Law, 877 Madison Plaza, Madison, WI 53727. Each attorney dictates his or her letters and then has them transcribed in draft form. After the attorneys read the drafts and make necessary alterations, the letters are given to you to type. The name of the attorney who dictated the letter as well as the name of the firm must be included in the signature block of each letter. Use modified block style with mixed punctuation and 5-space paragraph indentions.

Exercise 1

This letter was dictated by Lloyd F. Gwynn, Attorney-at-Law. Note the subject line. The letter is to be sent to Mr. Jordan at the address shown at the right. (There are 94 words in the body.)

Mr. Richard T. Jordan
847 Highland Avenue
Madison, WI 53713

November 20, 19--

Dear Mr. Jordan

SUBJECT: Estate of Mabel N. Jordan

As administrator of the estate of Mabel N. Jordan, you were ~~allowed~~ granted until ~~the end of this month~~ November 30 by the Surrogate's Court to submit your final accounting and distribution of the estate. If you ~~will not be~~ ~~are not~~ able to comply

(Continued on next page)

SENTENCE PRACTICE

The purpose of this drill is to help you develop a smoother typing style when typing numbers and symbols in context.

Drill 3

60-space line. Single spacing. Type each line twice; DS after each pair of lines.

1 The Harvester Building is 176 feet high. It has 14 stories.
2 The Economy Market has turkeys weighing from 9 to 17 pounds.
3 Last week I interviewed 88 job applicants but hired only 25.
4 David says he is 5 feet 6 inches tall and weighs 147 pounds.
5 Ship them 18 boxes, each containing 25 dozen pairs of socks.

6 The order reads: 9 rms. vellum ($8\frac{1}{2}$ × 11); 2 rms. legal bond.
7 Traffic is eastbound on 178th St. and westbound on 179th St.
8 This 20-piece silver service provides four 5-piece settings.
9 Robby no longer wears a size $15\frac{1}{2}$ shirt; he requires size 16.
10 Our ballpoint pens cost $2 each. Matching pencils cost 90¢.

11 On Monday, Atlantic Petroleum opened at $9\frac{1}{4}$ and closed at $8\frac{1}{2}$.
12 The series of 15 broadcasts is entitled "Famous New Yorkers."
13 *Interest rates: 10% (6 mos.); 11% (1 yr.); 12% (3 yrs.).
14 If I can deliver <u>today</u>, he will order a dozen of my $8 sets.
15 Though King & Lee ask $80 for the set, they may accept less.

16 *Solve:* (a + b) − (b + c) = 2(a − b) where a = 2 and b = 7.
17 "I'd like to be an executive secretary," said Suzie Jeffers.
18 "I studied English and typing; but I can't spell," she said.
19 Suzanne recognized her weakness (poor spelling) with regret.
20 Ad: Bargain office supplies! Tablets @ $1.39! Pens @ $.69!

21 Its value is still dropping! Will it ever zoom? I hope so.
22 Moral: Don't gamble—sometimes you win, but often you do not.
23 Hazel plans to apply for social security at 65 (not at 62).
24 Penn State University offered a 14-week session last summer.
25 Rooms were $9 per day—board extra. One freshman soon quit.

26 Was the 14-week experiment successful? Who knows? I don't.
27 I had 30 kids at the party. I expected all to obey quickly.
28 *Freshman grades: A (12%); B (22%); C (54%); D (10%); F (2%).
29 I send the dresses to her, c/o Mrs. Rite, with whom I board.
30 The supermarket sign read, "Bananas—41¢/lb. or 3 lbs./$1.15."

31 Just ask me (but do it tactfully); I'll be quite reasonable.
32 Stay on Route #28 to get to Queens Town; attempt no detours.

(Continued on next page)

Project A-4 REAL ESTATE AGENCY

You are working for Laura Robbins Harwick, partner in the firm of Harwick & Moody, Real Estate Brokers, 210 Smith Street, Schenectady, NY 12315. Mrs. Harwick has given you four letters to type. She prefers that you use full block style, open punctuation. Mrs. Harwick uses her social title, Mrs., in the signature block of all letters. Supply the missing salutations and complimentary closings.

Exercise 1

A copy of this letter is to be sent to John R. Warren.

June 17, 19— / The Silver Pen Company / 466 Market Street / Schenectady, NY 12317 / Attention Cynthia Silver / In accordance with the agreement reached at the recent conference between your representative, Frank Baxter, and our representative, John Warren, we are submitting for your approval the enclosed draft of a three-year lease on the fifth floor premises at 411 Front Street. ¶The terms and conditions of this lease have been prepared in accordance with Mr. Baxter's requests. They differ in some details from provisions usually found in agreements affecting the rental of business property. ¶Please have the draft signed by an authorized officer of your company. Indicate on it either approval or the changes that you believe should be made, and return it to us. If the draft is substantially correct, we shall then promptly prepare the lease in final form. The original copy will be executed by us as lessors and the duplicate copy by your company as lessee. Upon completion, the two papers will be exchanged for signatures. (152 words)

Exercise 2

June 19, 19— / Mr. and Mrs. J. P. Dorcas / 13 Carlysle Road / Scotia, NY 12302 / Last month you wrote to us asking whether we had in our listing file a six-bedroom house, Tudor style, on at least ten acres of wooded land. You stated at that time that you would be willing to pay up to $200,000 for the right place. ¶Our agency is now negotiating to obtain the exclusive listing of a property that seems to be just what you have in mind. The owners, John and Paula Carmine, have agreed to my bringing you out to take a tour of the house and grounds at a mutually agreed upon time. Please call me if you are interested and I will set up an appointment. P.S. Some of the extra features of this property include stables, a swimming pool, and a small greenhouse. (112 words in body; 18 words in postscript)

Exercise 3

June 25, 19— / Mr. and Mrs. J. P. Dorcas / 13 Carlysle Road / Scotia, NY 12302 / Our office has just received the exclusive listing for the Carmine property, and we will be moving quickly to secure a buyer. The listing price is $195,000. Since you had expressed such a great

(Continued on next page)

Drill 3 continued

33 If you are in doubt, ask, "How do I get back to Highway #28?"
34 Recipe for limeade: $1\frac{1}{2}$ cups of lime juice to $1\frac{1}{4}$ cups sugar.
35 Please ship it May 28 to our warehouse in West Philadelphia.

36 How could 54 men and 55 women use up 113 tickets so quickly?
37 Check on all orders numbered 41 to 1,265 as soon as you can.
38 A stalled engine delayed a train near the 125th St. station.
39 They employ 300 full-time workers and 190 part-time workers.
40 From May 4 to June 3, forward my mail to 68 East 9th Street.

PARAGRAPH PRACTICE

The purpose of the following drill is to give you practice in typing numbers and symbols more speedily and accurately.

Drill 4

65-space line. Double spacing. 5-space paragraph indention.

Note: Some of the numbers and symbols in these paragraphs would normally be used only in statistical copy. In standard copy they would be spelled out. They are included here only to provide practice on those keys.

1 Here's how we will help you with home improvements. We'll 13
give you suggestions; we'll show you samples; we'll demonstrate 26
methods—all without charge (we sell materials only). 37

2 We cordially invite you to come in and see our smart fall display 14
of men's suits and coats. Our store is open daily from 9 to 5 (open 27
evenings Thursday and Saturday until 8). 35

3 We are equipped with a complete line of custom-made ready- 13
to-wear clothes for men. Our credit terms of 4% discount if paid within 27
10 days or net in 90 days are the most liberal offered in the industry. 41

4 The only apartment still available in this building is on the 7th 14
floor. It has $4\frac{1}{2}$ rooms. The rent is reasonable for this type of luxury 28
apartment—$655 a month, with a month's rent in advance. A two- 41
year lease is required. 46

5 Do you enjoy boat rides? Our new paddle-wheel steamer leaves 13
from Pier 52 and makes daily trips up the Hudson (round-trip fare, 26
$16). For complete information, call us any day during the week 39
between the hours of 9 a.m. and 5 p.m. 47

6 When you buy corn oil, be sure to get Lorenzo's 100% pure corn 13
oil—the very best! Your salads will taste better; your cooking will 27
improve. Get it by the pint, by the quart, or by the gallon—in "the 41
can with the stars on top." 46

1 | 2 | 3 | 4 | 5 | 6 | 7 | 8 | 9 | 10 | 11 | 12 | 13 |

(Continued on next page)

issue us a new check for the amount of $156.21 to cover loan payment No. 19. Unfortunately, we must again assess a late charge of $6.54, which you may include with your payment or which we can add to your principal balance. ¶In order to avoid future problems with your loan payments, may I suggest that you make them in person at the teller's window and have your loan book receipted. This will assure that your payments are properly recorded and credited to your account on the day they are made. If we can be of further assistance to you, please do not hesitate to write or call. / Sincerely (492 words)

Exercise 4

This letter was also dictated by Paula Samson.

April 11, 19— / Mr. Harry Wells / Harry Wells and Associates / 384 Madison Avenue / New York, NY 10017 / Dear Harry / As we discussed in our telephone conversation last week, Central Savings and Loan is now well into the planning of its new accounts promotion. ¶We would definitely like you to put together a series of newspaper and magazine ads, two 30-second radio and television commercials, and a four-color illustrated brochure. John Clementi, my assistant, will be in touch with you shortly to discuss specifications and content. ¶We will require sample copy for each space ad and for each commercial. Once we have approved the samples, you will need to provide us with an estimate of the costs to develop and produce each one. The estimate should cover not only your fee, but all extra expenses such as fees for models and permissions. Also include an estimated schedule of the time required. For the brochure, please provide us with an estimate for printing in four colors in quantities of 25,000 and 50,000. ¶I know you will do a fine job for us. Call me any time you want to discuss ideas or get feedback on the materials as you develop them. / Cordially / SPECIAL DELIVERY (182 words)

Exercise 5

This letter was dictated by Thomas Smith, Accounts Officer. It is to be sent by registered mail.

April 12, 19— / Mrs. Kim Que Tran / 226 Cleeve Avenue / Jersey City, NJ 07316 / Dear Mrs. Tran / Your Regular Savings Account, No. 73625810, has been held inactive by our bank for a year. The last recorded transaction, made on April 11 of 19—, was a deposit of $250, which brought the balance of the account to $781.72. Interest at the rate of 5¼%, compounded daily, has increased the amount to $825.93. ¶These funds, as of today, have been transferred from this branch to our head office, located at 280 Loreli Avenue. The funds will remain there for six years. If, at the end of that time, we still have no response from you, the funds will be transferred to the state. ¶Please notify us of your intentions for the account. If you wish, you may instruct us to hold the account open indefinitely; or you may request that the account be closed and your funds withdrawn. We shall await your instructions. / Sincerely (144 words)

Drill 4 continued

7 Mother Emmy's Frozen Foods are the best you've ever tasted. 13
You can get them at Bee & Dee markets (and at many other stores). 26
Try them with this guarantee—if you feel they're not all that we claim, 40
send us the wrapper and we'll return your money. 50

8 Mauna Loa is the largest volcano in the world. It has been 13
built up from 10,000 cubic miles of lava. Mauna Loa has so-called 26
Hawaiian eruptions. These are relatively nonviolent. However, they 40
produce enormous lava flows and a broad, relatively flat mountain. 53

9 The famous cherry trees in Washington (a gift of the Mayor of 13
Tokyo) line the roadside for 2 miles in East Potomac Park. These 26
trees came from the original 3,000 trees which were propagated from 39
trees on the Arawaka River in a suburb of Tokyo. The first trees were 53
planted in 1912. 56

10 On May 2, 1927, Charles A. Lindbergh took off from Roosevelt 13
Field, Long Island. The 25-year-old airmail pilot had accepted the 26
challenge to fly solo and nonstop in his plane from New York to 39
Paris—an act as daring in its time as any that can be imagined. 52
Lindbergh completed the flight in 33½ hours. 61

11 At the shareholders' 45th annual meeting in Boston, several 13
issues were discussed. The first was an amendment to the bylaws 26
to enable the company to hold its meetings in various cities. A two- 40
thirds favorable vote was required for adoption; the amendment 52
passed by a vote of nearly 98%. Were you present at the meeting? 65

12 The Washington National Monument is a tapering shaft, almost 13
556 feet in height. It is covered in white Maryland marble in 2-foot 27
slabs. Eight small windows, two on each side, are located at the 500- 40
foot level, where points of interest may be viewed. Set into the 53
interior wall are 190 memorial stones received from states, foreign 67
countries, and organizations. 72

13 The #7 train was due at two o'clock. The crowd that had as- 13
sembled to meet the ambassador—the hero of the moment—was 25
becoming restless because the train was 45 minutes late. Some were 38
heard to murmur, "Let's go! Why wait any longer?" Others com- 51
mented, however, "We've waited so long; why not wait a little longer?" 65
When the train finally arrived, the ambassador had vanished. 77

1 | 2 | 3 | 4 | 5 | 6 | 7 | 8 | 9 | 10 | 11 | 12 | 13 |

planning a major new accounts promotion campaign. We would like to inquire about purchasing 10,000 copies of your book, *Keep Your Money Working for You,* to offer as a premium to customers opening new accounts during the promotion period. ¶ If you agree to supply these to us, we will want a special cover showing various kinds of currency. We would supply the art for this, subject to your approval. However, we would ask you to obtain the required permission from the U.S. Secret Service to reproduce currency for this purpose. ¶ Please give us a price quotation for an initial purchase of 10,000 copies as well as a price for an additional 10,000 copies, f.o.b. our Jersey City office. We anticipate needing delivery of the first 10,000 copies in eight weeks. / Very truly yours (140 words)

Exercise 3

Note that this letter will require two pages. It was dictated by Max Kosta, Manager, Consumer Loans.

April 10, 19— / Daniel R. Gallagher / 1411 Seward Avenue / Jersey City, NJ 07315 / Dear Mr. Gallagher / RE: Home Improvement Loan No. 128741 / I have your letter of April 4 in which you inquired about three late charges recently assessed against your home improvement loan. ¶ Our records show that payments Nos. 17 and 18 had both been received by us beyond the grace period allowed for loan payments, and that payment No. 19 so far has not been received at all. In your letter, you stated that all three payments had been made on time, and, therefore, no late charges should have been levied. ¶ Upon investigating the matter further, we found that loan payment No. 17, due on January 15, was not received until February 2, three days after the expiration of the fifteen-day grace period. Since this payment was not received in time to be credited on your monthly statement, a late charge of $6.54 was added to your principal balance. Although you state that you mailed the payment on January 21 and that poor mail service probably caused the delay in our receiving it, we cannot be held responsible for mail delivery. We regret, therefore, that no adjustment can be made for the late charge assessed against this payment. ¶ Our records concerning loan payment No. 18, due on February 15, show that it was received by our office on March 2, rather than on March 3, as shown on your statement. The late charge was erroneously assessed because the payment was not credited to your account until the day following its arrival. Accordingly, on the next monthly statement that you receive from us, this late charge of $6.54 will be shown as a miscellaneous credit, thus reducing the amount of principal balance owing. ¶ In regard to loan payment No. 19, due on March 15, as of the time of this writing, we have no record that it has ever been received by our office. Although you state that this payment was placed in our night depository box after closing hours on March 28, no trace of it can be found. Let me assure you that we have made a thorough check of the night depository box, and it is a complete mystery to us as to what might have happened to your check. May I suggest that you place a stop-payment order on the check to prevent its being cashed by another party and

(Continued on next page)

Topic 5 TIMED WRITINGS

Use the following selections to measure your typing speed and accuracy. Doing a timed writing periodically will help you keep track of your keyboarding progress. This, in turn, will give you an opportunity to set new goals for yourself so that you can reach the highest rate of speed and greatest degree of accuracy of which you are capable. (*Note:* For additional selections, use the Supplementary Practice section at the end of the book.)

IDENTIFYING TYPING ERRORS

Adapted from the International Typewriting Contest Rules

In assessing typing errors, charge only one error to a word, regardless of how many errors the word actually contains. The following are considered typing errors:

1. Variations from printed copy
   a. Misspellings (including changes in capitalization)
   b. Added or omitted words
   c. Substituted or transposed words
   d. Errors in punctuation*
   e. Errors in spacing*
2. Incorrect formatting
   a. Failure to indent or paragraph
   b. Irregular left margin or poor right margin
   c. Faulty line spacing
   d. Incorrect word division at the end of a line
3. Technique errors
   a. Flying capitals
   b. Crowded letters
   c. Strikeovers

*Charged to the immediately preceding word.

Directions:
65-space line. Double spacing.

1 There are living forms in water that are known to have been in 13
existence through the ages. These tiny life forms, too small to be 26
seen by the unaided eye, are made up of only one cell. This one cell 40
at frequent intervals divides into two. Each time the cell divides, 54
the two new cells are complete living things. As this division can go 68
on and on, apparently without end, these one-celled forms may be 81
said to live forever—if they do not make a meal for some larger 94
creature. It is quite possible that there are some one-celled animals 108
living now that have already had a life of a million years. SI 1.34 120

2 Just as there are different shades of beauty—one star differing 14
from another in glory—there are different degrees in our delight. 27
It is very pleasant to see the waving grain as the wind sweeps over 40
a wheat field, to sit idly by a stream and see it hurrying past, to lie 54
on the shore and look lazily at the tide coming in and at the gulls 67
sailing overhead. As we look longer and more intently, our delight 81
grows; what we see becomes clearer and takes on a deeper meaning. 94
We sense more vividly what we are looking at—the wheat field, the 107
stream, the tide and the gulls. As we look still longer, the scene 120
awakens memories. SI 1.33 123

1 | 2 | 3 | 4 | 5 | 6 | 7 | 8 | 9 | 10 | 11 | 12 | 13 |

Exercise 4

Note the subject line. This letter was dictated by Mrs. Knight.

February 12, 19— / PERSONAL / Mrs. Wanda Anderson / Anderson Catering Service / 54 Market Street / Columbus, OH 43220 / Dear Mrs. Anderson / Loan Against Life Insurance Policy No. GS 26307614 / In reply to your letter of February 7, I am sending a loan application form that you will need to complete in order to borrow $5,000 against your life insurance policy No. GS 26307614. Your husband, as beneficiary under the policy, must also sign the form to show consent to the loan, since it will become a charge against any claim payable under the policy. ¶Once we have received the completed forms from you, we will process them immediately. If everything is in order, you should have a check from us within one week after our receipt of the forms. Interest at the rate of 6 percent per year will be billed to you annually on the anniversary date of your policy. / Cordially (121 words)

Project A-3 SAVINGS AND LOAN ASSOCIATION

You are working in the general office of the Central Savings and Loan Association, 69 Hudson Boulevard, Jersey City, NJ 07322. As a member of a typing pool, you are required to type letters for a number of different executives. The firm prefers modified block style, mixed punctuation, with 5-space paragraph indentions.

Exercise 1

This letter was dictated by Roger T. Richman, Vice-President, Loan Department.

April 9, 19— / Froman & Sykes / 710 River Street / Jersey City, NJ 07317 / Gentlemen / We have received your application for a capital improvement loan to expand and modernize your warehouse facilities. ¶Before we can undertake to provide the financing you need, however, we must complete a review of your financial statements and your remodeling plans. To do this, we will require a certified copy of your firm's most recent income statement and balance sheet, and a detailed plan for the warehouse remodeling. Please send these to me at your earliest convenience. ¶In the meantime, we shall begin processing your application so that it will be ready for action when your statements arrive. / Sincerely (98 words)

Exercise 2

This letter was dictated by Paula Samson, Advertising Manager.

April 10, 19— / Premium Sales Manager / Savoy Publishing Company / 61 Harbor Street / Roanoke, VA 24010 / Dear Sir or Madam / Central Savings and Loan is now in the process of

(Continued on next page)

Timed Writings continued

3 Tides are a natural phenomenon. They are most visible at the 13
seashore as water rushes out to sea and then back toward land day 26
in and day out. This movement is caused by the gravitational pull 39
of the moon on the earth. As the earth rotates, exposing one side 53
to the moon, the oceans on that side bulge upwards, drawing water 66
away from the coastlands. The tide goes out. As the earth com- 78
pletes its turn away from the moon, the bulge in the ocean subsides, 92
and water flows back toward the land. The tide comes in. Although 105
tides occur over all the earth (in air and land as well as water), 119
the ocean tides are the most obvious because of their size. SI 1.31 130

4 Success in any business depends on the people who work for it. 13
This is especially true in the retail business. Customers will return 27
to a store where they have received courteous and efficient service. 41
In selling furniture, electrical appliances, or clothing, the 54
salesperson's job is to create an interest in the products the store 68
has to offer. The salesman or saleswoman may answer questions about 81
the construction of an item, demonstrate its use, explain how it is 95
cared for, show various models and colors, and otherwise help the 108
customer make a selection. In some stores (such as hardware stores), 122
special knowledge or skills may be needed to sell the merchandise; 135
but most selling does not require special skills or training. SI 1.55 147

5 We all know that water runs downhill. In the course of time, 13
water running down a hill may have an effect on whatever is in its 26
path. If it meets a hard, large stone during its course, it breaks against 41
that stone and moves around it. If part of the stone is weak, however, 56
the water is sure to find that weak spot. In the course of years, per- 70
haps ages, the water will wear away the weak part until it can pass 83
through the stone. Stones have been found that are little more than 97
shells because the water has made its way through a great hole in 110
what was once the heart of a stone. 117
The water also could break against the stone day after day, year 131
after year, until at last it cuts underneath it. Then it slowly makes a 145
new path for itself in the earth under the stone, through which it can 159
more easily pass. It may run under the ground this way, cutting a hole 173
hundreds of feet deep and several miles long, and then come to the 187
surface once again. SI 1.23 190

1 | 2 | 3 | 4 | 5 | 6 | 7 | 8 | 9 | 10 | 11 | 12 | 13 |

day to and from your place of work. Other updating changes have also been made. Please refer to the enclosed Declarations Page for a complete description of the coverages now in effect. ¶As a result of all the changes made, your new premium to cover the policy period from February 13, 19— to February 12, 19—, was increased by $93.00. Please remit this amount no later than March 1, to ensure continuous policy coverage. / Very truly yours (108 words)

Exercise 2

This letter was dictated by Mr. Dillon.

February 14, 19— / Ms. Roberta Vargo / 608 Cedar Avenue / Cleveland, OH 44112 / Dear Ms. Vargo / I have your recent letter requesting information about a policy to cover your cameras and recording equipment. ¶Our policies provide several forms of coverage for such personal effects, as described in the enclosed brochure. On page 3 you will see a policy that includes coverage for theft, loss due to carelessness on your part, and damage caused by someone other than yourself. Such coverage would apply no matter where the theft, loss, or damage occurred. ¶The cost of such a policy would depend on the value of the equipment being insured. However, the face value of the policy cannot exceed the current market value of the items. Any claims payable under the policy, therefore, would be based on the cost of the items less any depreciation for the time that you owned them. ¶I hope this information will answer your questions. If you require additional assistance in selecting a policy, please notify me and I will have one of our representatives in Cleveland call on you. / Sincerely yours (166 words)

Exercise 3

Note the subject line. This letter was dictated by Mrs. Knight.

February 15, 19— / Mr. Louis Parten / Box 119 / Springville, CA 93265 / Dear Mr. Parten / Claim No. 62 5496 114 / I have your letter of February 8 and shall respond to each question in the order listed in your letter. ¶It appears that the seven items on your claim sheet totaling $225.00, while a result of the collision, are not covered under your policy contract. The one exception may be the tire that blew out at the time of the collision. This would be listed at $39.45, less any applicable depreciation. Please advise us as to the length of time the tire had been in use so that we may make the adjustment and reimburse you. ¶Regarding your second question, the adjuster who reviewed the tow bill deducted for the changing of the tire. However, it appears that you do have emergency road service coverage, which would have paid for this. Therefore, I am enclosing a draft for $5.25, to bring the reimbursement to the full amount you paid Smith's Towing. ¶Please feel free to call this office, and, if necessary, we will have an adjuster work with you to conclude the remaining items in your claim. / Very truly yours (177 words)

Timed Writings continued

6 Home, to the average man or woman, means a house suitably 12
furnished, surroundings that please the eye, and perhaps a garden 25
in which to grow flowers or vegetables. It is a permanent retreat 38
that shelters its occupants from the world outside. 48

Most people would laugh at the idea that they might spend 60
their whole lives in a floating home. Yet there are hundreds of 73
thousands of men and women around the world who live on boats 85
either from choice or because of the way in which they earn their 98
livelihood. To them, home is a place that can be moved at will, at 111
any time. The hundreds of families that live and work on barges 124
on canals, for example, have a home in every sense of the word, 137
even though it is a home that is always moving from place to place. 150

SI 1.29

7 There are often occasions when you are faced with many dif- 13
ferent tasks, all of which seem urgent. When you undertake one of 26
them, you are troubled by the thought of a dozen other things that 39
you ought to be doing—things that cannot wait, you say. Or can they 53
wait? Of course they can; they have to wait. 62

Worry can never help you. It troubles your conscience and 75
distracts your attention from the work you are doing. Unless a real 89
emergency exists—and emergencies do come up—you must say to 101
your conscience, "Yes, that is important; but it must wait until this 115
more urgent matter has been disposed of. Then I will give it my full 129
attention." You will find that your conscience is easily satisfied if 143
you keep faith with it and really attend to each problem in its turn. 157

SI 1.32

8 In the traditional office, the job of typing was combined with 13
a number of other office chores. In a word processing system, how- 27
ever, correspondence secretaries and data entry clerks have no such 40
general duties. They are highly skilled people who produce typed 53
copy free of error. How do they do it? They use equipment that 66
records data on magnetic tape or disks. If they make an error, they 80
need only strike a correction key, and the error is erased. Then 93
they simply retype the correct word or number as though no mistake 106
had been made. In this way, they produce a tape or disk that is 119
free from error. Later the tape or disk is run through a printer 132
or automatic typewriter that can type the finished copy at speeds 145
no human could even approach. SI 1.42 150

1 | 2 | 3 | 4 | 5 | 6 | 7 | 8 | 9 | 10 | 11 | 12 | 13 |

Exercise 2

A copy of this letter is to be sent to Mrs. Marilyn Flowers.

January 10, 19– / Mr. Frederick Homer / Convention Chairperson / Massachusetts Cosmetology Association / 814 Clarendon Street / Boston, MA 02115 / Dear Mr. Homer / I am pleased to learn that your association has selected our establishment for its annual convention next year. ¶ You will find our prices, service, meeting rooms, banquet facilities, and guest accommodations the best in the Miami area. We are especially proud of the number of repeat convention bookings we have from our many satisfied guests. ¶ Mrs. Marilyn Flowers, our convention coordinator, will be available to answer your questions about the arrangements and to help insure the success of your convention. / Very truly yours (79 words)

Exercise 3

January 12, 19– / HOLD FOR ARRIVAL / Mr. and Mrs. Edward Tulbinski / Neptune Motel / 23 Ocean Boulevard / Virginia Beach, VA 23462 / Dear Mr. and Mrs. Tulbinski / One of our housekeepers turned in a baby blanket that was found in an unoccupied guest room today. In checking our records, we find that you were our last guests in that room. Since our records also show that you requested the use of a crib, we thought that the blanket probably belongs to you. ¶ If you find that you are, indeed, missing one of your baby's blankets, please telephone or write to my office and give us a description of the article. We will send the blanket to you as soon as we have positive identification. / Sincerely (98 words)

Project A-2 INSURANCE COMPANY

You are working at the Empire Insurance Company, 644 Weldon Avenue, Toledo, OH 43608, as a typist for Marilyn E. Knight, Vice-President, and John Dillon, Assistant Vice-President. Either Mrs. Knight or Mr. Dillon has given you the following letters to type. Mrs. Knight prefers modified-block style with mixed punctuation and no paragraph indention. She also wants her social title included in the signature blocks of her letters. Mr. Dillon prefers full block style with open punctuation.

Exercise 1

This letter was dictated by Mr. Dillon.

February 13, 19– / Mr. Joseph Hawthorne / 216 Rainbow Road / Youngstown, OH 44515 / Dear Sir / Subject: Updated Automobile Insurance Policy No. TRN 34681919 / The following important change in your policy has been made since your last premium notice. ¶ We have updated the information on how your car is used to include business travel of fifty miles a

(Continued on next page)

Timed Writings continued

9 There are no workers more sought after or more independent 13
than top-ranked, skilled mechanics. They are persons with a trade, 26
a practical skill. 30
If I were a young person of twenty with an ability to do 42
mechanical work, I would try first to get a job in a machine shop. 55
If I failed in that attempt, I would then try for placement as an 68
apprentice to an electrician. I would learn to work with my hands 81
because, in my opinion, the best-equipped person is the one who 94
combines book learning with hands-on experience. SI 1.42 103

10 You will find that more and more business firms are developing 13
speakers' bureaus and urging their people to speak to outside groups. 27
If you need a speaker, call several firms to determine who could 40
provide a speaker for a particular topic. 48
After making your selection, invite the speaker by telephone or 62
letter and include such information as the date, time and place, type 76
of speech or subject, length of speech, question and answer period, 89
type of class, size of class, and description of your class. 101
Once the speaker has accepted, begin the process of making him 114
or her feel welcome. Write another letter to express thanks and give 128
detailed information on how to get to your school; find out what 141
props or equipment are needed; and ask for a brief description of 154
the proposed talk and the speaker's background. SI 1.45 163

11 A watch needs attention if it is to give the best possible service. 14
Good watches are strong and will stand a certain amount of neglect 27
and abuse; but they will perform far better and last much longer if 40
they receive the care that they require. 48
A watch should be wound every day at about the same time. 60
It should be protected from jars and knocks, from dust and water. 73
Above all, it must never be dropped. It should be cleaned at regular 87
intervals, perhaps once a year; otherwise, its delicate parts may wear 101
away. Only an expert should ever be allowed to repair a fine watch; 115
an amateur handling it unskillfully may ruin it completely. 127
With proper care, a good watch may last a lifetime and may 140
even continue to give good service when handed down as an heir- 153
loom from parent to child. Many pocket watches made a century 165
ago still keep good time today. SI 1.40 171

1 | 2 | 3 | 4 | 5 | 6 | 7 | 8 | 9 | 10 | 11 | 12 | 13 |

Two Methods of Presenting a Completed Letter for Signature

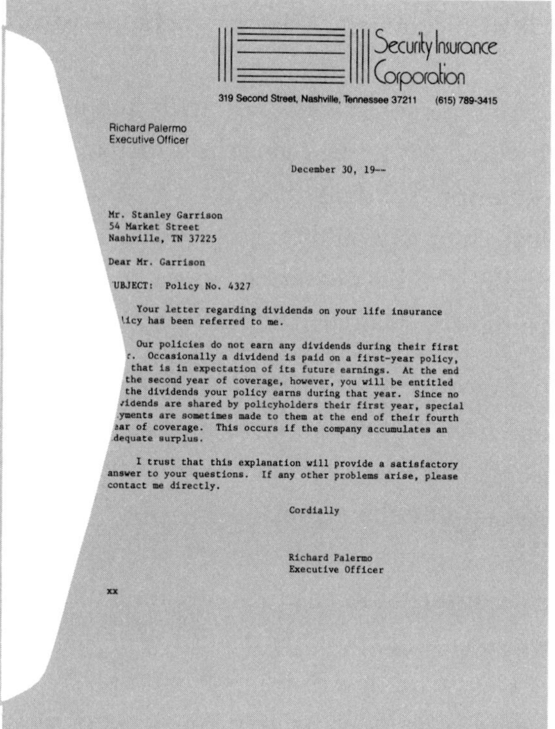

Security Insurance Corporation
319 Second Street, Nashville, Tennessee 37211 (615) 789-3415

Richard Palermo
Executive Officer

December 30, 19--

Mr. Stanley Garrison
54 Market Street
Nashville, TN 37225

Dear Mr. Garrison

UBJECT: Policy No. 4327

Your letter regarding dividends on your life insurance licy has been referred to me.

Our policies do not earn any dividends during their first r. Occasionally a dividend is paid on a first-year policy, that is in expectation of its future earnings. At the end the second year of coverage, however, you will be entitled the dividends your policy earns during that year. Since no vidends are shared by policyholders their first year, special yments are sometimes made to them at the end of their fourth ear of coverage. This occurs if the company accumulates an dequate surplus.

I trust that this explanation will provide a satisfactory answer to your questions. If any other problems arise, please contact me directly.

Cordially

Richard Palermo
Executive Officer

xx

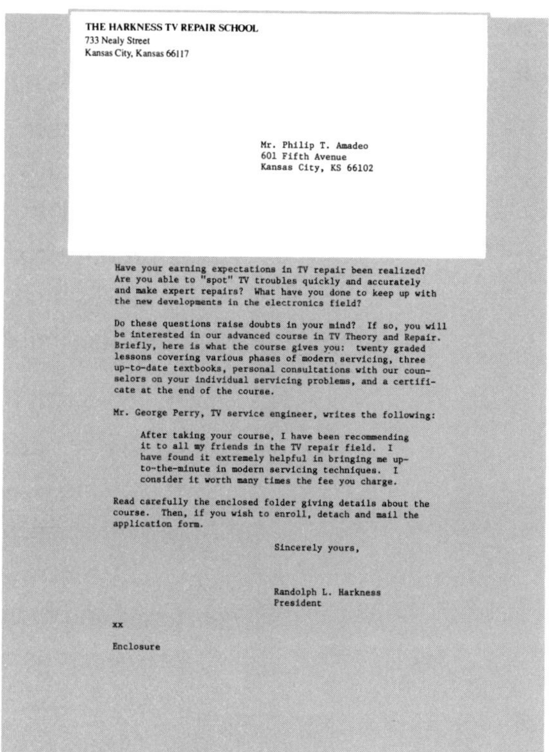

THE HARKNESS TV REPAIR SCHOOL
733 Nealy Street
Kansas City, Kansas 66117

Mr. Philip T. Amadeo
601 Fifth Avenue
Kansas City, KS 66102

Have your earning expectations in TV repair been realized? Are you able to "spot" TV troubles quickly and accurately and make expert repairs? What have you done to keep up with the new developments in the electronics field?

Do these questions raise doubts in your mind? If so, you will be interested in our advanced course in TV Theory and Repair. Briefly, here is what the course gives you: twenty graded lessons covering various phases of modern servicing, three up-to-date textbooks, personal consultations with our counselors on your individual servicing problems, and a certificate at the end of the course.

Mr. George Perry, TV service engineer, writes the following:

> After taking your course, I have been recommending it to all my friends in the TV repair field. I have found it extremely helpful in bringing me up-to-the-minute in modern servicing techniques. I consider it worth many times the fee you charge.

Read carefully the enclosed folder giving details about the course. Then, if you wish to enroll, detach and mail the application form.

Sincerely yours,

Randolph L. Harkness
President

xx

Enclosure

Project A-1 MOTOR INN

You are working for Frances S. Scully, Manager of the Good Neighbor Motor Inn, 212 Frasier Avenue, Miami, FL 33140. She gives you these letters to type for her. Ms. Scully prefers that her social title, Ms., be omitted from the signature block of each letter. Use a letter style of your choice, but use the same style for all letters in this project.

Exercise 1

January 9, 19– / League of Women Voters / 768 Magnolia Drive / Miami, FL 33144 / Attention Ms. Helen N. Hammond / Ladies / We wish to express our appreciation for your patronage in holding your annual business luncheon in our North Dining Room yesterday. We hope that you and your guests were completely pleased with the menu and the service. If you could spare a few minutes to write a note, we would appreciate your comments and criticisms. ¶As a service to the community, the inn is now making its Tower Room available, at a nominal charge, to civic groups that sponsor lectures and other educational programs. Coffee and other refreshments are included at no additional cost. We are now beginning to schedule events for February and March. Perhaps your group might want to book the facility for one of its upcoming programs. Please call me to discuss arrangements if you are interested. / Sincerely (130 words)

PART 2

PREPRODUCTION SKILLS

Topic 1 FIGURING SIDE MARGINS

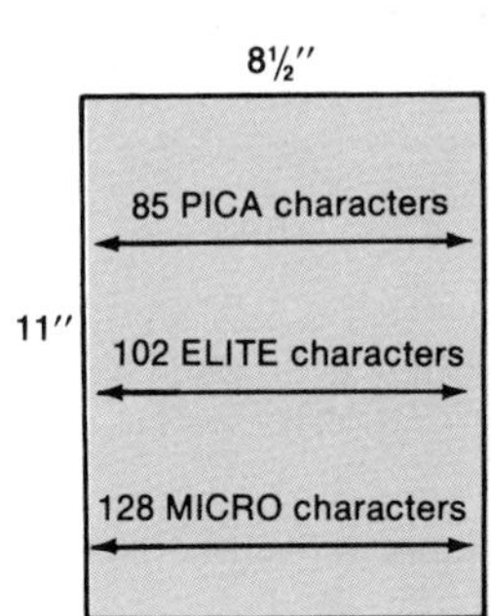

Two sizes of type are commonly found on typewriters. The larger size allows the typing of 10 characters to the horizontal inch. It is called *pica,* or sometimes 10-pitch. The smaller size allows the typing of 12 characters in the same space. It is called *elite,* or 12-pitch. Some newer model typewriters and word processing systems offer yet a third option. Called *micro,* it is an extremely small type that squeezes 15 characters into a horizontal inch. It is sometimes called 15-pitch.

Typing paper that is $8\frac{1}{2}$ inches wide has space for 85 pica, 102 elite, or $127\frac{1}{2}$ micro characters (rounded to 128). Dividing each of these numbers in half gives the center point of the horizontal scale—$42\frac{1}{2}$ for pica, 51 for elite, and $63\frac{3}{4}$ for micro. (For convenience, these numbers are usually rounded to 42, 50, and 64 respectively.)

Expressing Margins in Line Spaces

To figure margin settings so that the left and right margins will be equal, imagine a vertical line down the center of the page. One-half the typed material should be to the left of the line, one-half to the right. Using this principle, the margin stops for a 40-space line can be figured in this manner.

1. Divide the number of spaces in the line in half: $40 \div 2 = 20$. (This means there will be 20 characters on either side of the center point.)
2. Determine the left margin by subtracting 20 from the center point.

PICA	$42 - 20 = 22$	Left margin is 22.
ELITE	$50 - 20 = 30$	Left margin is 30.
MICRO	$64 - 20 = 44$	Left margin is 44.

3. Determine the right margin by adding 20 to the center point *plus* an additional 5. (The additional spaces are for ending words that exceed the ideal margin, not for beginning new ones. A good rule is to end lines within 3 to 6 spaces after hearing the end-of-line cue. That way you will avoid having to use the margin release.)

PICA	$42 + 20 + 5 = 67$	Right margin is 67.
ELITE	$50 + 20 + 5 = 75$	Right margin is 75.
MICRO	$64 + 20 + 5 = 89$	Right margin is 89.

SERIES A

TEMPA-TYPIST EMPLOYMENT AGENCY

Temporary employment agencies have become a widely used source of employment in recent years, especially for people who have valuable clerical skills. Applicants who register with a temporary employment agency are tested in its office; then they are sent out on jobs with different companies on a day-to-day (or even a week-to-week) basis. The temporary agency keeps a portion of the employee's hourly earnings as its fee for the service of finding the jobs. Such temporary employment assignments can provide a variety of work experience that is invaluable for the beginning office worker.

Each project in this series is set in a different office environment. You are to assume that after being tested and employed by the Tempa-Typist Agency, you are sent to work in each of these different offices. In each new office you must quickly learn the names of the people for whom you work and their preferences in letter style. Of course, it is assumed that all of your work must be mailable. This means that you must proofread carefully and make neat corrections of any errors before presenting finished work to your employers.

Directions for Series A

1. Type each letter accurately. If the company prefers a particular style, use it. Otherwise, use an acceptable style of your own choice.
2. The number of words in the body of each letter is given to help you determine good placement. As you progress through the projects, however, try to use eye judgment to set up some letters. With practice, this skill will come easily.
3. Always use your own reference initials. Type an enclosure notation when a reference is made to an enclosure within the body of the letter.
4. For each project in Series A, you need only prepare a copy of the first letter. In actual practice, of course, at least one copy of *each* letter would be prepared (for the files). In most instances, this copy would be a photocopy. For purposes of this series, however, a carbon copy may be substituted. An envelope should be typed for each letter.
5. When you have prepared a letter with a copy and an envelope, it should be submitted to your employer for signature in the following manner:
   a. Put the original (ribbon copy) on top, so that it can be easily read and signed.
   b. Place the copies underneath.
   c. Use the flap of the envelope to hold the package together. Place the envelope either at the top or along the side, as shown in the illustration on the next page.

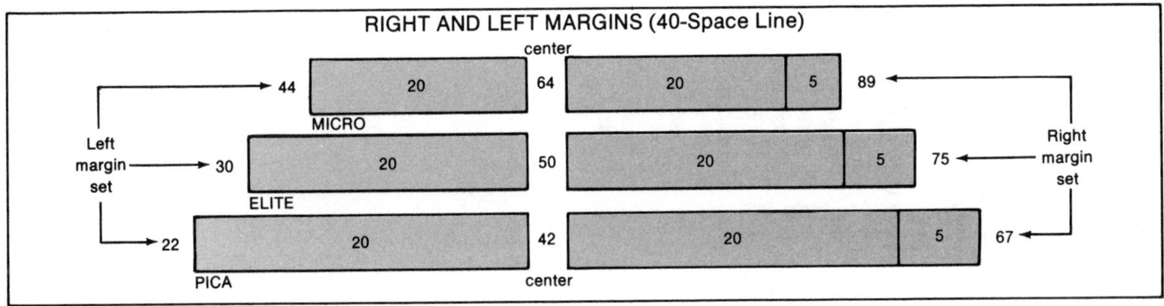

Expressing Margins in Inches

In some instances, the directions for setting margins may be expressed in inches. For example, you could be told to set 1-inch side margins for a report. If your machine had pica type, you would set your margins 10 spaces from either edge (because pica type has 10 characters to the inch). The actual margin settings would be 10 and 75 on a sheet of paper 8½ inches wide. If your machine had elite type, you would set your margins 12 spaces from either edge, or at 12 and 90. Finally, if you were using a micro type element (and your machine had the appropriate scale), you would set your margin stops 15 spaces in, or at 15 and 113.

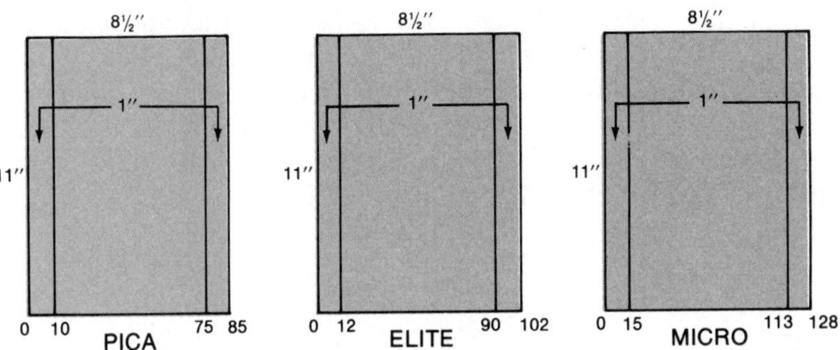

Exercise 1

Type the three paragraphs at the right, changing the margin settings for each. Type the first paragraph using a 40-space line, the second using a 50-space line, and the third using a 60-space line.

Full sheet. Single spacing. Begin on line 13.

The world's first large-scale computer, ENIAC, is now nearly 40 years old. Computers have come a long way, however, since 1946 when ENIAC made its debut. The changes that have taken place in terms of computer size, cost, and reliability are tremendous.

ENIAC, for example, weighed 30 tons and took up 15,000 square feet of space. Today computers sit on desktops and solve ordinary arithmetic problems 18 times faster than ENIAC. In the 1950s, a computer with a 180,000-bit capacity cost a quarter of a million dollars. Today desktop computers offer three times as much memory for less than $2,000.

Significant gains have also been made in recent years in the reliability of computer components. These improvements have led to fewer failures per component. They have also allowed computers to be placed in open environments with few restrictions on such things as temperature and humidity.

SECTION FOUR

Work Experience Simulations

The projects in this section offer exercises that integrate a variety of skills especially useful to students who are in the final stages of preparation for jobs as clerk-typists. The assignments simulate tasks typical of those performed on the job, giving students the opportunity to apply a wide range of skills, including English language skills. Work experience simulations will help students make the transition from classroom typing to on-the-job typing.

The projects are grouped into three *Series*, according to the complexity of the skills required to complete the assignments. In *Series A*, students work as clerk-typists for a temporary employment agency; their job is to type letters in a number of different business offices. *Series B* simulates the responsibilities given to clerk-typists who prepare business correspondence with supporting documents and enclosures. In *Series C*, students are expected to work more independently. They are given several different but related tasks and are expected to perform them without close supervision and direction.

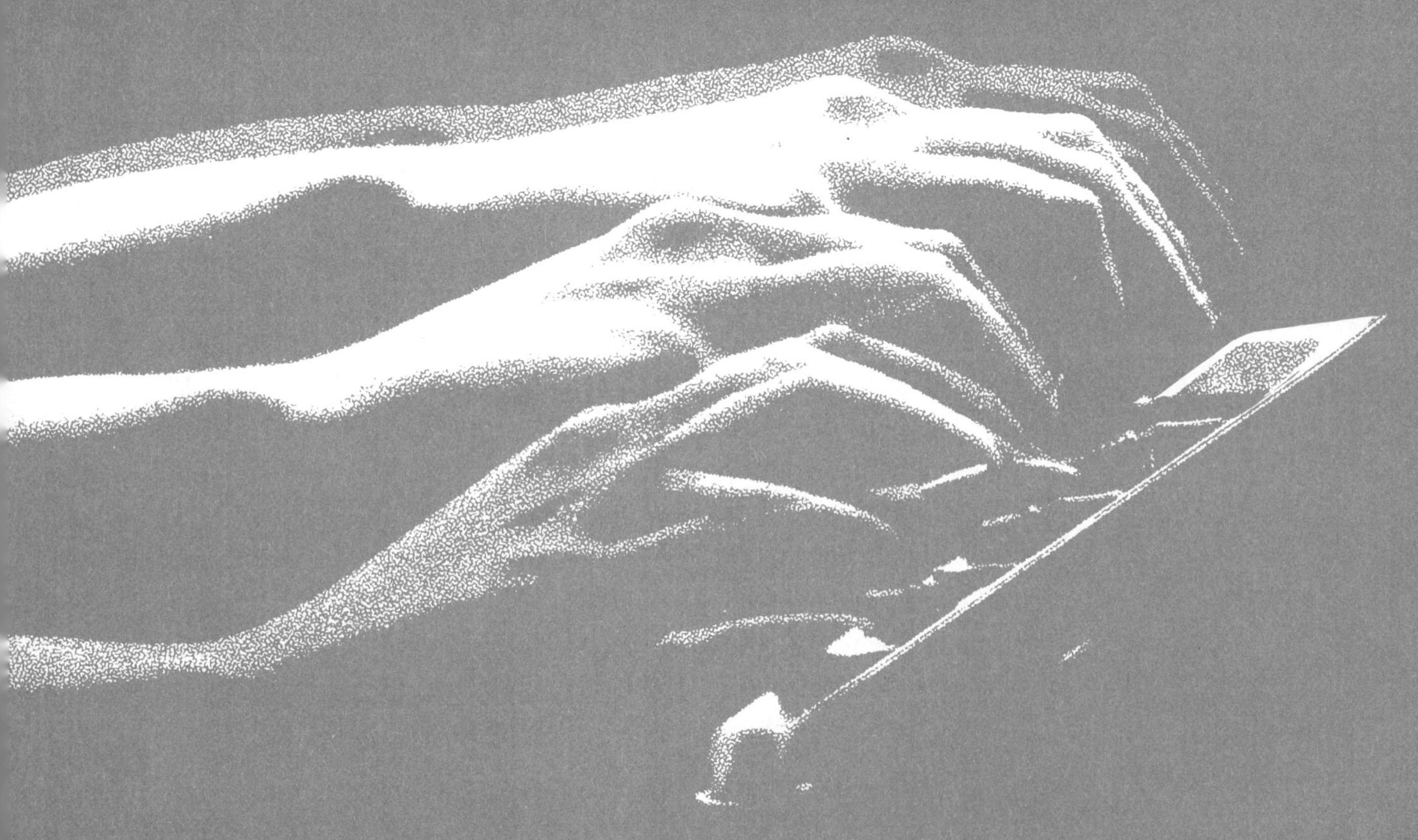

Topic 2 WORD DIVISION

Very seldom will you type from copy that can be reproduced exactly, line for line. Most typing is done from unarranged copy that requires the typist to decide, at the very least, when and where to end each line.

Even word processing systems do not relieve the operator of this responsibility. A processor's wordwrap feature merely ends each line with the last full word that will fit within the right margin (or sometimes with the first full word within the so-called hot zone—usually the last 5 to 7 spaces of the line). The result often is a document having some lines extremely long and others extremely short. Most word processing systems remedy this situation by allowing the operator to go back and manually eliminate the most glaring irregularities.

The only efficient way to accomplish this, of course, is to divide words at the ends of lines. Words cannot be divided just anywhere, however. Generally the only acceptable breaks are between syllables; but in typewriting, not even all syllable breaks are acceptable. You should follow these rules.

1. Do not divide one-syllable words.

   league — **through** — **walked,** *not* walk-
ed

2. Do not divide words having five or fewer letters.

   also, *not* al-
so — **diet,** *not* di-
et — **motor,** *not* mo-
tor

3. Do not divide words so that only the first letter appears on a line.

   around, *not* a-
round — **enough,** *not* e-
nough — **unique,** *not* u-
nique

4. Do not divide words so that only one or two letters are carried over to the next line.

   camper, *not* camp-
er;
but note: **camp-
ers** — **greatly,** *not* great-
ly;
but note: **great-
est** — **overdo,** *not* over-
do;
but note: **over-
due**

5. Whenever possible, divide words after a prefix or before a suffix.*

   bi-focals, *rather than* bifo-
cals — **vaca-tion,** *rather than* va-
cation — **read-able,** *rather than* reada-
ble

6. When the final consonant of a root word is doubled before adding a suffix, divide the word between the doubled letters *but only if* the suffix is sounded as a separate syllable.

   propel-ling, propel-lant, propel-ler
but note: **propelled,** *not* propel-
led — **quiz-zes, quiz-zing**
but note: **quizzed,** *not* quiz-
zed

7. When the root word to which a suffix is being added already ends in a double consonant, divide the word after the root and before the suffix.

   guess-able, *not* gues-
sable — **spill-age,** *not* spil-
lage — **stuff-ing,** *not* stuf-
fing

8. When a single vowel forms a syllable within a word, divide the word after that vowel.

   edu-cate, *not* ed-
ucate — **para-dox,** *not* par-
adox — **rati-fied,** *not* rat-
ified

* The suffixes *able* and *ible,* though sometimes shown as two syllables, should not be divided.

Topic 3 ELECTRONIC FILING

In Topic 1, you used index cards to set up files of data based on mailing lists, personnel records, and equipment inventories. Such manual card systems are more flexible than typed lists, but they do have limitations. Suppose, for example, in Exercise 5 (page 374), you wished to make a list of all equipment in the company's personnel department. Since your file is arranged alphabetically by item, simply finding all the cards for the personnel department would be a chore (the relevant card entry is three lines down). The process would require a painstaking card-by-card search of the entire file.

Fortunately there is an easier way. Software programs are now available that allow a word processing operator to store and manipulate such information electronically. The operator merely uses the keyboard and visual display to design a form containing spaces for all the information normally entered on an index card. Once designed, the form is stored and recalled whenever new entries need to be made (as, for example, when new equipment is acquired or old equipment moved or repaired).

The key advantage of such a system is accessibility. Keying information into the form amounts to putting it on file electronically. Once this is done, *all* of the data (not just the first, or key, word) is instantly accessible. An item can be found, for example, by date of purchase, supplier, serial number, or—as in the example above—by location (in the personnel department). The physical order in which the data is stored in no way limits or interferes with its access.

Electronic filing has another important advantage: it is extremely compact. Information is stored on diskettes that can hold 1,000 one-page forms. No bulky filing cabinets, boxes, or wheels are necessary.

Exercise 1
MANIPULATING DATA

If you have access to a word processor or microcomputer and filing software, design a blank form for the mailing list on page 371. Store the names in the order in which they appear. Then print out two lists—the first arranged in alphabetical order, the second arranged by ZIP Code.

Exercise 2
MANIPULATING DATA

If you have access to a word processor or microcomputer and filing software, design a blank form for the corporate customer list on page 372. Store the names in the order in which they appear. Then print out a list arranged by account number.

Exercise 3
MANIPULATING DATA

If you have access to a word processor or microcomputer and filing software, design a blank form for the personnel list on page 373. Store the names in the order in which they appear. Then print out two lists—the first of employees working in the accounting department, the second of employees who live in Cleveland.

Exercise 4
UPDATING A FILE

If you have access to a word processor or microcomputer and filing software, design a blank form for the equipment list on page 374. After you store the information in the list, update the file using the following information:

a. Copier in the advertising department moved to sales
b. Drum on the sales department duplicator replaced 8/19/—
c. Accounting department calculator replaced 8/27/— with a newer model from the same company (Serial No. 37-84099)
d. Service contract on transcriber switched to Triangle Office Repairs (476-2100)
e. Serial number on the sales department word processor found to be erroneously recorded; should be 3261A110

9. Divide words containing two separately sounded vowels in sequence between those two vowels.

abbrevi-ate, *not* abbre-viate | **medi-ocre,** *not* medio-cre | **recre-ation,** *not* rec-reation

10. Divide compound words spelled solid (without a hyphen) between the words making up the compound.

chair-person, *not* chairper-son | **inner-most,** *not* in-nermost | **there-after,** *not* thereaf-ter

11. Divide hyphenated compounds only at the hyphen.

in-service, *not* in-ser-vice | **self-control,** *not* self-con-trol | **tax-exempt,** *not* tax-ex-empt

12. Do not divide abbreviations and contractions.

NAACP, *not* NA-ACP | **M.D.,** *not* M.-D. | **wouldn't,** *not* would-n't

13. Do not divide numbers (including dates and addresses) and proper names unless absolutely necessary and then only at these points: (a) dates—between the day and year; (b) addresses—between the name of the street and the designation *street, road,* etc.; (c) names—between given names (including initials) and the surname.

May 8, 1984 *or* May 8, 1984 | **291 Oak Road** *or* 291 Oak Road | **Mary B. Ryan** *or* Mary B. Ryan

14. Do not divide the last word on more than two consecutive lines.

15. Do not divide the last word on a page.

Exercise 1

The words to the right have been divided into syllables. Assume that you have typed each word to the underscored letter. Use a hyphen to show the next acceptable word division point.

Half sheet. Left margin at 20. Tab stops at 32 and 49. Double spacing.

e nough	ex press ing	Ju ly 1986
stead y	tax pay er	self- re spect
looked	sep a rate	mul ti pur pose
USRDA	plan ning	ne ver the less
di al	ed i ble	grad u a tion
Ph. D.	pa per back	in ter state
un der	fol low- up	li a ble

Exercise 2

Assume that you have typed each of the phrases at the right to the underscored character. Find the next acceptable word break. Return at this point, hyphenating as necessary.

Full sheet. Left margin at 30. Type in one column. Single spacing for items; double spacing between items.

1. computer keyboard
2. computer keyboard
3. cooperative apartment
4. cooperative apartment
5. stretched into
6. stretched into
7. 1743 Del Rio Avenue
8. 1743 Del Rio Avenue
9. Linda Jo Arpel, D.D.S.
10. Linda Jo Arpel, D.D.S.
11. November 8, 1985
12. November 8, 1985
13. cross-country skiing
14. cross-country skiing
15. if I don't misspell
16. if I don't misspell

Exercise 7

STORAGE OF STANDARD PARAGRAPHS

You work in the credit office of Mickelmann's, a local department store chain. One of your duties is to handle routine correspondence relating to charge account applications. To simplify this task, a credit supervisor has written the standard paragraphs at the right. Prepare a master copy of this list, either for storage (if you have a word processor) or photocopying and distribution (if you lack such equipment).

MASTER REFERENCE FOR COMPOSITE CREDIT LETTERS

¶1 Thank you for requesting a charge account with Mickelmann's.

¶2 We have received and are currently considering your application for a charge account.

¶3 We are pleased to inform you that your application has been approved and that your new charge plate is enclosed.

¶4 We regret, however, that we cannot accommodate your credit needs at this time. In reaching this decision, we consulted the records of ABC Credit Bureau, 2355 Lahser Avenue, Dallas, TX 75241. If you wish to know the specific reasons for our decision, please contact our credit office within sixty days at 1-214-344-0400.

¶5 We expect to complete our processing within ten days. If you do not hear from us after this time, please contact our credit office at 1-214-344-0400.

¶6 We find, however, that there is insufficient information on your application form regarding your credit history. If you will therefore fill out and return the enclosed questionnaire, we should be able to complete our processing.

¶7 Initially your line of credit will be (*Stop Code*). After your account has been active for one year, you will have an opportunity to increase this amount.

¶8 If your charge plate should be lost or stolen, please notify us at once by calling our toll-free number, 1-800-325-1997.

¶9 We welcome you to our family of satisfied customers and look forward to serving you at any of our nine stores.

¶10 Should you wish to reapply for credit at a later date, we will be happy to consider your request.

Exercise 8

ASSEMBLY OF COMPOSITE LETTERS

Requests for credit letters routinely come to you on work requisition forms like the one at the right. Use this form and the paragraphs you stored (or keyboarded) in Exercise 7 to produce the requested letters.

Modified block style. Mixed punctuation. Note any enclosures.

WORK REQUISITION
Mickelmann's Department Store, Inc.

Originator Louise C. Ortiz, Credit Officer Date 9-17

Department Credit Extension 903

Item Credit letters (3) Input Stored [illegible] Priority Routine

Special Instructions Danita M. Bader, 351 West 19th St., Dallas, TX 75211
¶s 1,3,7 ($700 line of credit), 8,9

(2) Peter D'Amico, 99 Alameda St., Dallas, TX 75234 ¶s 1,4,10

(3) Mr. + Mrs. Irving W. Berg, 4796 Savage Court, Dallas, TX 75226 ¶s 2,6,1

Topic 3 TYPING FROM ROUGH-DRAFT COPY

Any copy that has been revised or edited is called a rough draft. Corrections to rough-draft copy are most often made using a standard set of symbols called *proofreaders' marks*. You should learn to recognize these symbols and use them yourself in correcting your own typewritten work. The most common proofreaders' marks are shown below and on the next page.

PROOFREADERS' MARKS

Symbol	*Meaning*	*Edited Copy*	*Corrected Copy*
	Delete, delete and substitute	a very short letters two a very short letters	very short letters two short letters
....	Stet (let original copy stand)	two short letters	two short letters
	Close up	in to	into
	Delete and close up	keyeboarding	keyboarding
	Transpose (letter, word)	Croix St. Hotle Croix St. Hotel	Croix St. Hotel St. Croix Hotel
≡	Capitalize (letter, word)	Stokes college Stokes College	Stokes College STOKES COLLEGE
/	Lowercase	the College	the college
	Spell out (number, abbreviation)	1 year one yr	one year one year
∧	Insert (letter, word, phrase)	the chid only the child	the child the only child
	Insert comma, semicolon	since then we since then we	since then, we since then; we
⊙ (:) (?)	Insert period, colon, question mark*	that day Monday that day Monday that day, Monday	that day. Monday that day: Monday that day. Monday?

* Circling a comma changes it to a period.

(Continued on next page)

Exercise 5

STORAGE OF STANDARD PARAGRAPHS

Your employer, Gulf Publications, wishes to use composite letters to reject unsolicited manuscripts sent to them for publication in their magazine. You are to prepare the master list of standard paragraphs to be used for this purpose. If you have word processing equipment, keyboard and store the paragraphs at the right. (Note the stop code that must be inserted for the article title/description at the end of ¶1.) If you do not have access to such equipment, simply type a master copy of the paragraphs for the office files. (Insert a 10-space blank at the end of ¶1.)

Standard Paragraphs for Unsolicited Manuscripts

¶1 Thank you for sending us your manuscript, (*Stop Code*).

¶2 As a result of marketing surveys that we have conducted, our editors feel that your subject matter—although interesting and imaginatively handled—will not appeal to our readership. We regret, therefore, that we are unable to consider your manuscript for publication.

¶3 Our policy in recent years has excluded poetry from the materials that we publish in our magazine. We regret, therefore, that we cannot consider your poems for publication. This decision is in no way related to the quality of your work. If you are serious about publication, we suggest that you seek out a publisher of one of the more prominent literary magazines.

¶4 We have reviewed your material carefully and find it both interesting and well written. The story, however, does not meet with our requirements for length and scope of coverage. To assist you in making the necessary revisions, our editors have made notes directly on your pages to indicate where they feel additional work is needed. We encourage you to prepare another draft and resubmit it to us for possible publication.

¶5 Thank you for giving us the opportunity to look at your material. The manuscript that you submitted for our consideration is being returned to you with this letter.

Exercise 6

ASSEMBLY OF COMPOSITE LETTERS

Using the list of standard paragraphs you stored (or keyboarded) in Exercise 5, prepare the letters described at the right. Complete paragraph 1; supply a complimentary closing; and include the name and title of Jerome S. Parker, Managing Editor, in the signature block.

Modified block style. Mixed punctuation. Use today's date. Note the enclosure.

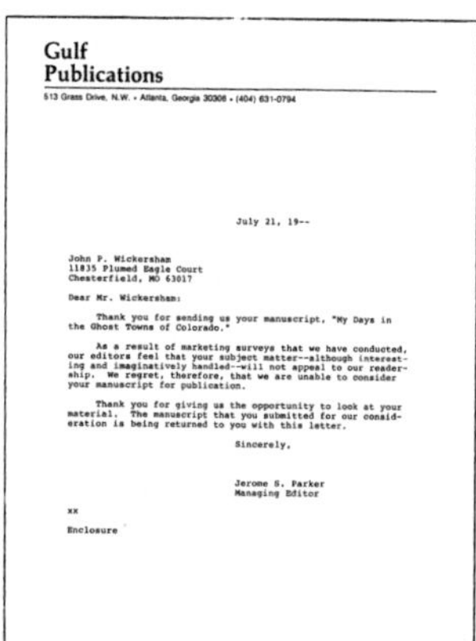

Gulf
Publications
513 Grass Drive, N.W. • Atlanta, Georgia 30308 • (404) 631-0794

July 21, 19--

John P. Wickersham
11835 Plumed Eagle Court
Chesterfield, MO 63017

Dear Mr. Wickersham:

Thank you for sending us your manuscript, "My Days in the Ghost Towns of Colorado."

As a result of marketing surveys that we have conducted, our editors feel that your subject matter--although interesting and imaginatively handled--will not appeal to our readership. We regret, therefore, that we are unable to consider your manuscript for publication.

Thank you for giving us the opportunity to look at your material. The manuscript that you submitted for our consideration is being returned to you with this letter.

Sincerely,

Jerome S. Parker
Managing Editor

xx

Enclosure

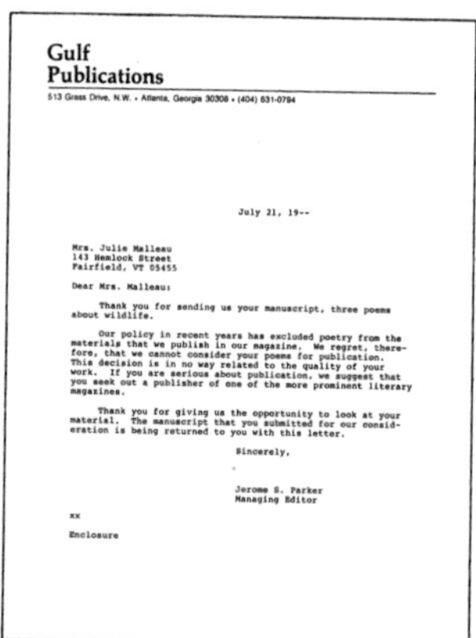

Gulf
Publications
513 Grass Drive, N.W. • Atlanta, Georgia 30308 • (404) 631-0794

July 21, 19--

Mrs. Julie Malleau
143 Hemlock Street
Fairfield, VT 05455

Dear Mrs. Malleau:

Thank you for sending us your manuscript, three poems about wildlife.

Our policy in recent years has excluded poetry from the materials that we publish in our magazine. We regret, therefore, that we cannot consider your poems for publication. This decision is in no way related to the quality of your work. If you are serious about publication, we suggest that you seek out a publisher of one of the more prominent literary magazines.

Thank you for giving us the opportunity to look at your material. The manuscript that you submitted for our consideration is being returned to you with this letter.

Sincerely,

Jerome S. Parker
Managing Editor

xx

Enclosure

1 A five-page article entitled "Nuclear Survival in the '80s" has been submitted for publication by Douglas Schiefer, 424 El Dorado Drive, San Marcos, TX 78666. Reply to him, using paragraphs 1, 4, and 5.

2 Send a reply to John P. Wickersham, 11835 Plumed Eagle Court, Chesterfield, MO 63017, who has submitted for publication an article entitled "My Days in the Ghost Towns of Colorado." Use paragraphs 1, 2, and 5.

3 Three poems about wildlife have been sent in by Mrs. Julie Malleau, 143 Hemlock Street, Fairfield, VT 05455. Send her a reply, using paragraphs 1, 3, and 5.

PROOFREADERS' MARKS (*continued*)

Symbol	*Meaning*	*Edited Copy*	*Corrected Copy*
# =	Insert space, hyphen	a job welldone a welldone job	a job well done a well-done job
↓ ↓↓	Insert apostrophe, quotation marks	childs play child's play	child's play "child's" play
]	Move right	$137.50 3.10]	$137.50 3.10
[	Move left	3 charts [4 tables	3 charts 4 tables
][	Center	]1985 [$3,417,283 4,008,921	1985 $3,417,283 4,008,921
	Move as shown	$244.75 14.82 2.93 137.00	$244.75 137.00 14.82 2.93
¶	Begin new paragraph	was set. ¶The next meeting we	was set. The next meet- ing we ....
	Run paragraphs together	was set. The next meet- ing we	was set. The next meeting we ....
___	Underscore; italics**	Type Right!	Type Right! *Type Right!*
~~	Boldface**	Type Right!	**Type Right!**
SS DS TS	Single-space, double-space, triple-space copy	I CAN KEYBOARD! Lloyd Bartholome DS Copyright 1985	I CAN KEYBOARD! Lloyd Bartholome Copyright 1985

** Possible only on machines with removable type elements.

Exercise 4

INSERTION OF VARIABLES

If you are using word processing equipment, recall from storage the letter you did in Exercise 3. Print out 10 copies, inserting the variables shown at the right and any others that are necessary. If you prepared a stencil in Exercise 3, use it to duplicate 10 mimeographed copies. Then type in the variable information on each. Date all letters May 16.

1 Ms. Irma Girard
241 Parks Avenue
South Lake Tahoe, CA 95705
Friday, May 23, 19—,
at 8:45 a.m.

2 Mr. Myron Volkstern
4212 Westland Way
South Lake Tahoe, CA 95705
Wednesday, June 4, 19—,
at 9:00 a.m.

3 Miss Marian Colson
54 Munroe Avenue
South Lake Tahoe, CA 95706
Monday, June 16, 19—,
at 11:15 a.m.

4 Ms. Stella Samuelson
503 Mercer Place
South Lake Tahoe, CA 95705
Friday, June 20, 19—,
at 11:30 a.m.

5 Ms. Delia DiGregorio
160 Center Park West
South Lake Tahoe, CA 95706
Tuesday, July 1, 19—,
at 9:00 a.m.

6 Mr. Brian Meredith
8011 Sherman Avenue
South Lake Tahoe, CA 95705
Thursday, July 10, 19—,
at 2:30 p.m.

7 Mrs. James Bronowski
1500 Waterside Plaza
South Lake Tahoe, CA 95706
Monday, July 14, 19—,
at 3:30 p.m.

8 Mr. George Smirnoff
121 Laurel Hill Terrace
South Lake Tahoe, CA 95705
Wednesday, July 23, 19—,
at 10:15 a.m.

9 Mr. John Falko
243 Third Avenue
South Lake Tahoe, CA 95705
Tuesday, July 22, 19—,
at 9:15 a.m.

10 Dr. Ellen Goodman
2401 Deckman Avenue
South Lake Tahoe, CA 95705
Friday, July 18, 19—,
at 4:00 p.m.

COMPOSITE LETTERS

A more complex form of repetitive typing is involved in the production of *composite letters.* Rather than being keyboarded and stored whole, these letters are compiled from *standard paragraphs.* The paragraphs are so written that they can be used in different combinations to produce different letters. This interchangeability accounts for the more colorful term *boilerplate* that is sometimes applied to such paragraphs or the documents that include them.

When doing a composite letter, the word processing operator first keys in variable information like the date, inside address, and salutation. Then he or she types in the numbers of the required standard paragraphs. Finally the remaining variables—the complimentary closing, signature block, reference line, and any special notations—are keyed in; and the letter is complete.

Clearly the most difficult part of this process is writing the standard paragraphs. These must be general enough to function in different contexts but not so general that they sound impersonal. They must also track—that is, move smoothly and logically from one thought to the next so that they form a unified document rather than a collection of disconnected thoughts. When these requirements are met, a composite letter can be as effective as one individually composed.

Exercise 1

Type the following sentences, making the corrections indicated.

Half sheet. Left margin at 15. Double spacing. Begin on line 6.

1. At the end the firm gave each ~~worker~~ a generuos bon us.
2. You willfind ti more conomical to let us buy the paperfor y ou
3. we never ~~no~~ the worth of water
4. I can not be you freind an your flatter too.
5. The botique is very expensive on Miller Ave.
6. Your party was a success ~~and~~ every body had a good time.
7. Please ~~e~~ the enclosed Form to us filled out and sign ed properly.
8. When i lent I had a friend but when I asked he was ~~not kind~~.
9. Manyschools now offer a place ment service to their students.

Exercise 2

Type the following sentences, making the corrections indicated.

Half sheet. Left margin at 15. Double spacing. Begin on line 6.

1. A well written telgeram must be breif but it must also beclear.
2. The GREATEST of faults I ~~should~~ say is to be consciuos of none.
3. These chairs made of fum oak an are strong and sturdy.
4. When I ~~do~~ well, I heard it ne ver when I did ill I herad it ever.
5. We are abound to for give ~~an~~ enemy, we arenot bound to trust
6. Merchandize must be shiped by ~~parcen~~post, by freight, or by ex press.
7. You ~~know~~ of course that we expect payment with in ~~too~~ days.
8. The even ing preformance began at 8 00 and ended at 10 54.
9. ~~Their~~ is no thing so powerfull as truth--and often Nothing so strangle.
10. The lamp is equpped with an Eye - Saver Shade (our own design).

SANGER HIGH SCHOOL

1285 Albion Drive, Salem, Oregon 97301
(503) 364-1452

Space down 15 times

V1 Date

V2 Name (address form)
V3 Number and street
V4 City, state, and ZIP

Dear V5 Name (salutation form)

Our annual Business Education Recognition Reception will be held on Friday, June 2, 19--, at 9 a.m. in the school auditorium. Among those being honored is your V6. (son/daughter, name)

At the reception, we recognize the achievements of those students who have excelled in business and distributive education classes. We also pay tribute to those students who have placed in state and regional business education competitions.

We cordially invite you to join us at the reception. In order to prepare properly, however, we need to know how many people will be attending. If you will be joining us, please fill out the bottom portion of this letter, and detach and return it to the school by the end of the week.

Sincerely

Carolyn E. Thomas
Department Chairperson
Business Education

xx/7.32.1

DS

Alternate underscores and spaces

\- -

DS

DETACH AND RETURN THIS PORTION

TS

Name of Parent ____

Name of Student ____

Yes, I will attend and bring _____ guests.

(*Shown in Elite Type*)

Model 35

Form Letter with Variables

Exercise 3

Type this rough-draft copy, making all the corrections indicated by the proofreaders' marks.

Half sheet. 1½-inch side margins. Double spacing. Begin on line 5.

SEASONS ARE IMPORTANT

TS

How do Sales vary by months and seasons? Statistic show little seasonla variation in some lines for exzmple, grocery stores and Drug store sales, too, are steady, expect for a great spurt before christmas. On the other hand, there is some variation in other lines of business. For example automobile dealers are very busier in the Spring months then they are in February and September. Fillling stations have their slackseason in Febrary; the climb steadily to a peak in july and then gradaually taper off. Ap parel stores, too have great variations.

--Small Business Series

Exercise 4

Type a copy of this memo, making all the corrections indicated by the proofreaders' marks. If boldface is not available as a function on your machine, use all capital letters instead.

Full sheet. 60-space line. Tab stop at 58 (elite) or 50 (pica). Double spacing. Begin on line 16.

To All Sales Representatives

Date: February 3, 19--

Subject: Sales Reports

TS

We have just sent you under separate cover an additional supply of our special Report Forms.

If your supply is insufficient, please let me know and additional copies will be sent you. A number of you are not making full use of these report forms. I want to point out again the vital necessity of making one of them for every call that you make. The information that we get from them is of great value to us in planing replacements and in developing new materials. I urge you, therefore to make out the reports regularly and get them to us as promptly as possible.

From: James T. Harris

Exercise 1

STORAGE OF FORM LETTER

Full sheet. 60-space line. Space as model.

Type the letter shown in Model 35. If you are using word processing equipment, refer to the operator's manual for the steps to follow in storing a letter with stop codes. If you do not have access to word processing equipment, prepare a mimeograph stencil instead. (If you use the second procedure, do not include the stop codes shown in the model; just leave the proper number of line spaces.)

Exercise 2

INSERTION OF VARIABLES

If you are using word processing equipment, recall from storage the letter you did in Exercise 1. Print out 10 copies, inserting the variables shown at the right. (*Note:* V1 is the date.) If you prepared a stencil in Exercise 1, use it to duplicate 10 mimeographed copies. Then type in the variable information on each.

1 (V2) Mr. and Mrs. Jerome Capretta
(V3) 3456 Union Road
(V4) Salem, OR 97302
(V5) Mr. and Mrs. Capretta
(V6) son, Joseph

2 (V2) Mr. and Mrs. Peter Gotfried
(V3) 702 St. Clair Avenue
(V4) Salem, OR 97303
(V5) Mr. and Mrs. Gotfried
(V6) son, Peter

3 (V2) Mr. and Mrs. Kenneth Lukas
(V3) 13415 Gainsboro Drive
(V4) Salem, OR 97301
(V5) Dear Mr. and Mrs. Lukas
(V6) daughter, Nancy

4 (V2) Mr. and Mrs. L. M. Mrozek
(V3) 2001 Reyburn Road
(V4) Salem, OR 97301
(V5) Mr. and Mrs. Mrozek
(V6) son, Larry

5 (V2) Mr. and Mrs. Wilbur Nelson
(V3) 13818 Emery Road
(V4) Salem, OR 97303
(V5) Mr. and Mrs. Nelson
(V6) daughter, Sandra

6 (V2) Mr. and Mrs. Paul Rice
(V3) 2813 Silverdale Avenue
(V4) Salem, OR 97301
(V5) Mr. and Mrs. Rice
(V6) son, Steven

7 (V2) Mr. and Mrs. Gerald Rocco
(V3) 4606 Chardon Road
(V4) Salem, OR 97302
(V5) Mr. and Mrs. Rocco
(V6) son, Vincent

8 (V2) Mr. and Mrs. Carl Swasey
(V3) 1011 Ashland Street
(V4) Salem, OR 97302
(V5) Mr. and Mrs. Swasey
(V6) daughter, Rose

9 (V2) Mr. and Mrs. Louis Ziska
(V3) 3958 Fairhill Drive
(V4) Salem, OR 97303
(V5) Mr. and Mrs. Ziska
(V6) daughter, Luella

10 (V2) Mr. and Mrs. Henry Smith
(V3) 1948 Kingston Avenue
(V4) Salem, OR 97303
(V5) Mr. and Mrs. Smith
(V6) daughter, Suzanne

Exercise 3

STORAGE OF FORM LETTER

Type the letter at the right, following the general instructions for Exercise 1 above. (*Note:* If you do not have word processing equipment, leave 43 blank spaces at the end of the first sentence.)

Full sheet. 50-space line. SS. 5-space paragraph indention. Date on line 16.

This letter is a confirmation of our appointment for (*Stop Code*). I'm looking forward to seeing you then. If, in the meantime, something arises to prevent your keeping the appointment, please call my office. My secretary will be glad to help you select an alternate meeting date. ¶ I'm enclosing with this letter a checklist of automobile insurance discounts and coverage options. Please review it, check those items that interest you, and return it to me. That way, when we meet, I'll have all the details you'll need to select the types of insurance and coverage limits you want. Cordially yours August DiVito General Agent AD:kp/9973 Enclosure

Exercise 5

Type the short paragraph at the right, making all the corrections indicated.

Half sheet. 2-inch side margins. Single spacing. Begin on line 11.

Problems of a Small Business

¶ Owners of small businesses has many problems. They must choose a location that customers can reach they must get to know the needs of their customer and win their good will. They must train their help. They must figure out store lay out and arrange window displays do their own record keeping and buying and attend to many management details that in a larger organization would be handled by several people.

Exercise 6

Type the rough-draft copy at the right, making all the corrections indicated by the proofreaders' marks.

Half-sheet. 1½-inch side margins. Double spacing. Begin on line 7.

¶ Students who consider dropping out of high school will be at a serious dis advantage when applying for better paying jobs with better chances for advancement.

However, a highschool diploma (or even a college degree) alone is not sufficient preparation. There are many jobs require technical special training work experience in a particular skill. Although the average college graduate deos earn more, many better jobs do not require college. A important part of career planing is to decide how much and what type of education to acquire after high school.

Exercise 6
FILE FOLDER LABELS

Type a label for each name in Exercise 4 (page 373). Type the name on the lower half of the label, 2 or 3 spaces from the left edge. Refer to the illustration on page 371 if necessary.

Exercise 7
MAILING LABELS FOR ENVELOPES

Type a label for each name and address in Exercise 3 (page 372). Center the name and address by estimating. *Use single spacing.*

Exercise 8
SHIPPING LABELS FOR PACKAGES

Type a shipping label for each of the first eight names and addresses in Exercise 2 (page 372). Center the name and address by estimating. Refer to the illustration on page 371 if necessary. *Use single spacing.*

Topic 2 REPETITIVE LETTERS

The cost of a business letter involves more than just the cost of stationery, postage, and time spent in typing. Someone must compose or dictate the letter; and that person's time could easily equal half, if not more, of the letter's total cost. To control such expenditures, many organizations use repetitive letters to handle correspondence of a routine nature.

Until recently, two duplicating processes were generally used to produce repetitive letters—mimeographing and offset printing. Today only the latter is used to any great extent in business. Mimeographing (like carbon paper) has largely been replaced by photocopying. The reason for the change is obvious: photocopying is faster and simpler. It does not require the careful, time-consuming preparation of a special master or stencil. All that is needed is one neat, reasonably clean original.

Photocopied documents, however, do have one key disadvantage. They look like what they are—copies. This can be a problem when, for business purposes, it is necessary to send an original (or something that could pass for an original) to a large number of people. To produce repetitive letters of this sort, many businesses use memory typewriters, text editors, microcomputers, or word processors. What all of these devices have in common is the capacity to store data electronically. Once stored, that data can be instantly recalled and printed out in quantity. The key term here is *printed out.* In other words, each document is individually typed—an original, not a copy.

Businesses most often employ repetitive letters to handle simple, recurring situations. For example, they use the letters to answer common inquiries, to follow up on payment requests, and to keep customers informed in the face of changes in the law. When typed individually, even such routine correspondence creates a favorable impression.

FORM LETTERS

A *form letter* is the simplest type of repetitive letter. As the name suggests, it is basically a form containing blanks to be filled in. These include (but are not limited to) the date, the inside address, and the salutation. In word processing terminology, these items are called *variables* because they are the only elements that change, or vary, each time the letter is used.

When keyboarding a form letter, the word processing operator puts in *stop codes* at points where variables are to be inserted. The codes can be symbols, letters, numbers, or any combination of these. Their effect when the document is recalled from storage is to stop the playback at those points to enable the operator to key in variable information.

Exercise 7

Type a correct copy of the following theme.

Full sheet. 1½-inch left margin; 1-inch right margin. Double spacing. Begin on line 11.

Taking It For Granted

All of us get many kinds of service which are necessary for our personal comfort and to which we give little thought; in fact, we generally take them as a matter of course. We turn on a faucet and are not surprised that water flows. In the morning, we open the front door and are not surprised the the dialy paper is ther. We leave home at a certain time to catch a bus or train to school or work, and we expect the bus or tain to be at our station at a given time. If we turn on a lightswitch and the light does not come on, we are surprised.

It is only when something goes wrong that we begin to think at all seriously about the services we usually take for granted. We expect our mail to be on time, our newspapers, our trains. When we pick up the phone and dia l a number, we know that our call will go through. We depend on these and many other services to transact our business and keep in order our affairs.

In turn we are expected to be at school or the office on time. If we are late to work, we may keep a customer or co-worker waiting. If we arrive late for a doctors appointment, other patients and the doctor may be inconvenince d. Being late wastes other people's time and delays work.

Many other people serve us and we serve many other people in this way. Throught our lives, we depend on people in all parts of the world to do their work, to do it well and to do it at the right time and they depend on us to do the same.

Exercise 5

OFFICE EQUIPMENT FILE

Type each of the eight items at the right on a 5″ × 3″ index card. Refer to Model 34 for correct placement of information. Arrange the cards in alphabetical order by item.

1 ITEM Calculator
DATE PURCHASED 5/3/—
DESCRIPTION Elec. Printing
SERIAL NO. 5A346701
LOCATION Payroll
NEW/USED New
PURCHASED FROM Olivetti Corp.
SERVICED BY Olivetti
PHONE 873-6051
SERVICE RECORD 9/2/—

2 ITEM Transcriber
DATE PURCHASED 12/1/—
DESCRIPTION Edisette
SERIAL NO. 35Z42110
LOCATION Personnel
NEW/USED New
PURCHASED FROM Roach-Reid Co.
SERVICED BY Dictating Equipment
PHONE 621-0733
SERVICE RECORD 4/22/—

3 ITEM Copier
DATE PURCHASED 7/15/—
DESCRIPTION 3M
SERIAL NO. 427850
LOCATION Advertising
NEW/USED New
PURCHASED FROM Business Products Sales
SERVICED BY Business Prod.
PHONE 741-6754
SERVICE RECORD 3/3/—

4 ITEM Calculator
DATE PURCHASED 7/21/—
DESCRIPTION Elec. Printing
SERIAL NO. 23-41377
LOCATION Accounting
NEW/USED New
PURCHASED FROM Data Devices Inc.
SERVICED BY Ohio Calc. Inc.
PHONE 252-4800
SERVICE RECORD 9/11/—; 11/2/—

5 ITEM Acc't. Mach.
DATE PURCHASED 6/10/—
DESCRIPTION NCR #36
SERIAL NO. 56Z4110
LOCATION Payroll
NEW/USED New
PURCHASED FROM NCR
SERVICED BY NCR
PHONE 881-9500
SERVICE RECORD 2/15/—; 4/30/—

6 ITEM Word Processor
DATE PURCHASED 10/3/—
DESCRIPTION Royal CTS
SERIAL NO. 3216A11
LOCATION Sales Dept.
NEW/USED New
PURCHASED FROM Royal Typewriter Co.
SERVICED BY Royal
PHONE 621-8100
SERVICE RECORD 12/3/—

7 ITEM Typewriter
DATE PURCHASED 2/4/—
DESCRIPTION IBM Cor. Sel.
SERIAL NO. 20-61772
LOCATION Personnel
NEW/USED New
PURCHASED FROM IBM
SERVICED BY IBM
PHONE 347-9870
SERVICE RECORD 4/3/—; 6/10/—

8 ITEM Duplicator
DATE PURCHASED 11/15/—
DESCRIPTION AB Dick
SERIAL NO. 467189
LOCATION Sales
NEW/USED Used
PURCHASED FROM Ace Office Equipment
SERVICED BY AB Dick
PHONE 775-1150
SERVICE RECORD 1/25/—

Topic 4 PROOFREADING TYPEWRITTEN COPY

To produce error-free work, you must proofread everything you keyboard. This is true even if you use a word processor equipped with dictionary software. Such equipment can detect errors but only certain kinds of errors. Were you to type the word *form* instead of the word *from,* for example, a word processor would not recognize the error since *form* also is a properly spelled English word.

How to Approach Proofreading

Proofreading involves more than giving your copy a quick review after removing it from the typewriter or printing it out. Proofreading well means reading slowly, carefully, and often repeatedly. Always remember these points. They will put you in the proper frame of mind to do a good job of proofreading.

1. *Try to read your own work as if it were typed by someone else.* We all tend to be more critical when reading someone else's work (finding errors is our "proof" that we've done a good job). We read our own work, however, with the opposite attitude, hoping to find no mistakes; and all too often that is exactly what we do find—whether it's true or not.
2. *Never assume that you will instinctively "feel" errors as you make them.* All mistakes do not automatically cause breaks in concentration or typing rhythm.
3. *Check reference materials as you proofread; don't guess.* Keep a dictionary or word division manual and a secretary's desk reference near at hand. Check any spelling, word division, or point of grammar of which you are unsure.

Proofreading Procedures

The second key to good proofreading is working systematically. To make detailed changes in the final page of a document when the first page may have to be redone is a waste of time. Mistakes of this nature can be avoided by observing a set procedure when proofreading. Follow these steps:

1. *Stop to proofread after each paragraph.* It is always easier to proofread a small rather than a large amount of copy. Be sure to include headings, inside addresses, complimentary closings, and similar document parts as "paragraphs."
2. *Read a first time for mechanical errors—typos, misspellings, incorrect word divisions, etc.* It is a good idea to read the copy from right to left (that is, backwards). This technique forces you to slow down and concentrate on each word. In this way, you see what is actually on the page. If you are using a typewriter, you might also find it helpful to use the paper bail to guide your eyes and keep your attention focused on a single line. If you are using a word processor and reading from a screen, you might use the cursor to keep your place.
3. *Read a second time for content errors.* Concentrate on meaning as you read. This will help you locate missing and/or substituted words and sentences.
4. *Store or put the document aside and reread it later a third time.* When proofreading technical, statistical, or legal material, you should make this third review an oral reading (that is, have another person follow your copy as you read aloud from the original).

Note that this procedure ensures that most changes will be made when they are easiest to make—before the copy is removed from the typewriter or (in the case of a word processor) before it is printed out. This, in turn, eliminates alignment problems and saves time that might otherwise be wasted on making multiple copies. The result is a document that is not only error-free but neatly done with a minimum expenditure of time and effort.

Exercise 4

PERSONNEL FILE

Type each of the 12 items at the right on a 5″ × 3″ index card. Use the employee's name as the key word. Arrange the cards in alphabetical order.

```
Koenig, Frank

4893 E. 97 Street
Cleveland, OH 44114

Phone:  (216) 621-2380

Position:  Receptionist

Dept.:  Personnel
```

	EMPLOYEE NAME	ADDRESS	
1	Koenig, Frank	4893 E. 97 Street Cleveland, OH 44114	Phone: (216) 621-2380 Position: Receptionist Department: Personnel
2	DiMarco, Tony	3440 Virginia Avenue Parma, OH 44134	Phone: (216) 842-3651 Position: Programmer Department: Data Processing
3	Michalski, Alicia	251 Plymouth Street Bedford, OH 44146	Phone: (216) 232-8461 Position: Buyer Department: Purchasing
4	Clough, Debbie	1555 Hilliard Avenue Lakewood, OH 44127	Phone: (216) 521-6628 Position: Coding Clerk Department: Accounting
5	Koch, Joan	224 Van Aken Boulevard Shaker Heights, OH 44125	Phone: (216) 921-4261 Position: Accountant Department: Accounting
6	Krall, Ed	5281 Sunset Drive Berea, OH 44128	Phone: (216) 234-7745 Position: Manager Department: Personnel
7	Hendricks, Paul	2919 Park Drive Cleveland, OH 44130	Phone: (216) 321-8950 Position: Accounts Payable Clerk Department: Accounting
8	Fanelli, Judith	2832 Mayfield Road Terrace Park, OH 45174	Phone: (216) 321-8950 Position: Salesperson Department: Sales
9	Chin, Jim Lee	679 Fernway Drive Cleveland, OH 44111	Phone: (216) 784-0652 Position: Salesperson Department: Sales
10	Chuppa, Stella	4650 Fleet Avenue Cleveland, OH 44118	Phone: (216) 561-1158 Position: Typist Department: Word Processing
11	Harris, Dennis	5281 Superior Avenue Euclid, OH 44122	Phone: (216) 884-2432 Position: Secretary Department: Personnel
12	Nemeth, Patricia	45 Erieview Towers Cleveland, OH 44111	Phone: (216) 696-2930 Position: Manager Department: Advertising

Exercise 1

Keyboard the sentences at the right exactly as they appear. Then turn to the continuation of the exercise at the top of the next page and proofread your sentences against the copy there.

Half sheet. 60-space line. Double spacing.

1. Mr. Rodgers is our new sale manger.
2. Any machine is only as acurate as teh operater.
3. Complete the from at your earliest conveneince.
4. I am now ready to re quest a immediate transfer.
5. The catalog will be print at the end of June.
6. Please send you resume to us as soon aspossible.
7. My Social Security number is 304-28-2176.
8. Todays meeting honored hight acadmic achievement.
9. The free of $50.00 will be due at the may session.
10. Flight 211 leaves today, at 7:30 a.m. for Brazil.

Exercise 2

Keyboard the paragraph at the right exactly as it appears. Then turn to the continuation of the exercise at the bottom of the next page and proofread your paragraph against the copy there.

Half sheet. 60-space line. Double spacing.

In this country we believe that the the opportunity to further ones education should not be limited by lack of fun s. The costof a postsecondary ed. is, however, prohibitive for families, so for this reason financial a has been made available to wupplement family resuorces when they prove inadequate. How do students apply for aid. Post-secondary institutions (public and private) provide Financial Aide Offices to help in filling most high schools. In most high schools, similar help is pro vided by guidance counselors.

Such assistence is necesary because the forms themselves are long, detailed, and complicated to fill out.

Exercise 3

Keyboard the columns at the right exactly as they appear. Then turn to page 64 and proofread your work against the copy there.

Left margin at 15; tab stops at 35 and 50. Double spacing.

Denver	Co	80291
Las Vegas	NM	89101
Mobile	FL	33193
Miami	AL	36601
Tapeka	KS	66601
Memphis	TE	31801
Baltimore	MA	21251
Milwaukee	Wi	53229
Boston	MA	02138
Salem	OR	97302
Pittsburg	PA	36608
Mobile	LA	17109

Exercise 2

MAILING LIST BY ZIP CODE

Type each of the 16 items at the right on a 5″ × 3″ index card. Use the ZIP Code as the key word. After you have typed the cards, arrange them in order by ZIP Code.

```
53401

Mr. Edward Ungers
631 Lincoln Drive
Racine, WI 53401
```

1	Mr. Edward Ungers	631 Lincoln Drive, Racine, WI 53401
2	Mr. Yung Koo	52 Morris Avenue, Fort Wayne, IN 46802
3	Miss Anna Yacobellis	8901 Harvard Avenue, Bay City, MI 48706
4	Ms. Carolyn Stinson	421 Case Avenue, Oak Park, IL 60301
5	Mrs. Lillian Wynn	782 E. 131 Street, Elkhart, IN 46514
6	Mr. Michael Voinovich	5600 Lander Road, Flint, MI 48502
7	Mr. Jerry Vittardi	344 Lake Shore Drive, Chicago, IL 60607
8	Ms. Doris Vollmer	831 Warner Building, Washington, DC 22013
9	Mr. George Trevino	475 Halle Drive, Corpus Christi, TX 78401
10	Mrs. Ralph Stokes	24 Regent Street, Macon, GA 31202
11	Mrs. Ruth Stein	1250 W. Clifton Drive, St. Louis, MO 63158
12	Mr. Tom Yamaha	3432 W. 25 Street, Cleveland, OH 44102
13	Ms. Linda Gray-Moin	753 Colorado Avenue, Palo Alto, CA 94306
14	Mr. R. H. Kocab	811 Ackley Street, Tulsa, OK 74111
15	Ms. Laura Donovan	3420 Lennox Drive, Albuquerque, NM 87101
16	Mr. Elvis Perkins	103 Triangle Court, Nashville, TN 38107

Exercise 3

CUSTOMER NAME FILE

Type each of the seven items at the right on a 5″ × 3″ index card. Refer to Model 34 for correct placement of information. Arrange the cards in alphabetical order.

	COMPANY	ADDRESS	CREDIT
1	Standard Construction Co.	14733 Grapeland Boulevard Floral Park, NY 11003 Account No. 76421	OK
2	Garcia Glass Works	26241 Pearl Road New Port Richey, FL 33552 Account No. 76502	Check Credit Manager
3	Hale Chisholm, Inc.	532 Bayfair Drive Passaic, NJ 07055 Account No. 76495	OK
4	Louis Gold & Sons	21 South Street Ellicott City, MD 21043 Account No. 76711	C.O.D. only
5	Oxford Iron Works	5521 Dalewood Road Allentown, PA 18105 Account No. 76552	OK
6	Matsumura Cycle Shop	2316 Bellfield Way San Jose, CA 95125 Account No. 76589	OK
7	Misch Electric, Inc.	4211 E. Sprague Street Huntsville, AL 35811 Account No. 76424	OK

Exercise 1 continued

Assume the sentences at the right are the original from which you typed your exercise copy. Read your sentences against the original and mark any errors you find on your copy. Use the proofreading techniques discussed on page 98 and the standard proofreaders' marks presented in the previous topic.

1. Mrs. Rogers is our new sales manager.
2. Any machine is only as accurate as the operator.
3. Complete the form at your earliest convenience.
4. I am not ready to request an immediate transfer.
5. The catalog will be printed at the end of July.
6. Please send us your resume as soon as possible.
7. My social security number is 340-28-2176.
8. Today's meeting honors high academic achievement.
9. The fee of $5.00 will be due at the May session.
10. Flight 211 leaves today at 7:30 p.m. for Basel.

Exercise 2 continued

Assume the handwritten copy at the right is the original from which you typed your exercise copy. Read your paragraph against the original material and mark any errors you find in your version. Use the proofreading techniques discussed on page 98 and the standard proofreaders' marks presented in the previous topic.

In this country, we believe that given the opportunity to further your education, you should not be limited by a lack of funds. The cost of postsecondary ed. is, however, prohibitive for most families, and so for this reason, financial aide has been made available to supplement family resources when they prove inadequate. How do students apply for aide? Postsecondary institutions (public and private) provide financial aide officers to help filling out financial aide application. In most high schools, similar help is provided by guidance personnel.

Such help is necessary because the forms themselves are long, detailed, and complicated to fill out.

LABELS

Names, subject titles, mailing addresses, and other items of information are often typed on labels. You may use these for identifying file folders or for addressing bulk mailings, parcels, or large envelopes.

The main difficulty labels present for the typist is their size. By themselves, most are too small to be inserted effectively in a typewriter. Therefore some way must be found to mount and hold them in place. One of the simplest ways to do this is to make a pocket by folding a sheet of typing paper, as shown at the left. The pocket, which should be taped at the edges to hold its shape, is inserted in the typewriter first. Then the label is placed in the pocket and the platen rolled back until the proper printing point is reached.

Adhesive-backed labels are simpler to prepare. These come in strips, rolls, or sheets. No mounting device is necessary because the label backing is usually large enough to wrap around the platen. Just be sure when detaching already typed labels to leave some excess backing (3 to 4 inches) in place.

Sheets of adhesive-backed labels are especially convenient for regular bulk mailings. Such labels are usually packaged with a special guide, a kind of stencil that shows the arrangement of the labels on their backing sheets. If a master mailing list is typed to the specifications on the guide, the placement of the addresses will conform exactly to the placement of the labels. Then, instead of being typed, the addresses can be photocopied. Sheets of labels are simply substituted for paper in the photocopier tray. This procedure saves an enormous amount of time and eliminates much tedious retyping.

Mailing or Shipping Label

Moss & Skelton
733 Sycamore Street, Yakima, Washington 98902

TO: Mrs. Lillian T. Sacks
466 Pearl Street
Yakima, WA 98902

Perforated File Folder Label

Hartford, Brazen & Company

Self-Adhesive File Folder Label

Johnson & Mapes, Inc.

Exercise 1

MAILING LIST BY NAME

Type each of the 12 names and addresses at the right on a 5″ × 3″ index card. Refer to Model 34 for correct placement of information. If cards are not available, cut paper to size. After you have typed the cards, arrange them in alphabetical order.

1	Mr. Gerald Jaworski	11810 Lake Avenue, Sherman Oaks, CA 91403
2	Mr. Jim Chan	1375 State Road, Garden City, NY 11530
3	Mr. Michael N. Adamo	24 Siebert Avenue, Freeport, NY 11520
4	Ms. Anne Balogh	137 Tivoli Avenue, Flint, MI 48506
5	Mr. Joseph Cawrse	842 S. Green Road, Shaker Heights, OH 44120
6	Mrs. Roslyn Evans	2425 North Park Drive, Chicago, IL 60628
7	Mr. Tito Cavalaro	883 E. 144 Street, Austin, TX 78757
8	Mrs. Linda Deitz	511 South Spring Street, Los Angeles, CA 90013
9	Ms. Katie James	9515 Buck Road, Wilmington, DE 19808
10	Ms. Violet Fressler	1684 Avalon Drive, St. Louis, MO 63110
11	Mr. Irwin Fishman	25 Van Ness Boulevard, San Francisco, CA 94106
12	Mr. Rupert Manley	48 Fernald Street, Columbus, OH 43204

Topic 5 CORRECTING ERRORS

Up to this point, you have not been required to correct your typing errors. This was done deliberately to minimize your concern, natural among beginning typists, about errors made on practice drills. As you start to produce typewritten material that others will read, however, you will need to produce copy that is error-free. This means not only correcting your errors but doing so in the neatest way possible.

If you are using word processing equipment or a self-correcting typewriter, correction of typing errors is greatly simplified. A word processor allows you to correct errors on the screen before your work is printed out on paper. A self-correcting typewriter has a special correction ribbon that "lifts off" errors as the machine backspaces. If you are not using equipment with built-in correction features like these, however, you will have to learn the most common methods of correcting errors manually. These include (a) erasing with a special typewriter eraser, (b) opaquing with either correction paper or correction fluid, and (c) covering an error with correction tape.

ERASING

When making corrections with a typewriter eraser, use the following procedure:

1. Turn the platen so that the paper is in a convenient position for erasing—with the error directly over the paper rest. (*Note:* To prevent the paper's slipping from the machine when a correction must be made at the bottom of a page, roll the paper *back* until the error can be brought around to the paper rest.)
2. If you are using a typebar machine, move the carriage to the right or the left so that eraser "crumbs" do not fall into the machine.
3. To protect the copy surrounding the error from smudging or flaking off, use an *eraser shield* if one is available. Position the shield so that the opening nearest in size to the error lies directly over it.
4. Apply the eraser lightly. Rub only in one direction to avoid making a hole in the paper or a noticeable mark.
5. When the error has been erased, return the carriage to the required printing point and type in the correction. Again, use a light touch. Otherwise the correction will appear darker than the surrounding copy.

OPAQUING

Using correction paper or correction fluid simplifies the above procedure and reduces the risk of damage to surrounding copy. The principle involved is just the opposite of erasing. The error is not rubbed away along with the top layer of paper. Rather it is covered over with an opaque, chalky substance that also provides a clean, new typing surface.

Correction Paper

When using correction paper to cover an error, follow this procedure:

1. Backspace until the letter or word to be corrected is at the printing point.
2. Insert the correction paper under the card holder, chalky side toward the paper.
3. Retype the incorrect character(s).
4. Remove the correction paper. The error should be completely covered with opaquing material. If not, reinsert the paper and retype the incorrect character(s) a second time.
5. Backspace to the proper point and type the correct word or letter over the error.

Correction Fluid

Correction fluid is an especially convenient way to cover errors. For this reason, it is easy to overuse. Remember, you should opaque out individual letters or words only. To make corrections of a line or more, you should normally retype the whole page.

When using correction fluid to cover an error, follow this procedure:

1. Turn the platen or move the carriage to the left or right so that the paper is in a convenient position for opaquing.
2. Apply a very small amount of correction fluid over the error and allow the fluid to dry.
3. Return to the required printing point and type in the correct copy.

PART 5 SPECIAL TYPING APPLICATIONS

Topic 1 INDEX CARDS AND LABELS

INDEX CARDS

Information of various kinds can be conveniently stored on index cards. Libraries, for example, keep card files of book titles, subject listings, and authors' names. You can check the card files to find a book you are looking for. In a business office, card files are kept so that information such as telephone numbers, addresses, and account numbers can be found quickly. Model 34, below, illustrates three different uses of index cards.

Index cards come in a variety of sizes: 5″ × 3″; 3″ × 2¼″; 6″ × 4″; and 8″ × 5″. The size used depends on the nature or amount of information to be recorded. After the information is put on the cards, they are either stored in open card file trays or drawers or mounted on a wheel. When stored, the cards are usually arranged alphabetically, with the key words clearly visible at the top.

Here are some general guidelines for typing on index cards:

1. Type the key words (a name or a number) on line 2, about 3 spaces from the left edge. It is acceptable either to use solid capitals or to capitalize only the first letter of each important word.
2. Leave 2 or 3 blank lines.
3. Type all other data in block style, aligning each new line with the key words.

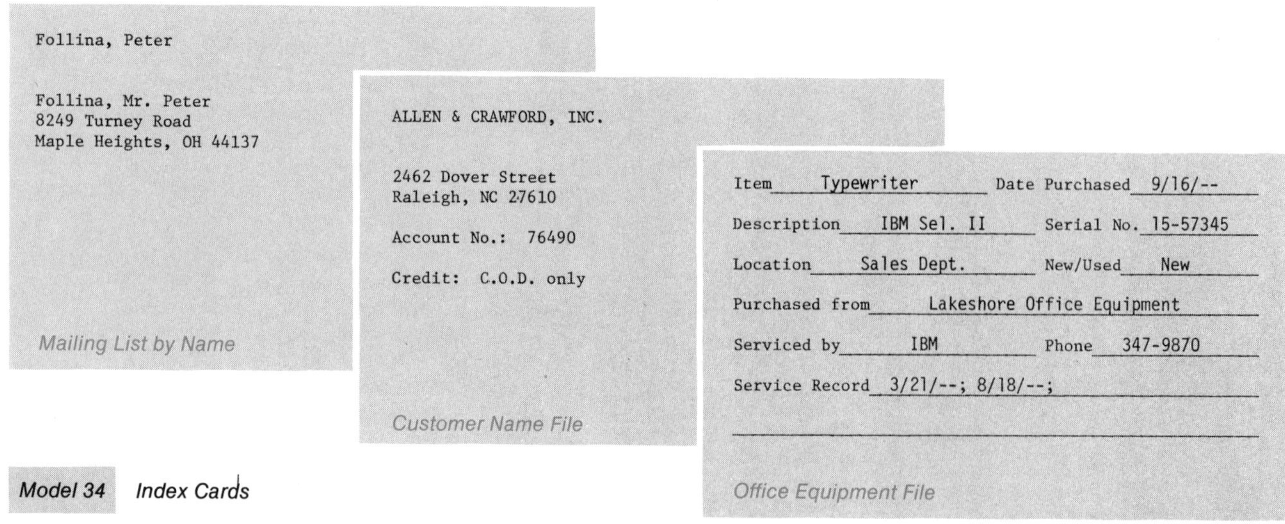

Follina, Peter
Follina, Mr. Peter
8249 Turney Road
Maple Heights, OH 44137
Mailing List by Name
ALLEN & CRAWFORD, INC.
2462 Dover Street
Raleigh, NC 27610
Account No.: 76490
Credit: C.O.D. only
Customer Name File
Item Typewriter Date Purchased 9/16/--
Description IBM Sel. II Serial No. 15-57345
Location Sales Dept. New/Used New
Purchased from Lakeshore Office Equipment
Serviced by IBM Phone 347-9870
Service Record 3/21/--; 8/18/--;
Office Equipment File

Model 34 *Index Cards*

USING CORRECTION TAPE

Correction tape also both covers an error and provides a new surface on which to type. With tape, however, the new surface is a separate strip of paper held to the page by an adhesive backing.

The main advantage of the tape method is that it can be used for extensive corrections (one, two, or even three lines). Its main disadvantage is that it cannot be used on correspondence—the tape covers the error but leaves the repair too obvious. Correction tape works well, however, for documents that will be photocopied for distribution.

When using correction tape to cover an error, follow this procedure:

1. Turn the platen so that the error is in a convenient position for correction—at least one or two lines above the card holder.
2. Remove a strip of correction tape from the roll. (The backing covering the adhesive should come away automatically.)
3. Mount the strip so that it covers the words or lines to be corrected. Tear off any excess tape and press the remainder firmly in place.
4. Return to the required printing point and type in the correct copy.

Exercise 1

Type the sentences at the right exactly as they appear. Then make the changes indicated using the correction method specified by your teacher.

Half sheet. Left margin at 15. Double spacing. Begin on line 7.

1. The boy said he had nine.
2. She felt better after the vacation.
3. Fourteen members were present.
4. Don has a high clerical attitude.
5. I bought a color tv for my bedroom.
6. Can I borrow your class lecture notes?
7. Their winter home is in Florida.

CORRECTIONS

1 Change *nine* to *none.*
2 Change *the* to *her.*
3 Change *fourteen* to *thirteen.*
4 Change *attitude* to *aptitude.*
5 Change *tv* to *TV.*
6 Change *Can* to *May.*
7 Change *Florida* to *Georgia.*

Exercise 2

Type the sentences at the right exactly as they appear. Then make the changes indicated using the correction method specified by your teacher.

Half sheet. Left margin at 15. Double spacing. Begin on line 7.

1. The salesman will attend a conference.
2. The stenographer mislaid her notebook.
3. The hurricane will probably travel west tonight.
4. They averaged a little over twenty miles an hour.
5. Dinner will be served in the Blue Room.
6. Tomorrow will be too late; we must see you today.
7. Many typists are needed to complete the work.
8. Helen was at first employed as a clerk.
9. The lecture will begin at half past seven.
10. The boy refused to give up before he finished.

CORRECTIONS

1 Change *salesman* to *salesmen.*
2 Change *her* to *his.*
3 Change *west* to *east.*
4 Change *twenty* to *thirty.*
5 Change *Dinner* to *Supper.*
6 Change *we* to *he.*
7 Change *Many* to *More.*
8 Change *Helen* to *Alice.*
9 Change *seven* to *eight.*
10 Change *boy* to *man.*

Exercise 6
Half sheet. SS body.

NATIONAL ANNUITY LIFE INSURANCE COMPANY

STATEMENT OF NET CURRENT ASSETS

June 30, 19—

CURRENT ASSETS:	
Common stocks at market value	$133,963,387
Cash in bank	3,011,849
Commercial paper	23,919,350
Receivable for securities sold	1,777,682
Investment income receivable	390,301
Total Current Assets	163,062,569
LESS CURRENT LIABILITIES:	
Payable for securities purchased	2,206,538
Balance due Company	27,576
Reserve for federal income tax	—
NET CURRENT ASSETS:	$160,828,455

Exercise 7
Full sheet. SS body.

R. R. KLINGER, INC.

CHANGES IN FINANCIAL POSITION

Year ended December, 31, 19—

Source of Funds	
Funds provided from operations	131,744
Dividends from investments	10,149
Net proceeds from issue of securities	
Long-term debt	73,499
Common shares	870
	216,262
Use of Funds	($000)
Additions to plant and equipment (net)	88,075
Arctic exploration project	5,495
Reduction of long-term debt	63,142
Purchase and cancellation of preferred shares	1,219
Purchase and cancellation of common shares	45,708
Other (net)	4,739
Increase in working capital during year	7,884
	216,262

Topic 6 REINSERTING PAPER

There are occasions when you must reinsert in your machine a page that was typed earlier. You may, for example, discover an error that you overlooked in proofreading; or your employer may wish you to stop the work you are doing and type some other material immediately. In either case, you will have to deal with the problem of aligning new type with old.

To learn how to recognize proper alignment, insert a sheet of paper in your machine and type this sentence:

```
I shall learn to reinsert my paper.
```

I shall learn to reinsert my paper.
B A

Notice how much space there is between the bottom of the typed line and the aligning scale (arrow A at the left). Memorize this spatial relationship. You will need to reproduce it when you reinsert the paper. Now look at the individual typed letters. Notice how the vertical marks on the aligning scale line up with the letters (arrow B at the left). On most typewriters, letters like *i*, *l*, or *m* are centered over the marks.

Now remove your paper from the machine and reinsert it. To find the correct alignment, follow these steps:

1. Turn the platen until the line of type appears just above the aligning scale. Then use the variable line spacer to reproduce the correct spatial relationship between the scale and the bottom of the typed characters.
2. Select a letter whose center is easy to locate and compare its position with the vertical marks on the scale. If necessary, use the paper release to move the paper slightly to the right or left to get the letter centered.
3. To check the accuracy of your alignment, set the ribbon control on stencil and type a period over the period in the practice sentence. If the two periods coincide, your paper is correctly aligned.
4. Reset the ribbon control and resume typing.

As a final test of your alignment, space twice after the period at the end of the practice sentence and add the following:

```
I shall learn today.
```

Exercise 1

Type the first sentence at the right. Then remove the paper from the machine and erase or cover the letters necessary for the correction indicated. Reinsert the paper, align, and type in the correction. Follow the same procedure for each of the other sentences.

Half sheet. Left margin at 15. Double spacing. Begin on line 6.

```
1. Late in the afternoon there was a hailstorm.
2. The men were promised a raise of 50 cents an hour.
3. A pupil in the fifth grade won the award.
4. We can prove that his signature is a forgery.
5. Few of the students passed the test.
6. I gave the beggar a nickel.
7. Sarah asked the guide for directions.
8. They wrote a short poem for the school assembly.
```

CORRECTIONS

1 Change *hail* to *snow*.
2 Change *50* to *65*.
3 Change *fifth* to *sixth*.
4 Change *his* to *the*.
5 Change *Few* to *All*.
6 Change *nickel* to *dollar*.
7 Change *Sarah* to *David*.
8 Change *poem* to *play*.

Exercise 4
Full sheet. DS body. Spread center second line of title.

GREAT LAKES PIPELINES

S U M M A R Y   B A L A N C E   S H E E T

(Thousands of U.S. Dollars)

ASSETS	1980	1979
Plant, property, and equipment	$362,317	$359,583
Less: accumulated depreciation	97,355	83,622
	264,962	275,961
Current assets	58,182	47,087
Deferred charges	262	392
	$323,406	$323,440
SHAREHOLDERS' EQUITY AND LIABILITIES		
Common stock	$ 50,000	$ 50,000
Retained earnings	27,761	30,079
First mortgage pipeline bonds	162,500	177,500
Current liabilities	67,972	60,284
Deferred credits	15,173	5,577
	$323,406	$323,440

Exercise 5
Full sheet. DS body.

TRANSWORLD INDUSTRIES
FINANCIAL HIGHLIGHTS

	1980	1979
Operations		
Operating revenues	1,870,325	1,499,137
Operating income	142,761	134,932
Net income	86,183	79,635
Funds provided from operations	131,744	127,161
Dividends declared		
Preferred shares	7,786	9,960
Common shares	37,922	31,414
Net income per common share		
Basic	$2.01	$1.92
Fully diluted	1.95	1.79
Dividends declared, per common share	.97	.85¾

Topic 7 CROWDING AND SPREADING

Sometimes after typing a line, or a whole assignment, you may find it necessary to substitute another word for one that you have typed. If the new word is not exactly the same length as the word already typed, some adjustment will have to be made.

CROWDING

If the new word is one letter longer than the space available, it can be *crowded* to fit. This is done by leaving less than the normal space before and after the new word. Practice crowding as follows:

```
We left him at the park.
We left them at the park.
```

1. On a half sheet, left margin at 15, type the following two sentences. Space exactly as shown.

```
We left him at the park.
          DS
We left      at the park.
```

2. To fit the word *them* in the space between the words *left* and *at* in the second sentence,

   If your machine has a half-space key:

   a. Move the printing point to the space following the word *left.*
   b. Depress *and hold down* the half-space key. The carriage will move forward a half space.
   c. Type the *t* in the word *them* as you hold down the half-space key. Release the half-space key.
   d. Continue depressing (and holding) the half-space key to type the remaining letters in the word *them.*

   If your machine does not have a half-space key:

   a. Position the printing point 2 spaces after the word *left.*
   b. Depress the backspace key slightly so that the carriage moves back a half space (manual machines only). If your machine is electric, move the carriage or element carrier back by hand.
   c. Hold the backspace key or element carrier steady and strike the letter *t.*
   d. Release the backspace key or element carrier.
   e. Repeat this operation for each of the remaining letters in the word *them.*

At the beginning or end of a word, it may be possible to insert an additional character (provided it takes up only a small amount of space) without erasing the entire word. Practice the technique of crowding without erasing as follows:

```
Today is Thursday May 17.
Today is Thursday, May 17.
```

1. Type the following sentence as shown here.

```
Today is Thursday May 17.
```

2. Add a comma after the word *Thursday.*

   If your machine has a half-space key:

   a. Bring the printing point to the position where the *y* in Thursday is typed.
   b. Depress and hold down the half-space key as you strike the comma.

   If your machine does not have a half-space key:

   a. Bring the printing point to the space after the *y* in *Thursday.*
   b. Depress the backspace key slightly and hold it steady as you strike the comma.

   (You can also push the carriage or element carrier back a half space manually instead of using the backspace key.)

SPREADING

If the word to be inserted is one letter shorter than the space available, the word is *spread* to fill the space. Practice spreading as follows:

1. On a half sheet, left margin at 15, type the two sentences at the top of the next page. Space exactly as shown.

Exercise 2

Full sheet, inserted with long (11-inch) side first. SS body.

MOLLY'S GIFT SHOPPE

Balance Sheet

December 31, 19—

ASSETS		LIABILITIES AND EQUITY	
Cash	$ 6,692	Notes Payable	$ 1,389
Notes Receivable	2,031	Accounts Payable	7,437
Accounts Receivable	9,930		
Merchandise Stock	26,500	Total Liabilities	8,826
Store Equipment	3,270		
Office Supplies	253	Owner's Equity	39,850
	$48,676		$48,676

Exercise 3

Full sheet. SS body.

FEDERAL FINANCE COMPANY

STATEMENT OF REVENUE AND EXPENSE

FOR THE YEAR 19—

Operating Revenues		
Interest on Loans	$192,000	
Interest and Dividends on Securities	313,000	
Fees and Commissions	123,000	
Total Operating Revenue		$628,000
Operating Expenses		
Salaries	244,000	
Taxes and Assessments	145,000	
All Other Current Expenses	153,000	
Total Operating Expenses		542,000
NET CURRENT EARNINGS		$ 86,000

The price is too high.
The cost is too high.

```
The price is too high.
             DS
The          is too high.
```

2. Fit the word *cost* in the space left in the second typing of the sentence. To avoid leaving an obvious extra letter space as you fit the shorter word *cost* into the empty space, proceed as follows:

If your machine has a half-space key:

a. Position the printing point 2 spaces after the word *The*.
b. Depress and hold down the half-space key.
c. Type the letter c in the word *cost*. Release the half-space key.
d. Continue depressing the half-space key and typing the remaining letters in the word *cost*.

If your machine does not have a half-space key:

a. Bring the printing point to the third space after the word *The*.
b. Depress the backspace key slightly so that the carriage moves back a half space (manual machines only). The same effect can be achieved on some machines by moving the carriage or element carrier back by hand instead of using the backspace key.
c. Hold the backspace key steady in this position as you strike the letter c in the word *cost*.
d. Release the backspace key.
e. Repeat the process for each of the remaining letters in the word *cost*.

Exercise 1

CROWDING

Type the first sentence at the right. Then make the correction indicated using the crowding technique. If your first attempt is not satisfactory, retype the sentence and try a second time before proceeding. Type and correct the remaining sentences in the same manner.

Full sheet. Left margin at 15. Double spacing. Begin on line 10.

```
1.  Jake's story was to fantastic for belief.
2.  I now work in the boys' clothing department.
3.  Our office is located on the fifth floor.
4.  I must buy four pears for a fruit salad.
5.  I recently started taking piano lessons.
```

CORRECTIONS

1 Change *to* to *too*.
2 Change *boys'* to *girls'*.
3 Change *fifth* to *fourth*.
4 Change *pears* to *apples*.
5 Change *piano* to *guitar*.

Exercise 2

SPREADING

Type the first sentence at the right. Then make the correction indicated using the spreading technique. If your first attempt is not satisfactory, retype the sentence and try a second time before proceeding. Type and correct the remaining sentences in the same manner.

Full sheet. Left margin at 15. Double spacing. Begin on line 10.

```
1.  The chorus is practicing for a concert.
2.  We would appreciate anything you do to help.
3.  The bowling tournament was held in June.
4.  Make a right turn into the school parking lot.
5.  You may want to add more sugar to the recipe.
```

CORRECTIONS

1 Change *chorus* to *choir*.
2 Change *would* to *will*.
3 Change *bowling* to *tennis*.
4 Change *right* to *left*.
5 Change *sugar* to *salt*.

Topic 4 FINANCIAL STATEMENTS

From time to time you may be asked to type tables that present financial data. Some of the more common forms of financial statements are presented in the exercises in this topic. Observe the following guidelines when typing them:

1. Center the statement title.
2. Single-space the body (although double spacing may be used occasionally). Leave a triple space before the side headings and a double space after them.
3. Align the amounts of money at the right.
4. Align the dollar signs at the top and bottom of a money column.
5. Double-space after a ruled line across a money column.
6. Type double rules under the final totals in a money column.
7. Single-space and indent runover lines.

Exercise 1

Full sheet. SS body.

THE ELITE LUGGAGE SHOP

BALANCE SHEET

December 31, 19--

TS

Assets:	
DS	
Cash	$ 1,450
Accounts receivable	2,750
Merchandise inventory	12,613
Store fixtures	2,500
Miscellaneous store supplies	58
Deposit on store lease	300
	DS
Total assets	$19,671
TS	
Liabilities and Capital:	
DS	
Accounts payable	$ 3,612
Notes payable	3,625
Unpaid expenses	74
	DS
Total liabilities	7,311
DS	
Capital	12,360
	DS
Total liabilities and capital	$19,671

Topic 8 CONSTRUCTING SYMBOLS

There are certain symbols for which there are no special keys on the standard keyboard. These symbols are made by using some of the characters on the standard keyboard in a special way or in a special combination. The table below lists some common examples. On some typewriters, the keyboard has additional keys for some of these symbols.

Symbol	*How Made*	*Illustration*
Ditto mark	Use quotation mark.	January 10 " 15
Fractions not on the keyboard	Use the slant to separate numerator and denominator. Leave a space before and after the fraction.	6 1/3 dozen
Minus sign	Use the hyphen. Leave a space before and after the minus sign.	6 - 4
Multiplication sign	Use the small *x*. Leave a space before and after the *x*. The *x* may also be used in measurements to indicate *by*.	3 x 2 a 9 x 12 rug
Division sign	Strike the hyphen, backspace, strike the colon. On some machines, it is necessary to turn the cylinder slightly before striking the colon in order to center the hyphen between the dots of the colon. Leave a space before and after the division sign.	6 ÷ 2
Degrees	Turn the cylinder down slightly by using the automatic line finder; strike small *o*.	32°
Feet and inches (after numbers)	Use apostrophe for feet and quotation marks for inches, each followed by a space.	6' 5" tall
Minutes and seconds (after numbers)	Use apostrophe for minutes and quotation marks for seconds, each followed by a space.	Time: 2' 4"
Exponents (raised numbers)	Turn the cylinder down slightly by using the automatic line finder; strike the desired key.	x^2
Chemical symbols (lowered numbers)	Turn the cylinder up slightly by using the automatic line finder; strike the desired key.	H_2O
Caret	Underscore the preceding letter; strike a slant in the space between words. Turn the cylinder down 1 line and center the word to be inserted over the slash.	good in/time
Brackets:		
Left bracket	Turn the cylinder back one line and strike the underscore. Turn the cylinder up one line; backspace twice; strike the slant. Backspace; strike the underscore.	/̲‾
Right bracket	Turn the cylinder back one line; strike the underscore. Turn the cylinder up one line; backspace; strike the slant. Backspace twice; strike the underscore.	‾/̲
Roman numerals	Use capital letters (occasionally small letters are used). Key to Roman numerals shown: 1, 5, 10, 50, 100, 500 and 1,000.	I V X L C D M

Exercise 7
LEADERS
Half sheet. DS body.

SAM LINDSAY NEW CAR SALES
SAMPLE FINANCE PLAN

Suggested retail price	$6,195.00
Down payment (20%)	1,239.00
Amount financed	4,956.00
Number of payments	60
Annual percentage rate	10.75%
Finance charge	1,472.18
Amount of each payment	107.14
Total amount of payments	6,428.18

Exercise 8
LEADERS
Full sheet. DS body. Pivot right column.

THE CHRISTMAS PLAY
CAST OF CHARACTERS

Mother	Sherrita Hightower
Father	Kevin Pugh
Raymond	Habib Sri
Hallie	Charles Griffin
Evie	Bridget Corley
Christmas Fairy	Connie Embry
Christmas Elves	Patrick Webb
	Michelle Labat
Santa	Wendell Green
Mrs. Claus	Allison Knight

---

Exercise 9
LEADERS
Full sheet. DS body.

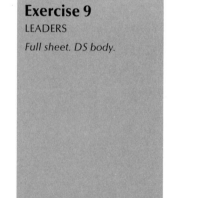

TABLE OF CONTENTS

Preface	ii
Chapter	
I. The Early Days of Opera	2
II. Italian Opera	40
III. French Opera	71
IV. Wagnerian Opera	94
V. Russian Opera	122
VI. American Opera	134
VII. Other Operas	155
VIII. Famous Opera Houses	187
IX. The Future of Opera	200
Bibliography	215
Index	233

Exercise 11

BOXED TABLE

Full sheet, inserted with long (11-inch) side first. DS body. SS runover lines. 6 spaces between columns.

PROJECT APOLLO
EARTH-TO-MOON MISSIONS

Date	Name of Mission	Significant Achievements	Hours on Moon	Mission Commander
July, 1969	Apollo 11	First manned landing; first moon walk	22	Neil Armstrong
Nov., 1969	Apollo 12	Second landing; two moon walks	31	Charles Conrad
Apr., 1970	Apollo 13	Explosion; mission aborted	—	James Lovell
Feb., 1971	Apollo 14	9-hour moon walk; craters inspected	33½	Alan Shepard
July, 1971	Apollo 15	Lunar roving vehicle; space walk	72	David Scott
Apr., 1972	Apollo 16	Lunar Rover inspects mountains and craters	72	John Young
Dec., 1972	Apollo 17	First scientist lands; last Apollo mission	75	Eugene Cernan

Topic 3 TABLES WITH PIVOTING AND LEADERS

PIVOTING

The appearance of some tables is improved if the items in the last column all align at the right. To accomplish this, a simple procedure known as *pivoting* is used. An example of a table with a pivoted right column is shown in the illustration below.

```
Favorite fruit                    Orange
Favorite color             Shocking Pink
Favorite sport               Ice Hockey
```

Follow these steps to pivot the right column of a table:

1. Type the first item in the left column (*Favorite fruit*).
2. Tab to the right margin. Then backspace once for every letter in the word to be typed (*O-r-a-n-g-e*).
3. Begin typing the word *Orange* where the backspacing ends.
4. Return to the left margin.

(Continued on next page)

Exercise 5

Type this ad for a free seminar. Center each line horizontally.

Half sheet. Double spacing except as noted. Begin on line 10.

Company Owners, Managers, Business Planners

Free Introductory Seminar

PROFIT SHARING AND BENEFITS PACKAGES

TS

Bachmann College of Business

Thursday, March 15, 19--

4–6 p.m.

TS

Space limited. For details call 255-2090.

SPREAD CENTERING

Directions:

Half sheet. Tab stop at center—42 (pica) or 50 (elite). Space down 4 lines between drills.

Sometimes it is desirable to stretch a centered word or phrase to cover a greater area. The process by which this is done is called *spread centering.* It involves leaving 1 space after each letter. The result has the same visual impact as using a larger or a boldface type.

To practice spread centering, keyboard the following drills.

Drill D

Spread center the word *GRADUATION.*

1. Tab to center.
2. Backspace once for *every* letter except the last one.

   G*space* R*space* A*space* D*space* U*space* . . . N
3. At the point where you stopped backspacing, lock the shift and type *GRADUATION* leaving 1 space after each letter.

Drill E

Spread center the phrase *MY BOOK REPORT.*

1. Tab to center.
2. Backspace once for every letter except the last one and for every space between words.
3. At the point where you stopped backspacing, lock the shift and type *MY BOOK REPORT* leaving 1 space after each letter and 3 spaces between words.

Exercise 6

COMPOSITION AT THE KEYBOARD

Type a birthday party invitation. Center each line horizontally. Spread center the second line.

Half sheet. Double spacing. Begin on line 8.

Exercise 7

Type the flyer at the right. Center each line horizontally; spread center the third line. Make the corrections indicated.

Full sheet. Triple spacing. Begin on line 20.

EXERCISE 6

You are invited to attend

A GALA BIRTHDAY PARTY

for

Your name

Sunday, *Your birthdate,* 19—

Your street address

Your city, state, and ZIP Code

8 p.m.

RSVP *your telephone number*

(on or before *date*)

EXERCISE 7

MARYSVILLE BOY SCOUTS

PRESENTS A

P A N C A K E   S U P P E R

All you can eat!

Friday, June 6, 19--

7 p.m.

Marysville Cafeteria

(392 Orville Avenue)

Tikcets, $1 (2)

Bringthe family!!

5. Type the second item in the left column (*Favorite color*).
6. Tab to the right margin. Then backspace once for every letter and space in the words to be typed (*S-h-o-c-k-i-n-g-space-P-i-n-k*).
7. Begin typing the words *Shocking Pink* where the backspacing ends. The words should end at exactly the same point where *Orange* ends.
8. Repeat this procedure with each additional line.

LEADERS

When there is a large space between two columns in a table, lines of alternating dots and spaces are sometimes used to connect the items in the columns. These are called *leaders* because they lead the eye across the space between the columns. The illustration below shows a table with leaders.

```
Main Floor . . . . . . . . . . . . . . . . . $15.00
Balcony, first 6 rows  . . . . . . . . . . .  12.50
Balcony, last 6 rows . . . . . . . . . . . .   9.00
```

Follow these steps to type leaders between two columns:

1. Type the first item in the left column (*Main Floor*). Space once after the last letter.
2. Check the printing point indicator to see whether it is on an even or odd number. Remember which it is. Begin typing periods, alternating with spaces, from this point.
3. End the line of leaders with either 1 or 2 spaces between the last period and the beginning of the second column.
4. Begin each succeeding line of leaders so that the first period is always typed on either an even or odd number to correspond with the first line.

Drill A

Type this table, following the instructions for pivoting given on page 361.

Half sheet. Double spacing. Margins at 15 and 50. Begin on line 7.

```
Favorite fruit                    Orange
Favorite color             Shocking Pink
Favorite sport                Ice Hockey
Favorite book                  Moby Dick
Favorite music           Country Western
```

Drill B

Space down 4 times after Drill A. Type this table following the instructions for leaders given above.

Half sheet. Double spacing. Margins at 10 and 65.

```
Main floor . . . . . . . . . . . . . . . . . . . $15.00
Balcony, first 6 rows  . . . . . . . . . . . . .  12.50
Balcony, last 6 rows . . . . . . . . . . . . . .   9.00
Second balcony . . . . . . . . . . . . . . . . .   7.50
Standing room  . . . . . . . . . . . . . . . . .   6.00
```

Exercise 1

PIVOTING

Half sheet. DS body. 10 spaces between columns.

RIVERVIEW CHARITIES, INC.

Board of Governors

January 1, 19— to December 31, 19—

President	Philip T. Westcott
Executive Director	Allan S. O'Hara
First Vice-President	Elvira A. Robertson
Second Vice-President	Herbert Hyde
Secretary	Andrew M. Trommer
Treasurer	Ida Modell

Drill C

Center horizontally the phrase *MY FAVORITE STORY.*

1. Tab to center.
2. Backspace once for every 2 letters or spaces:

   MY spaceF AV OR IT Espace ST OR (ignore Y)
3. At the point where you stopped backspacing, lock the shift and type *MY FAVORITE STORY* in solid capitals.

Exercise 1

Type this notice of a club meeting, centering each line horizontally.

Half sheet. Double spacing. Begin on line 11.

ATTENTION O.E.A. MEMBERS

Office Education Association

IMPORTANT MEETING

Wednesday, April 20, 19—

Room 121

Period 6

Carl Lever, Club Secretary

Exercise 2

Type a flyer announcing a dance club concert. Center each line horizontally.

Half sheet. Double spacing. Begin on line 10.

SPRING JAMBOREE

Featuring

Haley High-Steppers Dance Club

Mighty Meteors Marching Band

Saturday, May 7, 19--

Matinee, 1 p.m., $1

Evening Show, 8 p.m., $2

Haley High School Gymnasium

Exercise 3

Center horizontally the 15 lines at the right. You should be able to check your work easily!

Full sheet. Tab stop at center. Double spacing. Begin on line 7.

Exercise 4

COMPOSITION AT THE KEYBOARD

Center horizontally each item of information requested.

Full sheet. Tab stop at center. Double spacing. Begin on line 7.

EXERCISE 3

To

your

skills

now list

this skill

of centering

by backspacing

one for each two

items in every

line or name

or heading

or title

typing

like

so

EXERCISE 4

Your name

The name of your school

Your favorite class

Your career choice

Your three favorite records

(Center each on a separate line.)

Your favorite movie

The name of your local newspaper

Your favorite author

The oldest person in your family

Your favorite kind of ice cream

The city where you were born

A country you would like to visit

Your favorite TV show

The salary you would like to earn

Exercise 2
PIVOTING

Full sheet. DS body. 14 spaces between columns. Spread center secondary title. TS before and after divider lines.

OEA CLUB AWARDS ASSEMBLY

P R O G R A M

Greetings	Ms. Phyllis Edwards Chapter President

****

AWARDS	Mr. S. Dixon
Musical Selection	Men's Glee Club
CLUB RECOGNITIONS	Mrs. A. Hatton
Musical Selection	Women's Glee Club
OUTSTANDING BUSINESS STUDENT AWARD	Mr. E. Taneka

****

Closing Remarks	Ms. J. Reed Principal

Exercise 3
PIVOTING

Full sheet. DS body. SS indented lines. 14 spaces between columns.

METROPOLITAN HIGH SCHOOL

An Evening of Music

Sea Chanteys	Glee Club
Blow the Man Down	Henry Faber, Soloist
Codfish Chantey	Terry Plummer, Soloist
Rio Grande	Sylvan Corbin, Soloist
Instrumental Music	
Selections from Tales of Hoffmann	School Orchestra
Violin Solo—Estrellita	Helen R. Sebastian
Songs of the West	Madrigal Society
Poor Wayfaring Stranger	Marie Tesorio, Soloist
The Banks of the Sacramento	Ben Smith and Mike Fox, Duet
The Cowboy's Lament	Eric L. Westholm, Soloist
Contemporary Show Tunes	Mixed Ensemble
June is Bustin' Out All Over	
The Sound of Music	
Moon River	
Closing Song	
America the Beautiful	Laura Rolls and Audience

PART 3

HORIZONTAL AND VERTICAL CENTERING

Topic 1 HORIZONTAL CENTERING

Most typewritten material must be centered to be attractively formatted. Centering is achieved when all margins—left, right, top, and bottom—are approximately equal.

Electronic typewriters and word processing equipment center automatically. The operator merely depresses a special function key before typing the word or phrase to be centered. The machine then calculates the correct printing point at which to start typing and does so when the operator either returns (in the case of an electronic typewriter) or prints out a hard copy (in the case of a word processor).

If the equipment you are using does not have automatic centering, you should follow these steps to center a line horizontally.

Directions:
Half sheet. Tab stop at center—42 (pica) or 50 (elite). Space down 4 lines between drills.

1. Insert your paper with the left edge at 0 (zero) on the paper guide scale.
2. From the center of the paper, backspace once for every *two* letters or spaces in the line to be centered. (This will place half the typed characters on either side of the center point.) Do *not* backspace for an odd letter at the end of a line.
3. Begin typing at the point where you stopped backspacing.

To practice horizontal centering, keyboard the following drills.

Drill A

Center horizontally the word *SCHEDULE.*

1. Tab to center.
2. Spell out the word silently to yourself, backspacing once for every 2 letters.

   SC HE DU LE

3. At the point where you stopped backspacing, lock the shift and type *SCHEDULE* in solid capitals.

Drill B

Center horizontally the word *EDITORIAL.*

1. Tab to center.
2. Backspace once for every 2 letters, ignoring the odd letter left at the end.

   ED IT OR IA (ignore L)

3. At the point where you stopped backspacing, lock the shift and type *EDITORIAL* in solid capitals.

Exercise 4
PIVOTING

Full sheet. DS body. 10 spaces between columns.

INTERSCHOLASTIC FOOTBALL LINEUP

November 9, 19—

Greenleaf High School vs. Brady Academy

Greenleaf	Position	Brady
Lustman	Left end	Mansville
Gasperi	Left tackle	Barbieri
Brunswick	Left guard	McGuire
Leddington	Center	Sachs
Corby	Right end	Meadow
Tomlinson	Right tackle	Westerfield
Taylor	Right guard	Millet
Kearney	Quarterback	Grosvenor
Cunningham	Left halfback	Burgess
Zaner	Right halfback	Raleigh
Campbell	Fullback	McKeon

Exercise 5
PIVOTING

Full sheet. DS body. SS and indent runover lines. 20 spaces between columns.

ACKNOWLEDGMENTS		3
Honors Presentation		7
Coordinator	Mrs. Irma Vann	15
Class Sponsors	Mrs. Mary Kendziorski	27
	Anita Wessfann	33
	Theodore Lambret	40
Honors Presentation		44
Speaker	Wendy Laucks	51
Programs	Ms. Davida Cookes	60
Scholarships	Mrs. Irma Vann	68
Cover Design	Gerald Plett	75
Committee Chairperson	Ronald Drake	84

Exercise 6
LEADERS

Half sheet, inserted with short ($5\frac{1}{2}$-inch) side first. DS body. Pivot right column.

JOHN F. KENNEDY HIGH SCHOOL

SENIOR CLASS OFFICERS

19—

President .... Rudolph Carter
Vice President .... Kimberly Browning
Treasurer .... Inez Romero
Secretary .... Terry Mead

Exercise 1

Type the sentences at the right.

Full sheet. 70-space line. Single spacing; DS after each numbered item. Begin on line 13.

1. Week 1—The class average was 18 gross words, 14 net words.
   " 6— " " " " 24 " " , 20 " " .
   " 12— " " " " 31 " " , 24 " " .
   " 18— " " " " 33 " " , 29 " " .

2. The large box measured $8\frac{5}{8} \times 5 \times 4\frac{1}{8}$ inches. The small box measured $3 \times 2\frac{3}{4} \times 1\frac{7}{8}$ inches.

3. You should be able to give the answers to these examples without hesitation:
   $12 - 9 = ?$ $8 \times 7 = ?$ $42 \div 3 = ?$ $35 + 6 = ?$

4. One island was at 44° 18′ 22″ north latitude, the other at 16° 37′ 49″.

5. If x^2 equals 36 and x^3 equals 216, then x must equal 6.

6. He said, "I like all of you." [Applause.] He added, "In fact, I love you all!" [Laughter.]

7. The chemical symbol CO_2 represents carbon dioxide. The air you exhale contains CO_2.

8. The Magna Carta was dated MCCXV. What year was that?

9. The work/be completed today and sent/to Milwaukee. (must inserted above "work/"; airmail inserted above "sent/")

10. The lot is one hundred feet by forty feet (100′ × 40′).

11. The monument, when completed, will be 17′ 6″ high.

12. When the outdoor temperature is 30°C, is the weather cold or warm?

Exercise 2

CREATIVE KEYBOARDING

From this point on throughout this text, you will find advanced assignments like the one at the right. These exercises are designed to give you a chance to be creative. You should use your judgment and basic knowledge of keyboarding to complete them.

By carrying the technique of constructing symbols one step further—to superimposing characters—you can create dozens of unusual patterns. These can be employed for decorative purposes on greeting cards, announcements, reports, and similar documents.

1. Try these three examples:

   (**f** over **j**) (**6** over **0**) (**′** over =)

2. Now study these examples to see if you can discover the character combinations used to produce them. (*Hint:* Be sure to consider capital letters and symbols as possible components.) Experiment as necessary on your own machine.

3. Now try alternating any of the above combinations with punctuation marks and with each other. Examples:

In this way, create at least three distinctive patterns of your own.

BLOCK CENTERING

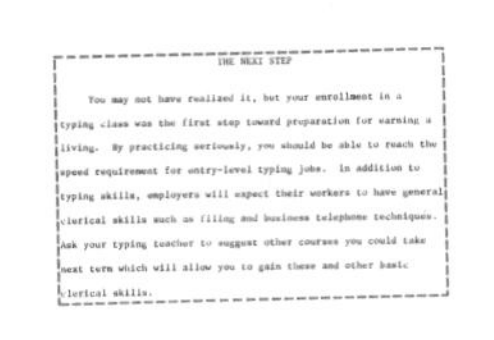

Instead of centering *each line,* it is sometimes desirable to center a *block* of material. Block centering is most often used to type lists of items line for line. Poems, for example, are usually block centered.

To center a block *horizontally,* begin by moving both margin stops to the ends of the typewriter scale. Then, find the longest line in the copy. From the center of the page, backspace once for every two letters or spaces in that line, and set the left margin at the point where you stopped backspacing. Every line in the paragraph or listing (except the paragraph lines with indentions) will start at the point where the left margin was set. If there is a title, center it horizontally over the block.

Exercise 8

Type the following paragraph and its title. Use block centering.

Half sheet. Double spacing. Begin on line 7.

THE NEXT STEP

TS

You may not have realized it, but your enrollment in a typing class was the first step toward preparation for earning a living. By practicing seriously, you should be able to reach the speed requirement for entry-level typing jobs. In addition to typing skills, employers will expect their workers to have general clerical skills such as filing and business telephone techniques. Ask your typing teacher to suggest other courses you could take next term that will allow you to gain these and other basic clerical skills.

Exercise 9

Type the following paragraph and its title. Use block centering.

Half sheet. Double spacing. Begin on line 7.

PROOFREADING TYPEWRITTEN COPY

TS

Businesses are now using specialized typewriters which can type copy at much faster rates than a typist using the traditional typewriter. Typewritten copy is produced in order to communicate, so businesses cannot afford to send communications containing errors. Remember that just as correctly keyboarded data is being processed at high speed, errors that were missed in proofreading are being processed at the same high speed. Accurate proofreading, then, is a skill you will want to develop as you prepare for a business career.

Exercise 8
BOXED TABLE
Half sheet. SS body. 7 spaces between columns.

CHARLES WEBBER & COMPANY
Years of Employment of Sales Staff

Years	Number	Percent
Over 20	3	7
15-20	3	7
10-15	6	14
5-10	12	29
0-5	18	43
Total	42	100

Exercise 9
BOXED TABLE
Half sheet. DS body. Block column headings.

POSTAGE AND HANDLING CHARGES

Total Material Ordered	Area 1	Area 2	Area 3	Area 4
$ 5.00 or less	$3.00	$3.00	$ 3.00	$ 3.00
$ 5.01 to $10.00	3.00	4.00	4.50	5.00
$10.01 to $25.00	4.50	5.50	7.00	8.50
$25.01 to $45.00	5.50	7.50	9.50	13.00
$45.01 to $75.00	7.00	9.50	12.50	19.50

Contact factory for charges on orders over $75.

Exercise 10
BOXED TABLE
Full sheet, inserted with long (11-inch) side first. DS body. SS runover lines. 5 spaces between columns.

COMPARISON OF REPROGRAPHIC PROCESSES

Process	Copies Expected	Error Correction	Copy Quality	Cost per Copy*
Carbon Paper	1–10	Difficult	Fair	Less than 1¢
Photocopier	1–200	Easy	Excellent	Up to 5¢
Fluid Duplicator	10–300	Difficult	Fair	Less than 1¢
Stencil Duplicator	50–1,000	Difficult	Good	Less than 1¢
Offset	200–5,000	Difficult	Excellent	Up to 4¢
Automatic Typewriter	1–10	Easy	Excellent	Less than 1¢
Facsimile Transmitter	1–5	Easy	Good	Up to 10¢

*Average cost of materials and equipment

Exercise 10
CREATIVE KEYBOARDING

Prepare a greeting card to give a friend or relative on a special occasion.

Front

1. Fold a half sheet of typing paper as shown at the left.
2. Open the sheet and insert the short (5½-inch) edge in the typewriter, turning the platen until the fold line is reached.
3. Set ½-inch side margins.
4. Keyboard a border for the front of the card as follows.
   a. Line 3: Keyboard a pattern of your choice for a full line. (See page 107 for some suggestions.)
   b. Lines 4–22: Repeat the pattern down the sides of the card. Keyboard in only the first and last spaces of each line.
   c. Line 23: Same as line 3.
5. Return to line 13 (the center of the card's front panel) and spread center the message *CONGRATULATIONS!* in all capital letters.
6. Remove the card from the machine.

Inside

7. Compose a message of 3 lines for the inside of the card.
8. Turn the card so that you are looking at the word *CONGRATULATIONS!* and reinsert the sheet in the machine, bordered portion first. Turn the platen until the fold line is reached.
9. Set a tab at the center point of the card.
10. Keyboard your message, beginning on line 11. Double space and center each line horizontally.
11. Remove your card from the machine and sign.

Topic 2 VERTICAL CENTERING

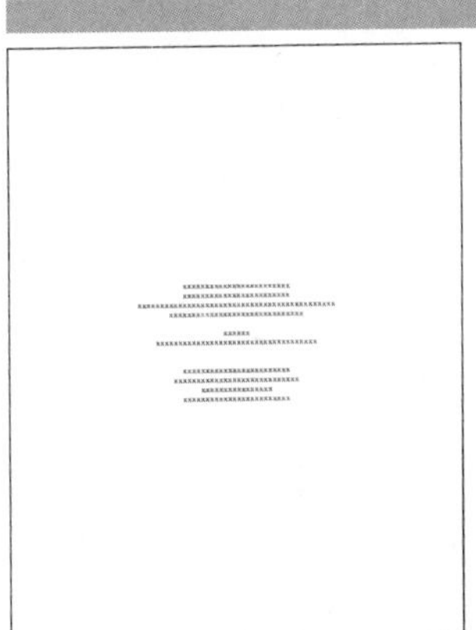

A piece of typewritten material looks more attractive if the typist starts typing far enough down on the paper so that there are equal amounts of blank space left at the top and bottom of the page. This is called *vertical centering*.

To center vertically, follow these steps:

1. Count the number of lines that will be used in typing the assignment. Include blank lines in your count. (Count 1 blank line when using double spacing and 2 blank lines when using triple spacing.)
2. Subtract the total lines counted from 66 (if you are using a full sheet) or from 33 (if you are using a half sheet). The remainder is the number of extra lines left to be divided between top and bottom margins.
3. Divide the remainder by 2 and add 1 to find the line on which to begin typing. Ignore fractions.

To practice the computations used in vertical centering, do the following drill.

Drill A

Compute the starting points for Exercises 1 and 2 on the following page.

EXERCISE 1

Lines available	= 33
Subtract lines in exercise	= 19
Lines remaining	= 14
Divide by 2	= 7
Add 1	= 8

Begin on line 8.

EXERCISE 2

Lines available	= 66
Subtract lines in exercise	= 20
Lines remaining	= 46
Divide by 2	= 23
Add 1	= 24

Begin on line 24.

Exercise 6

COMPOSITION
AT THE KEYBOARD

Expand the table at the right: (1) Divide the jobs listed into two categories—public sector (government) and private sector. (2) Visit the library and use the appropriate reference to make the two category lists equal in length. (3) In planning your table, add a subtitle; divide the body into two parts using internal subheadings and/or additional rules; alphabetize the entries in each category. (4) Type the expanded table on a full sheet; DS and center horizontally. (5) Write a paragraph-length caption summarizing the data in the table. Note any trends. TS and type this caption SS below the table.

PROJECTED GROWTH
OF SELECTED OCCUPATIONS

Job	Below Average	Average	Above Average
Bookkeeper	X		
Firefighter	X		
Postal Clerk	X		
Public Librarian	X		
Cashier			X
Computer Service Technician			X
Office Machine Repairer			X
Receptionist			X
Bank Teller		X	

Source: *Occupational Outlook Handbook.*

Model 33

Boxed Table

Extend horizontal rulings 2 pica or 3 elite spaces past sides of table.

MINIMUM SPEED REQUIREMENTS*
(5-Minute Typing Tests)

DS

School	DS Term 1 SS	Term 2	Term 3
	DS		
Cushman	20	30	35
Northbridge	25	35	45
Hanover	15	25	35
Maynor	20	30	40
Ovington	18	30	40
Stafford	25	40	50
Whitlock	22	35	45
	SS		

DS

*Gross words per minute

Exercise 7

BOXED TABLE

Half sheet. SS body. 5 spaces between columns.

Type the boxed table shown in Model 33 on this page. Remember to make a pencil mark to indicate the midpoint between the columns. Then, turn the paper sideways and use the underscore key to type the vertical rulings.

Exercise 1

Type the announcement at the right. Center each line horizontally and the whole announcement vertically.

Half sheet. Single spacing except as noted.

Exercise 2

Type the menu at the right. Center each line horizontally and the whole menu vertically.

Full sheet. Double spacing except as noted.

EXERCISE 1

BUSINESS TEACHERS' CLUB
DS
of
Metropolitan Detroit
TS
SPRING DINNER MEETING
TS
Friday, May 13, 19--
DS
6:00 p.m.
The LaSalle Room
DS
The Detroit Plaza Hotel
Renaissance Center
Detroit, Michigan
DS
RSVP 568-2001

EXERCISE 2

M E N U
TS
Assorted Relishes

Onion Soup

Salad Florentine

Roast Sirloin Tips of Beef

Baked Potato with Sour Cream

Seasoned Vegetables

Creme de Menthe Parfait

Bread and Butter

Coffee, Tea, Milk

Exercise 3

Type the membership roster at the right. Use block and vertical centering.

Half sheet. Double spacing except as noted.

Exercise 4

Type the course breakdown at the right. Use block and vertical centering.

Half sheet. Double spacing except as noted.

EXERCISE 3

PEP SQUAD MEMBERS
TS
Maria Portillo
Patrick Cotton
Sidney Johnson
Kristine Skorpen
Jeffrey Law
Patricia Brown
Penny Rosen
Kevin Johnson
Andrea Hill

EXERCISE 4

MEMORY TYPEWRITERS 201
Basic Skills Taught
TS
Storage and retrieval
Coding (dual-function keys)
Automatic formatting
Number alignment
Playback techniques
Log maintenance

Exercise 5

Type the attitude survey at the right. Use block and vertical centering.

Half sheet. Double spacing except as noted.

Should You Start Your Own Business?
TS
Are you willing to take moderate risks?
Do you have self-confidence?
Are you willing to work hard?
Can you set goals for yourself?
Are you open to new ideas?
Can you accept total responsibility?
Do you have special knowledge in some field?
Do you know how businesses operate?

Exercise 3

RULED TABLE

Full sheet. DS body. 8 spaces between columns.

SHAKESPEARE FESTIVAL AT HAYDEN PLAYHOUSE 8

Student Rates 11

Friday Evenings, February 3 through April 21, 19— 20

32

	Orchestra	Mezzanine	Balcony	
				38 50
Single Admission	$ 3.60	$ 2.40	$ 1.80	57
Any 4 Performances	13.00	8.50	6.50	65
Any 6 Performances	19.00	12.00	9.00	72
Any 8 Performances	25.00	15.00	11.50	80
Entire Series of 12	35.00	22.00	17.00	88

100

Exercise 4

RULED TABLE

Half sheet. SS body. 6 spaces between columns.

ADVENTURERS' ATHLETIC CLUB 6

AFTER-SCHOOL PICKUP SCHEDULE 12

April–May, 19— 16

30

TS Day	Schools	Starting Date	Ending Date	33 38
				52
Monday	McKenney, Lodge, Dow	4/17/—	5/08/—	61
Tuesday	St. Scholastica, St. Mary's	4/18/—	5/09/—	72
Wednesday	Holcomb, Burt, Cooke	4/19/—	5/10/—	82
Thursday	Emerson, Newton, Winship	4/20/—	5/11/—	92
Friday	Harding, Vetal, Dossin	4/21/—	5/12/—	101

115

Parents: Pack swimming and gym clothes. Buses will leave each school 129
between 3:30 and 4 p.m. and will return between 6 and 6:30 p.m. Please 144
arrange to meet your children at the main gate. 153

Exercise 5

RULED TABLE

Half sheet. SS body. 8 spaces between columns. DS before footnote.

ACCESSORY LIST FOR FLOOR POLISHER 7

GARWOOD MODEL NO. 100.7092 12

23

Key	Part No.	Part Name	
			28 39
93	691	Waxing and Scrubbing Brush	46
96	692	Polishing Brush	51
97	662	Rug Shampoo Brush	56
98	616	Buffing Pad	60
100	663	Wool Pad	63
107	666	Reconditioning Kit*	69

80

*Available on special order only 87

Exercise 6

Type this title page for a school report. Center the material vertically and each line horizontally.

Full sheet. Line spacing as shown.

A HISTORY OF THE VIOLIN

DS

(A Term Report)

Space down 13 times

Prepared by

DS

Jonathan H. James

Space down 13 times

Music Appreciation Class

SS

Mr. Adams, Instructor

SS

March 4, 19—

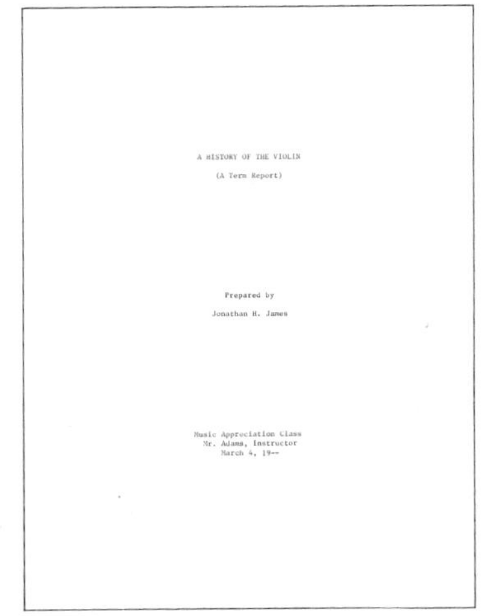

A HISTORY OF THE VIOLIN

(A Term Report)

Prepared by

Jonathan H. James

Music Appreciation Class

Mr. Adams, Instructor

March 4, 19--

Exercise 7

CREATIVE KEYBOARDING

Repeat Exercise 6, this time inserting a decorative border above and below the title. Center each line of the border horizontally. Be sure to adjust your vertical centering to compensate for the additional typed lines.

```
&&&&&&&&&&&&&&&&&&&&&&&

A HISTORY OF THE VIOLIN

    (A Term Report)

&&&&&&&&&&&&&&&&&&&&&&&
```

```
    ###############

#######################

A HISTORY OF THE VIOLIN

    (A Term Report)

#######################

    ###############
```

Topic 3 SPECIAL FORMATS

The exercises in this topic are designed to acquaint you with a number of special formats. These often combine vertical and horizontal centering with other formatting techniques. For this reason, they present a special keyboarding challenge. (*Note:* Each exercise shows only one solution to a given formatting problem. Others are possible.)

Exercise 1

SCRIPT WITH DIALOGUE

Full sheet. $1\frac{1}{2}$*-inch side margins. Tab stop 15 spaces in from left margin. Single spacing for dialogue but double spacing between character parts. Begin on line 11.*

ANSWERING THE BUSINESS TELEPHONE

TS

(Telephone rings)

BARNES: Murphy Products Company, Ms. Barnes.

BULKA: This is John Bulka of Uptown Radio. May I speak to Mrs. Murphy, please?

BARNES: I'm sorry, sir. Mrs. Murphy is out of the office. May I . . . (Mr. Bulka interrupts).

(Continued on next page)

RANDOLPH HIGH MOCK ELECTION RESULTS

Senior Class, 19--

DS

DS

Category	Male	Female
	SS	
	DS	
Best Dressed	Carl Ransom	Bernadine White
Class Clown	Kevin Smith	Regina Moreno
Class Cutie	Richard Roberts	Lesa Clarkston
Most Athletic	Carlos Ortego	Keisa Mitchell
Best Personality	Marathon Webb	Kim Vandenburg
Best Dancer	James Tammany	Kathy Murphy
	SS	

Model 32

Ruled Table

The line count given at the right will help you determine the vertical placement of the table.

Exercise 1

RULED TABLE

Half sheet. DS body. 6 spaces between columns.

Type a copy of the table shown in Model 32 above. Use the line count at the right when planning the vertical placement of the table. Follow the spacing guides given above and below horizontal rules.

Exercise 2

RULED TABLE

Half sheet. DS body. 6 spaces between columns.

FIRST FEDERAL SAVINGS AND LOAN

March 1, 19—

Type of Account	Minimum Amount	Annual Rate	Effective Annual Rate
8-year certificate	$1,000	8.00%	8.24%
6-year certificate	1,000	7.75%	7.98%
4-year certificate	1,000	7.50%	7.71%
2½-year certificate	1,000	6.75%	6.92%
1-year certificate	1,000	6.50%	6.66%
90-day certificate	500	5.75%	5.92%
Regular (Daily Interest)	None	5.25%	5.35%

Exercise 1 continued

BULKA: Do you know when she will return? She asked that I call and quote her some prices on CB radios. I would like to speak with her today.

BARNES: Well, I'm not certain of the time she will return, Mr. Bulka. May I take a message and relay the information to Mrs. Murphy?

BULKA: On second thought, maybe that would be better. I may not get a chance to call her later today.

BARNES: All right, sir.

BULKA: Please tell Mrs. Murphy that we have a special 40-channel radio at a 20 percent discount.

BARNES: Yes.

BULKA: There will be a small difference in price of only $20 between the 23-channel models and the new 40-channel models.

BARNES: (Repeats information to verify accuracy of the message.) I shall be glad to give this information to Mrs. Murphy. How is your name spelled, Mr. Bulka?

BULKA: B–U–L–K–A.

BARNES: Thank you. I shall give Mrs. Murphy your message.

BULKA: Thank you. Good-bye.

BARNES: You're welcome. Good-bye.

Exercise 2

MINUTES OF A MEETING

Full sheet. 1-inch side margins. Double spacing unless shown otherwise. Begin on line 7.

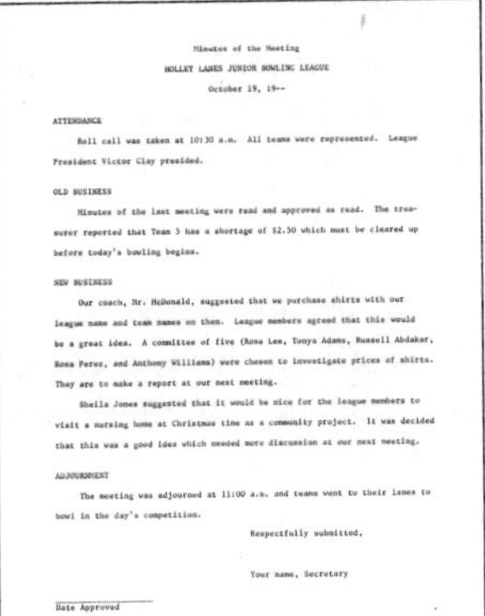

Minutes of the Meeting

HOLLEY LANES JUNIOR BOWLING LEAGUE

October 19, 19--

ATTENDANCE

Roll call was taken at 10:30 a.m. All teams were represented. League President Victor Clay presided.

OLD BUSINESS

Minutes of the last meeting were read and approved as read. The treasurer reported that Team 5 has a shortage of $2.50 which must be cleared up before today's bowling begins.

NEW BUSINESS

Our coach, Mr. McDonald, suggested that we purchase shirts with our league name and team names on them. League members agreed that this would be a great idea. A committee of five (Rose Lee, Tonya Adams, Russell Abdakar, Rosa Perez, and Anthony Williams) were chosen to investigate prices of shirts. They are to make a report at our next meeting.

Sheila Jones suggested that it would be nice for the league members to visit a nursing home at Christmas time as a community project. It was decided that this was a good idea which needed more discussion at our next meeting.

ADJOURNMENT

The meeting was adjourned at 11:00 a.m. and teams went to their lanes to bowl in the day's competition.

Respectfully submitted,

Your name, Secretary

Date Approved

Minutes of the Meeting

HOLLEY LANES JUNIOR BOWLING LEAGUE

October 19, 19—

TS

ATTENDANCE

Roll call was taken at 10:30 a.m. All teams were represented. League President Victor Clay presided.

TS

OLD BUSINESS

Minutes of the last meeting were read and approved as read. The treasurer reported that Team 5 has a shortage of $2.50, which must be cleared up before today's bowling begins.

TS

NEW BUSINESS

Our coach, Mr. McDonald, suggested that we purchase shirts with our league name and team names on them. League members agreed that

(Continued on next page)

Exercise 45
ROUGH DRAFT

Make all the corrections indicated by the proofreaders' marks. If necessary, review the symbols shown in the key on page 97.

Half sheet. DS body.

Crescent Furniture Exchange

Branch	Address	Telephone
Manhattan	321 East 108th Street	562-6011
Bronx	661 Front Street	927-1462
Jamaica	455 Hillside Avenue	866-3009
Newark	88 Grand Army Plaza	932-7411
Westchester	3211 Main Street	673-0776
Belleville	21732 Evans Rd.	735-2327
Cicero	9326 Telegraph Road	822-3670

Topic 2 TABLES WITH RULED LINES

Tables are often typed with horizontal and vertical rules. The rules can add to the attractiveness and clarity of the data presented.

RULED TABLES

Tables that have horizontal lines above and below the column headings and after the last line are called *ruled* tables. The underscore key is used to make these horizontal rulings. Look at Model 32 (page 357) and study the line spacing used before and after the typed lines in the table.

When a double horizontal rule is required, follow these steps:

1. Type the first line of the ruling in the usual way.
2. Before typing the second line, use the automatic line finder and turn the cylinder until the first typed line can be seen slightly above the aligning scale.
3. Type the second line and then release the automatic line finder to restore the paper to the original line of writing.

BOXED TABLES

Term 1 12345 Term 2	
20	30
25	35
15	25
20	30
18	30
25	40

Sometimes tables with horizontal lines also have vertical lines between the columns. These are called *boxed* tables. The horizontal lines in boxed tables extend $\frac{1}{4}$ inch past the sides of the tables. In planning a boxed tabulation, always leave an odd number of spaces between columns so that the vertical ruling can be placed at the midpoint between them. See Model 33, page 359, and the illustration at the left.

There is no special key on the standard keyboard for typing solid vertical lines. The vertical lines may be drawn with pen or pencil while the table is still in the typewriter. Most often, though, the vertical lines are added after the table is typed, complete with its horizontal rules. To do this, follow these steps:

1. Make a light pencil mark to indicate the placement of the vertical rules.
2. Remove the paper and reinsert it sideways.
3. Use the underscore key to type the vertical lines between the columns.

Exercise 2 continued

this would be a great idea. A committee of five (Rose Lee, Tonya Adams, Russell Abdakar, Rosa Perez, and Anthony Williams) will investigate prices and make a report at our next meeting.

Sheila Jones suggested that it would be nice for the league members to visit a nursing home at Christmas time as a community project. It was decided to pursue this idea at our next meeting.

TS

ADJOURNMENT

The meeting was adjourned at 11:00 a.m.

Respectfully submitted,

Space down 4 times

Your name, Secretary

____

Date Approved

Exercise 3

NEWS RELEASE

Full sheet. 1-inch side margins. Double spacing unless shown otherwise. Begin headings on line 13.

N E W S
R E L E A S E

SOUTHEASTERN HIGH SCHOOL
Chicago, Illinois
Release: Immediately
From: Roger Mills, Club Reporter
BOEC Club, Spartan Chapter

TS

BOEC SHINES AT STATE LEADERSHIP CONFERENCE

TS

SOUTHEASTERN HIGH, Chicago, May 14—With 38 members present, Southeastern had one of the largest delegations at the BOEC State Conference in Kankakee, Illinois, held May 7–9. With 104 financial members, Southeastern also has the largest total membership of all 89 BOEC chapters throughout the state of Illinois. In recognition of this, SE's delegation was allowed ten voting delegates—the highest number allocated any chapter.

On Friday evening at the conference, participants were entertained by BOEC members participating in the talent competition. Southeastern had two entrants in competition, April LaBeaux and Deborah Patrick.

The highlight of the two-day conference was the awards banquet held Saturday evening. At this banquet, winners of all competitions were announced. The Southeastern delegation was very proud when talent

(Continued on next page)

Exercise 43
ROUGH DRAFT

Make all the corrections indicated by the proofreaders' marks.

Half sheet. DS body. Block column headings. SS 2-line footnote.

REVISED TOUR RATES *

March 1, 19–

From	Canadian Rockies	Virgin Islands	Mexico
Boston	$480	$555	$575
Chicago	$450	570 500	[525
New York	475	545	570
Phila.	415	545	570
San Francisco St. Louis	425 450	590 510	500 490
Washington, D.C.	475	545	570

* Rates include all charges for air transportation fares, hotels accommodations and sight seeing.

Exercise 44
ROUGH DRAFT

Make all the corrections indicated by the proofreaders' marks.

Full sheet. DS body.

INDOOR PLANT DISTRIBUTORS

Retail price list

Name of Plant	Pot Size (inches)	Height (in feet)	Our Price
Croton	10	3	$17.95
Ficus Benjaminia	10	3½	15.95
Draceana Marginata	10	3½	17.95
Pilodendron Selloum	10	3	14.95
Areca palm	10	4	14.95
Schefflera	14 10	5	25.00 17.50
[Schefflera	17	12 11	75.00
Terrdium Plants	3	¼	.50
False Arelia	14 10	5	27.50 19.95
Ficus Benjamina	14	6	38.50

Exercise 3 continued

competition winners were announced because April LaBeaux had danced off with first-place honors.

Southeastern was even more elated when Shelly Thornwell was elected as the BOEC State Treasurer for the coming year. BOEC members are already looking forward to next year's state conference.

Exercise 4

MEMORANDUM

Half sheet. 6-inch line. Double-space heading; single-space body. Begin on line 7.

TO:	Graduating Seniors	DATE:	May 2, 19--
FROM:	H. Key, Sponsor	SUBJECT:	Caps and Gowns

TS

The Evans Rental Company will have a representative in our school auditorium on March 23 from 8 a.m. to 1:30 p.m. Measurements for caps and gowns will be taken at that time. Come prepared to pay a deposit of $2.50 when you are measured. Wear the height of shoes that you intend to wear at the graduation ceremony. An appointment is not necessary. You may go to the auditorium only before school, during your lunch period, or during a study period.

Your initials

Exercise 5

AGENDA

Full sheet. 5-inch line. Space heading as shown. Single spacing for items, double spacing between except as noted. Begin on line 22.

SEVENTH ANNUAL MIDWEST INVESTORS' FAIR

SS

National Investment Club Association

DS

Farren Court Hotel

SS

April 11, 19--

TS

9:45 a.m.	Registration/Breakfast (Geary Room)	
10:30 a.m.	Speaker:	Daniel G. Clarkson, President Mogul, Inc.
11:30 a.m.	Speaker:	Mary C. Hamburgh, CEO Graniff Corp.
	TS	
12:30 p.m.	Luncheon Buffet (South Terrace)	
	TS	
1:30 p.m.	Judging/Club Portfolios	
2:30 p.m.	Closing Remarks:	Orin Riley, Trustee NICA

Exercise 41

ROUGH DRAFT

Make all the corrections indicated by the proofreaders' marks.

Full sheet. DS body.

TALL BUILDINGS IN NEW YORK CITY

Building	Stories	Height Feet	Meters
World Trade Center	110	1353	412
Empire State Building	102	1,250	375
Chrysler Building	100	1,406	319
40 Wall Street	71	851	259
RCA Biulding	79	850	259
60 Wall Tower	66	826	252
One Chase Manhattan Plaza	60	814	248
PanAm Building	59	808	246
Woolworth Building	60	792	241

Exercise 42

ROUGH DRAFT

Make all the corrections indicated by the proofreaders' marks.

Half sheet. DS body.

MERCYGROVE ADULT EDUCATION PROGRAM

Work shop schedule

Course	Date	Time	Fee
Home Decrating Clinic	October 16, 19--	9:30 - 3:30	$20.00
Knowing Yourself	Oct. 16, 19--	9:00 - 3:30	$20.00
ComingAlive	October 23, 19--	10:00 - 2:30	$25.00
How to Get A Job!	October 23, 19--	1:30 - 4:30	23.00
Fall Photo graphy	October 30, 19--	9:30 - 3:30	35.00

Exercise 6

RESUME

Full sheet. 1½-inch margins. Line spacing as shown. Begin on line 10.

John Franklin
1345 Delaware Street
Chicago, Illinois 60611
(312) 833-1234

TS

OCCUPATIONAL OBJECTIVES

DS

Immediate:	Word Processing Trainee
Long-range:	Word Processing Manager

TS

WORK EXPERIENCE

DS

Summer 1985	Junior Clerk-Typist—Social Security Administration, Chicago, Illinois
1984–1985	Office Co-op Clerical Intern (part-time)—Word Processing Center, First Federal National Bank, Chicago, Illinois
1982–1984	Deliveryperson—Sun Times, Inc., Chicago, Illinois

TS

EDUCATION

DS

High School Diploma (Business), Miller Senior High, Chicago, Illinois

DS

Grade Average: B+

DS

Special Skills: Typing (50 wpm)
Shorthand (90 wpm)
Machine Operation (proficient with electronic memory typewriters and transcription machines)

TS

HONORS/ACTIVITIES

DS

President, Future Business Leaders of America Club
Treasurer, Youth Block Club
Member, National Honor Society

TS

REFERENCES

DS

Available on request

Exercise 7

COMPOSITION AT THE KEYBOARD

Using the format from Exercise 6 as a guide, compose a resume for yourself. Expand or omit categories as necessary. Limit the document to one page.

Exercise 39

Full sheet. DS body. Spread center secondary title.

EDUCATORS' AUDIOVISUAL EXCHANGE
C O M M U N I C A T I O N S

Title	Time in Minutes	Medium	Recommended Grade Levels
To Communicate Is First	30	Motion Picture	9-12
Everyday Champions	22	Filmstrip	4-8
Words Are Wonderful	10	Filmstrip	1-4
Lasers Unlimited	30	Motion Picture	10-12
Survival of the Fittest	48	Motion Picture	9-12

Exercise 40

ROUGH DRAFT

Make all the corrections indicated by the proofreaders' marks. (To review the symbols, refer to pages 92 and 93.)

Full sheet. SS body.

] SPECIAL ~~SELECTED~~ RADIO PROGRAMS [
] FOR MUSIC LOVERS [

] Time [	] ~~Radio~~ Station [	] Program [
10:30 a.m.	WNBC - AM	Madrigal Society
11:30 a.m.	WMCA - FM	The New Recordings
12:30 p.m.	WCBS - AM	Midday Concert
4:15 " p.m.	WQXR - FM	Symphonic Music
6:30 " p.m.	WHNE - FM	Dinner Music
7:30 " p.m	WORF - AM	Holiday for Strings
9:00 " p.m.	WABC - FM	Boston Pops in Concert ~~Selections for Aida~~
10:00 " p.m.	WAAT - FM	Gilbert and Sullivan Songs

Exercise 8

ENUMERATED LIST

Full sheet. 5-inch line. Single spacing for items, double spacing between. Begin on line 13.

CORRESPONDENCE SECRETARY

DS

Characteristics and Skills

TS

1. Possesses above-average verbal skills; expert in the application of spelling, grammar, and punctuation rules.
2. Practices good proofreading techniques; can recognize and use standard proofreaders' marks.
3. Formats with skill and ease a wide range of documents including letters, lists, reports, and financial statements.
4. Understands the concepts and basic procedures involved in word processing.
5. Appreciates the capabilities of machines and uses them to advantage.
6. Approaches learning experiences with enthusiasm; willingly upgrades skills.
7. Works well under deadline pressure.
8. Maintains concentration despite noise, interruptions, and other activities in the immediate environment.
9. Reacts positively to having work measured or monitored by supervisors.
10. Understands teamwork; cooperates with others to simplify and speed the completion of large or complicated typing projects.
11. Uses common sense to think through and solve recurring problems (deciphering poor handwriting, for example).
12. Tolerates well extended periods of sitting and constant demands for close reading under standard office lighting conditions.

Exercise 9

CREATIVE KEYBOARDING

Full sheet. 5-inch line. Single spacing for items, double spacing between. Begin on line 11.

Prepare a second version of the enumerated list in Exercise 8. This time vary the form by beginning each numbered point with a heading, as follows:

1. Language
2. Editorial Skills
3. Creativity
4. Training
5. Technology
6. Attitude
7. Pressure
8. Concentration
9. Supervision
10. Teamwork
11. Problem Solving
12. Stamina

Use the display format of your choice for the headings. Possibilities include underscored headings followed by a period or a colon; all capital headings followed by extra space; or (if you have equipment with the necessary features) boldface or italic headings followed by a period, a colon, or extra space.

Exercise 36
Half sheet.

BRENNER PAPER COMPANY 4

Price List of Carbon Copy Paper, 19— 12

List Number	Color	Size	Price per Ream	15 / 27
21a	White	8½ x 11	$2.10	32
21b	White	8½ x 13	2.50	37
32a	Canary	8½ x 11	2.70	42
32b	Canary	8½ x 13	3.00	47
41a	Pink	7½ x 11	2.70	51
41b	Pink	8½ x 13	3.00	56

Exercise 37
Half sheet. SS body.

REPUBLIC HIGH SCHOOL 4

Final Examination Results, Typewriting 1 12

June, 19— 14

Class	Register	Number Passed	Percent Passed	17 / 33
11	42	37	88	35
12	35	28	80	37
15	40	35	88	39
16	39	33	85	41
17	36	32	89	43

Exercise 38
Half sheet. SS body.

OVEN TEMPERATURE ROASTING CHART 6

	Temperature (°F)	Minutes (per pound)	10 / 21
Chicken	300	30-45	25
Leg of lamb	300	30-35	29
Veal shoulder	325	30-35	34
Pork, loin	350	30-40	38
Ham	325	25-30	41
Beef, rib	325	25-30	45

PART 4

SIMPLE TABULATIONS

Facts or figures may be presented in two different ways: (1) in the form of a paragraph and (2) in the form of a table, which is referred to as a *tabulation*.

The two illustrations below give the same information in two forms. Refer first to Illustration A and then to Illustration B to answer the following questions:

- On what day of the week does the Economics Club meet?
- Who is the faculty adviser of the Mathematics Club?
- Of what club is Mr. Pierson the faculty adviser?
- Which of the two illustrations more readily provides the information requested? Why?

Illustration A

PRATT HIGH SCHOOL

Schedule of Club Meetings
September, 19-- to June, 19--

The Anthropology Club meets on Wednesday, with Ms. Montgomery as faculty adviser. The Dramatic Society meets on Friday, with Mr. Pierson as faculty adviser. The Economics Club meets on Thursday, with Miss Farrell as faculty adviser. The Chorus meets on Tuesday, with Mr. Bradford as faculty adviser. The Mathematics Club meets on Friday, with Mr. Conway as faculty adviser. The French Club meets on Monday, with Mrs. Frawley as faculty adviser. The Business Education Club meets on Tuesday, with Ms. Lavery as faculty adviser.

Illustration B

PRATT HIGH SCHOOL

Schedule of Club Meetings
September, 19-- to June, 19--

Club	Day	Faculty Adviser
Anthropology Club	Wednesday	Ms. Montgomery
Dramatic Club	Friday	Mr. Pierson
Economics Club	Thursday	Miss Farrell
Chorus	Tuesday	Mr. Bradford
Mathematics Club	Friday	Mr. Conway
French Club	Monday	Mrs. Frawley
Business Education Club	Tuesday	Ms. Lavery

Topic 1 TYPING IN COLUMNS

The drills in this section will give you practice in typing material in tabulated form. When typing items in columns, always type ACROSS the page, line by line. To reach the starting point of the second, third, and following columns, depress the tab key or bar.

WORDS IN COLUMNS

When keyboarding the columns of words that follow, use this procedure.

1. Clear all old tab stops from machine.
2. Set only the *left margin* for the space line indicated.
3. Set tabs by spacing forward as indicated in the planning diagram under each drill.
4. Type each drill alone or as a class exercise from dictation by your teacher.
5. Use a full sheet and leave 3 lines between each drill.

Exercise 33

Be sure to align the program names in the last column.

Half sheet.

POLITICAL TALKS ON TV 4

Week Beginning Sunday, October 14, 19— 12

Channel	Day	Time	Program	
				25
11	Sunday	11:00 a.m.	Open Forum	31
4	Tuesday	2:00 p.m.	The Candidates Speak	39
32	Thursday	4:00 p.m.	Opinions of the Press	48
7	Sunday	1:00 p.m.	Meet the Press	55
5	Sunday	2:30 p.m.	Issues and Answers	63

Exercise 34

Half sheet.

EXHIBITION OF PAINTINGS 5

Thornton Galleries 9

Catalog Number	Title	Artist	
			11
			22
417	A Rainy Day	John C. Renschler	29
443	Abstraction	Sophie A. Gordon	36
500	Treasure Hunt	Gerald C. Forrester	44
554	Portrait of a Lady	Charles N. Buchanan	53
611	The Winner	Leonard N. Pearson	60
662	Street Scene	Vera Newton	66
771	The Village Store	Martin Reilly	73
888	Self Portrait	Mabel H. Stewart	80

Exercise 35

Half sheet. SS body. Block column headings.

OUTGOING LUXURY LINERS 5

leaving New York City 10

Week of October 10, 19— 15

Ship	Destination	Departs	Arrives	
				33
Olympia	Lisbon	Oct. 10	Oct. 23	39
Nordfels	Antigua	Oct. 12	Oct. 24	46
France	Naples	Oct. 13	Oct. 20	52
Jordeans	Le Havre	Oct. 15	Oct. 29	59
Mariposa	Athens	Oct. 16	Oct. 26	65

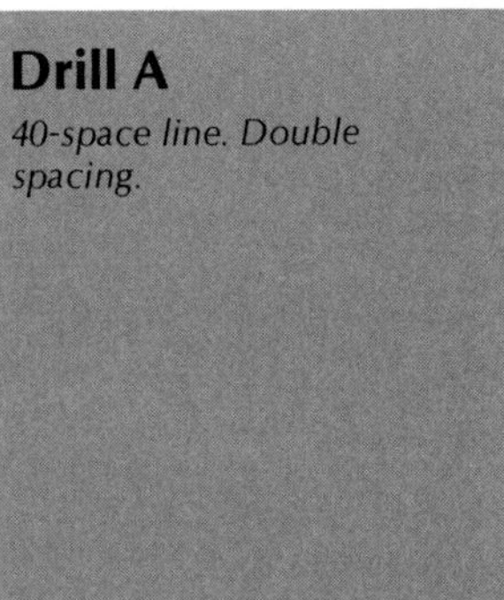

Drill A

40-space line. Double spacing.

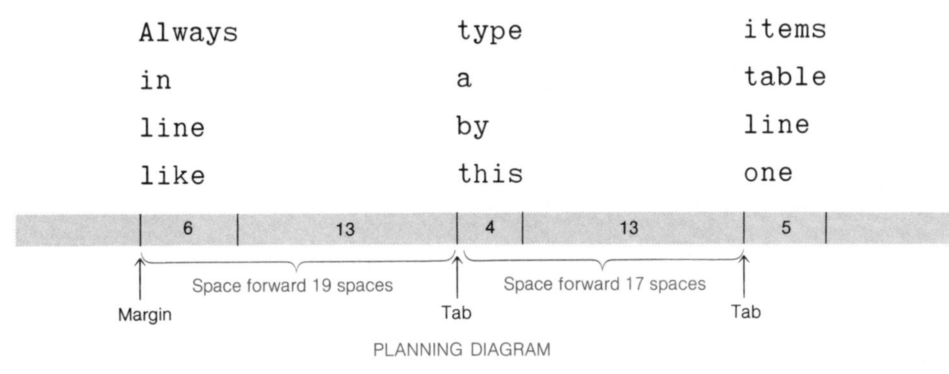

Drill B

60-space line. Single spacing.

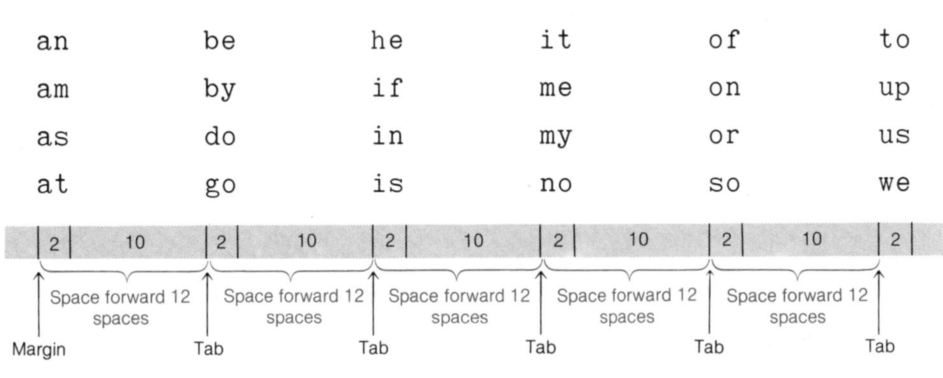

Drill C

40-space line. Line spacing as shown.

act	ask	far	law	oil
age	big	for	low	one
air	but	has	may	out
any	car	her	met	own
are	day	his	nor	put
arm	end	how	not	red

3	6	3	6	3	6	3	6	3

Drill D

50-space line. Single spacing.

oak	pine	maple	laurel
elm	cork	aspen	willow
fir	plum	birch	linden
yew	pear	cedar	spruce
ash	lime	larch	almond
bay	palm	apple	poplar

3	10	4	10	5	10	6

Directions for Exercises 31–45
HANDWRITTEN AND ROUGH-DRAFT COPY

In an office, you will often have to type material from handwritten and rough-draft copy. The following exercises will give you additional material to practice setting up tables from draft copy. If the draft copy has not been laid out in good tabular form, you, as typist, are expected to type the table in an acceptable style.

Exercise 31

Type the following table in an attractive style.
Half sheet.

DIRECTORY OF BRANCHES 4
Globe Manufacturing Company 10
January 10, 19— 14

Branch	Address	Manager	
			27
Boston, Mass.	114 Bay Street	Mark C. Dixon	35
Detroit, Mich.	59 Howard Avenue	Laura Trenton	44
Tucson, Ariz.	87 Lee Avenue	Leonard A. Kraus	53
Dallas, Tex.	212 Blanchard Street	Charles L. Haight	63
Newark, N.J.	338 Seventh Street	Warren Liang	72
Philadelphia, Penn.	170 Sebastian Road	Eugene Quinn	82
Richmond, Va.	55 Rose Place	Henry A. Front	91

Exercise 32

Arrange in tabular form a list of degrees awarded by Lincoln University in June, 19–. Be sure to include totals for the columns that require them.
Half sheet.

Liberal Arts College: Bachelor's Degrees, 430; Master's Degrees, 85; Doctorates, 15
School of Business: Bachelor's Degrees, 120; Master's Degrees, 57; Doctorates, 8
School of Education: Bachelor's Degrees, 86; Doctorates, 12
School of Journalism: Bachelor's Degrees, 135; Master's Degrees, 34; Doctorates, 3
School of Engineering: Bachelor's Degrees, 260; Master's Degrees, 76
School of Nursing: Bachelor's Degrees, 114; Master's Degrees, 32
Totals: Bachelor's Degrees, 1145; Master's Degrees, 284; Doctorates, 38

NUMBERS IN COLUMNS

Columns of words are normally aligned at the left. Numbers, however, receive varied treatment, depending on their form. Decimal fractions, for example, are aligned on their decimal points; numbers of four or more places, on their commas. All other figures are aligned at the right.

Most electronic typewriters and word processors have special features that align figures automatically. These features include the *decimal tab,* the *comma tab,* and the *flush right tab.* If your equipment has such features, use them to do Drills G and H below. Otherwise, follow the directions at the left.

Drill E

50-space line. Double spacing.

10	20	30	40	50	60
11	21	31	41	51	61
12	22	32	42	52	62
13	23	33	43	53	63
14	24	34	44	54	64

2	8	2	8	2	8	2	8	2	8	2

Drill F

50-space line. Double spacing.

555	666	777	888	999	000
515	616	717	818	919	010
525	625	725	825	925	025
121	232	343	454	787	898

3	6	3	6	3	6	3	6	3	6	3

Drill G

Notice that numbers in tables are aligned on the right. For numbers that have less than four digits (that is, those that don't take five spaces), space forward from the tab. To type 157 in column 2, for example, space forward twice from the tab.

50-space line. Single spacing.

1,205	1,003	2,208	3,103
1,290	157	412	368
51	67	64	46
1,639	1,464	1,294	2,121
415	1,337	507	694

5	10	5	10	5	10	5

Drill H

Notice that the dollar sign aligns with the largest amount in a column and that all decimal points also align.

50-space line. Single spacing.

$4.50	$11.80	$21.50	$ 4.20
6.00	8.75	11.70	21.22
6.90	13.70	7.25	35.00
4.23	5.45	78.43	6.99

5	8	6	8	6	8	6

Exercise 27

Half sheet.

MAIN TITLE DURANT REALTY CORPORATION

SECONDARY TITLE TRANSFERS, September, 19—

COLUMN HEADINGS Premises / Seller / Purchaser / Price

440 Hoe Avenue, sold by Hoe Avenue Corporation to Jason Kemp for $52,500
101 Corbin Street, sold by Empire Realty Company to James Morelli for $80,000
221 Forest Avenue, sold by Oscar Walden to George Taylor for $38,200
198 Monroe Avenue, sold by William T. Schreiber to Madge Noyes for $32,500
244 Halsey Street, sold by James T. Randolph to Rita Sayre for $36,000
167 Clark Street, sold by Leonore Ransom to Clive Estates for $67,500

Exercise 28

Arrange in tabular form a record of the commissions shown for Gardiner Furniture Company for the month ended October 31, 19—. Use 4 columns to list the name of the salesperson, the commission earned, the advances paid against the commission, and the balance due the salesperson.

Half sheet.

John Alterman earned $1045 in commissions, received $800 in advances, and has a balance of $245 due.

Susan Baxter earned $750 in commissions, received $500 in advances, and has a balance of $250 due.

Robert Lever earned $625 in commissions, received $600 in advances, and has a balance of $25 due.

Maria Hernandez earned $590 in commissions, received $480 in advances, and has a balance of $110 due.

Peter Walton earned $545 in commissions, received $440 in advances, and has a balance of $105 due.

Exercise 29

From the information given, prepare a table entitled WHERE OUR MONEY WENT. Arrange the data in 3 columns and provide appropriate column headings.

Half sheet.

Employees' and Officers' Salaries amounted to 50% of the company's revenue last year; to 45% this year.

Material Purchased amounted to 25% of revenue last year; to 24% this year.

Replacement of Facilities cost 2% last year; 5% this year.

All Taxes amounted to 15% last year; to 14% this year.

Dividends to Stockholders amounted to 6% last year; to 6% this year.

Reinvestment in Business amounted to 2% last year; to 6% this year.

Total in each percent column: 100

Exercise 30

From the data given, prepare a table for the Gotham City Employment Agency, listing openings they have for office employment as of May 12, 19—. Provide the necessary column headings.

Half sheet.

Accounting Clerk, 40-hour week, 5 years of experience, $215 a week
Data Entry Clerk, 40-hour week, 2 years of experience, $235 a week
File Clerk, 35-hour week, 5 years of experience, $200 a week
Receptionist, 35-hour week, no experience required, $180 a week
Stenographer, 35-hour week, 1 year of experience, $300 a week
Secretary, 40-hour week, 5 years of experience, salary open
Word Processing Operator, 40-hour week, 1 year of experience, $267 a week
Junior Typist, 40-hour week, no experience required, $215 a week

Topic 2 HORIZONTAL PLACEMENT OF A TABLE

Listen	while	we
learn	to	prepare
a	planning	diagram
for	tabulation	problems

The preparation of a well-arranged tabulation requires careful planning. The typist must decide where to set the left margin and where to set tab stops. In the drills in Topic 1, the planning was done for you. In completing the drills and exercises in this section, you must do your own planning. You will learn how to figure the left margin setting and where to set the tab stops by using the backspace centering method. Follow these steps:

1. Prepare the machine:
   a. Move margin stops to the ends of the typewriter scale.
   b. Clear all old tab stops left in the machine.
   c. Set the paper guide at 0 (zero).
   d. Insert a full sheet of paper. Space down to line 10.
   e. Move the carriage so that the printing point is at center.
2. Prepare a planning diagram:
   A planning diagram may be done on paper or it may be done mentally. A plan for typing the table shown in the left margin is described and shown below.
   a. Pick out the longest word in each column.

Column 1	Column 2	Column 3
Listen	tabulation	problems

   The longest word in a column determines the width of that column. By counting the number of characters in each of these words, you know how wide each column will be.

Column 1		Column 2		Column 3
6		10		8

   b. Decide how many spaces you want to leave *between* columns. In this example, we will leave 6 spaces between columns. (The amount of space between columns will vary from one table to another depending upon the number of columns in the table and the width of the columns. For most tables, from 6 to 10 spaces works well.)

Column 1		Column 2		Column 3
6	6	10	6	8

   Your planning diagram is now complete. You are ready to set a left margin stop for column 1 and tab stops for columns 2 and 3.
3. Set the left margin:
   With the carriage at center, backspace once for every *2 letters* and every *2 blank spaces* in your planning diagram. Spell out the letters and spaces in pairs as you backspace.

   Li st en *12 34 56* ta bu la ti on *12 34 56* pr ob le ms

   Set the left margin at the point where you finish backspacing.
4. Set the tab stops:
   a. Locate the tab stop for column 2 by spacing forward from the left margin. Strike the space bar once for each letter in the word *Listen* and for the 6 spaces that follow it. (Spell out the letters and spaces silently to yourself as you strike the space bar.)

   L i s t e n *1 2 3 4 5 6*
   ↑Set the tab for column 2 here.

   b. Locate the tab stop for column 3 by spacing forward from the tab stop you set for column 2. Follow the same procedure as outlined above.

   t a b u l a t i o n *1 2 3 4 5 6*
   ↑Set the tab for column 3 here.
5. Prepare to type:
   Pull the carriage back to the left margin and begin typing Drill A.

Exercise 25

TABULATED LISTING

Arrange this material attractively.

Full sheet. SS body. DS between items.

HAVE YOU A SAFE DEPOSIT BOX
TO PROTECT THESE VALUABLE BELONGINGS?

Legal documents	Trust agreements, contracts, deeds, mortgages, charters, leases, copyright papers. If legal papers are lost or destroyed, they may be impossible to replace; or replacing them may cost you many times the rental of a safe deposit box.
Important personal papers	Birth records, citizenship papers, income tax records, diplomas, marriage licenses, military discharge papers, wills. By keeping these papers in a safe deposit box, you will have them easily accessible for reference.
Insurance papers	Insurance policies and inventories of insured goods. Policies and related data kept together in a safe deposit box will be quickly available when needed.
Securities	Stocks and bonds. Securities need protection, especially if they are readily negotiable.
Valuable personal belongings	Jewelry, medals, heirlooms, rare stamps, valuable coins, treasured photographs. Valuable personal belongings kept in the home may be destroyed through fire, lost, misplaced, or stolen. Heirlooms are irreplaceable; other belongings may be replaced only at great cost.

Directions for Exercises 26–30

TABULATIONS FROM UNARRANGED COPY

The competent typist is able to plan tabulations from unarranged data. To give you practice in doing this, the copy for each of these exercises is given in unarranged form. Center each table attractively. Omit items in the body that are indicated or implied in the column headings. For example, in Exercise 26, the word *of* and the # sign are both implied in the column headings and should not be typed in the body of the table.

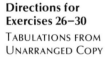

Exercise 26

Half sheet.

MAIN TITLE	LIST OF INACTIVE ACCOUNTS
SECONDARY TITLES	Atlantic Savings Bank December 31, 19—
COLUMN HEADINGS	Name / Address / Account No.

Charles N. Hoffman, of 62 Walnut Street, #11-440-0
Antoinette D. Hull, of 110 Johnston Street, #11-153-4
John H. Irvington, of 911 Marlowe Street, #11-336-6
Nicholas Lombardi, of 34 Wilson Boulevard, #12-271-1
Clinton S. McCloud, of 877 Pierce Avenue, #12-188-9
Hazel Pedersen, of 45 Tribune Square, #11-577-7
Gilbert A. Rondeau, of 776 West 15th Street, #11-478-8
Anita S. Savage, of 55 Coral Road, #12-378-9
Mary Wheeler, of 61 Exchange Place, #12-255-0

Full sheet. Leave 6 lines between drills. Center each drill horizontally. Begin on line 10. Continue on additional sheets if necessary.

Drill A

Double spacing. 6 spaces between columns.

Listen	while	we
learn	to	prepare
a	planning	diagram
for	tabulation	problems

Drill B

Single spacing. 10 spaces between columns.

receipt	receive	ceiling
perceive	deceive	their
freight	weight	conceive

Drill C

As you are backspacing to figure the left margin setting, ignore odd letters at the end of your counting.

Single spacing. 6 spaces between columns.

relieve	review	relief
scientist	believing	cashiers
audience	variety	yield

Drill D

Single spacing. 10 spaces between columns.

so	sew	sow
new	knew	gnu
karat	caret	carrot
their	they're	there
flu	flue	flew

Drill E

Double spacing. 8 spaces between columns.

mailable	valuable	advisable
salable	unusable	dependable
adaptable	excusable	available
durable	desirable	comparable

Drill F

Single spacing. 6 spaces between columns.

if he did	and the	their work
the man is	when they	she did
it is the	if it is	they both

Drill G

Double spacing. 8 spaces between columns.

may go	he did	for them
did they	and they	if they
he also	for it	turn it

Drill H

Single spacing. 6 spaces between columns.

ring	rang	had rung
go	went	had gone
do	did	had done
be	was	had been
know	knew	had known

Exercise 23 continued

FDA	Food and Drug Administration—Safeguards the health of the nation by enforcing laws and regulations that prevent the distribution of unsafe foods, drugs and medicines, medical devices, cosmetics, and veterinary products.
FIC	Federal Information Centers—Function as clearing houses for information about the federal government.
FRS	Federal Reserve System—As the nation's central bank, regulates the flow of money and credit; also provides supervisory services to the public, the U.S. Treasury, and commercial banks.
FTC	Federal Trade Commission—Promotes free and fair competition in the marketplace by enforcing antitrust and other laws.
NLRB	National Labor Relations Board—Prevents or eliminates unfair labor practices.
OEO	Office of Economic Opportunity—Administers funds to programs that reduce unemployment and poverty.

Exercise 24

TABULATED LISTING

Arrange this material attractively.

Full sheet, inserted with long (11-inch) side first. SS body. DS between items.

GREAT NORTHERN COTTON MANUFACTURING COMPANY 10

Boston, Massachusetts 14

May, 19— 16

Information about Directors 21

Thomas H. Bailey, Jr.	President, Bailey & Lester, Inc., Hartford, Connecticut	34 36
Claire S. Gibbons	Chairperson of the Executive Committee, Lacey Cotton Mills, Springfield, Massachu- setts. Member of the Board of Directors, McPhail Threads, Portland, Maine	48 56 65 71
Hubert N. Grover	President of the Company	79
George A. LeClerq	Vice President of the Company. Member of the Board of Directors, Ralph Chalmers & Company, Boston, Massachusetts	91 99 105
Margaret C. Morgenstern	Chemist, Rand Corporation, Santa Monica, California	118 120
Martin L. Rivera	President, Jeffries Cotton Works, Boston, Massachusetts. Member of the Board of Trustees, James Benton & Company, Boston, Massachusetts	131 139 148 150
Clifford J. Robinson	President, Blockton Cotton Goods, Inc., Atlanta, Georgia	163 166

Drill I

Double spacing. 7 spaces between columns.

MERCURY	VENUS	SATURN
MARS	JUPITER	EARTH
PLUTO	URANUS	NEPTUNE

Drill J

Double spacing. 7 spaces between columns.

New York	London	Paris
Tokyo	Sao Paulo	Rome
Moscow	Cairo	New Delhi

Drill K

Single spacing. 8 spaces between columns.

negligible	feasible	forcible
admissible	incredible	audible
responsible	invisible	sensible
reversible	eligible	flexible

Drill L

Double spacing. 5 spaces between columns.

1121	121	21	1
1232	232	32	2
1343	343	43	3

Drill M

Remember to align numbers at right.

Double spacing. 8 spaces between columns.

10.1	20.2	30.3	40.4
500.5	600.6	700.7	800.8
9.9	1.1	2.2	3.3

Drill N

Type in 3 columns.

Double spacing. 10 spaces between columns.

January, February, March
April, May, June
July, August, September
October, November, December

Topic 3 TITLES FOR TABLES

```
MAIN TITLE

Subtitle


Body of table     line 1
Body of table     line 2
```

A table should always have a title that describes what kind of information it contains. The title should be as concise as you can make it. A title is usually centered and it is separated from the body of the table by 2 (sometimes 1) blank lines.

If a title requires more than 1 line, *each* line of the title is centered. The main title is always typed first and secondary titles are placed afterward. When you type the exercises in this topic, follow this style for the titles:

1. Type the main title in solid capitals.
2. Type the secondary title (or titles) in lowercase, but capitalize the first letter of important words.
3. Double-space lines.

Exercise 21

LONG COLUMN HEADINGS

Columns 2 and 3 have headings of more than one line. Center each line separately and single-space.

Half sheet. SS body. Center vertically and horizontally.

TEMPERATURES AROUND THE WORLD

June 6, 19—

City	Local Time	Temperature (°F)
Acapulco	7 a.m.	84
Antigua	1 p.m.	75
Casablanca	12 noon	68
Hong Kong	8 p.m.	81
London	1 p.m.	65
Madrid	1 p.m.	73
Moscow	3 p.m.	46

Exercise 22

TABULATED LISTING

Arrange this material attractively.

Full sheet. DS body. TS between items.

STEPS IN CORRESPONDENCE FILING 6

INSPECTING The procedure of reading each piece of incoming mail 18
to see that it has been marked for release to filing. 29

INDEXING The procedure of deciding the name, subject, or other 42
caption under which a paper should be filed. The main 53
consideration here is how it will most probably be re- 64
quested from the files. 69

CODING The procedure of underscoring the caption selected in 81
the indexing. (Whenever a paper might be called for 91
under more than one caption, a cross-reference sheet 102
must be prepared.) 106

SORTING The process of arranging the material in order (alpha- 118
betic, numeric, and so on) after it has been coded. 128

STORING The process of inserting the papers into the files. 140

Exercise 23

TABULATED LISTING

Arrange this material attractively.

Full sheet. SS body. DS between items.

THE FEDERAL ALPHABET

(Government Department and Agency Abbreviations)

BLS Bureau of Labor Statistics—Collects and analyzes data on labor economics.

EEOC Equal Employment Opportunity Commission—Prevents or eliminates discriminatory practices in employment.

FCC Federal Communications Commission—Regulates interstate and foreign communications carried on by radio, telephone, and telegraph; also regulates radio and television stations.

(Continued on next page)

To practice centering table titles, do Exercises 1–9. Follow this general procedure:

1. Center each exercise vertically and horizontally. (To review vertical centering, see page 112; to review horizontal placement of a table, see page 123.)
2. Center the title of the table over the body.
3. Triple space after you type the title. (This will give you a 2-line separation between the body and the title.)

Exercise 1

Half sheet. Double spacing. 10 spaces between columns. Center vertically and horizontally.

INVESTMENT CLUB OFFICERS

TS

Patricia L. Carlton	President
Gilbert Ramirez	Vice-President
Raymond L. Wayland	Treasurer
Samuel Law	Secretary

Exercise 2

Half sheet. Double spacing. 10 spaces between columns. Center vertically and horizontally.

WESTVIEW NEWS EDITORIAL STAFF

TS

Anthony Beretti	Editor in Chief
Alma Rene Clark	Assistant Editor
Lloyd Hamilton	Executive Editor
Shelly Prillerman	News Editor
Alfred Monroe	Sports Editor
Thomas O'Brien	Social Editor
Claire Frankel	Clubs Editor

Exercise 3

Half sheet. Single spacing. 10 spaces between columns. Center vertically and horizontally.

WORDS USED IN APPLICATION FORMS

Surname	Last name
Maiden Name	Name before marriage
Marital Status	Single, married, etc.
Signature	Written (not printed) name
Spouse	Husband or wife
References	Adults who know your abilities
Dependents	People you support
Soc. Sec. No.	Social Security Number
Occupation	Type of work you do
Residence	Where you live
Telephone	Home telephone number
Citizenship	Name of country
Surety Bonding	Insurance against company losses

Exercise 18

LONG COLUMN HEADINGS

Half sheet. SS body. Center vertically and horizontally.

COMMODITY RECOMMENDATIONS

Friday, June 8, 19—

Commodity	Today's Price	Recommendation
Wheat	$3.48	Hold
Corn	2.56	Buy
Oats	1.51	Sell
Lard	.29	Hold
Cotton	.59	Hold
Wool	2.10	Sell
Copper	.95	Buy

Exercise 19

COMPOSITION AT THE KEYBOARD

Type a revised version of the table at the right: (1) Visit the library and update the employment figures. (2) In your planning, eliminate the *Main Offices* column; add a second *Employees* column (one for each year); rewrite subtitle and subheadings, as necessary; alphabetize entries. (3) Type your revised table on a full sheet inserted long side first. DS the body and block center the whole table. (4) Write a short paragraph describing the changes that have taken place over the period covered by the new table. Note any trends. Title your paragraph "Interpretation of Data."

TOP MICHIGAN MANUFACTURING COMPANIES

Number of Employees, 1979

Company	Main Offices	Product	Employees
General Motors	Detroit	Motor Vehicles	797,000
Ford	Dearborn	Motor Vehicles	479,292
Chrysler	Highland Park	Motor Vehicles	250,833
Dow Chemical	Midland	Chemicals, Plastics	53,002
Bendix	Southfield	Auto & Aviation Equip.	80,006
American Motors	Southfield	Motor Vehicles	29,519
Burroughs	Detroit	Bus. & Electronic Equip.	51,295
Whirlpool	Benton Harbor	Household Appliances	23,573
Fruehauf	Detroit	Transportation Equip.	29,400

Source: *The Million Dollar Directory.*

Exercise 20

LONG COLUMN HEADINGS

Note that column 4 has a 2-line heading; center each line separately and single-space.

Half sheet. SS body. Center vertically and horizontally.

HIGHEST MOUNTAIN ON EACH CONTINENT

Continent	Mountain	Location	Height in Meters
North America	Mt. McKinley	Alaska	6,193
South America	Mt. Aconcagua	Chile-Argentina	6,959
Europe	Mt. El'brus	Soviet Union	5,553
Asia	Mt. Everest	Nepal-Tibet	8,708
Africa	Mt. Kibo	Tanzania	5,802
Australia	Mt. Kosciusko	New South Wales	2,195
Antarctica	Mt. Vinson Massif	Antarctic	5,057

Exercise 4

PAIRED COLUMNS IN A TABULATION

When the relationship between two columns in a table is closer than between others, the spacing between columns is varied to show these relationships.

Full sheet. Double spacing. Follow the spacing shown in the planning diagram below this exercise. Center vertically and horizontally.

ABBREVIATIONS USED IN HELP-WANTED ADS

agcy.	agency	h.s.	high school
appt.	appointment	intvw.	interview
asst.	assistant	lic.	license
bkgd.	background	mo.	month
bus.	business	oppty.	opportunity
clk.	clerk	pd.	paid
coll.	college	refs.	references
dir.	director	sal.	salary
div.	division	secty.	secretary
eves.	evenings	sh.	shorthand
exp.	experience	swbd.	switchboard
ext.	extension	temp.	temporary
grad.	graduate	trnee.	trainee

5	6	11	16	6	6	11

Exercise 5

Half sheet. Single spacing. 16 spaces between columns. Center vertically and horizontally.

FREMONT HIGH SCHOOL

DS

Schedule of Football Games, 19—

TS

Oct. 12	McFee High School	At home
Oct. 22	Bayville Prep.	Away
Oct. 29	Fleer School of Business	At home
Nov. 5	Horace High School	Away
Nov. 11	Skelton High School	At home
Dec. 3	District Finals	Away

Exercise 6

Half sheet. Single spacing. 10 spaces between columns. Center vertically and horizontally.

VANDERWATER HIGH SCHOOL

19— Assembly Program Schedule

February 15	Current Events Club	Open Forum
March 1	English Department	Motion Pictures
March 15	School Orchestra	Musical Program
March 30	Glee Club	Easter Musical
April 27	Science Department	Demonstration
May 11	Counseling Department	Job Fair
May 25	Drama Club	A One-Act Play
June 8	Business Club	Awards Assembly

Exercise 15
LONG COLUMN HEADINGS

Half sheet. SS body. Center vertically and horizontally.

ELBERT TOURS, INC.
Rate Schedule*
St. Martin from Pittsburgh, June 15–22

Hotel	Double	Single	Child**
Coralita	$479	$509	$250
Great Bay, ocean view	455	—	245
Great Bay, mountain view	429	479	245
Le Galion	399	459	230
Le Bay, garden	449	559	280
Le Bay, beach	465	599	300
St. Tropez, lagoon view	425	519	260
St. Tropez, ocean view	445	539	270

*Rates are per person. They include airfares and 6 nights' hotel accommodations.
**Ages 2 to 11.

Exercise 16
LONG COLUMN HEADINGS

Full sheet, inserted with long (11-inch) side first. SS body. Center vertically and horizontally.

H. T. HARLAND COMPANY
Typewriter Inventory

Make	Model	Serial No.	Purchased
Adler	M-750	748-546	1975
IBM	Selectric	298-1646	1969
IBM	Self-Correcting	231-6658	1978
IBM	Executive II	191-8464	1969
Olympia	S-27	207-322	1977
Olympia	S-27	207-321	1978
Remington	EL-6	154-054	1974
Royal	J-300	869-1813	1974

Exercise 17
LONG COLUMN HEADINGS

Half sheet. SS body. Center vertically and horizontally.

SUMMARY OF COMMON METRIC CONVERSION FACTORS

If you know	And you want	Multiply by
inches	centimeters	2.54
feet	meters	0.30
yards	meters	0.91
miles	kilometers	1.61
quarts	liters	0.95
gallons	liters	3.79
ounces	grams	28.35
pounds	kilograms	0.45

Exercise 7

Half sheet. Double spacing. Spaces between columns are 5, 15, and 5. Center vertically and horizontally.

BIRTHSTONES

January	Garnet	July	Ruby
February	Amethyst	August	Sardonyx
March	Bloodstone	September	Sapphire
April	Diamond	October	Opal
May	Emerald	November	Topaz
June	Pearl	December	Turquoise

Exercise 8

Full sheet. Double spacing. Follow the spacing shown in the planning diagram below this exercise. Center vertically and horizontally.

TWO-LETTER STATE ABBREVIATIONS

Alabama	AL	Montana	MT
Alaska	AK	Nebraska	NE
Arizona	AZ	Nevada	NV
Arkansas	AR	New Hampshire	NH
California	CA	New Jersey	NJ
Colorado	CO	New Mexico	NM
Connecticut	CT	New York	NY
Delaware	DE	North Carolina	NC
District of Columbia	DC	North Dakota	ND
Florida	FL	Ohio	OH
Georgia	GA	Oklahoma	OK
Hawaii	HI	Oregon	OR
Idaho	ID	Pennsylvania	PA
Illinois	IL	Puerto Rico	PR
Indiana	IN	Rhode Island	RI
Iowa	IA	South Carolina	SC
Kansas	KS	South Dakota	SD
Kentucky	KY	Tennessee	TN
Louisiana	LA	Texas	TX
Maine	ME	Utah	UT
Maryland	MD	Vermont	VT
Massachusetts	MA	Virginia	VA
Michigan	MI	Washington	WA
Minnesota	MN	West Virginia	WV
Mississippi	MS	Wisconsin	WI
Missouri	MO	Wyoming	WY

20	6	2	12	14	6	2

Exercise 12
LONG COLUMN HEADINGS

Full sheet. DS body. Center vertically and horizontally.

WATCHING YOUR WEIGHT 4

"Junk" Food	Calories	
Cake, chocolate iced	356	17
Cola beverages, 8 oz.	90	22
Hot dog	124	24
Hamburger patty, 4 oz.	331	29
Ice cream, chocolate	385	34
Cashew nuts, 8 to 12	94	39
Potato chips, 7 large	108	44
Popcorn with butter, 1 cup	100	50

(Column heading line: 12)

Exercise 13
LONG COLUMN HEADINGS

Some tables have no heading for the first column, as illustrated here.

Full sheet. DS body. Center vertically and horizontally.

FOOTBALL STATISTICS 4

Lawton High School vs. Marlin High School 12

Game of November 11, 19— 17

	Lawton	Marlin	24
First downs	14	15	28
Yards gained (net)	413	355	33
Forward passes attempted	33	18	39
Passes completed	15	9	43
Passes intercepted	1	1	47
Punts (number)	3	5	51
Average distance of punts (yards)	39	44	59
Yards penalized	38	67	63
Fumbles lost	2	3	67

Exercise 14
LONG COLUMN HEADINGS

Remember to align the dollar sign with the longest amount in a column.

Full sheet, inserted with long (11-inch) side first. DS body. Spread center main title. Center vertically and horizontally.

S P E C I A L   S U M M E R   S A L E 7

SUNDECK REDWOOD FURNITURE 9

Week of June 1 Only 12

Item	Regular Price	Sale Price	29
Chair	$109.95	$ 99.88	33
Chaise lounge	149.95	124.88	39
Tete-a-tete	199.95	179.88	44
Coffee table	69.95	54.85	50
Ottoman	44.95	39.89	55
Rocker	119.95	99.88	59
Umbrella	89.95	69.88	64
Shell	9.95	8.88	68

Exercise 9
Half sheet. Single spacing. 8 spaces between columns. Center vertically and horizontally.

NATIONAL FOOTBALL LEAGUE

National Conference
Eastern Division

Dallas	Cowboys
Washington	Redskins
St. Louis	Cardinals
Philadelphia	Eagles
New York	Giants

Topic 4 TABLES WITH COLUMN HEADINGS

Column headings help a reader to understand the information in a table. A column heading may be centered over the column, or blocked, as shown in the illustrations below.

Blocked Column Headings

Instructor	Classes	Days
Mr. Cutting	Typewriting	Mon.-Fri.
Mrs. Shipworth	Clerk-Steno Training	Tues. & Thurs.
Ms. Rutledge	Data Processing	Mon. & Fri.
Margin 15	Tab 40	Tab 65

Centered Column Headings

Instructor	Classes	Days
Mr. Cutting	Typewriting	Mon.-Fri.
Mrs. Shipworth	Clerk-Steno Training	Tues. & Thurs.
Ms. Rutledge	Data Processing	Mon. & Fri.
Margin 15	Tab 40	Tab 65

SHORT COLUMN HEADINGS

A column heading that is blocked presents no difficulty in typing. Each heading begins at the point where the column starts. If the column headings are centered, however, you must first locate the midpoint of each column. The steps listed below describe how this is done for the table shown above.

1. To find the midpoint of the first column:
   a. Move the carriage to the point where the column is to begin. The first column begins at a left margin of 15.
   b. Find the longest item in the first column (*Mrs. Shipworth*).
   c. Divide the longest item in half by spacing forward once for every 2 letters in it. This will place the carriage at the center point of the column.
2. To type the column heading:
   a. With the carriage at the midpoint of the column, backspace once for every 2 letters in the heading of the column.

      In st ru ct or

   b. Begin typing the heading at the point where you stopped backspacing.
   c. Backspace and underscore the column heading.

(Continued on next page)

Exercise 9
CENTERED COLUMN HEADINGS

Half sheet. SS body. Center vertically and horizontally.

SCHEDULE OF PERFORMANCES
Grand Opera House
Fall Season, 19—

Date			Time	Opera
Saturday,	November	15	8:00	Magic Flute
Wednesday,	"	19	8:00	Lohengrin
Saturday,	"	22	8:15	Il Trovatore
Wednesday,	"	26	8:00	Don Giovanni
Saturday,	"	29	8:00	Faust
Wednesday,	December	3	8:30	La Traviata
Saturday,	"	6	8:00	Carmen
Wednesday,	"	10	8:15	Aida
Saturday,	"	13	8:00	Manon

Exercise 10
CENTERED COLUMN HEADINGS AND FOOTNOTE

Full sheet. DS body. Center vertically and horizontally.

MOODY PUBLISHING CORPORATION
White Plains, New York
BUSINESS TEXTBOOKS

Code	Author	Title	Price*
7114	Atkins, Adele	Office Practice	$7.65
7122	Bush, Ronald	Record Keeping	7.50
7125	Sobell, Richard	Elementary Accounting	8.65
7127	Sobell, Richard	Advanced Accounting	8.80
7131	Terhune, Edna	Learning to Typewrite	9.20
7137	Vann, Eva S.	Dictation Practice	7.85
7138	Vann, Eva S.	Transcription Practice	7.85

*All prices subject to a 25% discount on school orders

Exercise 11
LONG COLUMN HEADINGS

Full sheet. SS body. Center vertically and horizontally.

SUFFOLK ELECTRIC COMPANY, INC.
Members of the Board of Directors, May, 19—

Name	Principal Occupation	First Elected
Julian V. Cohen	Attorney at Law	1972
Edward Dellman	President, Dellman Brothers	1965
Joseph F. Elson	Secretary, Budd, Inc.	1973
Victor Fehr	Treasurer of the Company	1974
Evelyn A. Mason	Attorney at Law	1967
Daniel T. Remson	President of the Company	1979
Helen H. Sugimoto	Vice-President of the Company	1971

3. Repeat Steps 1 and 2 for centering the column headings in the remaining columns. The second column begins at a tab stop set at 40. The third column begins at a tab stop set at 65.
4. Double-space after typing all the column headings and return to the left margin.
5. Type the items in each column, typing across each line and using the tab stops.

Drill A

Type the table shown here. Center the column headings following the procedure outlined above.

Instructor	Classes	Days
Mr. Cutting	Typewriting	Mon.-Fri.
Mrs. Shipworth	Clerk-Steno Training	Tues. & Thurs.
Ms. Rutledge	Data Processing	Mon., Wed., & Fri.
↑ Margin 15	↑ Tab 40	↑ Tab 65

Drill B

Leave 10 lines after typing Drill A. Type the table shown here, centering each column heading over the column.

Player	Sport	School
Muriel Johnson	Tennis	Washington High
Richard Hamilton	Football	Northwestern High
Cecilia DuBois	Basketball	Peabody High

Center each table vertically and horizontally. Center column headings unless instructed otherwise by your teacher. Decide how many spaces you wish to leave between columns. Generally, from 6 to 10 spaces between columns work well in most tables. Columns should not be so widely spaced that it becomes difficult to read across, nor so close that the table looks cramped.

Exercise 1

Half sheet. Single spacing.

BASKETBALL SCHEDULE

DS

Abraham Lincoln High School

(19— Season)

TS

Date	Opponent	Borough
March 22	Grover Cleveland High	Queens
April 12	George Washington High	Manhattan
April 24	Sheepshead Bay High	Brooklyn

Exercise 2

Half sheet. Double spacing.

FAMOUS AMERICAN POETS

(19th Century)

Name	Famous Work
Walt Whitman	Leaves of Grass
Edgar Lee Masters	Spoon River Anthology
Edwin Markham	The Man with the Hoe

Exercise 6
BLOCKED COLUMN HEADINGS AND FOOTNOTE

Begin each column heading at the point where the column starts.

Half sheet. DS body. Center vertically and horizontally.

CRAWFORD CONSTRUCTION COMPANY
Consultant Fees, Year Beginning January 1, 19—*

Consultant	Specialty	Amount
Lopez & Garretson	Attorneys	$8,000
Maurice Burgess Associates	Engineers	4,500
R. N. Carson & Company	Accountants	3,500
Herbert S. Schell	Tax Advisor	800
Patricia N. Galvin	Architect	1,500

*Only those amounts in excess of $500 are included.

Exercise 7
CENTERED COLUMN HEADINGS

Full sheet. DS body. Center vertically and horizontally.

UNITY DISCOUNT STORES
Branch Locations

Branch	Address	Phone
West Warren Area	20430 Van Dyke	893-6750
Madison Heights	John R. Flagg Shopping Mall	542-4961
Lincoln Park	4142 Dix Highway	386-7611
Pontiac	Tel-Huron Shopping Center	333-7594
Mt. Clemons	Gratiot at Camden	791-0460
Northville	Northville Plaza	348-9820
Southfield	Tel-Twelve Mall	836-2133

Exercise 8
BLOCKED COLUMN HEADINGS

Begin each column heading at the point where the column starts.

Full sheet. SS body. Center vertically and horizontally.

NEW YORK STATE DEPARTMENT OF COMMERCE
FIELD OFFICES

City	Post Office Address	ZIP Code
Albany	112 State Street	12207
Binghamton	66 Chenango Street	13901
Buffalo	908 Ellicott Square Building	14209
Elmira	327 Baldwin Street	14901
Kingston	442 Broadway	12401
Mineola	33 Denton Building	11501
New York	342 Madison Avenue	10017
Ogdensburg	321 State Street	13669
Rochester	45 Exchange Street	14614
Syracuse	351 S. Warren Street	13202
Utica	185 Genesee Street	13501
Washington, D.C.	1026 - 17th Street N. W.	20036
White Plains	148 Martine Avenue	10601

Exercise 3

Half sheet. Double spacing.

METRIC CONVERSIONS

Corresponding Units of Measure

Quantity	English	Metric
length	foot	meter
weight	pound	kilogram
temperature	Fahrenheit	Celsius
volume	quart	liter

Exercise 4

TWO-LINE COLUMN HEADINGS

If there are several lines in the column heading, treat each line separately, following the same steps. Single-space the lines of a column heading.

Full sheet. Spread center fourth line of title. Double spacing.

KING SPORTING GOODS COMPANY

DS

165 Barnes Avenue

Seattle, Washington 98109

DS

S U P E R   S P R I N G   S P E C I A L S

TS

Equipment	Regular Price	Sale Price
Golf Clubs (Set)	$120.00	$75.00
Tennis Racket	25.50	15.00
Baseball Glove	32.75	17.50
Fishing Rod	19.00	12.50
Water Skis (Pair)	48.00	32.75
Backpack	60.00	49.90
Weight Bench	29.97	24.90

Exercise 5

ROUGH-DRAFT COPY

Type this table, making the corrections indicated.

Half sheet. Single spacing.

LECTURE SERI ES

Executive Trainign Course

Summer Session

[Date	Topics	Lecturer
June 10]	[Organization	James A. Ranedall
June 13	PublicRelations	Marian Thomas
June 18	Personnel	Frank Saunders
June 21	Purchasing	Herbert Rawls
June 25	Market Reserch	Charles Meyers
June 16	Advertising	Burton Welding

Exercise 2

THREE-COLUMN TABLE

Half sheet. SS body. Center vertically and horizontally.

SALVADOR FOOD COMPANY 5

Canned Products 8

Grapefruit Juice	Apple Sauce	Beets	15
Lemon Juice	Blueberries	Carrots	21
Mixed Vegetable Juice	Grapefruit Sections	Peas	30
Orange Juice	Halved Apricots	Spinach	37
Tomato Juice	Sliced Peaches	Green Beans	45
Guava Juice	Fruit Salad	Asparagus	52

Exercise 3

TABLE WITH PAIRED COLUMNS

Give columns 1 and 2 and columns 3 and 4 the "paired" look by leaving extra space between columns 2 and 3.

Half sheet. SS body. Center vertically and horizontally.

PENSION BENEFITS FOR RETIRED EMPLOYEES 8

Ludlow Chemical Plant 12

January 1, 19— 15

Edith T. Burnham	$ 825	Philip Lustig	$1,025	24
Joseph R. Clarke	800	Alice T. Manning	900	32
Nils A. Ericson	1,100	John Miracolo	700	40
Foster Garner	770	Harriet P. Stillwell	1,110	49
Martha Zender	965	Charles Waite	850	56

Exercise 4

TABLE WITH PAIRED COLUMNS AND FOOTNOTE

Leave 2 blank lines between the last line of the table and the footnote.

Full sheet. DS body. Center vertically and horizontally.

TIME IN OTHER CITIES 4

When It Is Noon in New York City 11

Berlin	6 p.m.	Moscow	8 p.m.	16
Chicago	11 a.m.	Paris	5 p.m.	21
Hong Kong	1 p.m.*	Rome	6 p.m.	27
London	5 p.m.	Sydney	3 a.m.*	32
Los Angeles	9 a.m.	Tokyo	3 a.m.*	38
Mexico City	11 a.m.	Washington	12 noon	46

*The following day 50

Exercise 5

BLOCKED COLUMN HEADINGS

Begin each column heading at the point where the column starts.

Half sheet. DS body. Center vertically and horizontally.

COMPOSITION OF METAL ALLOYS 5

Alloy	Component Metals	18
Brass	Copper and zinc	22
White gold	Tin, copper, and antimony	29
Bronze	Copper and tin	34
Pewter	Tin and lead or copper or brass	41
Plumber's solder	Lead and tin	47
Steel	Iron and carbon	51
Lynite	Aluminum and copper	56

Exercise 6
Full Sheet. Double spacing.

WELL-KNOWN BLACK WRITERS

Fiction	Poetry	Literary Criticism
Charles Chestnutt	Paul L. Dunbar	Alain Locke
Jean Toomer	James W. Johnson	Richard Wright
Rudolph Fisher	Fenton Johnson	Sterling Brown
Arna Bontemps	Claude McKay	James Baldwin
Langston Hughes	Jean Toomer	Darwin Turner
Richard Wright	Countee Cullen	Clarence Major
Ralph Ellison	Gwendolyn Brooks	Arthur P. Davis
Paul Marshall	Owen Dodson	Blyden Jackson
Frank L. Brown	Frank Home	Richard Stern

Exercise 7
UNARRANGED COPY
Half sheet. Double spacing.

BUSINESS DEPARTMENT AWARDS
Edison High School
June, 19—
Student / Subject / Award
Minnie Riggs / Stenography / Gold Medal
Jan Van den Bergh / Typewriting / Silver Pin
Willie Thomas / Bookkeeping / Gold Medal
Sarah Sykes / Office Machines / Silver Pin
Peter Dodge / Business Law / Silver Medal
David Knowles / DE Marketing / Gold Pin

Exercise 8
UNARRANGED COPY
Full sheet. Double spacing. Remember to align dollar amounts.

JUNIOR LEAGUE CHARITIES
19— Distribution of Funds
Facility / Total / Paid / Due
Lincoln Hospital / $4,300 / $3,100 / $1,200
Home for the Aged / 3,300 / 2,500 / 800
Hill Family Home / 1,000 / 800 / 200
City Zoo / 2,000 / 1,500 / 500
Braille School / 750 / 600 / 150
Children's Hospital / 700 / 500 / 200
Salvation Army / 2,000 / 1,500 / 500

PART 4

ADVANCED TABULATIONS

Listings of detailed data are easier to read and more attractive when they are arranged in the form of tabulations. Before beginning these more advanced tabulation exercises, you may want to review the information presented in pages 120 to 133 of *Simple Tabulations* and pages 108 to 112 of *Horizontal and Vertical Centering*.

Topic 1 TABULATION PRODUCTION PRACTICE

With practice, a good typist will be able to use eye judgment to set up tabulated material. After you have typed several of the exercises in this topic, see if you can estimate machine settings and achieve attractive layouts.

Directions for Exercises 1–25
TABULATION REVIEW

Exercises 1–25 review all the tabulating procedures taught in Section 2, Part 4. Word counts are provided for many exercises so that you may measure your production rate. As you progress through the exercises, you will find that they become more complex and demand increasingly higher levels of skill.

Exercise 1
TWO-COLUMN TABLE

Full sheet. DS body. Center vertically and horizontally.

		Words
HOTEL ATLANTIC		3
Convention Schedule, Spring, 19—		10
March 21–23	Paper Manufacturers Association	19
March 30–31	National Organization for Women	28
April 2–3	National Council of State Garden Clubs	38
April 4–6	Society of Automotive Engineers	46
April 18–24	National Public Health Association	55
April 27–29	Midwest Trial Lawyers Association	64
May 14–18	Conference of Postal Women	71
May 21–24	Court Reporters Association	79
June 4–8	National Council of Social Studies	88

LONG COLUMN HEADINGS

When a column heading is longer than any other item in the column, use the column heading as the longest column item when you prepare a planning diagram for the table. Backspace to find the left margin and space forward to set tab stops in the usual way (refer to page 123).

Name of Student	Typing Class	Words Per Minute
B. Pierce	11-A	70
C. Hotl	11-B	65
R. Neys	10-A	58

In this table assume that you have completed a planning diagram. You have set a left margin stop and two tab stops. The tabs are set to allow for 5 spaces between column headings. After you type the column headings, follow these steps to center each column under the heading:

1. To locate the center point of the first column: space *forward* from the left margin once for every 2 letters or spaces in the heading; select the longest item in the column (B. Pierce) and *backspace* once for each 2 letters or spaces in that item. Reset the left margin at this point.
2. To locate the center point of the second column: move the carriage to the first letter of the heading; space *forward* once for every 2 letters or spaces; select the longest item in the column and *backspace* once for every 2 letters or spaces. Reset the tab for the second column.
3. To reset the tab for the third column: use the same procedures outlined above. Now type the body of the table.

Drill C

Half sheet. Double spacing. 5 spaces between column headings. Begin on line 10.

Name of Student	Typing Class	Words Per Minute
B. Pierce	11-A	70
C. Hotl	11-B	65
R. Neys	10-A	58
↑ Reset margin	↑ Reset tab	↑ Reset tab

Exercise 9

Half sheet. Single spacing. Center column headings. Decide on the spacing between columns. Center vertically and horizontally.

MAJOR LEAGUE PENNANT WINNERS

1976–1984

Year	National League	American League
1976	Cincinnati	New York
1977	Los Angeles	New York
1978	Los Angeles	New York
1979	Pittsburgh	Baltimore
1980	Philadelphia	Kansas City
1981	Los Angeles	New York
1982	St. Louis	Milwaukee
1983	Philadelphia	Baltimore
1984	San Diego	Detroit

Exercise 6 continued

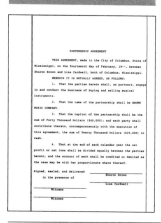

sum of Forty Thousand Dollars ($40,000); and each party shall contribute thereto, contemporaneously with the execution of this agreement, the sum of Twenty Thousand Dollars ($20,000) in cash. / 4. That at the end of each calendar year the net profit or net loss shall be divided equally between the parties hereto, and the account of each shall be credited or debited as the case may be with her proportionate share thereof.

Signed, sealed, and delivered
in the presence of

____
Sharon Brown

____
Witness

____
Lisa Cardwell

____
Witness

Exercise 7

SUMMONS WITH HEADING

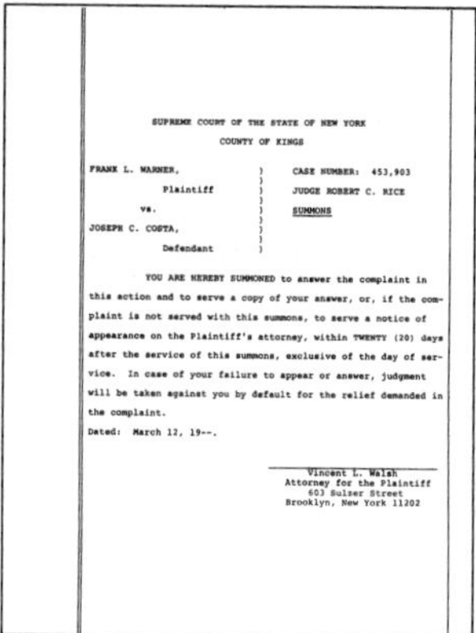

SUPREME COURT OF THE STATE OF NEW YORK
COUNTY OF KINGS

FRANK L. WARNER, Plaintiff vs. JOSEPH C. COSTA, Defendant

CASE NUMBER: 453,903
JUDGE ROBERT C. RICE
SUMMONS

YOU ARE HEREBY SUMMONED to answer the complaint in this action and to serve a copy of your answer, or, if the complaint is not served with this summons, to serve a notice of appearance on the Plaintiff's attorney, within TWENTY (20) days after the service of this summons, exclusive of the day of service. In case of your failure to appear or answer, judgment will be taken against you by default for the relief demanded in the complaint.

Dated: March 12, 19--.

Vincent L. Walsh
Attorney for the Plaintiff
603 Sulzer Street
Brooklyn, New York 11202

SUPREME COURT OF THE STATE OF NEW YORK / COUNTY OF KINGS / FRANK L. WARNER, / Plaintiff / vs. / JOSEPH C. COSTA, / Defendant / CASE NUMBER: 453,903 / JUDGE ROBERT C. RICE / SUMMONS / YOU ARE HEREBY SUMMONED to answer the complaint in this action and to serve a copy of your answer, or, if the complaint is not served with this summons, to serve a notice of appearance on the Plaintiff's attorney, within TWENTY (20) days after the service of this summons, exclusive of the day of service. In case of your failure to appear or answer, judgment will be taken against you by default for the relief demanded in the complaint. / Dated: March 12, 19—.

____
Vincent L. Walsh
Attorney for the Plaintiff
603 Sulzer Street
Brooklyn, New York 11202

Exercise 8

ASSIGNMENT

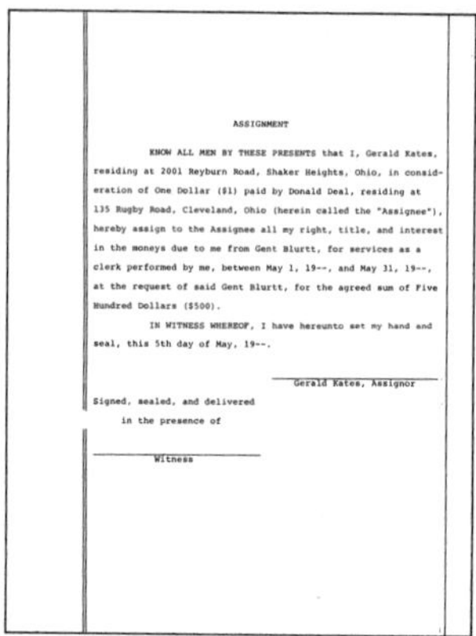

ASSIGNMENT

KNOW ALL MEN BY THESE PRESENTS that I, Gerald Kates, residing at 2001 Reyburn Road, Shaker Heights, Ohio, in consideration of One Dollar ($1) paid by Donald Deal, residing at 135 Rugby Road, Cleveland, Ohio (herein called the "Assignee"), hereby assign to the Assignee all my right, title, and interest in the moneys due to me from Gent Blurtt, for services as a clerk performed by me, between May 1, 19--, and May 31, 19--, at the request of said Gent Blurtt, for the agreed sum of Five Hundred Dollars ($500).

IN WITNESS WHEREOF, I have hereunto set my hand and seal, this 5th day of May, 19--.

Gerald Kates, Assignor

Signed, sealed, and delivered
in the presence of

Witness

ASSIGNMENT / KNOW ALL MEN BY THESE PRESENTS that I, Gerald Kates, residing at 2001 Reyburn Road, Shaker Heights, Ohio, in consideration of One Dollar ($1) paid by Donald Deal, residing at 135 Rugby Road, Cleveland, Ohio (herein called the "Assignee"), hereby assign to the Assignee all my right, title, and interest in the moneys due to me from Gent Blurtt, for services as a clerk performed by me, between May 1, 19—, and May 31, 19—, at the request of said Gent Blurtt, for the agreed sum of Five Hundred Dollars ($500). / IN WITNESS WHEREOF, I have hereunto set my hand and seal, this 5th day of May, 19—.

Signed, sealed, and delivered
in the presence of

____
Gerald Kates, Assignor

____
Witness

Exercise 10

Full sheet. Double spacing. Center column headings. Decide on the spacing between columns. Center vertically and horizontally.

CENTRAL NATIONAL BANK

260 Market Street

Philadelphia, PA 19104

Mortgagor	Location	Loan Value
John Abbott	483 Main Street	$10,000
Acker & Smith	25 Wing Street	12,000
Hazel Arthur	316 Court Street	4,000
Henry Gorchakov	22391 Columbia Turnpike	10,000
Patrick Kelly	258 Main Street	9,800

Exercise 11

ROUGH-DRAFT COPY

Type the table, making the corrections indicated.

Half sheet. Single spacing. Center column headings. Center vertically and horizontally.

CLASSES
FILMS FOR ^ IN SECRETARIAL Studies

Sound--16 mm

Title	Distributor	Time (Minutes)	Rental Fee (Per Month)
The Office Day	Business Bureau	20	~~Free~~
The Expert Typist	Visual Aids,^Inc.	15	$2.50
The Electronic Office ~~First Typing Lessons~~	Hugh A. Fiske & Co.	15	12.50
Stenographic Dictations	Visual Aids, Inc.	20	13.00
Applying for ^a Job	Hugh A. Fiske & Co.	23	9.50 ~~13.00~~
Electronic Mail ~~Postal Services~~	Business Bureau	20	Fere
Office Duties	Central Films	20	13.50

Exercise 5
WILL

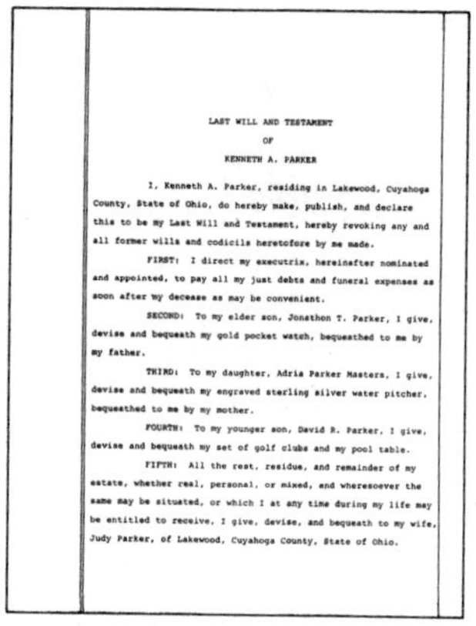

LAST WILL AND TESTAMENT

OF

KENNETH A. PARKER

I, Kenneth A. Parker, residing in Lakewood, Cuyahoga County, State of Ohio, do hereby make, publish, and declare this to be my Last Will and Testament, hereby revoking any and all former wills and codicils heretofore by me made.

FIRST: I direct my executrix, hereinafter nominated and appointed, to pay all my just debts and funeral expenses as soon after my decease as may be convenient.

SECOND: To my elder son, Jonathon T. Parker, I give, devise and bequeath my gold pocket watch, bequeathed to me by my father.

THIRD: To my daughter, Adria Parker Masters, I give, devise and bequeath my engraved sterling silver water pitcher, bequeathed to me by my mother.

FOURTH: To my younger son, David R. Parker, I give, devise and bequeath my set of golf clubs and my pool table.

FIFTH: All the rest, residue, and remainder of my estate, whether real, personal, or mixed, and wheresoever the same may be situated, or which I at any time during my life may be entitled to receive, I give, devise, and bequeath to my wife, Judy Parker, of Lakewood, Cuyahoga County, State of Ohio.

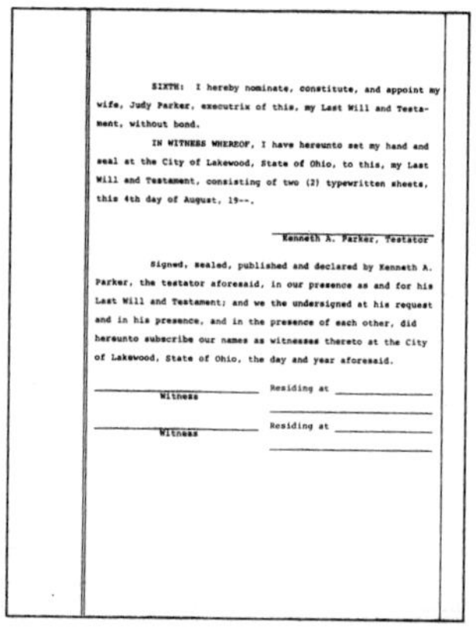

SIXTH: I hereby nominate, constitute, and appoint my wife, Judy Parker, executrix of this, my Last Will and Testament, without bond.

IN WITNESS WHEREOF, I have hereunto set my hand and seal at the City of Lakewood, State of Ohio, to this, my Last Will and Testament, consisting of two (2) typewritten sheets, this 4th day of August, 19--.

Kenneth A. Parker, Testator

Signed, sealed, published and declared by Kenneth A. Parker, the testator aforesaid, in our presence as and for his Last Will and Testament; and we the undersigned at his request and in his presence, and in the presence of each other, did hereunto subscribe our names as witnesses thereto at the City of Lakewood, State of Ohio, the day and year aforesaid.

Witness Residing at

Witness Residing at

LAST WILL AND TESTAMENT / OF / KENNETH A. PARKER / I, Kenneth A. Parker, residing in Lakewood, Cuyahoga County, State of Ohio, do hereby make, publish, and declare this to be my Last Will and Testament, hereby revoking any and all former wills and codicils heretofore by me made. / FIRST: I direct my executrix, hereinafter nominated and appointed, to pay all my just debts and funeral expenses as soon after my decease as may be convenient. / SECOND: To my elder son, Jonathon T. Parker, I give, devise, and bequeath my gold pocket watch, bequeathed to me by my father. / THIRD: To my daughter, Adria Parker Masters, I give, devise, and bequeath my engraved sterling silver water pitcher, bequeathed to me by my mother. / FOURTH: To my younger son, David R. Parker, I give, devise, and bequeath my set of golf clubs and my pool table./ FIFTH: All the rest, residue, and remainder of my estate, whether real, personal, or mixed, and wheresoever the same may be situated, or which I at any time during my life may be entitled to receive, I give, devise, and bequeath to my wife, Judy Parker, of Lakewood, Cuyahoga County, State of Ohio. / SIXTH: I hereby nominate, constitute, and appoint my wife, Judy Parker, executrix of this, my Last Will and Testament, without bond. / IN WITNESS WHEREOF, I have hereunto set my hand and seal at the City of Lakewood, State of Ohio, to this, my Last Will and Testament, consisting of two (2) typewritten sheets, this 4th day of August, 19—.

____
Kenneth A. Parker, Testator

Signed, sealed, published, and declared by Kenneth A. Parker, the testator aforesaid, in our presence as and for his Last Will and Testament; and we the undersigned at his request and in his presence, and in the presence of each other, did hereunto subscribe our names as witnesses thereto at the City of Lakewood, State of Ohio, the day and year aforesaid.

____________________ Witness	Residing at ______________
____________________ Witness	Residing at ______________

Exercise 6
PARTNERSHIP AGREEMENT

PARTNERSHIP AGREEMENT / THIS AGREEMENT, made in the City of Columbus, State of Mississippi, on the fourteenth day of February, 19—, between Sharon Brown and Lisa Cardwell, both of Columbus, Mississippi. / WHEREIN IT IS MUTUALLY AGREED, AS FOLLOWS: / 1. That the parties hereto shall, as partners, engage in and conduct the business of buying and selling musical instruments. / 2. That the name of the partnership shall be BROWN MUSIC COMPANY. / 3. That the capital of the partnership shall be the

(Continued on next page)

Exercise 12

Full sheet. Double spacing. Center column headings. Decide on the spacing between columns. Center vertically and horizontally.

University Conservatory of Music
Summer, 19—

Course Offering	Prof/Instructor	Class Hours
Composition	Mo Myer	10 MWF
Conducting	R. Smith	2 TTHF
Harmony	P. Deltz	9 TTHS
Music history	A. Lews	3 MWF
Music theory	R. Mead	9 MWTH
Opera	J. Kurtz	1 TTh
Sight Reading	M. Myer	4 MW
Orchestration	T. Po	10 TTh S

Exercise 13

Full sheet. Double spacing. Center column headings. Decide on the spacing between columns. Center vertically and horizontally.

WEST SIDE BOWLING LEAGUE
League Standings
February 7, 19--

Team	Won	Lost	Total Pins
The Bombers	47	13	47,340
Lucky Ones	45	15	47,126
The Strikers	41	19	46,560
Charlie's Angels	40½	19½	46,240
The Group	40	20	41,040
Thunderation	38	22	40,260
Chocolate Chips	38	22	40,100
Friday Fools	37	23	39,660

Directions for Exercises 3–8 Type Exercises 3–8 on legal paper. If legal paper is not available rule the proper margins on a plain, $8\frac{1}{2}'' \times 11''$ sheet. You should have a double line $1\frac{1}{2}''$ from the left edge and a single line $\frac{1}{2}''$ from the right edge.

Exercise 3

POWER OF ATTORNEY

POWER OF ATTORNEY / KNOW ALL MEN BY THESE PRESENTS that I, Frank T. Haynes, in Dauphin County, State of Pennsylvania, do appoint Raymond Garland of the same place my true and lawful attorney, for me and in my stead, to take charge of my business as manufacturer and vendor of gas stoves; to purchase and to sell all such articles as he may deem proper in connection with said business; to sign, accept, and indorse notes, drafts, and bills; to collect or settle all claims due or to become due in my favor; and to adjust, settle, or pay all claims that now exist or may hereafter arise against me; and in general do all other acts which he may consider useful or necessary connected with my business and interests. I hereby give Raymond Garland, my said attorney, full power to do everything necessary to be done connected with the business as fully as I could do if personally present, with full power of substitution and revocation, hereby ratifying and confirming all that my said attorney shall lawfully do by virtue hereof. / IN WITNESS WHEREOF, I have hereunto set my hand and seal, this 14th day of July, 19—.

Signed, sealed, and delivered
in the presence of

____
Frank T. Haynes

____
Witness

Exercise 4

EXECUTION WITH HEADING

When typing the exercise at the right, set the heading up in correct form.

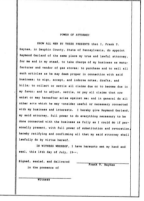

IN THE DISTRICT COURT OF THE STATE OF IDAHO / FOR THE COUNTY OF LUCAS / CIRINO RESTAURANT, INC., / Plaintiff / vs. / SAM HILL, / Defendant / STATE OF IDAHO / County of Lucas / CASE NUMBER: 486,910 / JUDGE SCOTT BRADY / EXECUTION / ss. / TO: SHERIFF OF LUCAS COUNTY, IDAHO: GREETING: / WHEREAS, on the 24th day of December, 19—, in the District Court of the State of Idaho for the County of Lucas, Cirino Restaurant, Inc., Plaintiff, recovered judgment against Sam Hill, Defendant, for the sum of $6,234.28 and court costs in the sum of $119.50. / THEREFORE, in the name of the State of Idaho, you are hereby commanded to seize the personal property of the said Sam Hill excepting such as the law exempts, and cause to be made by levy and sale, according to law, the amount of such judgment and disbursements and expenses that may accrue and of this writ make legal service and due return to me within sixty days from the date hereof. WITNESS my hand and seal of said Court. Dated: December 28, 19—.

____
Clerk

Exercise 14

Half sheet. Single spacing. Center column headings. Decide on the spacing between columns. Center vertically and horizontally.

Testing for College Entrance
Fall 19__

Examination	Examination Date	Registration Deadline
ACH	Dec. 20th	Nov. 13th
ACT	Oct. 29th	Sept. 30th
PSAT	Dec. 10	Nov. 11 3
SAT	Dec. 20	Nov. 14
NMSQT	Nov. 15	Oct. 20

Exercise 15

Half sheet. Double spacing. Center column headings. Decide on the spacing between columns. Center vertically and horizontally.

CARTER HIGH SCHOOL
D.E.C.A. Membership Roster

Name	Address	Phone	Dues Paid
Basil Willard	87 Hunter Avenue	893-4855	$5.00
Martha Dunn	12917 Ryan	366-7676	3.00
Evelyn Mason	19330 Edinborough	891-6913	1.50
Augusta Ellison	71 Vernier Road	882-5847	5.00
Daniel Remison	14230 Joy Road	772-0080	2.50
Richard Schmidt	23657 Hudson	565-9373	1.50

Bill of Sale

Know all Men by these Presents:

That we, JAMES R. PHELAN & COMPANY, of the Town of Babylon, in the County of Suffolk and State of New York------------------

*the part*ies *of the first part, in consideration of the sum of* Fifty Thousand Five Hundred-- ($50,500)-- *dollars,*

current lawful money of the United States of America, to ---------us----------- *in hand paid by* Daniel F. Newmark, of Mineola, New York------------------------- ---

*the part*y *of the second part, the receipt whereof is hereby acknowledged, do___ by these presents sell and convey unto the part*y *of the second part,* ------his-------- *executors, administrators, and assigns*

all the following GOODS, CHATTELS, and PROPERTY, to wit:

the gas and service station and automobile accessories business now conducted by us at 475 South Shore Drive, Babylon, New York, including the goodwill thereof, lease, stock in trade, fixtures, and appurtenances, as per inventory schedule attached, and each and every thing used by us therein.

To Have and to Hold *the same unto the part*y *of the second part,* ----his----- *executors, administrators, and assigns forever.*

And ---------we---------- *do___ for* ---------our--------- *heirs, executors, and administrators, covenant and agree with the part*y *of the second part,* ---his-- *executors, administrators, and assigns, to warrant and defend the sale of the said property, goods, and chattels, unto the part*y *of the second part,* ------his----- *executors, administrators, and assigns, against all and every person and persons whomsoever lawfully claiming or to claim the same.*

In Witness Whereof *the part*ies *of the first part ha*ve *executed these presents the* 28th----------------- *day of* August--------------- *one thousand nine hundred and* eighty-two---------------.

President

Secretary Treasurer

Exercise 16

UNARRANGED COPY

Arrange this material attractively. Half sheet. Double spacing. Type in four columns.

MOTION PICTURE ACADEMY AWARDS

1978–1984

Year / Best Actor / Best Actress / Best Picture

1978 / Jon Voight / Jane Fonda / The Deer Hunter
1979 / Dustin Hoffman / Sally Field / Kramer vs. Kramer
1980 / Robert De Niro / Sissy Spacek / Ordinary People
1981 / Henry Fonda / Katharine Hepburn / Chariots of Fire
1982 / Ben Kingsley / Meryl Streep / Gandhi
1983 / Jack Nicholson / Shirley MacLaine / Terms of Endearment
1984 / F. Murray Abraham / Sally Field / Amadeus

Exercise 17

UNARRANGED COPY

Arrange this material attractively. Omit any words in the body which are indicated or implied in the heading.

Full sheet. Spread center the main title.

CIVIL SERVICE EXAM SCHEDULE

City of Memphis

Job Opening   Date   Time   Room

The examination for Bookkeeper 1 will be given on June 21 at 9 a.m. in Room 415.

The examination for Data Entry Clerk will be given on June 21 at 9 a.m. in Rooms 419, 421.

The examination for Bookkeeper Trainee will be given on June 22 at 1 p.m. in Rooms 415, 417.

The examination for Word Processing Trainee will be given on June 22 at 9 a.m. in Room 417.

The examination for Stenographer 1 will be given on June 21 at 9 a.m. in Room 416.

The examination for Word Processing Secretary 1 will be given on June 21 at 1 p.m. in Room 416.

The examination for Word Processing Secretary 2 will be given on June 22 at 1 p.m. in Room 421.

Exercise 18

CREATIVE KEYBOARDING

Half sheet. Margins as necessary to center table vertically and horizontally. Double spacing for heading(s); single spacing for body.

What is the maximum number of columns with heads that you can arrange attractively and type on a half sheet of paper? Test yourself. Before coming to class, search newspapers, magazines, almanacs, encyclopedias, or similar sources for tables that have large numbers of columns. Select one table that you would consider a challenge to type. From it, copy 3 or 4 horizontal lines of data and, using this information, do a planning diagram. Then keyboard your version of the table. Include your planning diagram (handwritten) in the bottom margin. Compare your finished work with your classmates' to see who did the most complicated table.

Quitclaim Deed

This Indenture made the 27th-------------------- day of August---------------- one thousand nine hundred and eighty-one------------

Between

ELIZABETH ANN KOCSIS

the party____ of the first part,

and

WAYNE ROGER KOCSIS

the party____ of the second part,

Witnesseth: That the said party____ of the first part, in consideration of the sum of Ten and 00/100 ($10.00)------------------------------------ dollars, lawful money of the United States of America, to --------her-------- in hand paid by the party____ of the second part, the receipt whereof is hereby acknowledged, does hereby release and forever QUITCLAIM unto the party____ of the second part, and to-----his----- heirs and assigns, all that certain lot --, piece --, or parcel X of land situate in the City of Lyndhurst-------------------- County of Cuyahoga-------------------- State of Ohio------------------------, and bounded and described as follows, to-wit:

known as and being Sublot No. 193 in J. Marucik Co. Sunbay Subdivision No. 1 of part of original Sunview Township Lot No. 9, Tract 2, and part of original Sunview Township Lot No. 7, Tract 4, as shown by the recorded plat in Volume 36 of Maps, Page 98 of Cuyahoga County Records, and being 50 feet front on the west side of Cedar Road, and extending back of equal width 160 feet, as appears by said plat, but subject to all legal highways.

Together with the tenements, hereditaments, and appurtenances thereunto belonging or appertaining, and the reversion and reversions, remainder and remainders, rents, issues, and profits thereof.

To Have and to Hold the said premises, together with the appurtenances, unto the party____ of the second part, and to --his--- heirs and assigns forever.

In Witness Whereof the party____ of the first part has executed this conveyance the day and year first above written.

Signed and Delivered in the Presence of

____________________ ____________________

____________________ ____________________

Topic 5 REVIEW OF TABULATIONS

The exercises in this topic have been designed to build spelling as well as tabulation skills. The ability to spell correctly is one that employers frequently look for in prospective employees. The reason for this is clear: a beautifully typed piece of work that contains even one misspelled word is unacceptable in the business world.

Responsibility for the accuracy of spelling in final typed copy rests with the typist or word processing operator. He or she is expected to know the correct spelling of all commonly used words and to check the spelling of any words that are unfamiliar. The increased use of word processing equipment in offices is not likely to change this situation. Most dictionary software packages do not eliminate spelling errors. They merely locate them. It is up to the operator to determine the nature of the error and to make the proper correction.

The words used in the exercises that follow are those frequently misspelled in business correspondence. As you type the exercises, study the rules given and concentrate on learning to spell the words used. If you can master the spelling of just the 100 words in the Master Spelling List below, you will be that much closer to qualifying for a good job.

MASTER SPELLING LIST—PART 1

1	absence	26	autumn	51	difference	76	noticeable
2	accept	27	beginning	52	disappoint	77	occasionally
3	accommodate	28	believe	53	discuss	78	occurrence
4	accompany	29	benefited	54	dyeing	79	omitted
5	accomplish	30	breathe	55	effect	80	opportunity
6	accuracy	31	brought	56	efficient	81	personnel
7	achieve	32	business	57	eligible	82	planning
8	acquaint	33	calendar	58	embarrassment	83	possession
9	across	34	cancellation	59	employee	84	precede
10	advantage	35	cannot	60	equipment	85	privilege
11	affect	36	character	61	equipped	86	procedure
12	aisle	37	choose	62	essential	87	receive
13	almost	38	committee	63	exceed	88	recommend
14	already	39	competent	64	existence	89	reference
15	altogether	40	conscious	65	facilities	90	remittance
16	analysis	41	consistent	66	familiarize	91	representative
17	analyze	42	controlled	67	forty	92	separate
18	answer	43	convenience	68	further	93	shipment
19	apologize	44	correspondence	69	genuine	94	similar
20	apparently	45	counselor	70	immediately	95	stenographer
21	appointment	46	criticism	71	incidentally	96	surprise
22	appropriate	47	customer	72	knowledge	97	their
23	arrangement	48	decision	73	loose	98	tomorrow
24	assistance	49	describe	74	maintenance	99	undoubtedly
25	attendance	50	develop	75	necessary	100	volume

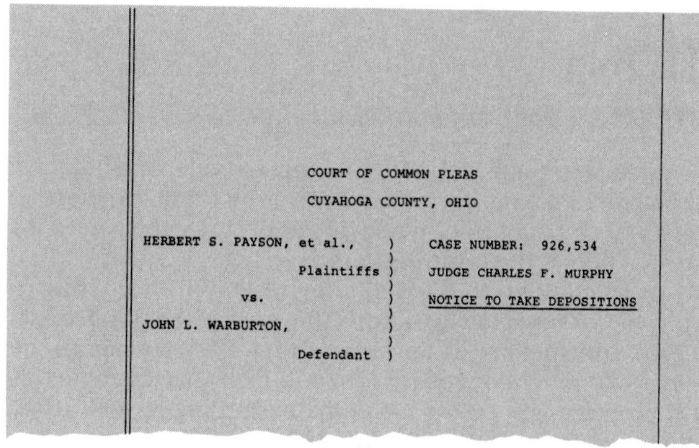
COURT OF COMMON PLEAS
CUYAHOGA COUNTY, OHIO

HERBERT S. PAYSON, et al.,) CASE NUMBER: 926,534
Plaintiffs) JUDGE CHARLES F. MURPHY
vs.) NOTICE TO TAKE DEPOSITIONS
JOHN L. WARBURTON,)
Defendant)

16. Legal documents that are used in court proceedings need formal headings. Although the documents may vary, there are some general rules for typing headings:
    - Center the name of the court 2 inches from the top of the page.
    - Type the names of the parties concerned at the left. The names are typed in solid capitals. The plaintiffs' names always appear first.
    - Type a line of parentheses as far down as the caption reads.
    - Type the case number, the judge's name, and the title of action in capitals at the right.

Look at the illustration of a heading at the left.

BACKING SHEETS

BACKING SHEETS Sometimes a legal document may be bound in a cover, called a *backing sheet.* The backing sheet is slightly heavier and larger than the paper on which the document is typed. The document is inserted under a 1-inch fold at the top of the backing sheet and stapled.

ENDORSEMENTS Sometimes information is typed on the backing sheet. This is called an *endorsement.* The information—such as the name of the document, the names of the parties, the date, and the name of the attorney—serves to identify the document.

FOLDING Most legal papers are filed in the standard way, without being folded. But if a legal paper is to go into a safe-deposit box or a special file, it is folded to fit.

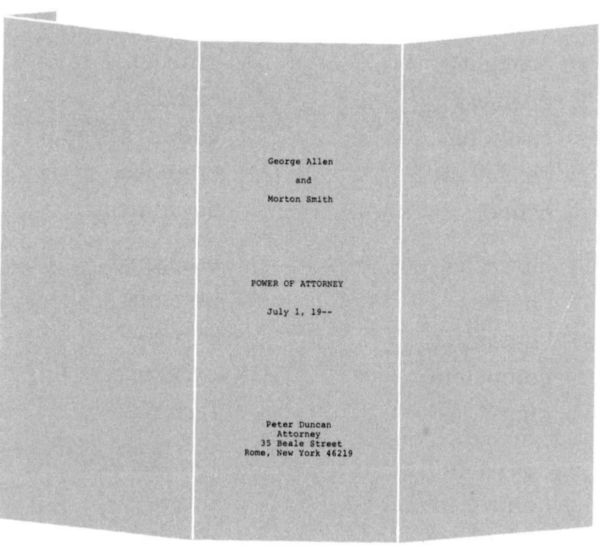

Backing Sheet Folded in Thirds with Endorsement on Center Panel

Exercise 1
QUITCLAIM DEED

Type the quitclaim deed shown on the following page. Use a printed legal form. If a form is not available, follow the procedures for typing the document in full given on page 332.

Exercise 2
BILL OF SALE

Type the bill of sale shown on page 335. Use a printed legal form. If a form is not available, prepare the document in fully typed form following the procedures outlined on page 332.

Exercise 1

Half sheet. Single spacing. Spaces between columns are 6, 12, and 6. Center vertically and horizontally.

WORDS FREQUENTLY CONFUSED

Learn to Use These Words Correctly

accept	except	lead	led
access	excess	lose	loose
advise	advice	patience	patients
affect	effect	personal	personnel
angle	angel	principal	principle
assistants	assistance	quiet	quite
choose	chose	recent	resent
council	counsel	stationery	stationary
course	coarse	than	then
dairy	diary	their	there
die	dye	to	too
forth	fourth	whether	weather
its	it's	whose	who's

Exercise 2

Full sheet. Single spacing. DS after each pair of similar words. 10 spaces between columns. Center vertically and horizontally.

COMMONLY MISSPELLED WORDS

List No. 1

Words	*Definitions*
accept	to receive
except	to exclude; but
advice	words of wisdom
advise	to give advice
assistants	those who give help
assistance	help
cite	to quote or refer to
sight	something seen
site	a location
coarse	rough in texture; not fine
course	direction of movement
choose	to select (present tense)
chose	past tense of *choose*
compliment	to praise
complement	to complete
council	an assembly to govern or advise
counsel	to advise; a lawyer
forth	forward; onward
fourth	4*th* spelled out

LEGAL DOCUMENTS TYPED IN FULL

Legal documents may also be typed in full, without the use of a printed form. When you type such a document, you must follow certain rules. Here are some general guidelines for typing legal documents in full:

1. Use legal paper that is $8\frac{1}{2}'' \times 11''$ or $8\frac{1}{2}'' \times 13''$. (Most courts require $8\frac{1}{2}'' \times 11''$ paper.) Legal paper has a double line at the left providing a $1\frac{1}{2}$-inch margin, and a single line at the right providing a $\frac{1}{2}$-inch margin.
2. Use pica type. For most legal documents, elite type is not acceptable.
3. Center headings between the vertical lines at the margins. To find the center, add the two numbers on your scale that fall on the vertical lines and divide by two.
4. Indent paragraphs 10 spaces.
5. Use double spacing, except for quotations, which are single spaced.
6. Triple-space after centered headings and titles.
7. Leave 2 inches for a top margin on the first page and $1\frac{1}{2}$ inches on other pages. Leave at least 1 inch for the bottom margin.
8. Leave 1 or 2 spaces between the typing and the ruled lines along the margins. If you do not have ruled paper, leave a $1\frac{1}{2}$-inch left margin and a 1-inch right margin.
9. Center the page numbers between the ruled margins and type them $\frac{1}{2}$ inch from the bottom edge of the paper. Do not number the first page.
10. Do not erase important data, such as dates, figures and names. Unavoidable additions (written between lines) should be initialed by the signers of the document.
11. Express numbers in figures. However, important numbers, such as prices and measurements, should be spelled out, followed by numerals in parentheses.
12. It is customary to use solid capitals for certain expressions that appear at the beginnings of paragraphs. Some examples are: WHEREAS, IN WITNESS WHEREOF.
13. Spell names exactly.
14. Include dates either at the beginning or at the end of the document.
15. Make signature lines about 3 inches long and triple-space before and after each line. Signatures must never appear by themselves on the last page. At least 3 lines of text should appear above the signatures.

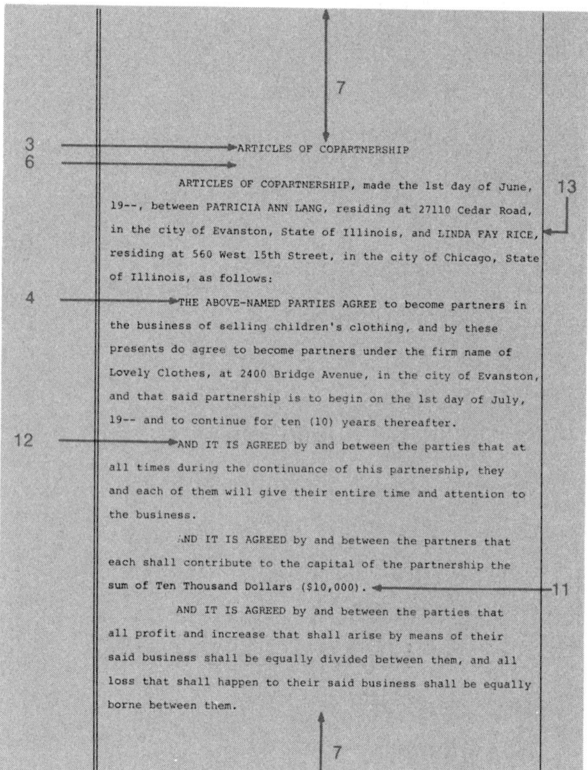

ARTICLES OF COPARTNERSHIP

ARTICLES OF COPARTNERSHIP, made the 1st day of June, 19--, between PATRICIA ANN LANG, residing at 27110 Cedar Road, in the city of Evanston, State of Illinois, and LINDA FAY RICE, residing at 560 West 15th Street, in the city of Chicago, State of Illinois, as follows:

THE ABOVE-NAMED PARTIES AGREE to become partners in the business of selling children's clothing, and by these presents do agree to become partners under the firm name of Lovely Clothes, at 2400 Bridge Avenue, in the city of Evanston, and that said partnership is to begin on the 1st day of July, 19-- and to continue for ten (10) years thereafter.

AND IT IS AGREED by and between the parties that at all times during the continuance of this partnership, they and each of them will give their entire time and attention to the business.

AND IT IS AGREED by and between the partners that each shall contribute to the capital of the partnership the sum of Ten Thousand Dollars ($10,000).

AND IT IS AGREED by and between the parties that all profit and increase that shall arise by means of their said business shall be equally divided between them, and all loss that shall happen to their said business shall be equally borne between them.

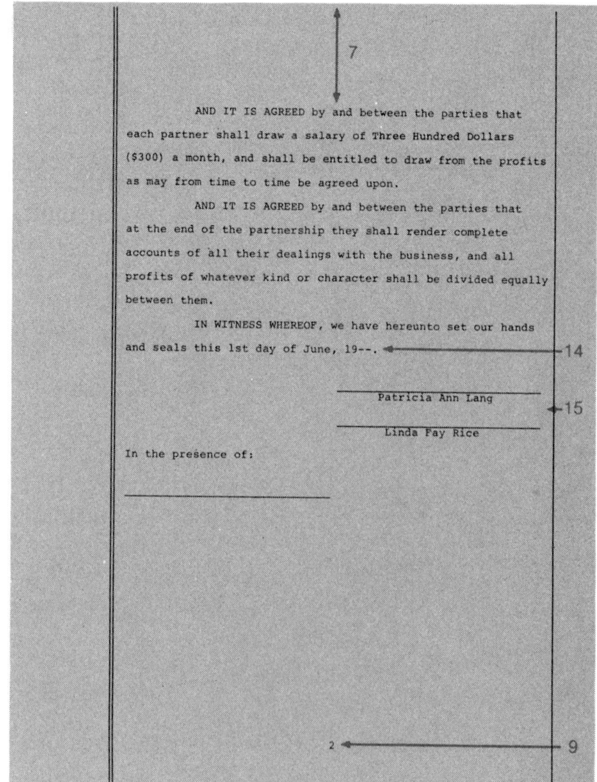

AND IT IS AGREED by and between the parties that each partner shall draw a salary of Three Hundred Dollars ($300) a month, and shall be entitled to draw from the profits as may from time to time be agreed upon.

AND IT IS AGREED by and between the parties that at the end of the partnership they shall render complete accounts of all their dealings with the business, and all profits of whatever kind or character shall be divided equally between them.

IN WITNESS WHEREOF, we have hereunto set our hands and seals this 1st day of June, 19--.

Patricia Ann Lang

Linda Fay Rice

In the presence of:

2

Exercise 3

Half sheet. Single spacing. DS after each pair of similar words. Spaces between columns are 4, 8, and 4. Center vertically and horizontally.

COMMONLY MISSPELLED WORDS

List No. 2

hear	to listen	principal	chief; school official
here	this place	principle	rule; general truth
know	to be familiar with	quiet	not noisy
no	opposite of *yes*	quite	completely
loose	not tight	their	belongs to them
lose	to mislay	there	that place
lead	heavy metal	too	in excess; or also
led	past tense of *to lead*	to	in the direction
passed	to go by	than	a comparison
past	a former time; beyond	then	at that time
personal	private	weather	the atmospheric state
personnel	employees	whether	alternative

Exercise 4

Half sheet. Single spacing. 6 spaces between columns. Center vertically and horizontally.

SIMILAR-SOUNDING TRIOS

to	too	two
quiet	quite	quit
cite	sight	site
counsel	council	consul
adapt	adept	adopt
holy	wholly	holey
clothes	cloths	close
martial	marshal	marital
loose	lose	loss
sent	scent	cent
rain	rein	reign
vain	vein	vane

Exercise 5

WORD-BUILDING PRACTICE

After typing this exercise as a tabulation, type the words in the last column from teacher dictation.

Half sheet. Single spacing. 4 spaces between columns. Center vertically and horizontally.

ANALYZING WORDS BY SYLLABLES

Five-Syllable Words

oc	occa	occasion	occasional	occasionally
rep	repre	represen	representa	representative
in	inci	inciden	incidental	incidentally
un	unnec	unneces	unnecessar	unnecessary
pro	pronun	pronunci	pronuncia	pronunciation
su	super	superin	superinten	superintendent

Topic 3 LEGAL DOCUMENTS

A typist in a law office must be familiar with certain typing practices unique to legal work. A typist in a business office also must occasionally type legal matter. You should, therefore, have a general working knowledge of the most common legal forms.

PRINTED LEGAL DOCUMENTS

Printed forms are available for many legal instruments. Here are some general guidelines for typing on printed legal documents:

1. Type insertions so that they align with the printed words on the line that you are filling in. To do this, use the variable line spacer or the automatic line finder.
2. Use hyphens to fill empty space that remains on either side of the item you type. This prevents alterations that might change the meaning of the document.

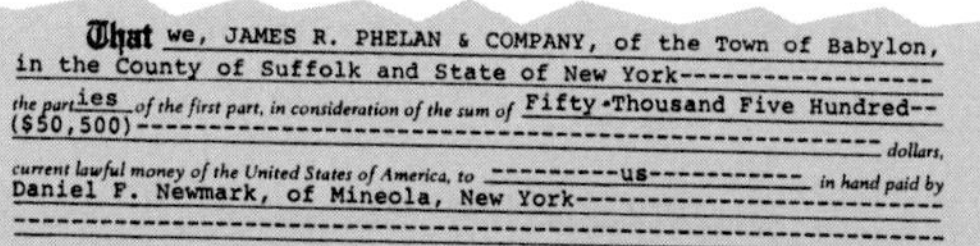

That we, JAMES R. PHELAN & COMPANY, of the Town of Babylon, in the County of Suffolk and State of New York------------------
the parties of the first part, in consideration of the sum of Fifty-Thousand Five Hundred--
($50,500)-- dollars,
current lawful money of the United States of America, to ----------us------------ in hand paid by
Daniel F. Newmark, of Mineola, New York--------------------------

3. Leave 1 space between the inserted word and the printed word that comes before it.

the party of the second part, the receipt whereof is hereby acknowledged, do___ by these presents sell and convey unto the party of the second part, ------his-------- executors, administrators, and assigns
all the following GOODS, CHATTELS, and PROPERTY, to wit:
the gas and service station and automobile accessories business
now conducted by us at 475 South Shore Drive, Babylon, New York,
including the goodwill thereof, lease, stock in trade, fixtures,

4. Line up left and right margins with those on the form.

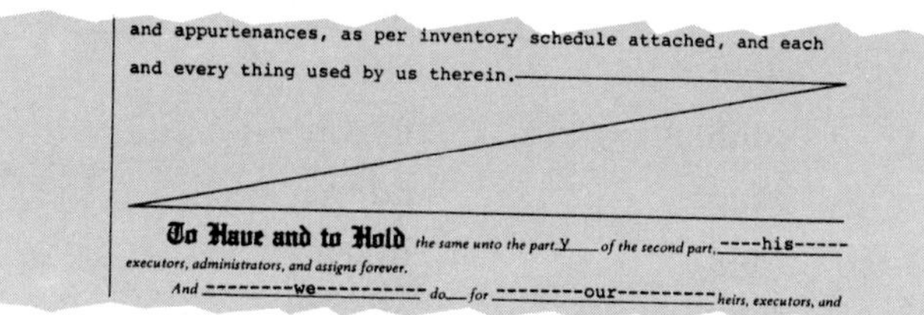

and appurtenances, as per inventory schedule attached, and each
and every thing used by us therein.

To Have and to Hold the same unto the party of the second part, ----his-----
executors, administrators, and assigns forever.
And --------we---------- do___ for ---------our---------- heirs, executors, and

5. Draw a "Z" rule to fill in large blank spaces.

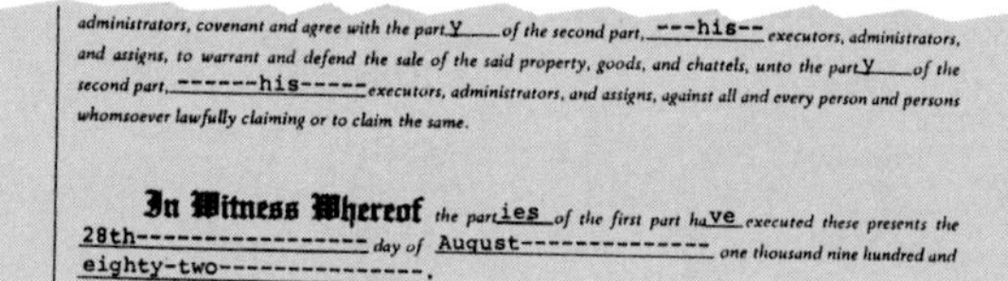

administrators, covenant and agree with the party of the second part, ---his--- executors, administrators, and assigns, to warrant and defend the sale of the said property, goods, and chattels, unto the party of the second part, ------his----- executors, administrators, and assigns, against all and every person and persons whomsoever lawfully claiming or to claim the same.

In Witness Whereof the parties of the first part have executed these presents the
28th----------------- day of August-------------- one thousand nine hundred and
eighty-two---------------.

6. Leave no space after incomplete words that you, as the typist, are to complete. Type the fill-in letters close to the printed letter.

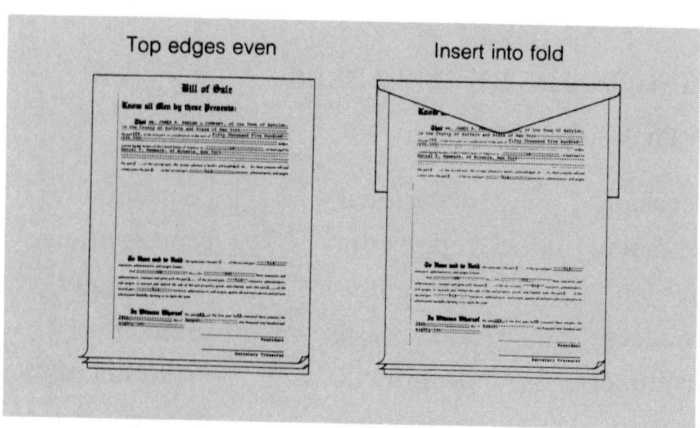

7. Make the top edges of the original and carbon copies exactly even. In that way, the typing on the copies will appear on exactly the same lines as the printing. Cover the tops of the original and carbon copies with a folded strip of paper or an envelope. Then insert them into the typewriter. This will keep the papers even.

Exercise 6

WORD-BUILDING PRACTICE

Full sheet. Double spacing. Decide on the spacing between columns. Center vertically and horizontally.

ANALYZING WORDS BY SYLLABLES

Four-Syllable Words

ac	accu	accura	accuracy
ap	appre	appreci	appreciate
grad	gradu	gradua	graduation
ac	accom	accommo	accommodate
ex	expe	experi	experience
im	imme	immedi	immediate
un	undoubt	undoubted	undoubtedly
can	cancel	cancella	cancellation
fa	famil	familiar	familiarize
ac	acknowl	acknowledg	acknowledgment
ben	bene	benefit	benefited

Exercise 7

WORD-BUILDING PRACTICE

Full sheet. Double spacing. Decide on the spacing between columns. Center vertically and horizontally.

ANALYZING WORDS BY SYLLABLES

Three-Syllable Words

crit	criti	criticism
main	mainte	maintenance
sep	sepa	separate
sim	simi	similar
per	person	personnel
cus	custom	customer
dif	differ	difference
an	ana	analyze
com	commit	committee
dis	disap	disappoint
de	deci	decision
de	devel	develop
ex	exis	existence
ex	excel	excellent
de	descrip	description
con	conve	convenient

Exercise 8

Can you find the silent letters in these words?

Half sheet. Double spacing. Decide on the spacing between columns. Center vertically and horizontally.

TRICKY SILENT-LETTER WORDS

know	handkerchief	campaign	mortgage
anxious	often	answer	island
whole	sword	guarantee	autumn
straight	minute	column	listen
ready	debt	doubt	rhythm

Exercise 12
EXPENSE REPORT

NAME: James Cutre WEEK ENDING: June 22, 19—

DATE	CITY AND STATE	LODGING	AIR	MEALS	ENTER-TAINMENT	MISC. EXPENSES	DAILY TOTAL
6/18	Grand Rapids, MI	48.70	68.42	60.00	15.40	6.00	198.52
TOTALS		48.70	68.42	60.00	15.40	6.00	198.52

ENTERTAINMENT EXPENSES:

DATE	ITEM	AMOUNT
6/18	Luncheon for Paula Briggs, President of U-STOR, Inc.	15.40
TOTAL		15.40

MISCELLANEOUS EXPENSES:

DATE	ITEM	AMOUNT
6/19	Registration fee for convention	6.00
TOTAL		6.00

EXPENSE SUMMARY:

TOTAL: 198.52 AMOUNT DUE EMPLOYEE: None

LESS ADVANCES: 225.00 AMOUNT DUE COMPANY: 26.48

Exercise 13
EXPENSE REPORT

NAME: Carol Barbour WEEK ENDING: August 7, 19—

DATE	CITY AND STATE	LODGING	AUTO EXPENSE	MEALS	MISC. EXPENSES	DAILY TOTAL
8/1	St. Louis, MO	28.50	54.00	29.75	3.65	115.90
8/2	Topeka, KS	25.00	58.50	27.50		111.00
8/3	Kansas City, KS	27.25	15.80	24.20		67.25
8/4	Augusta, KS	22.40	12.65	18.90	5.22	59.17
8/5	Springfield, MO	25.00	18.40	20.55		63.95
TOTALS		128.15	159.35	120.90	8.87	417.27

MISCELLANEOUS EXPENSES:

DATE	ITEM	AMOUNT
8/1	Parking	3.65
8/4	Telephone Calls	5.22
TOTAL		8.87

EXPENSE SUMMARY:

TOTAL 417.27 AMOUNT DUE EMPLOYEE: 417.27

LESS ADVANCES: None AMOUNT DUE COMPANY: None

Exercise 9

Be careful not to slur the vowels in these words.

Half sheet. Double spacing. Decide on the spacing between columns. Center vertically and horizontally.

WORDS THAT ARE OFTEN MISPRONOUNCED

arithmetic	probably	government	jewelry
separate	strength	athletic	family
across	library	length	empty
secretary	nuclear	generally	interest
quantity	treasurer	February	Wednesday

Exercise 10

Some word endings have a very similar sound. Take careful notice of the words listed at the right.

Arrange this material attractively on a full sheet.

WATCH OUT FOR THOSE WORD ENDINGS!

or	*er*	*ar*
administrator	messenger	grammar
ancestor	eraser	liar
doctor	consumer	scholar
visitor	employer	regular
distributor	subscriber	extracurricular
professor	manufacturer	calendar
collector	customer	collar
creator	receiver	peculiar

Exercise 11

Center attractively on a half sheet.

"UHBLE" ENDINGS

able	ible
changeable	invisible
agreeable	admissible
noticeable	terrible
unbelievable	responsible
usable	impossible
advisable	legible
comfortable	permissible
desirable	corruptible
probable	audible

Exercise 12

Learning one word ending can help you remember a similar one.

Center attractively on a half sheet. Don't forget to make a distinction in the spaces between the columns.

ANT/ANCE VERSUS ENT/ENCE

ant	*ance*	*ent*	*ence*
assistant	assistance	resident	residence
attendant	attendance	dependent	dependence
resistant	resistance	superintendent	superintendence
fragrant	fragrance	confident	confidence
reliant	reliance	correspondent	correspondence
radiant	radiance	prominent	prominence

EXPENSE REPORTS

Type each exercise following the style shown in Model 31. If forms are not available, prepare expense report forms similar to the one shown below.

Exercise 10
EXPENSE REPORT

Type an expense report using the information in Model 31.

Exercise 11
EXPENSE REPORT

Prepare an expense report using the information at the right. Then complete the expense summary, assuming no advances to the employee.

NAME: Marilyn Franklin WEEK ENDING: June 8, 19—

DATE	CITY AND STATE	LODGING	AUTO EXPENSES	MEALS	DAILY TOTAL
6/5	Duluth, MN	33.60	22.50	14.90	71.00
6/6	Duluth, MN	____	37.00	8.12	45.12
TOTALS		33.60	59.50	23.02	116.12

CORONA INDUSTRIES INCORPORATED
711 CHERRY STREET • ST. PAUL, MN 55121
(218) 792-8450

EXPENSE REPORT

NAME Thomas Kessler WEEK ENDING May 13 19--

Date 19--	City and State	Lodging	Transportation: Air, Rail, etc.	Transportation: Car Rental, Limo., Cab	Auto Expenses	Meals	Entertainment (See Detail)	Misc. Expenses (See Detail)	Daily Total
5/8	Chicago, IL	36 00	75 50	6 00		19 42		4 50	141 42
5/11	Baltimore, MD	64 65	92 70	11 40		36 50		15 00	220 25
TOTALS		100 65	168 20	17 40		55 92		19 50	361 67

NOTE: Attach all receipts.

ENTERTAINMENT EXPENSE DETAIL

Date	Name/Place	Amount
TOTAL		

MISCELLANEOUS EXPENSE DETAIL

Date	Item	Amount
5/8	Telephone call to home office	4 50
5/11	Laundry	15 00
TOTAL		19 50

EXPENSE SUMMARY

TOTAL	361 67
LESS ADVANCES	325 00
AMOUNT DUE EMPLOYEE	36 67
AMOUNT DUE COMPANY	None

Signature *Date* *Department Head Approval* *Date*

Model 31 *Expense Report*

Exercise 13

Arrange attractively on a half sheet.

REMEMBER "US" ENDINGS

ious	eous
cautious	courteous
curious	hideous
delicious	gorgeous
conscious	miscellaneous
gracious	simultaneous
religious	instantaneous

Exercise 14

Recognizing similar prefixes will improve your spelling.
Half sheet. Insert paper with the short side first.

STUDYING PREFIXES

For and Fore

for	fore
forget	foretold
forgive	forehead
forfeit	foreword
forbear	foreclosure
forward	forecast
forbid	forewarned

Exercise 15

These words have troublesome double letters.
Arrange attractively on a full sheet. Spread center title.

D O U B L E   T R O U B L E

co*ll*ection	emba*rr*assed	equi*pp*ed	nece*ss*ary
occu*rr*ing	acco*mm*odate	a*dd*re*ss*	mi*ss*pe*ll*
acro*ss*	a*cc*uracy	fulfi*ll*	a*pp*ointment
reco*mm*end	cance*ll*ation	perso*nn*el	po*ss*e*ss*
questio*nn*aire	omi*ss*ion	guarant*ee*	busine*ss*
i*mm*ediate	a*cc*ompany	c*oo*peration	co*mm*i*ttee*
especia*ll*y	boo*kk*eeper	remi*tt*ance	a*pp*arent
a*cc*eptance	o*cc*upation	exce*ll*ent	a*ss*istance

Exercise 16

There are only a few words with the "seed" ending.
Half sheet. Insert paper with the short side first.

STUDY LIST OF "SEED" ENDINGS

sede	ceed	cede
supersede	proceed	precede
	exceed	secede
	succeed	concede
		recede
		accede
		intercede

Exercise 17

Arrange attractively on a half sheet.

THE "EYES" ENDINGS

ise	*ize*	*yze*
advertise	criticize	analyze
supervise	apologize	paralyze
merchandise	familiarize	
surprise	equalize	
surmise	characterize	
devise	authorize	
advise	standardize	
revise	realize	

VOUCHER CHECKS

These voucher checks come from Glenwild Realty Corporation, Great Neck, NY 11023. Type each exercise following the style shown in Model 30. If forms are not available, prepare voucher checks similar to the one shown below.

Exercise 6
VOUCHER CHECK

Type a voucher check using the information in Model 30.

Supply an address from your own city or town for the payee of each check.

	VOUCHER CHECK NO.	DATE	PAYEE	DATE OF INVOICE	INVOICE NO.	AMOUNT
Exercise 7	0181	October 31	Best Landscaping	9/29/—	8942	512.92
Exercise 8	0183	November 3	Russo Bros.	9/2/—	7360	1469.40
Exercise 9	0195	November 19	Mays, Inc.	10/1/—	5289	367.85

GLENWILD REALTY
CORPORATION
GREAT NECK NEW YORK 11023

No. 0179 1-7130/2260

October 27, 19--

Pay to the Order of Shapiro & Associates, Inc. $687.12

Six Hundred Eighty-seven and 12/100---------------------------------- *Dollars*

SCIOTO NATIONAL BANK
GREAT NECK, NEW YORK 11027

TREASURER

⑆226071308⑆ 4038727⑈

DETACH THIS STUB BEFORE CASHING

No. 0179

TO

Shapiro & Associates, Inc.
781 Henry Street
New York, NY 10042

For payment of the invoice noted below:

Date	Invoice	Amount
8/15/--	6491	687.12

GLENWILD REALTY
CORPORATION
GREAT NECK, NEW YORK 11023

Model 30 *Voucher Check*

Exercise 18

Arrange attractively on a half sheet.

The Rule

I before *e* except after *c* or when sounded like *a* as in *neighbor* and *weigh*.

THE "IE/EI" COMBINATION

IE	EI	EXCEPTIONS
interview	ceiling	neither
believe	receipt	counterfeit
achieve	receive	foreign
fierce	sleigh	seize
niece	neighbor	height
convenient	weight	leisure
grievance	skein	ancient
piece	freight	weird
achievement	eight	efficient
brief	vein	their

Exercise 19

Arrange attractively on a full sheet.

The Rules

1. Words ending in a silent e usually drop the e before a suffix beginning with a vowel.
2. Words ending with a silent e usually keep the e before a suffix beginning with a consonant.

THE SILENT FINAL "E"

To Drop or to Keep?

Rule 1	Rule 2	Exceptions
using	hopeful	acknowledgment
desirable	announcement	judgment
noticing	arrangement	noticeable
changing	immediately	changeable
encouraging	statement	manageable
writing	sanely	dyeing
coming	movement	mileage
advertising	carefully	ninth
typing	falsehood	wholly
closing	likeness	truly
deciding	management	argument

Exercise 20

Arrange attractively on a half sheet.

The Rules

1. Words ending in *y* preceded by a consonant usually change the *y* to *i* before any suffix except one beginning with an *i*.
2. Words ending in *y* preceded by a vowel usually retain the *y* before all endings.

CHANGING FINAL "Y" TO "I"

Rule 1	Rule 2	Exceptions
ordinarily	annoyance	paid
easily	attorneys	laid
heaviest	enjoyable	daily
cities	delaying	said
beautiful	buyer	ladylike
supplying	employer	shyness

3. Place the amount in Arabic numerals close to the dollar sign, leaving no space.
4. Make no erasures or alterations.

Here are some guidelines for typing expense reports: (Refer to Model 31, page 329.)

1. Use the variable line spacer to adjust the cylinder. The preprinted rule should be very slightly below the top edge of the aligning scale.
2. Type the dollar amount close to the vertical line at the right. Space once before you type the cents. Do not type the decimal point.
3. You may need to turn the cylinder by hand when typing on several printed rules. To do this, disengage the line spacing mechanism by using the automatic line finder.

RECEIPTS

The following receipts come from the Glenwild Realty Corporation, Great Neck, New York 11023. Type each exercise following the style shown in Model 29. If forms are not available, prepare receipts similar to the one shown in Model 29.

Exercise 1
RECEIPT

Type a receipt using the information in Model 29.

	RECEIPT NO.	DATE	RECEIVED FROM	AMOUNT	PURPOSE
Exercise 2	196	July 2	Kollner & Budd	$450.00	Rent from 7/1 to 7/31
Exercise 3	274	Sept. 1	Frank Mancuso	$ 55.00	Office cleaning
Exercise 4	292	Oct. 15	Alice Kukar	$125.00	Typing services
Exercise 5	293	Oct. 16	C. J. Kolezynski	$376.50	2000 brochures

No. 148

GLENWILD REALTY CORPORATION GREAT NECK NEW YORK 11023

April 1, 19--

Received from Mayflower Dress Shop

One Hundred Eighty-five and 00/100-------------------- Dollars

Rent of store at 206 Main Street, from 4/1 to 4/30

GLENWILD REALTY CORPORATION

$ 185.00

By ______________________
AGENT

Model 29 *Receipt*

Exercise 21

Arrange attractively on a full sheet.

The Rules

1. If a one-syllable word ends with a consonant preceded by a vowel, *double* the final consonant before adding a suffix beginning with a vowel.
2. If a two-syllable word, accented on the last syllable, ends with a consonant preceded by a vowel, *double* the final consonant.
3. If a two-syllable word, accented on the first syllable, ends with a consonant preceded by a vowel, *do not* double the final consonant.
4. If a word ends with two consonants, keep both consonants when adding a suffix.

DOUBLING THE FINAL CONSONANT

Examples of the Rules

Rule 1	Rule 2	Rule 3	Rule 4	Exceptions
stopping	beginning	labeled	dismissing	questionnaire
shipping	occurred	traveling	skillful	cancellation
planning	controlling	canceled	installment	transferable
baggage	regretted	profited	addressing	gaseous
putting	equipped	credited	embarrassment	reference
digging	referred	counseling	fulfillment	programming
manned	enrolled	editing	possessing	buses
ripped	forgetting	legalize	stiffness	conferee
running	remittance	marketing	blissful	kidnapped
fitting	recurring	budgeted	passable	boxing

Exercise 22

Supply the correct *ie* or *ei* combination as you type the words in this exercise. Check your work against the answers provided on page 149. Do not write in the book.

Half sheet. Double spacing. 8 spaces between columns. Center vertically and horizontally.

APPLYING THE "IE/EI" RULE

ch■■f	n■■ther	l■■sure
rec■■ve	th■■r	effic■■nt
ach■■vement	bel■■ve	for■■gn
w■■rd	p■■ce	conven■■nt
■■ght	h■■ght	rec■■pt
n■■ghbor	n■■ce	interv■■w

Exercise 23

Supply the proper word endings as you type this table. Check your work against the answers provided (refer to page 149.) Do not write in the book.

Half sheet. Single spacing. 6 spaces between columns. Center vertically and horizontally.

WORD ENDING REVIEW

List No. 1

"eyes"	"seed"	"uhble"
advert■■■	pro■■■■	terr■■■■
surpr■■■	con■■■■	imposs■■■■
critic■■■	re■■■■	justifi■■■■
anal■■■	suc■■■■	respons■■■■
real■■■	super■■■■	leg■■■■
familiar■■■	ex■■■■	dur■■■■
merchand■■■	pre■■■■	notice■■■■

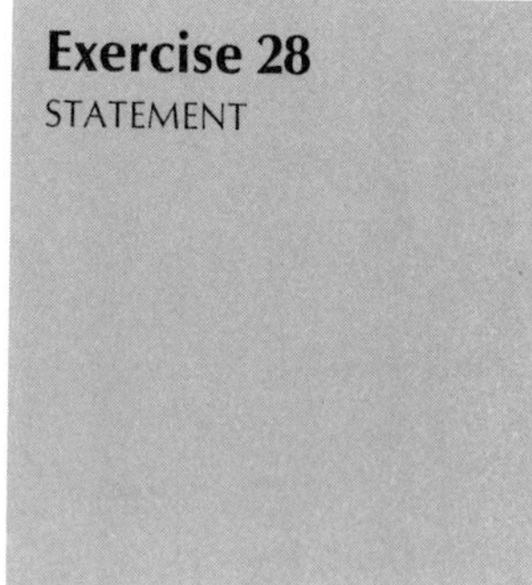

Exercise 28
STATEMENT

IN ACCOUNT WITH: Batista Bookshop, Tribune Square, Lansing, MI 48911 DATE: Jan. 30, 19—

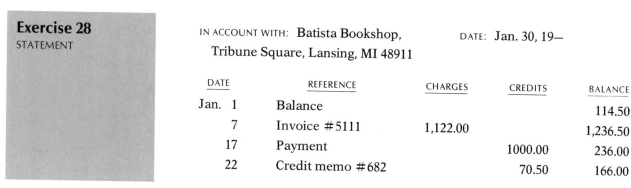

DATE	REFERENCE	CHARGES	CREDITS	BALANCE
Jan. 1	Balance			114.50
7	Invoice #5111	1,122.00		1,236.50
17	Payment		1000.00	236.00
22	Credit memo #682		70.50	166.00

Topic 2 RECEIPTS, VOUCHER CHECKS, AND EXPENSE REPORTS

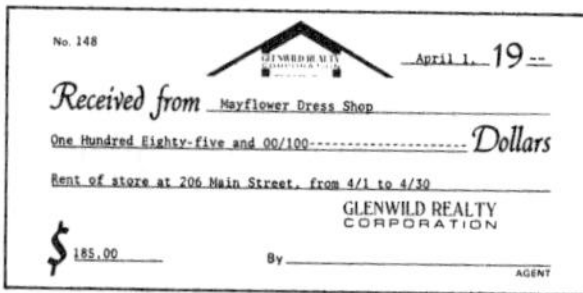

No. 148 April 1, 19--
Received from Mayflower Dress Shop
One Hundred Eighty-five and 00/100------------------ Dollars
Rent of store at 206 Main Street, from 4/1 to 4/30
GLENWILD REALTY CORPORATION
$ 185.00 By ______ AGENT

RECEIPT After making a payment, an individual or company may be given a receipt. This acknowledges that the money has been received. This form usually contains such information as:

- Date and an identifying number
- Individual or company who paid the money
- Amount of money involved
- Reason for payment

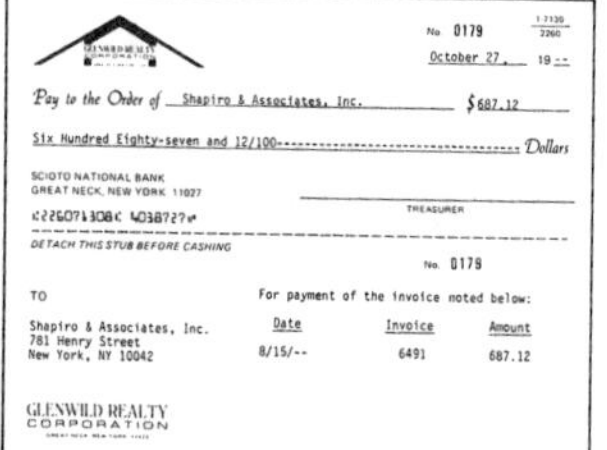

No. 0179
October 27, 19--
Pay to the Order of Shapiro & Associates, Inc. $687.12
Six Hundred Eighty-seven and 12/100------------------ Dollars
SCIOTO NATIONAL BANK
GREAT NECK, NEW YORK 11027
TREASURER
DETACH THIS STUB BEFORE CASHING
No. 0179
TO Shapiro & Associates, Inc. 781 Henry Street New York, NY 10042
For payment of the invoice noted below:

Date	Invoice	Amount
8/15/--	6491	687.12

GLENWILD REALTY CORPORATION

VOUCHER CHECK A voucher check is used by businesses to pay for merchandise and services. This form usually contains such information as:

- Date and an identifying number
- Individual or company to whom the money was paid
- Amount of money involved
- Reason for payment

EXPENSE REPORT An expense report is an itemized account of the expenditures made by an employee in the course of employment. It is prepared after a business trip, or routinely, every week. This form usually contains such information as:

- Dates the expenses were incurred
- Lists of such items as lodging, transportation, meals, entertainment, and miscellaneous items, with amounts spent on each
- Place of departure and destination

Notice that this group of forms requires you to type on printed lines or within boxes. This is easily accomplished using the variable line spacer and a little judgment. Your object is to duplicate the spatial relationship that exists between a typed word and an underscore. To do this, you engage the variable line spacer and turn the platen until the printed rule is just below the top edge of the aligning scale. If you then position the printing point at the beginning of the line, your typing should be both accurately and attractively placed.

Here are some general guidelines for typing receipts and voucher checks: (Refer to Models 29 and 30, pages 327 and 328.)

1. Use the variable line spacer to position the platen. (The preprinted rule should be just below the top edge of the aligning scale.) For each entry, position the printing point at the beginning (extreme left) of the line.
2. Type in the amount of money in words. Fill any space between the amount and the printed word *Dollars* with a row of hyphens.

Exercise 24

Supply the proper word endings as you type this table. (For answers, refer to page 149.)

Half sheet. Single spacing. 6 spaces between columns. Center vertically and horizontally.

WORD ENDING REVIEW

List No. 2

ance/ence	ious/eous	or/er/ar
attend■■■■	grac■■■■	gramm■■
depend■■■■	hid■■■■	calend■■
remitt■■■■	court■■■■	regul■■
superintend■■■■	delic■■■■	doct■■
exist■■■■	miscellan■■■■	administrat■■
accord■■■■	consc■■■■	custom■■
correspond■■■■	relig■■■■	visit■■
fragr■■■■	cur■■■■	schol■■
confid■■■■	simultan■■■■	creat■■
radi■■■■	caut■■■■	messeng■■
resid■■■■	instantan■■■■	ancest■■
resist■■■■	gorg■■■■	coll■■

Exercise 25

As you type this table (both columns), read the definitions in the first column and supply the missing letters in the second column. Check your work against the answers provided (refer to page 149). Do not write in the book.

Center attractively on a half sheet inserted with the short (5½-inch side) first.

HOW DO YOU SPELL THAT WORD?

Definition	Word
unchangeable	p■■man■nt
means of support	main■■■ance
words of wisdom	advi■e
definitely	specifi■■■ly
act of comparing	comp■■■son
second month	Feb■■ary
nonpresence	ab■■■ce
help	assist■■■■
ownership	po■■e■■ion
thankful	gr■■■ful
alike	sim■l■r
without a doubt	undo■■■edly
chief; school official	princip■■
study carefully	anal■■■
lawyer	coun■■l
rough in texture	c■■rse

Exercise 24
STATEMENT

IN ACCOUNT WITH: The Place Furniture Company, Northfield Plaza, Knoxville, TN 37906 DATE: July 31, 19—

DATE	REFERENCE	CHARGES	CREDITS	BALANCE
July 1	Balance			26.40
16	Payment		26.40	00.00
18	Invoice #4690	886.00		886.00
20	Credit memo #461		30.00	856.00

Exercise 25
STATEMENT

IN ACCOUNT WITH: The Neighborhood Store, 56 Lucas Avenue, Cranston, RI 02910 DATE: July 31, 19—

DATE	REFERENCE	CHARGES	CREDITS	BALANCE
July 1	Balance			188.25
8	Payment		100.00	88.25
9	Invoice #4674	76.00		164.25
16	Invoice #4687	419.75		584.00
29	Credit memo #463		35.00	549.00

Exercise 26
STATEMENT

IN ACCOUNT WITH: Garrett Office Equipment Co., 800 King Street, Garrett, IN 46738 DATE: Aug. 28, 19—

DATE	REFERENCE	CHARGES	CREDITS	BALANCE
Aug. 1	Balance			2569.42
4	Invoice #4699	3055.00		5624.42
7	Payment		5000.00	624.42
13	Credit memo #464		122.20	502.22
18	Invoice #4723	1945.56		2447.78
23	Payment		2300.00	147.78

Exercise 27
STATEMENT

IN ACCOUNT WITH: Glenmore Arms, 406 Adams Street, Minneapolis, MN 55408 DATE: Sept. 29, 19—

DATE	REFERENCE	CHARGES	CREDITS	BALANCE
Sept. 1	Balance			50.98
5	Invoice #4701	203.00		253.98
15	Payment		200.00	53.98
22	Invoice #4786	462.53		516.51
28	Payment		500.00	16.51

Exercise 26

Concentrate on spelling as you type this table. Three different words appear on each line. One of the three words in each line is misspelled. Correct and underscore the misspelled word as you type each line. Do not type the numbers. (For answers, refer to page 149).

Full sheet. Double spacing. 10 spaces between columns. Center vertically and horizontally.

CAN YOU FIND THE MISSPELLED WORDS?

1	seperate	performance	development
2	writting	proceed	familiar
3	priviledge	unnecessary	government
4	loose	prosedure	possession
5	answer	maintainence	reference
6	questionaire	undoubtedly	convenience
7	specifically	shiping	description
8	confident	opportunity	greatful
9	grammar	necessary	secetary
10	ommission	criticism	practically
11	personnel	ocassionally	forty
12	governor	responsable	across
13	cancelled	disappoint	difference
14	Wednesday	strickly	extraordinary
15	Febuary	conscientious	assistance
16	beginning	similiar	omitted
17	judgement	representative	bankruptcy
18	experience	beneficial	imediately
19	prominant	existence	merchandise
20	liesure	probably	quantity
21	incidentally	library	surprize
22	apparent	gracous	analysis
23	mortgage	paralize	athletic
24	rhythm	niece	forcast

711 CHERRY STREET • ST. PAUL, MN 55121
(218) 792-8450

DATE: June 30, 19--

STATEMENT

IN ACCOUNT WITH
Martin L. King High School
3842 Peachtree Street
Augusta, GA 30903

AMOUNT ENCLOSED

$ ________

PLEASE RETURN THIS STUB WITH YOUR PAYMENT

DATE	REFERENCE	CHARGES	CREDITS	BALANCE
June 1	Balance			500.42
5	Invoice #4583	175.89		676.31
11	Invoice #4589	342.50		1018.81
15	Payment		1000.00	18.81
20	Invoice #4594	2577.10		2595.91
25	Credit memo #439		125.75	2470.16
28	Payment		2300.00	170.16

PLEASE NOTIFY US PROMPTLY IF THIS STATEMENT DOES NOT AGREE WITH YOUR RECORDS

PLEASE PAY LAST AMOUNT IN THIS COLUMN

Model 28

Statement of Account

Exercise 23
STATEMENT

IN ACCOUNT WITH: Mrs. Susanne McGregor, 282 Ball Street, Fergus Falls, MN 56537

DATE: Mar. 31, 19—

DATE	REFERENCE	CHARGES	CREDITS	BALANCE
March 1	Balance			25.80
10	Invoice #5205	125.32		151.12
26	Invoice #5221	43.21		194.33

Exercise 27

WORD DIVISION REVIEW

Refer to the word division rules (pages 90–91) as you type this table. Complete columns 2 and 4 by inserting a hyphen to show the first acceptable division point after each slash. Type the word without a hyphen if there is no such division point. (For answers, refer to page 149.)

Full sheet. Double spacing. Follow the spacing shown in the planning diagram below this exercise. Center vertically and horizontally.

WORD DIVISION EXERCISE 1

Col. 1	Col.2	Col. 3	Col. 4
abs/ence		coul/dn't	
a/ccept		$31.5/5	
acce/ptance		se/lf-interest	
accid/entally		begi/nning	
acc/ommodate		bu/siness	
accord/ance		canc/ellation	
ac/curacy		for/ty	
achie/vement		immed/iately	
ackno/wledgment		lo/ose	
ac/ross		t/he	
af/fect		occu/rrence	
Pete/rson		noti/ceable	
stra/ight		ge/ography	
co/ward		mea/sure	
a/wkward		repre/sentative	

14	3	15	6	14	3	15

Exercise 28

As you type this table, complete columns 2 and 4. Use a hyphen to show the first acceptable division point after the slash in each word. (For answers, refer to page 149.)

Half sheet. Double spacing. Follow the spacing shown in the planning diagram below this exercise. Center vertically.

WORD DIVISION EXERCISE 2

Col. 1	Col. 2	Col. 3	Col. 4
expres/sed		descr/iption	
veri/fy		ali/gned	
th/eir		wal/ked	
su/rprise		pro/blems	
si/milar		si/tuation	
pla/nning		conve/nient	
ext/ension		addre/ssing	
buz/zard		pho/tographic	
cre/ative		pro/bable	
bea/utiful		suspi/cious	
U./S.A.		ra/dio	
all-a/round		lod/ging	
ad/ditional		fli/ghty	

10	6	11	10	12	6	13

Exercise 19
CREDIT MEMORANDUM

CREDIT TO: The Neighborhood Store,
56 Lucas Avenue, Cranston, RI 02910
NO.: 463

DATE: July 29, 19—
SOLD ON INVOICE NO.: 4687
YOUR ORDER NO.: 63421

QUANTITY	DESCRIPTION	UNIT PRICE	AMOUNT
1	Electric toaster, 4-slice	35.00	35.00

REASON FOR CREDIT: Short shipment on our Invoice No. 4687.

Exercise 20
CREDIT MEMORANDUM

CREDIT TO: Garrett Office Equipment Co.,
800 King Street, Garrett, IN 46738
NO.: 464

DATE: August 13, 19—
SOLD ON INVOICE NO.: 4699
YOUR ORDER NO.: 4228

QUANTITY	DESCRIPTION	UNIT PRICE	AMOUNT
			61.10

REASON FOR CREDIT: Wrong discount on our Invoice No. 4699.
Terms should read 4/10, n/60.

Exercise 21
CREDIT MEMORANDUM

CREDIT TO: Batista Bookshop,
Tribune Square, Lansing, MI 48911
NO.: 682

DATE: January 22, 19—
SOLD ON INVOICE NO.: 5103
YOUR ORDER NO.: 483910

QUANTITY	DESCRIPTION	UNIT PRICE	AMOUNT
1	Portable bookcase, #40	70.50	70.50

REASON FOR CREDIT: Returned—wrong color.

STATEMENTS

The following statements come from Corona Industries Inc., 711 Cherry Street, St. Paul, MN 55121. Type each exercise following the style shown in Model 28 (page 324). If forms are not available, prepare statements similar to the one shown in Model 28.

Exercise 22
STATEMENT

Type a statement of account for Martin L. King High School, as shown in Model 28 on the following page.

KEY TO EXERCISES 22–28

Exercise 22

chief	neither	leisure
receive	their	efficient
achievement	believe	foreign
weird	piece	convenient
eight	height	receipt
neighbor	niece	interview

Exercise 23

advertise	proceed	terrible
surprise	concede	impossible
criticize	recede	usable
analyze	succeed	responsible
realize	supersede	legible
familiarize	exceed	durable
merchandise	precede	noticeable

Exercise 24

attendance	gracious	grammar
dependence	hideous	calendar
remittance	courteous	regular
superintendence	delicious	doctor
existence	miscellaneous	administrator
accordance	conscious	customer
correspondence	religious	visitor
fragrance	curious	scholar
confidence	simultaneous	creator
radiance	cautious	messenger
residence	instantaneous	ancestor
resistance	gorgeous	collar

Exercise 25

permanent	possession
maintenance	grateful
advice	similar
specifically	undoubtedly
comparison	principal
February	analyze
absence	counsel
assistance	coarse

Exercise 26

1 separate	9 secretary	17 judgment
2 writing	10 omission	18 immediately
3 privilege	11 occasionally	19 prominent
4 procedure	12 responsible	20 leisure
5 maintenance	13 canceled	21 surprise
6 questionnaire	14 strictly	22 gracious
7 shipping	15 February	23 paralyze
8 grateful	16 similar	24 forecast

Exercise 27

Col. 2	Col. 4
absence	couldn't
ac-cept	$31.55
accep-tance	self-interest
acciden-tally	begin-ning
accom-modate	busi-ness
accordance	cancel-lation
ac-curacy	forty
achieve-ment	immedi-ately
acknowl-edgment	loose
across	the
af-fect	occur-rence
Peterson	notice-able
straight	ge-ography
cow-ard	measure
awk-ward	repre-sentative

Exercise 28

Col. 2	Col. 4
expressed	descrip-tion
verify	aligned
their	walked
sur-prise	prob-lems
simi-lar	situ-ation
plan-ning	conve-nient
exten-sion	address-ing
buz-zard	photo-graphic
crea-tive	prob-able
beau-tiful	suspi-cious
U.S.A.	radio
all-around	lodg-ing
addi-tional	flighty

CORONA INDUSTRIES INCORPORATED
711 CHERRY STREET • ST. PAUL, MN 55121
(218) 792-8450

CREDIT MEMORANDUM

NO. 439

CREDIT TO: Martin L. King High School
3842 Peachtree Street
Augusta, GA 30903

DATE June 25, 19--

SOLD ON INVOICE NO. 4594

YOUR ORDER NO. 98102

WE HAVE CREDITED YOUR ACCOUNT AS FOLLOWS:

QUANTITY	DESCRIPTION	UNIT PRICE	AMOUNT
1	File cabinet, 4-drawer, letter-size, Model 415	125.75	125.75

REASON FOR CREDIT: Returned--damaged in shipment.

AUTHORIZED BY ______________________

Model 27 Credit Memorandum

CREDIT MEMORANDUMS

These credit memos come from Corona Industries Inc., 711 Cherry Street, St. Paul, MN 55121. Type each exercise following the style shown in Model 27. If forms are not available, prepare credit memos similar to the one shown above.

Exercise 17
CREDIT MEMORANDUM

Type a credit memo to Martin L. King High School for a file cabinet that was returned to Corona Industries. Use the information shown in Model 27 above.

Exercise 18
CREDIT MEMORANDUM

CREDIT TO: The Place Furniture Company, Northfield Plaza, Knoxville, TN 37906

NO.: 461

DATE: July 20, 19—

SOLD ON INVOICE NO.: 4690

YOUR ORDER NO.: 63413

QUANTITY	DESCRIPTION	UNIT PRICE	AMOUNT
6	Table, Model 601 MT20, 60″ × 30″ (Credit of 5.00 per item)		30.00

REASON FOR CREDIT: Erroneous quotation of 65.00 per item on our Invoice No. 4690; price should have been 60.00 ea.

PART 5

OUTLINES, REPORTS, AND MANUSCRIPTS

This part will teach you the basic skills and rules involved in typing outlines, reports, and manuscripts. There is a natural progression from one to the other of these three topics. A topical outline expresses the "skeleton" of ideas and sequence of a report or speech. Reports and themes follow certain forms to make them attractive and easy to read. Manuscripts are typed in generally the same manner as reports, with a few important differences.

Topic 1 TOPICAL OUTLINES

A *topical outline* is a series of main topics and subtopics that form the framework for a speech or report. An outline guides a writer or speaker in presenting the information in an orderly and logical way. It may also aid the reader or listener in reviewing and remembering the outstanding points of a report or lecture.

The outline must be well arranged and its parts clearly identified. Refer to Model 1 on the next page and to the following rules when you type an outline.

1. Center the outline vertically and horizontally. Use the block centering method to determine margin stops. To do this, count the number of spaces from the Roman numeral "I" to the end of the line that extends farthest to the right. Set margins for that line length.
2. Center the title of the outline and type it in solid capitals.
3. Use single spacing, but double-space immediately before and after a topic identified by a Roman numeral. A short outline may be double spaced.
4. Use a combination of Roman numerals, Arabic numerals, and letters of the alphabet to identify different levels of topics. You may use up to six levels, as shown in the illustration at the left.
5. Put a period and 2 spaces after each numeral or letter, except those in parentheses. After a numeral or letter in parentheses, use no punctuation and leave only 1 space.
6. Indent each level of a new topic so that it aligns with the first word of the topic that precedes it. An *a*-level topic, for example, will align with the first word of a *1*-level topic. Set tabs at the places where each new level of topics begins.
7. If a topic requires more than one line, start the runover line under the initial letter of the first word of the preceding line.

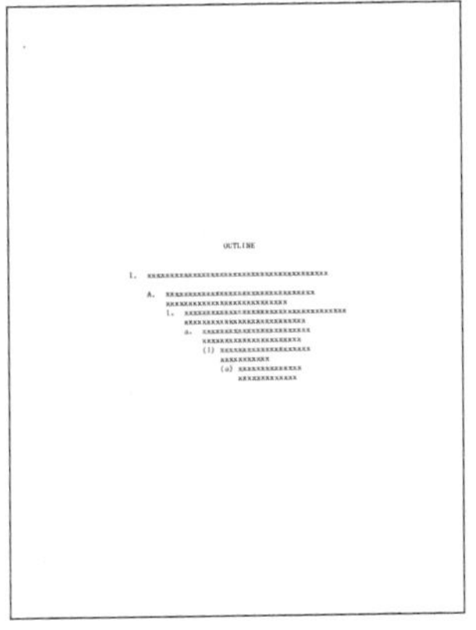

Exercise 14
INVOICE

SOLD TO: Garrett Office Equipment Co.
800 King Street
Garrett, IN 46738

INVOICE NO.: 4699

DATE: August 4, 19—
YOUR ORDER NO.: 4228
TERMS: 2/10, n/30
SHIPPED VIA: Amtrak

QUANTITY	DESCRIPTION	UNIT PRICE	AMOUNT
20	Book truck, Model WEP-20	41.25	825.00
40	Chair, with casters, Model 1A42	32.50	1300.00
30	Chair, with glides, Model 1A45	31.00	930.00
			3055.00

Exercise 15
INVOICE

SOLD TO: Batista Bookshop
Tribune Square
Lansing, MI 48911

INVOICE NO.: 5103

DATE: January 4, 19—
YOUR ORDER NO.: 483910
TERMS: 3/10, n/30
SHIPPED VIA: Conrail

QUANTITY	DESCRIPTION	UNIT PRICE	AMOUNT
5	Portable bookcase, tan texture, Cat. #40	70.50	352.50
2	Book truck, green, 36″ wide, 43″ high, Cat. #43-4	97.00	194.00
4	Magazine rack, tan texture, 21″ wide, 10″ deep, 36″ high, Cat. #36	55.75	223.00
			769.50

Exercise 16
INVOICE

SOLD TO: Mrs. Susanne McGregor
282 Ball Street
Fergus Falls, MN 56537

INVOICE NO.: 5221

DATE: March 26, 19—
YOUR ORDER NO.: 16025
TERMS: C.O.D.
SHIPPED VIA: UPS

QUANTITY	DESCRIPTION	UNIT PRICE	AMOUNT
1	Rubber link mat	6.00	6.00
16	Safety stair tread, brown	1.90	30.40
1	Sponge rubber mat	4.75	4.75
			41.15
		Sales tax	2.06
			43.21

8. Capitalize the first letter of each important word in topics that begin with Roman numerals or the capital letters A, B, C, D, and so forth. Capitalize only the first letter of the first word in all other topics.
9. Use no punctuation at the ends of lines.

Model 1

An Outline in Topical Form

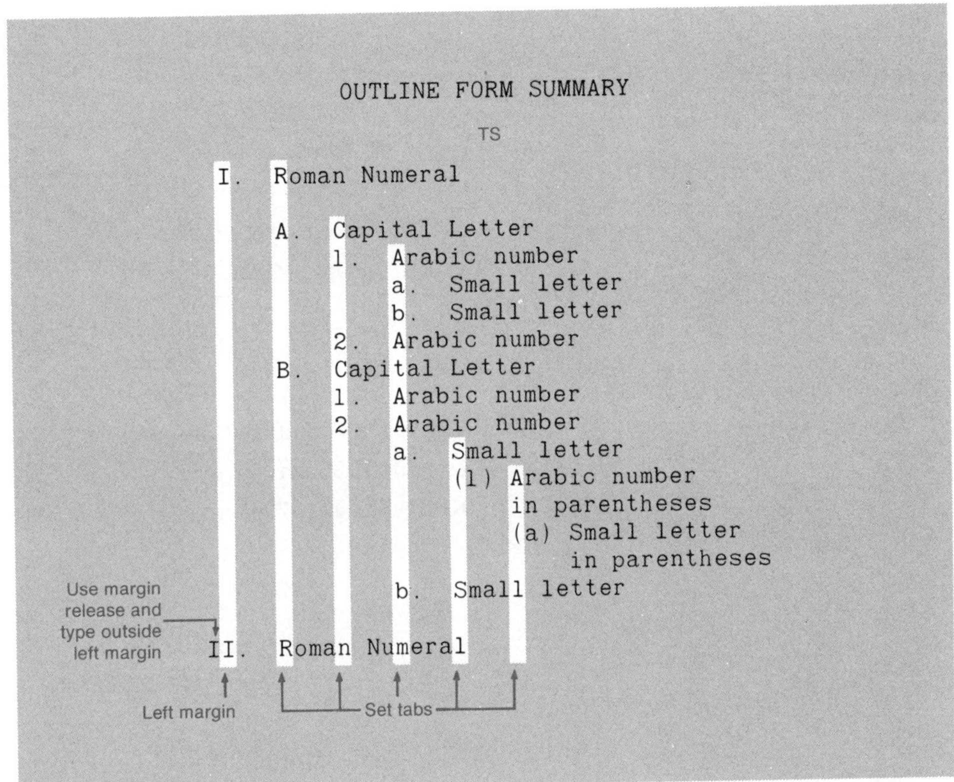

OUTLINE FORM SUMMARY
TS
I. Roman Numeral
A. Capital Letter
1. Arabic number
a. Small letter
b. Small letter
2. Arabic number
B. Capital Letter
1. Arabic number
2. Arabic number
a. Small letter
(1) Arabic number in parentheses
(a) Small letter in parentheses
b. Small letter
Use margin release and type outside left margin
II. Roman Numeral
Left margin
Set tabs

Before you begin Exercise 1, type Drills A–C to gain practice in aligning numbers. Remember that Arabic and Roman numerals align at the right. Repeat these drills if necessary.

Drill A

Half sheet. Double spacing. Align title at left margin. Begin on line 7.

Drill B

Half sheet. Double spacing. Block center the body. Center title. Begin on line 7.

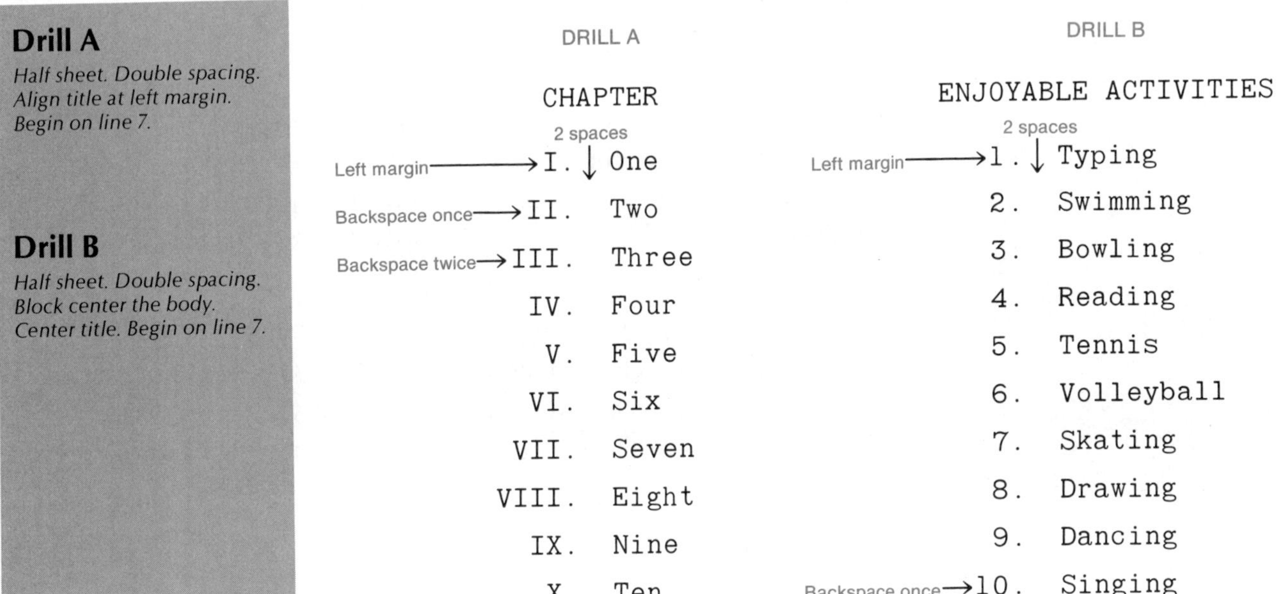

DRILL A
CHAPTER
2 spaces
Left margin→I. One
Backspace once→II. Two
Backspace twice→III. Three
IV. Four
V. Five
VI. Six
VII. Seven
VIII. Eight
IX. Nine
X. Ten
DRILL B
ENJOYABLE ACTIVITIES
2 spaces
Left margin→1. Typing
2. Swimming
3. Bowling
4. Reading
5. Tennis
6. Volleyball
7. Skating
8. Drawing
9. Dancing
Backspace once→10. Singing

Exercise 11
INVOICE

SOLD TO: The Neighborhood Store
56 Lucas Avenue
Cranston, RI 02910

INVOICE NO.: 4687

DATE: July 16, 19—
YOUR ORDER NO.: 63421
TERMS: 2/10, n/60
SHIPPED VIA: Yellow Freight Co.

QUANTITY	DESCRIPTION	UNIT PRICE	AMOUNT
5	Electric toaster, 2-slice	25.25	126.25
6	Electric toaster, 4-slice	35.00	210.00
3	Electric steam iron	9.50	28.50
1	Magic Mixer, 4-speed	55.00	55.00
			419.75

Exercise 12
INVOICE

SOLD TO: The Place Furniture Company
Northfield Plaza
Knoxville, TN 37906

INVOICE NO.: 4690

DATE: July 18, 19—
YOUR ORDER NO.: 63413
TERMS: n/30
SHIPPED VIA: Conrail

QUANTITY	DESCRIPTION	UNIT PRICE	AMOUNT
4	Credenza, Model 686 MC2D, 60″ × 19½″	86.50	346.00
6	Table, Model 601 MT20, 60″ × 30″	65.00	390.00
2	Table, Model 610 MT20, 72″ × 36″	75.00	150.00
			886.00

Exercise 13
INVOICE

SOLD TO: Glenmore Arms
406 Adams Street
Minneapolis, MN 55408

INVOICE NO.: 4786

DATE: September 22, 19—
YOUR ORDER NO.: 528198
TERMS: 2/10, n/30
SHIPPED VIA: Suppliers' Freightways

QUANTITY	DESCRIPTION	UNIT PRICE	AMOUNT
2	Arm chair, Model 64A	98.50	197.00
3	Arm chair, Model 60A	64.50	193.50
1	Desk chair, Model 5055	50.00	50.00
			440.50
		Sales tax	22.03
			462.53

Drill C

Type this agenda and align the items as shown.

Full sheet. 54-space line. Double spacing. Begin on line 13.

A G E N D A

Meeting of the BOEC Club

February 17, 19--

TS

A. Opening of the Meeting
   1. Roll call
   2. The BOEC creed and song
B. Old Business
   1. Reading of the minutes of the previous meeting
   2. Treasurer's report
   3. Report from the Membership Committee
C. New Business
   1. Planning for the State Leadership Conference
   2. Other new business
D. Adjournment and Socializing Time

Exercise 1

Type this topical outline using Model 1 (page 151) as a guide. Be sure to align numbers properly and set tabs for each series of indentions.

Full sheet. 55-space line. Center vertically.

DEVELOPMENT OF THE ELECTRONIC OFFICE

TS

I. Problems with Traditional Office Operation

DS

   A. Paperwork Explosion
   B. Increases in Letter Costs
      1. Dartnell Corporation study
      2. Office salaries higher
   C. Misuse of Time and Talent
      1. High skills demand
      2. Inconsistent career path
      3. High turnover rate

DS

II. Reorganization of Office Structure

DS

   A. Invention of Word Processing Typewriter (MT/ST)
      1. Marketing problems
      2. Expense
   B. Introduction of Word Processing "System"
      1. Definition of word processing
      2. Elements of the system
         a. People
         b. Machines
         c. Procedures
         d. Environment

Exercise 9
PURCHASE ORDER
Note that the *Amount* column is not provided in this exercise. As you type the purchase order, supply the missing figures.

VENDOR: G. McGroarty Office Equipment Co.
25 Zacco Street
Kansas City, KS 66103

PURCHASE ORDER NO.: 7522

DATE: May 13, 19—
DATE REQUIRED: June 27, 19—
TERMS: n/30
SHIP VIA: Your truck

QUANTITY	CAT. NO.	DESCRIPTION	PRICE
2 ea	PN42	File cabinet, 4-drawer, letter-size	110.00
4 ea	PN48	File cabinet, 4-drawer, legal-size	120.00
4 ea	LM12	Secretarial desk, black top, #348	200.00

INVOICES

The following invoices come from Corona Industries Inc., 711 Cherry Street, St. Paul, MN 55121. Type each exercise following the style shown in Model 26. If forms are not available, prepare invoices similar to the one shown below.

Exercise 10
INVOICE

Type an invoice for the items sold by Corona Industries to Martin L. King High School, as shown in Model 26 below.

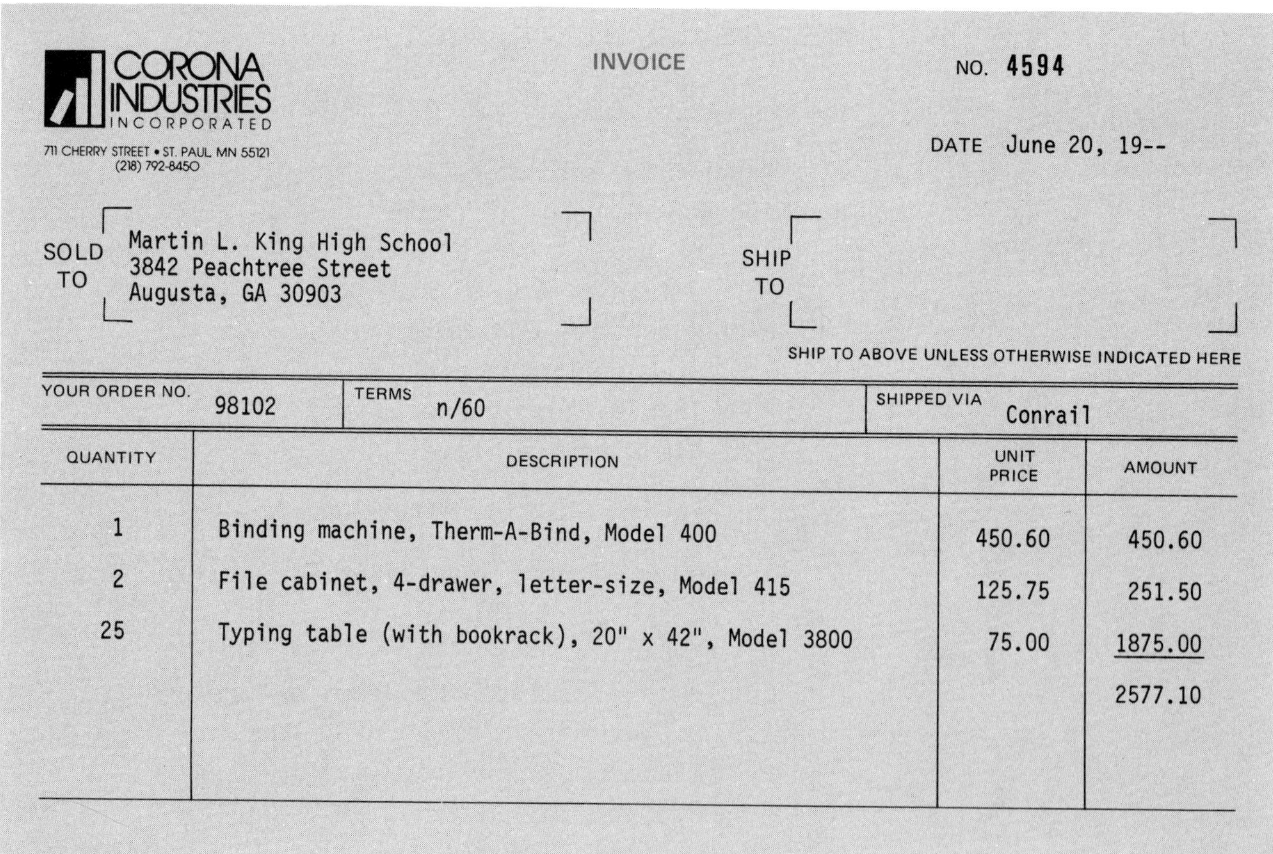
CORONA INDUSTRIES INCORPORATED
711 CHERRY STREET • ST. PAUL, MN 55121
(218) 792-8450

INVOICE

NO. 4594

DATE June 20, 19--

SOLD TO
Martin L. King High School
3842 Peachtree Street
Augusta, GA 30903

SHIP TO

SHIP TO ABOVE UNLESS OTHERWISE INDICATED HERE

YOUR ORDER NO.	TERMS	SHIPPED VIA
98102	n/60	Conrail

QUANTITY	DESCRIPTION	UNIT PRICE	AMOUNT
1	Binding machine, Therm-A-Bind, Model 400	450.60	450.60
2	File cabinet, 4-drawer, letter-size, Model 415	125.75	251.50
25	Typing table (with bookrack), 20" x 42", Model 3800	75.00	1875.00
			2577.10

Model 26 *Invoice*

Exercise 2

Type this outline, using the proper spacing. (If you are in doubt, refer to Model 1, page 151.)

Full sheet. 50-space line. Begin on line 10.

A SYSTEMATIC JOB SEARCH PROCEDURE

I. Organizing Information for Employers
   A. Social Security Number
   B. List of References (minimum: three)
   C. Data Sheet with Summary of Work History
   D. Notepad, Pen, and Pencil

II. Limiting Area to Be Covered
   A. Industrial Areas
   B. Downtown Areas
   C. Shopping Centers

III. Doing Your Homework
   A. Learning About the Company
   B. Learning the Managers' Names
   C. Investigating the Types of Jobs Available

IV. Planning Your Arrival Time
   A. Travel Time
      1. Check bus schedules
      2. Select best route
   B. The Company's Schedule
      1. Lunch time
      2. Closing time

V. Presenting Yourself
   A. Grooming
      1. Cleanliness
      2. Conservative, neat clothing
   B. Success Tips
      1. Relaxed, smiling manner
      2. Clear, pleasant voice
      3. Good posture
      4. Arrive alone

VI. Filling In an Application Form
   A. Complete and Correct
      1. No lines left blank
      2. Check for spelling errors
   B. Neat and Clean
      1. Legible writing or printing
      2. No scratched-out corrections

Exercise 6
PURCHASE ORDER

VENDOR: The Colburn Company
811 Franklin Road
Long Beach, CA 90811

PURCHASE ORDER NO.: 7519

DATE: May 7, 19—
DATE REQUIRED: May 31, 19—
TERMS: 2/30, n/60
SHIP VIA: Conrail

QUANTITY	CAT. NO.	DESCRIPTION	PRICE	AMOUNT
12 ea	2010	Mattress covers, twin, #2632	9.35	112.20
6 ea	3050	Mattress covers, full, #2640	11.80	70.80
8 ea	3089	Mattress covers, queen, #2679	13.59	108.72
				291.72

Exercise 7
PURCHASE ORDER

VENDOR: Selby-Costa Fabrics, Inc.
365 Maple Avenue
Tucson, AZ 85719

PURCHASE ORDER NO.: 7520

DATE: May 12, 19—
DATE REQUIRED: June 16, 19—
TERMS: n/30
SHIP VIA: Norwall Truck Lines

QUANTITY	CAT. NO.	DESCRIPTION	PRICE	AMOUNT
12 rolls	2010	Fabric, cotton, Rosebud pattern, #3480	42.40	508.80
15 rolls	2042	Fabric, cotton, Laurel pattern, #3645	42.40	636.00
10 ctns	52	Buttons, brass color, ½″, #22Y	15.32	153.20
				1298.00

Exercise 8
PURCHASE ORDER

VENDOR: Fleming Metal Spring Co.
245 Lincoln Avenue
Scranton, PA 18501

PURCHASE ORDER NO.: 7521

DATE: May 12, 19—
DATE REQUIRED: July 1, 19—
TERMS: 2/30, n/60
SHIP VIA: Kaplan Express, Inc.

QUANTITY	CAT. NO.	DESCRIPTION	PRICE	AMOUNT
2000 ea	12A1	Coil spring, heavy duty, #6 size	.25	500.00
4000 ea	12A5	Coil spring, regular, #8 size	.21	840.00
4000 ea	12A6	Coil spring, regular, #9 size	.22	880.00
1000 ea	25B	Metal bands, 1″ wide, #367	.55	550.00
				2770.00

Exercise 3

Type this handwritten outline.

Full sheet. 34-space line. Proper outline spacing. Center vertically.

THE STUDY OF FILING

I. Introduction
   A. Purpose of Filing
   B. History of Filing
II. The Filing Process
   A. Letter Preparation
      1. Releasing
      2. Indexing
      3. Coding
      4. Cross-referencing
      5. Preparing follow-ups
   B. Basic Filing Systems
      1. Alphabetic
      2. Numeric
      3. Geographic
      4. Subject
      5. Chronological
III. Electronic Filing
   A. Records Management Systems
      1. Centralized
      2. Decentralized
   B. Storage and Retrieval
      1. Magnetic media
         a. Cards
         b. Tape
         c. Diskettes
      2. Micrographics
         a. Microfilm
         b. Microfiche

Exercise 4
PURCHASE REQUISITION

DELIVER TO: Chris Federico, Reception Room
CHARGE TO: Budget No. 4862

REQUISITION NO.: 68421
DATE: September 5, 19—
DATE REQUIRED: September 30, 19—

RECOMMENDED VENDOR: Parson's Office Supply, Kansas City, KS

ITEM	QUANTITY	DESCRIPTION	UNIT PRICE
1	1 bx	Rubber bands, # 16	2.70 bx
2	2 bxs	Paper clips, 50 per box, #3	1.39 bx
3	4 bxs	Paper clips, 100 per box, #2	1.19 bx

PURCHASE ORDERS

The following purchase orders come from the Kassor Mattress Company, 3642 Payne Avenue, Kansas City, KS 66106. Type each exercise following the style shown in Model 25. If forms are not available, prepare purchase orders similar to the one shown below.

Exercise 5
PURCHASE ORDER

Type a purchase order using the information in Model 25. Notice that the "SHIP TO" space is not filled in when goods are to be sent to the same address printed on the purchase order form.

Telephone: (913) 481-7723

PURCHASE ORDER

KASSOR MATTRESS COMPANY
3642 PAYNE AVENUE • KANSAS CITY, KS 66106

NO. 7518
DATE May 5, 19--

TO Golubski Supply Co.
42 Truman Drive
Independence, MO 64051

SHIP TO

SHIP TO ABOVE UNLESS OTHERWISE INDICATED HERE

DATE REQUIRED: June 5, 19--	TERMS: n/30	SHIP VIA: Yellow Freight Company

QUANTITY ORDERED	QUANTITY RECEIVED	CAT. NO.	DESCRIPTION	PRICE	AMOUNT
20 ctns		426A	Nails, 1½", #38	4.52 ctn	90.40
10 ctns		113B1	Screws, ¼", brass, #42	6.40 ctn	64.00
3 ea		52B	Hammers, round head, claw-type, #6541	8.78 ea	26.34
					180.74

By: ______________________

Model 25 *Purchase Order*

Exercise 4

Type this topical outline, making the corrections indicated by the proofreaders' marks.

Full sheet. Proper outline spacing. Use block centering.

USE OF The BUSINESS TELEPHONE

I. The sound of your voice

A. Distance from the Mouthpiece

B. Clearness

1. Pronunciation

2. Volume of sound

3. Rate of speech

C. Manner and tone

II. Placinga call

A. Finding teh number

1. Telephone lists

2. Telephone directories

3. ~~Information~~ Directory assistance operator

B. Getting the connection

1. Dial and push button phones

2. Getting the person wanted

C. Sepcial types of calls

1. Long distance

a. Direct dial

(1) Rate schedules

(2) When an operator can help

(a) Poor connection

(b) Wrong number

b. Person to person

c. Collect

d. Credit card

2. Emergency

III. Receiving a call

A. Promptness answerin g

B. Preferred form of greeting

C. Correct Procedure

D. 1. Use of hold button

a. Keeping caller informed

b. Recovering from a cutoff

2. Taking messages ~~properly~~

PURCHASE REQUISITION

NO. 48162

DATE: May 3, 19--

DELIVER TO: Sam Salupo

DATE REQUIRED: June 5, 19--

CHARGE TO: Budget No. 4670

RECOMMENDED VENDOR: Golubski Supply Co., Independence, MO

ITEM	QUANTITY	DESCRIPTION	UNIT PRICE
1	20 ctns	Nails, 1½", #38	4.52 ctn
2	10 ctns	Screws, ¼", brass, #42	6.40 ctn
3	3 ea	Hammers, Lipstreuer & McGivern model with round head, claw-type, #6541	8.78 ea

Requisitioned by: ______________ Approved by: ______________

Model 24 Purchase Requisition

Exercise 2
PURCHASE REQUISITION

DELIVER TO: Roberto Mendoza
CHARGE TO: Budget No. 4670
REQUISITION NO.: 58164
DATE: Today's
DATE REQUIRED: Immediately
RECOMMENDED VENDOR: Jack's Tailoring & Upholstery Co., Kansas City, MO

ITEM	QUANTITY	DESCRIPTION	UNIT PRICE
1	7 doz	"C" Clamps, 4"	2.10 doz
2	50 yds	Lining material, type 02	1.59 yd

Exercise 3
PURCHASE REQUISITION

DELIVER TO: Shipping Department
CHARGE TO: Budget No. 4671
REQUISITION NO.: 59057
DATE: Today's
DATE REQUIRED: Immediately
RECOMMENDED VENDOR: Parson's Office Supply, Kansas City, KS

ITEM	QUANTITY	DESCRIPTION	UNIT PRICE
1	15 btls	Johnson's Glue-All, 8 fl. oz.	2.98 btl
2	10 rolls	Twine, extra-heavy, 500 ft. rolls	1.97 roll

Exercise 5

UNARRANGED COPY

Type the material at the right in correct topical outline form. Use Model 1 (page 151) as a guide.

Full sheet. 44-space line. Center vertically.

MAKING BETTER USE OF YOUR TIME / I. Your Time at Work / A. Organizing Your Day / 1. Planning what to do / 2. Avoiding interruptions / B. Using Short Periods of Time / II. Leisure Time / A. Filling Mental Needs / 1. Learning to relax / 2. Selecting appropriate activities / B. Filling Physical Needs / 1. Getting regular exercise / 2. Planning recreational outings / C. Filling Social Needs / 1. Meeting people / a. Group activities / b. Parties / c. Classes / 2. Building self-confidence / a. Community service / b. Hobbies

Exercise 6

UNARRANGED COPY

Type the material at the right in correct topical outline form. Use Model 1 (page 151) as a guide.

Full sheet. Block and vertical centering.

SUCCEEDING ON THE JOB / I. Your Appearance / A. What to Wear / 1. Conservative dress / 2. Simple accessories / B. Grooming / 1. Suitable hairstyle / 2. Nails trimmed and clean / 3. Teeth cleaned and flossed / II. Your Speech / A. Voice / 1. Pleasing tone / 2. Normal conversational level / B. Correct Grammar and Choice of Words / III. Your Attitude / A. Toward Work / 1. Alert / 2. Enthusiastic / 3. Willing to learn / B. Toward Fellow Employees / 1. Considerate / 2. Helpful / 3. Courteous / 4. Cooperative / 5. Patient / 6. Cheerful

Exercise 7

UNARRANGED COPY

Type the material at the right in correct topical outline form. Be sure to make any necessary changes in capitalization. Use Model 1 (page 151) as a guide.

Full sheet. Block and vertical centering.

Financial services / I. Savings accounts / A. Regular deposits / 1. Low interest rate / 2. Withdrawal on demand / B. Time deposits / 1. Minimum amount / 2. Fixed term / a. High interest rate / b. Early withdrawal penalty / C. Money market accounts / D. Retirement accounts / 1. Individual retirement accounts (IRAs) / 2. Keogh accounts / II. Checking accounts / A. Options / 1. Regular checking / a. No minimum deposit / b. No interest / c. Fee per check (service charge) / 2. NOW accounts / a. Minimum deposit / b. Interest / c. No service charge / B. Use / 1. Writing a check / a. Check number / b. Date / c. Payee / d. Amount / e. Purpose / f. Signature / 2. Endorsing a check / a. Blank endorsement / b. Special endorsement / c. Restrictive endorsement / 3. Reconciling a bank statement / a. Beginning balance / b. Deposits / c. Checks paid / d. Electronic fund transfers (EFTs) / e. Service charges / f. Ending balance

Exercise 8

UNARRANGED COPY

Type the material at the right in correct topical outline form. Be sure to make any necessary changes in capitalization. Use Model 1 (page 151) as a guide.

Full sheet. Block and vertical centering.

Life insurance / I. Types / A. Term / 1. Renewable / 2. Convertible / 3. Decreasing / B. Permanent / 1. Whole life / 2. Limited-payment life / 3. Endowment / II. Policy features / A. Beneficiaries / B. Premiums / C. Payments / 1. Cash value / 2. Dividends / 3. Proceeds / III. Provisions / A. Incontestable clause / B. Waiver-of-premiums clause / C. Automatic premium loan / D. Accidental death benefit / E. Assignment clause / F. Noncancelable clause / G. Guaranteed insurability option / H. Exclusions

- Date the materials are needed
- Terms of payment
- Quantity and detailed description of each item
- Unit prices, extensions, and total

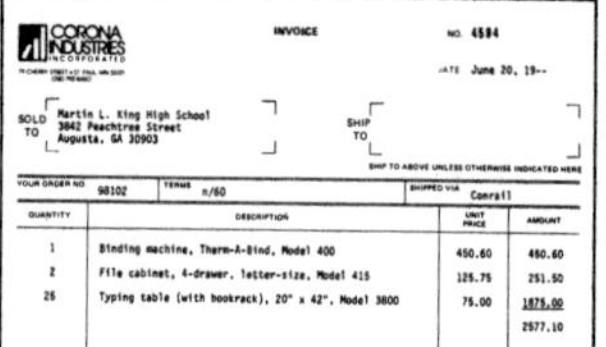
CORONA INDUSTRIES INCORPORATED

INVOICE

NO. 4594

DATE June 20, 19--

SOLD TO Martin L. King High School 3842 Peachtree Street Augusta, GA 30903

SHIP TO

YOUR ORDER NO. 98102 TERMS n/60 SHIPPED VIA Conrail

QUANTITY	DESCRIPTION	UNIT PRICE	AMOUNT
1	Binding machine, Therm-A-Bind, Model 400	450.60	450.60
2	File cabinet, 4-drawer, letter-size, Model 415	125.75	251.50
25	Typing table (with bookrack), 20" x 42", Model 3800	75.00	1875.00
			2577.10

INVOICE The vendor prepares an invoice (or bill) for the buyer. It is mailed at about the same time as the goods are shipped. An invoice shows the details of a sale and contains such information as:

- Name and address of the vendor and the buyer
- Buyer's purchase order number
- Terms of payment
- Method of shipment of the goods
- Quantity and detailed description of each item
- Unit prices, extensions, and total

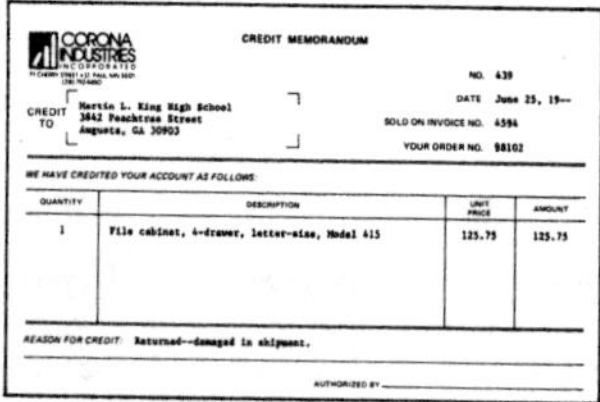
CORONA INDUSTRIES INCORPORATED

CREDIT MEMORANDUM

NO. 439

DATE June 25, 19--

CREDIT TO Martin L. King High School 3842 Peachtree Street Augusta, GA 30903

SOLD ON INVOICE NO. 4594

YOUR ORDER NO. 98102

WE HAVE CREDITED YOUR ACCOUNT AS FOLLOWS:

QUANTITY	DESCRIPTION	UNIT PRICE	AMOUNT
1	File cabinet, 4-drawer, letter-size, Model 415	125.75	125.75

REASON FOR CREDIT: Returned—damaged in shipment.

AUTHORIZED BY

CREDIT MEMORANDUM When the goods arrive, the buyer checks them against a copy of the invoice. If there are any shortages, damages, or overcharges, the vendor is notified. Sometimes short or damaged goods are replaced. If they are not to be replaced, and the buyer requests credit, the vendor prepares a credit memorandum and mails it to the buyer. This indicates that the buyer's account has been credited for the difference. Credit memorandums contain information similar to that on an invoice, with the addition of a statement indicating the reason for the credit.

CORONA INDUSTRIES INCORPORATED

DATE: June 30, 19--

STATEMENT

IN ACCOUNT WITH Martin L. King High School 3842 Peachtree Street Augusta, GA 30903

AMOUNT ENCLOSED $

PLEASE RETURN THIS STUB WITH YOUR PAYMENT

DATE	REFERENCE	CHARGES	CREDITS	BALANCE
June 1	Balance			500.42
5	Invoice #4583	175.89		676.31
11	Invoice #4589	342.50		1018.81
15	Payment		1000.00	18.81
20	Invoice #4594	2577.10		2595.91
25	Credit memo #439		125.75	2470.16
28	Payment		2300.00	170.16

PLEASE NOTIFY US PROMPTLY IF THIS STATEMENT DOES NOT AGREE WITH YOUR RECORDS

PLEASE PAY LAST AMOUNT IN THIS COLUMN

STATEMENT OF ACCOUNT Usually, at the end of the month, the vendor mails the buyer a statement of account. Although statements are often prepared on data processing equipment, in smaller firms they are still typed. The statement contains such information as:

- Amount owed at the beginning of the month
- The purchases, credits, and payments during the month
- Amount due at the close of the month

Here are some general guidelines for typing purchase requisitions, purchase orders, invoices, credit memorandums, and statements.

1. Clear all tab stops and margin stops.
2. Set the left margin and tab stops so that they can be used for as many items as possible.
3. Line up the typing line with the bottom of the key words printed on the form.
4. Leave 2 spaces after a key word, such as *Date.*
5. In the body of the form, leave one blank line before you type the first line of data.
6. Set tab stops for the data to be entered in each column. For narrow columns, set a tab so that the longest item is roughly centered. For wider columns, set the tab 2 spaces to the right of the vertical rule.
7. If an item requires more than 1 line, indent the second and succeeding lines 3 spaces.
8. Double-space items when you have only a few; otherwise, single-space.
9. Omit periods in abbreviations of quantity units.
10. Omit dollar signs; align columns of numbers at the right.

PURCHASE REQUISITIONS

The following purchase requisitions come from the Kassor Mattress Company, 3642 Payne Avenue, Kansas City, KS 66106. Type each exercise following the style shown in Model 24 (page 316). If forms are not available, prepare purchase requisitions similar to the one shown in Model 24.

Exercise 1
PURCHASE REQUISITION

Type a purchase requisition using the information in Model 24.

Topic 2 REPORTS WITHOUT FOOTNOTES

The ability to type attractive and well-planned reports is one of the most useful typing skills you can acquire. Reports, whether long or short, are an important part of almost every business. You can also apply your skills typing reports for schoolwork.

The following general rules should be followed when typing school themes, speeches, business and technical reports, and camera-ready copy (typewritten material that will be photographed for offset printing):

1. Use white, good-quality, $8\frac{1}{2}'' \times 11''$ paper.
2. Use double spacing for the general text and single spacing for lengthy quotations. Occasionally, for special reasons (such as to reduce the number of pages), reports are typed using single spacing throughout.
3. Leave a 2-inch top margin on the first page and a 1-inch top margin on each succeeding page. If the report will be bound at the top, increase the top margin to $2\frac{1}{2}$ inches on the first page and to $1\frac{1}{2}$ inches on succeeding pages.

Left-Bound Report

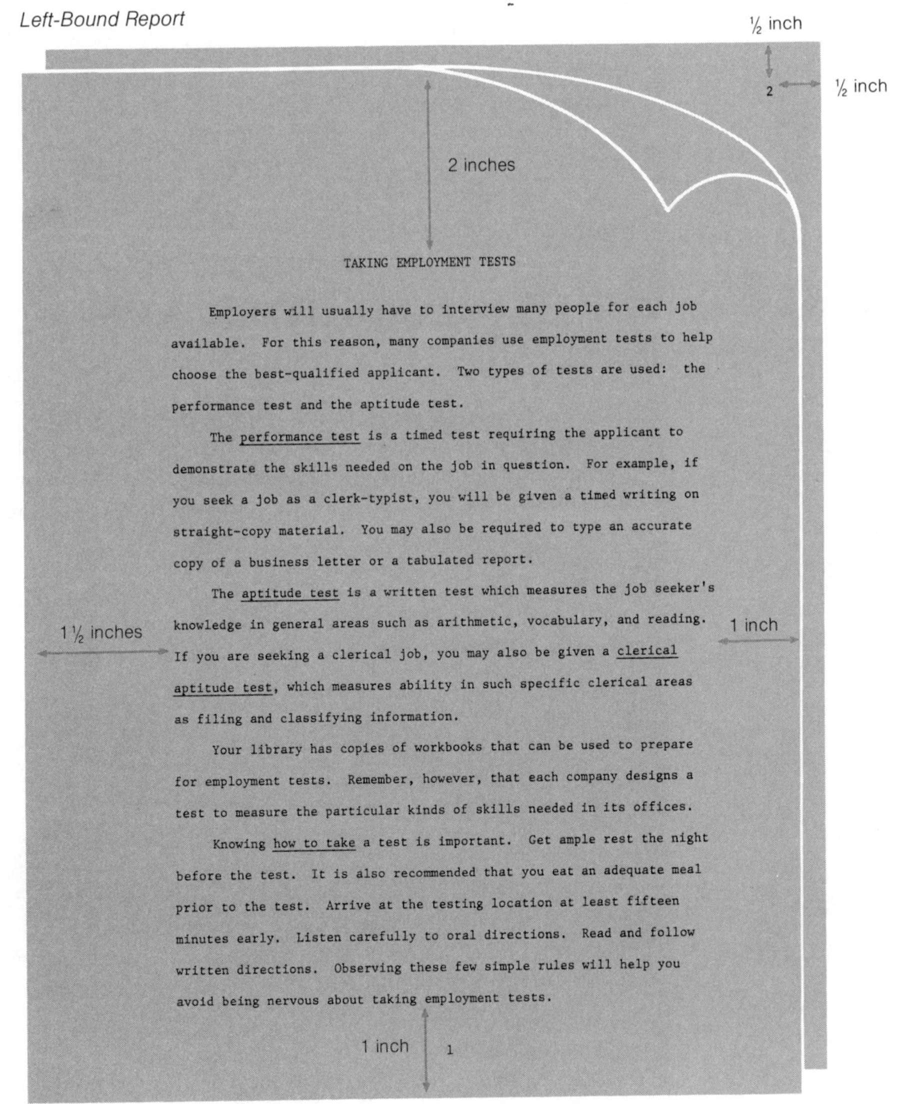

TAKING EMPLOYMENT TESTS

Employers will usually have to interview many people for each job available. For this reason, many companies use employment tests to help choose the best-qualified applicant. Two types of tests are used: the performance test and the aptitude test.

The performance test is a timed test requiring the applicant to demonstrate the skills needed on the job in question. For example, if you seek a job as a clerk-typist, you will be given a timed writing on straight-copy material. You may also be required to type an accurate copy of a business letter or a tabulated report.

The aptitude test is a written test which measures the job seeker's knowledge in general areas such as arithmetic, vocabulary, and reading. If you are seeking a clerical job, you may also be given a clerical aptitude test, which measures ability in such specific clerical areas as filing and classifying information.

Your library has copies of workbooks that can be used to prepare for employment tests. Remember, however, that each company designs a test to measure the particular kinds of skills needed in its offices.

Knowing how to take a test is important. Get ample rest the night before the test. It is also recommended that you eat an adequate meal prior to the test. Arrive at the testing location at least fifteen minutes early. Listen carefully to oral directions. Read and follow written directions. Observing these few simple rules will help you avoid being nervous about taking employment tests.

1

PART 3

BUSINESS FORMS AND LEGAL DOCUMENTS

In an office, you will often type information onto printed forms, such as invoices, purchase orders, receipts, and various kinds of legal documents. Knowing the purpose for which each form is used will aid you in filling it out.

Topic 1 INVOICES AND RELATED FORMS

Businesses use forms of all kinds to record a variety of data in an organized manner. Transactions with customers and suppliers are most commonly recorded on the forms given below. Some firms have computers to print the data on the forms; but others still depend on handwriting or typewriting. If you have to type such forms, follow the guidelines on page 315.

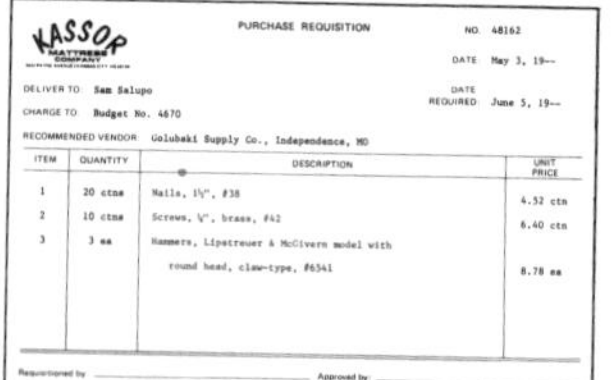

KASSOR MATTRESS COMPANY

PURCHASE REQUISITION

NO. 48162

DATE May 3, 19--

DELIVER TO Sam Salupo

DATE REQUIRED June 5, 19--

CHARGE TO Budget No. 4670

RECOMMENDED VENDOR Golubski Supply Co., Independence, MO

ITEM	QUANTITY	DESCRIPTION	UNIT PRICE
1	20 ctns	Nails, 1½", #38	4.52 ctn
2	10 ctns	Screws, ½", brass, #42	6.40 ctn
3	3 ea	Hammers, Lipstreuer & McCivern model with round head, claw-type, #6341	8.78 ea

Requisitioned by: ______ Approved by: ______

PURCHASE REQUISITION When supplies or other materials are needed, you may have to type a purchase requisition. This is then sent to the person responsible for ordering goods. The purchase requisition may contain such information as:

- Who is to receive the materials
- Department to be charged
- Recommended vendor
- Date the materials are needed
- Quantity and detailed description of each item
- Estimated unit prices

Telephone (913) 481-7723

PURCHASE ORDER

KASSOR MATTRESS COMPANY

NO. 7518

DATE May 5, 19--

TO Golubski Supply Co.
42 Truman Drive
Independence, MO 64051

SHIP TO

SHIP TO ABOVE UNLESS OTHERWISE INDICATED HERE

DATE REQUIRED June 5, 19-- TERMS n/30 SHIP VIA Yellow Freight Company

QUANTITY ORDERED	QUANTITY RECEIVED	CAT NO.	DESCRIPTION	PRICE	AMOUNT
20 ctns		426A	Nails, 1½", #38	4.52 ctn	90.40
10 ctns		113B1	Screws, ½", brass, #42	6.40 ctn	64.00
3 ea		52B	Hammers, round head, claw-type, #6541	8.78 ea	26.34
					180.74

By: ______

PURCHASE ORDER After the requisition has been approved, a purchase order is prepared. This is mailed to the vendor (the person who sells the goods). Or, if the goods are needed in a hurry, they can be ordered by telephone. After a telephone order has been placed, a confirming order is mailed to the vendor. The purchase order contains such information as:

- Name and address of the buyer and the vendor
- Shipping instructions, including method of shipment

4. Leave 1-inch side margins and a 1-inch bottom margin. If the report will be bound at the left, increase the left margin to $1\frac{1}{2}$ inches to allow for binding.
5. To avoid typing into the bottom margin, place a mark near the bottom of the page to warn you that the last line is approaching: Make two light pencil marks in the left margin, one at 1 inch and the other at 2 inches above the bottom edge. Don't forget to erase these marks before turning in your report.
6. Use Arabic numerals to number all pages within the body of the report. On the first page, the number is always centered in the bottom margin. (The first page of each major chapter or section is also numbered in this way.) If the report is unbound or bound at the left, other pages are numbered in the upper right corner. If the report is bound at the top, all page numbers are centered in the bottom margin.
7. Center the title of a report and type it in solid capitals. Triple space after the title. Type headings within the report at the left margin, underscore, or type in solid capitals. Triple space before each heading and double space after it.
8. Erase all errors carefully or use correction paper or fluid. (If a report is to be photocopied or offset printed, you may use correction tape.)
9. In multiple-page reports, avoid leaving fewer than two lines of a paragraph at the bottom of a page and avoid carrying over fewer than two lines of a paragraph to the next page. Do not divide a word at the end of a page.

Exercise 1

ONE-PAGE REPORT

Full sheet. 2-inch top margin. 1-inch side and bottom margins. Double spacing. TS after title. 5-space paragraph indention.

TAKING EMPLOYMENT TESTS

Employers will usually have to interview many people for each job available. For this reason, many companies use employment tests to help choose the best-qualified applicant. Two types of tests are used: the performance test and the aptitude test.

The *performance test* is a timed test requiring the applicant to demonstrate the skills needed on the job in question. For example, if you seek a job as a clerk-typist, you will be given a timed writing on straight-copy material. You may also be required to type an accurate copy of a business letter or a tabulated report.

The *aptitude test* is a written test that measures the job seeker's knowledge in general areas such as arithmetic, vocabulary, and reading. If you are seeking a clerical job, you may also be given a *clerical aptitude test.* It measures ability in such specific clerical areas as filing and classifying information.

Your library has copies of workbooks that can be used to prepare for employment tests. Remember, however, that each company designs a test to measure the particular kinds of skills needed in its offices.

Knowing *how to take* a test is important. Get ample rest the night before the test. It is also recommended that you eat an adequate meal prior to the test. Arrive at the testing location at least fifteen minutes early. Listen carefully to oral directions. Read and follow written directions. Observing these few simple rules will help you avoid being nervous about taking employment tests.

Exercise 22 continued

cap com Community. Many of our social political and religious leaders participated in the NYSL as youngsters. ¶Your company can help us continue our work by sponsoring a team. All it costs is the price of shirts and
ro trophies for your team you receive publicity when the youngsters wear
ab the shirts with your co.'s name printed on them. This and more is all explained in the enclosed booklet, *NYSL Sponsorship.* ¶We have openings for sponsorship of both boys' and girls' tennis and volleyball leagues. Without sponsorship, these youngsters will be left out of this year's
ep program. Can you please help. Call me at (208) 242-6177 any weekday
num before 5 o'clock, or write me at the address above. ¶On behalf of hundreds of area youngsters, thank you. *xx* (141 words)

Exercise 23

This letter was dictated by Janet Aiken, Public Relations Director of Morrell & Richardson Company. The date of the letter is March 18, 19—.

Mr. Harold P. Hodge, President Nampa Youth Sports Leagues 1927 Iris Street Nampa, ID 83640 Dear Mr. Hodge It would be our pleasure to sponsor a team in the Nampa Youth Sports Leagues. We regret that we have not done so already. ¶Our senior vice-president, Mrs. Barbara
num Holmes, played on 2 championship volleyball teams in the NYSL when
com she was a girl. Therefore we have decided to sponsor a girls' volleyball team. ¶I have read the booklet that you enclosed, but I will need your
col com assistance with two questions What kinds of shirts do you require and where is the best place to purchase them? Do we supply first-, second-, and third-place trophies? We would appreciate talking to someone from
ab the NYSL about these & other details. ¶Thank you for giving us this opportunity to support the youngsters of our community. *xx* (124 words)

Exercise 24

In this letter, Harold P. Hodge, President of the Nampa Youth Sports Leagues, answers the questions raised by Ms. Janet Aiken, Public Relations Director of Morrell & Richardson Company, 40 Granada Drive, Nampa, ID 83651. The letter is dated March 23, 19—.

sp Dear Ms. Aiken Thank you for your enthusiastic responce to our request for sponsorship. We hope the relationship between the NYSL and your company will be a long and enjoyable one. ¶The coach of the girls' volleyball team, Cindy Thorkelson, would be the best source of the information
frag you need regarding the purchase of shirts and trophies. Phone number 877-0426. Ms. Thorkelson has all the girls' sizes, as well as catalogs and
num ab price lists. ¶The season starts the 3rd week of next mo.; so contacting Ms. Thorkelson promptly is vital. If we can be of help in any other way, please let us know. ¶Again thanks for your support. *xx* (106 words)

Exercise 2

TWO-PAGE THEME

Type the following 2-page theme. Don't forget to mark in pencil the warning and final marks for a 1-inch bottom margin. Number the second page on line 3 at the right margin and continue the text on line 7. Block center your name, class, school, and date at the end of the theme.

Full sheets. Margins for an unbound report. Double spacing. TS after heading. 5-space paragraph indention.

THE OLD WOMAN AND HER MEMORIES

TS

The old woman sat by the fireside, thinking. Little by little, the light of day died away and the light given by the fire grew stronger until at last the room was full of its ever-changing light, a small haven of warmth and comfort cut off from the rest of the world. The few objects in the room, far from beautiful in the cold light of day, seemed to become lovely as the light of the fire touched them here and there. The old woman did not notice these changes. She was used to the room; she had lived in it for many, many years. She had lived there and she would die there if she had anything to say about the way of her going.

She was not thinking of dying just then, however. She was thinking of life, the most wonderful thing in the world. She was thinking of something that the young girl who lived next door had said that afternoon. The girl had come in, her face full of joy, eager to bring her happy news to the old woman. She was to be married next week. She was to marry a sailor, who was coming home from the seas. Her mother did not approve, for she said that the life of a young woman married to a sailor was a hard one; but the young girl said that old people know nothing of these things. She forgot that at that moment she was talking to a wise old woman who knew a great deal about such things.

The old woman continued to sit there, quite still, looking at the fire, but seeing other times and other people. The young always thought that the very old could know nothing and understand nothing; but she knew well what it was to be the wife of a sailor, sitting at home, waiting and waiting. She had been married to a sailor and she had three sons, and all of them in their turn had gone to sea. She remembered her husband as the young sailor she had first married—strong, light of heart, careless in the face of danger. Give him sails, he always cried, beautiful sails, and he would have nothing to do with the modern ships which were beginning to take the place of the sailing ships. He had lived, however, to see the change from the old sailing ships to the modern steamships and had learned to love them, too.

The old woman got to her feet with difficulty. The girl was right to be happy, she thought, for life was wonderful. She said to herself, "If I see the light of the morning tomorrow, I shall be ninety. Ninety years—a long time! I have often been lonely and sad. Yet I would gladly be as young as that girl and live my life all over again."

A Theme by *Your Name* / Creative Writing 1 / *Your school* / *Today's date*

Directions for Exercises 20–24
SPECIAL CHALLENGE LETTERS

In the next five exercises, you are to supply any missing complimentary closings and enclosure notations as you type the letters. For each letter, address a No. 10 envelope and fold and insert the letter.

Exercise 20

This letter was dictated by **Frank H. Torrance, Business Manager, HOME TOOL DISTRIBUTORS.** It is being sent to **Mr. Robert J. Cranbrook, 8832 Baymead Drive, Duluth, MN 55814.** The date of the letter is **June 20, 19—.**

Dear Sir SUBJECT: Strongiron Wrenches, Lot No. 9774 We have
num received your letter of June 17th, in which you informed us of your dis-
satisfaction with your Strongiron wrench. ¶Due to a crack in the manufacturer's mold for these wrenches, defective handles resulted in Lot No.
ab 9774. We have been assured by the Strongiron Tool Corpor. that this
mold has been replaced and that inspections are being made frequently
ep to prevent the recurrence of this problem ¶Your retailer, Fred's Hardware Company, has been shipped replacements for these defective
wrenches. If you will return your defective wrench to the retailer, he will
ww be most happy to replace it with one from a resent, approved lot. Yours
truly *xx* (105 words)

Exercise 21

The following letter was dictated by **Frank Penna, Advertising Editor, Household Magazine, Inc.** It is dated **November 1, 19—.** Be sure to add the notation for the enclosure mentioned in the letter.

Mr. Albert T. White White Household Appliance Company 474 Ward
Street Philadelphia, PA 19123 Dear Mr. White Are you making full use
ep sp of magazine advertising. Dealers have always reconized the value of the
com magazine market and many purchasers of your products are readers of
our magazine. ¶Won't you take a few minutes to look over this sample
copy of HOUSEHOLD MAGAZINE? Since you deal in products that
com appeal to homemakers note how many articles are written especially
ww for people who's interests lie in the home. Also note the advertisements
—many of them for products of the same general type as yours. ¶Don't
you agree with us that an advertisement in HOUSEHOLD MAGAZINE
sp would yeild substantial results? *xx* (99 words)

Exercise 22

This letter was dictated by **Harold P. Hodge, President** of the **Nampa Youth Sports Leagues,** and is dated **March 11, 19—.** Note the enclosure.

Public Relations Director Morrell & Richardson Company 40 Granada
Drive Nampa, ID 83651 Dear Sir or Madam The Nampa Youth Sports
Leagues (NYSL) help to build the characters of boys and girls in our

(Continued on next page)

Exercise 3

BOOK REPORT

Type this book report with subheads. Type the subheads at the left margin in solid capitals. DS before and after each subhead. Don't forget to place a warning mark at the bottom of the paper.

Full sheet. 2-inch top margin. 1-inch side margins. Double spacing. 5-space paragraph indention.

A BOOK REPORT

by *Your Name*

<u>The Old Man and the Sea</u>

Ernest Hemingway

ABOUT THE AUTHOR

Ernest Hemingway was born July 21, 1899, in Oak Park, Illinois. He went to the public schools in Oak Park. After working as a reporter for the *Kansas City Star,* he was an infantryman and ambulance driver in the Italian Army during World War I. He was a war correspondent during the Spanish Civil War and in World War II. In 1954 he was awarded the Nobel Prize for literature. He died in 1961.

ABOUT THE STORY

This short novel (only 140 pages) is the tragic story of Santiago, a Cuban fisherman, and of the giant fish he kills and loses in the Gulf Stream. The old man's only real friend in the village is a very young boy, Manolin, who believes in the old man's ability as a fisherman when everyone else has lost faith in him. When the boy's parents finally tell their son that he must go out fishing in a boat with other fishermen, the old man goes to sea alone.

The major part of the story takes place on the sea as the old man is alone with his thoughts. In his loneliness, he talks to a bird, to the fish, and even to the big marlin he catches. It takes the old man two long days to finally harpoon the giant fish. Then, the blood of the fish draws sharks who eat the old man's prize catch. He fights them off as best he can, but by the time he gets back to his village, only the skeleton of the great fish is left. The old man is sad about his loss, but he is a hero to the villagers when they see the skeleton of such a huge fish strapped to his boat.

REACTIONS TO THE STORY

It is a sad story, told very simply. It is easy to understand the feelings of the characters because of the straightforward way in which the story is told. It seems cruel that the old man loses his prize fish after he has fought so hard and waited so long to get it. I enjoyed the way the author told the story by letting the reader "listen in" on the old man's thoughts. After reading the book, I understand why it is called a literary "classic."

Report for *English 4*

Today's date

Exercise 19
BUSINESS LETTER

June 14, 19— Fred's Hardware Company 210 Lorbury Street Duluth, MN 55812

Attention: Ray Jackson

Gentlemen

SUBJECT: Complaints about Strongiron Wrenches

We are in receipt of your letter regarding the problems your
customers have encountered with Strongiron wrenches. I have
cap contacted the Company's customer service department in
sp Cincinati with respect to your comments. Their representative
informed me that they have received several complaints
com about these wrenches. As a result the company has conducted an investigation of the manufacturing process for
these tools. Evidently, a crack had developed in the mold
for the wrenches, and this produced a defect in the handles
cap of wrenches made under Lot no. 9774.

The broken mold has now been replaced, and the
sp company forsees no recurrence of this problem.

I have been authorized by the company to replace
all wrenches of Lot No. 9774 which we distributed to
num retailers. Therefore, we are shipping a carton of 3 doz-
en wrenches, Lot No. 9832, to you today. This shipment will replace the wrenches of Lot No. 9774, which
sp were shiped to you in April.

hy I trust that these steps will re-affirm your customers' faith in Strongiron products.

Sincerely yours

Frank H. Torrance Business Manager *xx* (169 words)

Exercise 4
TWO-PAGE REPORT

Type this report in proper report form. Refer to the guidelines in Rules 5 and 9 (page 158).

Full sheets. Margins for an unbound report. Double spacing. 5-space paragraph indention.

SELECTING MICROCOMPUTER SOFTWARE

The microcomputer is a versatile machine capable of manipulating both words and numbers electronically. The specific form of manipulation depends on the software package being used. Generally software takes the form of a magnetic disk on which special instructions are stored.

There are three main types of software. *Database software* allows a microcomputer to function as an electronic file manager. *Spreadsheet software* enables a microcomputer to forecast trends and analyze problems. Finally *word processing software* allows a microcomputer to function as a "super" typewriter.

Of these three types of software, the last is probably the most widely used. This is true despite the fact that word processing on a microcomputer is more complicated than word processing on a machine built especially for that purpose.

There are probably more than a hundred word processing packages on the market (some of the more popular ones include Bank Street Writer, Easywriter, WordStar, Display Writer, PFS: Write, and Applewriter). Before making a choice, you should therefore take the time to learn which special features are available. That way you can select the program best suited to your needs.

Generally word processing software helps the operator in two ways. First it enables the operator to edit copy before it is printed out on paper. Editing takes place while the material is still on the video display screen. The operator can scroll through the copy reviewing content or proofreading. If he or she finds any errors, these can be deleted and corrected immediately. For larger corrections, it is also possible to move whole lines or paragraphs of type. Capabilities such as these eliminate the need for cutting and pasting or extensive retyping, both awkward and time-consuming procedures.

The second way in which word processing software helps the operator is by simplifying formatting. Word processing programs enable a microcomputer to justify type, break and number pages, and insert headers and footers (the running titles that appear on pages at the top or bottom). They also allow the operator to merge stored paragraphs and variable data (like names and addresses) to produce form letters in volume.

Selecting software is a serious task but not a difficult one. Help is available from any number of sources, including catalogues that describe software packages and user publications that print articles comparing and evaluating them.

Exercise 18
BUSINESS LETTER

November 11, 19— Mr. Lincoln C. Rogers 728 Snyder Avenue Jersey City, NJ 07302

Dear Mr. Rogers

sp In accordance with the preferance you
com have expressed we shall be pleased to have you call at our office next Monday afternoon to discuss the matter of financing your purchase of a home.

Either Mr. Frank Linton or Ms. Joanne Bartsch will be available to confer with you. Please ask for one of them when you arrive. I have given each of them a memorandum setting
ww fourth the full particulars of the conversation we had last week, and since both Ms. Bartsch and Mr. Linton are specialists in home financing, they are therefore well qualified to advise you on the best procedure to follow.

ww I am confident that with the sound advise they can give, you will be able to arrange a loan with a payment plan that meets your
sp budjet requirements.

cap Thank you for giving Central Savings And Loan Association this opportunity to serve you.

Very truly yours

CENTRAL SAVINGS AND LOAN ASSOCIATION Roger T. Richman Vice-President *xx* (146 words)

Exercise 5

REPORT FROM ROUGH-DRAFT COPY

Type this report in proper report form. Make all corrections indicated by proofreaders' marks.

Full sheet. Margins for a top-bound report. Double spacing. 5-space paragraph indention.

The Legal secretary

One of the prized positions in the secretarial field is the one held by the legal secretary. The legal secretaries have long since been in short supply and the trend is likly to continue. This is because such secretaries need special skills, legal aptitudes, and training. To start, the legal secretary must familar with legal-ese. She must be able to read and understand (on at least anelementary level) the language found in complaints, contracts, conveyances, wills and similar documents. In addition, the legal secretary must have superlative secretarial skills. She must be able to type 60 wpm and take diction at 120 wpm plus.

Beyond these qualifications, there are 3 main requirement for successs as a letgal secretary. The first is accuracy. Where legal rights are at risk, there is no room for mistakes.

The second requirement is discretion. Most masters handled by attorneys are confidential. Fir example, they deal regularly with family relation ships, personal finances, and medical histories. The They carry out sensitive negotiations in areas like child-custody and criminal porsecution. The final documentation for these confidential matters must be prepared by the legal secretary.

The third and final requirement for a legal secretary is a good general edulcation. This should include constant training in english and languge skills, and some exposure to history, economics, the social sciences, and literature. All this in addition to basic officeskills.

Exercise 17
BUSINESS LETTER

December 4, 19— Mrs. Mary Kaufmann Eagle's Nest Ski Lodge Star Route 119 Jeffersonville, VT 05464

Dear Mrs. Kaufmann

I have spoken with the people in our
ab shipping and production depts. in regard to
the matter noted in your recent letter. As
you are aware, the turnover rate among
cap employees is quite large in the Fall due to
the replacement of "summer people" with
"winter people." As a result, we have several
sp new employes at the bakery.

I have impressed upon all our staff the
hy need for better stock control. All day old
products will be segregated and marked
with a large "X" on the wrapper. There will
ab be a 50% discount offered to those customers
for whom same-day freshness is not impor-
sp tant. All other customers will recieve only
goods that are baked the same day as they
are shipped.

I trust that these steps will assure the
freshness of our goods upon your receipt.
Please accept my sincere apologies for
frag any inconveniences to you. Or to your guests.

Sincerely yours

Rex Peterson PETERSON'S BAKERY *xx* (152 words)

Exercise 6

REPORT FROM ROUGH-DRAFT COPY

Type this report in proper report form. Make the corrections indicated by proofreaders' marks.

Full sheet. Margins for an unbound report. Double spacing. 5-space paragraph indention.

FINDING A JOB

Now that you ~~have acquired the skill of typing~~, you may feel that you are ready to use your skills ~~in~~ paid employment. Perhaps, you are considering summer or part-time work in an office. Be aware that finding a job ~~might~~ not be as easy as you think ~~unless~~ you do not use a approach ~~that is~~ systematic.

First you must decide where you will ~~go to~~ apply. Check with ~~your~~ relatives and friends about openingswhere they work. Many firms perfer to hire ~~those referred~~ by their employees. Your school, church, and state employment offices are also excellent sources. Ads in news papers and professional publications will give you some good leads. Of course, larger business and government ~~offices~~ maintain ~~a~~ regular ~~employment~~ office and welcome applicants every day.

Second, be sure that you are prepare when you ~~go to~~ look for work. Take important papers with you such as a social security card and ~~proof of birth~~. Be ready to complete an application blank asking for the names of ~~your~~ schools attended, ~~your~~ work experience, and ~~your~~ references. among other things. It is a good idea to take a ~~data sheet~~ with you ~~which~~ has all this information typed out ~~in a neat arrangement~~. Third, ~~groom yourself~~ for the interview. You ~~want to~~ make a good first impression. If you arrive for an interview ~~late~~, unprepared and unkempt, you are stacking the cards against yourself.

Finally, remembre that people rarely get the first job they interview ~~for~~. Do not be disappointed and stop looking.

Exercise 16
BUSINESS LETTER

November 28, 19— Mr. Rex Peterson Peterson's Bakery 14 Medusa Road Stowe, VT 05672

Dear Mr. Peterson

Until the past month, we were very pleased with the bakery goods which you have been supplying to our lodge. Since
cap the first part of november, however, we
sp have been recieving stale cookies,
hy com cakes, sweet-rolls and bread varieties. Many of the guests here have complained about the lack of freshness of these products.

I understand that you have had a large turnover in personnel recently; so perhaps you are unaware that shipments of stale bakery goods are
frag being made. Or that your quality control prior to shipment is faulty.

Please advise me as soon as pos-
ww sible weather you will be able to supply us once again with the delicious products we have come to expect from your company.

Sincerely

Mrs. Mary Kaufmann General Manager *xx* (118 words)

Exercise 7

REPORT FROM ROUGH-DRAFT COPY

Type this report in proper report form. Make all the corrections indicated by the proofreaders' marks.

Full sheets. Margins for a left-bound report. Double spacing. 5-space paragraph indention.

EARLY ART

DS

(A Report for History of Art Class)

DS

by Joanne Drew

TS

When did early humans first show an interest in art? In those far-off days, was the first artist held in high regrrd, as is the case today? These questions are not easy ot answer. It is possible to get a fairly satisfactory answer to the first, but it is difficult--herpahs impossible--to answer the second.

No records exist to tell us about the attitude of other man toward the artist. We can only guess. It seems probably that the art of making war and art of getting food wereemore highly valued than the art of getting figurs out of stone or the art ofpainting pictures.

It is however, known, within limits, when art began. Experts beleive that the first artistic creations appeared about fifty thou sand years agao. It was a very simple form of Art and for thousands of years it litt changed little. The earliest examples of artthat have been found are little more than great pieces of stone that were cut to animals. They have no clear lines; they have only a rough general form. It represents the first attempts of people to copy what they saw around them their in daily lives. In the next stage, here will were simple pictures of different animals. The details were poor, especially th head and the feet but it is possible to recognize what the artist meant to paint.

(Continued on next page)

Exercise 13
BUSINESS LETTER

Today's date Mr. Edward Khan Eastern Food, Inc. 730 Royce Street Peoria, IL 61612 Dear Mr. Khan We are very much pleased with our
sp customers' response to your products. Many of them allready know your
cap line well and need no encouragement. Others try a box of eastern fruit
com or vegetables at our suggestion and then come back for more. We hope
com hy Mr. Khan that you will continue to supply products of the same first class quality and that you will add other varieties. ¶Could you please send us about fifty copies of your pamphlet, *Eastern Foods for Your*
num *Family.* Our previous supply was exhausted in less than 1 month's time. Cordially GOLDBERG & MONAHAN Ms. Laura P. Kopec Purchasing Manager LK:*xx* (93 words)

Exercise 14
BUSINESS LETTER

April 21, 19— Mr. Samuel Morgan 41 Clark Street Brooklyn, NY 11212 Dear Mr. Morgan In answer to your question, we regret that we know of no store in your immediate neighborhood that carries our line of raincoats. You will, however, find a complete stock of our coats at the follow-
col ab ing stores, Baldwin Brothers' Shop, 1494 Swan Ave.; Smith Haber-
sem dashery, 128 D Street, and John's Downtown Store, 6940 Grove Street. We are certain that any of these stores will be able to fill your require-
ep ments ¶You may be interested to learn that these stores also carry our
frag new models in polyester gabardine. Which are slightly above the price range mentioned in our advertisement. Sincerely yours ROGERS, LLOYD AND COMPANY Durwood Rogers, Sales Manager *xx* P.S.
num Watch for our annual clearance sale of raincoats, beginning May 1st.
(97 words in body; 11 words in postscript)

Exercise 15
BUSINESS LETTER

May 29, 19— Mr. and Mrs. J. P. Wylie, Managers Coastside Apartments 4017 Robertson Avenue Virginia Beach, VA 23451 Dear Mr. and Mrs. Wylie We are required by law to notify you in writing of the results of our recent fire inspection. ¶We were generally pleased with the condition
ab of your apt. complex. We commend your concerned efforts to make
cap coastside a safer place to live. However, there are a few hazards we would
frag like you to eliminate. Before our next inspection on the 15th of next
num month. ¶These include a frayed wire on dryer #12 in the laundry room;
sem broken smoke detectors in apartments 4B, 42D, and 19C, open paint cans
sp in the storage shed; and a broken step on the fire excape for Building C. ¶When these problems are corrected, we will issue you a certificate of safety to present to your insurance company. Thank you for your cooperation. Sincerely Donald J. Wootten Fire Chief *xx* (126 words)

In the third stage--that is, about twenty thousand years ago--the pictures are masterpieces in attention to detail and in the clear outline of ~~stone~~ the figur~~s~~es.

~~You may ask~~ how it is possible to judge the age of pictures and figures so many centuries old? The answer is ~~to be found in the fact~~ that these works of art ~~are~~ have been covered with a ~~kind of stone~~ protective mineral buildup that took thousands of years to form. From this covering, the expert can tell ~~you,~~ beyond doubt, the age of the picture or of the figure.

Topic 3 REPORTS WITH FOOTNOTES

Footnotes are used (1) to identify the source of a statement that is quoted in the text of a report or (2) to include a thought or idea that the author of the report feels should be separated from the text. Remember the following general guidelines when typing reports with footnotes.

1. Footnotes are usually typed at the bottom of the same page on which they are referred to. They are numbered in order, using raised Arabic numerals. Type a divider line 1½ inches long at the left margin between the text and the footnote. Leave a single space below the text. Leave a double space after the divider line. (An alternative style is to type all footnotes on a separate page at the end of the report. This style is growing in popularity because it is much easier than the usual procedure.)
2. When typed at the bottom of the page, footnotes are single spaced. Double space between footnotes when more than one appears at the bottom of a page. Indent the first line of each footnote 5 spaces.

borders of China."[2] Then the Arabs captured some Chinese papermakers and from them the method was learned. Before this, the Arabs had used parchment, made from the skins of animals, but now they changed and used paper made chiefly from linen. They carried the use of paper to their colonies of Sicily and Spain. From these places it was carried to Europe. Early Europeans made paper of cotton and linen rags. When the great demand for paper and paper products created a

SS ______________ 1½ inch divider line

DS [1]L. J. Vonderkraft, Ancient Greek History, 6th ed. (New York: Holt, 1976), pp. 60-61.

DS [2]Campbell Shelby, "Our Marvelous Paper," Paper Industry Journal, vol. 4 (March 1973), pp. 78-80.

Exercise 9
BUSINESS LETTER

January 18, 19— N. A. Roberts, M.D. 4162 Wagner Street Pittsburgh,
ab PA 15204 Dear Doctor Roberts A doctor requires an attractive waiting
hy room and a comfortable, well appointed office. Furnishings in good taste
sp play an important role in creating a pleasent atmosphere and insuring
the comfort of patients. ¶We would be glad to have an opportunity to
com fill your requirements for new furniture draperies and floor coverings.
Perhaps you would like us to refinish or reupholster your worn furniture.
ro We have a large stock ready for immediate delivery our customer department will fill any special order you may have in mind. ¶Our consultant
com for interior decoration Lewis Vinings will be glad to call at your office
to discuss your furnishing needs with you. Sincerely HALLIDAY & COMPANY Millard Wong Executive Director *xx* (107 words)

Exercise 10
BUSINESS LETTER

Today's date Wilkins Food Products, Inc. 732 Birdwell Street Mobile,
AL 36617 Ladies and Gentlemen On opening the first case of your recent
num shipment of canned peaches, we found 7 swollen cans. We cannot risk
offering this merchandise to our customers. In fact, we feel doubtful
sem about the entire shipment therefore, we have not opened the other three
cases and we are returning the entire lot to you by freight today. ¶Please
ab credit our acct. with this return shipment and inform us at once whether
hy you can supply us with high quality goods. Sincerely yours HUGHES & RODMAN Walter Delapena, Buyer WD:*xx* (80 words)

Exercise 11
RECORD OF TELEGRAPH MESSAGE

Send this message as a direct telegram.

October 27, 19— 11:07 a.m. Charge Sender Ramies Pharmaceutical
Supplies, Inc. 1098 Maple Street Arlington, VA 22202 (703) 443-7070
ww sp Disregard message sent too you yesterday. Twenty-four cases of asprin
com arrived this morning and we no longer need the emergency order. Thank
you. Cathy Dodge, Manager Save-More Pharmacy No. 17 *xx*

Exercise 12
INTEROFFICE MEMO

SUBJECT Duluth Convention TO Frank Gallina, Art Department
FROM Frank H. Dreyer, President DATE August 5, 19— COPIES
Patricia Gallagher, Marketing Manager I want to express my apprecia-
sp tion for your excelent exhibit of our company's products at the Duluth
frag convention last week. ¶The booth was in a very desirable location. And
everything was set up exactly as we specified. Many people stopped by
com ro to examine the exhibit make inquiries and pick up brochures we are
hopeful this will result in increased business. ¶Your brochures, by the
way, are beautifully designed. I believe they will do a lot to promote
frag interest in our company. And in our products. Frank Dreyer *xx* (80 words)

3. Mark the bottom of your paper with a light pencil mark before you begin to type. As each raised footnote number is typed in the text, stop and make another light pencil mark approximately 4 lines above your last pencil mark. This will help you remember to stop typing in time to leave room for the footnotes and the bottom margin.

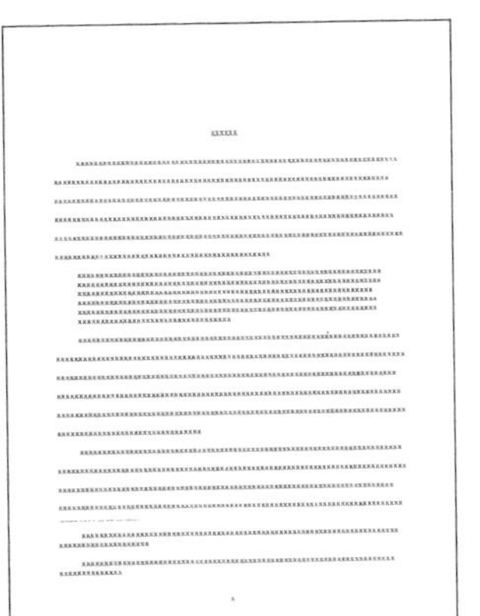

Often a report may include lengthy quotations and bibliographies. These items are handled in the following manner:

1. Lengthy quotations within the body of the text (more than 3 lines) are set off from the rest of the text by indenting them 5 spaces from both left and right margins. Such quotations do not need quotation marks since by setting them off you are already indicating that the material is a quotation. These longer quotations are single spaced.
2. A bibliography is placed at the end of the report on a separate page. The bibliography is an alphabetical list of books and articles that were referred to in the report or consulted by the author in preparing the report. Center the title, BIBLIOGRAPHY, in solid capitals on line 13 with a triple space after it. Single space within each entry in the bibliography and double space after an entry. The first line of each entry is typed at the left margin and the runover lines should be indented 4 spaces from the left margin.

The illustrations below contrast the formats used for footnotes and bibliographies. Study the differences in order of items, punctuation, and indention.

FOOTNOTE (BOOK):

```
     1Author's Name (first name first),
Title of Book, edition or volume (Place
of Publication:  Publisher's Name, date),
page number(s) of cited material.
```

FOOTNOTE (ARTICLE):

```
     2Author's Name (first name first),
"Title of Article," Magazine, volume
(date), page number(s) of cited material.
```

BIBLIOGRAPHY (BOOK):

```
Author's Name (last name first).  Title
    of Book.  Edition or volume.  Place
    of Publication:  Publisher's Name,
    date.
```

BIBLIOGRAPHY (ARTICLE):

```
Author's Name (last name first).  "Title
    of Article."  Magazine, volume, date,
    page number(s) of article.
```

Exercise 1

ONE-PAGE REPORT WITH FOOTNOTES

Type the first page of this report. (More copy is given here than will fit on the first page.) Type the footnotes, following the style shown in the example on page 165. For each footnote, make a warning mark 4 lines above your previous warning mark. When the text reaches a warning mark, roll the paper back and decide how many additional lines (if any) you will be able to type.

Remember to set off the quotation by indenting it 5 spaces from each side margin and by using single spacing.

Full sheet. 2-inch top margin. 1-inch side margins. Double spacing. 5-space paragraph indention.

THE STORY OF PAPER

TS

Paper serves us so constantly in our daily lives that it is difficult to picture a world without it. Most of our knowledge of the past comes to us on paper and most of our current information is printed on paper. Paper manufacturing today is a big industry which stemmed from a small beginning centuries ago.

The history of paper goes back to the time when history itself was first recorded. Vonderkraft states in his story of ancient times:

> Our word *paper* comes from the Greek word *papyrus*, which is the name of a certain kind of tall reed. The story of papyrus goes back four thousand years. This reed, called *bullrushes* in the *Bible*, is a plant that grows along the banks of the Nile.[1]

Paper as we know it, made from fiber pulp, originated in China. In the first century, the Chinese made paper from such materials as silk and old linen. Shelby states, "For six centuries the secret of this art lay locked within the borders of China."[2] The secret became known when the Arabs

(Continued on next page)

Exercise 5
BUSINESS LETTER

Today's date Joseph E. Silva & Company 381 Severn Street Jackson, MS 39204 Gentlemen We should like to know your wishes in regard to the method of payment for the shipment we made to you last week.
hy sp ¶Some of our out of town customers preffer to have us draw a sight draft
ww sem on them thorough their bank when payment is due, others favor sending us a check upon receipt of a monthly statement. Please let us know which
ep of the two methods is suitable for you Cordially HOLLAND COMPANY, INC. Steven C. Dullas Credit Department *xx* (72 words)

Exercise 6
BUSINESS LETTER

June 9, 19— Highway Trucking Company 12000 Fedorovich Road Springfield, MO 65807 Ladies and Gentlemen My tire shop has thou-
ww ro sands of old, treadless tires on the back lot. Their getting in the way,
ab therefore, I would like them removed. ¶A recycling plant in Macon, Ga., buys old tires, and I know that trucks from your company make regular runs to Macon. Would it be possible for one of your trucks to haul the
ep tires for us. Please write or call me with your answer or any questions. Thank you. Sincerely Morris Costello Service Manager *xx* (74 words)

Exercise 7
BUSINESS LETTER

Today's date Ms. Dorothy P. Henderson 408 Barnett Street Brockton, MA 02401 Dear Ms. Henderson We regret to inform you that the painting you wanted, "At the Fountain," has been sold since your visit to our
com gallery. We can however offer you another painting by the same artist,
ww entitled "Brook Scene." It's price is about the same as that of "At The Water's Edge" ($250). It was painted at the same period of the artist's
ww com life and is in the same colors. ¶If your interested in this painting we hope you will come to see it soon. It is the only painting by this artist that we have and is likely to be sold at any time. Yours truly G. Wellington Burke Gallery Director *xx* (101 words)

Exercise 8
INTEROFFICE MEMO

SUBJECT Claim Against Our Company TO S. Hanover, Legal Department FROM Thomas Metz, President DATE *Today's date* I am attach-
frag ing a letter received from Mr. Ronald Slater. Describing an accident
ww num involving his personnel automobile and 1 of our trucks. ¶Please take the appropriate steps (including getting an estimate of repair costs) to settle
cap this claim. ¶Yesterday, I spoke with Mr. Ricardo, the district Manager at Liberty Insurance Company. Their representative will get in touch with
sp you shortly to arrange for a meeting at a time conveneint for both you
ab and Mister Slater. TM *xx* Enclosure (75 words)

Exercise 1 continued

captured some Chinese papermakers and learned the method from them. Before this, the Arabs had used parchment, made from the skins of animals, but they soon adopted the Chinese art of making paper. They used chiefly linen. The Arabs carried the use of paper to their colonies in Sicily and Spain. From these places it was carried to Europe. Early Europeans made paper from cotton and linen rags. When the great demand for paper and paper products created a heavy drain on rag supplies, ways to make paper from wood pulp were discovered and made practical for mass production methods.

Footnotes to be typed with Exercise 1, "The Story of Paper"

[1]L. J. Vonderkraft, *Ancient Greek History,* 6th ed. (New York: Holt, 1976), pp. 60–61.

[2]Campbell Shelby, "Our Marvelous Paper," *Paper Industry Journal,* vol. 4 (March 1973), pp. 78–80.

Exercise 2

TWO-PAGE REPORT WITH FOOTNOTES

Type this 2-page report. Remember to place the footnotes at the bottom of the page where the raised numerals appear in the text. If a footnote falls on a partially filled page, place it at the bottom of the page with a divider line as you would if the text filled the page. Remember to indent the quotation.

Full sheets. Margins for an unbound report. Double spacing. 5-space paragraph indention.

THE BAT FAMILY

The bat flies, but it is not a bird; it is a mammal, similar to a mouse. Instead of wings, it has a thick membrane that connects its arms and legs and is spread when the bat is in flight. It flies as fast as a swallow, wheeling and darting about with remarkable skill, and without a sound. The bat guides itself by its sense of touch or of hearing, for it cannot see its way. Perhaps to make up for this lack of sight, its other senses are well developed. There is one species of bat that has ears so long that it folds them under its arms when it goes to sleep. All bats have very sensitive nerves that help them to avoid hitting objects as they fly.[1]

There are hundreds of kinds of bats, vastly different from one another. They vary in size from the common bat, which is as small as a mouse, to a huge bat that has a five-foot wingspan. Some eat fruit; others eat insects. They are found in many different regions—in the United States, in Europe, in India, in Egypt, and in Central and South America.

Vampire bats (which get their name from the vampire of old-time legends) are common to parts of Central and South America but are never found in the United States.

> At night the vampire bat goes forth in quest of its only food—the blood of defenseless animals sleeping in the open pasturelands or in

(Continued on next page)

Exercise 1
BUSINESS LETTER

September 4, 19— Mr. Calvin A. Hardy Advertising Manager Missouri Bus Company 82 Oakhurst Street St. Louis, MO 63104 Dear Mr. Hardy
sp num We have sent you under seperate cover approximately 20 sets of posters
com entitled "Appreciate St. Louis." If you find that you can make use of more we shall be glad to send you an additional supply. ¶We appreciate your
hy co-operation. We would be pleased if you would forward to us any
sp comments you recieve regarding the posters. Yours very truly ST. LOUIS BOARD OF TRADE D. Chu, Secretary *xx* (56 words)

Exercise 2
BUSINESS LETTER

Today's date Stockwell Landscaping Company 438 17th Street Burns, OR 97720 Ladies and Gentlemen In keeping with the town's spirit of
com urban renewal we at Robey Brothers are considering remodeling the
ro area around our building, the remodeling will include replacing the
frag shrubbery and constructing a brick wall. Also, a small duck pool. ¶We have seen your work and are impressed. Would you consider doing our
com sp remodeling? If so mail us an estimmate based on the enclosed drawings. Sincerely ROBEY BROTHERS CORPORATION Steven Robey, President SR:*xx* Enclosures (67 words)

Exercise 3
INTEROFFICE MEMO

SUBJECT Error in Shipping Order TO Supply Department FROM D. Bahr, Word Processing Training Supervisor DATE August 15, 19— We
num cap have just received twenty gross of no. 1 drafting pencils. We have no record of an order for these pencils. No one on our staff has any knowl-
sp ege of such an order. In addition, we would have no use for such pencils in this department. We use only the following—No. 1, No. 2, and special indigo blue No. 12. A mistake was made somewhere, probably in the
ww shipping department. ¶Please check your order file and advice us on what to do with the pencils. D. Bahr *xx* (86 words)

Exercise 4
BUSINESS LETTER

April 14, 19— Rudolph's Used Cars 747 Triumph Way Bloomington, IN 47401 Ladies and Gentlemen Would you like to double or triple your
num sp sales within 30 days? Our revolutionary new sales consept will help your
ab company increase sales at an amazing rate while teaching your reps to account properly for commissions and to keep accurate records. ¶ Send
cap now for our book, *Rapid Sales growth,* or ask for the cassette tape series. Use the enclosed order form for prompt service. If your sales do not increase in 30 days, we will return your money. Sincerely Miss Margery Ritter, Vice President MR/*xx* Enclosure (80 words)

Exercise 2 continued

corrals. Vampires are dreaded by farmers because they spread disease among cattle and horses, which are their victims.[2]

When the bat rests it usually hangs head down, suspended by its curved claws. Each front foot has only a single claw; the hind feet have five each. The bones of the forefeet or hands are very long, in some species longer than the body. A bat can walk, though very awkwardly, on its hind feet and on the tips of its forefeet, first on one side, then on the other. The mother bat either carries her little ones with her when she searches for food, or she suspends them from a branch by their claws.[3]

Bats are the themes of many tales, and they are often introduced into a story to add an atmosphere of mystery or dread. However, when people find out the facts about bats and their habits, it becomes obvious that there is no need for fear.

Footnotes to be typed with Exercise 2, "The Bat Family"

[1]*Compton's Encyclopedia,* vol. 3 (1975), s.v. "Birdlike Animals That Navigate by Radar," p. 90.

[2]J. L. Ranft, "Vampire Bats," *Americas Magazine* (September 1974), pp. 32–35.

[3]*Compton's,* p. 91.

Exercise 3

MULTIPLE-PAGE REPORT WITH FOOTNOTES

Type this report, paying special attention to footnotes. Prepare a title page for the report. (Refer to Exercise 6, page 114.)

Full sheets. Margins for a left-bound report. Double spacing, 5-space paragraph indention.

UNDERSTANDING DATA PROCESSING

Information (data) has been processed since human beings first decided to keep written records of their possessions. Even cave dwellers who scratched crude marks and drawings on the walls of their caves can be said to have been processing data. With the invention of paper and the resulting paper explosion, it was just a matter of time before machines were invented to help with this burden of paperwork.

Whether the processing of data is done by hand (such as with a simple adding machine) or with a complicated electronic machine, there should be no mystery surrounding it. Data processing is "the restructuring of data by man or machine to increase its usefulness and value."[1] It is any method used to accomplish accounting, statistical, and reporting functions for business.

No discussion of data processing is complete without a discussion of the computer. In fact, some people believe, incorrectly, that the terms

(Continued on next page)

Exercise 7

June 25, 19— Dear Joyce It's been more than six months since your last dental checkup. Please call to arrange an appointment. ¶Dr. McCardle will be on vacation the month of August. Susan Brent, Nurse H.C. McCardle, D.D.S.

RETURN ADDRESS H. C. McCardle, D.D.S., 1947 West Pico Boulevard Los Angeles, CA 90034

ADDRESSEE Ms. Joyce Rothschild 3978 Sunset Boulevard No. 8 Hollywood, CA 90028

Exercise 8

CREATIVE KEYBOARDING

Design a format for the meeting announcement at the right. Use your knowledge of centering and special display techniques to arrange the copy attractively on a postal card. Omit words or repetitious elements as necessary to fit the copy into your format.

Association of Garment Manufacturers
New York, New York
The Time: Friday evening, May 7, 8 o'clock
The Place: Wagner Building, 644 Elm Street
The Purpose: Business meeting

1. Annual election of officers
2. Decision on meeting dates
3. Plans for discussion topics
4. Introduction of new members

Arthur T. Gross
Secretary

RETURN ADDRESS Association of Garment Manufacturers 383 Monroe Avenue, Suite 700 New York, NY 10031

ADDRESSEE Mr. Herbert N. Ferguson 63 West 49th Street New York, NY 10023

Topic 10 APPLYING ENGLISH SKILLS

The exercises in this topic will give you practice in correcting errors in spelling, grammar, and punctuation. Before you type an exercise, read it carefully to find the errors. The symbols in the margin of each exercise provide clues to the kinds of errors to look for. After you have identified each error in an exercise, make a list of the corrections. Then type the exercise in an acceptable business style. *Do not mark the book.*

The key below gives the meaning of each symbol. Two new symbols (marked with an asterisk) have been added to those used in earlier sections of the text.

KEY TO SYMBOLS USED IN EXERCISES 1–24

*ab	abbreviation	ep	end punctuation	ro	run-on sentence
cap	capitalization	frag	sentence fragment	sem	semicolon
col	colon	hy	hyphen	sp	spelling
com	comma	*num	number style	ww	wrong word

Exercise 3 continued

data processing and *computer* mean the same thing. Maniotes and Quasney state:

> A computer is simply a machine capable of accepting information, processing the information at high speeds, and providing the results of these processes in an acceptable form for the user.[2]

As computers have become more widely used in processing data for business, they have made possible a vast expansion in data handling. In addition, they have taken over many routine clerical jobs. This, for obvious reasons, has caused a fear of the machine on the part of people who do not understand it. Actually, computers have opened new career possibilities in data processing, creating job openings for an increased number of trained personnel on many levels. Jobs are now available in the field in seven basic categories: management, programming and analysis, clerical, maintenance, design and manufacturing, marketing and sales, and education.[3] Many of these computer-oriented careers in data processing did not exist even a few years ago.

A study of the role of data processing and computers is of value to everyone. There are few people who can get through a complete day without some form of data processing touching their lives. The checks we write, the bill receipts we return, even the envelopes we address have been adjusted to allow for computer processing. Schools, courts, governments, banks, hospitals, police departments, industry—to name but a few—must all solve problems of processing the many names and account numbers to be handled each day.

Stories and jokes have been circulated portraying computers as monsters that may someday take over control of the entire world. But in fact, "without human direction the computer is quite useless."[4] Computers are only as capable as the men and women who program and maintain them.

Because of the volume of information to be handled and stored for reuse, more and more organizations are turning to the computer for help. We are fortunate to have the assistance of the computer in the job of processing data.

Footnotes to be typed with Exercise 3, "Understanding Data Processing"

[1]Gerald A. Silver and Joan B. Silver, *Data Processing for Business*, 3rd ed. (New York: Harcourt Brace, 1981), p. 5.

[2]John Maniotes and James S. Quasney, *Computer Careers* (New York: Hayden Book Co., 1974), p. 2.

[3]Ibid., p. 6.

[4]Ibid., p. 30.

Directions for Exercises 1–8

Use the copy in these exercises to type the address and message sides of eight postal cards. Position the contents of the message side attractively. If you need to, refer to Model 23.

Exercise 1

Today's date Dear Mr. Babcock This is to notify you that the cleaning of your rugs has been completed. The rugs will be delivered to your home on Saturday. Yours truly T. Towers

RETURN ADDRESS Crawford Cleaners 177 Montrose Street Bridgeport, CT 06608

ADDRESSEE Mr. John T. Babcock 733 Barclay Street Bridgeport, CT 06607

Exercise 2

February 5, 19— Ladies and Gentlemen Kindly send me one gallon of Gerber Liquid Floor Wax at $8.98, as advertised in today's *Trumpet.* Charge to my account and send promptly. Muriel Joice

RETURN ADDRESS 17 Orville Square Largo, FL 33540

ADDRESSEE Gerber Brush Company 98 Carter Street Tampa, FL 33617

Exercise 3

Today's date Dear John Please note that we have changed our address to 189 Highbridge Road. Our new telephone number is 446-1004. ¶We hope to see you at our new store. Mrs. Elizabeth Brooks

RETURN ADDRESS The Antique Shop 189 Highbridge Road Utica, NY 13503

ADDRESSEE Mr. John C. O'Toole 511 Hutton Place Utica, NY 13521

Exercise 4

Today's date Dear Mrs. Parsons This is to acknowledge your contribution of $25 to the Wildlife Fund. We thank you in behalf of those animals you have helped by your generosity. Best wishes Barbara Taylor

RETURN ADDRESS The Wildlife Fund 448 Halloran Avenue Wichita, KS 67214

ADDRESSEE Mrs. Jacqueline Parsons 76 Cartwright Street Wichita, KS 67210

Exercise 5

July 2, 19— Dear Mr. Marsden Thank you for your subscription to our magazine. The first copy will arrive in about three weeks. Sincerely L. Clark

RETURN ADDRESS Modern Fiction Magazine 59 Hill Street Nashville, TN 37208

ADDRESSEE Mr. Dennis L. Marsden 322 Sumner Road Nashville, TN 37208

Exercise 6

December 31, 19— Dear Ms. Byrne The glassware about which you inquired will be ready for shipment next Saturday. It should reach you the following Monday. Regards J. Horton

RETURN ADDRESS Felix Hart & Company 201 Bard Street Flint, MI 48511

ADDRESSEE Ms. Alison Byrne 766 Hoyt Square Detroit, MI 48025

Exercise 4

BIBLIOGRAPHY

Type this bibliography. (For proper style, refer to page 166.) Type the heading in solid capitals. Use single spacing when typing each entry. Double space after each entry. If there is more than one work by the same author, do not repeat the name but indicate it by typing an 8-character underscore followed by a period.

Full sheet. 2-inch top margin. 1-inch side margins. Single spacing. 4-space runover indention (set a tab). Center the heading on line 13.

BIBLIOGRAPHY

Campbell, William G., and Ballow, Stephen. *Form and Style: Theses, Reports, Term Papers.* 6th ed. Boston: Houghton Mifflin, 1981.

Carter, Colwell C., and Knox, James H. *The Complete Term Paper.* Reston, Va.: Reston Publishing, 1974.

Lester, James D. *Writing Research Papers: A Complete Guide.* 3rd ed. Glenview, Ill.: Scott Foresman, 1980.

McMahan, Elizabeth. *A Crash Course in Composition.* 3rd ed. New York: McGraw-Hill, 1980.

Manual of Style. 13th rev. ed. Chicago: University of Chicago Press, 1982.

Mulkerne, Donald, and Kahn, Gilbert. *The Term Paper—Step-by-Step.* Garden City, N.Y.: Doubleday, 1983.

Pierce, James F. *Organization and Outlining: How to Develop and Prepare Papers, Reports, and Speeches.* New York: Arco, 1971.

Taylor, Mildred G. *How to Write a Research Paper.* Palo Alto, Calif.: Pacific Books, 1974.

Turabian, Kate L. *A Manual for Writers of Term Papers, Theses, and Dissertations.* 4th ed. Chicago: University of Chicago Press, 1973.

________. *Student's Guide for Writing College Papers.* 3rd ed. Chicago: University of Chicago Press, 1977.

Exercise 5

REPORT WITH FOOTNOTES AND BIBLIOGRAPHY

Type this report with footnotes in the proper form. Type the bibliography on a separate page.

Full sheets. Margins for a left-bound report. Double spacing. 5-space paragraph indention.

BEES IN WINTERTIME

Bees have long been regarded as the symbol of industry. No other creatures deserve better the title of "hustler" than do these restless little insects. They are never idle when conditions permit them to carry on their work. Even when the weather is too cold for them to leave their hives, they work inside.[1]

Early in the winter, the queen—the mother of the hive—begins to lay eggs. These hatch into tiny grubs, or larvae, which are carefully fed. When twenty-one days have elapsed, the larvae have changed into full-grown bees.[2] They start to crawl out of the cells in which they were reared. At first they are weak and frail. After a few days they are full of the strength and energy of youth and are able to take up the work of the hive.

The queen continues to lay eggs, and what is called the *brood nest* grows steadily, but slowly, as the number of bees to look after it increases. The newly hatched bees devote themselves to the work of nursing and maturing the brood.

According to Rowland-Entwistle:

> Apart from size and better development of the ovaries, there is not a great deal of difference between the worker bumblebees and their

(Continued on next page)

Topic 9 POSTAL CARDS

Postal cards are used for brief messages, such as announcements and notices, when privacy is not important. The card is usually $5\frac{1}{2}$ by $3\frac{1}{2}$ inches, and there are only 21 lines on the message side of the card. Since the message space is so small, the inside address and reference initials are omitted. The salutation and complimentary closing may also be omitted to save further space. Since postal cards often have the stamp printed on the address side, it is important to type carefully and not to waste cards.

Model 23 on this page shows the proper placement of the address and message on a postal card. Always use at least $\frac{1}{2}$-inch margins on the message side, and type the message single spaced unless it is very short. Since you are limited to 21 lines, you will have to plan the proper spacing to arrange the contents of the message side attractively.

Before proceeding to the exercises, type Drill A to practice typing postal cards.

Drill A

Type the address and message sides of the postal card shown in Model 23. If no card is available, use paper cut to size.

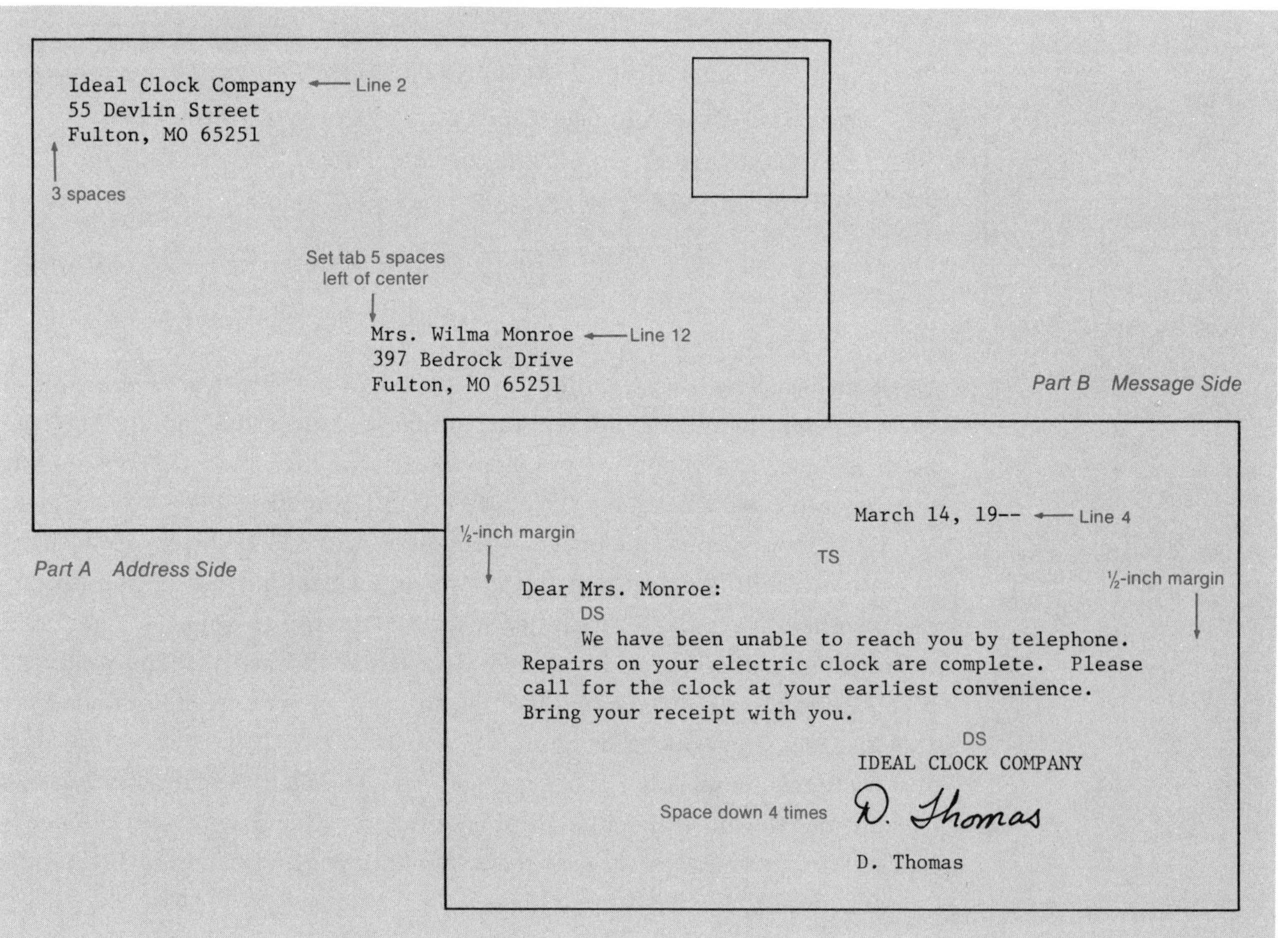

Ideal Clock Company
55 Devlin Street
Fulton, MO 65251
Line 2
3 spaces
Set tab 5 spaces left of center
Mrs. Wilma Monroe
397 Bedrock Drive
Fulton, MO 65251
Line 12
Part A Address Side
Part B Message Side
March 14, 19--
Line 4
½-inch margin
TS
½-inch margin
Dear Mrs. Monroe:
DS
We have been unable to reach you by telephone. Repairs on your electric clock are complete. Please call for the clock at your earliest convenience. Bring your receipt with you.
DS
IDEAL CLOCK COMPANY
Space down 4 times
D. Thomas
D. Thomas

Model 23 Address and Message Sides of a Postal Card

Exercise 5 continued

queen. There are size differences among the workers, however, and generally the larger bees go foraging, while the smaller ones tend the eggs and larvae.[3]

Honey is stored in the combs as a food reserve to be eaten during the winter and the spring, when nothing can be brought in from outside.[4] In winter the bees cluster together for warmth, eating only enough to keep themselves alive.

Early in the spring the bees fly about whenever the sun shines and the air is warm enough, although there are practically no nectar-bearing plants in bloom. You may well wonder what their object is. (Bees never do anything without a reason.) They have very important work to do outside. They need water, and plenty of it, at this time of the year. The older bees can get along with practically no water, but a great deal is needed to prepare the food for the young ones they are rearing in large numbers. Therefore, they must fetch all they can while the sun shines.

The young bees are fed on food prepared by the nurse bees from honey and pollen gathered the previous season. As both of these foods are highly concentrated, they are diluted with water before they are given to the larvae. That is why it is important to bring in so much water and why the bees go out by the hundreds whenever the weather permits.[5] On every journey, they bring back as much as their honey sacs will hold. In this way they store enough in the cells to last a few days.

Sometimes the weather becomes too cold for the bees to go out, and the water is used up. At other times the supply of honey in the hives runs short. Then the young are either destroyed or neglected.[6]

The bee benefits us more than any other insect does. It makes honey that we can eat; and in the process of making the honey, it helps farmers produce larger harvests of crops by serving as an excellent pollinator.[7]

Footnotes to be typed with Exercise 5, "Bees in Wintertime"

[1]Dorothy H. Patent, *How Insects Communicate* (New York: Holiday House, 1975), pp. 85–92.

[2]*The World Book Encyclopedia,* 1985 ed., s.v. "Bees: A Most Useful Insect," pp. 94–101.

[3]Theodore Rowland-Entwistle, *Insect Life: The World You Never See* (Chicago: Rand McNally, 1976), p. 93.

[4]Patent, *How Insects Communicate,* pp. 99–105.

[5]C. M. Larson and W. L. Gossett, "Some Facts about Bees," *Organic Gardening and Farming,* vol. 21 (May 1974), pp. 75–77.

[6]Ibid.

[7]*World Book Encyclopedia,* p. 103.

(Continued on next page)

Exercise 3

Full sheet. 1½-inch side margins. Begin on line 13. Use your own initials as reference initials.

Mailgram

November 12, 19—, 4:00 p.m.

Charge Sender

William S. Clapp
660 Bell Street
Jacksonville, FL 32202
(904) 622-9456

On return trip call on Norville Somerset, 22 Rand Road, Wilmington, DE. He wishes to see samples of our table-model radios.

B. Martin, Sales Manager
Albert Cortez and Company

Exercise 4

Full sheet. 1½-inch side margins. Begin on line 13. Use your own initials as reference initials.

Telegram
July 29, 19--, 1:00 p.m.
Charge Sender
Nicholas Aiken
Hotel Crosby
Meridian, MS 39301
(601) 667-9066

Change in coffee prices effective August 1. Continue taking orders at present prices through July 31. Customers will be notified by mail. New price list mailed to you today.

Henry Warden, Sales Manager
Griggs Wholesale Grocers, Inc.

Exercise 5 continued

Bibliography for Exercise 5, "Bees in Wintertime"

BIBLIOGRAPHY

Borror, Donald J., and White, Richard E. *A Field Guide to Insects of North America and Mexico.* Boston: Houghton-Mifflin, 1974.

Burton, Maurice, and Burton, Robert. *Encyclopedia of Insects and Arachnids.* London: Octopus Books, 1975.

Haguenoer, Michel. *World Treasury of Insects in Color.* New York: Galahad Books, 1975.

Klots, Alexander, and Klots, Elsie. *Insects of North America.* Garden City, N.Y.: Doubleday, 1971.

Larson, C. M., and Gossett, W. L. "Some Facts about Bees." *Organic Gardening and Farming,* vol. 21 (May 1974), pp. 75–77.

Patent, Dorothy H. *How Insects Communicate.* New York: Holiday House, 1975.

Romoser, William S. *The Science of Entomology.* 2nd ed. New York: Macmillan, 1981.

Rowland-Entwistle, Theodore. *Insect Life: The World You Never See.* Chicago: Rand McNally, 1976.

World Book Encyclopedia, 1985 ed., s.v. "Bees: A Most Useful Insect."

Exercise 6

REPORT WITH TITLE PAGE, FOOTNOTES, AND BIBLIOGRAPHY

Type the following report in proper report form. Type a separate title page for the report (refer to page 114 for guidelines). For examples of title page arrangement and correct arrangement of text, footnotes, and bibliography, refer to the three illustrations at the right.

Full sheets. Margins for a left-bound report. Double spacing. 5-space paragraph indention.

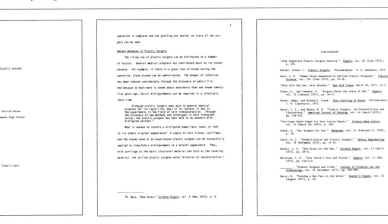

PLASTIC SURGERY

Patrick Moran
Normandy High School

Today's Date

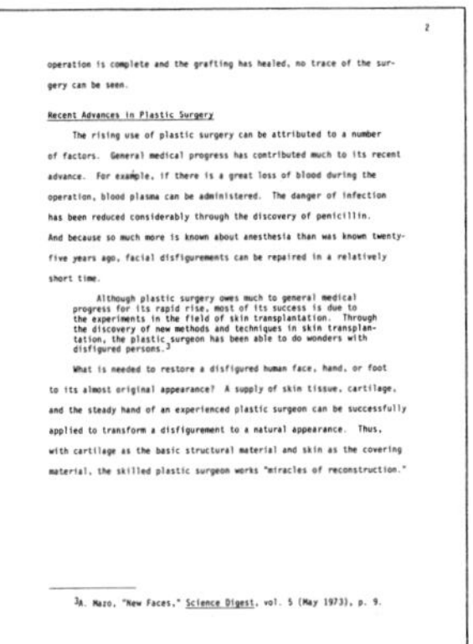

2

operation is complete and the grafting has healed, no trace of the surgery can be seen.

Recent Advances in Plastic Surgery

The rising use of plastic surgery can be attributed to a number of factors. General medical progress has contributed much to its recent advance. For example, if there is a great loss of blood during the operation, blood plasma can be administered. The danger of infection has been reduced considerably through the discovery of penicillin. And because so much more is known about anesthesia than was known twenty-five years ago, facial disfigurements can be repaired in a relatively short time.

> Although plastic surgery owes much to general medical progress for its rapid rise, most of its success is due to the experiments in the field of skin transplantation. Through the discovery of new methods and techniques in skin transplantation, the plastic surgeon has been able to do wonders with disfigured persons.[3]

What is needed to restore a disfigured human face, hand, or foot to its almost original appearance? A supply of skin tissue, cartilage, and the steady hand of an experienced plastic surgeon can be successfully applied to transform a disfigurement to a natural appearance. Thus, with cartilage as the basic structural material and skin as the covering material, the skilled plastic surgeon works "miracles of reconstruction."

[3]A. Mazo, "New Faces," Science Digest, vol. 5 (May 1973), p. 9.

3

BIBLIOGRAPHY

"Army Organizes Plastic Surgery Service." Hygeia, vol. 20 (June 1972), p. 435.

Barsky, Arthur J. Plastic Surgery. Philadelphia: W. B. Saunders, 1975.

Boon, A. R. "Human Faces Remodeled by Skilled Plastic Surgeons." Popular Science, vol. 124 (June 1974), pp. 24-26.

"Born with One Ear, Gets Another." New York Times, March 30, 1977, 44:3.

Brown, D., and Lumsden, R. "Surgery Heals the Scars of War." Hygeia, vol. 22 (January 1974), pp. 26-27.

Brown, James, and McDowell, Frank. Skin Grafting of Burns. Philadelphia: J. B. Lippincott, 1973.

Byars, L. T., and Kaune, M. M. "Plastic Surgery, Its Possibilities and Limitations." American Journal of Nursing, vol. 44 (April 1975), pp. 334-342.

"Cartilage Banks Urged for Face Injury Repair." Science News Letter, vol. 45 (March 18, 1974), p. 185.

Downs, W. "War Surgery for Sex." Newsweek, vol. 21 (February 8, 1976), p. 78.

Lewin, M. L. "Rehabilitation and Plastic Surgery." Safety Engineering, vol. 76 (November 1975), pp. 14-16.

Maisel, A. Q. "New Faces for New Men." Science Digest, vol. 13 (April 1973), pp. 28-32.

Maliniak, J. W. "Your Child's Face and Future." Hygeia, vol. 13 (May 1975), pp. 410-413.

________. "Plastic Surgeon and Crime." Journal of Criminal Law and Criminology, vol. 26 (November 1977), pp. 594-599.

Murry, M. "Turning a New Face to the World." Reader's Digest, vol. 31 (August 1977), p. 30.

PLASTIC SURGERY

Plastic surgery is the medical specialty that deals with the restoration of defects—congenital, hereditary, or acquired—to improve both function and appearance. The basis upon which this branch of surgery rests is the transplantation of tissues.[1]

Introduction

Although generally regarded as something new, plastic surgery is actually ancient. In fact, it was used by the Egyptians over three thousand years ago to repair disfigurements caused by war.[2] Since then the specialty has progressed; new methods and treatments have been developed, facilitated by the advance of medical technology. At present, plastic surgery is more necessary than ever because of the after-effects of wars and the high toll of automobile accidents.

(Continued on next page)

RECORD OF TELEGRAPH MESSAGE SUBMITTED BY TELEPHONE ← Center on line 13

TS

Class of service — Telegram

DS

Date/time sent — November 17, 19--, 10:15 a.m.

DS

Account charged — Charge Sender

DS

SS addressee's name, address, telephone number —
Happy Home Furniture Company
370 Congress Street
Dayton, OH 45414
(513) 224-7612

DS

1½-inch margin — 1½-inch margin

DS message

We urgently need at least 2 of the 12 cabinets ordered November 10. Do not delay shipment until all are ready. Send as many as you can immediately. Ship others as soon as possible. Wire dates we may expect arrival of first shipment and final shipment.

TS

Dictator/title — C. Rutgers, President

Company name — Charles Rutgers & Company

DS

Reference initials — xx

Model 22 *Typed Record of a Telegraph Message*

Exercise 6 continued

Procedures of the Plastic Surgeon

Contrary to the average point of view, there is nothing mysterious or occult about the procedures of the plastic surgeon. Deformities are diagnosed, photographed, studied, and corrected in much the same way as in any other surgical operation. For instance, the making of an entirely new nose is not difficult. The nose is formed from cartilage, taken from the hip or some other part of the body. Then flesh is removed from the scalp or forehead and grafted over the cartilage. When the operation is complete and the grafting has healed, no trace of the surgery can be seen.

Recent Advances in Plastic Surgery

The rising use of plastic surgery can be attributed to a number of factors. General medical progress has contributed much to its recent advance. For example, if there is a great loss of blood during the operation, blood plasma can be administered. The danger of infection has been reduced considerably through the discovery of penicillin. And because so much more is known about anesthesia than was known twenty-five years ago, facial disfigurements can be repaired in a relatively short time.

> Although plastic surgery owes much to general medical progress for its rapid rise, most of its success is due to the experiments in the field of skin transplantation. Through the discovery of new methods and techniques in skin transplantation, the plastic surgeon has been able to do wonders with disfigured persons.[3]

What is needed to restore a disfigured human face, hand, or foot to its almost original appearance? A supply of skin tissue, cartilage, and the steady hand of an experienced plastic surgeon can be successfully applied to transform a disfigurement to a natural appearance. Thus, with cartilage as the basic structural material and skin as the covering material, the skilled plastic surgeon works "miracles of reconstruction."

Footnotes to be typed with Exercise 6, "Plastic Surgery"

[1]Arthur J. Barsky, *Plastic Surgery* (Philadelphia: W. B. Saunders, 1975), p. 17.

[2]S. L. Haas, "Rise of Plastic Surgery," *Newsweek*, vol. 13 (February 20, 1974), p. 34.

[3]A. Mazo, "New Faces," *Science Digest*, vol. 5 (May 1973), p. 9.

Bibliography for Exercise 6, "Plastic Surgery"

BIBLIOGRAPHY

"Army Organizes Plastic Surgery Service." *Hygeia*, vol. 20 (June 1972), p. 435.

Barsky, Arthur J. *Plastic Surgery*. Philadelphia: W. B. Saunders, 1975.

(Continued on next page)

Topic 8 TELEGRAMS

When a written message must reach its destination as fast as possible, a telegram is sent. A direct telegram offers the fastest service. The message is sent immediately and is usually hand delivered to its destination within hours. For faster transmittal, the message is telephoned to the addressee after it reaches the local telegraph office.

A less expensive class of service is the overnight telegram, or "night letter." A message sent at the night letter rate may be delivered to the telegraph office at any hour, but it will not be sent until nighttime when the telegraph lines are less busy. A night letter is delivered by messenger to the addressee on the day following its transmittal.

A third class of service is the mailgram. The message is wired to a post office near the addressee where it is electronically printed and then placed in the mail. A mailgram offers next-day delivery at less than half the cost of a night letter. Since rates vary considerably, you should choose the class of service carefully. The minimum rate for a night letter or mailgram is based on a 100-word message; but for a direct telegram, it is based on a 10-word message. Each additional word adds to the cost.

To send a telegram or mailgram, businesses most often call in their messages by telephone to a local telegraph office. This is more convenient for them than arranging for hand delivery of messages typed on standard telegram forms. Model 22 (page 299) illustrates how to set up a record of a telegraph message submitted by telephone. Study the model carefully, and reread the interoffice memo in Exercise 11 of Topic 7 (page 296). Then, do Drill A to gain practice in typing a telegraph message.

Drill A

Type the record of a telegraph message sent by telephone shown in Model 22. Follow the spacing instructions given there. Make 1 carbon copy.

Directions for Exercises 1–4

The telegraph messages in these exercises were submitted by telephone. Type them following the style shown in Model 22. Be sure to include the heading for each one. Make 1 carbon copy.

Exercise 1

Full sheet. 1½-inch side margins. Begin on line 13.

Telegram July 19, 19—, 11:00 a.m. Charge Sender Atlantic Federal Bank 227 Morton Street Bangor, ME 04401 (207) 332-1788 Stop Check No. 10076 payable to Computer Service, Inc. written on our Account No. 3-035972-6. Check reported stolen from main office of Computer Service. L. Benton, Accountant SGS Investments *xx*

Exercise 2

Full sheet. 1½-inch side margins. Begin on line 13.

Night Letter May 24, 19—, 10:30 p.m. Charge Robert Leahy Agency 3702 Gold Street San Francisco, CA 94107 (415) 359-5085 Margaret Hatcher 138 Sweitzer Avenue Syracuse, NY 13213 (315) 531-3202 Please send remainder of art history manuscript immediately. Prince Publishers wants to see entire book. For reference, we have received Chapters 1 through 7 and are awaiting Chapters 8 through 10. Our art department is still waiting for slides that accompany Chapters 4 through 7. Must be complete for submission to publisher. Lynn Wilson, Agent R. Leahy Agency *xx*

Exercise 6 continued

Boon, A. R. "Human Faces Remodeled by Skilled Plastic Surgeons." *Popular Science,* vol. 124 (June 1974), pp. 24–26.

"Born with One Ear, Gets Another." *New York Times,* March 30, 1977, 44:3.

Brown, D., and Lumsden, R. "Surgery Heals the Scars of War." *Hygeia,* vol. 22 (January 1974), pp. 26–27.

Brown, James, and McDowell, Frank. *Skin Grafting of Burns.* Philadelphia: J. B. Lippincott, 1973.

Byars, L. T., and Kaune, M. M. "Plastic Surgery, Its Possibilities and Limitations." *American Journal of Nursing,* vol. 44 (April 1975), pp. 334–342.

"Cartilage Banks Urged for Face Injury Repair." *Science News Letter,* vol. 45 (March 18, 1974), p. 185.

Haas, S. L. "Rise of Plastic Surgery." *Newsweek,* vol. 13 (February 20, 1974), p. 34.

Lewin, M. L. "Rehabilitation and Plastic Surgery." *Safety Engineering,* vol. 76 (November 1975), pp. 14–16.

Maisel, A. Q. "New Faces for New Men." *Science Digest,* vol. 13 (April 1973), pp. 28–32.

Maliniak, J. W. "Your Child's Face and Future." *Hygeia,* vol. 13 (May 1975), pp. 410–413.

______. "Plastic Surgeon and Crime." *Journal of Criminal Law and Criminology,* vol. 26 (November 1977), pp. 594–599.

Mazo, A. "New Faces." *Science Digest,* vol. 5 (May 1973), p. 9.

Topic 4 MANUSCRIPTS

The procedures for typing manuscripts are essentially the same as those for typing reports. The differences lie in the fact that a report is a finished work to be read by someone seeking information, while a manuscript is more like a draft. It is read and corrected by editors. Then the edited manuscript is either retyped or set into type as the final copy.

Review the rules for typing reports (pages 157–158 and 165–166), noting these important differences for manuscript typing:

1. *All* copy must be double or triple spaced. *No* copy should be single spaced, including long quotations and footnotes. This is to make it easier for the editor to make corrections and to allow the text to be easily read by the typesetter.
2. Use generous margins to allow the editor to make notations or to write instructions on the pages. A 6-inch line with a 1½-inch left margin is desirable. Use right and bottom margins of at least 1 inch. Allow a 2-inch top margin on chapter-opening pages and a 1-inch top margin on succeeding pages.
3. Do not underline subheads; type them in both capitals and small letters. Differentiate between different levels of subheads by their placement. For instance, the most important head may be centered; the next level subhead may be at the left margin on a line by itself; and a third level subhead may start a paragraph, followed by 3 spaces.
4. Number all text pages in the upper right corner, starting with Arabic numeral 1 and proceeding in order to the last page.

Exercise 12 continued

6. The addressee will type the reply on the bottom part of the copies received. The original copy is removed for the addressee's department files. The last carbon copy is returned to the sender.

These forms are very convenient and easy to use—not only for the sender, but also for the receiver. They eliminate the need to handle separate sheets of carbon paper. Also, they encourage prompt replies simply because of the way in which they are designed—the person responding to such a memo need only fill in the blank spaces. The process of writing a response automatically generates a copy for the sender's files. Carbon set memo forms, therefore, offer several advantages over standard memorandum paper. *xx* (204 words)

Exercise 13

CARBON SET MESSAGE FORM

Use a carbon set message form to type this memo. Follow the instructions given in the memo in Exercise 12. (After you have finished the message, you may remove the first carbon copy and exchange memos with another student before typing the response.)

If memo forms are not available, use a full sheet ruled across the middle. Type the headings in solid capitals. Make 2 carbon copies.

Message

TO D. Greene AT Personnel Department SUBJECT Employee Social Security Number DATE June 16, 19— We have received papers for a temporary summer employee, Rhonda Patterson, who has been placed in the Word Processing Center. We find, however, that her social security number was omitted from the form sent us. Please supply us with this number as soon as possible so that Ms. Patterson's check will not be delayed. PLEASE REPLY TO—SIGNED S. Jenkins, Payroll Department

Reply

We are extremely sorry for this oversight. Rhonda Patterson's social security number is 382-77-3267. *xx* DATE June 17, 19— SIGNED D. Greene, Personnel Clerk

---

Exercise 14

CARBON SET MESSAGE FORM

Type this message on a carbon set form. If a form is not available, create your own, following the directions in Exercise 13 above. For more detail, refer to Model 21, page 289.

Message

TO Joyce Kaplan AT Advertising Department SUBJECT New Logo Design DATE October 5, 19— As you know, our merger with Sandsdown Industries will be finalized in the next few weeks. I've been put in charge of developing new logo, letterhead, and business card designs. I could hire an outside designer, but the budget in this department is very tight right now. Any ideas? *xx* PLEASE REPLY TO—SIGNED G. Celli, Public Relations

Reply

George: Why not hold an intercompany contest for the design of the new logo? Our merged name—Albright-Sandsdown Industries, Inc.—makes me think of all kinds of possibilities. We have some very creative people here, too. We could offer $100 as a prize for the person(s) whose design is accepted. *xx* DATE October 6, 19— SIGNED Joyce Kaplan, Advertising

Exercise 1

MANUSCRIPT

Type this manuscript in proper form. If you make any typing errors, correct them as you go. Any remaining errors may be corrected by using acceptable proofreaders' marks in pencil. Remember to double-space footnotes.

Full sheets. $1\frac{1}{2}$-inch side margins. 2-inch top margin and 1-inch bottom margin. Double spacing. 5-space paragraph indention.

WORD PROCESSING CAREERS

TS

Although the term *word processing* has been around since the mid-1960s, no one has yet come up with a universally accepted definition. Cecil defines it as "an efficient system of communicating one person's ideas to another in typewritten form."[1]

With the advent of word processing, a secretary need no longer work with only one executive. Now an "administrative secretary" serves a group of executives called "principals." In this new role, the secretary handles traditional secretarial duties, such as placing telephone calls, handling mail, and filing. In addition, he or she assumes a more administrative role, doing research, arranging meetings, and even dictating routine letters and messages.

When there is typing to be done for the principals, the administrative secretary sends it to the supervisor in the Word Processing Center. There, a "correspondence secretary" is given the assignment. The correspondence secretary is an expert in using an array of transcribing, high-speed duplicating, and electronic typewriters to produce perfect finished copy.

Not everyone will make a successful correspondence secretary. This specialist must have more than machine operation skills. He or she must also have a thorough knowledge of spelling, grammar, and punctuation.

Word processing has greatly altered career paths for clerical workers. A correspondence secretary with administrative abilities may want to switch to a job as an administrative secretary. An administrative secretary may want to make the switch to a position of correspondence secretary. Today, the secretarial career is becoming increasingly specialized, opening up new possibilities in the word processing field for those with technical skills.

Footnote to be typed with Exercise 1, "Word Processing Careers"

[1]Paula B. Cecil, *Word Processing in the Modern Office,* 2nd ed. (Menlo Park, Calif.: Cummings, 1980), p. 3.

Exercise 2

Use Exercise 1 (pages 166–167), "The Story of Paper," for additional practice in preparing typed copy for editing and printing. Retype the exercise, using the rules for manuscript typing. Remember to use wide margins and to double-space all lines.

Exercise 11

FULL-SHEET MEMO

When you type this interoffice memo, begin the numbered items at the left margin.

Full sheet. Memo form. No paragraph indention.

Partheno & Thomas, Inc.

MEMORANDUM

TO A. Katz, Correspondence Secretary DATE November 11, 19--

FROM D. Bahr, Word Processing Training Supervisor

SUBJECT Procedures for Handling Telegrams

Telegrams are sometimes typed on printed forms supplied by the telegraph company and then delivered to the local telegraph office. However, like many businesses today, we find it more convenient to telephone our messages to the telegraph office.

To type a record of a telegraph message submitted by telephone, follow this procedure:

1. Use a full sheet of plain paper to make a record of the message sent. Type the message in triplicate. Use 1½-inch side margins. On line 13, center the title, RECORD OF TELEGRAPH MESSAGE SUBMITTED BY TELEPHONE.

2. At the left margin, type the class of service used, a triple space below the title.

3. Double-space and type at the left margin the date and the exact time the message was sent.

4. Double-space and type at the left margin the name of the account to be charged.

5. Double-space and type at the left margin the addressee's complete name, address, and telephone number. Use single spacing for this address.

6. Double-space and begin the message, typing it in double-spaced form.

7. Triple-space after the message is complete and type at the left margin the name, title, department, and company of the dictator of the telegram.

8. Double-space and type your reference initials at the left margin.

DB

xx

TO A. Katz, Correspondence Secretary FROM D. Bahr, Word Processing Training Supervisor SUBJECT Procedures for Handling Telegrams DATE *Today's date* Telegrams are sometimes typed on printed forms supplied by the telegraph company and then delivered to the local telegraph office. However, like many businesses today, we find it more convenient to telephone our messages to the telegraph office. ¶To type a record of a telegraph message submitted by telephone, follow this procedure: 1. Use a full sheet of plain paper to make a record of the message sent. Type the message in triplicate. Use 1½-inch side margins. On line 13, center the title, RECORD OF TELEGRAPH MESSAGE SUBMITTED BY TELEPHONE. 2. At the left margin type the class of service used, a triple space below the title. 3. Double-space and type at the left margin the date and the exact time the message was sent. 4. Double-space and type at the left margin the name of the account to be charged. 5. Double-space and type at the left margin the addressee's complete name, address, and telephone number. Use single spacing for this address. 6. Double-space and begin the message, typing it in double-spaced form. 7. Triple-space after the message is complete and type at the left margin the name, title, department, and company of the dictator of the telegram. 8. Double-space and type your reference initials at the left margin. DB *xx*

(221 words)

Exercise 12

FULL-SHEET MEMO

Type an interoffice memo from the copy given at the right. Begin the enumerated items at the left margin.

Full sheet. Plain paper. No paragraph indention. Begin headings on line 7.

Memorandum SUBJECT Using New QUIKIMEMO Forms TO All Correspondence Secretaries FROM D. Bahr, Word Processing Training Supervisor DATE *Today's date* Ms. Allen in our Purchasing Department has informed me that we now have a supply of QUIKIMEMO interoffice forms. These forms allow for two-way communication on a single sheet. They come in sets of three sheets, consisting of an original and two copies. QUIKIMEMO forms should be used instead of the regular half-sheet memo forms when messages are short and replies are required.

Follow these steps in using the forms:

1. Complete the top section, which calls for the name of the addressee, the location of the addressee, the subject, and the date.
2. Type the message on the lines provided on the top half of the form. Add your reference initials at the end of the message.
3. Type the name and location of the sender on the line marked "Please Reply To." Leave room for the dictator's initials or signature.
4. Remove the first carbon copy sheet and file it in our department files for follow-up purposes.
5. Send both the original and the last carbon copy to the addressee. Leave the carbon paper intact.

(Continued on next page)

Exercise 3

MANUSCRIPT WITH HEADINGS

Type this manuscript in proper form. Number all pages on line 3 at the right margin. Remember to make light pencil marks at the left margin 1 inch and 2 inches from the bottom of the page as a warning that you are approaching the end of the page.

Full sheets. $1\frac{1}{2}$-inch side margins. 2-inch top margin and 1-inch bottom margin. Double spacing 5-space paragraph indention.

Unit I

TS

Chapter 1. Making Better Use of Your Time

Many of us complain that there is never enough time to do all the things we must do. Often we will find our situation greatly improved if we stop to be sure we are making wise use of the time we do have. Each of us has the same number of hours available in the day, yet some people seem to achieve so much more in those hours. Those of us who complain of lack of time will probably find that we have many hours of wasted time in our day that could be used more constructively with just a little bit of planning.

TS

Time on the Job

As a new employee, you will have to learn to organize work so as to make the best use of your time on the job. Employers pay for a certain number of hours' work from each employee. They expect that this time will be spent to produce the most work for the company. For this reason, coming to work late and taking long lunch breaks are costly to employers. An employee who wastes time cannot produce the expected quantity of work.

On most jobs there are short periods of time—just before lunch, break, or quitting time—in which there is not enough time to start a major project. During this time, however, you can be doing such jobs as changing a typewriter ribbon, cleaning file drawers, or getting fresh supplies. When these short periods are used constructively, there is more time available for major projects.

Leisure Time

The use of free time away from your work is important, too. If you do not plan to make the best use of this limited free time, it will just slip away. Many of us "procrastinate" (put off things until another time). We waste much time in thinking about what must be done instead of simply tackling the job. You can save time by making a list of the things that must be done—and then doing them.

Many of us waste time sitting inactively in front of a television set. Television has much to offer in the way of education and entertainment, but time you spend watching it should be planned.

Free Your Mind

On the job, you usually must work under the direction and supervision of another person. Your free time may be the only time that you

(Continued on next page)

Exercise 10

ROUGH DRAFT: FULL-SHEET MEMO

Type this interoffice memo, correcting the copy as indicated by the proofreaders' marks. Type your initials as reference initials. Then address an interoffice envelope.

Full sheet. Memo form. No paragraph indention. Large envelope.

Dept. 10, 19—

To: N. Adams

From: Glenda Harrison

Subject: CO-OP Program

Copies: Mary Samuels, John Capistro, Peter Matthews, Melanie Ames

At our ~~last~~ recent department Staff meeting, you spoke ~~of~~ to us about our company's ~~proposed~~ proposed involvement in a co-operative program with our local school system.

~~As~~ Since I started my office career ~~when I began~~ by working in a Co-op while in high school, I am thoroughly convinced of the value of this type of program.

Please add my dept. to the list of those ~~who~~ which will participate in the program. Persons who ~~working~~ work in ~~our offices~~ my department ~~would~~ require good typing skills, but speed is not as important as accuracy.

Please let me know further about the program as plans for it are developed and finalized.

Glenda Harrison

~~It would~~ It would be help~~ful~~ if ~~they~~ the Co-op students also have had a basic ~~accounting~~ course in accounting.

(114 words)

Exercise 3 continued

have to do what you *want* to do. Remember that your mind needs to relax and be free from pressures at regular intervals. It is important to your physical and mental well-being that leisure time be planned to include pleasant activities. Group activities should be included in your plan so that you have a chance to meet and talk with people in a nonwork setting. Hobbies, too, are good leisure-time activities because they build self-confidence.

Exercise 4

MANUSCRIPT—HANDWRITTEN COPY

Type this handwritten copy in proper manuscript form. Use your judgment about the placement and spacing of the subheads.

Full sheets. 1½-inch side margins. 2-inch top margin and 1-inch bottom margin. Double spacing. 5-space paragraph indention.

SECTION I PROBLEMS OF THE CREDIT MANAGER

COLLECTING OVERDUE BILLS

Collecting money from people who are not prompt payers is often a delicate, if not troublesome, matter. You must be careful not to offend. On the contrary, you must show the utmost courtesy, as some people are inclined to be sensitive. To collect bills from slow payers and still maintain their goodwill is a problem that calls for careful handling. Large firms handle this problem through their own credit departments. Small firms turn over their slow accounts to collection agencies that specialize in this kind of work.

In some cases, a tactfully worded letter will bring the response you wish. In other cases, you may have to send a series of short collection letters before the debt is finally settled. Sometimes a personal visit or a telephone call will solve the problem.

(Continued on next page)

Exercise 8 continued

her, and she will give you a draft for $200, together with the necessary forms to be sent with the draft to our London Branch.

Please bring this material to me as soon as you return, and I shall explain to you what I want done ~~you to do~~ with it.

(72 words)

Exercise 9

ROUGH DRAFT: HALF-SHEET MEMO

Type an interoffice memo from this handwritten copy, and make the corrections indicated by the proofreaders' marks. Type your initials at the end of the memo.

Half sheet. Memo form. No paragraph indention.

July 10, 19—

To: Madge Kidd
Office Manager

From: Laurence Werner
Supply Department Manager

Subject: Conserving Envelopes

At the present time, it is difficult to obtain the special paper used in the manufacture of our interoffice envelopes. Please ask your staff, ~~Therefore, it is important that you~~ therefore, to avoid wasting envelopes and ~~that you~~ to use a small ~~envelope~~ rather than a large ~~one~~ envelope whenever a small ~~envelope~~ one ~~would~~ will serve the purpose.

Envelopes with the imprinted word RUSH are to be sparingly used.

L. Werner

(59 words)

Exercise 4 continued

There are extreme cases where any measure you may take short of legal action is a waste of time.

TAKING LEGAL ACTION

Legal action exacts a heavy toll in time, money, and effort. Business people, therefore, when confronted with debtors who fail to pay their bills on time, try to collect their debts by means of correspondence.

WRITING COLLECTION LETTERS

The ability to write good collection letters is rated highly in the business world. The story is told of a young clerk in a wholesale house whose salary was $115 a week. During the slack period, she was given the task of following up some small accounts that were regarded as hopelessly bad. In each case she sought out the facts and looked into the record of the debtor. Then she went to work on her letters. Within a month she had collected more than 60 percent of the accounts turned over to her. She was promptly rewarded by an increase in salary. Today she is a highly paid credit manager.

Exercise 5

Use Exercise 4 (page 170) for practice in preparing typed copy for editing and printing. Retype the bibliography, using the rules for manuscript typing. Remember that all lines must be double spaced. Assume that the bibliography is page 7 of a manuscript.

Exercise 7 continued

Accordingly, will you please address documentation for all such shipments to my ~~personal~~ (attn.) In all cases, be sure to include the ^customer's purchase order number and the date ^on which ~~when~~ the goods were shipped. If a customer should pick up an order in person, ~~you must secure~~ ^obtain the customer's signature on the shipping ^document. This will serve ~~form~~ as proof that the goods were delivered.

When you ship parts, and wish to re-stock your inventory, please address your requisitions to me so that our inventory records ^can ~~may~~ be kept current. I shall make every effort to see that the part is shipped to you ^immediately. ~~right away~~.

Whenever~~y~~ you prepay shipping costs on any order that you fill for customers, please sen~~t~~d me the ^original ~~copy~~ of the freight bill receipted by the carrier.

xx (174 words)

Exercise 8

ROUGH DRAFT: HALF-SHEET MEMO

Half sheet. Plain paper No paragraph indention. Begin headings on line 7.

Type this interoffice memo from the handwritten copy. Make the corrections indicated by the proofreaders' marks. Use the standard headings, and arrange them in any order you prefer. The memo was written by **Oliver D. Church, Manager.**

May 19, 19—

Memo to ~~Mr~~. E. D. Loring, ^Special Messenger, concerning an urgent pickup at City Bank. Copy for Ms. L. D. Morris

Please call at the ^Exchange ~~foreign~~ department of ~~the~~ City Bank this afternoon before ^two ~~three~~ o'clock. Ask for (Ms. Morris), the exchange manager. Present ^your identification card ~~this note~~ to

(Continued on next page)

Exercise 6

MANUSCRIPT

Type the material at the right in proper manuscript form. Make the corrections shown in the copy.

Full sheet. 1½-inch side margins. 2-inch top and bottom margins. Double spacing. 5-space paragraph indention.

Buying Magazines

Magazines, issued weekly or monthly, can take up a good part of our reading time. Although less lasting *in interest* than books, they can occupy our attention for a considerably longer period of time than the daily newspaper. No matter what your tastes or hobbies are, you can probably find something to satisfy you in one or more of the magazines on the market. As with books, you should know where and how to secure the magazines that you wish to read.

Newsstands

Newsstands display a wide selection of current magazines for those who want to buy individual copies. The annual cost of ~~individual~~ copies *purchased individually* can be more than twice that of a yearly subscription mailed to your home. On the other hand, if you do not have the time or desire to read a periodical every week or month, it will be cheaper *in the long run* to pay the newsstand price.

Subscriptions

As already noted, ~~A~~ *a* yearly subscription is more economical if it suits your purpose. When you are sure that you will be a long-time permanent subscriber, you can save *a substantial amount of* money with a two-year or three-year subscription. Make certain, however, that you do not ~~load~~ *burden* yourself with more magazines than you have time to read~~,~~ or that ~~they~~ *you* do not ~~consume~~ *devote* time *to reading magazines* that would be better spent reading books.

Exercise 6

ROUGH DRAFT:
HALF-SHEET MEMO

Type the memorandum at the right, making the corrections indicated by the proofreaders' marks. Be sure to follow Model 18 for setting up the headings for a fully-typed memo.

Half sheet. Plain paper. No paragraph indention. Begin headings on line 7.

Memo Center

Subject: National Fund Contributions

To: Dept. Heads

From: Warren McPherson, Public Relations

Aug. 2, 19--

The National Fund soon will be starting its annual fund-raising campaign. Once again, we are encouraging our employees to give to this worthy charity. ¶ Please inform Make sure the employees in your department are aware of the various ways in which they may make their contributions. Discuss with them and the many activities ways the National Fund sponsors to helps those in need in our community. ¶ A representative from the National Fund will visit appear at Plant 2 sometime during later this month. I will give you more details on the date and time that later.

WM *xx* (88 words)

Exercise 7

ROUGH DRAFT:
FULL-SHEET MEMO

Type this interoffice memo, making the corrections indicated by the proofreaders' marks.

Full sheet. Memo form. No paragraph indention.

Memorandum

Date: November 5, 19--

To: All Branch Managers

From: B. Smith, Traffic Manager

Subject: Coordinating Invoices and Shipping Papers

From time to time we have make requested that you ship certain items to customers directly. Lately We have had difficulty in coordinating the invoices for these orders with the shipping papers. I have been asked to investigate it and organize a plan for eliminating this difficulty.

(Continued on next page)

PART

PUNCTUATION AND CAPITALIZATION

The typist or word processing specialist must know the basic rules of English grammar. This section reviews the most common rules of punctuation and capitalization. You can find a more complete discussion of these rules in a reference manual for typists and stenographers or in a standard handbook of English usage.

Topic 1 PERIOD

The period is used (1) at the end of complete sentences, (2) after abbreviations, (3) as a decimal point in writing numbers. This topic examines the use of the period at the end of complete sentences. Other uses of the period are presented in Section 3, Part 1.

Two serious errors commonly made in typing and transcribing are transcribing a part of a sentence (called a sentence fragment) as though it were a complete sentence and transcribing two complete sentences as though they were one sentence (called a run-on sentence).

By learning and applying the following four rules, you can avoid these two errors.

SENTENCE FRAGMENTS

Rule 1. A sentence must contain a subject and a predicate and must express a complete thought.

- *Fish swim.*
- *She will turn the page.*
- *Turn the page.* (Subject *you* is understood.)

Rule 2. Words such as *when, if, since,* and *because* signal a dependent clause. A dependent clause that stands alone is a sentence fragment. To make a complete sentence, the dependent clause must be preceded or followed by an independent clause (a group of words that could stand alone as a complete sentence), and the sentence must end with a period. If the dependent clause precedes the independent clause, use a comma to

Exercise 4
FULL-SHEET MEMO

Type an interoffice memo from this copy and address an interoffice envelope.

Full sheet. Plain paper. No paragraph indention. Begin headings on line 7. No. 10 envelope.

MEMORANDUM SUBJECT Stove Replacements DATE February 8, 19— 12
TO S. Cornwall, Sales Manager FROM Paul F. Kenny, Production Depart- 25
ment COPIES K. Hodge, Repair Department On several recent occasions, 39
we were informed that your salespeople had notified all customers that stoves 54
damaged in transit would be replaced with new ones. ¶This arrangement is 68
satisfactory only when damage is too serious to repair. When damage to a 82
stove is of a minor nature, the proper procedure is to use replacement parts 87
and make the necessary repairs. To replace all damaged stoves is much too 112
costly for the company. ¶We need your cooperation to make sure that all 126
claims are adjusted in our best interest. Although replacement is easier for the 142
salespeople, it is a much too expensive policy for the firm to follow in every 157
case. ¶Please bring this matter to the attention of the sales staff. Advise them 173
to use their judgment and to refrain from promising replacements of stoves 188
when repairs will serve the purpose. PFK *xx* (141 words) 197

Exercise 5
HALF-SHEET MEMO

Follow the style of Model 17 to type this interoffice memo. Remember to type your initials at the end of the memo.

Half sheet. Memo form. No paragraph indention.

March 1, 19—
To: All Sales Representatives
From: Anthony D. Fanning, Sales Manager
Subject: Imperial Oil Sales

It is very important that we make a concerted drive to boost the sales of the new Imperial Oil during March. Although each of us has written a few orders, sales, on the whole, have been disappointing.

Because this new oil is such a superior lubricant, we produced a large quantity in the belief it would almost sell itself. In view of its quality and reasonable price, I am sure that an earnest effort will quickly result in an excellent showing for every one of you.

(85 words)

Rule 2 continued

divide them. If the dependent clause follows the independent clause, this comma is not needed.

FRAGMENT: *When you go to the store.*
CORRECTED: *When you go to the store, buy bread and milk.*
FRAGMENT: *Because the train was late.*
CORRECTED: *She missed supper because the train was late.*

RUN-ON SENTENCES

Rule 3.

If there is a complete thought on both sides of a conjunctive adverb, such as *however, therefore, furthermore, consequently,* or *nevertheless,* use a period (or a semicolon—see Rule 13) to show the complete break.

RUN-ON: *Our teacher was absent, therefore we did not take the test.*
CORRECTED: *Our teacher was absent. Therefore, we did not take the test.*
OR: *Our teacher was absent; therefore, we did not take the test.*

Rule 4.

Watch for complete thoughts that run together without a conjunction, such as *and, or, but, for,* or *not.* Use a period (or a semicolon—see Rule 11) to separate the complete thoughts.

RUN-ON: *Do not be left out send in your application today.*
CORRECTED: *Do not be left out. Send in your application today.*
OR: *Do not be left out; send in your application today.*

Exercise 1

COMPOSITION AT THE KEYBOARD

Review Rules 1 and 2. As you type the material at the right, make complete sentences by adding independent clauses.

Half sheet. 70-space line. Single spacing. Begin on line 13.

1. When you see my friend.
2. Because his attendance record was poor.
3. After she completed her work.
4. When I looked down.
5. Once I read the book.
6. If you are an accurate speller.
7. Since she felt ill.
8. Before you begin to work.
9. When a letter is neatly typed.
10. If bowling and roller skating are ruled out.

Exercise 2

PERIOD

Review Rules 3 and 4. As you type the sentences at the right, use periods to correct the run-on sentences.

Half sheet. 70-space line. Single spacing. Begin on line 13.

1. Accidents are caused they don't just happen.
2. I fell asleep on the bus I missed my stop.
3. The job was difficult nevertheless, we got it done.
4. I saw the movie however, I did not like it.
5. She practiced daily therefore, she was very expert.
6. We are having a party of course, you are invited.
7. Try to remember names they are important to their owners.
8. Save your credit rating send us a check today.
9. Your business is appreciated we shall continue to serve you.
10. I couldn't mail the letter I lost my only stamp.

Exercise 1

HALF-SHEET MEMO

Type this interoffice memo following the style for the headings shown in Model 18. For the interoffice envelope, refer to Model 20, Style B.

Half sheet. Plain paper. No paragraph indention. Begin headings on line 7. Large envelope.

MEMORANDUM SUBJECT Customers' Complaints TO Louis E. Hastings 12
Manager, Sales Personnel FROM T. R. Vernon DATE *Today's date* Recently, 26
many customers have complained of poor service. Whenever a salesperson 40
was mentioned by name or number, I referred the matter to you to be dis- 54
cussed with the individual concerned. However, many complaints have been 68
general in nature. For example, there have been complaints that no sales- 83
person was available at the counter or that two salespeople were engaged in 98
conversation and did not respond promptly to waiting customers. ¶Please 112
take this matter up with the sales personnel, and instruct the floor supervisors 128
to be alert to these problems. T. R. Vernon *xx* (87 words) 137

Exercise 2

FULL-SHEET MEMO

Refer to Model 19 before typing this memorandum. If a memo form is not available, use plain paper and type the headings. Address an interoffice envelope.

Full sheet. Memo form. No paragraph indention.

TO Katherine S. Schultz Sales Manager FROM T. S. Armstrong Advertising 12
Manager SUBJECT Customers' Addresses DATE December 17, 19— Because 23
salespeople frequently omit customers' addresses on the sales slips, we are 38
having difficulty in compiling a customer card record for the purpose of 52
mailing circulars. ¶Please instruct all salespeople to fill in every customer's 68
complete address, even if it is not needed for credit or delivery purposes. This 84
will simplify our work and ensure that we are using current addresses. ¶We 99
shall probably have to send you, from time to time, some of your past sales 114
slips, requesting that you supply the customers' addresses from your own 128
records. At that time, please bring the omission to the attention of the sales- 141
people at fault. ¶This may seem to be a minor matter, but it is important in 156
assisting us to complete our records. We shall greatly appreciate your giving 171
it your careful attention. *xx* (133 words) 177

Exercise 3

FULL-SHEET MEMO

Type the memorandum at the right. Type headings like those shown in Model 18, page 286.

Full sheet. Plain paper. No paragraph indention. Begin the heading on line 7.

TO: All Sales Representatives FROM: Gladys Lahey, Controller SUBJECT: 15
Credit Cards DATE: January 27, 19— CC: Ronald Ritchie, Marketing Man- 30
ager In recent months our accounting staff has been having difficulty in 45
reconciling the company's monthly statement from Master Charge with the 59
items charged on your credit cards, as reported on your weekly expense 73
reports. ¶During the past three months there were 11 instances in which we 88
were unable to identify charges. In each case, we discovered that a sales 103
representative had misplaced or lost a sales draft and had neglected to include 119
the amount in his or her expense report. Without your copy of the draft, we 134
cannot identify a charge and have no means of knowing whether it is legiti- 149
mate. This forces us to ask Master Charge to send a copy of the draft to us for 165
verification. ¶We ask you, therefore, to treat your credit card purchases as 180
carefully as cash and to be sure to attach copies of your sales drafts to your 196
expense reports. *xx* (148 words) 200

Topic 2 COMMA

The comma is the most used (and misused) punctuation mark. If you master its two chief uses, you will be much closer to writing clear sentences. These two chief uses are (1) to set off an introductory dependent clause and (2) to set off words that interrupt the main thought of a sentence.

Rule 5.
INTRODUCTORY DEPENDENT CLAUSES

Words such as *if, as, when, because, since, before, after, unless, while, provided, whether,* and *although* introduce adverbial clauses. As mentioned in Rule 2, if these dependent clauses begin a sentence, a comma separates the dependent and independent (or main) clause. If the dependent clause follows the main clause, no comma is needed between them.

- *If you cannot be present, please notify me.*
- *Please notify me if you cannot be present.*
- *As I am sure you know, the store closes at five.*
- *When you finish your test, you may be excused.*

Rule 6.
PARENTHETICAL WORDS AND PHRASES

Use commas to set off all words and phrases that interrupt the main thought of the sentence.

- *I feel, therefore, that we should change our plans.*
- *Don't you think, Mr. Sanders, that the price is too high?*
- *He did not have the new orders, of course.*
- *The report, which was typed, caused a sensation.*

Rule 7.
WORDS IN APPOSITION

Use commas to set off explanatory words or phrases within a sentence.

- *My neighbor, Ms. Fischer, owns a sailboat.*
- *We couldn't find Larsdell, the secretary who wrote the report.*
- *That tree, the redwood, fell during a storm.*
- *Next Monday, January 6, is my birthday.*

Rule 8.
SERIES

Use commas to separate items when three or more are listed in a sentence. A comma is usually used before the conjunction preceding the last item of a series.

- *I bought a tie, a coat, and a pair of shoes.*
- *I talked to her on July 1, July 3, and July 18.*
- *This summer I plan to read five books, fix my car, and plant a garden.*
- *Please close the windows, turn off the light, and lock the door when you go.*

Rule 9.
CONJUNCTION

Use a comma before conjunctions such as *and, or, but, for,* or *nor* when they join two completely independent statements. The comma is optional between very short statements joined by *and, or, nor,* especially if the two thoughts are closely related.

- *Rita attends Central High School, and she is a cheerleader.* (comma optional)
- *Rita attended Central High School between 1975 and 1978, and she was a cheerleader in her senior year.*
- *I have tried several new cars, but I am still not sure which one to buy.*

Rule 10.
OMITTED WORDS

If a word or phrase is obviously missing, use a comma to indicate the omission.

- *He was a fast, efficient typist.* (*and* omitted)
- *Bill sold two cookies; Sandra, none.* (*sold* omitted)
- *A cold, frosty shake is good on a hot, sunny day.* (*and* omitted both times)

Drill D

Type an interoffice envelope for each person addressed in the memo in Model 18. Follow Style B shown in Model 20. On each copy of the memo, check the name of the person to whom it is being sent. Then fold the memos and insert them in the proper envelopes.

Drill E

Type the memo in Model 21 on a carbon set message form. Include both the message and the reply. Follow the spacing shown. If no printed form is available, prepare your own on ruled paper with 2 carbon copies. Type the headings in solid capitals.

QUIKIMEMO

TO
Grace Allen

AT
Purchasing Department

SUBJECT
Reorder of Interoffice Memo Forms

DATE
March 4, 19--

We are now running very low on our supply of half-sheet size interoffice memo forms. We need at least a ream of them immediately, since we use them daily. Also, the form on which I am typing this memo was sent to me as a sample. I think a supply of these forms would be very useful for all our departments.

xx

(The top half of the memo is completed by the originator.)

PLEASE REPLY TO

SIGNED
D. Bahr, Word Processing *D. Bahr*

I am sending you today the ream of half-sheet interoffice memo forms that you requested. I am also sending you a ream of the new carbon sets of QUIKIMEMO forms. I received a sample at the same time you did, and I immediately ordered a supply. Please instruct your typists in the proper use of these handy forms.

(The lower half of the memo is completed by the receiver.)

DATE
March 6, 19--

SIGNED
Grace Allen, Purchasing Department *Grace Allen*

ORIGINAL

COPY 1

COPY 2

Model 21 *Carbon Set Interoffice Message Form*

Exercise 3

COMMA

Review Rule 5 and type these sentences, adding a comma after each introductory clause. *Do not mark the book.*

Full sheet. 70-space line. Double spacing. Begin on line 6.

1. As we began to assemble the pages of the long report we found that many of the pages were very difficult to read.
2. While it is not our usual practice to grant discounts we feel it is in the best interest of good customer relations to do so this time.
3. If you find you will not be able to keep our luncheon date on Friday please call my secretary before closing time on Thursday.
4. Because she attended night school to acquire specialized skills she was qualified for promotion to a job in the Data Processing Center.
5. After allowing the contestants a few minutes to read the directions the test monitor gave the signal for them to begin.
6. Since my recent move downtown to a high-rise apartment building I no longer have to face a two-hour commuter train ride each day.
7. Whenever you are not completely sure about how to proceed on a new job it is a good idea to ask questions rather than do the job incorrectly.
8. As we grow older we realize how little we know.
9. By the time the boat had left the dock it was already past midnight.
10. As soon as you feel you are ready to apply for credit at our store simply complete the attached application form.

Exercise 4

COMMA

Review Rules 6 and 7. Type these sentences and use commas to set off the words and phrases that interrupt the main thought of the sentence or add explanatory details. *Do not mark the book.*

Half sheet. 70-space line. Double spacing. Begin on line 6.

1. Our company for example handles over a million checks daily.
2. I suggest therefore that you make a special effort to see them.
3. We shall see you on Monday November 5.
4. I am happy to recommend my former assistant Karen Franklin for the job.
5. Return this card Mr. Davis to receive your free copy.
6. We understand Ms. Palmer that you will return tomorrow.
7. My assistant Mr. Jenkins will be delighted as usual to show you around.
8. The dog which is named Rover was lost last Monday.
9. We knew of course that she had no sales experience.
10. Our new brochure I do believe will be helpful to you.

Exercise 5

COMMA

Review Rules 8 and 9. Type the sentences at the right and insert commas, as necessary, within a series of items and before conjunctions. *Do not mark the book.*

Half sheet. 70-space line. Single spacing. DS between sentences. Begin on line 6.

1. Mr. Hammond was visited by his son a neighbor and his insurance agent.
2. The resume includes sections on personal background education work experience and honors.
3. He did not know shorthand but he was an excellent typist.
4. Rona was very nervous but she won the contest.
5. It is a pleasure to have you for a customer and we hope to see you again soon.
6. We received your order but we are unable to fill it.
7. You are a good worker and we are sorry to lose you.
8. I went shopping and I bought a dress.
9. Typists must be accurate use good judgment and take pride in their work.
10. Nancy ran to the store bought some eggs and ran home.

Drill A

Type the memo in Model 17 on a printed half-sheet form. Follow the spacing shown. Notice that this memo is double spaced because it is so short. If no printed form is available, use a plain half sheet and type the headings in solid capitals and double spaced. Center the company name on line 5, and the words, INTEROFFICE MEMORANDUM, on line 7. Triple-space before typing the remaining headings. When typing your own form, remember to align the left margin of the body with the typed key words in the headings.

Drill B

Type the memo in Model 18 on a plain half sheet. Follow the spacing shown. Center the heading, MEMORANDUM, on line 7. Triple-space before typing the remaining headings. Type enough carbon copies to supply everyone addressed in the memo.

Drill C

Type the memo shown in Model 19, page 287, on a printed full-sheet form. If no printed form is available, use a plain full sheet and type the headings in solid capitals and double spaced. Center the heading, INTEROFFICE CORRESPONDENCE, on line 7, and triple space before typing the remaining headings. When typing your own form, remember to align the left margin of the body with the typed key words in the headings.

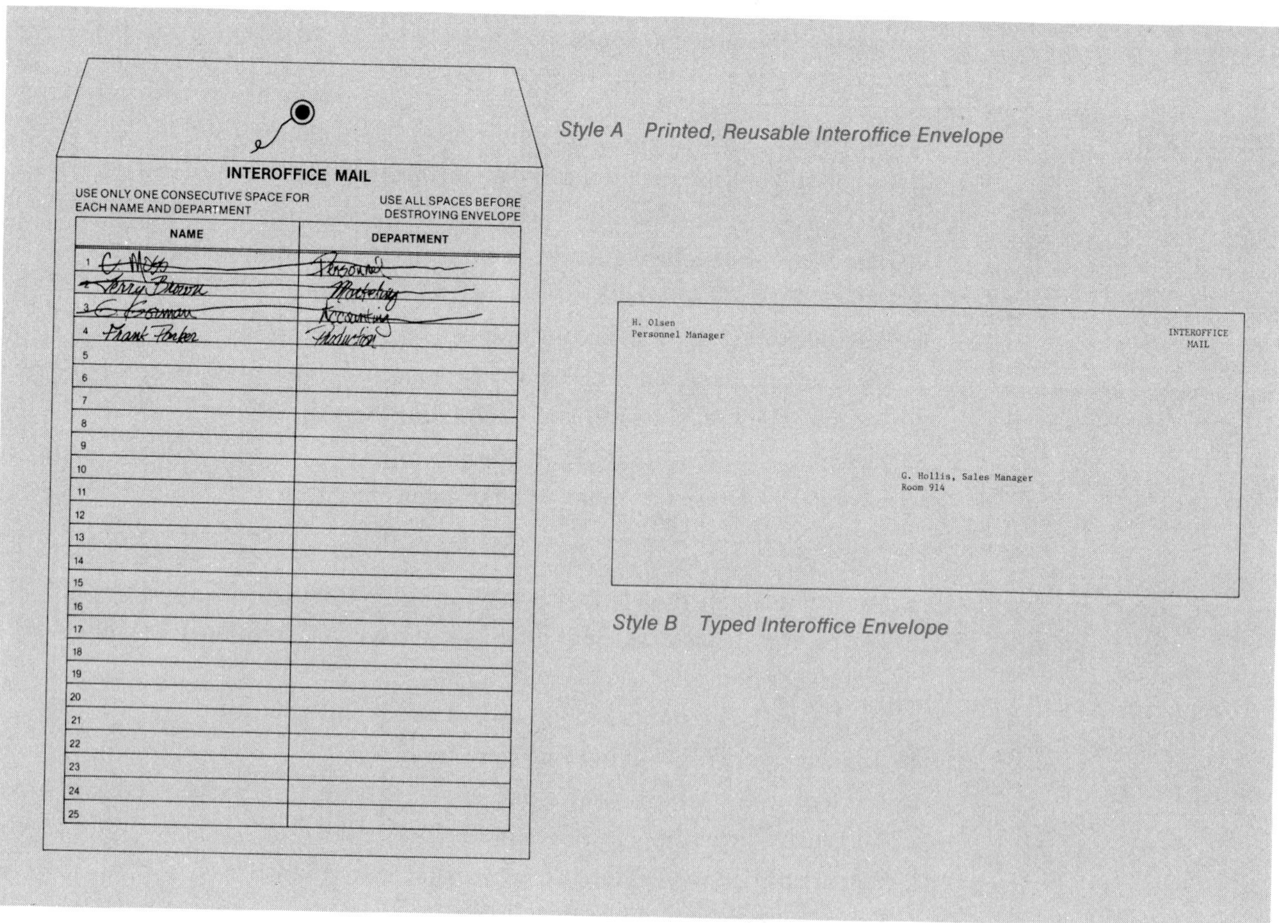

Style A *Printed, Reusable Interoffice Envelope*

Style B *Typed Interoffice Envelope*

Model 20 *Interoffice Envelopes*

Exercise 6

COMMA

Review Rule 10. Type these sentences and insert commas in the proper places to indicate omissions of words or phrases. *Do not mark the book.*

Half sheet. 70-space line. Double spacing. Begin on line 8.

1. Rex lives 40 miles from the city; Eleanor 50.
2. If you call from Ohio, dial 876-3232; otherwise (800) 947-6543.
3. A large bright pumpkin sat in the window.
4. We saw an entertaining thought-provoking film.
5. I found the old dusty book in the attic.
6. My recipe requires three eggs; his four.
7. Last year's trip took four hours; this year's three.
8. The voters called for new revolutionary legislation to lower taxes.
9. Our downtown store closes at six o'clock; our mall store at nine.
10. It was a pleasure to see her sweet smiling face.

Exercise 7

PERIOD AND COMMA

This exercise is a review of Rules 1–10. As you type these sentences, correct the punctuation as necessary. *Do not mark the book.*

Full sheet. 65-space line. Single spacing. DS after each sentence. Center title on line 6 and TS after it.

PERIOD AND COMMA REVIEW

1. On July 1 however I will be beginning a new job.
2. If you want to be sure that your car is adequately protected against theft install our burglar-proof alarm system.
3. Come in Mrs. Jones and have a seat.
4. I received the magazine in April May and June.
5. I received a birthday card it was very nice.
6. Our manager Mr. Wallace will not be in until Friday.
7. I am returning your call of Friday July 1.
8. My brother felt ill so he stayed home from school.
9. Whenever you are looking for a quality restaurant where you can entertain important customers you will find our employees eager to serve you.
10. Before you spend time retyping labels for a mailing list you use often ask about copier labels.
11. I went shopping today and I saw a sale-priced chair that you would like.
12. You are a good worker we are sorry to lose you.
13. When you learn a new skill. You qualify for a better job.
14. If a word cannot be divided. Type it whole.
15. Our Boston agent Teresa Reed will call on you soon.
16. On Sunday our opening day there was a capacity crowd.
17. This will be an attractive comfortable costume for the beach.
18. Because fares were so reasonable we decided to fly.
19. Everyone wants to live long but no one wants to be old.
20. This is a suitcase sir that will give you excellent service.
21. We have received the copy of your canceled check, therefore we will consider the matter closed.
22. He was therefore not able to meet the deadline.
23. Joe joined the union in 1961 and made big changes at first but he hasn't succeeded in changing the things he dislikes most.

Save-Rite Food Stores, Inc.

INTEROFFICE CORRESPONDENCE

Words

TO: All Employees ← Typed information is aligned horizontally with printed key words   DATE: March 4, 19-- 6

FROM: Marcia Domino, Personnel Manager 13

SUBJECT: New Vacation Policy 17

TS

Left margin of body aligns with typed information above

The corporate personnel office recently issued a new policy on 30
vacations. Happily, this policy increases the vacation benefits 43
previously in effect. You will find a copy of the new policy 56
attached to this memo. 61

Briefly, the new policy provides the following: 71

1. Vacation time is earned on an anniversary-year basis. A 83
maximum of ten days' vacation time may be earned in the first 96
year of employment. (This has been increased from five days.) 109
This paid vacation time is earned at the rate of one day per 121
month, exclusive of the first two months of employment. 132

2. For the following four anniversary years of employment 144
(years two through five), vacation time is earned at the rate 157
of ten days per year. 161

3. For the sixth through tenth anniversary years, vacation time 174
is earned at the rate of 15 days per year. (This was a maximum 187
of ten days per year under the old policy.) 196

4. During the eleventh anniversary year of employment, and 208
thereafter, vacation time is earned at the rate of 20 working 221
days per year. 224

Of course, all vacation time is separate from paid holidays noted 237
in the Holiday Schedule. 242

I am sure you will all be pleased with these changes. If you 255
have any questions, feel free to contact me or any member of my 268
staff. This policy is effective immediately. 277

MD

xx 278

Model 19 *Interoffice Memorandum on a Printed Full-Sheet Form*

Topic 3 SEMICOLON, COLON, AND DASH

These three punctuation marks are used to indicate a partial stop in thought, as opposed to a period, which indicates a complete stop in thought.

SEMICOLON

Rule 11.

Use a semicolon between two complete statements where there is no conjunction. Without a conjunction or a semicolon you would have a run-on sentence. Remember from Rule 4 that a period may also be used, but use of a semicolon between two related complete statements prevents short, choppy sentences.

RUN-ON: *Check your work carefully circle each typing error.*
CORRECTED: *Check your work carefully; circle each typing error.*
RUN-ON: *The play was very funny I could not stop laughing.*
CORRECTED: *The play was very funny; I could not stop laughing.*

Rule 12.

Use a semicolon when one (or both) of the complete statements on either side of a conjunction such as *and, or, but, for,* or *nor,* contain other commas. The semicolon helps to separate the two statements.

- *It was a warm, humid day; and since we had air conditioning, we used it.*
- *Since we were hungry, we stopped to eat; but the restaurant was about to close.*

Rule 13.

Use a semicolon before a conjunctive adverb, such as *however, therefore, of course,* or *namely,* when there are two complete statements (related in thought) on both sides of the expression. (Review Rule 3 regarding possible use of a period in such sentences.)

- *Time is limited; therefore, send your check today.*
- *Our supply is running low; of course, the price will increase.*
- *Students are excused on Friday; however, teachers must report as usual.*

Rule 14.

If the parts of a series are very long or contain commas, use semicolons to separate the parts.

- *I have lived in Detroit, Michigan; Cleveland, Ohio; and Chicago, Illinois.*
- *The boys amused themselves in the morning by taking walks; in the afternoon, by playing tennis; and in the evening, by playing cards.*

COLON

Rule 15.

Use a colon after the salutation in a business letter when mixed punctuation style (see Model 4, page 202) is used.

- *Dear Mr. Freeman:*

Rule 16.

Use a colon to introduce a long quotation or a list of items. Some of the words that may signal the need for a colon are: *as, as follows, the following, thus,* and *these.*

- *I am taking the following subjects: physics, typing, bookkeeping, English, and history.*
- *Remember this: "The race is not to the swift, nor the battle to the strong."*
- *It was decided thus: You and I will both attend the meeting.*

An interoffice memo may be typed on a half sheet or a full sheet, depending on its length. Double spacing can be used for very short messages. When a memo is addressed to several people, list their names in a single-spaced column after the heading, TO. Sometimes people not addressed will also receive copies. List their names after the heading, COPIES. If there is no such heading, type in CC, and then list their names (single spaced). Make enough carbon copies to supply everyone. On each copy, place a check mark beside the name of the person to whom that copy is being sent.

When a memo is addressed to many people (an entire department, for example), the usual procedure is to type the memo either on a carbon-backed master (for spirit process duplication) or mimeograph stencil. The memo is then duplicated in the quantity needed.

Some dictators prefer to have their initials typed at the end of their memos. Others like to sign their own initials or names. Follow the dictator's preference. Type your reference initials at the left margin, leaving room for the dictator's signature, if necessary. Add an enclosure notation as required.

Many businesses use printed envelopes for routing their interoffice correspondence. See Model 20, Style A (page 288). These envelopes can be reused many times. If no printed interoffice envelopes are available, the routing information may be typed on a standard No. 10 envelope. See Model 20, Style B.

For speed and convenience, many offices use printed carbon set message forms that provide space for a reply. See Model 21 (page 289). These forms usually have 2 carbon copies attached. The writer of the memo sends the original copy and the last carbon copy to the addressee and keeps the first copy as a file copy. For more details, read the memo in Exercise 12 (page 296). Notice that these memos are double spaced.

Words

MEMORANDUM ← Line 7 — 2

TS

Minimum 1-inch margins

SUBJECT Personal Telephone Calls DATE November 1, 19-- — 13

TO Mr. G. Hollis, Sales Manager — 19
Mr. R. Knight, Production Manager — 26
Ms. B. Massino, Office Manager — 32

FROM H. Olsen, Personnel Manager — 39

TS

Left margin aligns with typed headings

We have received many complaints recently about employees who tie up the — 54
telephone lines with private conversations. This creates costly delays — 69
for those who must place business calls. — 77

All employees, therefore, have been instructed to use only the telephone — 92
booths in the main hall for personal calls. Company telephones may be — 106
used for personal calls only in emergencies. — 115

Please cooperate by enforcing this rule in your department. — 127

DS

HO — 128

DS

xx — 129

Model 18 *Interoffice Memorandum on a Plain Half Sheet*

DASH

Rule 17.

Use a dash to indicate a sharp change in thought or to set off an explanatory phrase or enumeration. The dash is a more forceful punctuation mark than the comma, semicolon, or colon and should therefore be used sparingly. To make a dash, type two hyphens with no space before or after.

- *Imagination is as good as many voyages—and how much cheaper!*
- *The six-foot sofa—not the eight-foot one—is on sale.*
- *A, B, or C—the grade is not important.*

Exercise 8

SEMICOLON

Review Rules 11–14. Type these sentences, inserting semicolons or replacing commas with semicolons as necessary.

Half sheet. 70-space line. Single spacing. Center title on line 5 and TS after it.

PUNCTUATION: SEMICOLON

1. Leonard likes his food very plain I prefer mine with salt and pepper and a variety of spices and herbs.
2. You pay nothing into your pension the company pays for it all.
3. Leslie has training in this area moreover, she has a wealth of experience.
4. When I called, Josephine was out of the office so I left a message.
5. Our company did well last year but of course, we will do better this year.
6. Our current low prices will not be repeated therefore come in today.
7. You will like our polite, friendly salespeople and you will like our merchandise, which is beautifully displayed.
8. John has worked in New York, in a furniture store, in Chicago, in a men's clothing factory, and in Springfield, in a hardware store.
9. My favorite classes are swimming, where I get exercise, typing, where I am learning a skill, and math, where I am forced to think.
10. An effective letter can build goodwill a poor one may lose a customer.
11. Occasionally you will find employers who would like to hire you but they may not, at that time, have a job available.
12. He was competent and hardworking however, he was not very good at dealing with people.

Exercise 9

Colon and Dash

Review Rules 15–17. Type the sentences at the right, inserting a colon or dash at the indicated points.

Full sheet. Center title on line 12 and TS after it. 70-space line. Single spacing. DS after each sentence.

PUNCTUATION: COLON AND DASH

1. Dear Mr. Johnson ■ (mixed punctuation)
2. The patient could have only the following visitors ■ his son, his wife, his mother, or his father.
3. Join our family of customers ■ you won't regret it.
4. Employers consider all of the following ■ your appearance, your attitude, your work experience, and your test scores.
5. Our tableware ■ china, crystal, sterling, and stainless flatware ■ is all open stock.
6. The dates of the lectures are as follows ■ August 3, August 10, August 16, and August 23.

(Continued on next page)

Topic 7 INTERОFFICE CORRESPONDENCE

Some of the dictation given to you to type will be correspondence from one employee to another. These communications are called *interoffice correspondence*. They are typed in a style different from that used for business letters. Note the following differences:

1. The salutation and complimentary closing are omitted.
2. Standard headings—TO, FROM, DATE, SUBJECT—are used, but the arrangement may vary.

Memo forms bearing the company name and printed headings are often available. (See Model 17, this page, and Model 19, page 287.) When these forms are used, the typed information is aligned horizontally with the printed key words in the headings. A triple space is used between the last line of the heading and the body of the memo. On printed forms, the left margin of the body of the message is aligned with the typed information in the headings.

When an interoffice memo is to be typed on plain paper (see Model 18, page 286), the headings must be supplied. These are typed in solid capitals and are double spaced. Colons may be omitted after the typed headings. It is a good idea to begin with the SUBJECT heading, since it often requires the most information. Margins (top, bottom and sides) should be at least 1 inch, but may be increased depending upon the length of the memo. When memos are typed on plain paper, the left margin of the body of the message aligns with the left margin of the capitalized key words in the headings.

Spotless Dishwasher Company

INTERОFFICE MEMORANDUM

Words

TO: M. Meadows — DATE: June 22, 19-- 5
Sales Manager 8

FROM: E. Wheatley — COPIES TO: R. Finley 12
Production Manager — Warehouse Manager 19

SUBJECT: Electric Dishwashers 23

TS

The dishwashers that you wanted rushed to Mr. Hargraves in Dayton will 37
be ready for shipment in two days. They should reach Dayton within a 51
week. Please notify Mr. Hargraves so that he will have someone on hand 66
to take delivery. 70

Space down 3 or 4 times

Ellis Wheatley

xx 71

Model 17 *Interoffice Memorandum on a Printed Half-Sheet Form*

Exercise 9 continued

7. Save 30 percent ■ in addition to our usual low prices ■ on your winter coat during our March sale.
8. This is your chance to try our TV set in your home ■ and with no obligation!
9. Drama, dancing, scenery, music ■ this movie has it all.
10. The judge finally gave the verdict ■ "Guilty as charged."
11. We raise money through projects such as these ■ car washes, candy sales, doughnut sales, and bike races.
12. All my good friends ■ John, Mary, Sue, and Fred ■ came to the party.
13. Remember this saying ■ "One enemy is too many, whereas a hundred friends are too few!"
14. Don't wait until tomorrow ■ do it now!
15. The winners of the typing contest are as follows■ Rosie, 77 wpm; Ronald, 75 wpm; Alisha, 70 wpm; and David, 68 wpm.
16. Swimming, bicycling, and jogging ■ these are my summer pastimes.

Topic 4 QUESTION MARK AND EXCLAMATION POINT

These two punctuation marks are used at the ends of statements or sentences to indicate intent—questioning on the one hand, strong emotion on the other.

QUESTION MARK

Rule 18.

Use a question mark after a direct question.

- *Are you going out for lunch at noon?*

Sometimes a statement is deliberately phrased like a question to make a demand seem more courteous. These statements may be punctuated with a period.

- *May we have your check by return mail.*
- *Will you please send me an application for the job.*

When you punctuate a courteous request with a period, you are not *asking* a question; you are making a polite demand.

Rule 19.

When the sentence starts out as a statement and ends with a short question, a question mark should be used at the end.

- *You will be in class tomorrow, won't you?*
- *You received our latest price list, didn't you?*

EXCLAMATION POINT

Rule 20.

Use the exclamation point after a word, a phrase, or a sentence to express strong emotion.

- *We won!* • *At last! It's our graduation day!*
- *What a wonderful surprise your present was!*

Exercise 5 continued

use of a company car for all business travel, and you will be entitled to participate in the company's stock option plan after six months' service. Complete terms of your employment will be set forth in your employment contract, which will be ready for your signature early next week. ¶Welcome to Olympic Industries. We look forward to seeing you on Monday. Sincerely Frank Evans President *xx* (124 words)

Exercise 6

GOVERNMENT-SIZE STATIONERY

Your letter should look like the one shown on page 282. Cut paper to size if stationery is not available.

Full block style. Open punctuation. 1-inch side margins. Begin on line 15.

October 19, 19— Mrs. Linda Jones 225 Woodland Avenue Middlesex, NJ 08846 Dear Mrs. Jones We can well understand the growing anxiety of the "survivors" as the phasing out of your center proceeded. However, we do not understand the distinction you draw between termination and layoff. Perhaps you use "layoff" to mean temporary suspension from employment rather than dismissal, as is more common. Even so, the prospects of reemployment with the company would appear very dim. ¶If you have lost your job, you should register at the nearest state employment security office for suitable work and file for unemployment compensation. Since employer taxes are affected by the number of former workers who draw compensation, the company may contest your claim. Their argument would be that you were let go for good cause—namely, failure to meet the quota. You would have the right to appeal an adverse decision. At that time, you could note that the newly imposed quota represented a change in job conditions. The fact that the staff has been drastically reduced according to a deliberate schedule would also, it seems to us, be a point in your favor. Sincerely Alexis Herman Director *xx* (176 words)

Exercise 7

GOVERNMENT-SIZE STATIONERY

Select suitable margins. Be sure to indent the paragraph insert.

Modified block style. Mixed punctuation. 5-space paragraph indention. Begin on line 15.

Today's date Lambert & Jarvis, Inc. 849 Wilson Street Newark, NJ 07107 Ladies and Gentlemen We wish to call your attention to Part 131 of the U.S. Postal Service Manual, which covers the classification of first-class mail: *(Begin insert)* Typewritten originals and carbon and letterpress copies will be accepted for mailing only as first-class mail. Facsimile copies of typewriting produced by computer-assisted printout, duplicating machine, printing press, multigraph, and so forth, shall be accepted as third- or fourth-class mail, provided they are being sent in identical terms to several people and have none of the characteristics of actual and personal correspondence. *(End insert)* ¶The computer-printed matter you mailed as third-class should have been sent first-class, since it contained inserts which personalized the correspondence. It was, therefore, returned to you for collection of the additional fee. Always, when mail similar to this is sent, the first-class rate shall be charged. ¶Whenever you have questions about postal services and regulations, please telephone the post office before sending anything. We can help you in working out programs for the most efficient and least expensive mail delivery system. Sincerely yours R. E. Wright, Postmaster *xx* (175 words)

Exercise 10

QUESTION MARK AND EXCLAMATION POINT

Review Rules 18–20. As you type these sentences, supply the correct end punctuation marks.

Full sheet. 70-space line. Double spacing. Center title on line 6 and TS after it.

PUNCTUATION: QUESTION MARK AND EXCLAMATION POINT

1. Has the manager decided to include winter coats in the sale
2. That's enough Turn that stereo down now
3. Will you let us know your decision as soon as possible
4. May we have your answer soon
5. We will see you next week, won't we
6. Are you ready to take the test
7. Congratulations Your promotion is now official
8. What an experience that was
9. Why have you been ringing this bell
10. Will you please tell him I called
11. Shouldn't the bill total $37
12. Ouch I hurt my hand
13. Mr. Jones is still our area representative, isn't he
14. Do your salespeople know how to make forceful presentations
15. Would you kindly return the enclosed sample before June 30

Topic 5 PARENTHESES AND QUOTATION MARKS

PARENTHESES

Rule 21. Use parentheses for explanatory matter, for a reference, or for an expression that is not closely related to the main thought of the sentence.

- *Our check for the full amount ($35.00) is enclosed.*
- *The tools were used for scraping deer hides (Smith, 1971).*
- *Now (and forever, he hoped) he had the key that would unlock her heart.*

Rule 22. Use parentheses to enclose letters or numbers before lists within a sentence.

- *Be sure to (a) read directions, (b) ask questions, and (c) work quickly.*

QUOTATION MARKS

Rule 23. Use quotation marks around the exact words used by a speaker or writer.

- *"Have a wonderful time," she wrote.*

Rule 24. Use quotation marks to enclose titles of such works as songs, poems, paintings, and articles within books or periodicals. Titles of books, newspapers, periodicals, films, record albums, and plays should be underlined.

- *Sharon had to memorize the poem "Jabberwocky" from Alice's Adventures in Wonderland by Lewis Carroll.*

Exercise 2
HALF-SIZE STATIONERY
Select suitable margins.
Modified block style. Mixed punctuation. 5-space paragraph indention. Begin on line 8.

Today's date Mr. Charles Wikki 260 St. Helens Avenue Vancouver, WA 98602 Dear Mr. Wikki It is a pleasure to welcome you as a new credit customer. We know that you will enjoy the special store services that are now available to you. ¶Your credit card is enclosed. This card will make your shopping easier, quicker, and more convenient. All it needs is your signature. ¶Thank you, Mr. Wikki, for the confidence you have expressed in our store by opening an account with us. Sincerely Norman Avery Credit Manager *xx* Enclosure (71 words)

Exercise 3
EXECUTIVE-SIZE STATIONERY
Your letter should look like the one shown on page 282. Cut paper to size if stationery is not available.
Modified block style. Open punctuation. 5-space paragraph indention. 1-inch side margins. Begin on line 14.

December 30, 19— Mr. Stanley M. Garrison 54 Market Street Nashville, TN 37225 Dear Mr. Garrison SUBJECT: Policy No. 4327 Your letter regarding dividends on your life insurance policy has been referred to me. ¶Our policies do not earn any dividends during their first year. Occasionally a dividend is paid on a first-year policy, but that is in expectation of its future earnings. At the end of the second year of coverage, however, you will be entitled to the dividends your policy earns during that year. Since no dividends are shared by policyholders their first year, special payments are sometimes made to them at the end of their fourth year of coverage. This occurs if the company accumulates an adequate surplus. ¶I trust that this explanation will provide a satisfactory answer to your questions. If any other problems arise, please contact me directly. Cordially Richard Palermo Executive Officer *xx* (124 words)

Exercise 4
EXECUTIVE-SIZE STATIONERY
Select suitable margins.
Modified block style. Mixed punctuation. No paragraph indention. Begin on line 16.

Today's date Mr. James H. Carpenter 903 Webster Building 534 Spruce Street Reading, PA 19613 Dear Jim We find ourselves so absorbed in acquiring new customers that we wonder whether we neglect our old friends. So, we want to take time now to tell you how much we have appreciated your patronage over the years. ¶It has come to my attention that our sales representatives are sometimes late in making their calls because of their crowded schedules. If you experience any interruption in your service, please get in touch with me. I shall see that your needs are promptly taken care of. Best wishes Ralph Andrews Vice President *xx* (85 words)

Exercise 5
EXECUTIVE-SIZE STATIONERY
Select suitable margins.
Full block style. Open punctuation. Begin on line 14.

Today's date Ms. Annette Spear 627 Chester Street Tuckahoe, NY 10707 Dear Annette I want you to know how pleased I am that you have agreed to accept the position of Vice-President, Research and Development, at Olympic Industries. Having considered many candidates, we are confident that you possess the qualifications and personal attributes most suited for this demanding position. ¶As we discussed yesterday, your starting salary will be $48,000 per year. You will be given

(Continued on next page)

Rule 25.

Use quotation marks to call attention to a word or phrase, specifically to set off (a) the definition of a word; (b) a term used humorously or ironically; or (c) a word or phrase introduced by *marked, labeled,* or a similar expression.

- *Etc. stands for the Latin words meaning "and so forth."*
- *Mark's "new" car was really an old wreck.*
- *The door was marked "For Employees Only."*

Rule 26.

When quotation marks and other punctuation are used together, follow these placement rules:

a. Type a period or a comma *before* the closing quotation mark.
b. Type a semicolon or a colon *after* the closing quotation mark.
c. Type a question mark or an exclamation point *after* the closing quotation mark, except when the question mark or exclamation point is a part of the quoted material.

- *"I hate to go," she said, "but my plane leaves at 5:30."*
- *"Parting is such sweet sorrow"; that was his reply.*
- *Who said, "I shall return"? (The entire statement is a question.)*
- *He asked, "When will you return?" (Only the sentence in quotes is a question.)*

Exercise 11

PARENTHESES AND QUOTATION MARKS

Review Rules 21–26. Type the sentences at the right and insert parentheses and quotation marks as necessary.

Full sheet. 70-space line. Single spacing. DS after each sentence. Center title on line 5 and DS after it.

PUNCTUATION: PARENTHESES AND QUOTATION MARKS

1. Her article, English in the Typing Class, appeared in *Modern Education.*
2. When the temperature reached 40°C 104°F, the plant wilted.
3. The lie detector disproved the truth of his statements.
4. The lamp is equipped with a special shade our own design to give maximum light with minimum glare.
5. Quick action must be taken, Ms. Fleming said, on your nine pending bills.
6. The letter was stamped Special Delivery.
7. We regret, the credit manager wrote, that we cannot make a shipment until the present balance is reduced.
8. Have you ever read Frost's After the Apple Picking?
9. Look for sheets and towels that are marked irregular.
10. Did he say, We are going to increase tuition next semester?
11. It is a good idea to 1 brush your teeth twice a day, 2 avoid sweets, and 3 see your dentist regularly.
12. The students were improperly labeled radical.
13. The abbreviation *C.O.D.* means cash on delivery.
14. What an idea! said Mr. Brown.
15. Review the correct use of directional signals page 23.
16. Live each day to its fullest, advised the old man.
17. *Moonlighting* is defined as holding a second job.
18. Feudalism began following the Roman Empire's collapse Kay, 1970.
19. If a letter is medium length 100 to 200 words, use a 5-inch line.
20. You will find the information in the encyclopedia Volume 17.

Half-size stationery is best suited for short letters. Based on the length of the letter, the position of the date line may range from line 6 to line 13. The side margins vary from 1 inch to $\frac{3}{4}$ inches.

Side margins of 1 inch to $\frac{3}{4}$ inches are also used on executive-size stationery. The date line position may vary from line 10 to line 16, depending on the length of the letter.

The standard margin settings used for typing letters on $8\frac{1}{2}$ by 11 inch paper may also be used for typing letters on these special sizes of stationery. The paper guide, however, will need to be adjusted for each size of stationery so that the sheet is centered at 50 (or 42) on the carriage scale.

On government-size stationery, $1\frac{1}{2}$-inch to 1-inch side margins are used. The date line may be determined in the usual way or as directed in special government correspondence manuals.

Metric-size stationery is just slightly narrower than standard $8\frac{1}{2}$ by 11 inch stationery. The same side margins can therefore be used as for $8\frac{1}{2}$ by 11 inch paper. The main difference between the two sizes is the length. Metric-size stationery contains 70 line spaces—four more than $8\frac{1}{2}$ by 11 inch stationery. Short to medium letters, therefore, are started two lines lower on metric paper. For long letters, no date-line adjustment is necessary. (No exercises are given in this topic for letters typed on metric-size stationery, since any of the exercises in Topic 1 can be used for such practice.)

Before you begin to type the exercises, study the three letters illustrated below. They show finished letters for Exercises 1, 3, and 6. If stationery is not available in the sizes called for in the exercises, fold or cut paper to size.

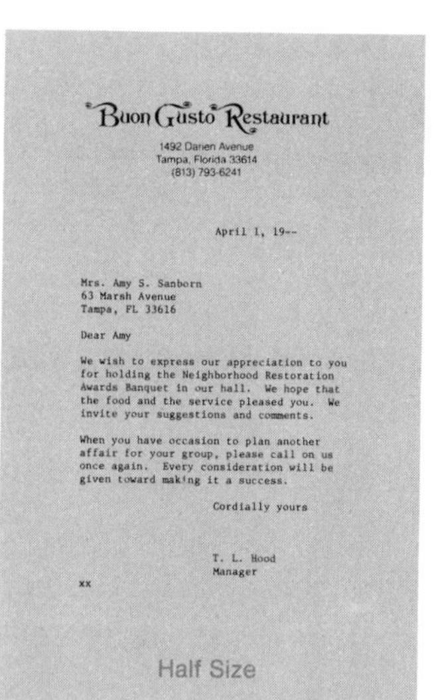
Buon Gusto Restaurant
1492 Darien Avenue
Tampa, Florida 33614
(813) 793-6241

April 1, 19--

Mrs. Amy S. Sanborn
63 Marsh Avenue
Tampa, FL 33616

Dear Amy

We wish to express our appreciation to you for holding the Neighborhood Restoration Awards Banquet in our hall. We hope that the food and the service pleased you. We invite your suggestions and comments.

When you have occasion to plan another affair for your group, please call on us once again. Every consideration will be given toward making it a success.

Cordially yours

T. L. Hood
Manager

xx

Half Size

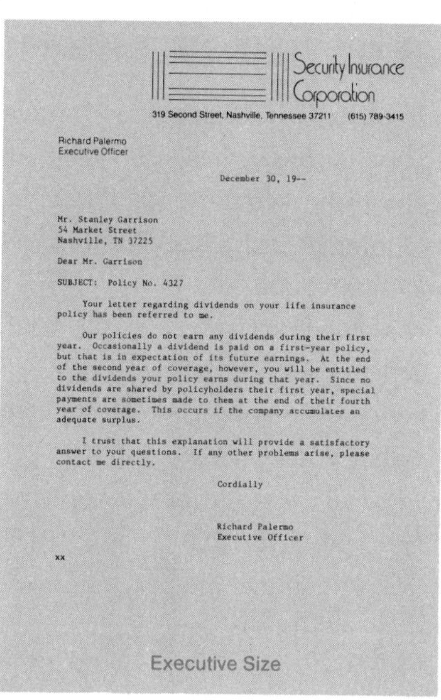
Security Insurance Corporation
319 Second Street, Nashville, Tennessee 37211 (615) 789-3415

Richard Palermo
Executive Officer

December 30, 19--

Mr. Stanley Garrison
54 Market Street
Nashville, TN 37225

Dear Mr. Garrison

SUBJECT: Policy No. 4327

Your letter regarding dividends on your life insurance policy has been referred to me.

Our policies do not earn any dividends during their first year. Occasionally a dividend is paid on a first-year policy, but that is in expectation of its future earnings. At the end of the second year of coverage, however, you will be entitled to the dividends your policy earns during that year. Since no dividends are shared by policyholders their first year, special payments are sometimes made to them at the end of their fourth year of coverage. This occurs if the company accumulates an adequate surplus.

I trust that this explanation will provide a satisfactory answer to your questions. If any other problems arise, please contact me directly.

Cordially

Richard Palermo
Executive Officer

xx

Executive Size

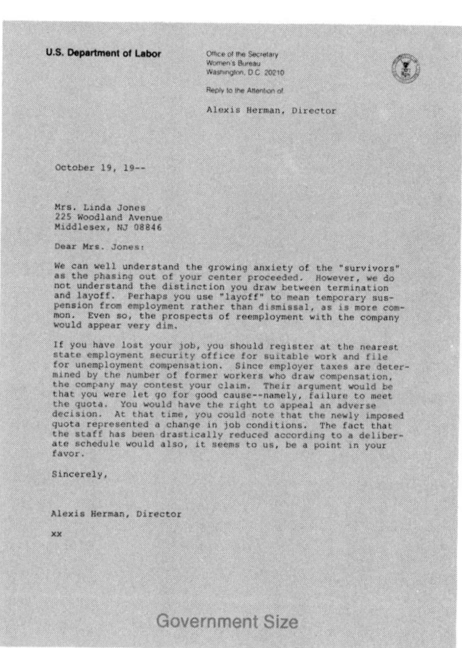
U.S. Department of Labor

Office of the Secretary
Women's Bureau
Washington, D.C. 20210

Reply to the Attention of

Alexis Herman, Director

October 19, 19--

Mrs. Linda Jones
225 Woodland Avenue
Middlesex, NJ 08846

Dear Mrs. Jones:

We can well understand the growing anxiety of the "survivors" as the phasing out of your center proceeded. However, we do not understand the distinction you draw between termination and layoff. Perhaps you use "layoff" to mean temporary suspension from employment rather than dismissal, as is more common. Even so, the prospects of reemployment with the company would appear very dim.

If you have lost your job, you should register at the nearest state employment security office for suitable work and file for unemployment compensation. Since employer taxes are determined by the number of former workers who draw compensation, the company may contest your claim. Their argument would be that you were let go for good cause--namely, failure to meet the quota. You would have the right to appeal an adverse decision. At that time, you could note that the newly imposed quota represented a change in job conditions. The fact that the staff has been drastically reduced according to a deliberate schedule would also, it seems to us, be a point in your favor.

Sincerely,

Alexis Herman, Director

xx

Government Size

Exercise 1

HALF-SIZE STATIONERY

Cut paper to size if stationery is not available.

Modified block style. Open punctuation. No paragraph indention. 1-inch side margins. Begin on line 13.

April 1, 19– Mrs. Amy S. Sanborn 63 Marsh Avenue Tampa, FL 33616 Dear Amy We wish to express our appreciation to you for holding the Neighborhood Restoration Awards Banquet in our hall. We hope that the food and the service pleased you. We invite your suggestions and comments. ¶When you have occasion to plan another affair for your group, please call on us once again. Every consideration will be given toward making it a success. Cordially yours T. L. Hood, Manager *xx* (61 words)

Topic 6 APOSTROPHE AND HYPHEN

APOSTROPHE

Rule 27.

Use an apostrophe with an *s* to show possession in a singular noun.

- *the student's book*
- *Shakespeare's plays*
- *boss's office*

Rule 28.

Use only an apostrophe to show possession in a plural noun ending in *s*.

- *my two aunts' children*
- *the students' notebooks*
- *the Smiths' car*

Rule 29.

Use an apostrophe with an *s* to show possession in an irregular plural noun (one that changes spelling to form the plural).

- *men's clothing*
- *children's toys*
- *the alumni's newsletter*

Rule 30.

When two or more persons own one item jointly, add an apostrophe to the final name. When two or more persons own different items individually, add an apostrophe to each name.

- *Alice and Mary's house* (Alice and Mary share possession of the house.)
- *Alice's and Mary's wigs* (Both Alice and Mary possess their own wigs.)

Rule 31.

The apostrophe is also used to form certain plurals, namely, those of abbreviations with periods, lowercase letters, and uppercase letters that might be misread if the apostrophe were not used.

- *Ph.D.'s*
  BUT: *GIs*
- *p's and q's*
- *I's and U's*
  BUT: *ABCs*

HYPHEN

A hyphen is used to connect two words. Some expressions are always hyphenated, while others are not. If you are in doubt about whether to hyphenate any expression, check in a dictionary.

Rule 32.
IN COMPOUND ADJECTIVES

Hyphenate compound adjectives when they come before the noun they describe.

- *A slow-moving van entered the driveway*
  BUT: *The van was slow moving.*
- *He is a well-known man.*
  BUT: *The man is well known.*

Do not use a hyphen after adverbs ending in *ly*.

- *a completely fresh inventory*
- *a poorly written book*

Rule 33.
IN A SERIES OF ADJECTIVES

Use the hyphen after each part of a compound adjective in a series of compound adjectives used to describe the same noun.

- *The flour is sold in one-, five-, and ten-pound bags.*

Rule 34.
IN NUMBERS

Use the hyphen in fractions (unless one of the elements contains a hyphen) and in compound numbers that are spelled out.

- *one-half*
- *thirty-three hundredths*
- *twenty-one*
- *nine-sixteenths*
- *one hundred forty-seven*

Exercise 4
AMS SIMPLIFIED STYLE

Following Model 16, type this handwritten letter in the AMS simplified letter style.

Today's date City Council City Hall 400 Main Street Cedar Rapids, IA 52401

TREE PLANTING ALONG INDUSTRIAL PARKWAY

We heartily approve of your proposal to plant trees in the grassy strip along the sidewalks of Industrial Parkway. The trees will add long-lasting beauty to the area and make our neighborhood a more pleasant place to live and work.

Our office staff has volunteered to help with planting the trees and landscaping the area. Please let us know when you will want to do this work.

We appreciate your concern for our neighborhood.

MICHAEL ROLLINS, OFFICE MANAGER (76 words)

Topic 6 LETTERS ON SPECIAL-SIZE PAPER

Most business correspondence is typed on standard (8½ by 11 inch) paper. However, four other sizes of stationery may also be used:

- Half size (5½ by 8½ in.)—sometimes used for miscellaneous, nonrecurring correspondence.
- Executive (7¼ by 10½ in.)—often used by top-ranking executives of an organization.
- Government (8 by 10½ in.)—used only by certain departments of the federal government.
- Metric (21 cm by 29.7 cm)—used by most foreign countries in all business letters.

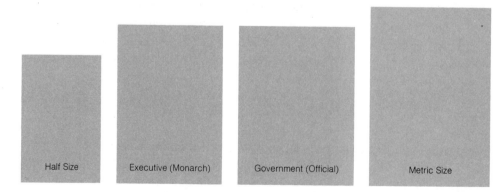

Half Size

Executive (Monarch)

Government (Official)

Metric Size

Exercise 12

APOSTROPHE

Review Rules 27–31. Type these phrases in two columns and add apostrophes where necessary.

Full sheet. Double spacing. 10 spaces between columns. Begin on line 10.

PUNCTUATION: APOSTROPHE

TS

1. several womens views
2. three authors books
3. both bicycles wheels
4. dot all *i*s and *j*s
5. Mrs. Smiths daughter
6. our neighbors believe
7. many students assignments
8. several days later
9. a shortage of M.D.s
10. our ladies department
11. one companys stock
12. twelve companies stock
13. my mothers parents
14. his childs playmates
15. anybodys guess
16. a messengers luggage
17. a ladys husband
18. several ladies husbands
19. childrens clothes
20. the Joneses business
21. TVs for sale
22. everyones favorite movie
23. Mr. Fines signature
24. Ron and Joans mother
25. the secretaries jokes
26. the bare trees
27. Rons and Joans mothers
28. his wifes club
29. my friends came
30. one hours sleep

Exercise 13

HYPHEN

Review Rules 32–34. Type the sentences at the right, supplying missing hyphens as necessary.

Full sheet. 70-space line. Double spacing. Center title on line 10 and TS after it.

PUNCTUATION: HYPHEN

1. The above mentioned report was mailed to you on Friday.
2. The letter was sent by first class mail.
3. A neatly typed letter of application will win the job.
4. I need about eighty five dollars for my senior trip.
5. Today we took one, three, and five minute timed writings.
6. Her term paper was clearly written.
7. Use the enclosed, self addressed envelope.
8. The woman was well dressed when she went for an interview.
9. Employers are impressed by a well groomed applicant.
10. He will soon reach his twenty first birthday.
11. One fourth of the students made the Honor Roll.
12. We use only up to date materials.
13. Be sure you maintain your self confidence.
14. He will be on vacation for a ten day period.
15. He always has a happy go lucky attitude.
16. The car has a finely tuned engine.
17. The long held notion that computers would completely take over and cause the loss of millions of jobs has not proven to be true.
18. More than three quarters of the report contained incorrect data.
19. She was recently promoted to a top level management position.
20. We will need shades for the first and second floor windows.

Exercise 1

STANDARD LENGTH LINE

Type the letter at the right in full block style using mixed punctuation and a standard (6-inch) line. Adjust vertical spacing as necessary for a short letter. Assign the finished letter a document code of 17. 14. 2.

April 4, 19– Mark Kleinschmidt, Distributor National Records 3000 Jackson Heights Boulevard Los Angeles, CA 90012 Dear Mr. Kleinschmidt The new album *Across the River* by King is selling in our store at a phenomenal rate. We sold more than 300 copies in just one week. It is the hottest album we have had in many years. ¶ Please send us 1,200 more copies of the album as soon as possible. Also send us 100 copies each of King's two other albums, as well as 50 posters of the band. Any promotional banners or decals would also be appreciated. ¶ I hope that National Records continues to produce albums as good as *Across the River* and to sign bands with the kind of appeal that King has. Cordially Denise Fry Manager *xx* cc: Jack O'Brien (106 words)

Exercise 2

STANDARD LENGTH LINE

Type the letter at the right in full block style using open punctuation and a standard (6-inch) line. Adjust vertical spacing as necessary for an average length letter.

Today's date Oklaco Corporation 700 Plaza Avenue Oklahoma City, OK 73127 Ladies and Gentlemen I'm sure that many of the letters you receive from station managers involve complaints and criticisms. This letter is different; I'm writing to thank you for the excellent service you have provided me through the years. ¶I have operated my Oklaco station here in Montpelier since 1946, and in all that time you have never treated me unfairly. The products and advertising posters have always been shipped promptly, and your truck drivers have been friendly and helpful. Whenever I've had a question or a problem, your representatives have provided thorough explanations. ¶I'm not the only one who has noticed the good service. My oldest son and his wife are so impressed with Oklaco that they are considering purchasing an Oklaco station in Nebraska. ¶I'm thankful to you for making my job easier and more pleasant. Keep up the good work. Respectfully yours Frank Carpenter, Station Manager *xx* (142 words)

Exercise 3

AMS SIMPLIFIED STYLE

For this exercise, use the AMS simplified letter style. Follow the spacing instructions indicated on Model 16. Check the placement points listed in the model carefully before you begin.

October 14, 19– Mr. John A. Hembree 1802 Higby Drive Cincinnati, OH 45207 CONSUMER ADVOCATES GETS RESULTS Consumer Advocates is concerned about what we eat, drink, drive, and see. We think that many of the foods and drinks we Americans consume are bad for our physical health. We feel that much of the television we view and a great percentage of the advertising we see and hear are bad for our mental health. ¶ In the last few years, greater emphasis has been placed on demanding more nutritious food, safer cars, and greater truth in advertising. Our group has been at least partly responsible for this greater awareness, but we must not be content with the changes already made. We must continue to make our demands known for a life-style that is safe, clean, and healthful. ¶ We need your support! If you want to work to change the world in which you live, please call us at 328-5188. Our staff will let you know how you can help. Thank you for your concern. SHEREE JANSEN, DISTRICT COORDINATOR *xx* (150 words)

Topic 7 CAPITALIZATION

Words are capitalized to specify the actual name or title of a special person or thing. Opinions on proper capitalization vary, but the following capitalization rules cover problems most likely to be encountered in business situations.

Rule 1. Capitalize the first word in a sentence.

- *They like ice cream.*
- *Tomorrow is my birthday.*

Rule 2. Capitalize the names (first, middle, and last) of persons. Also capitalize the personal pronoun *I* wherever it appears in a sentence. Capitalize geographic place names, the names of well-known landmarks, and the names of organizations.

- *John H. Jones*
- *Dallas, Texas*
- *The Grand Canyon*
- *Girl Scouts of America*

Rule 3. Proper adjectives—words derived from the names of specific people, places, or things—should be capitalized.

- *Shakespearean play*
- *French cuisine*
- *American offices*

Because of frequent usage, some words originally derived from proper nouns are not capitalized. If you are unsure about a word, consult a dictionary.

- *french fries*
- *india ink*
- *pasteurized milk*

Rule 4. Capitalize a title that comes immediately before a person's name; lowercase a title that follows. A title used alone, in place of a person's name, should also be capitalized.

- *A birthday party was given for Mayor Brookes.*
- *Ms. Roberts has been the president for seven years.*
- *What do you think, Governor, of the chicken salad?*

Rule 5. The first word of a quotation is capitalized when the quoted material is a complete sentence. When an expression such as *he said* interrupts the quoted material, however, the first word of the continuation is lowercased.

- *She reminded him, "A bird in hand is worth two in the bush."*
- *"A bird in hand," she reminded him, "is worth two in the bush."*

Rule 6. Capitalize the first and all important words in titles of books, plays, reports, periodicals, television shows, and so forth. The entire title may also be typed in solid capitals. (Refer to Rule 24, page 188, regarding quotation marks or underlining for titles.)

- *A Practical English Handbook*
- *"Introduction to the Keyboard"*
- *A PRACTICAL ENGLISH HANDBOOK*
- *"Typing for Personal Use"*

Rule 7. Capitalize the compass directions (east, west, north, south) only when they refer to sections of the country or of the world.

- *exploring the Old West*
- *go south on Parker Road*
- *Columbus sailed west in search of the Far East.*

Better Business Letters, Inc.

148 East Broadway, Manchester, N.H. 03102 (603) 922-1496

Words

January 4, 19-- 3

Space down 4 times

Ms. or Mr. Word Processor 8
The Eastern Secretarial Association 15
1 Main Street 18
New Haven, CT 06525 22

TS

HAVE YOU HEARD? 25

TS

There's a new movement under way to take some of the monotony out 38
of the letters given to you to type. The movement is symbolized 51
by the Simplified Letter being sponsored by AMS. 61

What is it? You're reading a sample. 69

Notice the left block format and the general positioning of the 82
letter. We didn't write "Dear ----," nor will we write "Yours 95
truly" or "Sincerely yours." Are they really important? We feel 108
just as friendly to you without them. 116

Notice the following placement points: 124

1. All lines blocked at left margin 131
2. Triple space before and after subject line 140
3. Subject line replaces salutation 147
4. Complimentary closing omitted 153
5. Dictator's name and title in solid capitals 163

Now take a look at the enclosed suggestions prepared for you. Talk 177
them over with your boss. But don't form a final opinion until 190
you've really tried out the AMS simplified letter style. That's 203
what our secretary did. As a matter of fact, she finally wrote most 217
of the suggestions herself. 223

Our secretary is sold on the idea. We hope you'll have good luck 236
with better (simplified) letters. 243

Vaughan Fry Space down 4 times

VAUGHAN FRY, RESEARCH & STANDARDS 250

DS

xx 251

DS

Enclosure 253

(Shown in Elite Type)

Model 16 *AMS Simplified Letter Style*

Rule 8.

Capitalize the name of a specific course title. Do not capitalize the name of a subject unless it is derived from a proper noun.

- *I am taking Typewriting II-A this semester.*
- *My English class is stimulating.*
- *I have taken typewriting.*

Rule 9.

Capitalize the first word in the salutation and the complimentary closing of a business letter.

- *My dear Mr. Evans*
- *Sincerely yours*
- *Very truly yours*

Rule 10.

Nouns followed by a number, either Roman or Arabic, are usually capitalized, except for page numbers. Examples:

- *Room 501*
- *Lesson 20*
- *Chapter II*
- *page 3*

Rule 11.

Capitalize the following: names of days of the week, months, holidays, races, religions, references to a deity, historical events, trade names of commercial products, and names of bodies of governments. Capitalize seasons only when they are personified, such as, "Old Man Winter."

- *Thursday*
- *November*
- *Fourth of July*
- *Vietnam War*
- *Asian*
- *Baptist*
- *God*
- *Kleenex*

Exercise 1

CAPITALIZATION

Review Rules 1–11. Type the sentences at the right, correcting any errors in capitalization.

Half sheet. 70-space line. Double spacing. Center title on line 6 and TS after it.

CORRECTING CAPITALIZATION ERRORS: ONE

1. The excelsior pen company has been in business for many years.
2. Avoid such high-calorie foods as french dressing.
3. Thank you, senator, for your interest in our efforts.
4. He said, "now is the time to learn all you can."
5. You will find this book, *a Trip through The Zoo*, entertaining.
6. The new furniture we bought was made in the east.
7. I am doing well in English, Algebra, and Music.
8. Yours Very Respectfully,
9. Her class is located in room 780.
10. Our family always has a cookout on memorial day.

Exercise 2

CAPITALIZATION

Type these sentences, correcting any errors in capitalization.

Half sheet. 70-space line. Double spacing. Center title on line 5 and TS after it.

CORRECTING CAPITALIZATION ERRORS: TWO

1. I am taking a course entitled principles of art.
2. She works for a well-known Company.
3. We were told to read chapter 9 tonight.
4. We had to read only one chapter of the book.
5. We lost our hubcap traveling north on interstate 95.
6. I will be happy when old man winter is gone.
7. I am now enrolled in Nursing Training II in night school.
8. You will need to complete form 1040 for income tax purposes.
9. My dear Mrs. Masten:
10. Thousands of people telephoned the white house to protest the speech.

Columbia Appliance Repair Association

703 HERRICK STREET
COLUMBIA, SOUTH CAROLINA 29203
(803) 334-7880

Words

December 12, 19-- 3

Space down 6 times to lengthen letter

Mr. David S. Sloan, Jr. 8
Victory Appliance Repair, Inc. 14
323 Jasmine Street 18
Columbia, SC 29212 21

Dear Mr. Sloan: 24

The Columbia Appliance Repair Association has a membership of more 37
than 60 percent of the appliance repair businesses in this city. Now 51
the association has set itself a membership goal of 100 percent, and 65
we would like to have <u>you</u> as a member. 72

Just consider these benefits of association membership: First, we 86
regularly conduct extensive advertising campaigns to bring in more 99
service calls to our members. Second, we sponsor a low-interest loan 112
service for the exclusive use of member businesses. Third, we pro- 126
vide members with up-to-date information on equipment and repair 139
techniques through our monthly newsletter and bimonthly workshops. 152

For all of this, the membership fee is only $140 per year, payable 165
either in full on application or in quarterly installments of $35 178
each. Just fill in the enclosed application form and mail it with 191
your check to association headquarters at the address above. 203

Very truly yours, 206

Space down 6 times to lengthen letter

Roderick M. Aylesworth 211
Secretary 213

ja/0137 214

Enclosure 216

(*Shown in Elite Type*)

Model 15 *Full Block Style with Standard Length Line*

Exercise 3

REVIEW

The following sentences contain errors identified by symbols in the margin. Find the errors before you type a corrected sentence. *Do not mark the book.*

Full sheet. 70-space line. Double spacing. Begin on line 10 and continue on a second sheet.

KEY TO SYMBOLS

ap	apostrophe	hy	hyphen
cap	capitalization	par	parentheses
col	colon	quo	quotation marks
com	comma	ro	run-on sentence
dsh	dash	sem	semicolon
ep	end punctuation	sp	spelling
frag	sentence fragment	ww	wrong word

REVIEW OF SPELLING, PUNCTUATION, AND CAPITALIZATION

TS

com, sp	1.	Since the project was needed the city acommodated our request.
cap, ep	2.	Are the painters expected to return friday.
sp, com	3.	When we listened to customer criticizm we avoided waste.
cap, sp	4.	After the Bank Manager recieved the report, he rejected it.
sp, com	5.	The representive in our area Ms. Jones was most helpful.
ro	6.	My cousin has an expensive hobby he builds model trains.
com	7.	I could not understand his hazy inadequate reasoning.
com	8.	It was however an extremely painful injury.
frag	9.	I recognized his handwriting. Which I had seen recently on a check.
com, sp	10.	My friend Jane Quinn has a seperate checking account.
com, hy	11.	My pearl necklace my jade ring and my diamond brooch are kept in a well secured vault.
sem, com	12.	The mechanic is qualified for the job however there are several reasons why she was not hired.
ro, com	13.	Some of the children were afraid others luckily ran back to warn the rest.
par	14.	We are offering excellent values two for the price of one.
sp, ep	15.	May we expect your remitance in a few days?
com, sp	16.	The plans were she felt quite similiar.
com	17.	Friday June 12 is the last day of the semester.
dsh	18.	Bank cards, charge accounts, loans all are forms of credit.
ap, cap	19.	Elizas decision to study spanish was made slowly.
col, com	20.	The menu includes the following deviled eggs baked beans potato salad and hot dogs.
com, ap	21.	Good work Patty! I knew you could make straight As!
sp, cap	22.	Are your children planing to attend camp this Summer?
com	23.	The woman was puzzled by the directions and so she asked the salesperson to explain them.
com, cap	24.	Ms. Zimmer the Supervisor at our factory developed the plan.
ww, quo	25.	It's to expensive for something labeled All Man-made Materials.

Topic 5 STANDARDIZED DOCUMENT FORMATS

In preceding topics, you learned to type letters in several styles. With the increased use of word processing equipment, however, the trend is away from such variety. Today most companies develop their own procedures, or style, manuals; and these usually specify a single format for all company correspondence.

The reason for this trend is obvious: it saves time and money. In the first place, routine but time-consuming decisions about such things as margins are eliminated. In the second place, training time for new personnel is cut. In the third place, errors caused by inconsistencies between different documents (or different versions of the same document) are diminished.

In this topic, you will be introduced to a new letter style called *AMS simplified* and a new formatting device—the use of a standard line for all correspondence, regardless of letter style or letter length. Both simplify document production. The AMS style eliminates most questions involving varied forms of address and closing. The use of a standard line (in combination with some standard spacing adjustments) simplifies placement of copy on a page.

Standard Line Length

Use of a standard length line eliminates the need for referring to a placement chart such as the one on page 197. The standard line most often selected for business purposes is 6 inches. When such a line is used, the date is always placed on line 13. (This puts it about 2 inches down from the top of the page, more than enough to clear most letterheads.) Letters are then centered vertically by adding or deleting space at two key points: (1) between the date and the inside address and (2) between the complimentary closing and the typed name of the document originator. A short letter, for example, would be centered by leaving as many as eight lines instead of the usual four in both places. A longer letter would be centered by leaving as few as three lines at these two points.

AMS Simplified Style

The letter format recommended by the Administrative Management Society has many time-saving features. These include a block format and a standard 6-inch line. The feature that distinguishes AMS simplified from most other letter styles, however, is its elimination of both the salutation and the complimentary closing. For the former, there is a substitute—a subject line in all capital letters. For the latter, there is merely an increased emphasis on the name and title of the document originator (these items also are presented in all capital letters).

Drill A
TYPING MODEL 15

Type Model 15, a business letter illustrating the use of a standard 6-inch line with the full block style. For spacing, follow the instructions given in the model. There are 144 words in the body of the letter.

Drill B
TYPING MODEL 16

Type the business letter illustrating the AMS simplified style shown in Model 16. Follow the spacing instructions given in the model. There are 187 words in the body.

PART 7

PERSONAL CORRESPONDENCE

In this part, you will learn to type personal notes, personal letters, and personal-business letters. You will gain experience centering a message on a page so that the typed copy is attractively framed by white space. You will also be introduced to the basic letter styles used for both personal and business correspondence.

Topic 1 PERSONAL NOTES AND LETTERS

PERSONAL NOTES

A personal note is generally very short and written to someone with whom the writer is well acquainted. Because of its nature, a personal note is usually typed on short stationery ($5\frac{1}{2}'' \times 8\frac{1}{2}''$). It is usually single-spaced, although a message of only one or two sentences may be double-spaced in order to stretch it out on the page.

Look at Model 2 on the next page. Notice that the return address, the date, and the complimentary closing start at the center of the page. This arrangement is called *modified block style*. Also notice that a comma is used after the salutation and the complimentary closing. When punctuation marks are used at these two points, the style of punctuation is called *mixed*.

Drill A
TYPING MODEL 2
Margins at 13 and 58 (elite) or 10 and 50 (pica). Single spacing.

Type the short personal note shown in Model 2 on the next page. Use a half sheet of paper, inserted short side first. Set a tab at center and begin typing on line 16.

Drill B
TYPING MODEL 2
Same format as Drill A.

Retype the note shown in Model 2 with the following changes:

1. Use your own street address, city, state, and ZIP Code.
2. Use today's date.
3. Write your own first name after the complimentary closing.

Exercise 7 continued

```
your plant until the time it returns.  This certificate
will insure your property against these risks

   While in Transit            While on Exhibition

   Theft                       Theft and Pilferage

   Fire                        Fire

   Colision                    Loading and unloading

   Overturning                 Malicious Mischief

   Storm                       Loss of Use of Space

   Loading and Unloading       Strikes or Riots

   The more exhibiters who take advantage of this
coverage, the lower will be the premiums. We hope that
you will decide to purchase your insurance through us.
Please use the enclosed application and send it today.
No application can be considered after April 10.

                              Sincerely
```

Handwritten corrections: coverage (for certificate); protect (for insure); the following (for these); colon after risks; In Transit, On Exhibition (capitalized); Collision; Unloading (capitalized); Overturning moved to follow Loading and Unloading; Fire moved left; exhibitors; no ¶; the premiums will be; ¶ We hope that.

John G. Newman Motorboat Committee *xx* (127 words)

Exercise 8

SPECIAL CHALLENGE
LETTER: NUMBERED PARAGRAPHS

Type this letter in any acceptable style and supply the missing parts. The letter is dated March 28, 19–. It was dictated by **Jacqueline Masters, President, The Mutual Bank of Pittsburgh.**

Peter S. Murillo 68 Reading Square Pittsburgh, PA 15203 The United Bankers Association recently sent questionnaires to 5,000 Pittsburgh residents, asking them what services they most want from a bank. Three responses appeared on almost every questionnaire: free checking, longer hours, and credit cards. ¶The Mutual Bank is anxious to serve its customers better. Beginning May 1, we will offer the new services described below. *(Begin insert)* 1. Free checking will be given to holders of regular accounts maintaining an average monthly balance of $200. All checking and service charges will be dropped on special accounts with an average balance of $500. 2. Banking hours on Thursday and Friday will be extended to 6 p.m. The bank will also be open on Saturdays from 9 until noon. 3. We have made arrangements to offer eligible customers a choice of two major credit cards. The enclosed pamphlets explain what these credit cards offer you. *(End insert)* We pledge, above all, to give you fast, courteous service. We want to be your banker; so we are listening to you. (165 words)

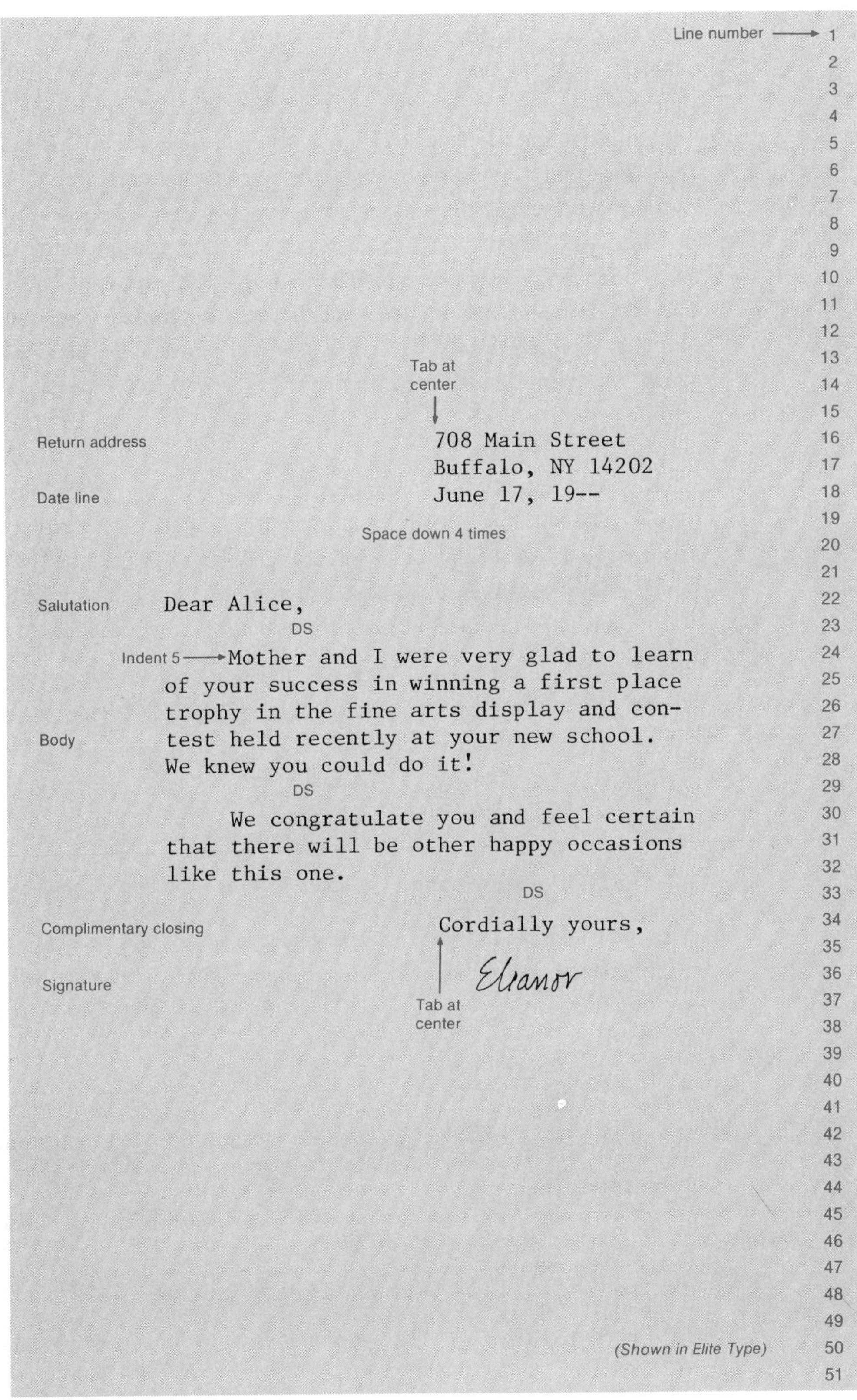

708 Main Street
Buffalo, NY 14202
June 17, 19--

Dear Alice,

Mother and I were very glad to learn of your success in winning a first place trophy in the fine arts display and contest held recently at your new school. We knew you could do it!

We congratulate you and feel certain that there will be other happy occasions like this one.

Cordially yours,

Eleanor

Model 2 *Short Personal Note • Modified Block Style with Mixed Punctuation and Indented Paragraphs*

Exercise 5
NUMBERED LIST

Modified block style. Mixed punctuation. 5-space paragraph indention.

Today's date Mrs. Eleanor Tsui Western High School 8970 South Fort Street Detroit, MI 48217 Dear Mrs. Tsui I applaud your efforts to prepare your students for the difficulties of job hunting after graduation. As a personnel interviewer, I see many young people who fail to get the jobs they want. This is often because they lack skill in presenting themselves to potential employers. ¶In response to your query, I suggest that you include the following in your lessons on job-hunting techniques: *(Begin insert)* 1. The letter of application 2. The data sheet or resume 3. The job interview 4. The employment test 5. The importance of grooming. *(End insert)* ¶I hope this information will help you in counseling your students. I would be glad to come to talk to them if you feel it would be beneficial. Cordially Arthur J. LaRue Personnel Interviewer *xx* (119 words)

Exercise 6
TABULATED INSERT

Modified block style. Mixed punctuation. 5-space paragraph indention.

Today's date Mr. David Bonnington Imperial House 10785 Dearborn Avenue Ripley, OK 74062 Dear Mr. Bonnington The unbelievably small St. Clair calculator is finally available—at an unbelievably small price. Now you can carry a calculator in your pocket while you keep more money in your wallet. ¶You will be impressed by the specifications of this hand-held machine listed below:

Display:	8 Digits, Floating Decimal
Functions:	Add, Subtract, Multiply, Divide
Constant:	4 Functions
Power:	4 AAA Batteries
Weight:	$3\frac{1}{2}$ Ounces
Size:	$4\frac{1}{2} \times 2 \times \frac{3}{4}$ Inches
Warranty:	1 Year

¶If you would like to try the new St. Clair for seven days with no obligation, just complete and return the enclosed card immediately. This offer will expire at the end of the month. Very truly yours M. Fillmore Sales Representative *xx*
(109 words)

Exercise 7
ROUGH DRAFT:
TABULATED INSERT

Modified block style. Open punctuation. No paragraph indention.

March 12, 19— Atlas Boat Corporation 598 Seventh Street Boston, MA 02169

Gentlemen

We have secured a Master insurance policy ~~covering~~ to cover exhibitors at the Thirty-~~Second~~ Third Annual Motor Boat Show, to be held in the Sixteenth Armory. A certificate can be issued to cover your exhibit from the time it leaves

(Continued on next page)

Exercise 1

Half sheet. Insert short side first. Modified block style. Mixed punctuation. Margins at 13 and 58 for elite; 10 and 50 for pica. Single spacing 5-space paragraph indention. Begin on line 16.

Type a personal note from the copy given below. (The symbol ¶ means to begin a new paragraph.)

Your address / *Today's date* / Dear Frank, Our social club is meeting next Wednesday evening, and we are planning an hour of entertainment beginning at eight o'clock. ¶We have invited three other people to provide entertainment. Several club members have requested that you play ragtime piano. Will you be good enough to play for us? Any selections you wish to play will be fine. / Sincerely, / *Your name* (57 words)

Exercise 2

COMPOSITION AT THE KEYBOARD

Same format as Exercise 1.

Compose and type a short note of congratulations or thanks to a friend or relative.

PERSONAL LETTERS

The personal letter differs from the personal note in that it is generally longer and is addressed to a person with whom the writer may not be as well acquainted. It is a communication written by one private individual to another. In typing personal letters, two parts may be added which were missing from the personal note. They are (1) the *inside address* and (2) the *typed name of sender*. Study Model 3, page 198. These two new parts are optional if the letter is written to a close friend.

Letters are usually single-spaced on standard-size paper (8½″ × 11″). It is acceptable however, to double-space a letter which has fewer than 50 words in the body.

As with personal notes, personal letters should be arranged on the page to give the impression of a picture in a frame. The Letter Placement Chart given here will help you decide on margin settings for letters of varying lengths. (Note that the word counts in the chart are based on actual, not typing, words.) With practice, you should be able to judge the placement of a letter on a page without using the chart.

LETTER PLACEMENT CHART

Length of Letter	*Actual Words in Body*	*Line Length* Inches	Pica	Elite	*Date Line*
Short	Up to 100	4	40	50	20
Average	101 to 200	5	50	60	18–15*
Long	201 to 300	6	60	70	13
2-Page	300+	6	60	70	13

*Exact placement of the date line in average length letters will depend on how close the number of words in the letter is to the maximum or minimum. The longer the letter, the higher the date line is placed on the page.

Drill C

TYPING MODEL 3

Modified block style. Mixed punctuation. 5-space paragraph indention.

Type the personal letter shown in Model 3 (page 198). Note that the return address and date line, complimentary closing, and typed name of sender all begin at center. Refer to the Letter Placement Chart above to determine the correct margins and placement of the date line. There are 104 words in the body of the letter shown.

Exercise 2

QUOTATION INSERT

Modified block style. Open punctuation. 5-space paragraph indention.

December 14, 19— Ms. Dolores Gessler, Store Manager Corner Market 727 B Street Jacksonville, FL 32216 Dear Ms. Gessler As you know, there has been a rash of late-night robberies at area Corner Markets recently. The enclosed packet contains artist's sketches of two of the robbers, and a photograph of a recent robbery taken by a hidden camera. ¶The police asked me to pass along the following instructions: *(Begin insert)* Post the drawings and photograph in a place where your employees will easily see them. If an employee spots one of these persons in the store, he or she should not approach him, but should immediately call the police. *(End insert)* ¶We hope to catch these criminals soon and put an end to the trouble and fear they are causing. Your cooperation might be the key to apprehending them. Sincerely Peter J. Tomlivich District Supervisor *xx*

(120 words)

Exercise 3

NUMBERED PARAGRAPHS

Full block style. Open punctuation. Begin each numbered paragraph at the left margin.

September 11, 19— Mr. Joseph L. Bowden Factory Superintendent Specialty Suppliers, Inc. 408 Haddon Street Lansing, MI 48921 Dear Mr. Bowden We find it necessary to call your attention to various practices causing inconvenience to our plants. *(Begin insert)* 1. The East plant complains that parts are shipped in oily barrels. 2. Both East and West plants report receiving unrelated parts in the same barrel. An operator has to take time to sort these parts. In the process, some may go into the scrap barrels. 3. All plants find that the quantity of finished casters in some barrels is short of the number marked on the tickets. *(End insert)* ¶Please give your attention to these problems at once and inform me of the steps you have taken to remedy them. ¶With respect to item No. 3 above, it is preferable to run over the specified count rather than under it. Sincerely yours Lawrence D. Niven, Manager *xx* (124 words)

Exercise 4

NUMBERED LIST

Modified block style. Open punctuation.

Today's date Charles N. Coffey 614 West 38th Street St. Louis, MO 63112 Dear Mr. Coffey You asked to be notified when we acquired any used office equipment in good condition. An insurance company, which recently closed its branch here, has sold us its complete installation of office furniture. Since the office had been open only a year, the furniture is in excellent condition. ¶The lot includes the following (all wood in walnut finish): *(Begin insert)* 1. Large and small flattop desks 2. Typewriter drop desks 3. Filing cabinets, sorters, and stools 4. Conference tables 5. Desk chairs and leather armchairs 6. Assorted portable partitions. *(End insert)* ¶Please let us know at once whether you are interested in purchasing any of these pieces. The furniture will be delivered to our warehouse on Franklin Street next Saturday. It would therefore be advisable for you to be there Monday when the selection will be best. Yours very truly Mrs. Frances C. Camden Sales Manager *xx* (133 words)

Line number

Tab at center

Words

Return address — 397 Grand Street 3
Boston, MA 02115 6

Date line — August 11, 19-- 9

Space down 4 times

Inside address — Mrs. Eva L. Andrus 13
119 Hawthorne Street 17
Boston, MA 02115 20

DS

Salutation — Dear Mrs. Andrus, 24

DS

Body —

For the past two months our neighborhood has 33
been invaded by motorcycles that have been using 43
the streets as raceways during the evening hours 53
when most of us are trying to relax. 60

I believe we can put a stop to this nuisance 69
if all of us who are affected would organize as a 79
group and make a formal complaint to the proper city 90
authorities. 93

On Tuesday evening, August 26, at 8 p.m., I 102
am holding a meeting at my home to discuss the prob- 113
lem and possible solutions. If you feel as most of 123
us do, I would be very pleased if you could attend 133
this meeting. 136

DS

Complimentary closing — Sincerely, 138

Signature — *Rebecca Shaw* — Space down 4 times

Typed name of sender — Rebecca Shaw 141

Tab at center

(Shown in Pica Type)

Model 3 *Personal Letter • Modified Block Style with Mixed Punctuation and Indented Paragraphs*

☆ North Star Stationers

7694 Twin Cities Parkway
St. Paul, Minn. 55110
(612) 572-2637

Words

November 30, 19-- 4

Mr. Walter T. O'Brien 8
676 Hobart Boulevard 12
Duluth, MN 55806 15

Dear Mr. O'Brien 18

In answer to your inquiry of November 20, we are 28
sending you under separate cover three samples of 38
carbon paper we believe compare well with the sam- 48
ples you sent us. The samples include: 56

DS — Set 3 tabs

Center table horizontally

10 Sheets	#8, Blue	Pencil Carbon	63
10 Sheets	#4, Black	Typewriter Carbon	72
10 Sheets	#6, Black	Typewriter Carbon	81

(DS between rows)

The No. 8 carbon comes packaged in envelopes of 100 91
sheets each; the No. 4 and No. 6 carbons are pack- 101
aged in boxes of 100 sheets. 107

We have made careful tests to match your samples, 117
and we shall be glad to receive your comments after 127
you have had an opportunity to test our selections. 137

Very truly yours 140

Rachel N. Perez

Rachel N. Perez 143
Production Manager 147

xx 148

(Shown in Pica Type)

Model 14 *Business Letter with a Tabulated Insert*
Modified Block Style with Open Punctuation

Drill D

TYPING MODEL 3

Modified block style. Mixed punctuation. 5-space paragraph indention.

Retype the letter shown in Model 3 with the following changes:

1. Use your own street address, city, state, and ZIP Code.
2. Use today's date.
3. Type your own full name as the sender, and sign the letter.

Drill E

OPENING PARTS OF MODEL 3

Begin on line 6. Fill the entire sheet.

Type Model 3 again, this time to see how far you can get in 3 minutes. Do not be concerned about accuracy (do not stop to correct errors). Instead, concentrate on the arrangement of the letter parts. Use the same format as Drill D. Repeat this exercise until the arrangement of the opening parts of a letter in modified block style becomes automatic for you.

Drill F

CLOSING PARTS OF MODEL 3

Begin on line 6. Fill the entire sheet.

This time type Model 3, beginning with the last paragraph. Try to complete the closing parts of the letter in 2 minutes or less. Use the same format as Drill D, and do not stop to correct errors. Repeat the exercise until the closing parts of this letter style become automatic for you.

Exercise 3

Type the letter at the right. Use Model 3 as a guide and refer to the Letter Placement Chart (page 197) to determine margins and date line.

Modified block style. Mixed punctuation. 5-space paragraph indention.

Your address / *Today's date* / Ms. Ruth Elwood / One Florida Drive / St. 19
Louis, MO 63155 / Dear Ms. Elwood, My mother told me this morning that 33
we will be taking a two-week vacation trip. We are going to fly to Florida and 48
board a ship for a Caribbean cruise. ¶As we are planning to leave on 63
Friday, I shall not be able to participate in the Piano Festival. (The two 78
events fall in the same two-week period.) I am sorry to have to disap- 93
point you. ¶I shall write you as soon as we return. Please let me know 108
about plans for the next festival. / Yours truly, / *Your name* (89 words) 120

Exercise 4

Type the letter at the right. Use Model 3 as a guide and refer to the Letter Placement Chart (page 197) to determine margins and date line.

Modified block style. Mixed punctuation. No paragraph indention.

Your address / *Today's date* / Mel Wilson / P.O. Box 125 / Gary, IN 46410 17

Dear Mr. Wilson, 20
The class of 19– held its five-year reunion last Friday. After all the excitement 38
of seeing so many old friends for the first time since graduation, we realized 54
that one of our favorite teachers was not with us. ¶ Our inquiries uncovered 69
the news that you were taken ill last July and have been confined to your 84
home now for several weeks. We are all extremely sorry to hear of this 98
and wish you a speedy recovery. ¶ We took some photos at the reunion. 112
As soon as they are developed, I will send you a few of them. 124
Sincerely, 126

Your name (101 words) 128

EVANS PUBLISHING COMPANY, INC.

177 Buckwald Street, Stamford, Connecticut 06904 • (203) 746-1000

Raymond T. Patterson
Business Manager

Words

December 21, 19-- 4

Dr. Rebecca D. Heymont, Dean 10
The Taylor School of Paralegal Studies 18
309 Myrtle Avenue 22
Stamford, CN 06901 26

Dear Dr. Heymont 29

We welcome the opportunity of sending you an examination 41
copy of INTRODUCTORY PARALEGAL STUDIES. It is being mailed 53
today under separate cover. 59

We hope that you will take the time to examine the book 70
carefully in order to see for yourself the many advanced ideas 83
and teaching methods it offers. We should like to call your 95
attention particularly to the following features: 105

Reset margin

DS

Use margin release and backspace

1. The book covers the basic subject matter taught 116
in standard courses of study. The material is 126
logically organized; at the same time, it is 135
graded, beginning with the simplest, most famil- 145
iar cases and progressing to less common ground. 155

DS

2. The writing is made as interesting as possible. 166
For example, each new subject is introduced by 176
a narrative history of an actual case. 184

DS

3. The treatment of all issues is totally unbiased. 195
Where differences of opinion exist, all sides 204
are presented and the prevailing law explained. 214

Reset margin

DS

We should be happy to add your school to the many that are 226
now using the book. We also supply a Teacher's Guide without 238
charge. 240

Yours truly 243

Raymond T. Patterson

Raymond T. Patterson 247
Business Manager 250

xx 251

(Shown in Elite Type)

Model 13 *Business Letter with Paragraph Inserts*
Modified Block Style with Open Punctuation

Exercise 5
ROUGH DRAFT
Modified block style. Mixed punctuation. 5-space paragraph indention.

Type this letter given in rough-draft form below. Use your own address for the heading and your own name as the sender. If you need to review proofreaders' marks, they are given on pages 92–93.

Your address / May 1, 19— / Mr. Allen Fitzgerald / Alston Printing Co. / 755 Market Way / South Bend, IN 46614

Dear Mr. Fitzgerald,

Although it had been more than a year since we shared some very plesant conversation on a cross-country fiight, I am hoping that you will still remember me. When we ~~left~~ ~~eachother~~ at the airport in Los Angeles, you gave me your card and invited me to ~~visit you~~ if ever I were to visit South Bend.

As it now happens, my company will be sending me ~~there~~ in two week's time to attend to some business for them. ~~Being a stranger in the area~~ I thought ~~how enjoyable it~~ would be for us to renew our ~~short~~ aquaintance. I will be in Suoth Bend for just ~~under a week~~.

Please let me extend an invitation to you ~~for your~~ joining me for dinner one ~~night~~ in a restaurant of your choosing. I will call you when I arrive at the Queen Anne Hotel on Tuesday, May15. I look forward to talking with you then.

Sincerely,

Your name (159 words)

Exercise 6
COMPOSITION AT THE KEYBOARD
Modified block style. Mixed punctuation. 5-space paragraph indention.

Compose and type a short letter requesting a recommendation from a teacher, counselor, friend, or long-standing acquaintance. You need the recommendation to receive a scholarship to a college in your state. You should mention the name of the college, the type of scholarship (athletic or academic), and the subject area that will be your major.

THE HARKNESS TV REPAIR SCHOOL

733 Nealy Street
Kansas City, Kansas 66117
(913) 651-2138

Words

July 10, 19-- 3

Mr. Philip T. Amadeo 7
601 Fifth Avenue 10
Kansas City, KS 66102 14

Dear Mr. Amadeo: 17

Have your earning expectations in TV repair been realized? 29
Are you able to "spot" TV troubles quickly and accurately 41
and make expert repairs? What have you done to keep up with 53
the new developments in the electronics field? 62

Do these questions raise doubts in your mind? If so, you will 75
be interested in our advanced course in TV Theory and Repair. 87
Briefly, here is what the course gives you: twenty graded 99
lessons covering various phases of modern servicing, three 111
up-to-date textbooks, personal consultations with our coun- 123
selors on your individual servicing problems, and a certifi- 135
cate at the end of the course. 141

Mr. George Perry, TV service engineer, writes the following: 153

Reset margin

DS

> After taking your course, I have been recommending 163
> it to all my friends in the TV repair field. I 173
> have found it extremely helpful in bringing me up 183
> to the minute in modern servicing techniques. I 193
> consider it worth many times the fee you charge. 203

Reset margin

DS

Read carefully the enclosed folder giving details about the 215
course. Then, if you wish to enroll, detach and mail the 227
application form. 231

Sincerely yours, 235

Randolph L. Harkness

Randolph L. Harkness 239
President 241

xx 242

Enclosure 244

(Shown in Elite Type)

Model 12 *Business Letter with a Quotation Insert*
Modified Block Style with Mixed Punctuation

Topic 2 PERSONAL-BUSINESS LETTERS

A personal-business letter, as its name suggests, is a business letter written by a private individual. Such correspondence could include letters to order merchandise, to apply for a job, to ask for a refund, or to handle any number of situations of a business nature.

Model 4 (page 202) is a sample of a personal-business letter. It is typed in modified block style, like that used in the preceding topic. Notice, however, that a colon rather than a comma is used after the salutation in a business letter. This style is still referred to as mixed punctuation.

SALUTATIONS If a letter is addressed to a specific person in a company or an organization, use that person's name in the salutation. If the person addressed is a man, the salutation should be *Dear Mr. — —;* if the person addressed is a woman, the salutation should be *Dear Ms. — —, Dear Miss — —,* or *Dear Mrs. — —.* On some occasions, you may be unsure of the sex of the addressee. For example, a letter signed *J. R. Jones,* or *Terry Lorenz* does not indicate whether the writer is male or female. In response, you may address the person without using a social title: *Dear J. R. Jones* or *Dear Terry Lorenz.*

When a business letter is addressed to a company or organization and not to an individual person, a more general salutation is required. Two salutations are commonly used in such cases: *Gentlemen* and *Ladies and Gentlemen.* Sometimes a letter is addressed to the Sales Manager, Personnel Director, or other individual, but the name of that person is not known to the writer. In such cases, the salutation should be *Dear Sir or Madam.*

COMPLIMENTARY CLOSINGS The complimentary closing for a business letter is largely determined by the preference of the writer. It usually indicates how familiar he or she is with the person being addressed. The most common closings are: *Sincerely yours, Sincerely, Cordially, Cordially yours,* and *Very truly yours.* More personal closings, such as *Regards, Best wishes, As ever,* and so on may be used at the writer's discretion.

ENCLOSURES Quite often a business letter is accompanied by a check, a form, or some other document the sender wishes to enclose. In such cases, an *enclosure* notation is typed at the left margin a double space after the typed name. This notation serves three purposes: (1) it tells the person who receives the letter that the sender has enclosed something in addition to the letter; (2) it reminds the typist to enclose the required material when the letter is prepared for mailing; (3) it provides a record on the file copy that something was sent along with the letter.

CARBON COPIES A copy of a business letter is very useful. The writer will often need to remember (sometimes weeks or months later) some facts included in the letter, such as the date, a price quoted, or an amount sent. For this reason you will be directed to make a carbon copy of letters in this topic. Although it is possible to obtain a photocopy of a letter, it is less expensive and less time-consuming to use carbon paper.

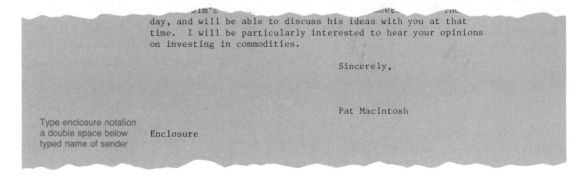

```
day, and will be able to discuss his ideas with you at that
time.  I will be particularly interested to hear your opinions
on investing in commodities.

                                     Sincerely,



                                     Pat MacIntosh

Enclosure
```

Type enclosure notation a double space below typed name of sender

Topic 4 LETTERS WITH INSERTS

An insert may be included within the body of a business letter. It could be a long quotation, a list of items, a series of numbered paragraphs, or a tabulation. An insert is set off from the rest of the letter by a double space above and below it. It is usually indented 5 spaces from the left and right margins. Tables, however, are centered horizontally. If an insert consists of a list of short items, the items may be double-spaced. If the items are long, however, the insert should be single-spaced with a double space between items.

When you plan the placement of a letter that contains an insert, determine the margins and date line in the usual way. When necessary, refer to the Letter Placement Chart (page 197). The date line, however, must be raised to allow for the blank lines left above, below, and within the insert. For each 2 line spaces added, raise the date line by 1 line.

Study Models 12, 13, and 14 (pages 271–273). They show examples of letters with different types of inserts. Before proceeding to Exercise 1, type Drills A–C to gain practice in placing inserts in letters.

Drill A

Type the business letter shown in Model 12, which includes a quotation insert. Follow the spacing instructions given in the model. There are 179 words in the body.

Drill B

Type the business letter shown in Model 13, which includes a series of numbered paragraphs as an insert. Follow the spacing instructions given in the model. There are 174 words in the body.

Drill C

Type the business letter shown in Model 14, which includes a tabulated insert. Follow the spacing instructions given in the model. There are 106 words in the body.

Directions for Exercises 1–7

As you type these business letters with inserts, refer to Models 12, 13, and 14. Remember to reset the left margin when you start and finish an insert. For very short inserts or those that are in table form, use tab stops. Watch for the mention of enclosures in the letters and add the necessary notation.

Exercise 1
PARAGRAPH INSERT
Full block style. Open punctuation.

March 10, 19— Rothrock Homes 1717 Commerce Street Birmingham, AL 35217 SUBJECT: Fixtures Sale Gentlemen A builder needs to save money and still give quality. Morrison fixtures are the best quality you can buy. And now the price will help you save those precious construction dollars. ¶Because you are a bulk buyer of Morrison fixtures, here is what we will do for you: *(Begin insert)* We are offering you anything in our inventory at 25 percent off our regular price. This offer is good for one week only, April 8 through 14. It is being made only to you and a handful of our other preferred customers. *(End insert)* This is our way of saying "thank you" for being a faithful customer. Cordially Andrew Rux, Manager *xx* (104 words)

Tab at center ↓ | Words

Return address — 1812 Overture Drive 4
St. Louis, MO 63117 8
Date line — March 18, 19-- 11

Space down 4 times

Inside address — Personnel Manager 15
The ACT Company 18
2311 Wilson Drive 21
St. Louis, MO 63101 25

DS

Salutation — Dear Sir or Madam: 29

DS

Please consider this letter as my application for a job as a 41
clerk-typist for your company. 47

My graduation from East End High School will occur this June, 59
and I shall have completed a three-year business course. I am 71
able to type a minimum of 65 words a minute accurately. 82

Body

The enclosed data sheet gives more details of my high school 94
training, previous work experience, and references. Many of 106
my summer vacations have been spent working in offices, and I 118
have a genuine liking for this type of work. If given an oppor- 131
tunity, I am sure I shall prove an asset to your company. 142

I would appreciate the opportunity to come to your office for 154
a personal interview at any time that would be convenient for 166
you. You may reach me at the above address or by telephone at 178
592-7810. 180

DS

Complimentary closing — Very truly yours, 183

Signature — *Jane S. Paxton* (Space down 4 times)

Typed name of sender — Jane S. Paxton 186

↑ Tab at center

DS

Enclosure notation — Enclosure 188

(Shown in Elite Type)

Model 4 *Personal-Business Letter • Modified Block Style with Mixed Punctuation and No Paragraph Indention*

Exercise 2 continued

shortly before Christmas. The envelope will be marked, "Do not open until Christmas." A few days later, the January issue of the magazine will be delivered in a special wrapper. Then, each month for a year, your friends will be reminded of your thoughtfulness by the arrival of another issue. It is an ideal Christmas gift. ¶Act now, while you have the opportunity to take advantage of this special offer. Yours sincerely Terry Pappas Subscription Department *xx* Enclosures P.S. Please notice on the enclosed price schedule that with gift subscriptions of ten or more, you receive an additional reduction of 33 percent off the already low Christmas rate. At this great price, you can hardly afford not to include all your friends. Why not get a subscription for yourself or your family as well?

Exercise 3

SPECIAL CHALLENGE LETTER

Type this business letter in any acceptable style, using either form of heading for the second page. Supply any missing parts. Address a large envelope. Don't forget to mark a 1-inch margin at the bottom of the first page. This letter was dictated by Martha S. Wendell, President of the Wendell Real Estate Company.

Today's date Mr. James F. Bancroft 604 Eustis Street Albany, NY 12206 I have your letter concerning the purchase of some property on Lake Champlain, where you wish to build a children's summer camp. ¶As it now happens, I have for sale an old estate covering 35 acres of level land on the western shore of the lake. The estate has a very beautiful large main house with 25 spacious rooms. This could easily be converted into a comfortable lodge for parents. The house is in an excellent state of repair and is very substantially built. The best materials and the finest workmanship went into its construction. ¶In addition to the main house, several other structures are situated on the property. There is a very large garage, fully equipped with a workshop. Several smaller buildings, which were formerly used as servants' quarters, are suitable for camper cabins. An old-fashioned artesian well adds an authentic rustic look. ¶The estate's lake frontage of more than 750 feet includes a beautiful white sandy beach. There is a well-constructed concrete dock and a two-story boathouse, large enough to hold 30 boats. ¶On the grounds are beautiful lawns and lovely old shade trees. A section of three acres, once used as a vegetable garden, could easily be converted into a ball field and tennis courts. The property is located about 25 miles from the airport at Burlington, Vermont. It is easily accessible by car over good roads. In town, it is possible for you to purchase all the supplies you will need for the camp. ¶I am of the opinion that this property would exactly suit your purpose. I am enclosing a recent set of photographs to give you an idea of the beauty and the layout of the estate. I think you will agree that the place is unusually attractive. ¶If Monday of next week is convenient for you, I should like you to meet me at my office at nine o'clock. We can drive over to the estate, and you may see for yourself how desirable it is. The price of the property and the terms of sale are open to negotiation. Cordially (349 words)

TYPING WITH CARBON PAPER

The paper used for carbon copies is either a cheaper grade of paper (called a *second sheet*), or a thinner grade of paper (called *onionskin*). Carbon paper has two sides: a glossy side and a dull side. The dull side sometimes has the brand name of the carbon paper printed on it. The following steps will aid you in using carbon paper:

1. To assemble the carbon pack, place the sheet on which you will type the original facedown on the desk. Next, place the carbon paper on top, glossy side up. Then place the copy sheet (second sheet or onionskin) on top of the carbon paper. Avoid touching the glossy side when you handle the carbon paper. The coating may rub off on your hands, and your fingerprints may be transferred to the original copy.
2. Pick up the pack with the second sheet facing you and insert it into your typewriter. Use a folded strip of paper (such as the flap of an envelope) over the top edge of a thick carbon pack. This will help keep the papers straight as they are inserted into the typewriter. Avoid wrinkling the carbon paper; it creases easily. At the first sign of wrinkling, pull the paper release lever forward and smooth out your papers. After the carbon pack is in the machine and rolled into position, the dull side of the carbon paper should be facing you. Check for this.
3. Check the carbon pack before you begin to type to be sure it has been assembled properly. This will avoid the possibility of typing an entire assignment and then discovering a useless "mirror" copy printed on the back of your original.
4. When making several carbon copies, look at the last 2 or 3 copies before you go too far. Are they readable? On electric typewriters, adjust the impression control lever to make a stronger impression. On manuals, use a heavier touch, especially on capital letters.
5. To make an erasure when using carbon paper, erase the last copy first. Use a carbon eraser. Insert a strip of paper between the copy and the coated side of the carbon paper to prevent smudging as you continue to erase each copy until you reach the original. The strip of paper inserted should extend beyond the edge of the paper, so you will remember to remove it.
6. Use the paper release to remove the carbon pack from the machine. To remove the carbon paper, grasp the carbon pack on the upper corner, where the carbon paper is notched, and pull out the carbon paper.
7. If a typing error is discovered after the carbon pack has been removed from the typewriter, correct each copy and the original, one at a time.

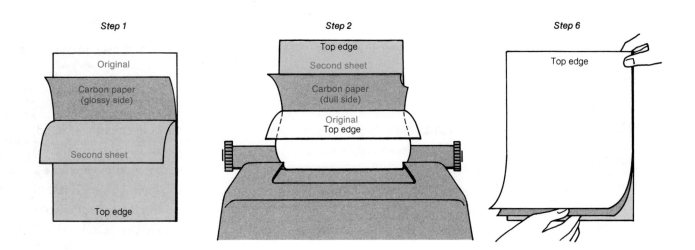

Step 1

Original
Carbon paper (glossy side)
Second sheet
Top edge

Step 2

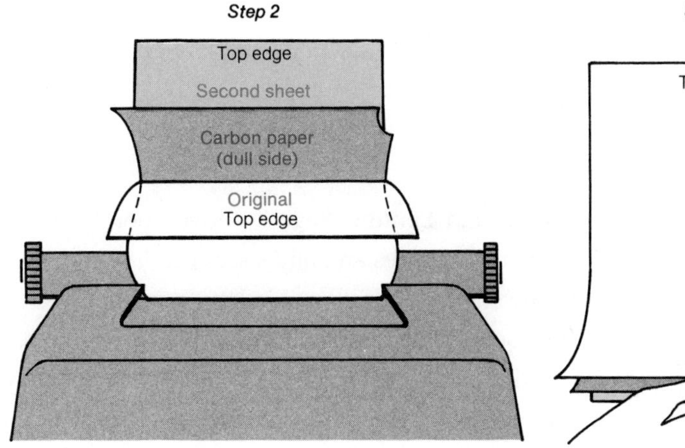

Step 6

Top edge

Exercise 1

ROUGH DRAFT

Type the second page of a letter from the rough-draft copy given at the right. Refer to page 97 if you need to review the proofreaders' marks. Use Style A heading shown in Model 11.

Modified block style. Mixed punctuation. 1-inch side margins. 5-space paragraph indention. Begin on line 7.

Lucian Electric Appliance Company 2 *Today's date*

Night Beacon retails for $7.50. The cost to you is $4.00. You can make a profit of $4.50 with an installation charge of $1.00.

As there is no official distributer of Night Beacon in your city, there are hundreds of possible sales waiting for you. We believe that you can increase your business considerably by carrying the Night Beacon. In fact we are so sure that you will find this venture profitible that we are willing to give you an attractive windowdisplay without charge and to supply you with 25 units on 30 days approval. You will not be obligated if, after a trial period of one month, you wish to return the merchandise.

On the other hand, if you decide to carry the Night beacon as a permanent item of stock we shall be glad to enter into a contract with you giving you the official agency in your city. We can then arrange credit terms to our mutual satisfaction.

Cordially,

NEWBOLD LIGHT FIXTURES, INC. Frederick S. Newbold, President *xx*

(158 words)

Exercise 2

Type the second page of a letter from the copy given here. For the heading, use Style B shown in Model 11.

Full block style. Open punctuation. 1-inch side margins. Begin on line 7.

Mr. Arnold Fenton Page 2 November 11, 19– letter is conveniently at hand, write their names and addresses on the order form enclosed. Then return the list in the stamped envelope we have provided for you. You may send payment now for your Christmas order, or, if you prefer, we can bill you later. ¶To each friend on your list, we will send an attractive Christmas card announcing your gift. Your name will appear on the inside fold. The card will be mailed so that it arrives

(Continued on next page)

Before you begin Exercise 1, practice the following drills to become familiar with handling a carbon pack and with making neat erasures on an original and carbon copy.

Drill A

Practice assembling and disassembling a carbon pack with one sheet of carbon paper. Repeat this several times. Follow the procedures outlined in Steps 1, 2, and 6 on page 203.

Drill B

Practice making an erasure. Follow the procedures given in Step 5.

1. Use the carbon pack assembled in Drill A.
2. Type the following sentence on line 15, exactly as it appears:

```
Ms. Livingston is the President of the firm.
```

3. Use the proper erasing technique to change the capital *P* in *President* to a small letter.

Drill C

Space down 5 lines from Drill B.

1. Type the following two sentences, exactly as they appear:

```
I was happy to receive there good news.
The mills will remain closed for four weeks.
```

2. Use the proper erasing technique to change *there* to *their* in the first sentence. In the second sentence, change *four* to *five*.

Exercise 1

TYPING MODEL 4

Modified block style. Mixed punctuation. No paragraph indention. 1 carbon copy.

Type the personal-business letter shown in Model 4 on page 202. There are 141 words in the body of the letter. Use the Letter Placement Chart (page 197) to determine the correct margin settings and placement of the date line. Remember to set a tab at center when modified block style is used.

Exercise 2

Modified block style. Mixed punctuation. 5 space paragraph indention. 1 carbon copy.

Study Model 4 (page 202) which illustrates the use of the enclosure notation. Then type a personal-business letter from the copy given below.

Your address / *Today's date* / Mr. Joseph Sykes / Personnel Manager / Parke-Davis Company / 7 Riverside Drive / *Your city, state, ZIP Code* / Dear Mr. Sykes: The Placement Coordinator at my school, Mr. Borovsky, has informed me of an opening in your word-processing center for a Transcription Machine Operator. Please consider me an applicant for that position. ¶ My advanced typewriting class visited your center last semester. I was interested in what I saw, and I should like very much to work for you. ¶ I have, therefore, enclosed my resume with this letter. However, I believe a personal interview would give you a better chance to evaluate my worth to your company as an employee. I shall be very glad to meet the appointment time you set. My telephone number is (*insert your number*). / Very sincerely yours, / *Your name* / Enclosure (102 words)

Center

Words

Line 7 → Heywood Associates 2 June 3, 19-- 8

TS

discounts allowed on many brands, even some which are not listed here. 22
Please take advantage of the many savings available to you by shopping 36
through our catalog. We shall be happy to furnish catalogs and prices 50
upon your request. 54

Sincerely yours, 58

JOHN DALY & SONS 62

R. L. Daly

R. L. Daly 64
Vice President 67

xx 68

Style A

Words

Line 7 → Heywood Associates 4
Page 2 5
June 3, 19-- 8

TS

discounts allowed on many brands, even some which are not listed here. 22
Please take advantage of the many savings available to you by shopping 36
through our catalog. We shall be happy to furnish catalogs and prices 50
upon your request. 54

Sincerely yours, 57

JOHN DALY & SONS 60

R. L. Daly

R. L. Daly 62
Vice President 65

xx 66

Style B

Model 11 *Second-Page Heading of a Business Letter*

Exercise 3

Modified block style. Mixed punctuation. 5-space paragraph indention. 1 carbon copy.

Your address / *Today's date* / Ocean Airlines / 4000 Roche Boulevard / San 19
Diego, CA 92104 / Ladies and Gentlemen: My marketing class is currently 33
learning how to design window displays. Each student has been given a theme 48
for creating an individual display. My theme is Hawaiian travel. ¶I've seen 63
your posters of Hawaii at the airport, and I'm impressed with your creativity 78
and bright colors. I believe a few of these posters would add the perfect touch 94
to my display. ¶Will you be so kind as to send me three or four of your posters? 110
I will be glad to pay any handling or postage charge. Thank you for your help. 126
/ Sincerely, / *Your name* (92 words) 130

Exercise 4

Modified block style. Mixed punctuation. 5-space paragraph indention. 1 carbon copy.

Your address / *Today's date* / Ms. Carol Rhodes / IBM Corporation / 11676 18
Southfield Road / *Your city, state, ZIP Code* / Dear Ms. Rhodes: Thank you 32
for spending time with me this morning discussing the position of Word Pro- 47
cessing Operator in your word processing center. I have given much thought 62
to the comments you made. ¶This type of work interests me very much. I 76
believe my strong background in punctuation, spelling, and grammar will 90
greatly reduce the time it will take to train me on the equipment in your office. 106
¶I shall telephone you on Wednesday afternoon, as you suggested. / Sincerely 121
yours / *Your name* (79 words) 124

Exercise 5

ROUGH DRAFT

Modified block style. Mixed punctuation. 5-space paragraph indention. 1 carbon copy.

Type a personal-business letter from the rough-draft copy given below. If you need to review proofreaders' marks, they are given on pages 92–93.

Your address / *Today's date* / Mr. R. B. Price / 1836 Ryan Road / Gary, IN 46406

Dear Mr. Price:

Enclosed is my check to confirm my reservation for dinner st the Spring mexting of the Business Teachers club which is being held next Friday evening. I prefer to the have menue featuring Lobster Newbarg. I understand that since my reservation is being sent in late, I will not recieve my ticket inadvance through the mail. Instead, I will expect to pick up my ticket at the door on Friday night.

Sincerely yours,

Della Thomas / Enclosure (71 words)

Exercise 19

SPELLING AND COMMA CHECKUP

Full block style. Open punctuation.

Today's date Barnett & Lowell 408 Manhattan East Orange, NJ 07019
Ladies and Gentlemen Subject: Your Purchase Order No. 02216 Please
sp notify us when you will be prepared to recieve deliveries at your new
warehouse. We are delaying shipment of your order for five cases of
continuous feed paper until we hear from you. After reading in your order
com that you wanted delivery this week we wondered whether we should hold
sp the merchandize until the warehouse is ready. ¶Since the goods are al-
sp ready packed, we would like to send them to you as soon as posible. We
sp would appreciate your sending us instructions immediatly. Cordialy
sp Ms. P. P. Froman Shipping Department Manger *xx* SPECIAL DELIVERY
P.S. Please verify the address of the new warehouse. Our records show it
as 37 Markland Drive, Paterson, New Jersey.

(80 words in body; 19 words in postscript)

Topic 3 TWO-PAGE LETTERS

Letters are often long enough to require more than one page. They are then continued on a second sheet of the same quality paper, but without a printed letterhead. Since the pages might become separated, each sheet after the first is headed with identifying information. This includes the name of the addressee, the page number of the letter, and the date. Study the two different styles of second-page headings shown in Model 11 (page 267).

When typing long letters of more than one page, remember to:

1. Use 1-inch side margins.
2. Avoid ending a page with the first line of a paragraph or with a hyphenated or divided word.
3. Mark the first page at least one inch from the bottom. This will remind you to stop in time to leave an acceptable bottom margin.
4. Carry over at least 2 lines of the body of the letter to the next page. This may require you to leave slightly more than a 1-inch margin at the bottom of the first page.
5. Begin the second-page heading on line 7. Triple space after you type the heading and then continue with the body of the letter.

Before you proceed to Exercise 1, type Drills A and B to gain practice in typing second-page letter headings.

Drill A

Full sheet. Modified block style. Mixed punctuation.

Assume that you have typed the first page of a business letter and are ready to complete it on a second sheet. Type the copy given in Model 11, Style A, which shows one way to position the second-page heading. Repeat the drill until you can type this arrangement of a second-page heading without hesitation.

Drill B

Full sheet. Full block style. Mixed punctuation.

Style B in Model 11 shows another way to arrange the second-page heading of a business letter. Type this letter several times until this arrangement of a second-page heading becomes familiar to you.

Exercise 6

Modified block style. Mixed punctuation. 5-space paragraph indention. 1 carbon copy.

Type a personal-business letter from the handwritten copy given below. Supply any missing opening or closing parts.

Your address / Today's date / Columbia Record Club / 55 Rochester Road / Columbus, OH 43215

For the past two years, I have been a member of your club. I have enjoyed receiving your monthly magazine and making my selections from your offerings.

I must cancel my membership at this time, however, because I am leaving the country for a year to participate in a student-exchange program in France.

I will write you when I return about reinstating my membership.

Your name (65 words)

Exercise 7

ROUGH DRAFT

Modified block style. Mixed punctuation. 5-space paragraph indention. 1 carbon copy.

Type a personal-business letter from the rough-draft copy given below. Supply the missing salutation and complimentary closing.

Your address / Today's date / **Alice Cohen, Director / Davis School of Art / 1120 Madison Avenue / New York, NY 10028**

Since junior high school I have ~~wanted to be~~ [been interested in a career as] an illustrator. I have decided [that] an ~~education at a top-notch~~ [art] school [education] is the best way to pursue this goal. My high school [art] teacher[, Mr. Gregson, is a] graduate[e] ~~from~~ [of] your school and highly recommends it. [¶ Will you] Please send me a catalog and an application for enrollment. In addition[,] I would appreciate [any] information ~~about~~ [you have concerning] scholarships, grants[,] loans[,] work-study programs[,] or ~~any~~ [stet] other type[s] of financial aid. [¶] I look forward to hearing from you soon.

Your name (96 words)

Directions for Exercises 16–19

Exercises 16–19 contain words that are misspelled. There are also missing commas in many of the letters. Before typing each exercise, find the misspelled word (or words) in each of the lines indicated by *sp* in the left margin. Make a list of their correct spellings on a separate piece of paper. Check each line that has the *com* symbol next to it and decide where on that line the comma (or commas) should go. Then type the letter in the style indicated with all the words spelled correctly and the missing commas in place. *Do not mark the book.*

Exercise 16

SPELLING CHECKUP

Modified block style. Mixed punctuation. 5-space paragraph indention. 2 carbon copies.

Today's date Mr and Mrs. David Lightfoot 372 Sand Street Youngstown,
OH 44517 Dear Mr. and Mrs. Lightfoot We deeply appreciate your
sp writting to us to express your satisfaction with our workmanship, and we
thank you for the picture you enclosed. ¶We would like to have your
sp permisson to show both the letter and the photograph to owners of
sp houses who come to us with problems similiar to yours. ¶Also, we would
like your permission to quote your letter and reproduce the picture in an
sp advertizement we are planning to run in an industrial journal. If you
prefer, we shall withhold your name. Sincerely yours RELIABLE HOME
IMPROVEMENTS Charles B. Arnez, Manager *xx* cc A. Sands (85 words)

Exercise 17

SPELLING AND COMMA CHECKUP

Modified block style. Mixed punctuation. 5-space paragraph indention.

Today's date Barton Printing Company 208 Dumont Street Decatur, IL
62506 Gentlemen Refer to: Purchase Order No. 02245 Three weeks ago
sp we ordered some original printing plates that were shiped to the Springer
Brick Company. The plates were later returned to you for some minor
com changes. As we understood the contract an additional charge was to be
made for the alterations to the plates. ¶We have not yet received a bill for
sp the exact amount of the aditional charge. Please forward this information
sp imediately so that we may submit our statment to the Springer Brick
Company and bring the transaction to a close. Yours truly PETERS &
DANZIG Jasper Austin, Director Accounting Department LBT:*xx*
(86 words)

Exercise 18

SPELLING AND COMMA CHECKUP

Full block style. Open punctuation.

June 9, 19– URGENT Craig Washing Machines, Inc. 555 Industrial
Court Wilmington, DE 19809 Attention Mr. Joseph Stanski Manager
sp Ladies and Gentlemen Last Wendsday we received a shipment of 32
sp com washers from your company. When we opened the crates we descovered
sp that you had sent us the wrong models. Our laundrymat is scheduealed to
com open next month but we will be forced to move back the opening date
unless you can quickly correct your mistake. We are returning the wrong
sp modles with a copy of our original order. Please send the correct washers
to us as quickly as possible. Sincerely DEL & FAYE'S WASH AND DRY
Del Kanter *xx* (77 words)

Exercise 8

Modified block style. Mixed punctuation. 5-space paragraph indention. 1 carbon copy.

Type a personal-business letter from the handwritten copy given below. Supply any missing opening or closing parts.

Your address / *Today's date* / Superintendent of Documents / Government Printing Office / Washington, D.C. 20402

I am presently enrolled in a class in which we are studying different careers. My teacher has assigned a term project which requires me to gather information on a career area of my choice.

I am interested in several occupational areas, so I would like to order one copy of each of the following reprints from the Occupational Outlook Handbook, Current Edition: No. 1955-5, Clerical Occupations; No. 1955-7, Banking Occupations; and No. 1955-26, Small Business Occupations.

I have enclosed a money order for $1.50 to cover the cost of the reprints. Thank you.

Your name (93 words)

Exercise 9

COMPOSITION AT THE KEYBOARD

Modified block style. Mixed punctuation. 5-space paragraph indention. 1 carbon copy.

Compose a letter of application in answer to the following classified advertisement.

OPPORTUNITIES FOR CLERKS, CLERK-TYPISTS, SECRETARIES, AND STENOGRAPHERS

We have several openings from starting positions requiring no experience to secretarial positions requiring 2-3 years' experience. If you have had high school or business college training in office procedures, have excellent grammar and spelling skills, and can type at least 40 wpm, we would be interested in talking with you.

APPLY BY LETTER TO: Box N-4420, Detroit News, Detroit, MI 48231.

Follow these guidelines when writing your letter:

1. State the purpose of the letter in the first paragraph. (Identify the exact job in question; tell where and how you heard about the job opening.)
2. Convince the employer that you are the one for the job by giving information about your education, training, experience, and skills that apply to the job.
3. List supplementary information about your special personal qualifications such as leadership roles in school, above-average grades, perfect attendance record, and so on.
4. Refer to a resume if one is to be enclosed.
5. Ask for an interview. (Supply necessary addresses and telephone numbers.)

Refer to the letters of application in this topic: Model 4 (page 202) and Exercises 2 and 4 (pages 204 and 205).

Directions for Exercises 13–15
SPECIAL CHALLENGE LETTERS

Before beginning these exercises, read the copy to decide on the placement of any parts that have been omitted and supply the missing parts. Use any acceptable style for each letter, but vary from one to the other. Use today's date.

Exercise 13

ATTENTION LINE, COMPANY NAME, AND MAILING NOTATION

Any acceptable letter style.

Address the letter to the attention of **Mrs. L. London.** The dictator of the letter is **Kale A. Sullivan, Sales Manager** of **Atlas Containers, Inc.** Include the company name in the signature block. The letter is being sent by certified mail.

Dickson Carton Corporation 730 Grand Street Omaha, NE 68102 The specifications of the large container that we submitted to you were intended only as suggestions. It is important to us to keep within the price limits given because of the competition with similar products now on the market. ¶If you can suggest a satisfactory container in that price range, we shall be glad to consider it. Please send us some samples and price quotations as soon as possible. ¶If you find, after receiving the new adhesive, that you can produce the container we originally specified at an acceptable price, we would prefer it. In that case, we would like to see additional samples. Sincerely yours (104 words)

Exercise 14

SUBJECT LINE AND POSTSCRIPT

Any acceptable letter style.

Include as the subject line: **Symphony Discount Tickets.** The letter was dictated by **Melvin Thompson, Ticket Manager.** Do not use postscript initials.

Ms. Georgia Templeton Cultural Resource Center 754 Comiskey Street Charlotte, NC 28212 Dear Georgia This year we will again be offering special discount tickets to performances of the Charlotte Symphony Orchestra. The discount is available to groups of 25 or more who purchase a block of tickets in the mezzanine section. Tickets normally costing $8 each cost only $5 under the special plan. ¶Your group may order tickets for any of the upcoming performances simply by phoning 364-5321. Thanks for your patronage. Cordially We hope to be able to offer this discount plan for the orchestra's next season. Our ability to do so will depend on this year's response. (67 words in body; 26 words in postscript)

Exercise 15

ATTENTION LINE, AND ADDRESSEE AND CC NOTATIONS

Any acceptable letter style. Small envelope.

Use the addressee notation **CONFIDENTIAL.** Direct the letter to the attention of **Dr. Harold Fraser, English Department.** The dictator is **Dr. Leila Huff, Dean of English, Maryville State University.** A copy is being sent to **Dr. Leo Bonini, Counselor.**

Los Grande College 4000 Mindanos Blvd. Santa Fe, NM 87501 Tonya Godfrey, a sophomore student at your college last year, is transferring to our school for the coming academic year. While her grades and her attitude are fine, we are having difficulty placing her in our program because your curriculum is so different from ours. ¶I am sending you a list of requirements for a B.A. in English from our university. Would you please note the courses you believe are equivalent to the classes Ms. Godfrey took in your program? Your cooperation will be invaluable in helping us place Ms. Godfrey in our program. Sincerely (95 words)

Topic 3 PREPARATIONS FOR MAILING

ADDRESSING ENVELOPES

The United States Postal Service now uses an automated machine called the Optical Character Reader (OCR) to speed the sorting of mail. The OCR can read printed or typewritten envelope addresses and sort letters with more speed and accuracy than is possible with manual sorting. To address envelopes in preparation for machine sorting, follow these guidelines:

1. Use single-spaced, blocked format for address lines.
2. The sender's return address may be printed on the envelope or it may be typed in the upper left-hand corner. Refer to Models 5 and 6 below for the exact placement of the return address.
3. The street or box number must be shown on the next to the last line, just before the city, state, and ZIP Code.
4. The city, state, and ZIP Code must appear on the last line of the address. Only one space is required between the two-letter state abbreviation and the ZIP Code on an envelope.
5. The recipient's address should be positioned roughly in the center of the envelope. Study this placement in Models 5 and 6. With practice, you should be able to judge placement of envelope addresses without consciously counting lines.

Model 5

No. 6 Envelope (6½″ × 3⅝″) Showing Address Placement (Standard Format)

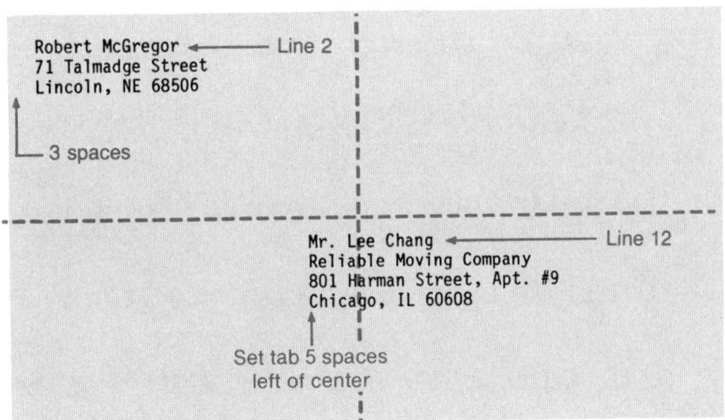

Model 6

No. 10 Envelope (9½″ × 4⅛″) Showing Address Placement (OCR Format)

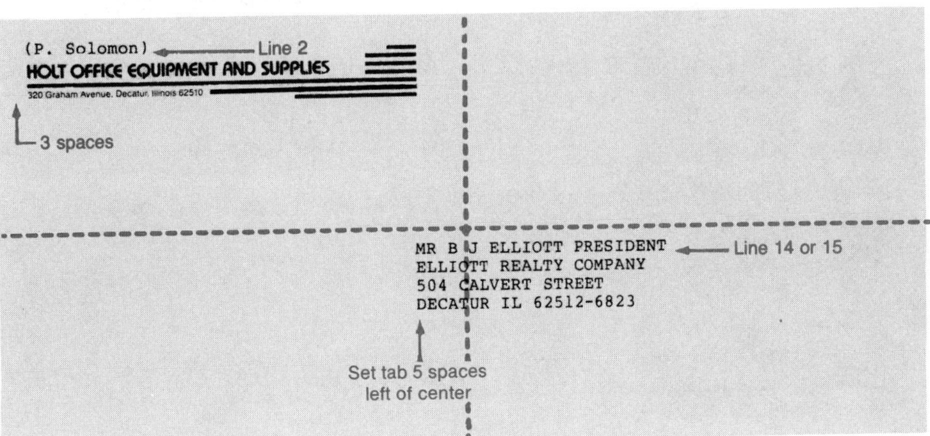

Exercise 12
ROUGH DRAFT:
SUBJECT LINE AND
COMPANY NAME

Any acceptable letter style.

August 2, 19— Mr. Randolph Gray, Vice President C & T Grocers 408 Abbott Street Kansas City, MO 64112

Dear Mr. Gray

SUBJECT: Printed ^Weekly^ Circulars

In reply to your letter ^of July 30^, I am sending you some samples of our ~~work~~ ^printing^ in a separate package. ^With this letter,^ I have enclosed a copy of our latest catalog, ~~that~~ ^which^ shows the different type faces and ~~papers~~ ^stocks^ we carry. ~~Also enclosed is~~ Our current price list, good through September 30, is also enclosed.

We would be pleased to furnish ^you with^ estimates for printing your weekly circular. We guarantee completion ^of all work^ within three working days. On rush orders of 1,000 copies ^or fewer^, we can provide 24-hour service.

If you have further questions, we shall be glad to send ~~a~~ ^our sales^ ~~representative~~ ^salesman^ to talk with you. Please contact my office directly to make an appointment.

Yours truly

OFFSET PRINTING SERVICE David L. Red Fox, President *xx* Enclosures

(120 words)

To speed mail through the special scanning equipment used by the postal service, businesses may elect to use the envelope format shown in Model 6. Note these differences from Model 5:

1. The return address is preprinted on the envelope.
2. The recipient's address is typed in solid capital letters with all punctuation marks eliminated.
3. A nine-digit ZIP Code is recommended. ("ZIP + 4" was implemented in 1983. The enlarged code consists of the original five digits plus a four-digit add-on designed to route mail to a particular building or city block. Use of the additional four digits is voluntary.)

Drill A

Using slips of paper cut to size or actual envelopes, type one copy of each envelope shown in Models 5 and 6.

Drill B

Using three small (No. 6) envelopes or slips of paper cut to size, address one envelope for each letter given in Exercises 3–5, Topic 1, pages 199–200. Use your own return address.

Drill C

Using four large (No. 10) envelopes or slips of paper cut to size, address one envelope for each letter given in Exercises 1–4, Topic 2, pages 204–205. Use your own return address.

Exercise 1

Address small (No. 6) envelopes, or slips of paper cut to size, for the addresses given at the right. Use your own return address.

1. Tudor Appliance Company / 719 Canal Street, Room 207 / New York, NY 10014
2. Gerald Yee / 308 Ingraham Street / Tulsa, OK 74151
3. Ms. Lydia T. Sobel / Ingersoll Metal Corp. / 57 Murray Avenue, Suite 7 / Evansville, IN 47706
4. Patricia St. John, President / Computer Professionals / 201 Convent Road / Minneapolis, MN 55405
5. Mr. Frank Carson / Hotel Shiawassee / 301 Court Street / Dallas, TX 75220
6. Lila's Boutique / 2764 Livonia Avenue / Warren, MI 48001

Exercise 2

Address large (No. 10) envelopes, or slips of paper cut to size, for the addresses given at the right. Use your own return address.

1. Mr. and Mrs. William B. Carroll / Roosevelt Apartments, #1305 / 191 Oak Street / Yonkers, NY 10707
2. Mr. David P. Cortez / Purchasing Department Manager / Lord & Gale / 67 Farley Street / Providence, RI 02906
3. Ms. Harriett Carstairs, President / American Air Conditioning / 149 Jackson Avenue / Dover, NJ 07801
4. Mr. Lawrence F. Kane / Kane Automobile Accessories Company / 1112 Lyman Street, Building B / Boston, MA 02108
5. Mr. Arthur M. Gordon / Hotel Westminster / 391 Clinton Avenue / Windsor, Ontario, Canada / N8X 1A7

Exercise 10 continued

items for office reception areas. We hope you will find something ~~to suit~~ *suitable for* your needs.

Cordially

PS Please be sure to use the stock numbers when ordering items from our catalog. They will assure ~~you of getting~~ *your receipt of* the correct items.

Mrs. Mary Ricker Product Supervisor *xx* Enclosure

(91 words in body; 23 words in postscript.)

Exercise 11

ROUGH DRAFT: ATTENTION LINE, SUBJECT LINE, AND MAILING NOTATION

Any acceptable letter style. Large envelope.

February 7, 19— Elite Window Designs, Inc. 64 Market Street Milwaukee, WI 53205

Attention: Shipping department Manager

Gentlemen

SUBJECT: Return of Venetian Blinds

This will confirm my telephone conversation on Tues. with Mrs. Edmunds, ~~where~~ she *has* agreed to accept ~~us~~ *our* returning *of* the 230 Venetian blinds we ordered last Dec. Mrs. Edmunds ~~confirmed~~ *assured me* that you will be able to supply us with Roman shades instead, as listed in our purchase order No. 0719 enclosed.

We will have the venetian blinds packed and returned *to you* by freight prepaid not later than ~~Saturday~~ *Friday*. To avoid *possible* confusion in our records, we would prefer ~~for~~ *that* you ~~to~~ issue us a credit for the Venetian blinds and bill us separately for the *Roman* shades.

Thank you for your cooperation in ~~this matter~~ *making this exchange for us*.

Yours sincerely

Calvin P. Ryder, President *xx* Enclosure CERTIFIED (109 words)

FOLDING LETTERS FOR INSERTION INTO ENVELOPES

Letters should be carefully folded before being inserted into envelopes. The method of folding a letter depends upon the size of the envelope to be used.

To fold and insert a full sheet into a small envelope (No. 6), refer to the illustration below and follow these steps:

1. Lay the letter faceup on your desk.
2. Bring the bottom edge to within $\frac{1}{4}$ inch from the top edge of the page and crease the fold.
3. Fold the letter from right to left approximately in thirds. First, fold the right-hand third of the paper toward the left and crease the fold. Then, fold the left-hand third over the right so that the edge is within $\frac{1}{4}$ inch of the first crease.
4. Pick up the folded letter with the last fold facing you. The crease should be at the bottom and the open edge at the top. Insert the letter into the envelope in this position.

Folding a Letter for a No. 6 Envelope

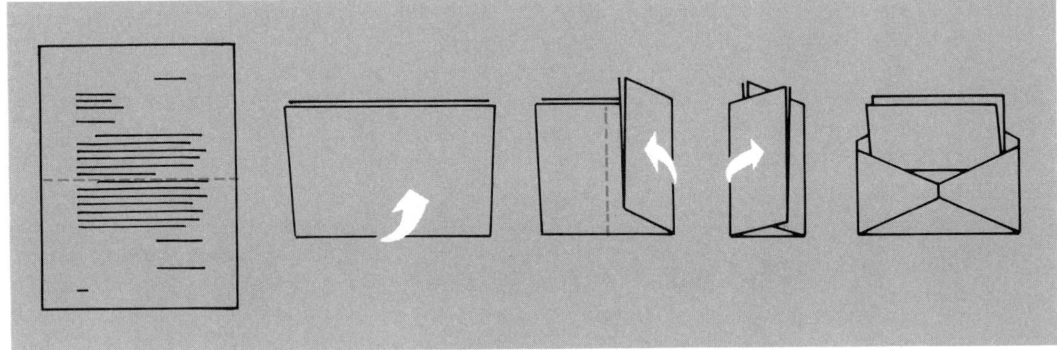

To fold and insert a full sheet into a large envelope (No. 10), refer to the illustration below and follow these steps:

1. Lay the letter faceup on the desk.
2. Fold the letter from bottom to top approximately in thirds. Begin by folding the bottom third of the paper toward the top and creasing the fold. Then, fold the top third down so that the edge is within $\frac{1}{4}$ inch from the bottom crease.
3. Hold the letter with the last fold facing you. The crease should be at the bottom as you insert the letter into the envelope.

Folding a Letter for a No. 10 Envelope

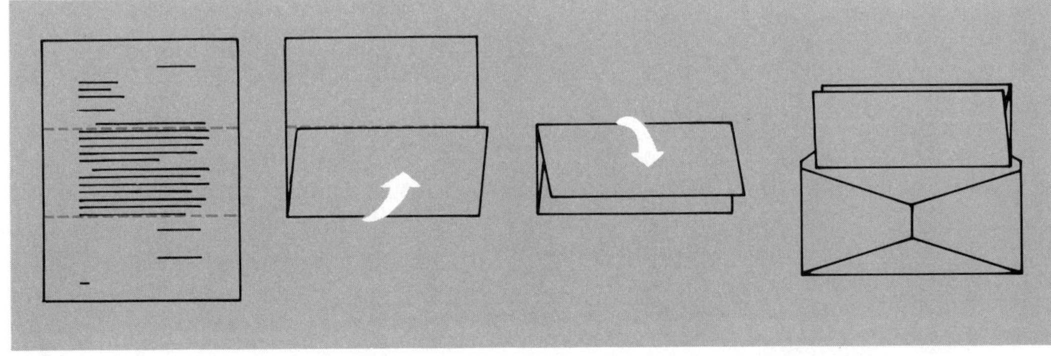

Drill D

Using either blank sheets or the letters previously typed in Topic 2, Exercises 1–4, (pages 204–205) fold them to fit a small envelope (No. 6).

Drill E

Using either blank sheets or the letters previously typed in Topic 2, Exercises 5–7 (pages 205–206), fold them to fit a large envelope (No. 10).

Exercise 9 continued

fund, is offering scholarships to women working to- 66
warda career in accounting. [I have] Enclosed ~~are~~ [several] announce- 79
ments for the scholarships [that we offer] ~~being offered. We hope~~ [and ask] 89
that you ~~will~~ post [them] ~~these brief announcements~~ on the 94
bulletin boards around your school. 101

Also enclosed is an application blank. We would 111
appreciate your dulpicating it to give to those stu- 122
dents who wish to [apply.] ~~have an application.~~ Your coopera- 130
tion will be appreciated by us as well as by those [women] 141
who qualify. 144

Sincerely ~~yours~~ 146

Cecily Madison, Trustee Mary Brookes Scholarship Fund CM:*xx* 158
Enclosures (87 words) 160

Exercise 10

ROUGH DRAFT: ADDRESSEE NOTATION, ATTENTION LINE, AND POSTSCRIPT

Modified block style. Open punctuation. No paragraph indention. Large envelope.

Today's date PLEASE FORWARD Brown, Clawson, and Ott 444 Brinton Street McAlester, OK 74501

Attention: Office Manager

Gentlemen

I trust that this letter will reach you at the newoffices recently opened , by your firm. ~~It is in regards to~~ the plastic plants [that] you ordered for the reception area. [were]

We have discontinued the [at] particular line [but] ~~that you~~ selected from our old catalog. We have several others that are similar, ~~however~~ and we highly recommend each of them.

Enclosed is a [current] catalog containing illustrations and information [about] ~~on each of~~ these new lines. It ~~also~~ includes in addition to plants, many other decorative

(Continued on next page)

Topic 4 PERSONAL-BUSINESS LETTER STYLES

So far, all letters in this part have been typed in modified block style. This topic introduces the *full block style* of typing letters. Look at the illustration on this page and compare the two letter styles. Notice that: (1) both styles have the same letter parts; (2) both styles follow the same placement rules for top, side, and bottom margins; (3) the two letter styles differ only in the placement of the heading and the *signature block* (which consists of the complimentary closing and the typed name of sender). Also, paragraphs are not indented in full block style. A letter typed in full block style, with *open punctuation* (no punctuation in salutation and complimentary closing), is shown in Model 7 on the following page.

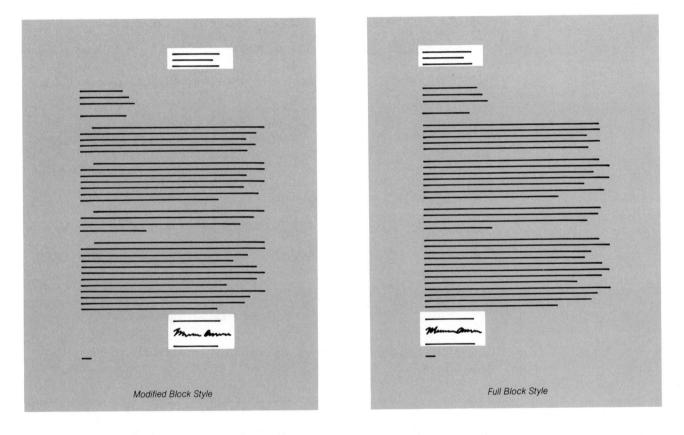

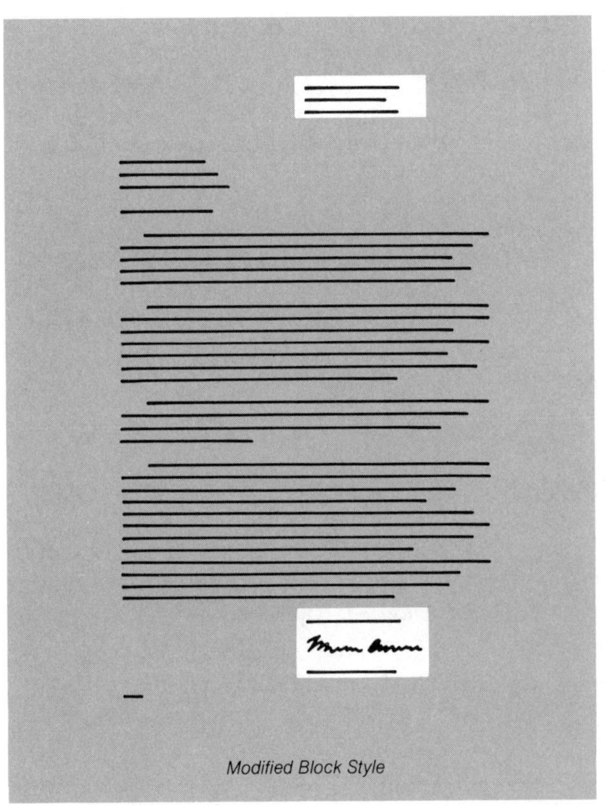

Modified Block Style

Full Block Style

Directions for Drills A–D

Type the letter shown in Model 7 (page 212) to practice the full block style and open punctuation in the following drills. There are 111 words in the body of the letter; use the Letter Placement Chart on page 197 to determine the proper margins.

Drill A

Begin typing with the return address and see how far you can type in 3 minutes. Repeat this drill several times.

Drill B

Begin typing with the word *committee* (third line of the third paragraph). Can you complete the letter in 2 minutes or less? Repeat this drill several times.

Exercise 8
SUBJECT LINE, CC AND MAILING NOTATIONS

Full block style. Open punctuation. Large envelope.

Today's date The Modern Pharmacy 283 Main Street Stillwater, MN 55082

Gentlemen

SUBJECT: Short Shipment

We have your letter reporting a shortage of two dozen bottles of aspirin in our recent shipment to you.

As you noted, eight dozen were packed, four dozen to a case, in one carton. According to our records, the remaining two dozen were shipped with other drugs later in the day.

Probably, at the time you wrote us, you had not received (or checked) the second shipment. We are certain that you will receive the full quantity indicated on the invoice. Please telephone our office immediately if you have further problems.

Sincerely yours

E. V. Mills Shipping Department *xx* SPECIAL DELIVERY cc: A. Kraft

(91 words)

Exercise 9
ROUGH DRAFT: ATTENTION LINE AND SUBJECT LINE

Modified block style. Open punctuation. No paragraph indention. Large envelope.

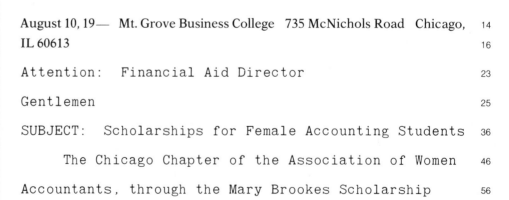

August 10, 19— Mt. Grove Business College 735 McNichols Road Chicago, 14
IL 60613 16

Attention: Financial Aid Director 23

Gentlemen 25

SUBJECT: Scholarships for Female Accounting Students 36

The Chicago Chapter of the Association of Women 46
Accountants, through the Mary Brookes Scholarship 56

(Continued on next page)

Words

Begin return address at left margin

139 Evergreen Avenue 4
Bethlehem, PA 18015 8
June 12, 19-- 11

Harris & Sons 14
75 Howe Street 17
Bethlehem, PA 18015 21

Ladies and Gentlemen ← No punctuation after salutation 25

No paragraph indention →

I am very happy to respond to your request for information 37
concerning the character of Mr. William Peters. 47

Mr. Peters has been my neighbor and friend for more than ten 59
years. During that time he has participated in many civic and 71
community activities. He served as president of our community 83
association for four years. 88

In my dealings with Mr. Peters, I have found him to be loyal, 100
responsible, and trustworthy. I recommend him highly for the 112
committee appointment that you mentioned in your letter. I 124
can think of no person who is better qualified and more de- 136
serving of this recognition. 142

Do not hesitate to contact me if you need more information. 154

Begin signature block at left margin

Sincerely ← No punctuation after complimentary closing 156

Charles J. Van Houten

Charles J. Van Houten 160

(Shown in Elite Type)

Model 7 *Personal-Business Letter*
Full Block Style with Open Punctuation

Exercise 5

ADDRESSEE NOTATION AND POSTSCRIPT

Full block style. Open punctuation. Small envelope.

May 8, 19— PERSONAL Ms. Ann Hernandez Executive Secretary Danton 13
and LaFarge, Inc. 39 Franklin Street Boise, ID 83702 Dear Ms. Hernandez 27
Congratulations on your new job! From your letter, it sounds like a great 42
opportunity for you. And, I'm sure the company was pleased to find someone 57
with your impressive background. ¶I'm sorry I was not more help to you in 71
locating a position. Call me, if you can, in the next few weeks to let me know 87
how the job is going. By the way, many exceptionally good openings are 101
coming in every day. If you have friends looking for work, please refer them 116
to me. ¶Best of luck to you as you continue your career. Sincerely Paul Barry, 132
Placement Counselor *xx* PS If you decide at a future time to look for another 147
job, you can be sure I will do everything I can to get you the best position at 163
the highest possible salary. (96 words in body; 33 words in postscript) 169

Exercise 6

SUBJECT LINE, BCC AND MAILING NOTATIONS

(Note the use of REFER TO in place of SUBJECT.)

Full block style. Mixed punctuation. Extra carbon copy. Large envelope.

February 18, 19— Mr. Raymond Speight 10938 Crandall Avenue Decatur, 14
GA 30031 Dear Mr. Speight REFER TO: Policy No. 637-033-039 I have 27
received important information from our company regarding your life insur- 42
ance policy as listed above. It is very urgent that I talk with you as soon as 58
possible about this important matter. ¶I have not been able to contact you by 73
telephone. Would you please call me at 354-8080, at your earliest convenience, 89
so that we may discuss this information. If you cannot reach me at that 103
number, please call me at home at 354-1695. Sincerely Jerome Ashley Sales 118
Representative *xx* bcc: T. Basker REGISTERED (76 words) 127

Exercise 7

ATTENTION LINE, COMPANY NAME, AND POSTSCRIPT

Modified block style. Mixed punctuation. No paragraph indention. Large envelope. Supply the salutation.

November 28, 19— Security Department Nevada Coliseum Las Vegas, NV 13
89108 Attention Mr. Fred Falletti In reference to your letter of November 21, 28
ABC Security Systems can supply the extra security guards you will need for 43
the rock concert scheduled for the evening of January 5. ¶We need to know, 58
however, the exact number of guards you will require, their precise duties 73
and responsibilities, and the kinds of equipment each guard should have. 87
The sooner we have this information, the sooner we can draw up a formal 101
agreement to send to you. ¶ABC can also provide trained medical assistants. 116
Our past experience in handling large concerts has repeatedly shown their 131
usefulness. Please notify me if you are also interested in having any of them 146
on hand. ¶Thank you for contacting us. I am sure our well-trained employees 161
will do the kind of efficient job you want done. Sincerely ABC SECURITY 175
SYSTEMS, INC. Lorene Hughes Business Manager *xx* PS Since the 188
concert is just over a month away, please send me the needed information for 203
the agreement at your earliest possible convenience. 214
(133 words in the body; 24 words in the postscript)

Drill C

Type the entire letter in 8 minutes or less. (You can complete it even if you type less than 20 wpm.) Compare your copy with the model. Are all the parts placed properly on the page in the full block style?

Drill D

Type the letter again, this time with one carbon copy and correct any errors that you make. Address a small envelope, fold the original letter, and insert it in the envelope.

Directions for Exercises 1–9

Type the following personal-business letters. Use the Letter Placement Chart (page 197) to determine the correct margins and date line position for each letter. Fold and insert each letter into a properly addressed envelope.

Exercise 1

Full block style. Open punctuation. 1 carbon copy. Small envelope.

Your address / *Today's date* / Jewel Glassware, Inc. / 830 Eighth Avenue / 19
Glendale, CA 91209 / Ladies and Gentlemen / This is the third time I have 33
written to you concerning the set of monogrammed glasses which I ordered 47
from you four months ago. When I wrote you last, you said they were prob- 62
ably lost in transit; you promised to put a tracer on the shipment. That was 77
a month ago! I still haven't heard or seen anything of the glasses. ¶I have, 92
however, received the canceled check to show that you have received and 106
deposited my payment. I think four months is long enough to wait patiently 121
for a set of glasses. ¶Please cancel my order for the glasses and issue me a full 137
refund for the amount I have paid. I would appreciate your taking immediate 152
action on my refund. ¶ I am sorry that this incident has changed my formerly 168
good opinion of your company. / Yours truly / *Your name* (137 words) 178

Exercise 2

Full block style. Open punctuation. 1 carbon copy. Large envelope.

Your address / *Today's date* / Mr. Gregory A. Hearn / Hearn & Slate, Inc. / 740 Emerson Avenue / *Your city, state, ZIP Code* / Dear Mr. Hearn / Last Friday I found that I had an immediate need for a pair of faucets I had ordered from you. I could not wait for the delivery of the entire order I had given you. I telephoned and explained the situation and offered to come by shortly after five o'clock for the faucets in question. You told me to ask for them in the shipping room where they would be ready for me. ¶When I arrived, only one clerk was in the shipping room. He said he had no package for me and had been given no instructions. When I asked him to see whether he could locate the package, he became very rude and offensive. I had no choice but to leave, and at considerable inconvenience, I had to get the faucets elsewhere. ¶I thought you should know of this incident. I cannot give you the name of the clerk (he refused to identify himself) but he was the only one on duty at the time. / Yours truly / *Your name*

(167 words)

Exercise 2

ATTENTION LINE AND CC NOTATION

Modified block style. Mixed punctuation. 5-space paragraph indention. Small envelope.

December 3, 19— Coloma Realty Company 5120 West Duneland Highway 13
Coloma, MI 49038 Attention: Clara DeSoto Ladies and Gentlemen As we 26
discussed last week, the rent increases for the apartments at Garden Manor 41
will be based on several improvements. These include installing new 55
showers, painting the living rooms, and remodeling the kitchens. ¶I have 69
engaged Mr. Anthony Harper, a local contractor, and he will call on you soon 84
to estimate the cost of the repairs. ¶I'd like to mention that I was very 99
pleased with the way the building looked. I feel you are managing it well. 114
Thanks. I appreciate it! Best wishes Delmont Kent *xx* cc: Anthony Harper 128
(85 words)

Exercise 3

ATTENTION AND SUBJECT LINES, AND CC NOTATION

Modified block style. Mixed punctuation. 5-space paragraph indention. Large envelope.

March 24, 19— McCullum & Fielder Accountants Suite 21 Dreyfuss Build- 14
ing, 231 Chase Drive Akron, OH 44310 Attention Wendy McCullum Ladies 28
and Gentlemen SUBJECT The Omni Account Some of your clients need 41
many banking services. Perhaps they now have several types of accounts to 56
take care of their different banking needs. Here is good news for them and 71
for you in your capacity as financial adviser. ¶The People's Bank has 85
developed a new account for customers with diverse banking needs. It is 100
called the Omni Account. The Omni provides every banking service our 114
institution offers for only one small monthly fee. ¶We think your company 128
should know about the Omni Account, since many of your clients do their 142
banking with us. The enclosed brochure describes the account in detail. If 157
you have any questions concerning the Omni, please call Mrs. Jennifer 171
Walker at our main office. Yours very truly Albert Santini Branch Manager 186
xx Enclosure CC Jennifer Walker (119 words) 192

Exercise 4

SUBJECT LINE, COMPANY NAME, AND MAILING NOTATION

Modified block style. Mixed punctuation. 5-space paragraph indention. Large envelope.

July 5, 19— Mr. E. D. Osgood Osgood & Rider, Inc. P.O. Box 27 Beverly, MA 15
01915 Dear Mr. Osgood SUBJECT: Construction of Factory Parking Lot 28
We have your letter expressing concern about the interruption in our work 42
on the parking lot of your new factory. Let us assure you that we will do 57
everything we can to meet the completion date agreed upon. ¶The con- 71
struction of the parking lot has been slowed by the rain and wind storms 85
during the past two weeks. In order to speed up the work, we will therefore 100
shift five men from another project to work with our crew at your factory. 115
With the additional crew, the job should be finished in three weeks, in accor- 130
dance with our contract. ¶Please do not feel that we are forgetting our agree- 145
ment with you. If you have further concerns, please call to discuss the 159
problems with me. Cordially yours ACME CONSTRUCTION COMPANY 171
Charles M. Floyd Vice-President *xx* CERTIFIED (131 words) 180

Exercise 3

Full block style. Open punctuation. 1 carbon copy. Small envelope.

Your address / *Today's date* / National BanKard Corp. / 156 New Portland / Memphis, TN 38107 / Ladies and Gentlemen / I have your letter requesting that I send you a financial statement on the form that you enclosed. ¶I am very much surprised at this request. I can understand why you might desire such information from someone who is applying to you for credit when previous credit has not been established or from a customer who wishes to have a credit limit greatly increased. ¶I cannot understand, however, why anything of the sort is necessary in my case. I have dealt with your company for almost a year and have always met my obligations promptly when they became due. I consider your request unwarranted and can see no reason why I should comply with it. / Very truly yours / *Your name* (115 words)

Exercise 4

ROUGH DRAFT

Full block style. Open punctuation. 1 carbon copy. Large envelope.

Your address / *Today's date* / Reader's Review / Treasurer's Office / Pleasantville, NY 10570

```
Ladies and gentlemen

Your invoice for $11 covering a three-year ~~pre~~(sub)scription
to your magazine ar^(r)ived today.  This invoice is ~~cer-
tainly~~ in error^(,) since I am certain that I asked for a
(1)-year trial subscription. ¶A copy of your invoice and
my check for ^($)4.57 are ^(e)inclosed.  This am~~m~~ount will
cover my one-year subscription(.) please check your rec-
ords and write ^(me) if you have any further questions.

Sincerely yours
```

Your name / Enclosures (65 words)

Exercise 5

Modified block style. Open punctuation. No paragraph indentions. 1 carbon copy. Large envelope.

Your address / *Today's date* / Mr. Charles Floyd / Floyd Construction 18
Company / 160 Third Street / *Your city, state, ZIP Code* / Dear Mr. Floyd / 34
According to our contract, you were to complete the stone driveway from the 49
public curb back to my garage in return for setting up your stone-crushing 64
equipment on my property located at Sawyer and Third Streets. ¶You have 78
now had your machinery on my property for almost a year, you have com- 92
pleted the work you were doing in the area, and you appear to be preparing 107
to leave. ¶This letter is written to remind you of your part of the contract. 122
Please write or call me to confirm when you will begin construction of my 136
driveway. / Very truly yours / *Your name* (97 words) 143

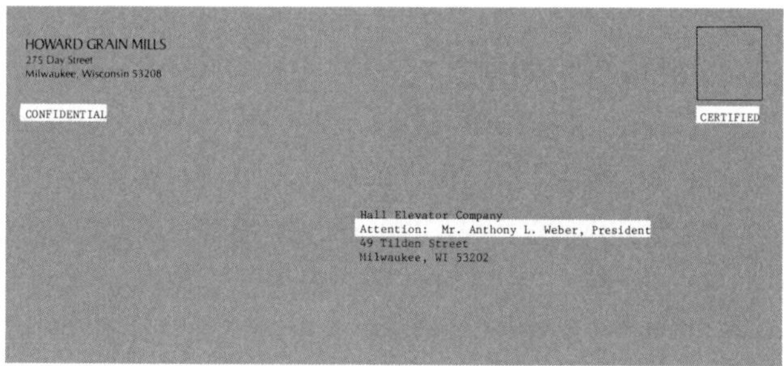

This illustration shows the preferred placement of special notations on an envelope. Note that the attention line is included as part of the address block; it is not placed in the lower left corner of the envelope. Since most mail is sorted by machines designed to scan the last two lines on an envelope, those lines should be reserved for the street address and ZIP Code. Addressee notations, attention lines, and mailing notations must, therefore, be placed in the upper half of the envelope where they will not interfere with machine sorting.

Letters that include special notations will require some adjustment for the placement of the date line. For each notation, the date line is raised one line above that indicated in the Letter Placement Chart on page 197. The number of words in a postscript must also be considered before figuring the date line placement. For each twenty words in a postscript, the date line should be raised one line.

Drill A

TYPING MODEL 10

Type the letter shown in Model 10 (page 256). Assume that you are typing on letterhead stationery. Follow the spacing instructions given in the model. Determine the proper margins and position of the date line by referring to the Letter Placement Chart (page 197). Remember to count the postscript. Remember also to raise the date line one line for each special notation. Type your initials in place of *xx*. The body of the letter contains 156 words.

Drill B

OPENING PARTS OF MODEL 10

See how much of Model 10 you can type in 3 minutes. Use the same margin settings and date-line placement as in Drill A. Repeat the drill until you can type the opening parts of the letter without hesitation.

Drill C

CLOSING PARTS OF MODEL 10

Now start with the last paragraph of Model 10. Use the same margin settings as in Drill A. Try to finish the letter in 3 minutes or less. Repeat the drill until you can type the closing parts of the letter without hesitation.

Drill D

AN ENVELOPE FOR MODEL 10

Address a large envelope for the Model 10 letter you typed in Drill A. Copy the return address from the letterhead in Model 10. Add all the special notations from the letter that belong on the envelope. Then fold and insert the letter correctly.

Exercise 1

ATTENTION LINE AND SUBJECT LINE

Modified block style. Mixed punctuation. No paragraph indention. Large envelope.

Today's date Career Placement Office Eaton School of Management Training 29 Paint Street Circleville, OH 43113 Attention: Mrs. Sarah Ryan Ladies and Gentlemen SUBJECT: Job Applicants We want to thank you for sending two of your students to be interviewed for the administrative assistant's position available at DuPres Associates. Although their interviews and applications were very positive, we found someone whose qualifications better met our needs. We had many applicants for the position, and this decision was not reached easily. ¶We enjoyed meeting and talking with your students, and we wish them luck in their endeavors. Sincerely J. I. Krasnov Personnel Manager *xx* (70 words)

Exercise 6

ROUGH DRAFT

Modified block style. Mixed punctuation. 5-space paragraph indention. 1 carbon copy. Small envelope.

Your address / *Today's date* / United Art Suppliers / 116 Hoyt Street / Duluth, MN 55811

Ladies and Gentlemen:

Last week I send you an order for merchandice which included three dozen tubes of assorted oil paints. The goods arrived this morning. In the carton, however, I find only two cases, each containing only eight tubes. There is therefore a shortage of 20 tubes. Please send the additional tubes which are included in my original order. Or if you prefer you may credit me with the twenty tubes, as my present supply will be sufficient enough until I send you my next order. Yours truly,

Your name (81 words)

Exercise 7

Full block style. Mixed punctuation. 1 carbon copy. Large envelope.

Your address / August 20, 19— / Metz Brothers / 491 South Street / Rochester, NY 14612

Gentlemen:

Last month I was in your city for a convention. On July 24, a truck belonging to your firm and operated by your driver, Larry Steel, ran into my car while it was legally parked in front of Crompton Assembly Hall. I filed a report at that time with the Rochester Police Department.

Since that time, I have had my car repaired at a cost to me of $387. However, my insuring agent at Coastal Insurance Co.

(Continued on next page)

275 Day Street, Milwaukee, Wisconsin 53208

(415) 275-4030

Words

March 18, 19-- 3

DS

Addressee notation CONFIDENTIAL 6

DS

Hall Elevator Company 10
49 Tilden Street 13
Milwaukee, WI 53202 17

DS

Attention line Attention: Mr. Anthony L. Weber, President 26

DS

Gentlemen: 28

DS

Subject line SUBJECT: Elevator Inspection 34

DS

Since your company installed the elevators in this plant, the 46
service provided by your inspectors has been efficient and cour- 59
teous. However, I must call your attention to an incident that 72
occurred during the last inspection. 79

Prior to the inspection date, I had prepared a list of problems 92
that had arisen since the last inspection. Most of them were 104
minor and required only small adjustments to correct them. When 117
I handed the list to the inspector, he pocketed it without read- 130
ing it. I pointed out that my list would certainly save him time 143
and would assure us that the problems were corrected. He became 156
indignant at this and seemed to think I was interfering with his 169
work. Now, only five days after the inspection, we find that 181
several problems were not corrected. 188

Would you please schedule another inspection without delay. I 201
would appreciate your calling my office to confirm the date and 214
time your inspector will arrive. 221

Yours very truly, 225

DS

Company name in signature block HOWARD GRAIN MILLS 229

John R. Rabin

John R. Rabin 232
Plant Manager 235

JRR:xx 236
Mailing notation CERTIFIED 238
Carbon copy notation cc: Carl Reese 241
Postscript P.S. Our plant is available for your inspection only on Thursdays 254
and Fridays. 257

(Shown in Elite Type)

Model 10 *Business Letter with Special Notations*
Modified Block Style with Mixed Punctuation

Exercise 7 continued

has so far been unsuccessful in collecting this sum from you. The fact that your employee, Larry Steel, was using your truck to run a personal errand does not, in my opinion, relieve you of your responsibility.

I shall appreciate receiving your check for $387 without further delay. I think you will agree that settlement of this claim out of court would be better for both of us.

Yours truly,

Your name (137 words)

Exercise 8

Modified block style. Open punctuation. 5-space paragraph indention. 1 carbon copy. Small envelope.

Your address / *Today's date* / Ann Riley, Credit Manager / Morales and Reiss / 1098 Maple Drive / Madison, WS 53705

Dear Ms. Riley:

I have your letter requesting information on the whereabouts of Patrick O'Connell, but I'm afraid I cannot help you.

It was a surprise to me to learn that Mr. O'Connell had listed me as a credit reference. During the seven months that he lived in my apartment building, I saw so little of him that I barely got to know him. You will want to know, however, that Mr. O'Connell was three months

(Continued on next page)

Topic 2 SPECIAL NOTATIONS

The opening parts of a business letter may contain any of three *special notations.* These notations are described below and are illustrated in Model 10 on page 256.

```
PERSONAL

CONFIDENTIAL
```

1. ADDRESSEE NOTATIONS. Special instructions are sometimes given for handling a letter when it arrives at its destination. These instructions include PERSONAL, CONFIDENTIAL, HOLD FOR ARRIVAL, and PLEASE FORWARD. Such notations should always appear on the envelope. They are typed a triple space below the return address. On the letter, notations for PERSONAL or CONFIDENTIAL may be typed at the left margin, in solid capitals, a double space below the date.

```
Attention:  J. M. Ross

ATTENTION  Carla Cortez
```

2. ATTENTION LINE The word *Attention* is used to direct a letter to a particular person or department in a company. It may be typed with the first letter capitalized, and sometimes it is followed by a colon. The attention line is usually placed at the left margin, a double space below the inside address and a double space above the salutation. It may also be the second line of the inside address. The salutation *Ladies, Gentlemen,* or *Ladies and Gentlemen* is used, since the letter is addressed to the company, not to the person named in the attention line. On the envelope, the attention line is the second line of the address, immediately following the company's name, as shown in the illustration on page 257.

```
SUBJECT:  Dental Care
```

3. SUBJECT LINE The word *Subject* is used to identify the main topic of the letter. (You might think of it as a title for the body of the letter.) Generally, it is placed at the left margin, a double space below the salutation and a double space above the body. Often, it is typed in solid capitals with a colon following it.

Four other special notations are sometimes included as part of the closing of a business letter. They are shown here and in Model 10 on the following page.

```
Yours very truly,

HOWARD GRAIN MILLS
```

4. COMPANY NAME IN SIGNATURE BLOCK The firm name is included as part of the signature when it is necessary to emphasize that the signer is speaking on behalf of the company. It is typed a double space after the complimentary closing in solid capital letters.

```
REGISTERED

CERTIFIED
```

5. MAILING NOTATIONS When a letter is sent REGISTERED, CERTIFIED, or SPECIAL DELIVERY, this fact should be noted on the letter and on the envelope. On the letter, the notation is usually typed in solid capitals directly below the enclosure notation (if any) or on the line below the reference initials. On the envelope, the mailing notation is typed below the stamp, as shown in the illustration on page 257.

```
cc:  Eleanor Mennick
```

6. CARBON COPY NOTATION The notation for carbon copy is used when a copy of the letter is made for someone other than the addressee. It may be typed either as cc, cc:, CC, or CC:, and it is followed by the name of the person who is to receive the copy. If the dictator does not wish the addressee to know that another person is receiving a copy of the letter, a *blind carbon copy* notation is typed in the upper left corner of the file copy. Either of the following forms may be used: bcc or bcc:, followed by the name of the person to whom the copy is sent.

```
P.S.  or  PS
```

7. POSTSCRIPT A postscript is typed at the very end of the letter as an afterthought or to give special emphasis to a particular point of information. Postscript initials may be typed either as P.S. or PS, followed by two spaces, or they may be omitted altogether. The postscript is typed in full block style or indented, following the style of the letter. It is always the last item on the page.

Exercise 8 continued

behind in his rent at the time he moved. All my attempts to collect his rent had failed, and I was, quite frankly, pleased when I discovered he had left.

Mr. O'Connell left no forwarding address. If you should succeed in locating him, I would appreciate your sending me his current address.

Sincerely,

Your name (130 words)

Exercise 9

ROUGH DRAFT

Full block style. Open punctuation. 1 carbon copy. Large envelope.

Your address / *Today's date* / Sun-Ray Solar Heating / 1700 South Serbin Street / Dallas, TX 75224

Ladies and Gentlemen

I picked up one of your brochures at the Home and garden Exposition in Cleveland last month and I ~~am~~ was impressed with the rapid technological advancement in your Solar Heating systems. I am seriously considering instaling solar heating in my new house, but I still have a few unanswered questions: Will solar heating work well in areas where it is often cloudy? Do you provide long-term financing? Is it possible to ad one of your systems to my existing blueprints or will I have to have new ones drawn? If possible, I would like one of your representatives to visit me and discuss these and other questions. feel free to contact me at (419) 282-5663 and make an appointment.

Sincerely

Your name (121 words)

Exercise 35 continued

sp on a person's abillity. Previous experience in
sp dealing with people is desireable.

We shall be very grateful for your prompt response so that we may reach a decision as soon as possible.

Cordially

Helen R. Cooke Personnel Manager *xx* Enclosure (131 words)

Exercise 36

SPELLING CHECKUP

Modified block style. Open punctuation. 5-space paragraph indention.

Today's date Ms. Helen R. Cooke Personnel Manager Camp Woodland Asheville, NC 28806

Dear Ms. Cooke

sp Jordan Drake was an assisstant in this office last
sp year from Febuary through August. In accordance with an understanding we had when he entered our employ, he left to return to school.

His duties in the office were fairly simple; he
sp acted as a receptionist and ocassionaly did some typing. His work was entirely satisfactory. He had a pleasing manner and was courteous, will-
sp ing, and cooporative. His duties were not of such a
sp nature as to give him much oportunity to show leadership qualities. However, he exercised good
sp judgement and got along well with our employees.

Had he again applied for the same position the next summer, he would have been hired
sp immediatly.

Very truly yours

Elizabeth Wolfe Office Manager *xx* (114 words)

Exercise 10
COMPOSITION
AT THE KEYBOARD

Modified block style. Mixed punctuation. 5-space paragraph indention. 1 carbon copy.

Compose and type a short business letter to Mr. Isaac Goldberg, Editor, *The Daily Herald,* 3200 Lafayette Avenue, *Your city, state, and ZIP Code.* Use your own school address and today's date as the heading. Include the following information in your letter:

- You are writing as president of your senior class.
- Class members and class sponsors have suggested Mr. Goldberg as an interesting speaker.
- You have been given the task of writing to ask him to deliver a 10- to 15-minute address at your commencement exercises, which will be held on Wednesday, June 10, at 7 p.m. in your high school auditorium.
- Your class has budgeted an amount of $100 as a stipend to cover any expenses of the speaker.
- You would like Mr. Goldberg to address his reply to your graduating class sponsor, Mrs. Jewel Fischer.

Topic 5 LETTERS FOR REVIEW

Exercises 1–6 in this topic provide additional practice on the skills learned in the previous topics.

Exercises 7–12 contain errors in spelling, punctuation, grammar, and word usage. Each of these exercises contains *editing alerts* that provide clues to the errors you are expected to find. Locate the errors and list the necessary corrections on a separate sheet before you begin to type these exercises. *Do not mark the book.*

In all exercises where you are instructed to type letters, refer to the Letter Placement Chart (page 197), if necessary, to determine the proper margins.

Exercise 1
PERSONAL NOTE

Half sheet. Insert short side first. Modified block style. Mixed punctuation. Margins at 13 and 53 for elite; 7 and 47 for pica. Single spacing. Begin on line 12.

Your address / *Today's date* / Dear Sis, I'll bet you are surprised to get this note from me! Well, Dad was a little upset when our telephone bill arrived yesterday. He insisted that Mom and I begin to write more letters and make fewer long-distance telephone calls to chat. ¶Tell me all about your new lifestyle. It seems so exciting. I can hardly wait two more years until I can go off to college. ¶I am starting to save more of my allowance so I can afford to call you at least once every two weeks. Write soon. / Love, / *Your name* (92 words)

Exercise 2
PERSONAL LETTER

Modified block style. Mixed punctuation. 5-space paragraph indention.

12076 Oakman / Dearborn, MI 48122 / *Today's date* / Dear Aunt Suzy and Uncle Don, I had so much fun during your visit. The only bad part was that you had to leave so soon. Perhaps you can stay longer next time. ¶Daphne finally had her puppies—nine days late. Yesterday, we found her and eight tiny, brown and white babies squeezed into that rag box that Mom keeps in the furnace room. I guess Daphne didn't like the nice basket we bought her. If you know anyone who would like a springer spaniel puppy, we have plenty. ¶I want especially to thank you for taking me to the baseball game. It was the first major-league game I had ever attended. I tacked the pennant you bought me to my door, and I think of you every time I look at it. / With much love, / *Your name* (128 words)

Exercise 34 continued

sp always payed his bills promptly. We have granted him credit to the extent of $3500. We would not hesitate to give him a
sp favorable recomendation. We believe you will find him a very desirable customer.
Let us know if we can be of further
sp assistence to you.
sp Sincerly

Philip F. Chandler Business Manager *xx* (85 words)

Exercise 35

SPELLING CHECKUP

Modified block style. Mixed punctuation. 5-space paragraph indention.

August 23, 19— Ms. Elizabeth Wolfe Office Manager Sherman, Spears & Company 4 Franklin Square Charleston, SC 29408

Dear Ms. Wolfe

sp Jordan Drake has submited your name as
sp a referance on his application for a position as trainee in our recreational camp. Will you be good enough to give us your appraisal of his
sp qualifications and charater? We are enclosing our regular reference form. If you prefer to provide additional comments, we shall find that helpful also.

A trainee in our camp is equivalent to an
sp apprentice councilor. the duties involve food service, receiving guests, and clerical work. Although these duties do not require leadership, we prefer to hire employees with ability in that direction. Camp work makes unusual demands

(Continued on next page)

Exercise 3
PERSONAL LETTER
Modified block style. Mixed punctuation. 5-space paragraph indention. 1 carbon copy.

Your address / *Today's date* / Mr. Richard Holley, President / National Association of School Secretaries / 51 Michigan Avenue / Grand Rapids, MI 49509 Dear President Holley: I was delighted to receive your kind invitation to serve as Recorder at the annual conference of the National Association of School Secretaries. I accept this invitation with great pleasure ¶ If the NASS has made any special arrangements with the Hilton Hotel for accommodations and meals, will you kindly send me this information so that I may make reservations as soon as possible? I have attended many of these conferences, and I know that it is often difficult to secure reservations at the hotel serving as conference headquarters unless one applies well in advance. ¶ Many thanks for your invitation. I am looking forward to seeing you at the conference. / Sincerely, / *Your name* (109 words)

Exercise 4
PERSONAL-BUSINESS LETTER
Full block style. Mixed punctuation. 1 carbon copy. Small envelope.

Your address / *Today's date* / Dr. Janet Nottingham / 1670 Harper Avenue / Billings, MT 59101 / Dear Dr. Nottingham: / As you can tell from my return address, my family has relocated. I am now applying for a clerical position with medical offices in this city. ¶ Since I worked part-time in your office for six months last year and received excellent training, I should like your permission to use your name as a reference. ¶ I am enclosing a self-addressed postal card for your convenience in replying. Your approval would be greatly appreciated. / Sincerely, / *Your name* / Enclosure (74 words)

Exercise 5
PERSONAL-BUSINESS LETTER
Modified block style. Mixed punctuation. 5-space paragraph indention. 1 carbon copy. Large envelope.

Your address / *Today's date* / Dr. Janet Nottingham / 1670 Harper Avenue / Billings, MT 59101

Dear Dr. Nottingham:

Thank you for allowing me to use your name as a reference. I am sure you will be pleased to learn that I have accepted a position at Mercy Hospital as a Ward Clerk. I shall begin work next Monday.

I appreciate your kindness, and I hope that someday I may have the opportunity to repay you.

Gratefully,

Your name (57 words)

Exercise 32

SPELLING CHECKUP

Modified block style. Mixed punctuation. No paragraph indention.

June 25, 19— Garner & Bruce Associates 41 Sother Street Brockton,
MA 02045 Gentlemen Ms. Epstein has sent us the samples of carpet you
sp chose for your new offices. ¶It is our oppinion that the carpets you chose
sp are not apropriate for the daily wear and tear of an office. We feel you
sp would do better to use a higher quality, more dureable material. This,
sp of course, will be more expenssive now but will save you money in the
long run. ¶If you desire help in choosing carpeting, I will be in town next
sp Tuesday. I will be glad to stop by to help you in your descision. Cordialy
Mel Dantzler Sales Manager (92 words)

Exercise 33

SPELLING CHECKUP

Full block style. Mixed punctuation.

Today's date Ms. Sylvia T. Bryant Superintendent Broderick Building
781 Henry Street New York, NY 10006 My dear Ms. Bryant We were
glad to receive your recent letter. ¶We include in our services any and
every kind of cleaning you desire, anywhere in the building. This even
sp includes windows, both inside and outside. Our responsabilities cover
sp hiring a crew of well-trained workpeople and providing all neccesary
sp supplies and equipment. Our supervisers make daily checks of the work
sp performed and submit reports and sugestions. ¶We cannot quote you any
rates until we inspect your premises and determine the exact nature of the
work to be done. We cheerfully furnish estimates without imposing any
obligation on you. The cost of our service is usually considerably less than
sp that of a self-managed staff. We sincerly believe we offer a practical and
economical solution to all your cleaning needs. ¶Please fill out the
sp enclosed postal card. We shall have our representative call imediately to
give you an estimate. Yours very truly John M. McMurray, Manager
xx Enclosure (146 words)

Exercise 34

SPELLING CHECKUP

Full block style. Open punctuation.

Today's date Ms. Eve L. Rivers Credit Manager Reliance Mortgage
Corporation 183 Wharf Street Boston, MA 02118

Dear Ms. Rivers

We are pleased to comply with your request
sp for confedential information concerning our
business dealings with Mr. Robert T. Leyden.

Our records show that in the four years
during which he has dealt with us, he has

(Continued on next page)

Exercise 6

PERSONAL-BUSINESS LETTER

Modified block style. Open punctuation. 5-space paragraph indention. 1 carbon copy. Large envelope. Supply any missing parts of the letter.

Your address / October 1, 19— / Barnett Auto Parts / 960 Carpenter Street / Jackson, MI 49280 / On July 6, I sent your company full payment for a pair of custom mud flaps for my MG. I received my canceled check on July 16, but I didn't receive my order until September 24, even though your catalogue promises delivery within four weeks. ¶When I opened the package, I discovered you had sent me a set of hubcaps for a Lincoln Continental. Not only that, I also received a bill for $78. ¶I am returning the hubcaps and the unpaid bill, and I want you to cancel my original order and return my money. Please do not take as long to return my money as you did to send me the hubcaps. / *Your name* (114 words)

English Editing Alerts

Refer to page 194 for a list and an explanation of the editing alerts shown beside Exercises 7–14. Each symbol will give you a clue as to what kind of error is in that line. Read the copy carefully and locate the errors before you begin to type. *Do not mark the book.*

Exercise 7

PERSONAL NOTE WITH EDITING ALERTS

Half sheet. Insert short side first. Modified block style. Mixed punctuation. 5-space paragraph indention.

Your address / *Today's date* / Dear Aunt Belle, It was very thoughtful of
com you to remember my birthday. I thank you very much for the card the
com sp novel and the good wishes. ¶I have allready started to read the book. It
cap is most interesting. I am really enjoying it. / Yours Sincerely, / *Your name*
(41 words)

Exercise 8

PERSONAL-BUSINESS LETTER WITH EDITING ALERTS

Modified block style. Mixed punctuation. 5-space paragraph indention.

Your address / *Today's date* / The Honorable Max Fentwick / House of
Representatives / Washington, DC 20515 / Dear Mr. Fentwick: I am
com strongly opposed to the building of a new highway, through our congres-
sional district. The construction would be a waste of money and a terrible
sp inconveniance to those whose homes would be destroyed to make way
for the road. I think our tax dollars could be better spent on things such
as improving present roads, building a new library, or adding a park. ¶I
sp incourage you to speak out against this proposed highway. If I can help
cap by writing to other members of Congress, Please let me know. / Sincerely,
/ *Your name.* (89 words)

Exercise 9

PERSONAL-BUSINESS LETTER WITH EDITING ALERTS

Modified block style. Mixed punctuation. 5-space paragraph indention.

Your address / *Today's date* / Kelley Pen Company / 400 Rosemary Circle
sp cap / Pittsburgh, PA 15230 / Ladies and Gentlemen: I recieved your model
ww 200 fountain pen for my birthday. Its a beautiful pen, and I was extremely
happy to receive it. I had the pen in the front pocket of my white work
ro uniform when the pen began leaking this made both me and my uniform blue. My uniform is ruined, and I must buy another to replace it.

(Continued on next page)

Exercise 30
ROUGH DRAFT
Any acceptable letter style.

Mr. Gene M. Campbell 826 Doane Street Sayville, NY 11782

Dear Mr. Campbell

We sincerely regret the mistake that was made in your purchase order No. 7634. We appreciate your willingness to keep the cans shipped in error. Our truck will deliver to you this week the five ~~two~~ 2-gallon cans of White Premium Enamel ~~which~~ that you originally ordered. They will probably have reached you by the time you recieve this letter.

Enclosed is our invoice No. 1288 for the two 5-gallon cans ~~which~~ that were shipped in error. Invoice No. 1253 (for five 2-gallon cans) you have already received.

Yours very truly

Sally F. Harris, Traffic Manager *xx* Enclosure (86 words)

Directions for Exercises 31–36
SPELLING CHECKUPS

The following business letters contain words that are misspelled. Before typing each exercise, find the misspelled word (or words) in each of the lines indicated by *sp* in the left margin. Refer to the Master Spelling Lists on pages 138 and 230, and to a dictionary. Make a list of the correct spellings on a separate piece of paper. Then, type the letter in the style indicated, spelling all the words correctly. *Do not mark the book.*

Exercise 31
SPELLING CHECKUP
Modified block style. Open punctuation. 5-space paragraph indention.

Today's date Clark Appliance Company 270 Bay Street Boston, MA
02107 Ladies and Gentlemen We have an application for credit from Mr.
sp Robert T. Leyden of 44 Front Street. He has refered us to you concerning
sp his record as one of your custamers. ¶He applied for credit with our
company recently. At that time, we ran a credit check through Credit Data
Bureau and received a negative report. Mr. Leyden states that the infor-
sp mation contained in Credit Data's files discribing his payment history is
sp incorrect. ¶We would be greatful for any information you can give us.
sp We are especially intrested to know how much credit you have extended
to him. We assure you that the information you give us will be kept in
sp strict confidance. Yours truely Ms. Eve L. Rivers Credit Manager *xx*
(112 words)

Exercise 9 continued

com ¶Since the malfunction of your pen has caused this problem I believe
that your company should reimburse me for my loss. The cost of the
uniform was $37. I would appreciate your prompt attention in this
matter. / Sincerely, / *Your name* (97 words)

Exercise 10

PERSONAL-BUSINESS LETTER WITH EDITING ALERTS

Full block style. Open punctuation. 1 carbon copy. Small envelope.

Your address / *Today's date* / Mr. Edmundo Oneggo / 1267 Clarity Way /
sp Philadelphia, PA 19138 / Dear Mr. Onego / When I returned home from
com sp work yesterday I was surprized to find a package from you waiting for
ro ww me I didn't expect you too be so prompt in responding to my request
ww to borrow your camera flash unit. The biggest surprise, however, come
ww when I opened the package and discovered you also sent me you best
com telephoto lens! Thanks to your generosity I know my school science
project will be a success. ¶I will be sure to take good care of your equipment
ep ment and return it promptly? I will also send you a few of the pictures
sp from the project and a leter telling you how everything turned out.
Thanks again for your kindness. / Sincerely / *Your name* (116 words)

Exercise 11

PERSONAL-BUSINESS LETTER WITH EDITING ALERTS

Any acceptable letter style. 1 carbon copy. Large envelope.

cap *Your address* / *Today's date* / Mr. Larry Norman, program director /
WARQ-TV / 44 Brock Building / Little Rock, AR 72207 / Dear Mr.
sp Norman / Your station has always been exceptionaly responsive to the
community's needs and wishes. I'm sure I speak for many when I say,
cap "Thank You." ¶Your latest action is a perfect example of responsiveness
sp ep and ture concern for the public you serve, Dropping three programs
ww because they are to violent or demeaning to certain groups shows respon-
sp sibility, courage, and strong principle. I aplaud this action. ¶Your decision may stir protest among some, but I believe it will bring better quality
cap television to the american people. / Sincerely / *Your name* (84 words)

Exercise 12

PERSONAL-BUSINESS LETTER WITH EDITING ALERTS

Any acceptable letter style. 1 carbon copy. Large envelope.

Your address / *Today's date* / Ms. Dawn Mercer / Mercer Travel Agency /
518 Pierazzi Street / Tacoma, WA 98438 / Dear Ms. Mercer / My family
cap and I are considering a vacation in your state in august and september.
sp We are totally unfamilir with the area and would like to get some ideas
ww cap fore an interesting trip. Our family is especially interested in american
com ww history swimming, and water skiing, so a trip to a recreational lake or a
ww ro historical sight might be appropriate we are open to other ideas, however.
sp ¶Please send us any information on tours or travel packages which mihgt
frag suit our needs. Your prompt attention will be appreciated. Because we
need to make our final plans within the next four weeks. / Sincerely /
Your name (100 words)

Exercise 29
ROUGH DRAFT
Any acceptable letter style.

The Ryder Theater 710 Lane Street St. Joseph, MO 64506

Ladies and Gentlemen

If you are having problems with your present heating system and are tired of paying those high fuel bills each month let Phoenix Solar Systems help you cut your heating costs!

In the past 12 months we have installed solar heating units in eight public buildings, including motion picture houses. These units were installed to supplement existing conventional heating systems. The solar unit takes over whenever sunlight falls on the panels and it automatically shuts down your other heating system. Many of our customers report savings of over 60 percent on their fuel bills this year—and that's in spite of two rate increases in the past eight months.

The enclosed phamphlet describes how solar heat works and describes our most popular units. If you would like more information please fill out the postal card at the back of the pamphlet.

Sincerely yours

Stanley T. Foxx, President *xx* Enclosure (147 words)

SECTION THREE

Typing for Vocational Use

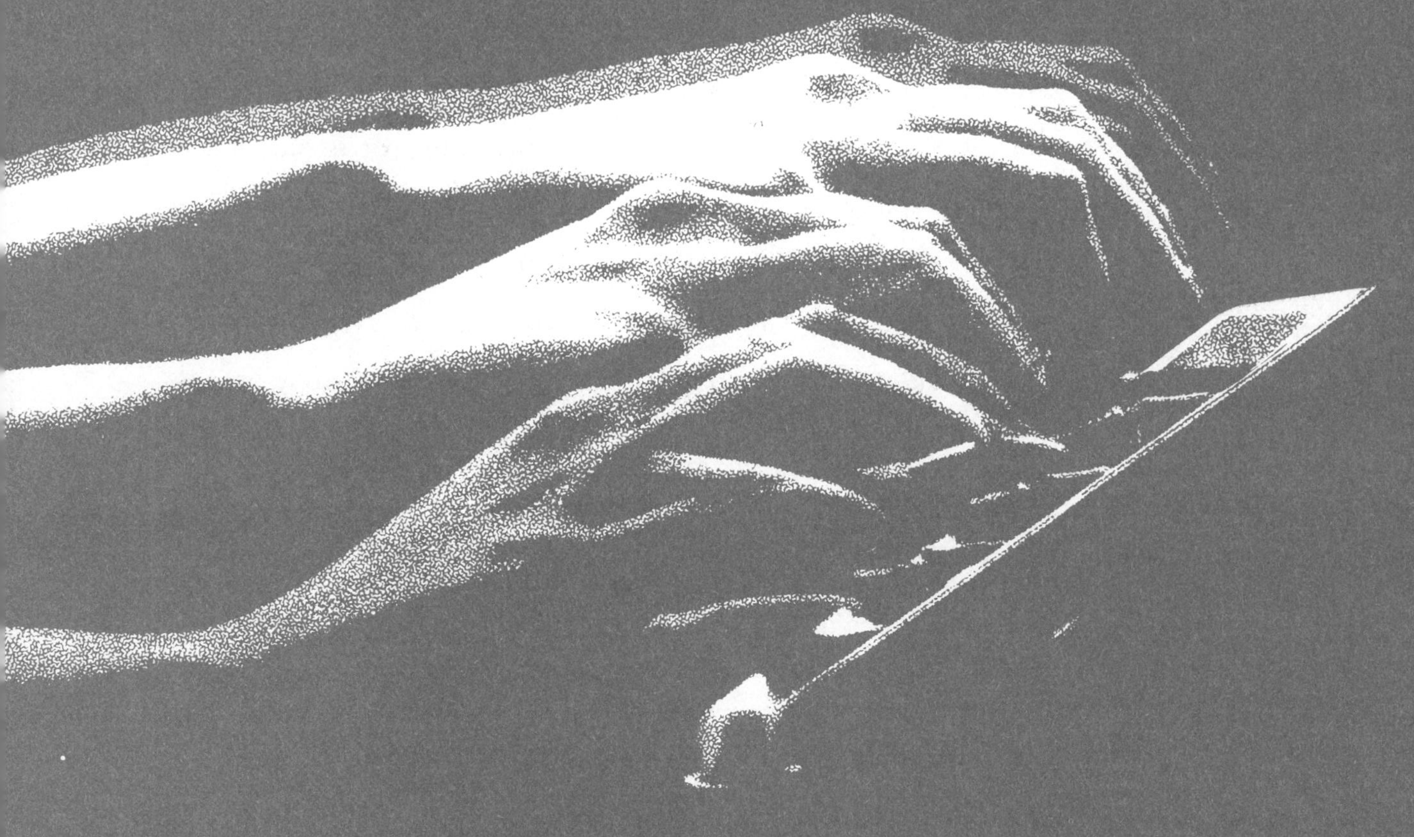

Exercise 27
ROUGH DRAFT
Any acceptable letter style.

Mr. James L. Dalton 692 Fourth Avenue Wilmington, DE 19808

Dear Sir

Since you have not yet received the watch we repaired for you and mailed almost 2 weeks ago, we must assume that it was lost in the mail. We have asked the post office to trace it. Thw watch was insured for $60 dollars (it's list price). If it is not recovered, we shall send you a check for the ammount less our repair costs. We hope this adjustment will be satisfactory.

Sincerely

Otis Simms, Manager SMB/*xx* (76 words)

Exercise 28
ROUGH DRAFT
Any acceptable letter style.

Miller Advertising, Inc. 42 West Jason Avenue New York, NY 10064

Dear Mr. Miller

Along with this letter are enclosed our first thoughts on our "Keep Cool This Summer" ad campaign that I already discussed with you. The ideas we want to stand out have been circled in red ink. Since it's your business to know what people find appealing, I leave all the rest of the design up to you.

When you have some rough sketches and copy ready, give me a call. Then I can confirm your ideas and give the "go-ahead" on the campaign. Since we have to run the first ads in 2 weeks, there is little time remaining.

Thanks so much.

Cordially

Penny Maxwell, Advertising Manager *xx* Enclosure (103 words)

PART 1

STYLE GUIDELINES

This section includes information on rules of English usage that are needed by typists, writers, secretaries, word processing specialists, and anyone else who works with words. These rules are intended to cover only the problems most commonly encountered in nontechnical typing. For a more thorough treatment of this subject, refer to a good style manual or office handbook.

Topic 1 GUIDELINES FOR TYPING NUMBERS

Figures, rather than words, are generally preferred to express numbers in business typing. This is especially true in typing forms and tables. There are, however, many occasions when numbers are expressed in words to conform with accepted customs of English usage. The following rules cover the more common problems you will encounter in expressing numbers. For a complete guide to typing numbers, refer to a style manual or office handbook.

Rule 1. Spell out exact numbers from zero through ten. Use figures for all others.

- *two desks* • *ten copies* • *15 pens*

Rule 2. Treat all related numbers the same way within a paragraph. If any of the related numbers is above ten, use figures for all.

The secretary ordered 5 staplers, 10 desk calendars, and 24 typewriter ribbons. Her two colleagues ordered 8 tablets as well.

Rule 3. Spell out numbers that represent approximate quantities but use figures for exact amounts.

- *The plant employs about five hundred workers.*
- *The stadium can seat 27,410 spectators.*

Exercise 25
SPECIAL CHALLENGE LETTER
Any acceptable letter style.

The date of this letter is **May 27, 19—**. The dictator is **Don Brody, Personnel Interviewer.** Address a small envelope and fold and insert the letter. Supply any missing letter parts.

Mr. James McCarthy 12047 Woodingham Gary, IN 46416 I received your letter and resume inquiring about job openings for clerk-typists in our company. We are now accepting applications from qualified individuals for entry-level positions that will be vacant in late June. These positions require no business experience. ¶Your clerical skills and the courses you have taken in the business area appear to meet the minimum qualifications for the jobs in question. In addition, your letter of inquiry and fine resume speak well of your formatting and typing skills. I am therefore placing your correspondence in our applicants file. ¶If you are still interested in working here after you graduate in June, please telephone me at 556-1780, Extension 114. I would like to arrange an appointment for you to come in to take our typing and clerical aptitude tests. You can also complete our job application form at that time. (134 words)

Directions for Exercises 26–30

As you type the next five business letters, make all the corrections indicated. If you need to refresh your memory of the proofreaders' marks, refer to pages 92 and 93. Use today's date for all the exercises, and include your reference initials. These letters are to be set up in any acceptable style, but be sure to vary the styles.

Exercise 26
ROUGH DRAFT
Any acceptable letter style.

Mrs. Isabel T. Johnson 80 Park Lane Cincinnati, OH 54216

Dear Mrs. Johnson

We ~~'re~~ *are* sorry *that* the table we sent to your home was delivered in such poor condition. All furniture manufactured by our firm is approved by our quality control inspection division *(as indicated by the attached inspection tag)* ~~(note attached tag)~~ prior to shipment. ~~and~~ *The goods are then* packaged with great care. The damage was probably caused by careless handling by the freight company ~~which~~ *that* delivered the table.

We will send an expert cabinetmaker to your home, ~~He~~ *who* will make the repairs to your satisfaction. There will be no charge for this service. *If you will call me at 891-7800,* I will personally make all the arrangements. ~~My phone number is 891-7800~~.

Yours very truly

Loretta Berman Sales Manager *xx* (105 words)

Rule 4. Spell out a number when it begins a sentence.

- *Twenty people applied for the job.*

Rule 5. Spell out the smaller of two numbers that come together as part of the same construction.

- *three 15-cent stamps* • *20 two-story buildings.*

Rule 6. Spell out the hour when *o'clock* is used.

- *eleven o'clock*

Rule 7. Spell out numbers for most time periods, but use figures to express exact quantities.

- *I'll be back in twenty minutes.* • *The train will leave in 18 minutes.*

Rule 8. Spell out ordinal numbers, except when part of a date.

- *third fourth twentieth*
- *12th of May* BUT: *May 12*

Rule 9. Spell out simple fractions, but use figures for quantities made up of a whole number and a fraction.

- *one-half mile three-quarters cup*
- *6½ feet*

Rule 10. Use figures: (1) to express sums of money when the dollar sign is used; (2) to express percentages; (3) with abbreviations and symbols; (4) to express measurements; (5) to express numbers in an address; and (6) to express numbers that identify buildings, rooms, pages, flights, documents, and so forth.

- *I paid $8 for a front-row seat.*
- *Ken owes me five dollars.*
- *The interest rate on city bonds rose to 8 percent.*
- *#3 12 doz. 7 a.m. 26¢*
- *She is 5 feet 4 inches tall.*
- *103 Russell Street*
- *Passengers for Flight 9 should go to Room 405 for customs inspection.*
- *Use Form 1053a to file the S.E.C. report.*

Exercise 1

NUMBER STYLE

Review Rules 1–10 on business style for typing numbers. These sentences show correct application of these rules. Type each sentence once.

Half sheet. 60-space line. Single spacing. Center title on line 7 and TS after it.

NUMBER STYLE GUIDE: ONE

1. Our office has eight new employees.
2. She has 24 tropical fish, 4 dogs, and 2 cats.
3. About five hundred members are expected to attend.
4. Four persons were on vacation in July.
5. You must pass 12 five-minute timings during the school year.
6. He will arrive at six o'clock this evening.
7. Roger studied piano for five years.
8. Your first payment is due on the 12th of the month.
9. The table measures 6¼ feet by 5½ feet.
10. She formerly lived at 5900 Fifth Avenue.

Exercise 22 continued

new machinery, and enlarged our labor force. Now we are in a position to 72
produce a much larger quantity of hardcover and paperback bindings than in 87
the past. ¶Frankly, our problem is this: Until additional orders come in from 102
our increased staff of sales representatives, some of our machinery will be 117
idle. To meet this situation, we are offering a 25 percent price reduction on 133
orders placed within the next 30 days. ¶If you will send us your specifications, 149
we shall quickly submit quotations. Sincerely yours Ivan Stanislaus Sales 164
Manager *xx* (114 words) 166

Exercise 23

Any acceptable letter style.

February 19, 19— Mr. Thomas S. Burke 11532 Meyers Street Allentown, PA 14
18141 Dear Mr. Burke I am pleased to announce a new program of personal 28
accident insurance. It will provide AUTOMATIC protection for all dues- 42
paying members of the Communication Workers of America, AFL-CIO (CWA). 56
Each member's coverage (at no additional cost) will be effective one month 71
following the date of membership in the CWA local. ¶Coverage of $5,000 is 86
provided against accidental death and dismemberment. An extra $5,000 will 101
be paid if accidental death occurs on a common carrier. The master policy 116
with details of the policy coverage will be on file at the national CWA office. 132
The insurance carrier is IMA Life Insurance Company of New York. ¶In order 147
to let you name a beneficiary on your policy immediately, we have enclosed 162
an enrollment form. Please complete the form and send it to your local 177
CWA office. Fraternally yours Kenneth J. Kagler Executive Secretary *xx* 190
Enclosure (136 words) 192

Exercise 24

SPECIAL CHALLENGE LETTER

Any acceptable letter style.

Use today's date for this letter. The dictator is Herbert L. Edmundson, President. Note that an enclosure is mentioned in the first paragraph. Address a large envelope and fold and insert the letter. Supply any missing letter parts.

Bennett Engineering Works World Headquarters 30 Reynolds Circle Amityville, NY 11106 We are enclosing a folder explaining how our Fairview Lights meet all the requirements of modern lighting. ¶ The importance of lighting in factories and offices is being widely acknowledged today. It has an important influence on the health of employees and on the quality of work that they do. To be most effective, lighting must be of the right intensity and in the right position. Here, our expert knowledge can be of great value to you. ¶We suggest that you have one of our consultants survey your existing lighting system. The consultant can determine whether your system is the best one for your workers and the kind of work they do. Careful consideration will be given to such points as the location of machines, the position of the operators, and the kinds of work done. ¶We perform this consulting service without charge. Let us also assure you that any recommendations we make are offered in your best interests. (158 words)

Exercise 2

These sentences show correct application of Rule 10 on business style for typing numbers. Type each sentence once.

Half sheet. 60-space line. Single spacing. Center title on line 7 and TS after it.

NUMBER STYLE GUIDE: TWO

1. She is 5 feet 2 inches tall.
2. Turn to page 7 in your textbook.
3. The charge on the shipment was 79¢.
4. The interest charge on extended payment accounts is 18 percent.
5. The suit now sells for $53.
6. That blender, Stock #7562, is on special order.
7. Janet saved thirty dollars on the carpet installation.
8. A check for $5.35 is enclosed.
9. The bank paid 5 percent interest, compounded daily.
10. We had to report for registration at 9 a.m.

Exercise 3

NUMBER STYLE

Type these sentences, inserting the number in parentheses in the space where the colored mark appears. Decide, according to Rules 1–10, whether to use figures or words. *Do not mark the book.*

Full sheet. 70-space line. Double spacing. Center title on line 13 and TS after it.

NUMBER STYLE GUIDE: THREE

1. I am the youngest of ■ children. (3)
2. ■ students went on the field trip. (60)
3. My favorite TV program begins at ■ o'clock. (9)
4. The basketball star was ■ feet tall. (7)
5. Our state has a ■ percent tax on sales. (4)
6. This is her ■ job in the past two years. (5th)
7. We drove ■ miles on our vacation trip. (3,500)
8. Plan to return on the ■ of July. (12th)
9. Please buy ■ two-cent stamps. (35)
10. The stadium is only ■ full. (2/3)

Key to Exercise 3

1. three 2. Sixty 3. nine 4. 7 5. 4 6. fifth
7. 3,500 8. 12th 9. 35 10. two-thirds

Topic 2 GUIDELINES FOR TYPING ABBREVIATIONS

For the sake of clarity, abbreviations should be used sparingly in business correspondence. When in doubt, spell out words. When you do abbreviate, use the standard forms listed in a dictionary. Be consistent in the abbreviations you do use.

There are some general rules you can follow when using abbreviations:

Rule 1. Always abbreviate the titles Mr., Mrs., Ms., Messrs., and Dr. before a name. Spell out other titles when they are used with only a last name. Note that the title Miss does not require a period.

- *Governor Greene*
- *Mayor Mahoney*
- *Dr. Harriet Washington*
- *Ms. Yee*
- *Captain Hale*
- *Colonel McGuiness*

Exercise 20
Full block style. Open punctuation.

Today's date / Messrs. J. R. Tobin and P. T. Ford / T&F Equipment 13
Leasing / 1501 Jackson Street / Seattle, WA 98108 22

Gentlemen 24
We regret to inform you that we cannot accept 33
a cancellation of your order for 500 notebooks 43
imprinted with your company's name. 50
Inasmuch as the printing has been completed, 59
the notebooks are of no value to anyone else 68
except as scrap. We must, therefore, insist upon 78
your acceptance of them in accordance with 87
the terms agreed upon in our contract. 95
Cordially yours 98

K. S. Fields, Manager / *xx* (60 words) 104

Directions for Exercises 21–25

Type the following exercises using a variety of acceptable letter styles. Note that in all exercise letters from this point until the end of Topic 1, line breaks for the opening and closing parts are not indicated. You are to decide yourself how these parts are to be set up.

Exercises 24 and 25 are Special Challenge Letters. You must supply the opening and closing parts. Remember to add your initials as reference initials.

Exercise 21
Any acceptable letter style.

October 12, 19— David Margulies, Manager Ko-Zee Motel 3610 Page Street 14
Beckley, WV 25801 Dear Mr. Margulies Three months ago, we shipped you 28
six dozen monogrammed bath towels and ten dozen hand towels. ¶On that 41
particular order, we had used a special material for making the monograms. 56
We would appreciate it if you would send us a note telling us how the material 72
has endured with constant use. In return for your sending us this information, 88
we will send you a set of six of our best-quality water tumblers. Thank you. 103
Sincerely Rick Davis, Marketing Manager *xx* (75 words) 111

Exercise 22
Any acceptable letter style.

December 9, 19— Mr. Henry F. Akioto Van Dyke Publishing Company 1057 14
Walnut Street Salt Lake City, UT 84101 Dear Mr. Akioto We have a problem 28
that we think you can help us solve, and, by doing so, you can save your 42
company money. ¶We have recently leased additional floor space, installed 57

(Continued on next page)

Rule 2. Do not abbreviate such words as *Street* or *Avenue* unless you must save space, as on an envelope or in a list.

- *613 Grand Avenue*

Rule 3. Spell out words indicating direction in street addresses, such as *East* or *West.* Abbreviations are acceptable on envelopes.

- *29 West Main Street*
- *8534 North Highland Parkway*

Rule 4. Abbreviate academic degrees, professional designations, and *Junior* or *Senior* when they follow the name. (Be careful not to use two titles that have the same meaning. It is *incorrect* to write *Dr.* John V. Brown, *M.D.*)

- *Hedley J. Burke, Jr.*
- *Hilda J. Lyons, C.P.A.*
- *Jack Robbins, Ph.D.*

Rule 5. Spell out names of localities, days of the week, and months of the year in formal writing.

- *October*
- *New York*
- *Wednesday*

Rule 6. Abbreviate the word *Saint* when it is part of an address or a place name.

- *2976 St. Stephens Drive*
- *St. Paul, Minnesota*

Rule 7. Abbreviate the words *Number* and *Numbers* when they precede a figure.

- *Model No. 880*
- *Model Nos. 880 and 881*

Rule 8. Abbreviate words such as *Company, Incorporated,* and *Corporation* only when they are abbreviated on the company's letterhead.

- *General Motors Corporation*
- *Macmillan, Inc.*

Rule 9. Do not space after periods within abbreviations made up of the first letters of two or more words.

- *Ph.D.*
- *M.D.*
- *F.O.B.*

However, space once after the periods in the initials of a person's name.

- *Mr. R. M. Stone*

You may omit periods in abbreviations that stand for an organization's name or a country.

- *USA USSR YMCA NBC NASA*

Rule 10. Always use the two-letter state abbreviations in addresses on letters and envelopes. When an address occurs within a sentence, however, the name of the state should be spelled out. If the ZIP Code is also included in a sentence, one space should be left between it and the name of the state.

Rule 11. Avoid using symbols and abbreviations in business letters and other general writing.

- *Use percent instead of %.*
- *Use equals instead of =.*
- *Use hour instead of hr.*
- *Use cents instead of ¢*
- *Use number instead of #.*
- *Use pound instead of lb.*

You may use symbols and abbreviations, however, in tables, in such business forms as invoices and purchase orders, and in technical writing when these units are used with figures.

Exercise 18
Full block style. Mixed punctuation.

March 14, 19— / Mr. and Mrs. Charles Olsen / 3057 Outer Drive / Saginaw, 13
MI 48611 / Dear Mr. and Mrs. Olsen / Spring is indeed welcome this year, and 27
we are already thinking about your lawn. First, we would like to thank you for 43
last year's business. Second, we would like to include you in this year's pro- 59
gram. ¶We are pleased to announce that our prices per treatment are the same 74
as last year's. We have enclosed the monthly breakdown for your summer 88
program. Your payment is due only as the monthly treatments are completed. 103
You might, however, want to take advantage of the discounted prepayment 117
offer. ¶Please sign the enclosed schedule and send it back in the self-addressed 133
envelope. Then relax—your lawn-feeding and weed-control chores belong to 148
us. / Sincerely / Miss Doris Ingram, President / *xx* / Enclosures (111 words) 159

Exercise 19
Full block style. Open punctuation.

Today's date / Mr. Ralph T. Furman / Assistant Merchandise Manager / 13
L. M. Robbins Company / 68 Wakefield Road / Kansas City, KS 66104 25

Dear Mr. Furman 28
Andrew J. Rockland has applied for a 36
position with our company as a clerk-typist. 44
He has given us your name as a ref- 52
erence. 55
We would like to have confirmation 63
from you of the dates of his employment with 71
your firm. In addition, we would be grateful 80
for any comments you may have concerning 89
his job performance, his abilities, and his 99
character. We would especially like to 107
know whether you found his work satis- 115
factory and whether he had a good atten- 124
dance record while in your employ. 130
Your reply will be kept in strict confidence. 139
Sincerely 141

Carl Avery / Personnel Interviewer / *xx* (95 words) 148

Exercise 1
ABBREVIATIONS

Type this list of common business abbreviations.

Half sheet. Double spacing. Spaces between columns are 4, 8, and 4. Center vertically and horizontally. Center title on line 7 and TS after it.

SOME COMMON BUSINESS ABBREVIATIONS

acct., a/c	account	int.	interest
amt.	amount	inv.	invoice
bal.	balance	mgr.	manager
C.O.D.	cash on delivery	mdse.	merchandise
c/o	care of	Messrs.	plural of Mr.
cat.	catalog	misc.	miscellaneous
cr.	credit	mtg.	mortgage
dr.	debit	pd.	paid
dept.	department	recd.	received
F.O.B.	free on board	wt.	weight

Exercise 2
ABBREVIATIONS

These sentences show correct application of Rules 1–11. Type each sentence once.

Half sheet. 70-space line. Double spacing. Center title on line 6 and TS after it.

ABBREVIATION STYLE GUIDE: ONE

1. I saw President Reagan when he campaigned in our town.
2. My summer address is 234 Lasher Street.
3. I recently moved to 76 North Maple Road.
4. His heir, William Ford, Jr., was present for the reading of the will.
5. The convention was held on the last Thursday in September.
6. She graduated from St. Gerard School in 1978.
7. Area No. 7 is our sales territory in Maine.
8. The clerical employees at Falvey Company are on strike.
9. My sister will receive her Ph.D. in June.
10. Send the bill to 12 Pine Street, Salem, Oregon 97302.
11. Eighty percent of the employees were female.

Exercise 3
ABBREVIATIONS

Type these sentences, inserting the information in parentheses where the colored square appears. Decide according to Rules 1–11, whether to use an abbreviation or spell out the word. *Do not mark the book.*

Full sheet. 70-space line. Double spacing. Center title on line 13 and TS after it.

ABBREVIATION STYLE GUIDE: TWO

1. Our manager, ■ Ryan, will retire in March. (Ms.)
2. She went to visit her sister in Los Angeles, ■. (Calif.)
3. I remember living at 37 Chestnut ■ when I was a child. (Ave.)
4. My insurance Policy, ■ 113-467, will mature next year. (No.)
5. There has been a 5 ■ increase in the price of silver. (%)
6. Have you been to ■ Louis, Missouri? (St.)
7. Gene King, ■, won the lottery prize last week. (Sr.)
8. Wednesday, ■ 12 is our absolute deadline. (Aug.)
9. She is manager of the Wilson ■ branch in Dallas. (Co.)
10. ■ Millben will not run for office in this year's election. (Gov.)
11. In one ■, the messenger will pick up the package. (hr.)

Key to Exercise 3

1. Ms. 2. California 3. Avenue 4. No. 5. percent 6. St.
7. Sr. 8. August 9. Company 10. Governor 11. hour

Exercise 14 continued

the line of machinery you offer for use in wheel alignment and brake service 102
will be extremely helpful to us. We are open to all options, including the use 118
of rebuilt or used equipment. ¶Thank you for your kind assistance in this 133
matter. / Cordially / Andrew Jost / President / *xx* (104 words) 142

Exercise 15

Full block style. Open punctuation.

Today's date / Manhattan Paint Company / 503 West 14th Street / New York, 14
NY 10009 / Ladies and Gentlemen / There was an error made on your recent 28
shipment to us. Our Purchase Order No. 7634 called for five 2-gallon cans of 43
White Premium Enamel. Instead, you sent us two 5-gallon cans. ¶We are able 58
to use the cans you sent; so we will keep them. However, please ship the five 74
2-gallon cans that we originally requested as soon as possible. A customer has 90
ordered them for a job he must begin shortly. / Yours truly / Gene M. 103
Campbell, Manager / *xx* (75 words) 107

Exercise 16

Full block style. Open punctuation.

June 14, 19– / Mr. Howard Leyton / 711 Plaza Building / 834 Third Avenue / 13
Little Rock, AR 72201 / Dear Mr. Leyton / We shall, of course, comply with 27
your request to cancel your life insurance policy if you wish it. We urge you, 43
however, to reconsider. If you decide to take out another policy later, you will 59
have to pay a higher premium. You will also have to undergo a physical exam- 74
ination. ¶We hope you will be able to meet with our representative for your 89
area, Ms. Goldman. She can discuss with you the possibility of converting 104
your present policy into one that better suits your present needs. Ms. Goldman 120
will telephone you to arrange a convenient appointment. We hope that you 135
will consider her information carefully in making your final decision. / Yours 150
sincerely / Ms. Marilyn P. Young / Branch Administrator / *xx* (108 words) 162

Exercise 17

Full block style. Open punctuation.

January 24, 19– / Drummond Brothers / 189 Linton Avenue / Scranton, 12
PA 18502 / Gentlemen / Since we always try to please our customers, we are 26
glad to make an adjustment such as you request. Since your present payment 41
date is not convenient for you, another arrangement can be made to our 55
mutual satisfaction. ¶ Unfortunately, we cannot vary our cash discount 69
period. The reason is that we feel it is only fair to give all our customers the 85
same time limit. We can, however, arrange to send your monthly statements 100
on the 15th of the month. They will cover all transactions from the 16th of 115
the preceding month. This will entitle you to our cash discount if payment 130
is made no later than the 25th. ¶Please let us know whether you wish us to 145
make this change. / Cordially yours / David L. Foster / Credit Manager / 158
xx (108 words) 159

Topic 3 GUIDELINES FOR TYPING METRIC UNITS

The National Bureau of Standards has set standards to aid our transition to the metric system. The metric system is formally called the International System of Units. Our conversion to it will require some changes in the style we use for typing numbers. Here are the rules you are most likely to need in daily use of the metric system.

Rule 1.
CAPITALIZATION

a. Use lowercase letters for all metric units, unless they begin a sentence. Exception: a metric unit that comes from the name of a person is always capitalized. (Celsius, for example, was the person who created the metric unit for measuring temperature.)

- *They walked 25 kilometers.*
- *It was 18 degrees Celsius on graduation day.*

b. Use lowercase letters for most metric symbols.

- g *for gram*
- kg *for kilogram*
- mg *for milligram*
- m *for meter*
- cm *for centimeter*
- mm *for millimeter*

There are three exceptions to this rule: (a) Use a capital L to symbolize liter, since a lowercase l might be confused with the numeral 1; (b) capitalize the symbol for a metric unit that comes from the name of a person; and (c) capitalize the symbol for a metric term that stands for a million or more.

- L *for liter*
- C *for Celsius*
- kH *for kiloHertz*
- Mc *for megacycle*

Rule 2.
PLURALS

a. Use plurals only when the quantity expressed is zero, greater than one, or less than minus one.

- *0 degrees Celsius*
- *1 degree Celsius*
- *−5 degrees Celsius*

b. Symbols for metric units do not add *s* to form plurals.

- *250 mL for 250 milliliters (not mLs)*
- *15 kg for 15 kilograms (not kgs)*

Rule 3.
SPACING

a. Leave one space between a number and a metric symbol.

- *7* m
- *33.4* kg

b. Leave one space—not a comma—between groups of numbers in the thousands, on either side of the decimal point.

- *7 540 321, not 7,540,321*
- *0.613 75, not 0.61375*

c. Do not leave a space between the degree symbol (°) and the symbol for Celsius (C).

- *20°* C

Rule 4.
PERIOD AND DECIMAL POINT

a. Do not use a period after a metric symbol, except at the end of a sentence. Examples:

- *15* cm
- *3* kg

b. Use the dot (or period) as a decimal point within numbers. In numbers less than one, type a zero before the decimal point.

- *0.38*

Directions for Exercises 11–20

Following the letter style shown in Model 9, type the letters in these exercises in full block style. Use the Letter Placement Chart on page 197 to determine the proper margins and position of the date line. Substitute your own initials for the *xx* at the end of each letter.

Exercise 11

Full block style. Open punctuation.

March 10, 19– / June Gibson, Financial Manager / Good Heart Charities / Box 2000 / Concord, NH 03301 / Dear Miss Gibson / Our company is preparing tax returns and financial statements for Goetz Brothers Manufacturing of St. Louis. ¶In reviewing our records, we have discovered that you failed to send Goetz Brothers a statement of contributions for the first and third quarters of last year. We cannot complete our work until we receive those statements. Your prompt attention to this matter would be most appreciated. / Sincerely / Dennis Brendel / Accountant / *xx* (63 words)

Exercise 12

Full block style. Open punctuation.

Today's date / Ms. Judith Nilsson / Computer Equipment Company / Housing Division / 305 Canton Road / San Diego, CA 92109 / Dear Ms. Nilsson / We are happy to submit a bid on installing a new heating and air conditioning system in your facility. The specifications you have outlined are receiving our careful attention. ¶We will want to send a representative to inspect the premises shortly, and we will call you to make an appointment. Our estimate will be completed within a week after the inspection. We can assure you that our materials and workmanship will meet the highest standards. / Cordially / Philip P. Logan, President / *xx* (75 words)

Exercise 13

Full block style. Open punctuation.

August 8, 19– / National Calculators, Inc. / 84 Cyril Street / Rochester, NY 14617 / Ladies and Gentlemen / Several weeks ago we purchased three dozen pocket electronic calculators from you. At that time, you offered us some attractive window posters. We did not believe that we could make use of them, and so we did not accept your offer. ¶We now find, however, that we have a place for two of these posters. Will you please send them to us as soon as possible? We are sure they will help to increase our sales of the calculators. / Sincerely / Ms. I. A. Golden / Store Manager / *xx* (79 words)

Exercise 14

Full block style. Mixed punctuation.

February 10, 19– / Minnesota Machines / 4100 Simmons Road / Duluth, 12
MN 55807 / Gentlemen / Until now, our small tire shop has specialized in 25
the sale of tires exclusively. At this time, we are considering expanding our 41
operations to include related services. We are especially interested in adding 57
wheel alignment and brake service. ¶We would like a representative from 71
your company to visit us or to give us a call at (218) 762-8196. A knowledge of 87

(Continued on next page)

Rule 5.
COMPOUND UNITS

a. Type square or cubic symbols with raised numbers.

- *8* `cm`^{2} *for 8 square centimeters* • *9* `cm`^{3} *for 9 cubic centimeters*

b. Use the term "per" to form compound units spelled out. Use the diagonal to stand for "per" in the symbols for compound units.

- `m/s` *for meters per second* • `km/h` *for kilometers per hour*

Exercise 1
METRIC STYLE

Type these sentences to gain practice in expressing amounts in metric terms.

Half sheet. 70-space line. Double spacing. Begin on line 6.

1. The small box measured 9.4 cm by 7.6 cm by 5.2 cm.
2. The lengths of the chains are 1.50 m, 2.20 m, and 3.50 m.
3. It takes a jet four hours to fly from Phoenix to New York, at an average air speed of 963 kilometers per hour (km/h).
4. Of this amount, $14 329 was spent for nonbusiness purposes.
5. What will the carpet cost if it sells at $14.50 per m^2?
6. It's a hot day when the mercury hits 32°C.
7. The jug of milk holds 3 L; the container of butter weighs 0.5 kg.
8. The old saying now goes, "Give them a centimeter and they'll take a kilometer."
9. Sandra's prescription is for 200 milliliters of cough medicine.
10. Driving home, we traveled over 1 600 km in two days.

Exercise 2
METRIC STYLE

Follow the directions given for Exercise 1.

1. The cake recipe called for an oven setting of 160°C.
2. Water freezes at 0°C and boils at 100°C on the Celsius scale.
3. The large size weighs 1.25 kg and sells for 99 cents.
4. The letter I mailed today weighed 28 g.
5. The living room measures 9 m by 5 m.
6. The cubic meter (m^3) is the base unit for measuring volume.
7. The swimming pool is 15 m long, 9 m wide, and 3 m deep.
8. Soft drinks now come in 1-liter (L) bottles.
9. The measuring cup shows that 250 mL equal 8 fluid ounces.

Topic 4 REVIEW OF ENGLISH EDITING SKILLS

Study the words given in the Master Spelling List, Part 2 (page 230), in groups of fives or tens. Then type the words from dictation daily for a week. Take a test on them at the end of the week. Work to add this list of words to those you are able to spell accurately. Watch out for these words (and the words in the first spelling study list on page 138) as you type assignments that are given in unedited form.

A good command of spelling is an asset for any office worker. Equipment is constantly being improved to increase efficiency in processing paperwork; you, too, should expect to increase your skills steadily during your working years. If you have learned the basics of English grammar, punctuation, and spelling, you need not fear being replaced by a machine; there is always a demand for office workers who have good language skills.

Letterhead	**ALBURY'S** **WHOLE-GRAIN CEREAL, INC.** 34 Virginia Avenue, New Orleans, La. 70122 (504) 525-3611	
		Words
Date line	February 17, 19--	4
	Space down 4 times	
Inside address	Mrs. Alberta Bonnard	8
	109 Crippen Avenue	12
	Baton Rouge, LA 70807	16
	DS	
Salutation	Dear Mrs. Bonnard	20
	DS	
	We are pleased to send you a copy of our booklet, THE CARE OF	32
	CHILDREN. It offers many practical suggestions to help you	44
	in looking after the daily needs of infants and small children.	57
	DS	
	For more than thirty years, nutritionists have recommended our	70
Body	whole-grain cereal as one of the first solid foods that babies	83
	may have and as the hot breakfast cereal for every growing	95
	child. Adults, too, find Albury's Whole-Grain Cereal nourish-	108
	ing and delicious.	112
	DS	
	We hope that you will try some of the excellent recipes sug-	124
	gested in the booklet. They add variety and good nutrition	136
	to the daily menu and are easy and economical to prepare.	148
	DS	
Complimentary closing	Sincerely yours	151
Signature	Paul T. Daly — Space down 4 times	
Typed name and title of sender	Paul T. Daly, President	156
	DS	
Dictator's and typist's initials	MVT:xx	157
	DS	
	Enclosure	159

(Shown in Elite Type)

Model 9 *Business Letter • Full Block Style with Open Punctuation*

MASTER SPELLING LIST—PART 2

1 addresses	26 enclosure	51 interview	76 recognize
2 advertise	27 engagement	52 jewelry	77 referring
3 angle	28 enough	53 leisurely	78 regular
4 argument	29 especially	54 library	79 responsibility
5 association	30 exhibit	55 losing	80 restaurant
6 authorized	31 experienced	56 manager	81 secretary
7 bargain	32 familiar	57 marital	82 sincerely
8 bookkeeper	33 February	58 merchandise	83 specialize
9 calculate	34 finalize	59 mileage	84 specifically
10 career	35 financial	60 misspell	85 statistics
11 celebration	36 fiscal	61 mortgage	86 stepping
12 churches	37 foreign	62 ninety	87 strength
13 clerical	38 forward	63 ninth	88 studying
14 column	39 fulfill	64 paid	89 suggestion
15 conferring	40 gentlemen	65 pamphlets	90 superintendent
16 congratulate	41 government	66 permitted	91 supervise
17 consumer	42 graduation	67 physical	92 therefore
18 cooperation	43 grammar	68 probably	93 thirtieth
19 corporation	44 grateful	69 profited	94 thorough
20 criticize	45 guarantee	70 prompt	95 twelfth
21 definitely	46 happiness	71 quality	96 twentieth
22 desirable	47 height	72 quantity	97 using
23 dessert	48 incorporated	73 questionnaire	98 Wednesday
24 duplicate	49 individual	74 quite	99 weird
25 eighth	50 interest	75 receptionist	100 writing

Exercise 1

PUNCTUATION AND CAPITALIZATION REVIEW

As you type these sentences, make any necessary corrections in punctuation and capitalization.

Full sheets. 70-space line. Double spacing. Begin on line 10.

Comma

1. You want a comfortable home good food and time for recreation.
2. In another ten years in fact we shall be firmly established.
3. We know the shipment was wrong but we are puzzled about the error.
4. They complain of poor housing poor water supply and few stores.
5. I believe therefore that we are not responsible.

(Continued on next page)

Exercise 10 continued

M & R Trucking, Daniels Bottling, Ourston Auto Customizing, or Minkelson's Toys. Enclosed are copies of these and other logos we have created.

Many of the firms now using our logos have reported positive customer reaction to our designs. Several of our clients have written us letters to tell us of improved name recognition that has resulted from use of a logo.

We believe your business deserves the chance to get one step ahead of the competition. We will be glad to visit your office and explain the services we offer. If you prefer, you may visit our offices at any time to inspect our work firsthand.

Cordially

Rebecca LeBret / Art Director / *xx* / Enclosures (129 words)

Drill D
TYPING MODEL 9

Type the letter shown in Model 9 on the following page. If letterhead stationery is not available, use a plain sheet. Follow the spacing instructions given in the model. Determine the proper margins and position of the date line by referring to the Letter Placement Chart. Type your initials in place of *xx*. The body of the letter contains 109 words.

Drill E
OPENING PARTS OF MODEL 9

Type the beginning of the letter shown in Model 9 to see how far you can type in 3 minutes. Use the date line placement and margin settings determined for Drill D. Repeat the drill until you can type the opening parts of this letter without hesitation.

Drill F
CLOSING PARTS OF MODEL 9

Type the letter shown in Model 9 starting with the last paragraph. Use the same margins you set for Drill D. Try to finish the letter in 3 minutes. Repeat the drill until you can type the closing parts of this letter without hesitation.

Exercise 1 continued

6. Our superintendent Mr. Walker graduated from Fisk University.
7. When your supply is low please telephone our order department.
8. She gave us some wise sound advice.
9. My newest book Along the Way is a novel.
10. Sgt. Riley Sgt. Holmes and Sgt. Fisher were promoted recently.

Semicolon

11. The neighborhood was poor the house was old the room was small.
12. The change has been beneficial for us it has also helped you.
13. We tried to explain the problem however, he refused to listen.
14. I arrived late nevertheless, I heard the entire sermon.
15. I have lived in Detroit, Michigan Chicago, Illinois and Akron, Ohio.

Colon

16. I need the following information name, date, age, file number.
17. I have one question to ask why are you so eager for the change?
18. His reasoning was as follows he had never meant to stay there.
19. This investment has one great advantage it is absolutely safe.

Apostrophe

20. One hours sleep before midnight is worth three after.
21. Everybodys business is nobodys business.
22. Several students cars were ticketed for illegal parking.
23. Mrs. Abbott spells her name with two bs and two ts.
24. My youngest brothers name is Harold.

Dash

25. You and I have a great heritage the heritage of a free democracy.
26. The piano was very large too large to fit into the room.
27. We rose bright and early or, at any rate, early that morning.

Parentheses

28. That method trial and error was the only one she had ever tried.
29. That is the main purpose perhaps the only purpose of his visit.
30. He referred to the house our house as their legal property.

Hyphen

31. Our ready to wear dresses have been reduced for the sale.
32. Thirty eight cases were delivered this morning.
33. Canned tuna comes in three, six, and nine ounce sizes.
34. Mail us the form in the enclosed, self addressed envelope.

Exercise 8 continued

to conduct himself properly. We do not excuse his action but are merely 85
explaining it. We have spoken to him about the matter and believe he sincerely 101
regrets his rudeness. ¶This employee did not know where your package was 115
because he had changed assignments with another clerk. It is most unfortu- 130
nate that these circumstances resulted in so much annoyance to you. ¶Here- 145
after, should arrangements be made for anyone to call for a package, we shall 160
leave it at the front desk. We trust you will have no further cause for com- 175
plaint. We want you to know we value your patronage and will do our best 190
to please you. / Yours very truly / G. A. Hearn, President / *xx* (154 words) 201

Exercise 9

Modified block style. Open punctuation. No paragraph indention.

Today's date / Hoffman & Sons / 36 Water Street / Rochester, NY 14615

Gentlemen

We regret that we are unable to comply with your request for two posters advertising GOLDEN umbrellas. Since there was little demand for these posters, we did not reorder them when our supply was exhausted.

Perhaps you would be interested in purchasing copies of another poster we print. We are sending you, under separate cover, our latest catalog and a revised price list.

Sincerely

Mrs. M. W. Doss, Director / Public Relations Department / MWD:*xx* (64 words)

Exercise 10

Modified block style. Open punctuation. No paragraph indention.

May 8, 19— / Mr. Gordon Hethcock / Hethcock & Parapoulos / 63 Dodge Street / Providence, RI 02907

Dear Mr. Hethcock

Our graphics firm specializes in creating eye-catching logos for businesses in this area. You may have seen the ones we designed for

(Continued on next page)

Quotation Marks

35. The prisoner cried, I am not guilty!
36. We began by singing The Star Spangled Banner.
37. He stamped the package Fragile and then weighed it carefully.
38. Which officer said, Let's appoint Klepper to the post?

Capitals

39. Read chapter 6, page 115, of your english book.
40. Mr. Alexander, who is President of the company, works on saturdays and sundays.
41. I saw you driving West on Russell street last Spring.

Numbers and Abbreviations

42. Miss. Roberts was born May fourth.
43. Professor Joan Martin had to pay a ten-dollar parking ticket.
44. I found 3 valuable stamps in a store in Saint Louis, MO.

Exercise 2

COMMA REVIEW

Review Rules 5–10 on comma usage (refer to page 182). Type these sentences, adding any necessary punctuation as you type. *Do not mark the book.*

Full sheet. 70-space line. Double spacing. Begin on line 8.

1. No two people look alike dress alike or work alike.
2. A personable efficient secretary is a valuable asset.
3. When you are looking for new office furniture let us know.
4. As we have not received your approval we cannot take any action.
5. It was a pleasure meeting you and we hope to see you again soon.
6. Thank you for the check to cover your water gas and telephone bills.
7. The school of course will pay all your expenses.
8. All you need do Ms. Gates is save a small amount each week.
9. When you apply for a job be sure to take a resume with you.
10. I lost my new textbook <u>Personal Typing</u>.
11. If I found myself in such a predicament I would quit.
12. Our representative in your area Ms. E. Thomas will handle your problem.
13. We were on vacation for two weeks; our neighbors for three.
14. You can therefore be certain of good service from us.

(*Continued on next page*)

Exercise 5 continued

7,500 books will be hardbound using a low-priced cloth. It will also be perfect bound, and the cover and spine will be imprinted. ¶Under separate cover, we are sending two sample books with bindings similar to what we want. Please use these in preparing the cost estimates. When submitting your estimates, let us know how soon you can make delivery after the order is placed. We would also like to see sample materials and some books you have done to these specifications. / Sincerely / Otto Q. Karman / Purchasing Agent / *xx* (135 words)

Exercise 6

Modified block style. Open punctuation. 5-space paragraph indention.

August 19, 19— / Mr. Julius Watson / Watson and Lewis Contracting, Inc. / 13
42 La Salle Street / New Orleans, LA 70113 / Dear Mr. Watson / We are pleased 27
to inform you that we have accepted your bid for the construction of our new 42
warehouse. Even though some lower bids were submitted, management did 56
not choose the lowest bidder. Past experience in working with you has led us 71
to trust your estimates and rely on your ability to complete a job as agreed. 86
¶Our lawyer felt it necessary to make some minor changes in the terms of the 101
contract. It will be ready for your inspection early next week. If you would 116
like to meet to discuss any of the revisions, feel free to call me at any time. 132
You can reach me at 949-3112. Cordially / Baldwin Brooks / Financial Vice- 146
President / *xx* (109 words) 148

Exercise 7

Modified block style. Open punctuation. No paragraph indention.

March 5, 19— / Miss Felicia Curtis / Edsel Ford High School / 14337 Rotunda 14
Drive / Dearborn, MI 48122 / Dear Miss Curtis / Thank you for your interest 28
in attending our typewriting conference to be held in Dearborn next month. 43
As you know, the authors of our newest typing textbook, *Modern Office Type-* 58
writing, will be on hand. They will make presentations and discuss the latest 74
innovations in typing instruction. ¶Your letter states that you will be able to 90
attend only the sessions held after the luncheon. Therefore, you need not send 106
in the registration form and the $5 fee. The fee is intended to cover the cost 122
of the luncheon only. ¶I am sorry you will not be able to be with us for the 137
entire day. However, I am certain you will find the afternoon sessions valuable 153
to you in your classroom instruction. / Cordially / Charles L. Lester / Regional 168
Manager / *xx* (119 words) 170

Exercise 8

Modified block style. Open punctuation. 5-space paragraph indention.

November 1, 19— / Mr. Victor Stephens / Manor Plumbing Company / 40 12
Main Street / Ayer, MA 01432 / Dear Mr. Stephens / We deeply regret the inci- 26
dent about which you wrote us. We try to engage only courteous help, but we 41
do not always succeed. The people in our shipping room have little contact 56
with our customers. The man of whom you speak evidently did not know how 71

(Continued on next page)

15. When your resume is neatly typed it makes a good first impression.
16. I lived in Detroit Michigan until the age of 17.
17. He made a great number of errors; however he made neat corrections.
18. Visit the Downriver Bank the friendly savings place.
19. I was happy to receive the shipment of Friday May 15.
20. It is you must admit a beautiful day today.
21. Because of its great value you should insure that package.
22. If you don't understand read the directions more carefully.
23. I will admit incidentally that I was very nervous.
24. He asked me when I worked last where I worked and why I left.
25. She is a bright conscientious student.

Exercise 3

CAPITALIZATION REVIEW

Review Capitalization Rules 1–11 (pages 192–193). Type these sentences, correcting any capitalization errors as you type.

Full sheet. 70-space line. Double spacing. Begin on line 13.

1. We are now located in the bradford building on lycaste street.
2. I would like to buy a set of turkish towels.
3. "Do you know," she asked, "what happened to my favorite fountain pen?"
4. You will find the answers on page 75 of chapter 2.
5. My neighbors attend the chinese community church.
6. Our store's busiest season runs from thanksgiving to Christmas.
7. The frenchman spoke english with a strong accent.
8. An honest person is the noblest work of god.
9. Her first novel, Off On A Holiday, was republished last year under a new title, Lost In A Proud Land.
10. The painting, "a visit to mars," shows vivid imagination.
11. The Olympia Cruise Ship sails on wednesday, July 18.
12. The secretary of state made an address at the meeting.
13. I prefer to wait and speak to president Lowell.
14. Mrs. Bahr, our school secretary, drove to florida on vacation.
15. I believe that Kensington park is located just east of us.
16. Many students still find mathematics a difficult subject.
17. The nurse put a band-aid strip on the child's finger.
18. I saw a joint session of the senate and house of representatives.

Exercise 2
Modified block style. Mixed punctuation. No paragraph indention.

Today's date / Mr. Albert Wheeler / 68 Elm Road / Rochester, NY 14605 / Dear Mr. Wheeler / We expect to open our new salesroom at 73 Hartford Avenue in about a month. ¶We have planned a private showing for our regular customers next Monday from 10 a.m. to 1 p.m. On display will be a number of new home appliances, which we are sure will interest you. ¶We hope you will join us and be our guest at a luncheon following the showing. / Cordially / Herbert Dean, President / *xx* (66 words)

Exercise 3
Modified block style. Mixed punctuation. 5-space paragraph indention.

Today's date / Atlas Containers, Inc. / 481 Dalton Avenue / Omaha, NE 68106 / 14
Gentlemen / We regret that we cannot immediately submit samples of the 28
container for which you have sent specifications. As you have planned this 43
container, the manufacture will involve a very difficult gluing job. ¶We hope 58
to be able to send you a sample soon. We are awaiting delivery of a special 73
adhesive for a container ordered by another firm. We shall advise you as soon 89
as the adhesive arrives and we have had an opportunity to try it. ¶We doubt, 104
however, that we will be able to produce the container within the price limits 120
you mention. The expense involved in using the special adhesive will add to 135
the cost considerably. / Yours very truly / Samuel P. Lewis / Production 148
Manager / *xx* (109 words) 150

Exercise 4
Modified block style. Mixed punctuation. 5-space paragraph indention.

January 6, 19— / Mr. Alvin Collins / Collins Furnishings, Inc. / 318 Washington 15
Street / Memphis, TN 38106 / Dear Mr. Collins / We are happy to have the 28
opportunity to explain our recent request for a financial statement. But first, 44
let us assure you that you have a most excellent credit rating. No reflection 60
whatever was intended by the request. ¶When revising our credit files, we 75
routinely send a standardized form to all customers—even those of long stand- 91
ing. That we have faith in your financial standing is indicated by the unlimited 107
credit we have extended you. We shall continue to serve you as we have done 123
in the past. Our service will not be affected by a decision on your part not to 139
furnish us a financial statement. / Cordially / Ms. Rachel Engel / Credit 152
Manager / BNL / *xx* (107 words) 155

Exercise 5
Modified block style. Open punctuation. No paragraph indention.

Today's date / Mr. Norman L. Inman / Orville Book Bindery / 74 Raviolo Place / Auburn, ME 04210 / Dear Mr. Inman / We have two books in the process of being printed and are soliciting bids from several binderies. ¶Both volumes contain 432 pages and have a trim size of 6 by $9\frac{1}{4}$ inches. One lot of 10,000 copies requires an inexpensive two-color paper cover with a perfect binding. The second lot of

(Continued on next page)

Exercise 4

REVIEW

The following sentences contain errors identified by the symbols in the margin (see page 194). Find the errors; then type the corrected sentence.

Full sheet. 70-space line. Use single spacing, but double-space between sentences. Center title on line 8 and TS after it.

TYPING FROM UNEDITED SENTENCES

com	1.	If you agree we shall act at once.
ww, com	2.	Weather you buy from us or not we desire to please you.
com, ww	3.	If delivery is not made soon we will not except the goods.
ro, com	4.	The road sloped gently downward on one side on the other side
		there was a steep drop.
sp, com	5.	Our job is to produce better merchandice but we can succeed
ww		only with your corporation.
dsh	6.	It takes two people to make a good photograph the one behind the
ep		camera and the one who makes the print
com, sp	7.	An efficient well-planned road system is especialy important
		for the progress of the country.
sem, cap	8.	We want our taxes to be low however, we must pay for any Public
cap		Services that we want.
cap, com	9.	Last Autumn we had to change the contract because no matter how
com, ww		hard we tried we found it impossible to meat the deadlines.
com, sp	10.	We believe you will find the material to be strong of good qual-
com		ty and reasonably priced.
ro, com	11.	Supplies in our line will be limited for a few months we shall
com		therefore accept orders for future delivery only.
sp, com	12.	We are greatful to you Mr. Evans for the way in which you have
sp		met the many dificult situations that have arisen during the
ww		passed year.
par	13.	That step using fire for cooking as well as warmth was first taken
ap		by modern mans remote ancestors.
com	14.	We hesitated to bring up this matter but then we decided that
sp		you should be aware of all the finantial facts.
com, cap	15.	Mary Drake our Committee Chairperson will make a favorable
cap		report at our annual meeting in the Fall.
cap	16.	Our East coast branch is fully equipped to handle your export
sp		shipments just as soon as we receive your authorisation.
com	17.	Last summer for the first time in more than five years we pro-
cap		duced a shakespearean play.

HOLT OFFICE EQUIPMENT AND SUPPLIES

320 Graham Avenue, Decatur, Illinois 62510 ▪ (217) 964-1076

Tab at center

		Words
Date line	February 6, 19--	3
	Space down 4 times	
Inside address	Mr. B. J. Elliott, President	9
	Elliott Realty Company	14
	504 Calvert Street	18
	Decatur, IL 62512	22
	DS	
Salutation	Dear Mr. Elliott:	26
	DS	
	As we discussed in our telephone conversation this	36
	morning, my company is expanding very quickly, and	46
Body	it is likely that within six months it will double	56
	its present stock. Consequently, we will require	66
	additional warehouse storage space, preferably at a	76
	location as near to our main store as possible.	86
	DS	
	Since I will be out of town for a few days, I will	96
	not be available until early next week to look at	106
	warehouse properties. I'm sure you have among your	116
	current listings some that you would recommend for	126
	our storage needs. I will call you upon my return	136
	to arrange an appointment with you to look at your	146
	properties.	148
	DS	
Complimentary closing	Cordially,	151
Signature	Paul Solomon (Space down 4 times)	
Typed name and title of sender	Paul Solomon	154
	Business Manager	155
	DS	
Typist's initials	xx	

Tab at center

(Shown in Pica Type)

Model 8 *Business Letter • Modified Block Style with Mixed Punctuation and No Paragraph Indention*

PART 2

ADVANCED BUSINESS CORRESPONDENCE

Topic 1 BUSINESS LETTERS ON LETTERHEAD PAPER

Business letters typed on letterhead paper differ only slightly from the personal-business letters in Section 2. These differences are described and illustrated below.

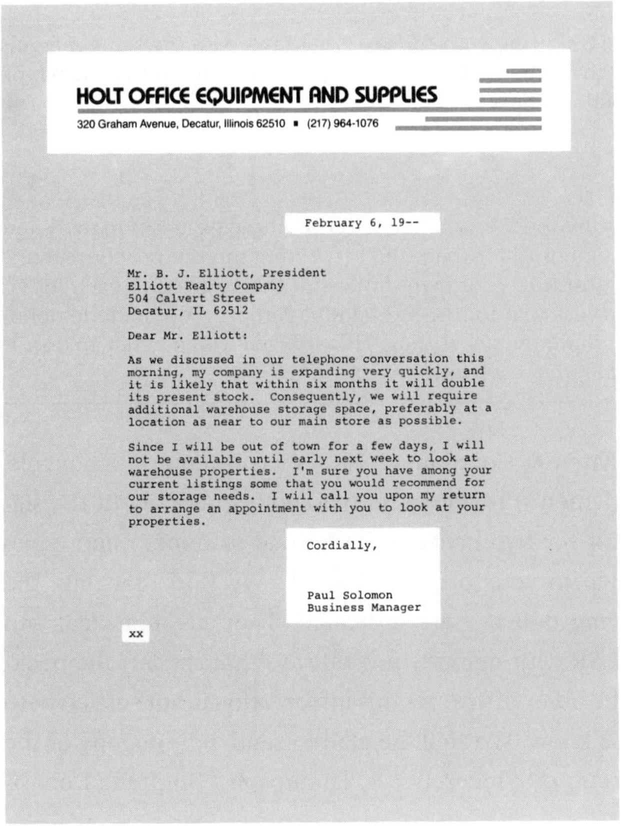

HOLT OFFICE EQUIPMENT AND SUPPLIES
320 Graham Avenue, Decatur, Illinois 62510 ▪ (217) 964-1076

February 6, 19--

Mr. B. J. Elliott, President
Elliott Realty Company
504 Calvert Street
Decatur, IL 62512

Dear Mr. Elliott:

As we discussed in our telephone conversation this morning, my company is expanding very quickly, and it is likely that within six months it will double its present stock. Consequently, we will require additional warehouse storage space, preferably at a location as near to our main store as possible.

Since I will be out of town for a few days, I will not be available until early next week to look at warehouse properties. I'm sure you have among your current listings some that you would recommend for our storage needs. I will call you upon my return to arrange an appointment with you to look at your properties.

Cordially,

Paul Solomon
Business Manager

xx

THE PRINTED LETTERHEAD Businesses use special stationery printed with the company's name, street address, city, state, and ZIP Code and, usually, telephone number.

THE DATE LINE Letters typed on letterhead stationery begin with the date line, typed a minimum of three lines below the letterhead information.

SIGNATURE BLOCK This contains the signature, the typed name of the sender, and the title of the position held by that person. The sender's name is placed on the fourth line under the complimentary closing, as in personal business letters. The position title may follow on the same line, separated from the name by a comma. More often, however, it is placed on the next line, directly under the name.

REFERENCE INITIALS These are the initials of the person who prepared the letter. They are typed at the left margin a double space below the signature block, usually in lowercase with no internal periods or spacing. In some organizations, the initials of the word originator are included as well. These are usually typed in solid capitals and separated from the preparer's by a colon. See Model 9 (page 242).

DOCUMENT CODE Organizations employing word processing systems need a fast, dependable way to locate and recall stored documents. The usual method is to assign a code to each document as it is being prepared. The exact form of the code varies from company to company. When used, however, the code appears on the same line as the reference initials. See Model 15 (page 278).

COURTESY TITLES Use of courtesy titles in business letters poses a problem for the typist. The titles *Ms., Mrs.,* and *Miss* in the signature block are optional. If the letter writer prefers to include one of these, it is typed without parentheses in front of the name. (In the handwritten signature, however, the courtesy title is enclosed within parentheses.) The courtesy title, *Mr.,* is seldom used in the signature block.

In responding to a letter in which the writer has not used a courtesy title, it is acceptable to address that person in reply without a title. For example, a salutation might read *Dear N. Wilson, Dear Laura Martin,* or *Dear Earl R. Scanlon.*

The business letters that follow will cast you in the role of typist for the writers or dictators of the letters. Study Models 8 and 9 (pages 237 and 242) and notice the placement of the new letter parts. Then practice Drills A–F. Drills A–C should be mastered before you begin Exercise 1; Drills D–F, before you begin Exercise 11.

Drill A

TYPING MODEL 8

Type the letter shown in Model 8 on the following page. If letterhead stationery is not available, use a plain sheet and begin with the date line. Follow the spacing instructions given in the model. Determine the proper margins and position of the date line by referring to the Letter Placement Chart on page 197. Type your initials in lowercase letters in place of *xx*. The body of the letter contains 109 words.

Drill B

OPENING PARTS OF MODEL 8

Type the letter shown in Model 8 to see how far you can type in 3 minutes. Use the date line placement and margin settings determined for Drill A. Repeat the drill until you can type the opening parts of this letter without hesitation.

Drill C

CLOSING PARTS OF MODEL 8

Type the letter shown in Model 8 starting with the last paragraph. Use the same margins you set for Drill A. Try to finish the letter in 3 minutes. Repeat the drill until you can type the closing parts of this letter without hesitation.

Directions for Exercises 1–10

Following the letter style shown in Model 8, type the letters in these exercises in modified block style. Use the Letter Placement Chart (page 197) to determine the proper margins and position of the date line. Substitute your own initials for the *xx* given in each letter. (Note that these exercises, and those that follow throughout Part 2, do not include punctuation for the salutation and complimentary closing. This will give you practice in deciding the correct punctuation required in each letter.)

Exercise 1

Modified block style.
Mixed punctuation.
No paragraph indention.

Today's date / Bernard McKuen & Company / 146 Lewis Avenue / Knoxville, TN 37906 / Ladies and Gentlemen / This is in reply to your query about the signature on the delivery receipt for two boxes of letterhead stationery and envelopes. The delivery was made to your office last week. We find that only the initials of the person receiving delivery are indicated. They are not clear but appear to be either TSR or LSR. Our delivery person says that she left the package with the receptionist in the outer office. ¶If this information is not sufficient to help you trace delivery, let us know. We shall be glad to send a photocopy of the signed receipt for your inspection. / Sincerely / R. Thompson / Shipping Department / *xx* (111 words)